LOVE'S KNOWLEDGE

LOVE'S KNOWLEDGE

Essays on Philosophy and Literature

MARTHA C. NUSSBAUM

OXFORD UNIVERSITY PRESS
New York   Oxford

Oxford University Press

Oxford   New York   Toronto
Delhi   Bombay   Calcutta   Madras   Karachi
Petaling Jaya   Singapore   Hong Kong   Tokyo
Nairobi   Dar es Salaam   Cape Town
Melbourne   Auckland

and associated companies in
Berlin   Ibadan

Copyright © 1990 by Martha C. Nussbaum

First published by Oxford University Press, 1990
First issued as an Oxford University Press paperback, 1992

Oxford University Press, Inc.,
200 Madison Avenue, New York, New York 10016

Oxford is a registered trademark of Oxford University Press

Library of Congress Cataloging-in-Publication Data
Nussbaum, Martha Craven, 1947–
Love's knowledge : essays on philosophy and literature /
Martha C. Nussbaum.
p.   cm.
Includes bibliographical references.
ISBN 0-19-505457-1
ISBN 0-19-507485-8 (pbk)
1. Ethics.   2. Literature and morals.   3. Philosophy in
literature.   I. Title.
BJ46.N87   1990
170—dc20   89-39728

9 8 7 6 5 4 3

Printed in the United States of America

The essays in this collection have been previously published as follows:

"The Discernment of Perception: An Aristotelian Conception of Private and Public Rationality," *Proceedings of the Boston Area Colloquium in Ancient Philosophy* 1 (1985): 151–201. (The present volume contains a revised and expanded version.)

"Plato on Commensurability and Desire," *Proceedings of the Aristotelian Society,* suppl. vol. 58 (1984): 55–80.

"Flawed Crystals: James's *The Golden Bowl* and Literature as Moral Philosophy," *New Literary History* 15 (1983): 25–50.

"'Finely Aware and Richly Responsible': Literature and the Moral Imagination," in *Literature and the Question of Philosophy,* ed. A. Cascardi (Baltimore: The Johns Hopkins University Press, 1987), 169–91. (An earlier and briefer version was published as "'Finely Aware and Richly Responsible': Moral Attention and the Moral Task of Literature," *Journal of Philosophy* 82 [1985]: 516–29.)

"Perceptive Equilibrium: Literary Theory and Ethical Theory," in *The Future of Literary Theory,* ed. R. Cohen (London: Routledge, Chapman, and Hall, 1989), 58–85. (An earlier version was published in *Logos* 8 (1987): 55–83) (revised).

"Perception and Revolution; *The Princess Casamassima* and the Political Imagination," in *Method, Language, and Reason: Essays in Honour of Hilary Putnam,* ed. G. Boolos (Cambridge, Eng.: Cambridge University Press, 1990).

"Sophistry About Conventions," *New Literary History* 17 (1985): 129–39.

"Reading for Life," *The Yale Journal of Law and the Humanities* 1 (1988): 165–80 (revised).

"Fictions of the Soul," *Philosophy and Literature* 7 (1983): 145–61.

"Love's Knowledge," in *Perspectives on Self-Deception,* ed. B. McLaughlin and A. Rorty (Berkeley: University of California Press, 1988), 487–514.

"Narrative Emotions: Beckett's Genealogy of Love," *Ethics* 98 (1988): 225–54. (A French version was published in *Littérature* 71 (1988), 40–58.)

"Love and the Individual: Romantic Rightness and Platonic Aspiration," in *Reconstructing Individualism,* ed. T. Heller et al. (Stanford, Calif.: Stanford University Press, 1986), 257–81.

For my mother and grandmother,
Betty W. Craven and Gertrude J. de Quintal

Preface

This volume collects my published papers on the relationship between literature and philosophy, especially moral philosophy. It adds to the previously published material expanded and revised versions of three essays, two entirely new essays, and a substantive Introduction. The essays explore some fundamental issues about the connections between philosophy and literature: the relationship between style and content in the exploration of ethical issues; the nature of ethical attention and ethical knowledge and their relationship to written forms and styles; the role of the emotions in deliberation and self-knowledge. The essays argue for a conception of ethical understanding that involves emotional as well as intellectual activity and gives a certain type of priority to the perception of particular people and situations, rather than to abstract rules. They argue that this conception, rather than being imprecise and irrational, is actually superior in rationality and in the relevant sort of precision. They argue, further, that this ethical conception finds its most appropriate expression and statement in certain forms usually considered literary rather than philosophical—and that if we wish to take it seriously we must broaden our conception of moral philosophy in order to include these texts inside it. They attempt to articulate the relationship, within such a broader ethical inquiry, between literary and more abstractly theoretical elements.

In their original places of publication, the papers were not accessible to non-specialist readers, since most of them appeared in journals and collections that do not have wide circulation. Some are difficult to obtain even for the academic reader. Equally troublesome was the question of disciplinary location. These papers cross traditional disciplinary boundaries. They also argue that certain important questions cannot be well addressed unless those boundaries are crossed. And yet ironically, because of the very separations they criticize, they have on the whole been separated from one another, appearing in publications some of which are read by philosophers, others by literary scholars. The present collection should remedy that problem, enabling readers of all backgrounds and interests to assess them as a group.

This project has close affiliations with much of my work on ancient Greek philosophy: especially with *The Fragility of Goodness: Luck and Ethics in Greek Tragedy and Philosophy* (Cambridge, Eng.: Cambridge University Press, 1986), and with *The Therapy of Desire: Theory and Practice in Hellenistic Ethics,* based on the Martin Classical Lectures 1986, and forthcoming. The discussions of literary and ethical topics in these books are continuous with many of the arguments here. I have included in this volume two published articles on ancient Greek topics written at the same time as *The Fragility of Goodness:* "The Discernment of Perception" and "Plato on Commensurability and Desire." These articles develop in greater detail than some of the literary papers some important parts of the ethical conception that I am investigating in the collection as a whole. (The former has been revised and expanded for this collection.) "Transcending Humanity," not previously published, links some of my work on Greek philosophy to the contemporary issues of this collection. Two earlier pieces on the connection between philosophy and literature in ancient Greek texts are not included: "Consequences and Character in Sophocles' *Philoctetes,*" *Philosophy and Literature* 1 (1986–87): 25–53, and "Aristophanes and Socrates on Learning Practical Wisdom," *Yale Classical Studies* 26 (1980): 43–97. I still endorse the arguments of these pieces, and hope to collect them in a different sort of volume at some point. But since they discuss ethical issues *in* the literary works without asking about the relationship of ethical content to literary form, they seemed less closely linked than the two included papers to the central argument of this collection.

Several recent articles on Greek topics that are very closely linked to the themes of this volume are not included because they will appear, in revised form, in *The Therapy of Desire.* These articles are: "Therapeutic Arguments: Epicurus and Aristotle," in *The Norms of Nature,* ed. M. Schofield and G. Striker (Cambridge, Eng.: Cambridge University Press, 1986), 31–74; "The Stoics on the Extirpation of the Passions," *Apeiron* 20 (1987): 129–75; "Beyond Obsession and Disgust: Lucretius' Genealogy of Love," *Apeiron* 22 (1989); "Mortal Immortals: Lucretius on Death and the Voice of Nature," *Philosophy and Phenomenological Research* (1989); and "Serpents in the Soul: a Reading of Seneca's *Medea,*" forthcoming in a volume in honor of Stanley Cavell, ed. T. Cohen and P. Guyer. The Stoic piece develops at length the view of the connection between emotion and belief developed more briefly in several of these essays. The Seneca piece explores the relationship between love and morality, and has especially close links with "Perceptive Equilibrium" and "Steerforth's Arm." The Lucretius piece is closely related to "Narrative Emotions." In an Introduction to a new translation of Euripides' *Bacchae* by C. K. Williams, to be published in 1990 by Farrar, Straus, and Giroux, I develop further some of the issues about humanity and transcendence discussed in "Transcending," and comment further on the relationship between Aristotle and Greek tragedy.

From my writing on contemporary issues about the relationship between philosophy and literature, I have omitted the reply to Richard Wollheim, Patrick Gardiner, and Hilary Putnam that accompanied "Flawed Crystals" in its original publication in *New Literary History.* The main points are covered in the Introduction and in the endnote to "Flawed Crystals" here. I also omit my comments on Paul Seabright's paper on *Portrait of a Lady* that appeared in the same volume of *Ethics* as "Narrative Emotions." I plan to expand this into an independent paper. Several of my reviews and review articles have dealt with literary/philosophical questions. The only one of these that I have included here is a review article on Wayne Booth's *The Company We Keep*—both because it is a rather self-sufficient article and because the book with which it deals is a major book that will be read for years to come.

I have written endnotes as well as an Introduction, because I felt that there were more issues requiring comment and clarification than could easily be covered in a cohesive Introduction with a single line of argument. The endnotes make many specific remarks about the relationships of the articles to one another, and direct the reader who has not yet read the Introduction to some of the central theoretical issues that are discussed there.

All footnotes have been adjusted for uniformity of reference. References have been brought up to date where necessary.

Providence, R.I. M.C.N.
October 1989

Acknowledgments

Since these papers have been written over a period of ten years, I owe thanks to many people and organizations. Work on various parts of this volume has been supported by a Guggenheim Fellowship, an NEH Fellowship, and a Visiting Fellowship at All Souls College, Oxford. The writing of the Introduction was supported in part by the World Institute for Development Economics Research, Helsinki, which provided an atmosphere that was marvelously secluded and free from distraction. Brown University generously supported the final preparation of the collection by assigning me a research assistant; and I owe thanks to Kurt Raaflaub, who, as Chair of the Classics Department, made that possible. Equally important, the University, by allowing me to function as a member of three departments—Philosophy, Classics, and Comparative Literature—has contributed immeasurably to the development of this interdisciplinary work.

The ideas in this collection have been developing for many years, as the Introduction relates; and I owe thanks to the following teachers who, early in my intellectual life, encouraged me to go on asking philosophical questions of works of literature: Marion Stearns, Marthe Melchior, Edith Melcher, Seth Benardete. The formal and public life of the project began with an invitation from the Pacific Division of the American Philosophical Association to present a paper on "philosophy and literature." This was the incentive for the writing of "Flawed Crystals," the earliest of these papers. And the excellent written commentary at that session by Richard Wollheim—followed shortly after by similarly stimulating written comments by Patrick Gardiner at the Oxford Philosophical Society—reinforced my conviction that there was an important issue here and that it ought to be pursued further. Warm thanks are due to Ralph Cohen, editor of *New Literary History,* who arranged for the publication of these exchanges in an issue devoted to "Literature and Moral Philosophy," commissioning additional written comments from Hilary Putnam and Cora Diamond. Cohen has supported this work from its inception in many ways, publishing three of the papers, commissioning two of these, and giving me, throughout, the benefit of his insight and encouragement. Once begun, my work on these issues was further assisted by an invitation to participate in a conference on Styles of Fictionality organized by Thomas Pavel; by a second invitation from the American Philosophical Association (this time the Eastern Division), in response to which I wrote "'Finely Aware,'" which had the benefit of a valuable written commentary by Cora Diamond, whose insightful writing on these topics has been especially valuable; and by the various other invitations from journals and collections in response to which the rest of the papers were written. (In that connection I would like to thank the Boston Area Colloquium for Ancient Philosophy, the Stanford Humanities Center, the Aristotelian Society, the National Humanities Center, Lawrence Becker, George Boolos, Anthony Cascardi, Brian McLaughlin, and Amelie Rorty.) During the final stages of work on several of the papers, I had the privilege of delivering them as Luce Seminars at Yale University; I wish to thank Peter Brooks and the Whitney Humanities Center for this invitation and for the helpful discussions it promoted. Other portions of the book were delivered as Read-Tuckwell Lectures at the University of Bristol, England; and I am grateful to the Philosophy Department there for their warm hospitality. (See the separate Acknowledgments page.)

Many particular debts are expressed in the notes to the particular essays. But here, in addition to those mentioned above, I wish to thank several people whose support and conversation have been especially valuable at various times during my work: Julia Annas, Sissela Bok, Stanley Cavell, Denis Dutton, David Halperin, Anthony Price, Hilary Putnam, Henry Richardson, Christopher Rowe, Amartya Sen. And I am especially grateful to the many graduate and undergraduate students at Harvard, Wellesley, and Brown who have participated in the development of these ideas and whose comments, questions, and papers have been a most valuable source of insight.

My efforts to make these papers into a uniform collection were enormously assisted by Christopher Hildebrandt, Jonathan Robbins, and Gwen Jones, who spent many tedious hours checking references and changing the Henry James texts and page numbers to those of the New York Edition. Gale Alex impeccably typed several of the papers, and Ruth Ann Whitten resourcefully provided many kinds of assistance. To Angela Blackburn and Cynthia Read of the Oxford University Press I am grateful for their efficiency, warm support, and wise advice.

Half of the author's proceeds from the sale of this book will be given to the AIDS Action Committee of Boston. The other half will be given to the John J. Winkler Memorial Trust.

The READ-TUCKWELL LECTURESHIP was established by a residual bequest to the University of Bristol made by Alice Read-Tuckwell, who directed in her will that income deriving from the trust funds should be used to establish and maintain the lectureship and that the lecturer should deliver a course of lectures on Human Immortality and related matters, the course of lectures to be printed and published. The material in chapters 1, 2, 6, 7, 14, and 15 was delivered as the fourth set of Read-Tuckwell Lectures in 1989, and other material was presented in an associated seminar.

Contents

List of Long and Short Titles

"Discernment" "The Discernment of Perception: an Aristotelian Conception of Private and Public Morality"

"Plato on Commensurability" "Plato on Commensurability and Desire"

"Flawed Crystals" "Flawed Crystals: James's *The Golden Bowl* and Literature as Moral Philosophy"

"'Finely Aware'" "'Finely Aware and Richly Responsible': Literature and the Moral Imagination"

"Perceptive Equilibrium" "Perceptive Equilibrium: Literary Theory and Ethical Theory"

"Perception and Revolution" "Perception and Revolution: *The Princess Casamassima* and the Political Imagination"

"Sophistry" "Sophistry About Conventions"

"Reading" "Reading for Life"

"Fictions" "Fictions of the Soul"

"Love's Knowledge" "Love's Knowledge"

"Narrative Emotions" "Narrative Emotions: Beckett's Genealogy of Love"

"Love and the Individual" "Love and the Individual: Romantic Rightness and Platonic Aspiration"

"Steerforth's Arm" "Steerforth's Arm: Love and the Moral Point of View"

"Transcending" "Transcending Humanity"

Fragility *The Fragility of Goodness: Luck and Ethics in Greek Tragedy and Philosophy*

LOVE'S KNOWLEDGE

"It isn't playing the game to turn on the uncanny. All one's energy goes to facing it, to tracking it. One wants, confound it, don't you see?" he confessed with a queer face, "one wants to enjoy anything so rare. Call it then life," he puzzled it out, "call it poor dear old life simply that springs the surprise. Nothing alters the fact that the surprise is paralyzing, or at any rate engrossing—all, practically, hang it, that one sees, that one *can* see."

Henry James, The Ambassadors

Style for the writer, no less than colour for the painter, is a question not of technique but of vision: it is the revelation, which by direct and conscious methods would be impossible, of the qualitative difference, the uniqueness of the fashion in which the world appears to each one of us. . . . And it is perhaps as much by the quality of his language as by the species of . . . theory which he advances that one may judge of the level to which a writer has attained in the moral and intellectual part of his work. Quality of language, however, is something the theorists think they can do without, and those who admire them are easily persuaded that it is no proof of intellectual merit.

Marcel Proust, Remembrance of Things Past

You may know a truth, but if it's at all complicated you have to be an artist not to utter it as a lie.

Iris Murdoch, An Accidental Man

He shook his head sadly.

"I glanced over it," said he. "Honestly, I cannot congratulate you upon it. Detection is, or ought to be, an exact science and should be treated in the same cold and unemotional manner. You have attempted to tinge it with romanticism, which produces much the same effect as if you worked a love-story or an elopement into the fifth proposition of Euclid."

"But the romance was there," I remonstrated. "I could not tamper with the facts."

"Some facts should be suppressed, or, at least, a just sense of proportion should be observed in treating them. The only point in the case which deserved mention was the curious analytical reasoning from effects to causes, by which I succeeded in unravelling it."

Sir Arthur Conan Doyle, The Sign of Four

Introduction: Form and Content, Philosophy and Literature

"Ma dì s'i' veggio qui colui che fore
trasse le nove rime, cominciando
'Donne ch'avete intelletto d'amore.'"

E io a lui: "I'mi son un che, quando
Amor mi spira, noto, e a quel modo
ch'e' ditta dentro vo significando."

"And tell me if the man I see here
is the one who published the new poem, beginning
'Ladies, you who have the knowledge of love.'"

I said to him: "I am one who, when Love breathes
in me, takes note. And in whatever way
he dictates within, that way I signify."

Dante, *Purgatorio,* Canto XXIV

How should one write, what words should one select, what forms and structures and organization, if one is pursuing understanding? (Which is to say, if one is, in that sense, a philosopher?) Sometimes this is taken to be a trivial and uninteresting question. I shall claim that it is not. Style itself makes its claims, expresses its own sense of what matters. Literary form is not separable from philosophical content, but is, itself, a part of content—an integral part, then, of the search for and the statement of truth.

But this suggests, too, that there may be some views of the world and how one should live in it—views, especially, that emphasize the world's surprising variety, its complexity and mysteriousness, its flawed and imperfect beauty—that cannot be fully and adequately stated in the language of conventional philosophical prose, a style remarkably flat and lacking in wonder—but only in a language and in forms themselves more complex, more allusive, more attentive to particulars. Not perhaps, either, in the expositional structure conventional to philosophy, which sets out to establish something and then does so, without surprise, without incident—but only in a form that itself implies that life contains significant surprises, that our task, as agents, is to live as good characters in a good story do, caring

3

about what happens, resourcefully confronting each new thing. If these views are serious candidates for truth, views that the search for truth ought to consider along its way, then it seems that this language and these forms ought to be included within philosophy.

And what if it is love one is trying to understand, that strange unmanageable phenomenon or form of life, source at once of illumination and confusion, agony and beauty? Love, in its many varieties, and their tangled relations to the good human life, to aspiration, to general social concern? What parts of oneself, what method, what writing, should one choose then? What is, in short, love's knowledge—and what writing does it dictate in the heart?

A. Expressive Plants, Perceiving Angels

> He chose to include the things
> That in each other are included, the whole,
> The complicate, the amassing harmony.
> Wallace Stevens
> "Notes Toward a Supreme Fiction"

In his preface to *The Golden Bowl,* Henry James describes the author's selection of appropriate terms and sentences, using two metaphors. One is a metaphor of plant growth. Focusing on his theme or idea, the author causes it "to flower before me as into the only terms that honorably expressed it."[1] And elsewhere in the prefaces, James frequently compares the author's sense of life to soil, the literary text to a plant that grows out of that soil and expresses, in its form, the soil's character and composition.

James's second metaphor is more mysterious. The fully imagined text is next compared (in its relation, apparently, to whatever simpler, more inert, less adequate language may have been, before its invention, on the scene to cover the subject) to some creatures of the air, perhaps birds, perhaps angels. The novelist's imagined words are called "the immense array of terms, perceptional and expressional, that, after the fashion I have indicated, in sentence, passage and page, simply looked over the heads of the standing terms—or perhaps rather, like alert winged creatures, perched on those diminished summits and aspired to a clearer air."[2]

These two metaphors point to two claims about the writer's art that seem worth investigating. To investigate and defend them is a central purpose of these essays. The first is the claim that there is, with respect to any text carefully written and fully imagined, an organic connection between its form and its content. Certain thoughts and ideas, a certain sense of life, reach toward expression in writing that has a certain shape and form, that uses certain structures, certain terms. Just as

---

1. Henry James, Preface to *The Golden Bowl,* in *The Art of the Novel* (New York, 1907), 339 (hereafter *AN*). In the volumes of the New York Edition (Scribners, 1907–9) containing *The Golden Bowl,* this passage occurs on I.xvi. James is actually talking here of the activity of "revision," the author/reader's re-imagining of the language and form of his text.

2. James, *AN* 339.

the plant emerges from the seeded soil, taking its form from the combined character of seed and soil, so the novel and its terms flower from and express the conceptions of the author, his or her sense of what matters. Conception and form are bound together; finding and shaping the words is a matter of finding the appropriate and, so to speak, the honorable, fit between conception and expression. If the writing is well done, a paraphrase in a very different form and style will not, in general, express the same conception.

The second claim is that certain truths about human life can only be fittingly and accurately stated in the language and forms characteristic of the narrative artist. With respect to certain elements of human life, the terms of the novelist's art are alert winged creatures, perceiving where the blunt terms of ordinary speech, or of abstract theoretical discourse, are blind, acute where they are obtuse, winged where they are dull and heavy.

But to understand that metaphor fully, we clearly need to connect it with the first. For if the novelist's terms are angels, they are also earthly and of the soil of finite human life and feeling. In the canonical medieval conception, angels and separated souls, lacking immersion in earthly ways of life and the body that is a necessary condition for such immersion, are able to apprehend only abstract essences and general forms. Lacking concrete sensuous imaginings, they cannot perceive particulars. On earth, they have only an imperfect cognition, as Aquinas says, "confused and general."[3] James, here, alludes to that conception and inverts it. His angelic beings (his words and sentences) are beings not without but of the imagination, "perceptional and expressional," drawn from the concrete and deeply felt experience of life in this world and dedicated to a fine rendering of that life's particularity and complexity. His claim is that only language this dense, this concrete, this subtle—only the language (and the structures) of the narrative artist, can adequately tell the reader what James believes to be true.

The essays in this volume examine the contribution made by certain works of literature to the exploration of some important questions about human beings and human life. Their first claim is that in this contribution form and style are not incidental features. A view of life is *told.* The telling itself—the selection of genre, formal structures, sentences, vocabulary, of the whole manner of addressing the reader's sense of life—all of this expresses a sense of life and of value, a sense of what matters and what does not, of what learning and communicating are, of life's relations and connections. Life is never simply *presented* by a text; it is always *represented as* something. This "as" can, and must, be seen not only in the paraphrasable content, but also in the style, which itself expresses choices and selections, and sets up, in the reader, certain activities and transactions rather than others.[4] The responsibility of the literary artist, then, as James conceives it and as

3. Thomas Aquinas, *Summa Theologica* 1 q.89 a.1.

4. On the work of art as a shaping of life, see Nelson Goodman, *Languages of Art* (Indianapolis, Ind., 1968, chaps. 1, 6; also his *Ways of Worldmaking* (Indianapolis, Ind., 1978). The literature on the activity of the reader is by now vast, but see especially Wayne Booth, *The Company We Keep: An Ethics of Fiction* (Berkeley, 1988); Peter Brooks, *Reading for the Plot: Design and Intention in Narrative* (New York, 1984); W. Iser, "Interaction Between Text and Reader," in *The Reader in the Text,* ed. Susan R. Suleiman and Inge Crossman (Princeton, N.J., 1980), 106–19; see also his *Act of Reading: A Theory of Aesthetic Response* (Baltimore, Md., 1978).

this book will conceive it, is to discover the forms and terms that fittingly and honorably express, adequately state, the ideas that it is his or her design to put forward; and to bring it about that the reader, led by the text into a complex artistic activity "in his own other medium, by his own other art," is active in a way suited to the understanding of whatever is there for understanding, with whatever elements of him or herself are suited to the task of understanding. And we should bear in mind that all writers about life are, in James's view, literary artists, except those too inattentive to care at all about their formal choices and what these express: "The seer and speaker under the descent of the god is the 'poet,' whatever his form, and he ceases to be one when his form, whatever else it may nominally or superficially or vulgarly be, is unworthy of the god: in which event, we promptly submit, he isn't worth talking of at all."[5] The writer of a philosophical treatise, if the treatise is thoughtfully narrated, expresses, just as much as the novelist, in his or her formal choices, a sense of what life is and what has value.

This first claim is not unique to James. As we shall shortly see, it has very deep roots in the Western philosophical tradition, in the "ancient quarrel" between the poets and philosophers presented in Plato's *Republic* and continued in many subsequent debates. But, to confine ourselves for the present to the modern protagonists of this collection, we can point out that Marcel Proust develops, explicitly and in detail, a very similar thesis. Proust's hero Marcel holds that a certain view of what human life is like will find its appropriate verbal expression in certain formal and stylistic choices, a certain use of terms. And since the literary text is seen as the occasion for a complex activity of searching and understanding on the part of its reader, Marcel also holds that a certain view of what understanding and self-understanding are will appropriately issue in certain formal choices aimed both at stating the truth adequately and at eliciting, from the reader, an intelligent reading of life.

But Proust and James, and this volume with them, claim more than this. The first claim directs us to look for a close fit between form and content, seeing form as expressive of a view of life. But this already leads us to ask whether certain forms might not be more appropriate than others for the true and accurate depiction of various elements of life. This all depends, obviously, on what the answers actually are or may be to various questions about human life and about how we come to know it. The first claim implies that each available conception will be associated with a form or forms that fittingly state it. But at this point both James and Proust make a second claim, the claim expressed in James's second metaphor. This claim, unlike the first, depends on their particular ideas about human life. The claim is that only the style of a certain sort of narrative artist (and not, for example, the style associated with the abstract theoretical treatise) can adequately state certain important truths about the world, embodying them in its shape and setting up in the reader the activities that are appropriate for grasping them.

One might, of course, hold that the truths in question *can* be adequately stated in abstract theoretical language and also hold that they are most efficiently communicated to readers of a certain sort through colorful and moving narrative. Young children, for example, frequently learn some types of mathematics more

5. James, *AN* 340.

easily through amusing word problems than through abstract computations. But this hardly implies that the truths of mathematics have themselves any deep or intrinsic connection with the word problem form, or that they are deficiently stated in their abstract form. Where our questions about how to live are concerned, a similar claim has frequently been made for literature: it is held to be instrumental to the communication of truths that could in principle be adequately stated without literature and grasped in that form by a mature mind. This is not the position taken by Proust and James, or by this book. Literature may indeed have an important instrumental role to play in motivation and communication, and this is itself significant; but far more is claimed for it. My first claim insists that any style makes, itself, a statement: that an abstract theoretical style makes, like any other style, a statement about what is important and what is not, about what faculties of the reader are important for knowing and what are not. There may then be certain plausible views about the nature of the relevant portions of human life that cannot be housed within that form without generating a peculiar implicit contradiction. The second claim is, then, that for an interesting family of such views, a literary narrative of a certain sort is the only type of text that can state them fully and fittingly, without contradiction.

Two examples will make this clearer. Suppose one believes and wishes to state, as Proust's Marcel does, that the most important truths about human psychology cannot be communicated or grasped by intellectual activity alone: powerful emotions have an irreducibly important cognitive role to play. If one states this view in a written form that expresses only intellectual activity and addresses itself only to the intellect of the reader (as is the custom in most philosophical and psychological treatises), a question arises. Does the writer really believe what his or her words seem to state? If so, why has this form been selected above others, a form that itself implies a rather different view of what is important and what dispensable? One might get an answer to this question that would rescue the author from the charge of inconsistency. (For example, the author may believe that the psychological thesis itself is not among the truths that must be grasped through emotional activity. Or she may believe that it is among those truths, but be indifferent about whether the reader grasps it.) But it seems at least *prima facie* plausible to suppose that the author has either been oddly inattentive or is actually ambivalent about the view in question. Proust's text, by contrast, states in its form exactly what it states in its paraphrasable philosophical content; what it tells about knowledge it also commits itself to in practice, alternating between emotive and reflective material in just the way that Marcel holds to be appropriate for telling truth.[6]

Take, again, Henry James's belief that fine attention and good deliberation require a highly complex, nuanced perception of, and emotional response to, the concrete features of one's own context, including particular persons and relationships. Again, one could try to state this position abstractly, in a text that displayed no interest in the concrete, in emotional ties, or in fine-tuned perceptions. But the same difficulty would then arise: the text is making a set of claims, but its formal choices seem to be making a different and incompatible set of claims. It seems *prima facie* plausible to hold, as James does hold, that the terms of the novelist's

6. For a fuller discussion of this point, see "Love's Knowledge" in this volume.

art can state what James calls "the projected morality" more adequately than any other available terms.[7] Again, more needs to be said—especially about Aristotle, who makes statements about particularity that lie close to James's, but in a very different style (see §§E, F). But the general sense of the second claim is, I hope, by now emerging.

The predominant tendency in contemporary Anglo-American philosophy has been either to ignore the relation between form and content altogether, or, when not ignoring it, to deny the first of our two claims, treating style as largely decorative—as irrelevant to the stating of content, and neutral among the contents that might be conveyed. When philosophy's style is not ignored or declared irrelevant, a more interesting position, respectful of the first claim, has occasionally made its appearance. This view is that the truths the philosopher has to tell are such that the plain clear general non-narrative style most frequently found in philosophical articles and treatises is in fact the style best suited to state any and all of them.[8] Both positions will be disputed in this book. The first (the repudiation of the whole question of style) will be my primary target. I wish to establish the importance of taking style seriously in its expressive and statement-making functions. But the second must be confronted as well, if we are to make, inside philosophy, a place for literary texts. For if all significant truths or candidates for truth about human life really are such that the abstract philosophical style states them at least as well as the narrative styles of writers such as James and Proust, then even the acceptance of the first claim will do nothing on behalf of *those* styles, except to link them with illusion. We can hardly hope to settle here the question of truth about matters of such importance, or even to investigate more than a small fraction of the topics in which the question of truth and style arises. So the narrower and more modest claim of these essays will be that with respect to several interrelated issues in the area of human choice, and of ethics broadly construed (see §§C, E, G), there is a family of positions that is a serious candidate for truth—and which deserves, therefore, the attention and scrutiny of anyone who seriously considers these matters—whose full, fitting, and (as James would say) "honorable" embodiment is found in the terms characteristic of the novels here investigated. (Clearly there are differences among the novels, and we shall investigate them also.)

Throughout this book, I shall be speaking of author and reader: so a brief comment is necessary at the start to clarify what I do and do not mean by this. I view these literary texts as works whose representational and expressive content issues from human intentions and conceptions. This feature is, in fact, prominently dramatized in the novels studied here, in all of which the voice of an authorial consciousness is to be heard, and in all of which the making of the text is an explicit theme of the narrative itself. Moreover, all of them—especially James and Dickens—closely connect the stance of the author with the stance of the reader—as the authorial presence occupies in thought and feeling the reader's position, asking what the reader will be able to feel and think. It is important to distinguish,

7. On this point, see "'Finely Aware'" and "Discernment" in this volume. The phrase "the projected morality" is from the Preface to *The Portrait of a Lady, AN* 45.

8. Especially influential here are the views of John Locke; they are discussed in "Fictions" and "Love's Knowledge."

here, three figures: (1) the narrator or author-character (together with this character's conception of the reader); (2) the authorial presence that animates the text taken as a whole (together with the corresponding implicit picture of what a sensitive and informed reader will experience); and (3) the whole life of the real-life author (and reader), much of which has no causal relation to the text and no relevance to the proper reading of the text.[9] The first and the second pair are what will concern me here: that is, I will be concerned with intentions and thoughts that are realized in the text, and that may appropriately be seen in the text, not with other thoughts and feelings the real-life author and reader may find themselves having.[10] Both James and Proust insist on the difference between any real author's whole daily life, with its routines, its inattentions, its patches of deadness, and the more concentrated attention that produces and animates the literary text. On the other side, they correctly notice that the reader, too, may in many ways lapse, and may fail to be what the text demands. I am concerned with what is embodied in the text and what the text, in turn, requires of the reader. Thus nothing I say about the author here implies that critical statements made by the writer have any particular authority in the interpretation of the text. For such statements may very well be dissociated from the intentions that are actually fulfilled in the text. Nor, in speaking of intentions fulfilled in the text, am I thinking simply of conscious volitions to make an art-work of such and such a sort. Such a notion of intention would indeed direct us away from a scrutiny of all that is in fact realized in the text; and such narrow notions of intention have brought the entire notion of intention into discredit.[11] I am interested, then, in all and only those thoughts, feelings, wishes, movements, and other processes that are actually there to be seen in the text. On the other hand, seeing something in a literary text (or, for that matter, a painting) is unlike seeing shapes in the clouds, or in the fire. There the reader is free to see whatever his or her fancy dictates, and there are no limits on what she may see. In the reading of a literary text, there is a standard of correctness set by the author's sense of life, as it finds its way into the work.[12] And the text, approached as the creation of human intentions, is some fraction or ele-

9. For similar distinctions, see Wayne Booth, *The Rhetoric of Fiction* (Chicago, 1961; 2nd ed., 1983), and *The Company We Keep,* where the distinctions are connected with an analysis of ethical assessment.

10. An excellent account of the role of intention in interpretation is presented in Richard Wollheim's *Art and Its Objects,* 2nd ed. (Cambridge, Eng., 1980) and his *Painting as an Art* (Princeton, N.J., 1987). Wollheim argues that the standard of correctness for the spectator's (or reader's) activity must be found by reference to the artist's intention; but that only those intentions are relevant that are causally involved in the production of the work. He also insists on the close interweaving at every stage of the artist's role with the spectator's; these are not so much two people as two roles, and the artist frequently occupies the spectator's role during the process of making.This account is very close to James's subtle analysis of the author's rereading in the Preface to *The Golden Bowl.* On intention, see also E. D. Hirsch, Jr., *Validity in Interpretation* (New Haven, Conn., 1967).

11. A similarly broad notion of intention, with similar constraints, can be found in Wollheim's *Art and Its Objects* and *Painting as an Art;* see also Stanley Cavell, *Must We Mean What We Say?* (New York, 1969; repr. Cambridge, Eng., 1976).

12. For this contrast, see Wollheim, *Art and Its Objects* (especially the supplementary essay "Seeing-In and Seeing-As") and *Painting as an Art,* chap. 2.

ment of a real human being—even if the writer manages to see what she sees only in her work.

A problem seems to be raised by my use of Henry James's prefaces. In appealing from novels to prefaces, don't I after all confound the author-in-the-text with the real-life author, and give the statements of the latter an inappropriate authority? Here, three things may be said. First, an author need not be a bad judge of what has in fact been realized in his text. This is very often the case, for complex psychological reasons; but there are exceptions, and I think that James is one. Second, I do not treat the prefaces as infallible. Like most critics, I find them inaccurate at times in their claims about the reader's viewpoint, and on other related matters. But they remain remarkably perceptive and helpful guides to the novels. Finally, James strongly suggests that, once published together with the novels, they have become a part of the literary enterprise they introduce. It is, then, perhaps too simple to view them as comments by the real-life author. They are closely linked to the authorial consciousness of the novels, and link the novels together into a larger narrative structure, with discursive and narrative parts, and a connecting authorial presence of its own. I suggest, then, that in bringing his life's work together and linking its component parts with a more or less continuous discussion of literary art and its "projected morality,"[13] James has moved in the direction in which Proust moves in the creation of his own hybrid text, combining commentary and narration into a larger whole.

B. The Ancient Quarrel

> My father had left a small collection of books in a little room upstairs, to which I had access (for it adjoined my own), and which nobody else in our house ever troubled. From that blessed little room, Roderick Random, Peregrine Pickle, Humphrey Clinker, Tom Jones, the Vicar of Wakefield, Don Quixote, Gil Blas, and Robinson Crusoe, came out, a glorious host, to keep me company. They kept alive my fancy, and my hope of something beyond that place and time—they, and the *Arabian Nights,* and the *Tales of the Genii*—and did me no harm. . . . This was my only and my constant comfort. When I think of it, the picture always rises in my mind, of a summer evening, the boys at play in the churchyard, and I sitting on my bed, reading as if for life. . . . The reader now understands, as well as I do, what I was when I came to that point of my youthful history to which I am now coming again.
>
> Charles Dickens, *David Copperfield*

To show more clearly the nature of this philosophical/literary project, it will be useful (since it is in some ways so anomalous) to describe its beginnings and motivations, the soil from which it has grown. It grew, then, immediately and recently from my sense of the force and inevitability of certain questions, and from my bewilderment at finding these questions, on the whole, not addressed in the academic contexts I encountered, a bewilderment that only increased my obsession

13. James, *AN* 45.

with the questions. More remotely, however, it began, I can only suppose, from the fact that, like David Copperfield, I was a child whose best friends were, on the whole, novels—a serious and, for a long time, a solitary child.[14] I can recall sitting for hours in the brown and silent attic, or in the tall grass of any field that was left unaltered by the chilly clear opulence that Bryn Mawr in general offered—reading with love, and thinking about many questions. Taking enormous delight at being in an open field, bewildered, reading, with the wind blowing round my shoulders.

In my school there was nothing that Anglo-American conventions would call "philosophy." And yet the questions of this book (which I shall call, broadly, ethical) were raised and investigated. The pursuit of truth there was a certain sort of reflection about literature. And the form the ethical questions took, as the roots of some of them grew into me, was usually that of reflecting and feeling about a particular literary character, a particular novel; or, sometimes, an episode from history, but seen as the material for a dramatic plot of my own imagining. All this was, of course, seen in relation to life itself, which was itself seen, increasingly, in ways influenced by the stories and the sense of life they expressed. Aristotle, Plato, Spinoza, Kant—these were still unknown to me. Dickens, Jane Austen, Aristophanes, Ben Jonson, Euripides, Shakespeare, Dostoyevsky—there were my friends, my spheres of reflection.

In several projects of early adolescence I find (rereading them with a sense more of continuity than of rupture) some germs of later preoccupations. I find a paper about Aristophanes, discussing the ways in which ancient comedy presents social and ethical issues and inspires recognition in the audience. I find a paper on Ben Jonson, and the depiction of character and motive in the "comedy of humors." I find, somewhat later, a long play about the life of Robespierre, focusing on the conflict between his love of general political ideals and his attachments to particular human beings. The plot concerns his decision to send Camille Desmoulins and his wife, both loved friends, to death for the sake of the revolution. For Robespierre's asceticism and incorruptible idealism there is profound sympathy, and love, even as there is also horror at his ability to lose the vision of the particular and, losing that, to do terrible things. The questions of "Perception and Revolution" are there already—preparing me, no doubt, for a certain ambivalence toward the revolutionary movements that I soon after encountered. Finally, there is a long paper about Dostoyevsky and the whole question of whether the best way to live was one that seeks to transcend one's finite humanity; here, once again, I see some of the very problems and even distinctions that I still investigate.

As for Proust, my French literature courses meticulously surveyed the centuries, one each year, arriving by twelfth grade at the nineteenth; and he remained unknown to me. And Henry James. I read *The Portrait of a Lady* too early, with only moderate enthusiasm. *The Golden Bowl,* lent to me by a teacher, lay on my desk for two years, with its cover of white, black, and gold, the evidently cracked

14. If this alerts the reader to the possibility that a particular, not altogether immersed sense of life may have a role to play in writing these essays, this will begin to open up a central question of several of the essays themselves: In asking us to identify with and recognize ourselves in the sense of life expressed in his or her writings, where are authors of various kinds leading their readers, and how disposing them to various forms of human love? (See "Perceptive Equilibrium," "'Finely Aware,'" "Steerforth's Arm," in this volume.)

bowl, silent, feared, holding in its curve the apples of the Garden. I returned it, unread, at graduation.

What I find worth emphasizing about this time is, first of all, the obsessive quality of my focus, then as now, on certain questions and problems, which seemed simply to have arrived, and concerning which I seem hardly ever to have been able, from then on, not to think. And, second, the fact that by far the most natural and also fruitful way to pursue them seemed to me to be, then as now, to turn to works of literature. I was pursuing questions usually called philosophical; there is little doubt of that. And each of these early essays contains a fair amount of general analysis and discussion. But it seemed to me best to discuss the issues in connection with a text that displayed concrete lives and told a story; and to discuss them in ways that responded to these literary features. In part, this can be attributed to the absence of alternative texts; in part to the ambitions of the teachers at my exigent and feminist girls' school, who were powerful intellects somewhat confined and constrained in their high school role, and who sought to break through the boundaries of what was then taken to be a literary education suited for young women.

In college, already loving ancient Greek literature, I learned Greek. And, while beginning the study of the admitted philosophers (especially Plato and Aristotle), I focused above all on Greek epic and Greek drama, where I found problems that profoundly moved me. I learned to look closely at words and images; at metrical structures; at narration and organization; at intertextual reference. And I always wished to ask, What does all this mean for human life? What possibilities does this recognize or deny? Here again, as in my earlier studies, this questioning was encouraged, both as an appropriate way of approaching a literary text and as an appropriate place to pursue one's philosophical concerns and perplexities.

In graduate school, however, the situation was different. I encountered, in my effort to pursue this complex philosophical/literary interest, a threefold resistance: from the conceptions of philosophy and moral philosophy then dominant in the Anglo-American tradition; from the dominant conception of what ancient Greek philosophy included and what methods its study ought to use; and, finally, from the dominant conception of literary study, both within Classics and outside it. This was at Harvard in 1969; but these problems were in fact typical of their time, and by no means unique to Harvard.

To begin with the literary resistance, which I encountered soonest: ancient literary works were then being studied with an eye on philological and to some extent aesthetic issues, but not with an emphasis on their connections with the ethical thought of the philosophers, or, indeed, as sources of ethical reflection of any kind. Indeed, the ethical works of the philosophers did not figure as an essential part of graduate study in the Classics at all. On the reading list, of Aristotle, was only the *Poetics,* which was assumed to be a work that one could profitably study without any acquaintance with other Aristotelian works; of Plato, only those works, for example *Symposium* and *Phaedrus,* which were seen as having importance for the history of literary style, and which were deemed not to be *philosophical* works in any case. (Most philosophers agreed with this.) In the broader world of literary study to which Classics was occasionally linked, aesthetic issues were understood (following, on the whole, standards set by New Critical formalism) to be more or less divorced from ethical and practical issues. One rarely found anything but contempt for ethical criticism of literature.[15]

On the side of philosophy, there was resistance too. Here Harvard was more pluralistic than most major philosophy departments, especially since Stanley Cavell was already teaching there and beginning to publish some of his remarkable work bridging literature and philosophy. But most of Cavell's work on literature was produced after that time; and at that time his work (largely concerned with Wittgenstein) did not address itself explicitly to questions in moral philosophy, or influence the way in which moral philosophy was taught and written by others.[16] For these reasons I remained for some years more or less ignorant of Cavell's work, and focused on the dominant positions in ethics. By this time, the positivist/metaethical movement in ethics that had for a long time discouraged the philosophical study of substantive ethical theories and practical ethical issues, confining ethics to the analysis of ethical language, was dying. Already, the revival of interest in normative ethics that has by now generated so much excellent work was beginning, led by John Rawls.[17] But the leading approaches to ethical theory in that revival were Kantianism and Utilitarianism—both positions that were, for good internal reasons, hostile to literature. These two approaches were taken to divide the field more or less exhaustively.

In the study of ancient philosophy the situation was even less hospitable to a philosophical study of works of literature. My supervisor, the wonderful scholar G.E.L. Owen,[18] had no veneration for conventional ways of proceeding in scholarship. To the study of ancient dialectic, logic, science, and metaphysics, he brought precise and deep historical learning and an iconoclastic temperament. Frequently, he overturned cherished distinctions and methods, to the end of constructing an account of the ancient thinkers both historically richer and philosophically deeper than those currently on the scene. But Owen had little interest in ethical problems; or, if any, only in issues about the logic of ethical language. This being the case, he never asked whether the conventional way of writing the history of Greek ethics was in fact fruitful and correct.

That way, familiar by now to many generations of students, was to begin Greek ethics with Democritus—perhaps with a backward glance to Heraclitus and

15. Somewhat after this time, Gregory Nagy (who was at that time working on Indo-European linguistics and metrics) began to produce, at Harvard, his now well-known work on connections between traditional genres and views of the hero: see *The Best of the Achaians* (Baltimore, 1979).

16. Cavell's earliest work in this area is collected in *Must We Mean What We Say?* (above, n. 11); for later work, see especially, *The Claim of Reason: Wittgenstein, Skepticism, Morality, and Tragedy* (New York, 1979) and *Disowning Knowledge in Six Plays of Shakespeare* (Cambridge, Eng., 1987).

17. John Rawls, *A Theory of Justice* (Cambridge, Mass., 1971); Rawls's views are futher discussed in "Perceptive Equilibrium." On Rawls's, and my, use of the term "moral philosophy," see "Perceptive Equilibrium," n. 2. Rawls's influence has been enormous; but in fairness it should also be said that some philosophers of the immediately preceding period whose work focused on the analysis of ethical language were also concerned with substantive ethical questions: in particular, this is true of the work or R. M. Hare (*The Language of Morals* [Oxford, 1952]; *Freedom and Reason* [Oxford, 1963]; *Moral Thinking* [Oxford, 1981]).

18. See G.E.L. Owen, *Logic, Science, and Dialectic: Collected Papers in Greek Philosophy* (London and Ithaca, N.Y., 1986).

Empedocles—and to proceed onward with Socrates and the sophists; to focus most of one's attention on Plato and Aristotle; and to end with barely a nod to the Hellenistic philosophers. The ethical contribution of literary works was not taken to be a part of Greek ethical thought as such—but, at most, a part of the background of "popular thought" against which the great thinkers worked. "Popular thought" was taken to be a very different subject from philosophical ethics; and even this subject did not, it was thought, require the close study of literary forms or of whole literary works.[19] An interest in whole works of literature was therefore assumed to be a "literary" interest—by which was meant an aesthetic interest and not a philosophical interest. Aristotle, then, was inside philosophical training and Sophocles outside. As for Plato, he was split conveniently into two figures or sets of issues, to be studied in two different departments with different supervisors, whose own intellectual communication was typically slight. Some entire works (e.g. *Symposium*)[20] were, as I say, taken to be literary rather than philosophical; the others were taken to contain both excerptible arguments and literary decoration; it was thought that these two elements could, and should, be studied apart from one another, and by different people.[21]

But by this time I was already too set in my ways not to find this situation puzzling and disturbing. My interest in certain philosophical questions did not diminish; and I still found that the questions led me as much to works of literature as to works of admitted philosophy. And in a sense more so. For I was finding in the Greek tragic poets a recognition of the ethical importance of contingency, a deep sense of the problem of conflicting obligations, and a recognition of the ethical significance of the passions, that I found more rarely, if at all, in the thought of the admitted philosophers, whether ancient or modern. And I began, as I read more and more often the styles of the philosophers, to have a sense that there were deep connections between the forms and structures characteristic of tragic poetry and its ability to show what it lucidly did show.

Therefore, when I was advised to pursue the project of studying ethical conflict in Aeschylus by finding as my supervisor a literary expert in the Classics Department, I felt both assent and dissent. Dissent, because I was convinced that these were philosophical questions, whatever that meant; at any rate, some of the very

19. See, for example, the approach to the study of "popular morality" exemplified in A.W.H. Adkins, *Merit and Responsibility* (Oxford, 1960). K. J. Dover's *Greek Popular Morality* (Oxford, 1974) is a methodologically far more adequate work, and its argument does not in any way rule out the possibility that literary works might have something to contribute to ethics studies as wholes and in their own right. But it is not that project that the book attempts.

20. K. J. Dover's edition of the *Symposium* (Cambridge, 1980) has on the back jacket a blurb reading: "Plato's *Symposium* is the most literary of all his works and one which all students of classics are likely to want to read whether or not they are studying Plato's philosophy." No matter who wrote this text, it is typical of approaches to that dialogue in the period I describe and, in fact, is consistent with the approach adopted by Dover himself.

21. See my discussion of these trends in Plato scholarship in a review of a group of new books on Plato in *The Times Literary Supplement,* June 1987; see also *Fragility* chaps. 6–7, Interlude 1. For examples of stimulating recent attempts to undo these separations, see Charles Kahn, "Drama and Dialectic in Plato's *Gorgias*," *Oxford Studies in Ancient Philosophy* 1 (1983) 75–121; C. Griswold, *Self-Knowledge in Plato's Phaedrus* (New Haven, Conn., 1986); G. Ferrari, *Listening to the Cicadas* (Cambridge, 1987).

same questions the philosophers were discussing, if not the same answers. It therefore seemed to make sense to pursue them right there, in conversation with the philosophers, and not off in some other department—all the more since the prevailing methods and aims in literary study made literary experts not very interested in such questions. Dissent, as well, because I loved philosophy in all of its forms, and sensed that the questions would be more clearly focused, even where literature was concerned, if they were studied in a dialogue with other philosophical thought. Assent, however, because I did perceive that any good study of these questions in tragedy would have to treat the poets not simply as people who might have written a treatise but didn't, nor yet simply as repositories of "popular thought," but as thinker-poets whose meanings and whose formal choices were closely linked. To that end, a close study of literary language and form was going to be essential.

But even more important than my own ambivalence about these disciplinary separations was the fact that by now my study of the Greeks was showing me that most of them would have found the separations unnatural and unilluminating. For the Greeks of the fifth and early fourth centuries B.C., there were not two separate sets of questions in the area of human choice and action, aesthetic questions and moral-philosophical questions, to be studied and written about by mutually detached colleagues in different departments.[22] Instead, dramatic poetry and what we now call philosophical inquiry in ethics were both typically framed by, seen as ways of pursuing, a single and general question: namely, how human beings should live. To this question both poets such as Sophocles and Euripides and thinkers such as Democritus and Plato were seen as providing answers; frequently the answers of poets and non-poets were incompatible. The "ancient quarrel between the poets and the philosophers," as Plato's *Republic* (using the word "philosopher" in Plato's own way) calls it, could be called a quarrel only because it was about a single subject. The subject was human life and how to live it. And the quarrel was a quarrel about literary form as well as about ethical content, about literary forms understood as committed to certain ethical priorities, certain choices and evaluations, rather than others. Forms of writing were not seen as vessels into which different contents could be indifferently poured; form was itself a statement, a content.

Before Plato came on the scene the poets (especially the tragic poets) were understood by most Athenians to be the central ethical teachers and thinkers of Greece, the people to whom, above all, the city turned, and rightly turned, with its questions about how to live. To attend a tragic drama was not to go to a distraction or a fantasy, in the course of which one suspended one's anxious practical questions. It was, instead, to engage in a communal process of inquiry, reflection, and feeling with respect to important civic and personal ends. The very structure of theatrical performance strongly implied this. When we go to the theater, we usually sit in a darkened auditorium, in the illusion of splendid isolation, while the dramatic action—separated from the spectator by the box of the proscenium arch—is bathed in artificial light as if it were a separate world of fantasy and mystery. The ancient Greek spectator, by contrast, sitting in the common daylight,

---

22. For a more extensive treatment of this issue, see *Fragility,* Interlude 1.

saw across the staged action the faces of fellow citizens on the other side of the
orchestra. And the whole event took place during a solemn civic/religious festival,
whose trappings made spectators conscious that the values of the community were
being examined and communicated.[23] To respond to these events was to acknowledge and participate in a way of life—and a way of life, we should add, that prominently included reflection and public debate about ethical and civic matters.[24] To
respond well to a tragic performance involved both feeling and critical reflection;
and these were closely linked with one another. The idea that art existed only for
art's sake, and that literature should be approached with a detached aesthetic attitude, pure of practical interest, was an idea unknown in the Greek world, at least
until the Hellenistic age.[25] Art was thought to be practical, aesthetic interest a practical interest—an interest in the good life and in communal self-understanding.
To respond in a certain way was to move already toward this greater
understanding.

As for the study of ethical matters by the people whom we now call philosophers, this too was taken to be a practical and not just a theoretical enterprise. It
was seen as tragedy was seen: as something that had as its goal the good human
life for its audience. From Socrates and Plato straight through to the Hellenistic
schools, there was deep agreement that the point of philosophical inquiry and discourse in the area of ethics was to improve, in some manner, the pupil's soul, to
move the pupil closer to the leading of the good life.[26] This goal was taken to
require a good deal of reflection and understanding; so producing understanding
was itself an important part of the practical project. The philosophers were forced,
then, to ask, and did ask, how *does* the pupil's soul seek and attain ethical understanding? What elements does it have that promote and impede understanding
and good ethical development? What state is the soul in when it recognizes a
truth? And what is the content of the most important evaluative truths it will
learn? Having arrived at some (at least provisional) conclusions about these matters, they would then go on to construct discourses whose form would suit the
ethical task, enlivening those elements in the souls of the pupils that seemed to be
the best sources of progress, forming the pupils' desires in accordance with a correct conception of what matters, confronting them with an accurate picture of
what has importance.

Both the ethical philosophers and the tragic poets, then, understood themselves
to be engaging in forms of educational and communicative activity, in what the
Greeks called *psuchagōgia* (leading of the soul),[27] in which methodological and

23. See *Fragility,* chaps. 2, 3, 13, and Interludes 1 and 2. On the tragic festivals and their social
function, see John J. Winkler, "The Ephebes' Song," *Representations* 11 (1985) 26–62.

24. On the connection between Athenian fondness for public critical debate and the development of rational argument, see G.E.R. Lloyd, *Magic, Reason, and Experience* (Cambridge,
Eng., 1981).

25. See Nussbaum, "Historical Conceptions of the Humanities and Their Relationship to
Society," in *Applying the Humanities,* ed. D. Callahan et al. (New York, 1985), 3–28.

26. See Nussbaum, "Therapeutic Arguments: Epicurus and Aristotle," in *The Norms of
Nature,* ed. M. Schofield and G. Striker (Cambridge, Eng., 1986), 31–74.

27. On this idea, see my "Therapeutic Arguments," and also *The Therapy of Desire* (Martin
Classical Lectures, 1986), forthcoming. See also P. Rabbow, *Seelenführung* (Munich, 1954); I.
Hadot, *Seneca und die griechisch-römische Tradition der Seelenleitung* (Berlin, 1969).

formal choices on the part of the teacher or writer were bound to be very important for the eventual result: not just because of their instrumental role in communication, but also because of the values and judgments they themselves expressed and their role in the adequate stating of a view. An ethical discourse addressed to the soul expresses certain ethical preferences and priorities in its very structure; it represents human life as being this way or that; it shows, well done, the shape of a human soul. Are those representations truthful and illuminating? Is that the soul we want our pupils to confront as their teacher? That was the question that generated the ancient quarrel.

In Plato's attack upon the poets we find a profound insight: that all of the ways of writing that were characteristic of tragic (and much of epic) poetry are committed to a certain, albeit very general, view of human life, a view from which one might dissent.[28] Tragedies state this view in the very way they construct their plots, engage the attention of their audience, use rhythm and music and language. The elements of this view include at least the following: that happenings beyond the agent's control are of real importance not only for his or her feelings of happiness or contentment, but also for whether he or she manages to live a fully good life, a life inclusive of various forms of laudable action. That, therefore, what happens to people by chance can be of enormous importance to the ethical quality of their lives; that, therefore, good people are right to care deeply about such chance events. That, for these same reasons, an audience's pity and fear at tragic events are valuable responses, responses for which there is an important place in the ethical life, since they embody a recognition of ethical truths. That other emotions as well are appropriate, and based upon correct beliefs about what matters. That, for example, it is right to love certain things and people that lie beyond one's own control, and to grieve when these people die, when these things are removed. The tragic genre depends on such beliefs for its very structure and literary shape: for its habit is to tell stories of reversals happening to good but not invulnerable people, and to tell these stories as if they matter for all human beings. And the form sets up in its audience responses, particularly those of pity for the characters and fear for oneself, that presuppose a similar set of beliefs. It feeds the tendency of the spectator to identify with a hero who weeps uncontrollably over the body of a loved one, or goes mad with rage, or is terrified by the force of an insoluble dilemma.

But one may or may not accept these beliefs, this view of life. If one believes, with Socrates, that the good person cannot be harmed,[29] that the only thing of real importance is one's own virtue, then one will not think that stories of reversal have deep ethical significance, and one will not want to write as if they did, or to show as worthy heroes people who believe that they do. Like Plato's *Republic,* we will omit the tears of Achilles at Patroclus' death, if we wish to teach that the good person is self-sufficient.[30] Nor will we want works around that make their connection with the audience through the emotions—since all of them seem to rest on

28. See *Fragility,* Interludes 1 and 2.
29. *Apology* 41 CD; Socrates claims knowledge of this, although in general he denies that he has any knowledge.
30. *Republic* 387–88.

the belief (a false belief, from this point of view) that such external happenings do have significance. In short, one's beliefs about the ethical truth shape one's view of literary forms, seen as ethical statements.

It seemed to me then, as it does now, that this ancient debate approached these issues at the right level of depth, asking the right questions about the relationship between forms of discourse and views of life. By contrast, it seemed to me that the contemporary Anglo-American treatment of the elements in this quarrel—which compartmentalized the forms of discourse in such a way that there seemed to *be* no debate and no quarrel—prevented these important questions from being properly raised and discussed. It seemed to me important to begin to recover for the study of ancient Greek philosophy an account of these questions about luck, and of their implications for philosophical form. I began to pursue that task. One portion of this project became *The Fragility of Goodness;* I am currently working on the Hellenistic continuation of that ethical debate.

In this work a central role has been played by Aristotle, the nonliterary philosopher whom I most love, and who creates both illumination and a puzzle at the center of this project.[31] For Aristotle defends the claim of tragedy to tell the truth; and his own ethical view, as I have argued, is close to views that can be found in the tragedies. And yet Aristotle does not write tragedies. He writes philosophical and explanatory commentaries that are concrete, close to ordinary language, intuitive, but, still, not literary in their style. This led me to wonder whether there was not a form of philosophical writing that was both different from the expressive literary forms and also, at the same time, their natural ally—explanatory rather than itself expressive, and yet at the same time committed to the concrete, directing us to attend to the particulars rather than itself showing them in their bewildering multiplicity. I have tried to exemplify such a form here (see pp. 48–49).

But my interest in the ancient debate was motivated by an interest in philosophical problems whose force I felt, and feel, in life. I therefore began, while pursuing these historical issues, to look for ways of continuing the ancient debate in the contemporary philosophical context. The ancient debate had helped me to articulate much that I had sensed long before about the novels of Dickens and Dostoyevsky, what I was at that very time discovering in Henry James and in Proust. And through the pursuit of these connections a continuation of the debate began to take shape, one that would bring the lucid bewilderment and the emotional precision of these writers into conversation with the very different styles and forms that were and are most common in the philosophical pursuit of the very questions with which the novels are also occupied. I finished reading *The Golden Bowl* in a small flat in London's Lincoln's Inn on Christmas Day of 1975, alone. And the pity and dread of the indelible final lines became, from then on, interwoven with, and expressive of, my reflection about tragedy and its effect, about chance, conflict, and loss in the personal life.

At this time I began to teach philosophy. And turning to the contemporary philosophical scene with these concerns about form and style, I still discovered

---

31. See *Fragility,* chaps. 8–12; on Aristotle's style, Interlude 2. See also my "Aristotle," in *Ancient Writers,* ed. T. J. Luce (New York, 1982), 377–416.

little there that addressed them. The ethical debate was becoming more complex; interesting criticisms of both Kantianism and Utilitarianism were beginning to be heard—sometimes with appeal to ancient Greek questions and debates. But so far as the *form* of ethical writing was concerned, there had been little further work. One could still observe, in the literary choices made, an odd mixture of antitragic depth with unreflective conventionality. That is, on the one hand, one saw in certain then influential moral philosophers of the past—in Kant, Bentham, and Spinoza, for example, and also in the most perceptive of their contemporary followers—a concern with the suitability of form to content, combined with an ethical view that could never find its fitting expression in novels or tragic dramas: the acceptance, that is, of my first claim, combined with a rejection of the second. One can see in the stylistic choices of such figures issues closely related to the ancient issues.[32]

On the other hand, however, most disciples and descendants of these philosophers on the contemporary scene did not (and still do not) give the impression of having chosen their styles with these philosophical questions about style in view. Nor did the opponents of these ethical positions, who might seem to have a special reason for reflecting on these matters. Whether Kant's views about inclination were being defended or attacked, whether the emotions were being praised or blamed, the conventional style of Anglo-American philosophical prose usually prevailed: a style correct, scientific, abstract, hygienically pallid, a style that seemed to be regarded as a kind of all-purpose solvent in which philosophical issues of any kind at all could be efficiently disentangled, any and all conclusions neatly disengaged. That there might be other ways of being precise, other conceptions of lucidity and completeness that might be held to be more appropriate for ethical thought—this was, on the whole, neither asserted nor even denied.

This situation resulted in part from the long predominance of ethical views that really did underwrite the conventional style—so that it had by then become second nature, as though it was *the* style for ethics. It owed much, as well—and one can hardly overestimate this—to the long-standing fascination of Western philosophers with the methods and the style of natural science, which have at many times in history seemed to embody the only sort of rigor and precision worth cultivating, the only norm of rationality worth emulating, even in the ethical sphere. That issue is as old as the debate between Plato and Aristotle over the nature of ethical knowledge. And it is certainly possible to make a substantial argument that the true nature of the ethical domain is such that it can best be conveyed in the style we usually associate with mathematics or natural science. This has been done, for example, by Spinoza, with great philosophical power; in a different way it has been done by the best of Utilitarian thought.

But there is a mistake made, or at least a carelessness, when one takes a method and style that have proven fruitful for the investigation and description of certain truths—say those of natural science—and applies them without further reflection

32. This is no mere coincidence, since most of these figures were close readers of the ancient Greek philosophers. The influence of the Stoics and their theory of emotion is especially pervasive.

or argument to a very different sphere of human life that may have a different geography and demand a different sort of precision, a different norm of rationality. Most of the moral philosophy I encountered lacked these further reflections and arguments. And frequently stylistic choices appeared to be dictated not by any substantial conception at all, not even by the model of science, but by habit and the pressure of convention: by Anglo-American fastidiousness and emotional reticence, and above all by the academicization and professionalization of philosophy, which leads everyone to write like everyone else, in order to be respectable and to be published in the usual journals. Most professional philosophers did not, I found, share the ancient conception of philosophy as discourse addressed to nonexpert readers of many kinds who would bring to the text their urgent concerns, questions, needs, and whose souls might in that interaction be changed. Having lost that conception they had lost, too, the sense of the philosophical text as an expressive creation whose form should be part and parcel of its conception, revealing in the shape of the sentences the lineaments of a human personality with a particular sense of life. As Cora Diamond writes, with wonderful clarity: "the pleasure of reading what has been written under the pressure of content shaping form, form illuminating content, has to do with one's sense of the soul of the author in the text, and . . . such pleasure, and such a sense of the soul of the author, is precisely what is irrelevant or out of place in the writing of professionals for professionals."[33]

So thoroughly were these issues lost from view that one found—and found

---

33. Cora Diamond, letter, August 30, 1988. See also the witty discussion of this question in Michael Tanner, "The Language of Philosophy," in *The State of Language,* ed. Leonard Michaels and Christopher Ricks (Berkeley, 1980), 458–66. Tanner's paper begins with a commentary on the following passage of philosophical prose for professionals, taken from an article entitled "A Conceptual Investigation of Love":

Having defined the field of investigation, we can now sketch the concepts analytically presupposed in our use of 'love'. An idea of these concepts can be gained by sketching a sequence of relations, the members of which we take as relevant in deciding whether or not some relationship between persons A and B is one of love. These are not relevant in the sense of being evidence for some further relation 'love' but as being, in part at least the material of which love consists. The sequence would include at least the following:

   (1) A knows B (or at least knows something of B)
   (2) A cares (is concerned) about B
       A likes B
   (3) A respects B
       A is attracted to B
       A feels affection for B
   (4) A is committed to B
       A wishes to see B's welfare promoted

The connection between these relations which we will call 'love-comprising relations' or 'LCRs' is not, except for 'knowing about' and possibly 'Feels affection for' as tight as strict entailment. (W. Newton-Smith, in *Philosophy and Personal Relations,* ed. Alan Montefiore (London, 1973), 188–19. One should point out that the author is actually an outstanding specialist in the philosophy of space and time, where this style would seem to be more at home.)

This passage should illustrate, for readers unfamiliar with professional philosophical prose, what I am talking about in this section. Tanner admirably concludes, "What is needed is a recognition that there are other modes of rigor and precision than quasi-formal ones, and ways of being profound that do not require near-unintelligibility."

increasingly as criticism of Kantianism and Utilitarianism mounted—writings in which there appeared to be the peculiar sort of self-contradiction between form and thesis that I have already mentioned. An article, for example, argues that the emotions are essential and central in our efforts to gain understanding on any important ethical matter; and yet it is written in a style that expresses only intellectual activity and strongly suggests that only this activity matters for the reader in his or her attempts to understand. There might have been some interesting reason for writing this way; but usually, in cases of this kind, the whole issue had just not arisen. Such articles were written as they were because that was the way philosophy was being written, and sometimes because an emotive or literary style would have evoked criticism, or even ridicule. Sometimes, too, because philosophers are not trained to write that way, and did not wish to admit that they might lack a relevant piece of equipment. In fact, it was clear that one could not regain for our community the ancient questions concerning style without both training oneself in professionally irrelevant ways and risking ridicule—although there were already courageous pioneers, especially Stanley Cavell, who took the risk.

The side of literature was not, even at this later time, any more hospitable. For, once again, there was change; but again, the views that were then reigning—as the New Criticism waned and Deconstruction took over—continued to be largely hostile to the idea of bringing a broad range of human concerns into connection with literary analysis. The ancient quarrel was rejected as old-fashioned and uninteresting, along with the work of some modern writers, such as F. R. Leavis and Lionel Trilling,[34] who had tried to continue it. It was assumed that any work that attempts to ask of a literary text questions about how we might live, treating the work as addressed to the reader's practical interests and needs, and as being in some sense about our lives, must be hopelessly naive, reactionary, and insensitive to the complexities of literary form and intertextual referentiality.[35]

To be sure, the "ancient quarrel" was sometimes defective in its *exclusive* focus on the practical. It sometimes ignored the fact that literature has tasks and possibilities other than that of illumination about our lives. (We should, however, remember that the ancient concept of the ethical was extremely broad and inclusive, taking in all ways in which texts shape mind and desire, and alter life by their pleasure.) And in many cases, too, the literary discourse of ancient writers could be insufficiently sensitive to the ways in which a literary text as a whole hangs together, both with itself and with other texts, to the play of metaphor and allusion, the self-conscious patterning of language. These same criticisms can sometimes be accurately made against more recent practitioners of ethical criticism. Sometimes they did force the text into a narrow moral straitjacket, neglecting other ways in which it speaks to its reader, neglecting, too, its formal complexities. Too often there were excessively simple theories about "the" moral role of literature, views that concealed many complexities. Nor can there be any doubt that

34. See especially F. R. Leavis, *The Great Tradition* (New York, 1948); L. Trilling, *The Liberal Imagination: Essays on Literature and Society* (New York, 1950).
35. This position is effectively criticized in Arthur Danto, "Philosophy And/As/Of Literature," *Proceedings and Addresses of the American Philosophical Association* 58 (1984), 5–20.

literary work of recent years has done an enormous amount to make readers more precisely and firmly aware of subtleties of literary structure and intertextual reference.

But the failure of what was oversimple in the ancient project, and in some—though certainly not all—of its recent continuations, should not have been taken as the failure of the entire ancient approach, and as an excuse for dismissing its motivating questions.[36] For clearly the ancient approach was not, at its best, insensitive to literary form. Form was, indeed, what it was all about. And it argued plausibly, moreover, that some of the most interesting and urgent questions about literary form itself could not be well pursued unless one asked about the intimate connections between formal structures and the content they express. Ethical criticism of this sort actually demands an exacting formal inquiry.

Nor is the charge that such criticism must inevitably be wooden and moralistic any more plausible, even in light of the ancient situation.[37] For frequently the view of human life expressed in the literary works, dealing, as they so frequently did, with the passionate love of particulars, with grief, pain, and bewilderment, seemed to its critics to be subversive of morality narrowly construed. That was what its defenders legitimately saw as one of its most essential ethical functions. Recent examples of fine ethical interpretation—for example, F. R. Leavis's essay on Dickens's *Hard Times* or Trilling's on *The Princess Casamassima*[38]—show the same point, turning to literature and its forms in order to subvert oversimple moralisms.

Again, far from insisting that all literature must play some single, simple role in human life, the best ethical criticism, ancient and modern, has insisted on the complexity and variety revealed to us in literature, appealing to that complexity to cast doubt on reductive theories.[39] It is, in fact, criticism that focuses exclusively on textual form to the exclusion of human content that appears to be unduly narrow. For it appears to take no account of the urgency of our engagements with works of literature, the intimacy of the relationships we form, the way in which we do, like David Copperfield, read "as if for life," bringing to the text our hopes, fears, and confusions, and allowing the text to impart a certain structure to our hearts.

The project I undertook was, then, to begin to recover, in the domain of the ethical, very broadly and inclusively construed, the sense of the deep connection between content and form that animated the ancient quarrel and that has usually been present in the greatest ethical thinkers, whether they were friends of literature or not and whether or not they wrote in a "literary" way.

36. Wayne Booth argues eloquently for a revival of a broad and flexible ethical criticism in *The Company We Keep* (Berkeley, 1988), criticizing oversimple versions and showing that ethical criticism need not have these defects. See my review in "Reading," this volume. For another defense of ethical criticism, see Martin Price, *Character and Moral Imagination in the Novel* (New Haven, Conn., 1983). Booth's book contains a comprehensive bibliography of ethical criticism.

37. This issue is discussed at length in Booth, with references to modern examples.

38. F. R. Leavis, "*Hard Times:* An Analytic Note," in *The Great Tradition,* 227–48; L. Trilling, "*The Princess Casamassima,*" in *The Liberal Imagination,* 58–92. On these critics, see also "Perceptive Equilibrium," in this volume.

39. This is plainly true of Trilling, Leavis, and Booth.

This is, clearly, not a single inquiry but a complex family of inquiries,[40] even if one considers only questions that are ethical in this broad sense, and not the many others with respect to which the relationship between content and form might profitably be studied. The essays here represent, then, simply a beginning of one small part of this larger inquiry, a beginning rooted in my love for certain novels and in my closely related concern with certain problems: with the role of love and other emotions in the good human life, with the relationship between emotion and ethical knowledge, with deliberation about particulars. No claim about novels in general, far less about literature in general, could possibly emerge from this book. But I believe that these larger questions can best be approached through the detailed study of complex particular cases—all the more since it is the importance of complex particularity that we shall, in these studies, be trying to make clear.

C. The Starting Point: "How Should One Live?"

> It is no chance matter we are discussing, but how one should live.
>
> Plato, *Republic*

> Here, as in all other cases, we must set down the appearances and, first working through the puzzles, in this way go on to show, if possible, the truth of all the deeply held beliefs about these experiences; and, if this is not possible, the truth of the greatest number and the most authoritative.
>
> Aristotle, *Nicomachean Ethics*

The "ancient quarrel" had an exemplary clarity, since the participants shared a view of what the quarrel was about. However much Plato and the poets disagreed, they agreed that the aim of their work was to provide illumination concerning how one should live. Of course they were at odds concerning what the ethical truth was, and also concerning the nature of understanding. But still, there was some roughly single goal, however much in need of further specification, that they did share, some question to which they could be seen as offering competing answers.

One obstacle to any contemporary version of the ancient project is the difficulty of arriving at any account of what we are looking for that will be shared by the various parties. My aim is to establish that certain literary texts (or texts similar to these in certain relevant ways) are indispensable to a philosophical inquiry in the ethical sphere: not by any means sufficient, but sources of insight without

40. For other related philosophical work, see Stanley Cavell (works cited above, n. 15); Richard Wollheim (see n. 10); Bernard Williams, *Problems of the Self* (Cambridge, 1973); *Moral Luck* (Cambridge, 1981), *Ethics and the Limits of Philosophy* (Cambridge, Mass., 1983); Hilary Putnam, *Meaning and the Moral Sciences* (London, 1979); Cora Diamond, "Having a Rough Story About What Moral Philosophy Is," *New Literary History* 15 (1983), 155–70, "Missing the Adventure," abstracted *Journal of Philosophy* 82 (1985), 529ff; Iris Murdoch, *The Sovereignty of Good* (London, 1970); David Wiggins, *Needs, Values, Truth* (Oxford, 1987); Bas van Fraassen, "The Peculiar Effects of Love and Desire," in *Perspectives on Self Deception,* ed. B. McLaughlin and A. Rorty (Berkeley, 1988), 123–56; Peter Jones, *Philosophy and the Novel* (Oxford, 1975).

which the inquiry cannot be complete. But then it is important to have some conception, however general and flexible, of the inquiry inside which I wish to place the novels, the project in which I see them as helping to state a distinctive alternative to Kantian and Utilitarian conceptions. A difficulty here is that some influential accounts of what moral philosophy includes are cast in the terms of one or another of the competing ethical conceptions; thus they will prove unsuitable, if we want to organize a fair comparison among them. For example, if we begin with the Utilitarian's organizing question, "How can one maximize utility?," we accept, already, a certain characterization of what is salient in the subject matter of ethics, of the right or relevant descriptions for practical situations—one that would rule out from the start, as irrelevant, much of what the novels present as highly relevant. Similarly, reliance on a Kantian characterization of the domain of the moral, and of its relation to what happens in the empirical realm, together with reliance on the Kantian's organizing question "What is my moral duty?," would have the effect of artificially cutting off from the inquiry some elements of life that the novels show as important and link to others—all in advance of a sensitive study of the sense of life that the novels themselves have to offer. So we would, it seems, be ill advised to adopt either of these methods and questions as architectonic guides to the pursuit of a comparison among different conceptions, different senses of life—among these the views of life expressed in the novels. It seems that we should see whether we can find an account of the methods, subject matter, and questions of moral philosophy (ethical inquiry) that is more inclusive.

And here, it must be stressed, what we really want is an account of ethical inquiry that will capture what we actually do when we ask ourselves the most pressing ethical questions. For the activity of comparison I describe is a real practical activity, one that we undertake in countless ways when we ask ourselves how to live, what to be; one that we perform together with others, in search of ways of living together in a community, country, or planet. To bring novels into moral philosophy is not—as I understand this proposal—to bring them to some academic discipline which happens to ask ethical questions. It is to bring them into connection with our deepest practical searching, for ourselves and others, the searching in connection with which the influential philosophical conceptions of the ethical were originally developed, the searching we pursue as we compare these conceptions, both with one another and with our active sense of life. Or rather, it is to recognize that the novels are in this search already: to insist on and describe, the connections the novels have already for readers who love them and who read, like David Copperfield, for life.

No starting point is altogether neutral here. No way of pursuing the search, putting the question, fails to contain some hint as to where the answers might lie.[41] Questions set things up one way or another, tell us what to include, what to look for. Any procedure implies some conception or conceptions of how we come to know, which parts of ourselves we can trust. This does not mean that all choices of procedure and starting-point are merely subjective and irrational.[42] It does mean that in order to attain to the rationality that *is* available (as the chimera of

---

41. See the further discussion of this in "Perceptive Equilibrium," this volume; also "Therapeutic Arguments" (see n. 26). And see Diamond, "Having a Rough Story" (see n. 40).

42. See "Therapeutic Arguments" (see n. 26).

total detachment is not) we need to be alert to those aspects of a procedure that might bias it unduly in one direction or another, and to commit ourselves to the serious investigation of alternative positions.

Here both life and the history of philosophy combine to help us. For we do, in life, bring our experience, our active sense of life, to the different conceptions we encounter, working through them, comparing the alternatives they present, with reference to our developing sense of what is important and what we can live with, seeking a fit between experience and conception. And in the history of moral philosophy we also find an account of an inclusive starting point, and an open and dialectical method, that is, in effect, the philosophical description of this real-life activity and how it goes, when done with thoroughness and sensitivity. For the proponents of rival philosophical conceptions in ethics have usually not concluded that their inquiries and results were non-comparable with those of their opponents, or comparable only by a method of comparison that already throws the judgment to one or another side. They have, instead, frequently appealed to the inclusive dialectical method first described by Aristotle, as one that (continuous with the active searching of life) can provide an overarching or framing procedure in which alternative views might be duly compared, with respect for each, as well as for the evolving sense of life to which each is a response. Philosophers as different as Utilitarian Henry Sidgwick and Kantian John Rawls have appealed to Aristotle's conception of philosophical procedure as one that can, in its inclusiveness, be fair to the competing positions.[43] I concur in this judgment and follow this example—insisting, as well, that one of the salient virtues of this method is its continuity with "our actual adventure" as we search for understanding. (It is important to distinguish the Aristotelian procedure and starting point from Aristotle's own ethical conception, which is just one of the conceptions it considers.)

The Aristotelian procedure in ethics begins with a very broad and inclusive question: "How should a human being live?"[44] This question presupposes no specific demarcation of the terrain of human life, and so, *a fortiori,* not its demarcation into separate moral and nonmoral realms. It does not, that is, assume that there is, among the many ends and activities that human beings cherish and pursue, some one domain, the domain of moral value, that is of special importance and dignity, apart from the rest of life. Nor does it assume, as do utility theorists, that there is a more or less unitary something that a good agent can be seen as maximizing in every act of choice. It does not assume the denial of these claims either; it holds them open for inquiry within the procedure—with the result that, so far, we are surveying everything that Aristotle surveys, that we do actually survey: humor alongside justice, grace in addition to courage.

The inquiry (as I describe it more fully in "Perceptive Equilibrium") is both empirical and practical: empirical, in that it is concerned with, takes its "evidence" from, the experience of life; practical, in that its aim is to find a conception by which human beings can live, and live together.

The inquiry proceeds by working through the major alternative positions

43. John Rawls, *A Theory of Justice,* 46–53; Henry Sidgwick, *The Methods of Ethics,* 7th ed. (London, 1907), especially the preface to the sixth edition (republished in the seventh).
44. Bernard Williams presents an effective defense of this starting point in *Ethics and the Limits* (above, n. 40); see also *Fragility,* chap. 1, and "Perceptive Equilibrium," this volume.

(including Aristotle's own, but others as well), holding·them up against one another and also against the participants' beliefs and feelings, their active sense of life. Nothing is held unrevisable in this process, except the very basic logical idea that statement implies negation, that to assert something is to rule out something else. The participants look not for a view that is true by correspondence to some extra-human reality, but for the best overall fit between a view and what is deepest in human lives. They are asked to imagine, at each stage, what they can least live well without, what lies deepest in their lives; and, again, what seems more superficial, more dispensable. They seek for coherence and fit in the web of judgment, feeling, perception, and principle, taken as a whole.[45]

In this enterprise, literary works play a role on two levels.[45] First, they can intervene to make certain that we get a sufficiently rich and inclusive conception of the opening question and of the dialectical procedure that pursues it—inclusive enough to hold all that our sense of life urges us to consider. "Perceptive Equilibrium" discusses this question, showing how John Rawls's conception of the Aristotelian procedure might be enlarged by consideration of our literary experience.[46] And the style of this Introduction illustrates the inclusiveness of the Aristotelian approach.

But according to the terms of the ancient quarrel the very choice to write a tragic drama—or, we can now say, a novel—expresses already certain evaluative commitments. Among these seem to be commitments to the ethical significance of uncontrolled events, to the epistemological value of emotion, to the variety and non-commensurability of the important things. Literary works (and from now on [see §F] we shall focus on certain novels) are not neutral instruments for the investigation of all conceptions. Built into the very structure of a novel is a certain conception of what matters. In the novelists we study here, when we do find a Kantian character, or some other exponent of an ethical position divergent from the one that animates the narrative taken as a whole (James's Mrs. Newsome, Dickens's Agnes and Mr. Gradgrind[47]), those characters are not likely to fare well with the reader. And we are made aware that if the events in which we, as readers, participate had been described to us by those characters, they would not have had the literary form they now do, and would not have constituted a novel at all. A different sense of salience would have dictated a different form. In short, by consenting to see the events in the novel's world as the novel presents them, we are, as readers, already breaking ethically with Gradgrind, Mrs. Newsome, and Agnes.

My second interest in the novels, then, is an interest in this link between a distinctive conception of life (or a family of conceptions) and the structures of these novels. I shall argue, in fact, that there is a distinctive ethical conception (which I shall call the Aristotelian conception) that requires, for its adequate and complete investigation and statement, forms and structures such as those that we find in these novels. Thus if the enterprise of moral philosophy is understood as we have

45. A third function for literature in this inquiry is described in the Notes to "Plato on Commensurability," this volume.

46. See also H. Richardson, "The Emotions of Reflective Equilibrium," forthcoming.

47. On Mrs. Newsome, see "Perceptive Equilibrium"; on Agnes, "Steerforth's Arm," on Mr. Gradgrind "Discernment," this volume.

understood it, as a pursuit of truth in all its forms, requiring a deep and sympathetic investigation of all major ethical alternatives and the comparison of each with our active sense of life, then moral philosophy requires such literary texts, and the experience of loving and attentive novel-reading, for its own completion. This involves, clearly, an expansion and reconstruction of what moral philosophy has for a long time been taken to be and to include.

Nothing could be further from my intentions than to suggest that we *substitute* the study of novels for the study of the recognized great works of the various philosophical traditions in ethics. Although this may disappoint some who find moderate positions boring, I have no interest in dismissive assaults on systematic ethical theory, or on "Western rationality," or even on Kantianism or Utilitarianism, to which the novels, to be sure, display their own oppositions. I make a proposal that should be acceptable even to Kantians or Utilitarians, if, like Rawls and Sidgwick, they accept the Aristotelian question and the Aristotelian dialectical procedure as good overall guides in ethics, and are thereby methodologically committed to the sympathetic study of alternative conceptions. The proposal is that we should *add* the study of certain novels to the study of these works, on the grounds that without them we will not have a fully adequate statement of a powerful ethical conception, one that we ought to investigate. It will be clear that I sympathize with this ethical conception and that I present, in alliance with the novels, the beginning of a defense of it. But that's just it, it is the beginning, not the completion. And in the full working out of the inquiry the investigation of alternative views, in their own styles and structures, would play a central role. In fact, work on this larger inquiry will, as "Perceptive Equilibrium" argues, play a role even in the understanding of the novels, since one sees something more deeply and clearly when one understands more clearly that to which it is opposed.

There will be those who will object that no question and no procedure can possibly be fair both to the sense of life we find in a novel of James and to the very different view of, say, Kant's second Critique. And of course we have admitted that the procedure is not empty of content. In fact, the procedures of Aristotelian dialectic and the insights of the Aristotelian ethical view, though importantly distinct, are in many ways continuous with one another, in that the sense of life that leads us to build into the overall procedure an attention to particulars, a respect for the emotions, and a tentative and non-dogmatic attitude to the bewildering multiplicities of life will incline us also to have some sympathy with the Aristotelian conception, which emphasizes these features. But, first of all, the procedure as a whole simply *includes* these features: it does not, yet, tell us how to value them. And it instructs us to consider sympathetically all the significant positions, not only this one. In its inclusiveness and its flexibility, and above all its open-endedness, it can plausibly claim to be a balanced philosophical inquiry into all alternatives, not simply a partisan defense of this one. Furthermore, the procedure did not include these features for arbitrary theoretical reasons: it got them from life, and it included them because our sense of life seemed to include them. So if a procedure that includes what life includes is distant from certain theoretical alternatives, this is, or may be, a sign of narrowness in those theoretical alternatives.

But surely, some will say, any conception of procedure that has any content at all will incorporate a conception of rationality that belongs to one tradition of

thought rather than another, and which cannot therefore contain or sympathetically explore the thoughts of any other tradition. Traditions each embody norms
of procedural rationality that are part and parcel of the substantive conclusions
they support.[48] This is no small worry; but I think that a great deal, here, depends
on what one makes of it, how determined one is or is not to make progress on the
opening question. The Aristotelian procedure tells us to be respectful of difference;
but it also instructs us to look for a consistent and sharable answer to the "how
to live" question, one that will capture what is deepest and most basic, even
though it will, of necessity, to achieve that aim, have to give up certain other
things. To this extent its flexibility is qualified by a deep commitment to getting
somewhere. It is built into the procedure itself that we will not simply stop with
an enumeration of differences and with the verdict that we cannot fairly compare,
cannot rationally decide. It instructs us to do what we can to compare and choose
as best we can, in the knowledge that no comparison is, perhaps, altogether above
somebody's reproach, since we must translate each of the alternatives, in effect,
into our own evolving terms and hold them up against the resources of our own
imaginations, our own admittedly incomplete sense of life. (We must note here
that it is exactly that determination to compare and to arrive at something sharable that motivates both Rawls's and Sidgwick's choice of the Aristotelian procedure.) So why pursue this flawed method, instead of simply concluding that every
ethical tradition is altogether noncomparable with every other, and that there is
no single starting point, no single procedure?

The Aristotelian's answer to this is that this is what we actually do—and what
we must most urgently do more, and do better. We do ask how to live. We do
compare and assess one tradition, one way, one answer against another—though
each one contains norms of procedural rationality—undeterred, in our neediness,
by the messiness of that enterprise. What I propose here is not a merely theoretical
undertaking, but one that is urgently practical, one that we conduct every day,
and must conduct.[49] If we wish to regard the obstacles against fair comparison of
alternatives as insuperable for reasons of methodological purity, we can always do
so; but at enormous practical cost. And our common experiences, our active practical questions, give a unity and focus to the search that it might not seem to have
when we regard it solely on the plane of theory. As Aristotle said, "All people seek,
not the way of their ancestors, but the good."[50] The Aristotelian procedure gives
explicit form to that search and urges its continuation. We want to know how the
different ethical conceptions—including those distant from us in time and place—
do or do not fit with our experience and our wishes. And in a world in which

48. For this challenge, see Alasdair MacIntyre, *Whose Justice? Which Rationality?* (Notre
Dame, 1988); I discuss MacIntyre's argument in a review article in *The New York Review of
Books,* (December 7, 1989).

49. See also Nussbaum, "Non-Relative Virtues: an Aristotelian Approach," *Midwest Studies
in Philosophy* 13 (1988), 32–53; "Aristotle on Human Nature and the Foundations of Ethics,"
in a volume on the philosophical work of Bernard Williams, ed. J. Altham and R. Harrison,
Cambridge University Press, forthcoming, 1991. For one sketch of the political outcome of such
an inquiry, see Nussbaum, "Aristotelian Social Democracy," in *Liberalism and the Good,* ed. H.
Richardson and G. Mara (New York, 1990).

50. Aristotle, *Politics,* 1268a 39ff, discussed in "Non-Relative Virtues" (above, n. 49).

practical discourse is and must be increasingly international, we need to do this all the more urgently, as flexibly and attentively as we can, no matter how hard it is to do this well. As Charlotte Stant says to the Prince (before embarking on a project that is messy, urgent, and full of love), "What else can we do, what in all the world else?"[51]

But why, a different objector might ask, do I wish to dragoon literature into this practical/philosophical enterprise? And must this enterprise not make too many concessions to the philosophical demand for explanation to be altogether fair to literature? Isn't literature being turned, here, into a chapter in a textbook on ethics, and thus flattened and reduced? To this, the reply must first of all be that literature is there in the practical search already; and that it is not ordinary readers, but theorists, who have sometimes felt that the pressure of a practical question would, rather like a sweaty hand on an exquisite leather binding, sully the text's purity of finish.[52] Our actual relation to the books we love is already messy, complex, erotic. We do "read for life," bringing to the literary texts we love (as to texts admittedly philosophical) our pressing questions and perplexities, searching for images of what we might do and be, and holding these up against the images we derive from our knowledge of other conceptions, literary, philosophical, and religious. And the further pursuit of this enterprise through explicit comparison and explanation is not a diminution of the novels at all, but rather an expression of the depth and breadth of the claims that those who love them make for them. Depth, because the Aristotelian practical procedure shows with what they are to be compared, to what they are taken to be the rivals: namely, to the best and deepest of the other philosophical conceptions. Breadth, because the result of the dialectical enterprise should be to convince not only people of an already Jamesian sensibility, but all people interested in serious ethical reflection and in fair scrutiny of alternatives, that works like these contain something that cannot be fully stated otherwise and should not be omitted.

Nor, we must insist again, does this dialectical approach to works of literature convert them from what they are into systematic treatises, ignoring in the process their formal features and their mysterious, various, and complex content. It is, in fact, just this that we wish to preserve and to bring into philosophy—which means, for us, just the pursuit of truth, and which therefore must become various and mysterious and unsystematic if, and insofar as, the truth is so. The very qualities that make the novels so unlike dogmatic abstract treatises are, for us, the source of their *philosophical* interest.

51. James, *The Golden Bowl*, III, 5.
52. It is striking that in the last few years literary theorists allied with deconstruction have taken a marked turn toward the ethical. Jacques Derrida, for example, chose to address the American Philosophical Association on the topic of Aristotle's theory of friendship (*Journal of Philosophy* 85 (1988), 632–44); Barbara Johnson's *A World of Difference* (Baltimore, 1987) argues that Deconstruction can make valuable ethical and social contributions; and in general there seems to be a return to the ethical and practical—if not, perhaps, to the rigorous engagement with ethical thought characteristic of the best work in moral philosophy, whether "philosophical" or "literary." No doubt a part of this change can be traced to the scandal over the political career of Paul de Man, which has made theorists anxious to demonstrate that Deconstruction does not imply a neglect of ethical and social considerations.

D. Form as Content: Diagnostic Questions

> The exposition of the letter is nothing other than the development of
> the form.
>
> Dante, Letter to Can Grande

The Aristotelian procedure tells us a good deal about what we are searching for
and how, in general, the search might go. But so far it has told us little about how
to inquire into the whole question of literary form and form's expression of content: what questions we might ask to delve more deeply into that question, what
categories we might recognize in organizing the comparison between the novels
and admitted philosophical texts. Such questions may be asked about any text and
in any area, not only the ethical domain. And to be asked well they must be asked
about the entire form and structure of each text, not only about a brief excerpt.
But in order to have some place to begin ourselves, let us simply listen to several
beginnings—beginnings, all of them, of texts in pursuit of questions having to do
with human life and how to live it. And, listening to the texts and the differences
among them, listening to the shape of the sentences and the tone of the voices, let
us see what questions start to arise, what questions seem as if they will lead us
further toward an understanding of the ways in which content and form shape
one another. I choose, here, only examples of high literary excellence, in which
the fit between content and form seem to me to be particularly well realized and
particularly artful.

TEXT A   DEFINITIONS

1. By that which is self-caused I mean that whose essence involves
existence; or that whose nature can be conceived only as existing.

2. A thing is said to be finite in its own kind when it can be limited
by another thing of the same nature. For example, a body is said to be
finite because we can always conceive of another body greater than it.
So, too, a thought is limited by another thought. But body is not limited by thought, nor thought by body.

3. By substance I mean that which is in itself and is conceived through
itself; that is, that the conception of which does not require the conception of another thing from which it has to be formed.

4. By attribute I mean that which the intellect perceives of substance
as constituting its essence.

5. By mode I mean the affections of substance; that is, that which is
in something else and is conceived through something else.

6. By God I mean an absolutely infinite being; that is, substance consisting of infinite attributes, each of which expresses eternal and infinite essence.

TEXT B   Whether I shall turn out to be the hero of my own life, or whether
that station will be held by anybody else, these pages must show. To

begin my life with the beginning of my life, I record that I was born (as I have been informed and believe) on a Friday, at twelve o'clock at night. It was remarked that the clock began to strike, and I began to cry, simultaneously.

In consideration of the day and hour of my birth, it was declared by the nurse, and by some sage women in the neighbourhood who had taken a lively interest in me several months before there was any possibility of our becoming personally acquainted, first, that I was destined to be unlucky in life, and secondly, that I was privileged to see ghosts and spirits: both these gifts inevitably attaching, as they believed, to all unlucky infants of either gender born towards the small hours on a Friday night.

TEXT C   Strether's first question, when he reached the hotel, was about his friend; yet on his learning that Waymarsh was apparently not to arrive till evening he was not wholly disconcerted. A telegram from him bespeaking a room "only if not noisy," reply paid, was produced for the enquirer at the office, so that the understanding they should meet at Chester rather than at Liverpool remained to that extent sound. The same secret principle, however, that had prompted Strether not absolutely to desire Waymarsh's presence at the dock, that had led him thus to postpone for a few hours his enjoyment of it, now operated to make him feel he could still wait without disappointment. They would dine together at the worst, and, with all respect to dear old Waymarsh—if not even, for that matter, to himself—there was little fear that in the sequel they shouldn't see enough of each other. The principle I have just mentioned as operating had been, with the most newly disembarked of the two men, wholly instinctive—the fruit of a sharp sense that, delightful as it would be to find himself looking, after so much separation, into his comrade's face, his business would be a trifle bungled should he simply arrange for this countenance to present itself to the nearing steamer as the first "note" of Europe. Mixed with everything was the apprehension, already, on Strether's part, that it would, at best, throughout, prove the note of Europe in quite a sufficient degree.

TEXT D   You have implored me, Novatus, to write to you telling you how anger might be allayed. Nor does it seem to me inappropriate that you should have an especially intense fear of this passion, which is of all the passions the most foul and frenzied. For in the others there is some element of peace and calm; this one is altogether violent and headlong, raging with a most inhuman lust for weapons, blood, and punishment, neglecting its own so long as it can harm another, hurling itself on the very point of the sword and thirsty for a revenge that will drag the avenger down with it. For these reasons some of the wisest thinkers have called anger a brief insanity; for it is just that lacking in self-control, forgetful of decency, unmindful of obligations, persistent and undeflected in what it begins, closed to reasoning and advice, stirred up by empty causes, ill suited for apprehending the just and true—altogether like a ruin that crushes those beneath it while it itself is shattered.

As we read on in these works,[53] listening to the prose and following its structures, large and small, we might begin—especially in light of these juxtaposi-
tions—to ask ourselves some, or all, of the following questions.

Who is speaking here (in each case)? What *voice* or voices are addressing us and/
or one another in the text? Here we would ask about the overt characters and
narrators, but also about the whole presence of the author in the text as a whole.
What sorts of human beings are confronting us, and do they, indeed, present
themselves as human at all (rather than, say, as quasi-divine, or detached and
species-less)? What tone do they use, what shape do their sentences have? What
do we learn about their relationship to the other participants in the text, and to
the reader? How do they seem to compare to one another, and to our own sense
of ourselves, in security, knowledge, and power? (Who is it who tells us about
Strether, and what sort of character is that? Who is Novatus, and what sort of
person is addressing him? Who is presenting himself as the author of the life story
we are about to read, and how secure does he seem to be in his knowledge? Where
do those definitions come from, and who is the "I" that speaks them? Is there in
each of the texts, taken as a whole, an implied consciousness distinct from that of
each of the characters and speakers?)

Then, too, we might notice that these voices speak to us, and to one another,
from different places or *points of view,* vis-à-vis their subject matter and vis-à-vis
the reader's own position. And another family of questions would begin to take
shape. Do they (in each case) present themselves, for example, as immersed in the
matter at hand as in a present experience in which they are personally involved?
As reflecting on it from some posture of detachment—either temporal, or emotional, or both? As having no concrete position at all, but as seeing the world
"from nowhere"?[54] (What is the letter writer's practical relation to the anger of
which he speaks? What does the form of David's text show us about his own position vis-à-vis the story of his life? From what position does the "I" of "I have just
mentioned" watch Strether? Is the "I" of the definitions immersed in daily life?)
One and the same voice may occupy, at different times, different points of view
toward the narrated material; so these questions must be followed through the
text. And here, once again, we will also ask about the point(s) of view of the
authorial consciousness, insofar as it animates the text, and also about the point(s)
of view the reader is invited to take up toward the subject matter. (Does Seneca's

53. These passages are Spinoza, *Ethics,* opening section; Dickens, *David Copperfield,* opening
paragraphs; Henry James, *The Ambassadors,* opening; and Seneca, *De Ira (On Anger),* Book I,
opening. The translation of Spinoza is that of Samuel Shirley (Indianapolis, Ind., 1982), that of
Seneca my own. Notice that I have, here, admitted a certain sort of paraphrase, namely, a good
translation, as having, for our purposes, a style similar enough to that of the original to be dis-
cussible in its place. One cannot always do this well, especially with poetic works; and in every
case the questions introduced here should be asked of the translation to see how well it reconstructs the stylistic message of the original. There is an excellent discussion of the style of the
James paragraph in Ian Watt, "The First Paragraph of *The Ambassadors:* An Explication," in
Essays in Criticism 10 (1960), 254–68; a revised version appears in A. E. Stone, Jr., ed., *Twentieth-Century Interpretations of The Ambassadors* (Englewood Cliffs, N.J., 1969), 75–87.

54. This phrase is used by Thomas Nagel to characterize a certain conception of scientific
objectivity and the perspective appropriate to it: see *The View from Nowhere* (Oxford, 1986).

text make the reader experience anger? Does James's text invite the reader to see the world, more or less, through the eyes of Strether? And what point of view exactly is that? Is the point of view of Spinoza's implied reader, or that of the implied author in the text, one from which the world seems to contain interesting stories?)[55]

Asking all this might lead us to ask, as well—concerning the overall speech of the authorial presence, concerning the represented activity of the characters, and concerning the reader's own activity—about the *parts of the personality involved.* What is active, or rendered active, in each case? Intellect alone? Or also emotions, imagination, perception, desire? There may, in principle, be different answers on the different levels we have mentioned. For Seneca's text represents anger, but in a way that seems neither to express anger nor to arouse it in the reader. In fact, the force of the ugly representation is surely to distance the reader from it. On the other hand, the answers frequently are held together through an invitation to identify with the represented experiences—as Strether's curiosity and his complex feeling become the reader's own adventure; as Spinoza's reader embarks, herself, on the intellectual activity represented in the text; as David's love and fear, because we are led to love and to identify with him, become our very own.

Then, too, *what overall shape and organization* does the text seem to have, and what type and degree of control does the author present himself as having over the material? Does he, for example, announce at the outset what he is going to establish and then proceed to do just that? Or does he occupy, instead, a more tentative and uncontrolling relation to the matter at hand, one that holds open the possibility of surprise, bewilderment, and change? Do we know at the outset what the format and overall shape of the text is going to be? And how does it construct itself as it goes, using what methods? Is there a story? An argument?

Then, insofar as the voices that converse with us make assertions, what status seems to be claimed for them, implicitly or explicitly? That they are known to be true? Or simply believed? What is shown to be the basis of the knowledge or belief? Are the truths claimed to hold for all time, or for some period of time? And over the entire universe? Or only the human world? Or just certain societies? And so forth. How far, and in what ways, does the text express perplexity or hesitation?

Then again, does the text give pleasure?[56] If so, what sort of pleasure does its texture afford? What is implied in and through the text about this pleasure, its varieties, its connections with goodness, with action, with knowledge? How does it lead us to feel about our own experiences of delight? David Copperfield's narrative both gives the reader vivid sensory pleasure and (later) comments upon the importance of sensory pleasure in the ethical life. The pleasure of the text seems warm and generous—but also dangerously seductive: we sense that it is in tension with a certain type of moral firmness. Seneca's text offers a more severe and solid satisfaction, with its powerfully crafted rhetoric of condemnation. It is the satis-

---

55. On point of view and related concepts in the analysis of narrative, see the probing discussion of G. Genette, *Narrative Discourse,* trans. J. E. Lewin (Oxford and Ithaca, N.Y., 1980).

56. For illuminating comments on this point, I am indebted to Cora Diamond. On the relationship between the text and patterns of desire, see Peter Brooks *Reading for the Plot* (see n. 4).

faction of self-command; and it comes, we feel, at a cost, since it involves giving up a part of ourselves.[57] Spinoza's text imparts a particularly keen intellectual pleasure, the pleasure of knowing exactly what each thing is and how they are all connected. This pleasure, too, exacts a price: for it asks us to distance ourselves from most of our current relations to objects, to texts, to one another. James's text affords the pleasure of lucidly and subtly confronting our own bewilderment, our love of particulars, our sense of life's adventure. And it too asks us, in its very form, to give up something: the claim to know for sure and in advance what life is all about. In all these cases of form shaping content, we find, then, that the text gives pleasure of an appropriate sort. (Many texts in contemporary moral philosophy, by contrast, give no pleasure at all, of any kind, relevant or irrelevant.)

Each of these texts has a subject or subjects; and its treatment of its subject is marked by certain formal features. We want, then, to know how it speaks about whatever it selects. *Consistency* first: How much concern does the text display for giving a contradiction-free story of whatever its subject might be? If there are apparent contradictions, how are they treated, and what are they taken to show?

Then, *generality:* To what extent is the subject matter characterized in general terms and made the object of general claims? On the other hand, to what extent do particular people, places, and contexts figure in the claims, and how do they figure? As examples of something more general, or as irreducibly unique? Are Novatus and Seneca particulars in the same way in which David and Strether are particulars? Why does Seneca, in any case, write to his own brother in this highly general and abstract way? What is the significance of the fact that Spinoza's text does not tell a story of particulars at all?

Then, *precision:* How precise does the text attempt to be concerning its subject? How much vagueness or indeterminacy does it allow? And what *sort* of precision does it display as its proper concern? Precision in a philosophical text written *more geometrico* is just one sort of precision. The sentences of Dickens and James have another sort that is absent (deliberately) from Spinoza's sentences. For they capture, with vivid and subtle nuance, complexities of ethical experience that the more abstract text does not (or not yet) convey. There may even be, as Dickens's beginning suggests, a relevant sort of precision in the lucid characterization of the mysterious or unclear.

Texts ask and answer questions, offer *explanations* of the phenomena they address. How much of this concern for explaining does the text in question show? What sorts of explanations does it seek, and where does explaining come to an end? Natural science, history, psychoanalysis—each of these offers a different model of explaining. How are our texts related to these, and to other norms?[58]

---

57. On Seneca, see Nussbaum, "The Stoics on the Extirpation of the Passions," *Apeiron* 20 (1987), 129–77, and "Serpents in the Soul: A Reading of Seneca's *Medea*," forthcoming in a festschrift for Stanley Cavell, ed. T. Cohen et al., (Texas Tech University Press, 1990).

58. The relationship between literature and psychoanalytic theory is a large and important topic. For two approaches to it, see Brooks, *Reading for the Plot,* and Wollheim, *Art and Its Objects.* See also Wollheim, "Incest, Parricide, and the Sweetness of Art," lecture delivered at Brown University, February 1989, and forthcoming. Two representative collections of work in this area are *Literature and Psychoanalysis,* ed. Shoshana Felman (Baltimore, Md., 1982) and *Literature and Psychoanalysis,* ed. E. Kurzweil and W. Phillips (New York, 1983).

How is David Copperfield's scrupulous concern to tell the reader how each event in his life came about different from Spinoza's concern with deductive explaining? What does each offer us, for understanding and for life?

In all of this we must be asking, in close conjunction with these and other formal questions, questions about what is usually called content. What does the text in question seem to say, or show, *about* human life, *about* knowledge, about personality, about how to live? And how are these claims related to the claims made in and by the form itself? Frequently (as in all of these cases) we find consistency, and mutual illumination. David Copperfield writes with the kind of attention that he also praises. Seneca leads the interlocutor (and the reader) away from passion even while he condemns it. Spinoza cultivates the intellectual joy of which he will speak. James's text exemplifies, as a whole, a kind of consciousness of which it frequently speaks with praise. But clearly this need not always be the case. A text can make claims while its style makes rather different claims. Sometimes this is due to sloppiness. Sometimes, however, there are most interesting tensions: for texts may, in their form and manner, in the desires they express and nourish, actively subvert their own official content, or call its livability into question.

This questioning should be followed through using several different levels of formal analysis. We need to think of *genre,* and of the texts as extensions (or redefinitions or subversions) of an existing genre.[59] The decision to write a novel rather than a treatise already implies some views and commitments. But the relationship of the particular work to its predecessors and rivals in its own genre must also be considered: for there is no such thing as "the novel"; and some of the novels we shall discuss are critical of received ways of writing in that genre. This does not mean that we should after all discard the concept of genre. For even Beckett, whose assault on the novel is radical, writes against the background of certain expectations and desires that only a concept of genre can enable us to decode. It does mean that we must look beneath this general concept and analyze, much more concretely, the formal and structural features of the work before us in each case. We ask certain large-scale structural questions here—for example, about the role of the hero or heroine, the nature of the reader's identification, about the way in which the authorial consciousness is present in the text, about the novel's temporal structure. We also ask questions that are more often called stylistic, such as: What are the shape and rhythm of the sentences? What metaphors are used, and in what contexts? What vocabulary is selected? In each case, the attempt should be to connect these observations to an evolving conception of the work and the sense of life it expresses.

E. The Aristotelian Ethical View

Our craving for generality has another main source: our preoccupation with the method of science. I mean the method of reducing the explanation of natural phenomena to the smallest possible number of prim-

---

59. For an eloquent defense of the concept of genre, and its ineliminability, I am indebted to a fine lecture by Ralph Cohen at the University of California, Riverside, May 1988.

itive natural laws; and, in mathematics, of unifying the treatment of
different topics by using a generalization. Philosophers constantly see
the method of science before their eyes, and are irresistibly tempted to
ask and answer questions in the way science does. This tendency is the
real source of metaphysics, and leads the philosopher into complete
darkness.

Ludwig Wittgenstein, The Blue Book

I have said that the novels studied in this volume make their claim to be philosophical in connection with a particular set of answers to the question, "How
should one live?" This conception is developed and supported in several of the
essays, especially "Discernment," "Finely Aware," and "Transcending." Its role
in public, as well as private reflection is defended in "Discernment" and "Perception and Revolution." Here, therefore, I shall only enumerate briefly its most
prominent features, commenting on the links between those featurs and the structure of the novel as a literary genre. The sense of life expressed in the structuring
of these novels seems, then, to share the following features, which are also features
of an Aristotelian ethical position.[60]

1. Noncommensurability of the Valuable Things

It is not surprising that we find in these novels a commitment to qualitative distinctions; one could hardly imagine a *literary* art without that commitment. But
the novel is committed more deeply than many other forms to a multiplicity and
fineness of such distinctions. The organizing vision of the novels shows that one
thing is not just a different quantity of another; that there is not only no single
metric along which the claims of different good things can be meaningfully considered, there is not even a small plurality of such measures. The novels show us
the worth and richness of plural qualitative thinking and engender in their readers
a richly qualitative kind of seeing. The novelist's terms are even more variegated,
more precise in their qualitative rightness, than are the sometimes blunt vague
terms of daily life; they show us vividly what we can aspire to in refining our
(already qualitative) understanding. The tendency to reduce quality to quantity
appears in the novels (in the Ververs in the first half of *The Golden Bowl,* in Dickens's Mr. Gradgrind and Mr. McChoakumchild); but, at best, it is seen as ethical
immaturity—at worst, callousness and blindness. Mr. Gradgrind's aversion to the
novel was well-grounded.[61]

---

60. Other contemporary philosophers who defend positions closely related to the position I
describe here include David Wiggins (see n. 40); Bernard Williams (above, n. 40); Cora Diamond
(see n. 40); John McDowell, "Virtue and Reason," *The Monist* 62 (1979), 331–50; and, on certain issues, Charles Taylor, *Sources of the Self* (Cambridge, 1989). For related discussion of Aristotle, see *Essays on Aristotle's Ethics,* ed. A. Rorty (Berkeley, 1980) and N. Sherman, *The Fabric
of Character* (Oxford, 1989). See also L. Blum, *Friendship, Altruism, and Morality* (London,
1980).

61. For argument against commensurability, see "Discernment," "Plato on Commensurability," "Flawed Crystals"; also *Fragility,* Chaps. 4, 6, 10. In "Discernment," the claim that values
are commensurable is broken down into several more specific theses, whose relationship to one
another is investigated; notes refer to contemporary philosophical analyses.

1a. Pervasiveness of Conflicting Attachments and Obligations

For the agent for whom "nothing will ever come to the same thing as anything else," there are few easy trade-offs, and many choices will have a tragic dimension. The choice between $50 and $200, when one cannot have both, is not terribly wrenching: what one forgoes is simply a different quantity of what one also gets. The choice between two qualitatively different actions or commitments, when on account of circumstances one cannot pursue both, is or can be tragic—in part because the item forgone is not the same as the item attained. The novel as form is deeply involved in the presentation of such conflicts, which spring straight from its commitment to non-commensurating description and to the ethical relevance of circumstances. One might, of course, describe some such dilemmas briefly, giving a vividly written example. But in "Flawed Crystals" I argue that it is only by following a pattern of choice and commitment over a relatively long time—as the novel characteristically does—that we can understand the pervasiveness of such conflicts in human efforts to live well.[62]

2. *The Priority of Perceptions (Priority of the Particular)*

In these essays, and in the novels, much is made of an ethical ability that I call "perception," after both Aristotle and James. By this I mean the ability to discern, acutely and responsively, the salient features of one's particular situation. The Aristotelian conception argues that this ability is at the core of what practical wisdom is, and that it is not only a tool toward achieving the correct action or statement, but an ethically valuable activity in its own right. I find a similar case made out in James, with his constant emphasis on the goal of becoming "finely aware and richly responsible." Once again, this commitment seems to be built into the very form of the novel as genre.

Much needs to be said about the relationship of these concrete perceptions to general rules and general categories: for here the view could easily be misunderstood. It is very clear, in both Aristotle and James, that one point of the emphasis on perception is to show the ethical crudeness of moralities based exclusively on general rules, and to demand for ethics a much finer responsiveness to the concrete—including features that have not been seen before and could not therefore have been housed in any antecedently built system of rules. The metaphor of improvisation is used by both Aristotle and James to make this point. But rules and general categories still have enormous action-guiding significance in the morality of perception, as I try to show in "Discernment" and "'Finely Aware.'" It is all a question of *what* significance they are taken to have, and how the agent's imagination uses them.[63]

---

62. On conflict and its connection with commensurability, see "Discernment," "Plato on Commensurability," this volume; *Fragility,* chap. 4.

63. On perception of the particular, see "Discernment," "'Finely Aware,'" "Perceptive Equilibrium," "Perception and Revolution," and "Steerforth's Arm," this volume. For related philosophical discussion, see the work of Wiggins and McDowell cited earlier; also M. de Paul, "Argument and Perception: The Role of Literature in Moral Inquiry," *Journal of Philosophy* 85 (1988) 552–65; L. Blum, "Iris Murdoch and the Domain of the Moral," *Philosophical Studies* 50 (1986) 343–67, and "Particularity and Responsiveness," in *The Emergence of Morality in Young Children,* ed. J. Kagan and S. Lamb (Chicago, 1987).

The particular perception that takes priority, in this conception, over fixed rules and principles, is contrasted, both in Aristotle and in my discussions of him, with both the *general* and the *universal*.[64] It is important to distinguish these two ideas and to see precisely how "the priority of the particular" works with respect to each. Aristotelian arguments against *generality* (against general rules as *sufficient* for correct choice) point to the need for fine-tuned *concreteness* in ethical attention and judgment. They insist on the need to make ethical attention take into account, as salient, three things that general principles, fixed in advance of the particular case, omit.[65]

(a) *New and unanticipated features.* Aristotle used analogies between ethical judgment and the arts of the navigator or doctor to argue that general principles designed to cover a wide range of cases seen in the past will prove insufficient to prepare an agent to respond well to new circumstances. Insofar as we train agents to think of ethical judgment as consisting simply in the application of such antecedently formulated rules (so long as we train doctors to think that all they need to know is contained in textbooks) we prepare them badly for the actual flow of life, and for the necessary resourcefulness in confronting its surprises.

(b) *Context-embeddedness of relevant features.* Aristotle and James suggest that to see any single feature of a situation appropriately it is usually essential to see it in its relations of connectedness to many other features of its complex and concrete context. This is another way in which surprise enters the ethical scene; and, here again, general formulations frequently prove too crude.

Notice that neither of these features prevents the Aristotelian ethical view from having a deep interest in the universal and in the universalizability of ethical judgments. So far as these features go, the Aristotelian might well hold, and usually does, that should the very same circumstances, with all the same relevant contextual features, present themselves again, it would again be correct to make the same choice.[66] This is frequently, indeed, part of the justification of the choice as correct. The Aristotelian will point out that, once we recognize as relevant as many features of context, history, and circumstance as this view actually does, the resulting (highly qualified) universals are not likely to be of much action-guiding usefulness. Certainly they will not play the role of codifying and simplifying that ethical universals have played in numerous philosophical views. But when we recognize that complex Jamesian judgments are, in many cases, universalizable, we recognize something important about the way in which a novel offers ethical education and stimulates the ethical imagination. But difficulty for even the highly concrete universal comes with the third Aristotelian argument for particular perceptions.

(c) *Ethical relevance of particular persons and relationships.* Responding to a novel of Henry James, the reader may often implicitly conclude: "If a person were to be in circumstances sufficiently similar to those this character is in here, the same words and actions would again be warranted." But these inferences can take

64. On general and universal, see also "Discernment," and "'Finely Aware,'" endnote.
65. See "Discernment" and *Fragility* ch. 10.
66. In this respect, the position resembles the one defended by R. M. Hare (above n. 16), who demands universalizability, but insists on very concrete universals. There is further discussion of Hare's position below, and in "'Finely Aware'", Note, this volume.

two different forms. If we consider, for example, the scene between Maggie and her father that is the subject of "'Finely Aware,'" we might have an inference of the form, "If a person were like Maggie and had a father exactly like Adam, and a relationship and circumstances exactly like theirs, the same actions would again be warranted." But we might also have a judgment of the form: "One should consider the particular history of one's very own relationship to one's particular parents, their characteristics and one's own, and choose, as Maggie does, with fine responsiveness to the concrete." The first universal, though not of much help in life, is significant: for one has not seen what is right about Maggie's choices unless one sees how they respond to the described features of her context. But the second judgment is an equally important part of the interaction between novel and reader—as the readers become, in Proust's words, the readers of their own selves. And this judgment tells the reader, apparently, to go beyond the described features and to consider the particulars of one's own case.

But suppose one found the description of one's own case—would that give rise, in turn, to a concrete universal that would incorporate everything that was of ethical relevance? The novels suggest that this is not always so. The account of Maggie's relationship to her father suggests that the describable and universalizable properties are not all that is of relevance. For we sense in Maggie and Adam a depth and quality of love that would not, we feel, tolerate the substitution of a clone, even one who had all the same describable features. She loves *him,* not just his properties, or him beyond and behind the properties—however mysterious that is.[67] And the reader is invited to love in the same way. Furthermore, it is a salient feature of human life, as the novels present it, that it is lived only once, and in one direction. So to imagine the recurrence of the very same circumstances and persons is to image that life does not have the structure it actually has. And this changes things. As Nietzsche points out, recommending such a thought experiment in the context of practical choice, it attaches a weight to our actions that the actual contingency of life rarely does: the weight of making the world for all eternity. On the other hand, Aristotle suggests that a certain *sort* of intensity will be subtracted: for he holds that the thought that one's children (for example) are "the only ones one has" is an important constituent of the love one has for them, and that without this thought of non-replaceability a great part of the value and motivating force of the love will be undercut. The absence of this intensity in a society (Plato's ideal city) gives us, he holds, a sufficient reason to reject it as a norm.[68] Maggie, then, has to realize that it is a part of her love that no qualitatively similar replacement would be acceptable; and a part of her human situation that the very same things will never come around again; that there is just one father for her, who lives only once. So the universalizable does not, it would seem, deter-

---

67. Much depends here on the conception of the individual and what it includes as essential: for discussion of the mystery and difficulty we get into here, see "Love and the Individual," this volume.

68. Nietzsche, *The Gay Science,* trans. W. Kaufmann (New York, 1974), Sect. 341. See the discussion of this view in Milan Kundera, *The Unbearable Lightness of Being,* trans. Michael Henry Heim (London & Boston, 1984). For the Aristotelian view, see *Pol.* 1262b22–3, discussed in "Discernment" and in *Fragility* chap 12.

mine every dimension of choice; and there are silences of the heart within which its demands cannot, and should not, be heard. (See also "Discernment," and endnote to "'Finely Aware.'")

These reflections about love bring us directly to the third major feature of the Aristotelian conception.

3. Ethical Value of the Emotions[69]

"But novels both represent and activate the emotions: so our dealings with them are marred by irrationality. They are not likely, therefore, to contribute to rational reflection." No other objection has been so frequently made against the literary style, and no other has been so damaging to its claims. Emotions, it is said, are unreliable, animal, seductive. They lead away from the cool reflection that alone is capable of delivering a considered judgment.[70] Certainly the novel as form is profoundly committed to the emotions; its interaction with its readers takes place centrally through them. So this challenge must be confronted.

A central purpose of these essays is to call this view of rationality into question and to suggest, with Aristotle, that practical reasoning unaccompanied by emotion is not sufficient for practical wisdom; that emotions are not only not more unreliable than intellectual calculations, but frequently are more reliable, and less deceptively seductive. But before we can go very far with this issue, it is very important to notice that the traditional objection is actually two very different objections, which have been confused in some contemporary versions of the debate. According to one version of the objection, emotions are unreliable and distracting because they have nothing to do with cognition at all. According to the second objection, they have a great deal to do with cognition, but they embody a view of the world that is in fact false.

According to the first view, then, emotions are blind animal reactions, like or identical with bodily feelings, that are in their nature unmixed with thought, undiscriminating, and impervious to reasoning. This version of the objection relies on a very impoverished conception of emotion that cannot survive scrutiny. It has had a certain influence; but by now it has been decisively rejected by cognitive psychology, by anthropology, by psychoanalysis, and even by philosophy— not to speak of our sense of life itself.[71] However much these disciplines differ about the further analysis of emotions such as fear, grief, love, and pity, they agree

---

69. "Discernment" makes a parallel argument about the imagination, again with reference to Aristole; the full elaboration of the position requires this.

70. This argument begins, in the Western philosophical tradition, with Plato's attack on rhetoric in the *Gorgias;* it is influentially continued in Locke (see n. 8) and Kant. For effective summaries of some of these traditions of argument, see Blum, *Friendship, Altruism* (see n. 60), and C. Lutz, *Unnatural Emotions* (Chicago, 1988).

71. For different types of criticism of this position, see, from anthropology, Lutz, and R. Harré, ed., *The Social Construction of the Emotions* (Oxford, 1986); from psychoanalysis, the work of Melanie Klein; from cognitive psychology, among others, the work of James Averill (see Harré, ed. for a representative article); in philosophy, R. de Sousa, *The Rationality of Emotion* (Cambridge, Mass. 1987), B. Williams, "Morality and the Emotions," in *Problems of the Self* (see n. 40). A good collection of recent work from various disciplines is in *Explaining Emotions,* ed. A. Rorty (Berkeley, 1980).

that these emotions are very closely linked to beliefs in such a way that a modification of beliefs brings about a modification of emotion. In drawing this conclusion, they are in fact returning to the conception of emotion that Aristotle shared with most of the other Greek philosophers. For they all held that emotions are not simply blind surges of affect, recognized, and discriminated from one another, by their felt quality alone; rather they are discriminating responses closely connected with beliefs about how things are and what is important.[72] Being angry, for example, is not like experiencing a bodily appetite. Hunger and thirst do seem to be relatively impervious to changes in belief, but anger seems to require and to rest upon a belief that one has been wronged or damaged in some significant way by the person toward whom the anger is directed. The discovery that this belief is false (either that the event in question did not take place, or that the damage is after all trivial, or that it was not caused by that person) can be expected to remove the anger toward that person. Feeling grief presupposes, in a similar way, a family of beliefs about one's circumstances: that a loss has taken place; that the loss is of something that has value. Once again, a change in the relevant beliefs, either about what has happened or about its importance, will be likely to alter or remove the emotion. Love, pity, fear, and their relatives—all are belief-based in a similar way: all involve the acceptance of certain views of how the world is and what has importance.

There are various subtly different positions available (in both the ancient discussion and the contemporary literature) about the precise relationship between emotions and beliefs. But the major views all make the acceptance of a certain belief or beliefs at least a necessary condition for emotion, and, in most cases, also a constituent part of what an emotion is. And the most powerful accounts, furthermore, go on to argue that if one *really* accepts or takes in a certain belief, one will experience the emotion: belief is sufficient for emotion, emotion necessary for full belief. For example, if a person believes that X is the most important person in her life and that X has just died, she will feel grief. If she does not, this is because in some sense she doesn't fully comprehend or has not taken in or is repressing these facts. Again, if Y *says* that racial justice is very important to her and also that a racially motivated attack has just taken place before her eyes, and yet she is in no way angry—this, again, will lead us to question the sincerity, either of Y's belief-claims, or of her denial of emotion.[73]

Because the emotions have this cognitive dimension in their very structure, it is very natural to view them as intelligent parts of our ethical agency, responsive to the workings of deliberation and essential to its completion. (Dante's *intelligenza d'amore* is not an intellectual grasp of emotion; it is an understanding that is not available to the non-lover, and the loving itself is part of it.) On this view, there will be certain contexts in which the pursuit of intellectual reasoning apart from emotion will actually prevent a full rational judgment—for example by preventing an access to one's grief, or one's love, that is necessary for the full understanding of what has taken place when a loved one dies. Emotions can, of course,

---

72. On this see *Fragility,* Interlude 2; "The Stoics on the Extirpation"; and in this volume, "Narrative Emotions."

73. For extended discussion of this, and the concept of belief involved, see "The Stoics."

be unreliable—in much the same ways that beliefs can. People get angry because of false beliefs about the facts, or their importance; the relevant beliefs might also be true but unjustified, or both false and unjustified. "Narrative Emotions" argues that certain entire emotional categories—in that case, guilt about one's birth and one's embodiment—are always irrational and unreliable, whenever they occur. But the fact that some beliefs are irrational has rarely led philosophers to dismiss all beliefs from practical reasoning. So it is not easy to see why parallel failings in the emotions should have led to their dismissal. And the Aristotelian view holds, in fact, that frequently they are more reliable in deliberation than detached intellectual judgments, since emotions embody some of our most deeply rooted views about what has importance, views that could easily be lost from sight during sophisticated intellectual reasoning.[74]

This brings us to the second objection. For although the greatest writers on emotion in the Western philosophical tradition (Plato, Aristotle, Chrysippus, Dante, Spinoza, Adam Smith) agree in finding in emotions this cognitive dimension, and although all deny that they are by nature unreliable in the way that the first objector has claimed, some of them still urge us to leave emotions out of practical reasoning, or even to get rid of them altogether. The objections of Plato, the Stoics, and Spinoza are very different from the objection that identifies emotions with bodily feelings; yet they, too, banish emotions from philosophy. On what grounds? Because they believe that the judgments on which the major emotions are based are all *false*. "Transcending" explores this issue in detail, as does my related work in Greek philosophy. But the core of the objection is that the emotions involve value judgments that attach great worth to uncontrolled things outside the agent; they are, then, acknowledgments of the finite and imperfectly controlled character of human life. (For the same reason Augustine held, against the Stoics, that they were essential to Christian life.) In other words, their dismissal has, in this case, nothing to do with the fact that they are "irrational" in the sense of "non-cognitive." They are seen as pieces of reasoning that are actually false, from the perspective of certain aspirations to self-sufficiency. But those aspirations and the views that support them may be called into question—as they are in this book. And if one takes up a different view of the human being's situation and proper ends, emotions will return as necessary acknowledgments of some important truths about human life.

Nothing in this project should (I repeat) be taken to imply a foundationalism concerning the emotions.[75] They can be unjustified or false just as beliefs can be. They are not self-certifying sources of ethical truth. But the project does try to show the inadequacy of the first objection, by showing the richness of the connections between emotion and judgment. And by its exploration of love and other precarious attachments, it shows an ethical conception that is at odds with the second objector's, and shows this sense of life as good.[76]

74. See "Discernment," this volume and *Fragility,* chap. 3 on Creon; also C. Diamond, "Anything But Argument?" *Philosophical Investigations* 5 (1982) 23–41.

75. For criticism of this idea, see "Narrative Emotions" and "Love's Knowledge," this volume.

76. The rehabilitation of emotion in practical reasoning has, for obvious cultural reasons, been a prominent theme in contemporary feminist writing: see, for example, Carol Gilligan, *In a Dif-*

This brings us to the fourth and final element of the Aristotelian conception, in some ways the most fundamental one.

4. Ethical Relevance of Uncontrolled Happenings

In the ancient quarrel, dramatic poetry was taken to task for implying, in the way it constructed its plots, that events that happen to the characters through no fault of their own have some serious importance for the quality of the lives they manage to live, and that similar possibilities were present in the lives of the spectators. Attackers and defenders of the literary agreed that the attention given to plot expressed, in itself, an ethical conception that was at odds with the Socratic claim (accepted by Plato in the *Republic's* attack on tragedy) that a good person cannot be harmed. So much seems to be true, as well, of our more modern fictional examples. The structure of these novels, as members and extenders of that genre, has built into it an emphasis on the significance, for human life, of what simply happens, of surprise, of reversal. James links his own interest in contingency with that of ancient tragedy, referring to the pity and fear of the characters before their situation. (And his readers are to be "participators by a fond attention," regarding the happenings as important, even as the characters do.) Proust tells us that one of the primary aims of literary art is to show us moments in which habit is cut through by the unexpected, and to engender in the reader a similar upsurge of true, surprised feeling. The ability of their texts to give insight is seen by both authors to depend on this power to display such uncontrolled events as if they matter to the characters, and to make them matter to the reader. And the Aristotelian conception holds that a correct understanding of the ways in which human aspirations to live well can be checked by uncontrolled events is in fact an

---

ferent Voice (Cambridge, Mass., 1982). The argument of this book has many connections with this and other related work in feminism, presenting the issues as important for all human beings who wish to think well.

There has recently been a very interesting body of work developing concerning the role of emotion in the law and in legal judgment. For two different recent examples, see Paul Gewirtz, "Aeschylus' Law," *Harvard Law Review* 101 (1988) 1043–55, and Martha L. Minow and Elizabeth V. Spelman, "Passion for Justice," *Cardozo Law Review* 10 (1988) 37–76. Both of these articles are deeply concerned with the role of literature and literary styles in the law, and see the connection of this issue with the issue of emotion's role. (Not incidentally, both are also concerned with feminism.) Gewirtz' eloquent conclusion draws these interests together:

> ... But while the nonrational emotions can distort, delude, or blaze uncontrollably, they have worth in themselves and can also open, clarify, and enrich understanding. The values and achievements of a legal system—and of lawyers, judges, and citizens involved with a legal system—are shaped by what the emotions yield.... These observations suggest one important connection between literature and law that is rarely made explicit. Literature makes its special claims upon us precisely because it nourishes the kinds of human understanding not achievable through reason alone but involving intuition and emotion as well. If, as the *Oresteia* suggests, law engages nonrational elements and requires the most comprehensive kinds of understanding, literature can play an important role in a lawyer's development. The inclusion of the Furies within the legal order—an inclusion that represents the linking of emotional spheres to law—links literature itself to law and underscores the special place literature can have in developing the legal mind to its fullest richness and complexity. (p. 1050)

On these issues, see also James Boyd White, *The Legal Imagination* (Chicago, 1973), *When Words Lose Their Meaning* (Madison, Wisc., 1984), and *Heracles' Bow* (Chicago, 1985).

important part of ethical understanding—not, as the Platonist would have it, a deception.[77]

The Aristotelian conception contains a view of learning well suited to support the claims of literature. For teaching and learning, here, do not simply involve the learning of rules and principles. A large part of learning takes place in the experience of the concrete. This experiential learning, in turn, requires the cultivation of perception and responsiveness: the ability to read a situation, singling out what is relevant for thought and action. This active task is not a technique; one learns it by guidance rather than by a formula. James plausibly suggests that novels exemplify and offer such learning: exemplify it in the efforts of the characters and the author, engender it in the reader by setting up a similarly complex activity.[78]

There is a further way in which novels answer to an Aristotelian view of practical learning. The Aristotelian view stresses that bonds of close friendship or love (such as those that connect members of a family, or close personal friends) are extremely important in the whole business of becoming a good perceiver.[79] Trusting the guidance of a friend and allowing one's feelings to be engaged with that other person's life and choices, one learns to see aspects of the world that one had previously missed. One's desire to share a form of life with the friend motivates this process. (We see this in the Assinghams, who find the basis for a shared perception of their situation through the loving desire to inhabit the same picture, to bring their abilities to one another's need.) James stresses that not only relationships represented within the novels, but the entire relation of novel-reading itself, has this character. Both certain characters, and, above all, the sense of life revealed in the text as a whole become our friends as we read, "participators by a fond attention." We trust their guidance and see, for the time, the world through those eyes—even if, as in the case of Dickens's Steerforth, we are led, by love, outside the bounds of straight moral judgment.

One might, if one were skeptical, wonder about this—thinking that love distorts as much as, or more than, it reveals. But the essays grow out of an experience in which the ability of love to illuminate has been a marked reality. One sees this, in the essays, in straightforward autobiographical ways—in the way in which my love for my daughter and my daughter's view of Steerforth led me to a revised conception of the connection between love and morality; in the way in which Hilary Putnam's changes of view illuminated, through friendship (which is not to say agreement, but something deeper than agreement), my own evolving views of the political life. One sees this, too, in the way in which still other figures and events, unnamed and absent, take form within the text, and lead the text to its perceptions. But above all one sees this in the story of my relationships with the novels themselves, which began earlier than almost any other love and are loves as intimate as any. The evolving story of those relationships is the story, as well, of the unfolding of thought, the shaping of sympathy.

77. See *Fragility,* chaps. 8–12.
78. On learning, see "Discernment" and "'Finely Aware,'" this volume.
79. See *Fragility,* chap. 12, and Sherman (see n. 60).

F. Novels, Examples, and Life

> . . . I spoke of the novel as an especially useful agent of the moral imag-
> ination, as the literary form which most directly reveals to us the com-
> plexity, the difficulty, and the interest of life in society, and best
> instructs us in our human variety and contradiction.
>
> Lionel Trilling, *The Liberal Imagination*

One might grant that some text other than an abstract treatise is required if we
are going to investigate the claims of the Aristotelian conception clearly and
fully—both because of what a treatise can and cannot state and because of what
it does and does not do to and for its reader. And yet one might still be far less
certain that novels are the texts required. A number of different questions arise:
Why these novels and not others? Why novels and not plays? biographies? histories? lyric poetry? Why not philosophers' examples? And above all, why not, as
James's Strether says, "poor dear old life"?

Here we must insist again that what we have on our hands is a family of inquiries; and not all our questions, even about how to live, will be well pursued in
exactly the same texts. If, for example, we should want to think about the role of
religious belief in certain lives that we might lead, none of the novels chosen here
will help us much—except Beckett's, and that only in a somewhat parochial way.
If we want to think about class distinctions, or about racism, or about our relationships with other societies different from our own—again, these particular novels will not be sufficient—although, as "Discernment" argues, most novels focus
in some manner on our common humanity, through their structures of friendship
and identification, and thus make some contribution to the pursuit of those projects. My choices of texts express my preoccupation with certain questions, and do
not pretend to address all salient questions.[80] (For some curricular thoughts in
connection with my position, see the endnote to "Perception and Revolution.")

Next, we should insist that neither all nor only novels prove appropriate, even
for this small portion of the project. Not all novels are appropriate for reasons
suggested by both James and Proust in their criticisms of other novel writers.
James attacks the omniscient posture of George Eliot's narrator as a falsification
of our human position. He also indicates that the conventional springs of dra-

---

80. Nor, of course, do they claim to represent the only places where one might turn for understanding on these issues. It will be obvious that I have confined myself to only one small part of
one literary tradition; but in so doing I do not mean to imply that there are not other traditions,
other perspectives, whose inclusion would be important for the full completion of this inquiry.
And if one turns from these questions to others, this is even more important to remember. For
there will be some issues whose investigation is absolutely essential to the full completion of our
dialectical project that could not possibly be well studied using only literary texts from the high
literary tradition of Europe and North America. We will need, before our project is anywhere at
all, to get as good an understanding as we can of the ways of life of people very different from
ourselves, and of minorities and oppressed groups in our own society. And although I would not
concede that the works studied here are doomed to narrowness and bias by their origins, it is
reasonable to suppose that the full and precise investigation of such issues would require turning,
as well, to texts from other origins.

matic interest played upon by many novels may, if we are not careful, corrupt our relation to our own daily lives with their more humdrum searches for precision of thought and feeling, their less dramatic efforts to be just.[81] Proust's Marcel is critical of much of the literary writing he encounters, holding that it is insufficiently concerned with psychological depth. Both Proust and James write in a way that focuses attention on the small movements of the inner world. So the account I develop with reference to them cannot automatically be extended to all other novelists. On the other hand, I also believe that James has good arguments for the view that the novel, among the available genres, best exemplifies what he calls "the projected morality."[82] I have suggested some of these connections between the structure of the novel and the elements of the Aristotelian view; the essays develop them further.

Not only novels prove appropriate, because (again, with reference only to these particular issues and this conception) many serious dramas will be pertinent as well, and some biographies and histories—so long as these are written in a style that gives sufficient attention to particularity and emotion, and so long as they involve their readers in relevant activities of searching and feeling, especially feeling concerning their own possibilities as well as those of the characters. In one case ("Love's Knowledge") I find in a short story sufficient structural complexity for the issues I am investigating there. Lyric poetry seems to me to raise different issues. They are important to the continuation of the larger project; I leave them to those who are more involved than I am in the analysis of poems. I leave for a future inquiry, as well, the ethical role of comedy and satire, both in the novel itself and in other genres.

But the philosopher is likely to be less troubled by these questions of literary genre than by a prior question: namely, why a literary work at all? Why can't we investigate everything we want to invest. ate by using complex examples of the sort that moral philosophers are very good at inventing? In reply, we must insist that the philosopher who asks this question cannot have been convinced by the argument so far about the intimate connection between literary form and ethical content. Schematic philosophers' examples almost always lack the particularity, the emotive appeal, the absorbing plottedness, the variety and indeterminacy, of good fiction; they lack, too, good fiction's way of making the reader a participant and a friend; and we have argued that it is precisely in virtue of these structural characteristics that fiction can play the role it does in our reflective lives. As James says, "The picture of the exposed and entangled state is what is required."[83] If the examples do have these features, they will, themselves, be works of literature.[84]

81. See "Flawed Crystals"; and my "Comment on Paul Seabright," *Ethics* 98 (1988) 332–40.

82. See n. 7. It is clear that I am confining my discussion to available forms of *verbal* expression, and not even attempting to consider the relation of the verbal to the pictorial, the musical, and so forth.

83. H. James, *AN* 65. On James's view of morality, see also F. Crews, *The Tragedy of Manners: Moral Drama in the Later Novels of Henry James* (New Haven, Conn., 1957).

84. Close to this is Iris Murdoch's use of examples in *The Sovereignty of Good*. Other philosophers who begin to approach this degree of complexity include Bernard Williams (see n. 40); Thomas Nagel, *Mortal Questions* (Cambridge, 1979); and Judith Jarvis Thomson, *Rights, Restitution, and Risk: Essays in Moral Theory* (Cambridge, Mass., 1986).

Sometimes a very brief fiction will prove a sufficient vehicle for the investigation of what we are at that moment investigating; sometimes, as in "Flawed Crystals" (where our question concerns what is likely to happen in the course of a relatively long and complex life), we need the length and complexity of a novel. In neither case, however, would schematic examples prove sufficient as a substitute. (This does not mean that they will be totally dismissed; for they have other sorts of usefulness, especially in connection with other ethical views.)

We can add that examples, setting things up schematically, signal to the readers what they should notice and find relevant. They hand them the ethically salient description. This means that much of the ethical work is already done, the result "cooked." The novels are more open-ended, showing the reader what it is to search for the appropriate description and why that search matters. (And yet they are not so open-ended as to give no shape to the reader's thought.) By showing the mystery and indeterminacy of "our actual adventure," they characterize life more richly and truly—indeed, more precisely—than an example lacking those features ever could; and they engender in the reader a type of ethical work more appropriate for life.

But why not life itself? Why can't we investigate whatever we want to investigate by living and reflecting on our lives? Why, if it is the Aristotelian ethical conception we wish to scrutinize, can't we do that without literary texts, without texts at all—or, rather, with the texts of our own lives set before us? Here, we must first say that of course we do this as well, both apart from our reading of the novels and (as Proust insists) in the process of reading. In a sense Proust is right to see the literary text as an "optical instrument" through which the reader becomes a reader of his or her own heart. But, why do we need, in that case, such optical instruments?

One obvious answer was suggested already by Aristotle: we have never lived enough. Our experience is, without fiction, too confined and too parochial. Literature extends it, making us reflect and feel about what might otherwise be too distant for feeling.[85] The importance of this for both morals and politics cannot be underestimated. *The Princess Casamassima*—justly, in my view—depicts the imagination of the novel-reader as a type that is very valuable in the political (as well as the private) life, sympathetic to a wide range of concerns, averse to certain denials of humanity. It cultivates these sympathies in its readers.

We can clarify and extend this point by emphasizing that novels do not function, inside this account, as pieces of "raw" life: they are a close and careful interpretative description. All living is interpreting; all action requires seeing the world *as* something. So in this sense no life is "raw," and (as James and Proust insist) throughout our living we are, in a sense, makers of fictions. The point is that in the activity of literary imagining we are led to imagine and describe with greater precision, focusing our attention on each word, feeling each event more keenly— whereas much of actual life goes by without that heightened awareness, and is thus, in a certain sense, not fully or thoroughly lived. Neither James nor Proust thinks of ordinary life as normative, and the Aristotelian conception concurs: too

85. I am thinking of Aristotle's claims, in both *Rhetoric* and Poetics, about the connection between our interest in literature and our love of learning: see *Fragility,* Interlude 2.

much of it is obtuse, routinized, incompletely sentient. So literature is an extension of life not only horizontally, bringing the reader into contact with events or locations or persons or problems he or she has not otherwise met, but also, so to speak, vertically, giving the reader experience that is deeper, sharper, and more precise than much of what takes place in life.

To this point we can add three others that have to do with our relation, as readers, to the literary text, and the differences between that relation and other relations in which life involves us. As James frequently stresses, novel reading places us in a position that is both like and unlike the position we occupy in life: like, in that we are emotionally involved with the characters, active with them, and aware of our incompleteness; unlike, in that we are free of certain sources of distortion that frequently impede our real-life deliberations. Since the story is not ours, we do not find ourselves caught up in the "vulgar heat" of our personal jealousies or angers or in the sometimes blinding violence of our loves. Thus the (ethically concerned) aesthetic attitude shows us the way. Proust's Marcel concurs, making a far stronger (and, perhaps, to that extent less compelling) claim: that it is only in relation to the literary text, and never in life, that we can have a relation characterized by genuine altruism, and by genuine acknowledgment of the otherness of the other. Our reading of Dickens complicates this point, as we shall see; but it does not remove it. There is something about the act of reading that is exemplary for conduct.

Furthermore, another way in which the enterprise of reading is exemplary is that it brings readers together. And, as Lionel Trilling emphasized, it brings them together in a particular way, a way that is constitutive of a particular sort of community: one in which each person's imagining and thinking and feeling are respected as morally valuable.[86] The Aristotelian dialectical enterprise was characterized as a social or communal endeavor in which people who will share a form of life try to agree on the conception by which they can live together. Each person's solitary scrutiny of his or her own experience may, then, be too private and non-shared an activity to facilitate such a shared conversation—especially if we take seriously, as the novels all do, the moral value of privacy regarding one's own personal thoughts and feelings.[87] We need, then, texts we can read together and talk about as friends, texts that are available to all of us. The ubiquity of "we" and the rarity of "I" in James's later novels, where the authorial voice is concerned, is highly significant. A community is formed by author and readers. In this community separateness and qualitative difference are not neglected; the privacy and the imagining of each is nourished and encouraged. But at the same time it is stressed that living together is the object of our ethical interest.

I have insisted, so far, on the inseparability of form and content in thoroughly written works. But I have also defended the novels as part of an overall search that will clearly require, for its completion, the explicit description of the contribution of the literary works and comparison of their sense of life with that involved in

---

86. See *The Liberal Imagination* (see n. 34), esp. vii–viii—Preface added 1974.
87. A subtle analysis of issues of privacy in the novel of consciousness is in D. Cohn, *Transparent Minds* (Princeton, N.J., 1978).

other works. In pursuit of this search, the essays themselves use a style that responds to the literary works and, to some extent, continues their strategies; but it also shows an Aristotelian concern for explanation and explicit description. And several of the essays (especially "Love's Knowledge") discuss the idea of a philosophical style that is the ally of literature, one that is not identical to the styles of the literary works, but directs the reader's attention to the salient features of those works, setting their insights in a perspicuous relation to other alternatives, other texts. It was already obvious in our account of the dialectical procedure that the comparison among conceptions must be organized by a style that is not entirely committed to one conception; but now we can see that even to begin that dialectical task, where literature is concerned, we need—even before we get to the investigation of alternative conceptions—a type of philosophical commentary that will point out explicitly the contributions of the works to the pursuit of our question about human beings and human life, and their relation to our intuitions and our sense of life.[88] The novels and their style are, we have argued, an ineliminable part of moral philosophy, understood as we have understood it; but they make their contribution in conjunction with a style that is itself more explanatory, more Aristotelian. In order to be the ally of literature, and to direct the reader to that variety and complexity, rather than away from it, this Aristotelian style itself will have to differ greatly from much philosophical writing that we commonly encounter: for it will have to be non-reductive, and also self-conscious about its own lack of completeness, gesturing toward experience and toward the literary texts, as spheres in which a greater completeness should be sought.[89] But it will need to differ from the novels as well, if it is going to show the distinctive features of the novels in a way that contrasts them with features of other conceptions. Both the literary works and the "philosophical criticism" that presents them are essential parts of the overall philosophical task.

Such a combination of literary richness with explanatory commentary could take many forms. Some writers—for example, Plato and Proust—incorporate both elements into a single literary whole. Some—for example, Henry James—connect their literary texts with an explicit commentary of their own. Other practitioners of philosophical commentary—from Aristotle to such present-day figures as Stanley Cavell, Lionel Trilling, Cora Diamond, and Richard Wollheim—write commentaries on works of art made by others. There is no single rule as to how this should be done. Much depends on the philosopher's degree of narrative ability, and on the type and degree of his or her commitment to the overall project of investigating alternative ethical conceptions. But in every case one must be careful that the form and the stylistic claims of the commentary develop and do not undercut the claims of the literary text. And one must not rule out the possibility that the literary text may contain some elements that lead the reader outside of the dialectical question altogether; that, indeed, might be one of its most significant contributions.

88. This point was first made to me by Richard Wollheim, in his comments on "Flawed Crystals," *New Literary History* 15 (1983) 185–92. See, in this volume, "'Finely Aware,'" p. 162.

89. For a more extensive account of this point, see "Love's Knowledge," with reference to William James. On Aristotle's own style, see *Fragility,* Interlude 2.

G. The Boundaries of Ethical Concern

And for what, except for you, do I feel love?
Do I press the extremest book of the wisest man
Close to me, hidden in me day and night?
                                          Wallace Stevens
                             "Notes Toward a Supreme Fiction"

This inquiry takes as its starting point the question, How should one live? And all the books I study here address themselves, in one or another way, to that question. But several of them also deal with love; and love, or its intelligence, is a connecting theme in these essays. This means that it is necessary, as well, to ask how far the novels invite or permit themselves to be enclosed by the bounds of the ethical question—to what extent, on the other hand, they express, and seduce the reader into, a consciousness that steps outside it. In these essays and in the novels, there is a recurrent conception (or conceptions) of an ethical stance, a stance that is necessary for properly asking and answering that inclusive ethical question. That stance is closely connected, frequently, with the stance of the author and reader. Our question, in each case, must then be, is this stance the organizing stance of the novel taken as a whole? Or (to put the point more dynamically) does the literary work constitute its reader (at times) as a consciousness that transgresses the bounds of that question? And if it does so, how does this bear on the novel's ethical contribution?

An author's answer to this question (and one's assessment of that answer, as reader and critic) will depend upon and express a view about the relationship between the ethical point of view and certain important elements in human life—especially forms of love, jealousy, need, and fear—that seem to lie outside of the ethical stance and to be in potential tension with it. The authors I discuss here vary (and also, perhaps, shift) in their views on this question. And my own view about the issue has also undergone a shift, leading me to focus on, or to turn for illumination to, one novel or author rather than another at different times. To clarify certain questions that the essays, taken together, will raise, I want to divide this evolution into three periods (although in reality they are not altogether temporally discrete). I shall focus on the example of erotic/romantic love.

In the first period, then, I believed that the Aristotelian ethical stance was inclusive enough to encompass every constituent of the good human life, love included. If one moves from a narrow understanding of the moral point of view to the more inclusive Aristotelian understanding, with its question about the good human life, one could, I then argued, think and feel about everything that is a plausible part of the answer to that question, passionate love included, asking how it fits with other elements and how one might construct a balanced life out of all of them. (I pointed, here, to the fact that Aristotle's ethical works include many aspects of human life that for Kant and many others would lie outside of morality: joke-telling, hospitality, friendship, love itself. All these elements are securely inside the search for the good human life as Aristotle understands it, and can be evaluated and further specified by that search.)

In this period I emphasized the fact that James's conception of the ethical stance appears to be similarly inclusive; that his novels are shaped by, and constitute in their reader, a consciousness that is always aware of the bearing of everything—the fortunes of the characters, the structure of the plot, the very shapes of the sentences—on the question about human life and how to live it. This consciousness is aware of non-ethical and even antiethical elements in life—such as jealousy, the desire for revenge, and erotic love insofar as it is linked to these. But the nature of its awareness of these elements is itself powerfully ethical. The reader is urged always to look at their bearing on the "projected morality," and to evaluate them as elements of (or impediments to) a good human life. My own belief that the Aristotelian ethical stance was complete as an attitude toward the various elements in life was the guiding idea in the writing of *Fragility;* and one sees it here in "Flawed Crystals," "'Finely Aware,'" and "Discernment," with their assimilation of Aristotle and James.

Richard Wollheim, in his written commentary on "Flawed Crystals," argued that one of the salient contributions of the novel to our self-understanding was to lead its readers, at certain times and in certain ways, "outside of morality," making them accomplices of extra-moral projects, especially those based on jealousy and revenge.[90] In this way, he argued, the novel, showing us the boundaries of morality and its roots in more primitive attitudes, shows us something important about morality that we could not have seen from a moral treatise itself. My reply to Wollheim at that time, in the printed response, was to argue that our difference was merely verbal, the result simply of a difference in the use of the words "moral" and "ethical." He was using a narrower Kantian understanding of the moral, I a broader Aristotelian understanding. What was outside the ethical or moral in the former sense was inside it in the latter. Even (I said) if one did grant that at times *The Golden Bowl* does allow its readers to glimpse the boundaries of even this broader ethical stance, showing them a love that is, in its exclusiveness, incompatible with fine awareness and rich responsibility, and even if the novel does, up to a point, implicate its readers in that love's guilty partiality of vision, still it does so in a way that permits them always to retain a keen awareness of what the characters lose from view; and so in this way the novel remains always inside the ethical stance.

During a second period, I held more or less constant my view of Jamesian readership and its ethical features, but expressed a different attitude to love, in its relation to the Aristotelian ethical viewpoint. Or rather, I developed more deeply some elements of my view that had already been suggested in my reading of the ending of *The Golden Bowl,* though not in my reply to Wollheim. Here I insisted that certain significant human relationships, erotic love above all, demand a kind of attention that is in a deep and pervasive tension with the ethical viewpoint, even when that viewpoint is understood in the broad Jamesian/Aristotelian way. The demand of the relationship for both exclusivity and privacy is held to be ethically problematic, since even the inclusive Aristotelian understanding of the ethical stance emphasizes the connection of that stance with wide and inclusive attention and with the public giving of reasons. Thus, in "Perceptive Equilibrium," above all (and in the sections of "Steerforth's Arm" dealing with Adam Smith and

90. Wollheim (see n. 88).

with James) I argued, following James and Strether, that there is a pervasive tension between love and the ethical, and between the sorts of attention required by each. Any life that wishes to include both cannot aim at a condition of balance or equilibrium, but only at an uneasy oscillation between the ethical norm and this extra-ethical element. (This point was first suggested in the brief remarks at the end of the reading of *The Golden Bowl* in "Flawed Crystals," about the need to improvise concerning when to hold onto the norm of fine awareness, and when to let it go.) As for James, my argument was that he sets his readers up in the point of view that is most favorable to morality, making them allies of Strether and showing Strether's viewpoint as the fruit of his own long engagement with literature. But James complicates the reader's attachment to Strether just enough to make the reader perceive, around the margins of the novel, the silent world of love, and to wonder, therefore, whether a more complete human good might not be "perceptive oscillation," rather than "perceptive equilibrium." To this extent, the novel would not, as such, contain a representation of that complete human good.

In this period I did not insist on any positive contribution that love might make to ethical understanding. I saw it as part of a complete human life, but a part that was, where ethical vision was itself concerned, subversive rather than helpful. Here I had lost confidence in, or lost sight of, the arguments contained in the reading of Plato's *Phaedrus* in chapter 7 of *Fragility,* which claimed that love's "madness" is essential not only for a full life, but also for understanding and pursuit of the good. "Love and the Individual" again recorded those arguments, but with some skepticism; and that heroine's evident absorption in the face and form of a particular individual is *shown* there as incompatible with broader ethical concern, even though she *talks* a lot about ethical concern.

Another argument influenced me at that time; it helps to explain my emphasis on the gulf between love and ethical attention. This argument is mentioned briefly in "Flawed Crystals" and "Perceptive Equilibrium," in my references to jealousy; but it is not developed at length, although it was a major theme in Wollheim's reply to "Flawed Crystals." It is worked out in detail in an account of Senecan tragedy that is part of my book in progress on Hellenistic ethics. This argument looks at the way in which erotic love, betrayed or disappointed, converts itself into anger and evil wishing toward the object, or the rival, or both. I argue that erotic love cannot be "domesticated" within an Aristotelian scheme for balanced and harmonious action toward the complete life, but must always be potentially subversive of the Aristotelian pursuit, because of this love's connection with anger and the wish to harm. In loving erotically, one risks not only loss, but also evil.

The third view is found in "Steerforth's Arm," the most recent of the articles. Here, led by my reading of Dickens (or perhaps also led again to Dickens by my interest in this possibility) I suggest that the non-judgmental love of particulars characteristic of the best and most humane ethical stance contains within itself a susceptibility to love, and to a love that leads the lover at times beyond the ethical stance into a world in which ethical judgment does not take place. Dickens presents a version of the morality of sympathy that is kinetic and romantic in a way that Strether's is not. Strether's "non-judgmental love of particulars" is not, at bottom, ever really non-judgmental. The insistent Aristotelian question, the question about how all this now before me fits into some plan of how a human being ought to live, the question of whether the appropriate acts and feelings are being chosen, is never inaudible. The tradition into which Dickens fits his hero has different ancient roots. It is in Roman Stoic ideas of mercy and the waiving of straight judgment, developed further in Christian thought, that we see, I think, one origin of David Copperfield's conception of love. (Another origin is surely Romantic, as we see in David's preference for exuberant onward movement and in his association of stasis with death.)

According to this conception, love and ethical concern do not exactly have an equilibrium, but they support and inform one another; and each one is less good, less complete, without the other. Proust could certainly not accept this idea, since he believes that all personal love is necessarily solipsistic, indifferent to the well-being of the loved. It is more difficult to know whether, and how far, James could accept it. *The Ambassadors* and some parts of *The Golden Bowl* seem too preoccupied with getting it right, too much still in the grip of the demand for fine awareness and rich responsibility, to welcome love, with its exclusivity and its tumult, as a nourishing influence in the ethical life—even though it might at the same time be seen to be a central part of a rich or full human life. And yet, in the love of Hyacinth Robinson and Millicent Henning, in the way in which both Hyacinth and Lady Aurora mercifully love the Princess, in the portrait of the Assinghams in *The Golden Bowl*—and perhaps in Maggie Verver's tender refusal of judgment at that novel's end, where we see a deep link between erotic attachment and a new, more yielding sort of moral rightenss—we do find elements of this picture, signs that there is a grace in the yielding of tight control, and that indeed, as Maggie reflects, "the infirmity of art [is] the candor of affection, the grossness of pedigree the refinement of sympathy."[91]

Philosophy has often seen itself as a way of transcending the merely human, of giving the human being a new and more godlike set of activities and attachments. The alternative I explore sees it as a way of being human and speaking humanly. That suggestion will appeal only to those who actually want to be human, who see in human life as it is, with its surprises and connections, its pains and sudden joys, a story worth embracing. This in no way means not wishing to make life better than it is. But, as "Transcending" argues, there are ways of transcending that are human and "internal," and other ways that involve flight and repudiation. It seems plausible that in pursuit of the first way—in pursuit of human self-understanding and of a society in which humanity can realize itself more fully—the imagination and the terms of the literary artist are indispensable guides: as James suggests, angels of and in the fallen world, alert in perception and sympathy, lucidly bewildered, surprised by the intelligence of love.[92]

91. H. James, *The Golden Bowl* (New York, 1907–9) II.156; and see "Flawed Crystals," this volume.

92. For comments on an earlier draft of this Introduction, I am very much indebted to Sissela Bok, Cora Diamond, Anthony Price, Henry Richardson, Christopher Rowe, Paul Seabright, and Amartya Sen. I am also grateful to the Columbia Law School and the Boston University Law School for the opportunity to discuss it in colloquia, and to the members of the audiences on those occasions for their challenging questions.

The Discernment of Perception:
An Aristotelian Conception of
Private and Public Rationality

What one acquires here is not a technique; one learns correct judgements. There are also rules, but they do not form a system, and only experienced people can apply them right. Unlike calculating-rules.
    What is most difficult here is to put this indefiniteness, correctly and unfalsified, into words.

Ludwig Wittgenstein, Philosophical Investigations, II.xi

Of these States the poet is the equable man . . .
He bestows on every object or quality its fit proportion, neither more
    nor less . . .
He judges not as the judge judges, but as the sun falling round a
    helpless thing . . .
He sees eternity in men and women, he does not see men and
    women as dreams or dots.

Walt Whitman, from By Blue Ontario's Shore

Is practical reasoning scientific?[1] If it is not, as it is ordinarily practiced, can it be made to be? And would it be a good thing if it were?[2] Much contemporary writing in moral philosophy and in the social sciences gives a vigorously affirmative answer either to the first question or to the conjunction of the second and third. Aristotle's ethical and political writings present powerful negative arguments. "It is obvious," he writes, "that practical wisdom is not scientific understanding *(epistēmē)*" (*EN* 1142a24). And this is not just an admission of a defect in contem-

---

1. This topic was first addressed in my *Aristotle's De Motu Animalium* (Princeton, N.J., 1978) Essay 4; it was developed further in *Fragility* chap. 10. For related development of the ideas about literature, see, in this collection, "Flawed Crystals," "'Finely Aware'" and "Perception and Revolution."
    2. On "scientific," see further below; and, for a discussion of ancient conceptions of science, see *Fragility* chap. 4.

porary theory. For he makes it clear elsewhere that it is in the very nature of truly rational practical choice that it cannot be made more "scientific" without becoming worse. Instead, he tells us, the "discernment" of the correct choice rests with something that he calls "perception."[3] From the context it is evident that this is some sort of complex responsiveness to the salient features of one's concrete situation.

Aristotle's position is subtle and compelling. It seems to me to go further than any other account of practical rationality I know in capturing the sheer complexity and agonizing difficulty of choosing well. But whether we are in the end persuaded by it or not, the need to study it is urgent. Even more in our time than in his, the power of "scientific" pictures of practical rationality affects almost every area of human social life, through the influence of the social sciences and the more science-based parts of ethical theory on the formation of public policy. We should not accept this situation without assessing the merits of such views against those of the most profound alternatives. If we do not finally accept Aristotle's conception, at least we will have found out more about ourselves.

This paper is a sympathetic presentation of the Aristotelian conception. In the process it sketches some ways in which Aristotle argues against his actual opponents, and some ways in which his views might provide us with arguments against some contemporary proposals for "scientific" conceptions of rationality. But since its aim is to remain rather close to Aristotle and to the ethical problems to which his view responds, it does not provide a detailed exegesis of opposing positions or, therefore, detailed arguments against them. It offers a direction for further inquiry.

In the paper the word "scientific" will be used as Aristotle used it, to designate a family of characteristics that were usually associated with the claim that a body of knowledge had the status of an *epistēmē*. Since the aspiration to *epistēmē* took different forms in the projects of different opponents, Aristotle's attack on scientific conceptions of rationality is a family of attacks, directed at logically distinct positions—although these positions are in some forms mutually consistent and were combined into a single conception in certain works of Plato. I shall suggest that Aristotle's attack has three distinct dimensions, closely interwoven. These are: an attack on the claim that all valuable things are commensurable; an argument for the priority of particular judgments to universals; and a defense of the emotions and the imagination as essential to rational choice. Each of the three features he attacks was prominent in the ancient ethical debate; and each has been important in contemporary writing on choice. Once we have understood the three features of Aristotle's criticism separately, and understood the corresponding features of his own positive conception, we shall see how the parts of his conception fit together, and confront the charge that this norm is empty of content. In order to see its content more clearly, we will turn to a complex literary case that presents its salient features more fully. Finally we shall move from the area of personal choice, where Aristotle's picture has an immediate intuitive appeal, to the more difficult task of commending his view as exemplary for public choice.

---

3. *EN* 1109b18–23, 1126b2–4—on which see below.

I. Plural Values and Noncommensurability

Aristotle knew of the view that a hallmark of rational choice is the measurement of all alternatives by a single quantitative standard of value. Such a "science of measurement,"[4] in his day as in ours, was motivated by the desire to simplify and render tractable the bewildering problem of choice among heterogeneous alternatives. Plato, for example, argues that only through such a science can human beings be rescued from an unendurable confusion in the face of the concrete situation of choice, with its qualitative indefiniteness and its variegated plurality of apparent values. Plato even believed, and argued with power, that many of the most troublesome sorts of human irrationality in action were caused by passions that would be eliminated or rendered innocuous by a thoroughgoing belief in the qualitative homogeneity of all the values. The weak (akratic) agent will be less tempted to deviate from the path of greater known good if he or she understands that the less good, but prima facie alluring, item simply contains a smaller quantity of the very same value that can be found by going toward the better item. The proposed "science" relies on the idea that the some such single standard of value can be found and that all rational choice can be recast as a matter of maximizing our quantities of that value.

We can break the "science of measurement" down into four distinct constituent claims. First, we have the claim that in each situation of choice there is some one value, varying only in quantity, that is common to all the alternatives, and that the rational chooser weighs the alternatives using this single standard. Let us call this claim *Metricity*. Next, there is the claim of *Singleness*: that is, that in all situations of choice there is one and the same metric. Third is a claim about the end of rational choice: that choices and chosen actions have value not in themselves, but only as instrumental means to the good consequences that they produce. We call this *Consequentialism*. If we combine Consequentialism with Metricity, we have the idea of maximization: that the point of rational choice is to produce the greatest amount of the single value at work in each case. Combining both of these with Singleness, we have the idea that there is some one value that it is the point of rational choice, in every case, to maximize.[5] Finally, there are in Aristotle's opponents, as in modern Utilitarian writers, various accounts of the content of the end that is to serve as the metric and the item to be maximized. Pleasure, for Aristotle as for us, is the most familiar candidate.[6] Aristotle rejects all four of these components of the "science of measurement," defending a picture of choice as a

---

4. This phrase is taken from Plato, *Protagoras,* 356. For a full discussion of the claims made in this paragraph, see *Fragility,* chap. 4, and also, in this collection, "Plato on Commensurability." I do not believe that Plato is the only proponent of the "science" that Aristotle has in view; on some of the other relevant background, see my "Consequences and Character in Sophocles' *Philoctetes,*" *Philosophy and Literature* 1 (1976–7) 25–53.

5. It is, of course, not necessary to accept or reject all of these as a single package. We could have Metricity without any of the others; Metricity and Singleness without Consequentialism (if a metric could be found, for example, in the actions themselves); Consequentialism without either Metricity or Singleness.

6. On the role of hedonism in Plato and its relationship to the historical context, see *Fragility,* chap. 4, which includes full references to the secondary literature.

quality-based selection among goods that are plural and heterogeneous, each being chosen for its own distinctive value.

Arguments against pleasure as a single end and standard of choice occupy considerable space in his ethical works. The other available candidate, the useful or advantageous, is criticized only implicity, in many passages that treat it as a non-homogeneous, nonsingle item. Presumably this is because it had no prominent defenders. The popularity of hedonism as a theory of choice called, on the other hand, for detailed criticism. There are numerous well-known difficulties surrounding the interpretation of Aristotle's two accounts of pleasure.[7] What we can confidently say is that both accounts deny that pleasure is a single thing yielded in a qualitatively homogeneous way by many different types of activity. According to *EN* VII, my pleasures just are identical with the activities that I do in a certain way: viz., the unimpeded activations of my natural state. Pleasures, then, are just as distinct and incommensurable as are the different kinds of natural activity: seeing, reasoning, acting justly, and so forth (1153a14–15, b9–12). According to *EN* X, pleasure supervenes upon the activity to which it attaches, like the bloom on the cheek of a healthy young person, completing or perfecting it. Here pleasure is not identical with the activity; but it cannot be identified without reference to the activity to which it attaches. It cannot be pursued on its own without conceptual incoherence,[8] any more than blooming cheeks can be cultivated in isolation from the health and bodily fitness with which they belong.[9] Still less could there be a single item, Pleasure, that is separable from *all* the activities and yielded up by all of them in differing quantities. To these criticisms, Aristotle adds the observation that pleasures "differ in kind" as the associated activities differ (1173b28ff.). Some are choiceworthy and some are not, some are better and some are worse. Some, furthermore, are pleasures only for corrupt people, while some are pleasures for good people (1173b20ff.). Thus the *way* in which pleasure is not single provides us with additional reasons not to set it up as the end of practical choice.

Pleasure does not fall short by lack of singleness alone. It fails, as well, in inclusiveness: that is, it does not cover or contain everything that we pursue as choiceworthy. For, Aristotle writes, "there are many things that we would eagerly pursue even if they brought no pleasure, such as seeing, remembering, knowing, having the excellences. And even if pleasures follow upon these of necessity, it makes no difference; for we *would* choose them even if no pleasure came from them" (*EN* 1174a4–8). Even if in fact pleasure is firmly linked to excellent action as a necessary consequence, it is not the end *for which* we act. We choose the action for its own sake alone. Deliberative imagination can inform us that we would do so even if the link with pleasure were broken. Elsewhere Aristotle shows us cases

---

7. These difficulties include: the question whether the two accounts are answers to a single or to two different questions; the question whether the two accounts are compatible or incompatible; the question whether *EN* VII (= *EE* VI) belongs with the *Nicomachean* or the *Eudemian* work, and what difference this makes to our analysis. Some important items in the vast literature on these questions are discussed in *Fragility,* chap. 10.

8. For one account of the relationship between the conceptual and the empirical in Aristotle, see *Fragility,* chap. 8.

9. The interpretation given here is the most common one; a recent reinterpretation is discussed in *Fragility,* chap. 10, n. 12.

where the link is in fact broken: for example, a good person will sometimes choose to sacrifice life itself, and therefore all possibility of present and future pleasure, for the sake of helping a friend or acting courageously (1117b10ff.). Aristotle shows us, then, that we do in fact pursue and value ends that are not reducible to pleasure; we shall later see that he makes an implicit argument for the value and goodness of these plural commitments.

Argument against pleasure is strong argument against Singleness, since no other plausible candidate for a homogeneous single standard was being put forward. But it is plain that Aristotle's opposition to Singleness is general. In his attack on the Platonic notion of the single Good,[10] he insists that "the definitions of honor and practical wisdom and pleasure are separate and different *qua* goods" (*EN* 1096b23–25); from this he draws the conclusion that there can be no single common notion of good across these things. What he seems to be saying is that what we pursue or choose when we deem each of these items choiceworthy is something distinct, peculiar to the item in question; there is no single thing that belongs to all of them in such a way as to offer a plausible unitary account of their practical value. In the *Politics* he rejects even more explicitly the view that all goods are commensurable. In this important passage he has been describing a theory about the basis of political claims according to which any and all differences between persons are relevant to political distribution. If A is the same as B in all other respects but excels B in height, A is *eo ipso* entitled to a greater share of political goods than B; if A excels B in height and B excels A at playing the flute, we will have to decide which excels the other by more. And so on. Aristotle's first objection to this scheme is specific: it recognizes as relevant to political claims many features that are totally irrelevant to good political activity. But his second objection is general. The scheme is defective because it involves treating all goods as commensurable with one another: height and musicianship are measured against wealth and freedom. "But since this is impossible, it is obvious that in politics it is reasonable for men not to base their claim upon any and every inequality" (1283a9–11).[11]

Clearly this, like the *EN* argument, is an argument against Singleness: there is no one standard in terms of which all goods are commensurable *qua* goods. It looks like an argument against Metricity as well: for it suggests that there is something absurd in supposing that even in each single pairwise comparison of alternatives we will find a single relevant homogeneous measure. And in fact the *EN* remarks about definition, when linked to other observations about the intrinsic

10. See further discussion of this passage in *Fragility,* chap. 10, with notes. I argue there that several other interesting and profound arguments in this chapter of the *EN* are not really pertinent to the criticism of Plato with reference to the notion of a single good in a human life: this is the argument that seems to do the important work on that topic.

11. For further discussion of this passage, and of Aristotle's arguments that the goal of political distribution should be capability to function, see my "Nature, Function, and Capability: Aristotle on Political Distribution," *Oxford Studies in Ancient Philosophy,* Supplementary Volume 1988. On the need to recognize qualitatively heterogeneous ends in political planning, see Robert Erikson, "Descriptions of Inequality: the Swedish Approach to Welfare Research," paper for the Quality of Life Conference arranged by the World Institute for Development Economics Research in Helsinki, and forthcoming in *The Quality of Life*, Oxford University Press, ed. M. Nussbaum and A. Sen.

value of activity according to excellence, do yield arguments against Metricity, and Consequentialism as well, in favor of a picture in which the end or good consists of a number of distinct component activities (associated with the several excellences), each of these being an ultimate end pursued for its own sake. The good life for a human being consists, Aristotle argues, in activity according to the excellences; repeatedly he insists that it is these activities, not either their consequences or the states of soul that produce them, which are the ultimate bearers of value, the ends for which we pursue everything else that we pursue. It is actually part of the definition of activity according to excellence that it should be chosen for its own sake and not for the sake of something else (*EN* 1105a28–33), so to choose good activity only for the sake of some further consequences will not only be to misunderstand the relative value of actions and consequences, it will actually be to fail to act well. If I eat healthy food simply in order to have my parents' approval, or act justly simply in order to be rewarded (*or,* we must add, simply in order to produce the best consequences for the city), my action fails to be virtuous at all. To act temperately or justly requires, evidently, an understanding of the intrinsic value of temperance and justice; I cannot treat them as tools and still act in accordance with them. But now if, in addition, each of the excellences is, as Aristotle has argued, a distinct item, different in its nature from each of the others, then the choice to act according to any one of them will require an appreciation of that distinct nature as an end in itself; choice among alternatives will involve weighing these distinct natures as distinct items, and choosing the one that gets chosen for the sake of what it itself is. Suppose that, offered a choice between playing music and helping a friend, I decide by selecting some single metric over these two cases and asking about quantities of that. Then either the metric will be identical with the nature of the distinctive value of one or the other of the alternatives, or it will be something distinct from them both—let us say, for example, pleasure or efficiency. But in all three of these cases we will, according to Aristotle, be neglecting the nature of some genuine end or value: in the first two cases we will be neglecting one, in the third case both. By reducing music and friendship to matters of efficiency, for example, I will be failing to attend properly to what they themselves *are*. By assessing friendship in terms of artistic creativity, or artistic creativity in terms of other-regarding virtue alone, I still neglect some genuine value.

At this point, the proponent of Metricity will press questions. First, how can non-metric choice really be rational? If in choosing between A and B I do not choose so as to maximize one single item, and do not even compare the two in terms of a single item, then how on earth *can* I rationally compare the diverse alternatives? Isn't choice without a common measure simply arbitrary, or guesswork? Second, suppose that Aristotle has correctly described the way in which most people do in fact make choices, seeing their values as plural and incommensurable. Why should we think this a particularly good way to choose? Why shouldn't this messy state of things motivate us to press for the development of Metricity, and even of Singleness, where these currently do not exist?[12] The questions are connected. For if we feel that choice without at least this limited com-

---

12. On this ambition as a theme in early Greek ethics, see *Fragility,* chaps. 3 and 4.

mensurability is not rational, this will be a strong reason to favor the development of a superior technique.

The Aristotelian position does not simply describe the status quo. It also makes a strong implicit case for the preservation of our current ways of deciding, as both genuinely rational and superior in richness of value. We begin to see this if we return to the idea of difference of definition. To value each of the separate types of excellent activity as a constituent of the good life is tantamount, in Aristotle's conception, to saying that a life that lacked this item would be deficient or seriously incomplete, in a way that could not be atoned for by the presence of other items, in however great a supply. To value friendship (for example) in this way is to say (as Aristotle explicitly does) that a life that lacked this one item, even though it had as much as you like of every other item, would fall short of full value or goodness in an important way.[13] Friendship does not supply a commodity that we can get elsewhere; it is that very thing, in its own peculiar nature, that is the bearer of value. This is what it means to judge that something is an end, not simply a means to an end: there are no trade-offs without loss.

To value each separate constituent of the good life for what it is in itself entails, then, recognizing its distinctness and separateness from each of the other constituents, each being an irreplaceable part of a composite whole. A rational Aristotelian adult will have a reasonably good understanding of what courage, justice, friendship, generosity, and many other values are. He or she will understand how, in our beliefs and practices, they differ from and are noninterchangeable with one another. Suppose now that a proponent of ethical progress suggests that things can be made neater by doing away with some or all of this heterogeneity. He or she will reply that to do away with this is to do away with the nature of these values as they are, and hence with their special contribution to the richness and fullness of the good life. The proposal threatens to impoverish our practical world: for we have said that each of these items makes its own distinctive contribution, one that we will not get by trading it in for something else. Can it be rational to deliberate in a way that effaces this distinctness? To purchase neatness at such a price appears irrational rather than rational. Would we want to be, or to have, friends who were able to deliberate efficiently about friendship because they could get themselves to conceive of it as a function of some other value? The really rational way to choose, says Aristotle with great plausibility, is to reflect on and acknowledge the special contribution of each item, and to make the understanding of that heterogeneity a central part of the subject matter of deliberation. Evasiveness is not progress.

As for the first question: The Aristotelian should begin by objecting to the way it is posed; for the opponent suggests that deliberation must be either quantitative or a mere shot in the dark.[14] Why should we believe this? Experience shows us a

13. In Book I of the *EN*, in discussing the criterion of "sufficiency," Aristotle suggests that we ask, concerning a candidate for component membership in *eudaimonia*, whether a life that was complete with respect to every other item, but lacked this one alone, was truly complete without it. The argument in *EN* IX for the role of friendship in *eudaimonia* works the same way: see *Fragility*, chap. 12.

14. This is a deep and pervasive thought, from ancient Greek times until the present. For a critical discussion, see Amartya Sen, "Plural Utility," *Proceedings of the Aristotelian Society* 83

further alternative: that it is qualitative and not quantitative, and rational just because it is qualitative, and based upon a grasp of the special nature of each of the items in question. We choose this way all the time; and there is no reason for us to let the rhetoric of weighing and measuring bully us into being on the defensive here, or supposing that we must, if we are rational, be proceeding according to some hidden metric.[15]

I mean to speak later on of social reasoning. So I need to do more now to begin bringing out the contrast between the Aristotelian picture and some pictures of deliberation that are used in contemporary social science.[16] We can readily see how Aristotelianism is at odds with the foundations of classical utilitarianism, and indeed any contemporary Utilitarianism that relies on Singleness or even Metricity. But so far it looks perfectly compatible with a decision procedure that makes use of a purely ordinal ranking of preferences, where the alternatives ranked would prominently include situations in which the agent either does or does not perform some excellent action, or some combination of such actions.[17] Why

---

(1982–3). Sen argues plausibly that utility cannot adequately be understood as a single metric, since not all qualitative distinctions can be reduced to quantitative distinctions. Then, however, he comes to the conclusion that utility must be understood as a plurality of vectors, along each of which there is full quantitative commensurability, and between which there is total non-comparability. This view is still, then, in the grip of the picture that Aristotle attacks. In more recent work, Sen has defended a more thoroughly Aristotelian conception. See especially *Commodities and Capabilities,* a Hennipman Lecture (Amsterdam, 1985), in which the valuation function is an incomplete partial ordering based on qualitative comparison and not on reduction to any single metric.

15. I do not discuss here the apparent difficulties caused by the presence in most translations of the phrase, "We deliberate not about the end, but about the means to the end." The mistranslation is discussed in *Fragility,* chap. 10, with references, especially to David Wiggins, "Deliberation and Practical Reason," *Proc. Arist. Soc.* 76 (1975–6) 29–51, to which my understanding of Aristotle on these issues is much indebted. Deliberation about "what pertains to the end" (the correct translation of the Greek) includes, as well, the further specification of what is to count as the end. Starting, for example, from the valued end of love and friendship, I can go on to ask for a further specification of what, more precisely, love and friendship *are* and for an enumeration of their types, without implying that I regard these different relationships as commensurable on a single quantitative scale, either with one another or with other major values. And if I should ask of justice or of love whether both are constituent parts of *eudaimonia,* I surely do not imply that we can hold these two things up to a single measuring standard, regarding them as productive of some one further thing. The question whether something is or is not to count as part of *eudaimonia* is just the question whether that thing is a valuable component in the best human life. Since Aristotle holds that the best life is inclusive of all those things that are choiceworthy for their own sake, this is equivalent to asking whether that item has intrinsic value. But in his discussion of Plato on the good, Aristotle has argued that valuing a virtue for its own sake not only does not require, but is incompatible with viewing it as qualitatively commensurable with other valuable items. To view it in that way would not be to have the proper regard for the distinctness of *its* nature.

16. On the relevance of Aristotelian conceptions to contemporary social thinking, see "Perception and Revolution," this volume. See also "Non-Relative Virtues: an Aristotelian Approach," *Midwest Studies in Philosophy,* 1988.

17. So far, too, it appears compatible with a single-valued ranking in terms of the strength of agents' desires, the view defended by James Griffin in "Are There Incommensurable Values?" *Philosophy and Public Affairs* 7 (1977) 34–59, and discussed by Dan Brock in his commentary on the original version of this paper in *Proceedings of the Boston Area Colloquium for Ancient Philosophy* 1 (1985); for an Aristotelian criticism of that view, see below.

should we not envisage the rational agent as proceeding according to some such ordering, and social rationality as aggregation of such individual orderings?

We shall soon see how Aristotle objects to the idea of any antecedently fixed ordering or ranking of ends; I therefore defer discussion of the implications of these arguments for social choice. I am also unable to discuss at length two other ways in which Aristotle's ethical approach is at odds with models dominant in social science. I mention them briefly. First, as we have begun to see, Aristotle does not make the sharp distinction between means and ends that is taken for granted in much of social science literature, in economics, perhaps, above all (see n.15). Nor does he hold that ultimate ends cannot be objects of rational deliberation. We can ask concerning each ultimate end not only what the instrumental means to its realization are, but also what *counts* as realizing this end. Furthermore, against the background of our (evolving) pattern of ends, we can always ask of some putative constituent, for example friendship, whether or not it really belongs there as a constituent of the end: that is, whether life would be less rich and complete without it. All this is a part of rational deliberation; and by extending the sphere of practical rationality in this way, Aristotelianism certainly diverges from much that economic accounts of rationality either assume or explicitly state. I cannot enter further here into this highly important and complex subject.[18]

Another evident difference between Aristotle and the theorist who proceeds by ordering preferences concerns the relationship between desire and value. Aristotle does not think that the bare fact that someone prefers something gives us any reason at all for ranking it as preferable. It all depends who the someone is and through what procedures the ranking has been effected. The rankings of the person of practical wisdom will be criterial of our norms, both personal and social; what the bad or mad or childish person prefers counts little or nothing. Nor are the judgments of severely deprived people to be trusted: for frequently they will adjust their preferences to what their actual situation makes possible. Value is anthropocentric, not fixed altogether independently of the desires and needs of human beings;[19] but to say this is very far from saying that every preference of every human being counts for evaluative purposes.

Aristotle would be even more strongly opposed, clearly, to any proposal in which alternatives are ranked in terms of a metric of desire strength. If the fact that someone desires something gives us, all by itself, no good reason to value it, a fortiori the strength or quantity of someone's actual desire give us no good reason for valuing it proportionally to that strength. Even if Aristotle should grant that desire strength *can* be measured and numbered in the unitary way required by this theory—as he almost certainly would not—he would surely view it as an

18. For the bare beginnings of a discussion, see n. 15, *Fragility,* chap. 10, and *De Motu,* Essay 5. On this subject, in addition to the Wiggins article cited in n. 15, see also his "Claims of Need," in *Morality and Objectivity,* ed. T. Honderich (London, 1985) 149–202. An excellent discussion of this whole topic is in Henry Richardson, *Deliberation Is of Ends,* Harvard Ph.D. dissertation, 1986.

19. On this anthropocentricity, see *Fragility,* chaps. 10 and 11, and "Aristotle on Human Nature and the Foundations of Ethics," forthcoming in a volume in honor of Bernard Williams, ed. R. Harrison and J. Altham, Cambridge University Press, 1991.

even more perverse and less plausible version of commensurability than the one that locates commensurability in the object or alternative chosen. The Platonic thesis errs by making values commensurable; but at least it locates value in the right place, in objects and activities, not in our feelings about these. This proposal, by contrast, says something no more plausible, and locates value in the wrong place.[20]

But instead of pursuing this important subject further, I want to turn now to one of its offshoots, one that will focus the difference between Aristotelianism and some forms of technical social theory in a particularly interesting way. In the theory of ordered preferences, when there is a choice (personal or collective) to be made between A and B, only one question is typically asked and considered salient, namely, which alternative is preferred. (Sometimes, as in the Griffin proposal, questions of the weight or intensity of preference are raised, but this is notoriously difficult and controversial.) The agent works with the picture of a single line or scale, and the aim is simply to get as high up on this line as possible. Although the line does not imply, in this case, the presence of a unitary measure of value in terms of which all alternatives are seen as commensurable, there is still a single line, the ranking of actual preferences from among the available alternatives. All alternatives are arranged along this line, and the agent is to look to nothing else in choosing. Aristotelianism asks about overall preferability. But its rather difficult picture of the choice situation also encourages us to ask and to dwell upon a further question about A and B. We have said that the Aristotelian agent scrutinizes each valuable alternative, seeking out its distinct nature. She is determined to acknowledge the precise sort of value or goodness present in each of the competing alternatives, seeing each value as, so to speak, a separate jewel in the crown, valuable in its own right, which does not cease to be separately valuable just because the contingencies of the situation sever it from other goods and it loses out in an overall rational choice. This emphasis on the recognition of plural incommensurable goods leads directly and naturally to the perception of a possibility of irreconcilable contingent conflicts among them. For once we see that A and B have distinct intrinsically valuable goods to offer, we will also be prepared to see that a situation in which we are forced by contingencies beyond our control to choose between A and B is a situation in which we will be forced to forgo some genuine value. Where both A and B are types of virtuous action, the choice situation is one in which we will have to act in some respect deficiently; perhaps even to act unjustly or wrongly. In such situations, to decide that A is preferable to B is sometimes the least of our worries. Agamemnon saw that between the sacrifice of his daughter Iphigenia and an impiety that would bring in its wake the death of all concerned, there was hardly a question of *how* to choose for a rational agent. But here the further problems have only begun. What can be done, thought, felt, about the deficiency or guilt involved in missing out on B? What actions, emotions, responses, are appropriate to the agent who is trapped in such a situation?

---

20. Nor would the Griffin view solve the difficulties that Plato wishes to solve by the introduction of metricity and singleness. On these see "Plato on Commensurability," this volume. Sen's *Commodities and Capabilities* (see n. 14) contains a very illuminating discussion of this issue.

What expressions of remorse, what reparative efforts, does morality require here? The individual cannot neglect these concerns without grave moral deficiency. Agamemnon neglected them, in the belief that the problem of preference was the only one to be solved by rationality. The chorus of elders regard this not as wisdom, but as madness.

I have written much more about these situations elsewhere.[21] They are the core of Greek tragedy; they are also a regular part of most human lives. Aristotelianism acknowledges them and treats them as salient; indeed, as inextricable from the richness and diversity of the positive commitments of a good person living in a world of uncontrolled happening. Economic theory does not explicitly rule them out by definition, as does a great part of modern moral philosophy. But it treats them as irrelevant to what the theory is about, namely, choosing rationally.[22] We can go further. It may be an indirect and unnoticed consequence of one prominent formulation of an axiom of the theory of social choice that we are not to recognize such situations. Consider the principle known as the independence of Irrelevant Alternatives: "The social choice made from any environment depends only on the orderings of individuals with respect to the alternatives in that environment. . . . It is never necessary to compare available alternatives with those which are not available at a given moment in order to arrive at a decision."[23] In a case of the type I have been considering, the social choice theorist must, apparently, then refuse to consider the relation of Agamemnon's situation to another situation in which he could have kept all of his commitments without atrocious wrongdoing. He must consider only the ordering of the options in the situation itself, and regard it as irrelevant that all the available options are hideous by comparison to what a good person would wish to choose. This is not the intent of the principle, clearly; but it does seem to be a consequence of this formulation—and one that is of a piece with the more general denial of the distinction between value and desire that I have described above. For the Aristotelian, "unavailable" does not imply "irrelevant" (these two words are used interchangeably in Arrow's formulation of this principle, with confusing effect). Aristotelianism fosters attention to the ways in which the world can impede our efforts to act well; it indicates that caring about many things will open us to the risk of these terrible situations. It asks us, as people committed to goodness, to notice it when none of our options

21. See *Fragility,* Chap. 2; also *Aristotle's De Motu,* essay 4; and "Flawed Crystals," this volume. Aristotle himself gives less weight to such conflicts than his theory seems to demand, but he does in principle recognize them: see *Fragility,* chaps. 11–12 and Interlude 2.

22. *Fragility,* chap. 2 contains discussion of the views of Kant, Hare, and Sartre, and extensive reference to the secondary literature.

23. This formulation is cited from K. Arrow, "Values and Collective Decision Making," from P. Laslett and W. G. Runciman, eds., *Philosophy, Politics and Society,* Third Series (Oxford, 1967), repr. in E. Hahn and M. Hollis, eds., *Philosophy and Economic Theory* (Oxford, 1979), 110–26, on pp. 113, 120. Arrow explicitly links the principle, thus stated, to a rejection of any cardinal measure of utility: "Any cardinal measure, any attempt to give a numerical representation of utility, depends basically on comparisons involving alternative actions which are not, or at least may not be, available, given the environment prevailing at the moment" (113). I think it fair to say, then, that at least he holds the principle in a form that would rule out the sort of proper recognition of moral dilemmas that I am describing here.

is good.[24] It encourages us to develop appropriate ways of thinking and feeling about these possibilities, telling us that all this is a part of living well for a human being. Agamemnon's decision, even under these terrible constraints, will be better and more rationally made if he considers the relation of these constraints to his wishes and choices as a person of virtue. Social choice theory, however, insists that only his ordinal ranking of the actual possibilities is relevant; he can choose rationally and well without thinking that the sacrifice of a daughter is an absolutely bad thing.[25]

Does this matter for a theory of public rationality? I would argue that it matters deeply. Frequently leaders, like private citizens, will be confronted with unpalatable moral choices, choices in which there is no loss-free, and perhaps even no guilt-free course available. We want leaders who will be able to make tough necessary choices in such situations, preferring A to B or B to A. We do not want the presence of recognized dilemma to prevent them from evincing a preference. But we also want them to preserve and publicly display enough of the Aristotelian intuitions of the ordinary private person that they will say, here is a situation in which we are violating an important human value. Suppose, for example, we are in agreement that on balance Truman was correct in choosing to bomb Hiroshima; that this was the best available exit to the horrible dilemma in which he and the nation had been placed by factors beyond their control. Still, it matters deeply whether the bombing is to be treated simply as the winning alternative, or, in addition, as a course of action that overrides a genuine moral value. It matters whether Truman takes this course with unswerving confidence in his own powers of reason, or with reluctance, remorse, and the belief that he is obligated to make whatever reparations can be made. Whether all his attention is directed toward picking the top point on a single ordered line, or whether he attends, as well, to the intrinsic ethical character of the claim that on balance is not preferred.[26] The Aristotelian leader, cherishing each separate value and attaching to each the appropriate emotions and feelings of obligation, behaves in the second of these ways. What is more, he or she holds that it is good, in a more general way, to focus on these dilemmas and not to go beyond them, or "solve" them, because to do so

24. If the agent is deliberating well about this situation, the negative utility he or she attaches to the two bad courses will show up in some way in his or her desires and preferences; but, first, since she is only allowed to compare possible alternatives, and not to compare all the possible ones with all the good and unavailable ones, the bad one that is the least bad will still show up as the top point on a free-floating (not cardinally anchored) line; second, if, like Agamemnon, he is deliberating evasively, the badness of the chosen course will not be reflected in his desires and so, if the *selection* is correct, the presence of badness on both sides will have made no difference; third, this procedure does not allow us to distinguish between evasive and nonevasive deliberation, as long as the alternative selected remains the same.

25. By "absolutely" I do not and cannot mean one that is never to be done; for part of my point is to insist that there are circumstances in which anything that one might do will be just this bad. I mean that whenever it is done, it is bad: though sometimes it may be the least bad thing available.

26. For a good discussion of this topic, and this case, see M. Walzer, "Political Action and the Problem of Dirty Hands," *Philosophy and Public Affairs* 2 (1973) 160–80. *Fragility,* chap. 2, gives other references.

reaffirms and strengthens attachment to the values in question, in such a way that one will be less likely to violate them in other circumstances. The leader who is brought up to disregard the contrast between one's actual situation and a situation that is, for better or worse, not available will not learn through that education that there is a salient difference between these two ways, and so he or she will be all too likely to prefer the former, as easier on the conscience.[27]

In R. M. Hare's recent book *Moral Thinking,* two stylized reasoners are introduced. They are called the Archangel and the Prole.[28] The Prole, stuck with ordinary daily intuitive rationality, sees moral dilemmas as real and indissoluble, requiring remorse and reparative efforts. The Archangel, a Utilitarian philosopher, is able to see that from the critical perspective of this theory (as Hare describes it) such dilemmas vanish. She learns to rise above them, and has disdain for those who continue to recognize them. Hare presents his position, as always, with vigor and subtlety. He qualifies his contrast by arguing that there are many reasons why, in most daily choices, we should behave like proles. And yet the Archangel is a norm for practical reasoning, when it is at its best. And it is clear that the Archangel is Hare's answer to his own urgent motivating questions about how a theory of choice can actually make things better in human life. I believe, with Aristotle, that the Archangel's superior clarity and simplicity does not make things better; that rising above a human problem does not solve it. I believe that we want more proles and fewer Archangels, not only in daily choice, but as leaders and models. Angels, Thomas Aquinas held, cannot perceive what is there for perceiving in this world of contingency. And thus they are, as Aquinas concluded, poor guides indeed for getting around in this world, however well off they might be in heaven. It is, said Aristotle, the human good that we are seeking, and not the good of some other being.

II. Priority of the Particular

"The discernment rests with perception." This phrase, from which my title is taken, is used by Aristotle in connection with his attack on another feature of pseudo-scientific pictures of rationality: the insistence that rational choice can be captured in a system of general rules or principles which can then simply be applied to each new case. Aristotle's defense of the priority of "perception," together with his insistence that practical wisdom cannot be a systematic science concerned throughout with universal and general principles, is evidently a defense of the priority of concrete situational judgments of a more informal and intuitive kind to any such system. Once again he is attacking an item that is generally taken to be criterial of rationality in our day, particularly in the public sphere. His attack on ethical generality is closely linked to the attack on commensurability. For the two notions are closely related, and both are seen by their defenders as progressive

---

27. There is an excellent discussion of this in S. Hampshire, "Public and Private Morality," in *Morality and Conflict* (Cambridge, Mass., 1983), 101–25, at 123; I discuss his position in the later (political) sections of this essay.

28. R. M. Hare, *Moral Thinking* (Oxford, 1981).

stratagems that we can use to extricate ourselves from the ethical vulnerability that arises from the perception of qualitative heterogeneity. Too much heterogeneity leaves the agent who sees it open to the possibility of surprise and perplexity. For a new situation may strike her as unlike any other. A valuable item may seem altogether distinct and new. But if she tells herself either that there is only a single item in terms of which all values are commensurable—or that there is a finite number of general values, repeatedly instantiated, under which all new cases are bound to fall as instances—by either of these routes she will escape from the burden of the intractable and unexpected. She will come to each new situation prepared to see only those items about which she already knows how to deliberate.

The perception of heterogeneity brings another problem with it: vulnerability to loss. To view a beloved person (country, occupation) as not unique but an instance of a homogeneous general concept is to view it as potentially replaceable by another similar instance, should the world take from us the one we now have. Plato's Diotima argues that making the general prior in this way to the particular brings a "relaxing" and "easing" of the strains involved in planning a life. With value-generality, as with commensurability's more radical reduction to a single value, if the world removes something you love there is likely to be a ready supply of other similarly valuable items. Many Greek thinkers believed that a hallmark of a truly rational decision procedure would be that it should remove some of our ethical perplexity and vulnerability, putting us more securely in control of the more important things. This idea still has a powerful appeal.

Here we must begin to distinguish, as Aristotle himself does not, or does not with clarity, the *general* from the *universal*. The *general* is opposed to the *concrete;* a general rule not only covers many cases, it applies to them in virtue of some rather non-concrete characteristics. A *universal* rule, by contrast, applies to all cases that are in the relevant ways similar; but a universal may be highly concrete, citing features that are not very likely to be replicated. Many moral views that base correct choice on universal principles employ principles of broad generality. And this is a natural link, if one is interested in the codifying and action-guiding force of principles. One could not teach a child what to do using rules whose terms were too concrete to prepare the child for new cases as yet unseen; and one epistemological role for rules in morality has traditionally been to simplify and systematize the moral world, a task that highly refined and concrete universals have difficulty performing. But universals may also be concrete; and some philosophers, notably R. M. Hare,[29] who have a deep interest in the universalizability of moral prescriptions have also insisted that principles should often be highly context-specific. Aristotle's claims that the "particular" is "prior" in ethical reasoning are directed, in different ways and with different arguments, at both general principles and universal principles. His attack on the general is more global and more fundamental. Universalizability he accepts up to a point, though I believe that in certain cases he denies its moral role, holding that it is not, in these cases, correct to say that were the same circumstances to occur again, the same choice would again be correct. So to give a clear description of the view and the arguments that

29. See *Moral Thinking;* and for further discussion of his position in this volume, see Introduction, and "'Finely Aware,'" endnote.

support it, we must insist on this distinction more forcefully than does Aristotle, whose primary opponent is a Plato whose universals are also highly general.

Aristotelian arguments against commensurability do not by themselves imply that particular judgments are prior to general rules. His attack on commensurability, as we have described it, relied on the picture of a plurality of distinct values, each generating its own claims, but each having, as well, its own general definition and being instantiable in any number of particular situations and actions. So the bare fact that, for example, courage and justice and friendship are plural and distinct does little to support the priority of particular perceptions to systems of rules or principles. On the contrary, our talk of distinctness in definition suggested that Aristotle might have had a strong interest in such a system. On the other hand, Aristotle does insist, as we have seen, that practical wisdom is not *epistēmē,* that is, systematic scientific understanding. He defends this claim by arguing that it is concerned with ultimate particulars *(ta kath'hekasta)* and that these particulars cannot be subsumed under any *epistēmē* (a system of universal principles) but must be grasped with insight through experience (*EN* 1142a11ff.). In praising perception, he is praising the grasping of particulars contained in this sort of experienced judgment. His statement seems to be an assault on the priority of the *general,* and probably of the *universal* as well. We need, then, to ask how the further moves from plurality to specificity or concreteness, and sometimes also from concreteness to singularity, are defended. And we need to know, as well, what role rules, of various sorts, actually do play in Aristotelian rationality.

We must notice first that rules could play an important role in practical reason without being prior to particular perceptions.[30] For they might be used not as normative for perception, the ultimate authorities against which the correctness of particular choices is assessed, but more as summaries or rules of thumb, highly useful for a variety of purposes, but valid only to the extent to which they correctly describe good concrete judgments, and to be assessed, ultimately, against these. On this second picture, there is still room for recognizing as ethically salient the new or surprising feature of the case before us, features that have not been anticipated in the rule, or even features that could not in principle be captured in any rule. If Aristotle's talk of rules is of this second kind, there need be no tension at all between his evident interest in rules and definitions, and his defense of the priority of perception. I shall now argue that this is, in fact, the situation, and explore his reasons for giving priority to the particular.

We can begin with the two passages in which our title phrase is introduced. In both he explicitly claims that priority in practical choice should be accorded not to principle, but to perception, a faculty of discrimination that is concerned with apprehending concrete particulars:

> The person who diverges only slightly from the correct is not blameworthy, whether he errs in the direction of the more or the less; but the person who diverges *more* is blamed; for this is evident. But to say to what point and how much someone is blameworthy is not easy to determine by a principle: nor in fact is this the case with any other perceptible item. For things of this sort are among

---

30. For a longer account of this point, see *Fragility,* chap. 10.

the concrete particulars, and the discernment rests with perception. (*EN* 1109b18–23)

Again, in a discussion of one of the specific virtues, mildness of temper, Aristotle writes: "What degree and type of divergence is blameworthy, it is not easy to express in any general principle: for the discernment lies in the particulars and in perception" (1126b2–4). The subtleties of a complex ethical situation must be seized in a confrontation with the situation itself, by a faculty that is suited to address it as a complex whole. Prior general formulations lack both the concreteness and the flexibility that is required. They do not contain the particularizing details of the matter at hand, with which decision must grapple; and they are not responsive to what is there, as good decision must be.

These two related criticisms are pressed repeatedly, as Aristotle argues for the ethical priority of concrete description to general statement, particular judgment to general rule. "Among statements about conduct," he writes in an adjacent passage, "those that are universal *(katholou)* are more general *(koinoteroi,* common to many things),[31] but the particular are more true—for action is concerned with particulars, and statements must harmonize with these" (1107a29–32). Principles are authoritative only insofar as they are correct; but they are correct only insofar as they do not err with regard to the particulars. And it is not possible for a formulation intended to cover many different particulars to achieve a high degree of correctness. Therefore, in his discussion of justice Aristotle insists that the experienced judgments of the agent must both correct and supplement the general and universal formulations of law:

> All law is universal; but about some things it is not possible for a universal statement to be correct. Then in those matters in which it is necessary to speak universally, but not possible to do so correctly, the law takes the usual case, though without ignoring the possibility of missing the mark. . . . When, then, the law speaks universally, and something comes up that is not covered by the universal, then it is correct, insofar as the legislator has been deficient or gone wrong in speaking simply, to correct his omission, saying what he would have said himself had he been present and would have legislated if he had known. (*EN* 1137b13ff.)

The law is authoritative insofar as it is a summary of wise decisions. It is therefore appropriate to supplement it with new wise decisions made on the spot; and it is also appropriate to correct it where it diverges from what a good judge would do in this case. Here again, we find that particular judgment is superior both in correctness and in flexibility.

Aristotle illustrates the idea of ethical flexibility in a vivid and famous metaphor. He tells us that a person who makes each choice by appeal to some ante-

---

31. Note here the slide from universal to general: but the point is that the moment it covers many particulars it gets too unspecific to be the best way of approaching a concrete context. A universal need not abstract from contextual features (see below); but the sort of universal principle that can be fixed in advance and applied to many cases will have to do this too much for Aristotle. I translate *katholou,* for consistency, as "universal" throughout, though in my interpretive remarks I try to make clear exactly which issue Aristotle has in mind.

cedent general principle held firm and inflexible for the occasion is like an archi-tect who tries to use a straight ruler on the intricate curves of a fluted column. No real architect does this. Instead following the lead of the builders of Lesbos, he will measure with a flexible strip of metal, the Lesbian Rule, that "bends to the shape of the stone and is not fixed" (1137b30–32). This device is still in use, as one might expect. I have one. It is invaluable for measuring oddly-shaped parts of an old Victorian house. (The Utilitarian who recently wrote that "we" prefer ethical sys-tems in the style of the Bauhaus[32] had fortunate architectural tastes, given his view of rules.) It is also of use in measuring the parts of the body, few of which are straight. We could anticipate our point, not too oddly, by saying that Aristotle's picture of ethical reality has the form of a human body or bodies rather than that of a mathematical construct. So it requires rules that fit it. Good deliberation, like the Lesbian Rule, accommodates itself to the shape that it finds, responsively and with respect for complexity.

But perhaps Aristotle is speaking here only of the defectiveness of actual systems of rules; perhaps he says nothing against the idea that an ethical science could come into being if its rules were made precise or complicated enough. The image of the Lesbian Rule does not encourage this thought. But we can go further in answering this objection, showing, first, that he believes that correct choice can-not, even in principle, be captured in a system of rules, then going on to point out three features of the "matter of the practical" that show why not.

In this same section of *EN* V, Aristotle tells us that practical matters are in their very nature indeterminate or indefinable *(aorista)*—not just so far insufficiently defined. The universal account fails because no universal can adequately capture this matter. "The error is not in the law or in the legislator, but in the nature of the thing, since the matter of practical affairs is of this kind from the start" (1137b17–19). Again, in Book II, discussing the role of universal definitions and accounts in ethics (and preparing to put forward his own definitions of the virtues) he writes:

> Let this be agreed on from the start, that every statement about matters of practice ought to be said in outline and not with precision, as we said in the beginning that statements should be demanded in a way appropriate to the matter at hand. And matters of practice and questions of what is advantageous never stand fixed, any more than do matters of health. If the universal definition is like this, the definition concerning particulars is even more lacking in precision. For such cases do not fall under any science or under any precept, but the agents themselves must in each case look to what suits the occasion, as is also the case in medicine and navigation. (1103b34–1104a10)

The general account *ought*[33] to be put forward as an outline only, and not the precise final word. It is not just that ethics has not yet attained the precision of science; it should not even try for such precision.

---

32. J. Glover, quoted in D. Wiggins, "Deliberation and Practical Reason" (see n. 18).

33. This "ought to" is sometimes mistranslated as "will have to." On this, see *De Motu,* Essay 4, *Fragility,* chap. 10.

Three reasons for this are suggested in this brief passage. First, practical matters are mutable, or lacking in fixity. A system of rules set up in advance can encompass only what has been seen before—as a medical treatise can give only the recognized pattern of a disease. But the world of change confronts us with ever new configurations, ever new situations for the determining of the virtuous course. What is more, since the virtues themselves are individuated and defined with reference to contingent circumstances that may themselves undergo change (for example, Aristotle himself points out that there will be no virtue of generosity in a city with communistic property institutions),[34] the good agent may need not only to locate the virtuous action among strange new events, but also to deal with an evolving and situation-relative list of virtues. Even natural justice for human beings, Aristotle says, is "all mutable," i.e. historically rooted, relative to circumstances of scarcity and also of personal separateness that are relatively stable, but still in the natural world.[35] A doctor whose only resource, confronted with a new configuration of symptoms, was to turn to the textbook would be a poor doctor; a pilot who steered his ship by rule in a storm of unanticipated direction or intensity would be incompetent. Even so, people of practical wisdom must meet the new with responsiveness and imagination, cultivating the sort of flexibility and perceptiveness that will permit them, in the words of Thucydides (articulating an Athenian ideal of which Aristotle is the heir and defender) to "improvise what is required" (I.118). In several contexts, Aristotle speaks of practical wisdom as an ability concerned with *stochazesthai*. This word, which originally means "to take aim at a target," comes to be used of an improvisatory conjectural use of reason. He tells us that "the person who is good at deliberation without qualification is the one who takes aim *(stochastikos)* according to reason at the best for a human being in the sphere of things to be done" (1141b13–14); he associates this ideal closely with the observation that practical wisdom is concerned with particulars and not universals (1141b14–16).

In the *EN* V passage, and implicitly in the one from Book II, Aristotle alludes to a second feature of the practical, its indeterminate or indefinable character *(to aoriston)*. It is difficult to interpret this feature; it seems to be connected with the variety of practical contexts and the situation-relativity of appropriate choice. One example is revealing. There is no definition *(horismos)* of good joke-telling, Aristotle writes, but it is *aoristos,* since it is so much a matter of pleasing the particular hearer, and "different things are repugnant and pleasant to different people" (1128a25ff). To extrapolate from this case, excellent choice cannot be captured in general rules, because it is a matter of fitting one's choice to the complex requirements of a concrete situation, taking all of its contextual features into account. A rule, like a manual of humor, would do both too little and too much: too little,

---

34. *Pol.* 1263b7–14. Here, however, Aristotle actually concludes that the Platonic scheme should be blamed for eliminating the virtue, a response that appears to run counter to his overall position (on which see *Fragility,* chap. 10, 11). The remark is probably best understood as saying that Plato has not eliminated property itself, he has just eliminated individuals' control over property; thus, there is still the conceptual space for the virtue, but there is no sphere of choice in which individuals can exercise the virtue. See also "Non-Relative Virtues."

35. *EN* 1134b28–33; on Aristotle's arguments as to why laws should be made difficult to change, see *Fragility,* chap. 10.

because most of what really counts is in the response to the concrete; and this would be omitted. Too much, because the rule would imply that it was itself normative for response (as a joke manual would ask you to tailor your wit to the formulae it contains), and this would impinge too much on the flexibility of good practice. The Lesbian Rule is called *aoristos,* presumably because, unlike such precepts, it varies its own shape according to the shape of what is before it. In speaking of mutability Aristotle stresses change over time and the moral relevance of surprise; in speaking of the *aoriston* he stresses complexity and context. Both features call for responsiveness and yielding flexibility, a rightness of tone and a sureness of touch that no general account could adequately capture.

Finally Aristotle suggests that the concrete ethical case may simply contain some ultimately particular and non-repeatable elements. This is one part of what he means when he says that they simply do not fall under any general science or precept. Complexity and variety already yield a high degree of situational particularity, for the occurrence of properties that are, taken singly, instantiated elsewhere in an endless variety of combinations can make the whole context a unique particular. But Aristotle also recognizes the ethical relevance of non-repeatable components. The moderate diet for Milo the wrestler is not the same as the moderate diet for Aristotle (indeed, for any other human being), because Milo's concrete, and presumably unique combination of size, weight, needs, goals and activity are all relevant to determining the appropriate for him. This is a contingent limitation on the universal; we could try to say that we have here a universal principle with only a single instance, in that if anyone else should turn up with that precise size, weight, etc., the ethical prescription would be the same. Even so, this would not be the sort of universal principle that would satisfy most devotees of principles, since it is rooted in the particulars of Milo's historical context in such a way that it could not have been anticipated with precision in advance; and perhaps (indeed, very likely) will be of no further use in the future. An ethical science with "principles" this context-specific would have to have a vast and infinitely extensible series of principles; and this is not a science that will satisfy those who are looking for science.

But Aristotle goes further still in some cases. The particularity of love and friendship seems to demand nonrepeatability in yet a stronger sense. Good friends will attend to the particular needs and concerns of their friends, benefiting them for the sake of what they are, in and of themselves. Some of this "themselves" consists of repeatable character traits; but features of shared history and of family relationship that are not even in principle repeatable are allowed to bear serious ethical weight. Here the agent's own historical singularity (and/or the historical singularity of the relationship itself) enter into moral deliberation in a way that could not even in principle give rise to a universal principle, since what is ethically important (among other things) is to treat the friend as a unique nonreplaceable being, a being not like anyone else in the world.[36] "Practical wisdom is not con-

36. On the types of individuality recognized as relevant to love and friendship, see *Fragility,* chaps. 6, 7, 12. For some doubts as to whether the Aristotelian position really satisfies all our intuitions about this individuality, see this volume, "Love and the Individual." Further remarks are in the Introduction in the section entitled "The Aristotelian Ethical View," and in the endnote to "'Finely Aware.'"

cerned with universals only; it must also recognize particulars, for it is practical, and practice concerns particulars" (1141b4–16).[37]

In all of these ways, rules, general and/or universal, seen as normative for correctness of judgment, fail in their very nature to measure up to the challenge of practical choice. And Aristotle's arguments are strong not only against the normative use of a systematic hierarchy of rules, but in general against any general algorithm for correct choice. The defense of the Lesbian ruler and the account of the context-relativity of the mean imply not only that the good judge will not decide by subsuming a case under antecedently fixed rules, but also that there is no general procedure or algorithm for computing what to do in every case. The appropriate response is not arrived at mechanically; there is no general procedural description that can be given concerning how to find it. Or if there is, it is about as useful as a joke manual, and as potentially misleading. Here again, Aristotle's picture breaks sharply with contemporary attempts to describe a general formula or technique of choice which can then be applied to each new particular. Aristotle has no objection to the use of general guidelines of this sort for certain purposes. They have a useful role to play so long as they keep their place. Rules and general procedures can be aids in moral development, since people who do not yet have practical wisdom and insight need to follow rules that summarize the wise judgments of others. Then too, if there is not time to formulate a fully concrete decision in the case at hand, it is better to follow a good summary rule or a standardized decision procedure than to make a hasty and inadequate contextual choice. Again, if we are not confident of our judgment in a given case, if there is reason to believe that bias or interest might distort our particular judgment, rules give us a superior constancy and stability. (This is Aristotle's primary argument for preferring the rule of law to rule by decree.) Even for wise adults who are not short of time, the rule has a function, guiding them tentatively in their approach to the new particular, helping them to pick out its salient features. This function we shall later examine in more detail.

But Aristotle's point in all these cases is that the rule or algorithm represents a falling off from full practical rationality, not its flourishing or completion. The existence of a formal choice function is not a condition of rational choice, any more than the existence of a navigation manual is a condition (surely not sufficient and usually not even necessary) of good navigation. Either the choice function is simply the summary of what good judges do or have done in situations so far encountered—in which case it will be true but posterior, and the more posterior the more it simplifies[38]—or it is an attempt to extract from that which they do and have done some more elegant and simple procedure that can from then on be normative for what they do—in which case it will be false and even corrupting.

An important thing to remember, in assessing this claim, is that Aristotelian deliberation does not confine itself to means–end reasoning. It is, as we have insisted, concerned as well with the specification of ultimate ends. But this means

37. For a list of passages in which Aristotle speaks this way, see *Fragility*, chap. 10, n. 29. Compare the illuminating discussion of these issues in Andrew Harrison, *Making and Thinking: A Study of Intelligent Activities* (Hassocks, Sussex, 1978), esp. chap. 3.

38. See *Aristotle's De Motu*, Essay 4.

that the contextual and nonrepeatable material can enter into the agent's deliberation at a much more basic level than at the level of means calculation and (for
example) the reckoning up of probabilities in connection with this. A great part
of *rational* deliberation will be concerned with questions about whether a certain
course of action here and now really counts as realizing some important value
(say, courage or friendship) that is a prima facie part of her idea of the good life;
or even whether a certain way of acting (a certain relationship—type or particular)
really counts as the sort of thing she wants to include in her conception of a good
life at all. Whether this friendship, this love, this courageous risk, really is something without which her life will be less valuable and less complete. For this sort
of question, it seems obvious that there is no mathematical answer; and the only
procedure to follow is (as we shall see) to imagine all the relevant features as well
and fully and concretely as possible, holding them up against whatever intuitions
and emotions and plans and imaginings we have brought into the situation or can
construct in it. There is really no shortcut at all; or none that is not corrupting.
The most we have by way of a theory of correct procedure is the account of good
deliberation given by Aristotle himself, which is deliberately thin, referring for its
content to the account of character. It not only does not tell us how to compute
the mean, it tells us that there is no general true answer to this question. Beyond
this, the content of rational choice must be supplied by nothing less messy than
experience and stories of experience. Among stories of conduct, the most true and
informative will be works of literature, biography, and history; the more abstract
the story gets, the less rational it is to use it as one's only guide. Good deliberation
is like theatrical or musical improvisation, where what counts is flexibility, responsiveness, and openness to the external; to rely on an algorithm here is not only
insufficient, it is a sign of immaturity and weakness. It is possible to play a jazz
solo from a score, making minor alterations for the particular nature of one's
instrument. The question is, who would do this, and why?

If all this is so, Aristotle must also refrain from giving any formal normative
account of the properties of adult deliberative rationality. For, like its subject matter, it is too flexible to be pinned down in a general way. Instead, he stresses the
importance of experience in giving content to practical wisdom, developing a contrast between practical insight and scientific or mathematical understanding:

> It is obvious that practical wisdom is not deductive scientific understanding *(epis-
> tēmē)*. For it is of the ultimate and particular, as has been said—for the matter of
> action is like this. It is the analogue of theoretical insight *(nous)*: for *nous* is of the
> ultimately first principles, for which there is no external justification; and practical
> wisdom is of the ultimate and particular, of which there is no scientific under-
> standing, but a kind of perception—not, I mean, ordinary sense-perception of the
> proper objects of each sense, but the sort of perception by which we grasp that a
> certain figure is composed in a certain way out of triangles. (1142a23)[39]

Practical insight is like perceiving in the sense that it is noninferential, nonde-
ductive; it is an ability to recognize the salient features of a complex situation.

---

39. See the excellent discussion of this passage in Wiggins, "Deliberation." I am to some
extent indebted to his translation-cum-explication here, as in 1143a25–b14 below.

And just as the theoretical *nous* comes only out of a long experience with first principles and a sense, gained gradually in and through experience, of the fundamental role played by these principles in discourse and explanation, so too practical perception, which Aristotle also calls *nous*, is gained only through a long process of living and choosing that develops the agent's resourcefulness and responsiveness:

> Young people can become mathematicians and geometers and wise in things of that sort; but they do not appear to become people of practical widsom. The reason is that practical wisdom is of the particular, which becomes graspable through experience, but a young person is not experienced. For a quantity of time is required for experience. (1142a12–16)

and again:

> We credit the same people with possessing judgment and having reached the age of intuitive insight and being people of understanding and practical wisdom. For all of these abilities are concerned with the ultimate and the particular . . . and all practical matters are concerned with the particular and the ultimate. For the person of practical wisdom must recognize these, and understanding and judgment are also concerned with practical matters, i.e. with ultimates. And intuitive insight *(nous)* is concerned with ultimates in both directions . . . [There follows a development of the parallel between grasp of first principles and grasp of ultimate particulars.] . . . This is why we should attend to the undemonstrated sayings of experienced and older people or people of practical wisdom not less than to demonstrations. For since experience has given them an eye they see correctly. (1143a25–b14)

By now we are inclined to ask what experience can possibly contribute, if what practical wisdom sees is the idiosyncratic and the new. Our emphasis on flexibility should not, however, make us imagine that Aristotelian perception is rootless and ad hoc, rejecting all guidance from the past. The good navigator does not go by the rule book; and she is prepared to deal with what she has not seen before. But she knows, too, how to use what she has seen; she does not pretend that she has never been on a boat before. Experience is concrete and not exhaustively summarizable in a system of rules. Unlike mathematical wisdom it cannot be adequately encompassed in a treatise. But it does offer guidance, and it does urge on us the recognition of repeated as well as unique features. Even if rules are not sufficient, they may be highly useful, frequently even necessary. We shall return to this important issue in section V, working with a concrete example of Aristotelian deliberation. We turn now to the third feature of his conception, which will further illuminate the others.

III. The Rationality of Emotions and Imagination

So far the Aristotelian picture has attacked two items that are commonly alleged to be criterial of rationality. His third target is even more broadly so held: the idea that rational choice is not made under the influence of the emotions and the imag-

ination. The idea that rational deliberation might draw on and even be guided by
these elements has sometimes even been taken (in both ancient and modern
times) to be a conceptual impossibility, the "rational" being defined by opposition
to these "irrational" parts of the soul. (This is especially true of emotion, but
important writers in both ancient and modern times have included imagination
in their blame of the irrational. This is, surprisingly, true even of some philosophers, like Stuart Hampshire, who are otherwise sympathetic to Aristotle's conception of choice.)[40] Plato repudiated emotion and appetite as corrupting influences, insisting that correct practical judgments are reached only by encouraging
the intellect to go off "itself by itself," free from their influence as far as possible.
The condition of the person in which they lead or guide intellect is given the pejorative name of "madness," which is definitionally contrasted with rationality or
soundness of judgment.[41] The two dominant moral theories of our own time,
Kantianism and Utilitariansim, have been no less suspicious of the passions;
indeed, this is one of the few things on which they (usually) agree. For Kant, the
passions are invariably selfish and aimed at one's own states of satisfaction. Even
in the context of love and friendship, he urges us to avoid becoming subject to
their influence; for an action will have genuine moral worth only if it is chosen
for its own sake; and given his conception of the passions he cannot allow that
action chosen only or primarily because of passion could be chosen for its own
sake. The Utilitarian believes that a passion like personal love frequently impedes
rationality by being too parochial: it leads us to emphasize personal ties and to
rank the nearer above the further, obstructing that fully impartial attitude toward
the world that is the hallmark of Utilitarian rationality.

Imagination fares no better. Plato's rejection of the influence of sensuous cognition is part and parcel of his general rejection of the influence of the bodily.
Without attempting to characterize Kant's own complex view of imagination, we
may say that modern Kantians have shown considerable interest in curbing flights
of deliberative imagination that they see as potential strong impediments to action
in accordance with duty. Imagination is thought to be too often egoistic and self-
indulgent, too concerned with particulars and with their relation to the self. One
can be correctly motivated by duty without developing imagination; therefore its
cultivation is at best a luxury, at worst a danger.

Nor do Utilitarians approve of imagination's vivid portrayal of alternatives in
all their color and singularity; again this faculty is suspected of being wedded to
particularity and the recognition of incommensurables, therefore of being a threat
to the impartial assessment of facts and probabilities. Whatever the faults of Dickens's *Hard Times* as a portrait of Utilitarianism—and they are many—he is surely
correct in depicting the Benthamite father as holding the view that "fancy" is a
form of dangerous self-indulgence, and that reason (conceived of as that fact-stor-
ing and calculative power in virtue of which Mr. Gradgrind is always "ready to

40. See, for example, Hampshire, *Morality and Conflict*, pp. 130–135—where imagination is
contrasted with the "rational" and said to be a faculty inappropriate for judgments about justice.
(Here I should say, "sympathetic to the picture of choice that I have ascribed to Aristotle"—since
Hampshire and I do not have altogether the same interpretation of Aristotle.)

41. See *Fragility,* chaps. 5, 7. The *Phaedrus,* I argue, modifies this picture.

weigh and measure each parcel of human nature, and tell you exactly what it comes to") is the only faculty to which education is properly addressed, if we are to build a properly impartial society. (Concerning Louisa, from the cradle starved in fancy, he reflects with moral satisfaction, "would have been self-willed . . . but for her bringing-up.") Contemporary theorists follow these leads, either explicitly repudiating imagination and emotion as irrational or offering a picture of rationality in which they play no positive role.

I have sketched these motivations for the rejection of imagination and emotion in order to indicate that Aristotelian perception may have corresponding motives for their cultivation. If these faculties are indeed closely linked with our ability to grasp particulars in all of their richness and concreteness, then perception will disregard them at its peril. As we pursue this lead, we shall at the same time see how Aristotle answers the charges that these faculties are invariably distorting and self-serving.

Aristotle does not have a single concept that corresponds exactly to our "imagination." His *phantasia,* usually so translated, is a more inclusive human and animal capability, that of focusing on some concrete particular, either present or absent, in such a way as to see (or otherwise perceive) it *as* something, picking out its salient features, discerning its content.[42] In this function it is the active and selective aspect of perception. But *phantasia* also works closely in tandem with memory, enabling the creature to focus on absent experienced items in their concreteness, and even to form new combinations, not yet experienced, from items that have entered sense-experience. So it can do much of the work of our imagination, though it should be stressed that Aristotle's emphasis is upon its selective and discriminatory character rather than upon its capability for free fantasy. Its job is more to focus on reality than to create unreality.

Phantasia appears to be a faculty well suited to the work of deliberation as Aristotle understands it, and it is no surprise to find him invoking it in connection with the minor premise of the "practical syllogism," that is, the creature's perception of an item in the world *as* something that answers to one of his or her practical interests or concerns. Elsewhere he shows imagination working closely with an ethical conception of the good: our imaginative view of a situation "marks off" or "determines" it as presenting elements that correspond to our view of what is to be pursued and avoided.[43] It is also no surprise that he ascribes to human beings the capacity for a special sort of imagining, which is called "deliberative *phantasia,*" and which involves the ability to link several imaginings or perceptions together, "making a unity from many." All thought, for Aristotle, is of necessity (in finite creatures) accompanied by an imagining that is concrete, even where the thought itself is abstract. This is just a fact of human psychology. But whereas the mathematician can safely disregard the concrete features of his or her imagined triangle when she is proving a theorem about triangles, the person of practical

---

42. See *De Motu,* Essay 5, where I discuss all the relevant texts, and the secondary literature.
43. See *De Anima,* 431b2ff, discussed in greater length in *Fragility,* chap. 10. In "Changing Aristotle's Mind" (forthcoming in M. Nussbaum and A. Rorty, eds., *Essays on Aristotle's "De Anima"* [Oxford, 1991]), Hilary Putnam and I bring forward evidence that Aristotle regards emotion, as well as imagination, as a selective form of cognitive awareness.

wisdom will not neglect the concrete deliverances of imagination when thinking about virtue and goodness. Instead of ascending from particular to general, deliberative imagination links particulars without dispensing with their particularity.[44] It would involve, for example, the ability to recall past experience as one with, as relevant to, the case at hand, while still conceiving of both with rich and vivid concreteness. We are now prepared to understand that the Aristotelian will hold this concrete focusing to be not dangerously irrational, but an essential ingredient of responsible rationality, to be cultivated by educators.

As for the emotions, Aristotle notoriously restores them to the central place in morality from which Plato had banished them. He holds that the truly good person will not only act well but also feel the appropriate emotions about what he or she chooses. Not only correct motivation and motivational feelings but also correct reactive or responsive feelings are constitutive of this person's virtue or goodness. If I do the just thing from the wrong motives or desires (not for its own sake but, say, for the sake of gain), that will not count as virtuous action. This much even Kant could grant. More striking, I must do the just thing without reluctance or inner emotional tension. If my right choices always require struggle, if I must all the time be overcoming powerful feelings that go against virtue, then I am less virtuous than the person whose emotions are in harmony with her actions. I am assessible for my passions as well as for my calculations; all are parts of practical rationality.

Lying behind this is a picture of the passions as responsive and selective elements of the personality. Not Platonic urges or pushes, they possess a high degree of educability and discrimination. Even appetitive desires for Aristotle are intentional and capable of making distinctions; they can inform the agent of the presence of a needed object, working in responsive interaction with perception and imagination.[45] Their intentional object is "the apparent good." Emotions are composites of belief and feeling, shaped by developing thought and highly discriminating in their reactions. They can lead or guide the perceiving agent, "marking off" in a concretely imagined situation the objects to be pursued and avoided. In short, Aristotle does not make a sharp split between the cognitive and the emotive. Emotion can play a cognitive role, and cognition, if it is to be properly informed, must draw on the work of the emotive elements.[46] It is no surprise that choice is defined as an ability that lies on the borderline between the intellectual and the passional, partaking of both natures; it can be described, says Aristotle, either as desiderative deliberation or as deliberative desire (*EN* 1113a10–12, 1139b3–5).

Putting all this together, and allowing ourselves to extrapolate from the text in a way that appears to be consistent with its spirit, we might say that a person of

44. This view of deliberative *phantasia* is not certain, but it has a long and venerable history; see, for example, Aquinas's fascinating discussions of why God equipped humans with *phantasia* for life in this world, and why an angel who lacked it would be confused and at a loss in a world of particulars. (The numerous references in the *Summa Theologica* to this topic are brought together and discussed in Putnam and Nussbaum.)

45. See *Fragility,* chap. 9 (an earlier version of which was published as "The 'Common' Explanation of Animal Motion," in P. Moraux and J. Wiesner, eds., *Zweifelhaftes im Corpus Aristotelicum* [Berlin, 1983], 116–57.)

46. See my "The Stoics on the Extirpation of the Passions," *Apeiron,* 1987.

practical insight will cultivate emotional openness and responsiveness in approaching a new situation. Frequently, it will be her passional response, rather than detached thinking, that will guide her to the appropriate recognitions. "Here is a case where a friend needs my help": this will often be "seen" first by the feelings that are constituent parts of friendship, rather than by pure intellect. Intellect will often want to consult these feelings to get information about the true nature of the situation. Without them, its approach to a new situation would be blind and obtuse. And even where correct choice is reached in the absence of feeling and emotional response, Aristotle will insist that it is less virtuous than choice that is emotional. If I help a friend unfeelingly, I am less praiseworthy than if I do so with appropriate love and sympathy. Indeed my choice may not really be virtuous at all; for an action to be virtuous, it must not only have the same content as the virtuously disposed person's action, it must be done "in the same manner" as the manner in which a person whose passions love the good would do it. Without feeling, a part of correct perception is missing.

I believe that such statements imply that perception is not merely aided by emotion but is also in part constituted by appropriate response. Good perception is a full recognition or acknowledgment of the nature of the practical situation; the whole personality sees it for what it is. The agent who discerns intellectually that a friend is in need or that a loved one has died, but who fails to respond to these facts with appropriate sympathy or grief, clearly lacks a part of Aristotelian virtue. It seems right to say, in addition, that a part of discernment or perception is lacking. This person doesn't really, or doesn't fully, *see* what has happened, doesn't recognize it in a full-blooded way or take it in. We want to say that she is merely saying the words. "He needs my help," or "she is dead," but really doesn't yet fully *know* it, because the emotional part of cognition is lacking. And it isn't just that sometimes we need the emotions to *get to* the right (intellectual) view of the situation; this is true, but not the entire story. Neither is it just that the emotions supply extra praiseworthy elements external to cognition but without which virtue is incomplete. The emotions are themselves modes of vision, or recognition. Their responses are part of what knowing, that is truly recognizing or acknowledging, *consists in.* To respond "at the right times with reference to the right objects, toward the right people, with the right aim, and in the right way, is what is appropriate and best, and this is characteristic of excellence" (*EN* 1106b21–3).

To read Aristotle this way offers a surprising exegetical and philosophical dividend, which can be only briefly described here. It has long troubled interpreters that, just after rejecting Socrates' account of *akrasia,* according to which all action against ethical knowledge is produced by intellectual failure, Aristotle goes on to offer an account of his own that itself characterizes *akrasia* as an intellectual failure. The ordinary belief that it is possible to know the better and to do the worse because one is overcome by pleasure or passion was flouted in Socrates' account, which claimed that these failures were really due to ignorance. Aristotle, having set himself to preserve the ordinary belief, does indeed mention the motivating role of the desire for pleasure in *akrasia,* but says that this desire would not overpower knowledge but for a simultaneous intellectual failure, the failure of the agent to grasp the "minor premise" of the practical syllogism. He or she has general ethical knowledge, and uses it, but either lacks or fails to use the concrete perception of the nature of this particular case. How, then, has he escaped his own criticism?

Without becoming too deeply entangled in the interpretative issues surrounding this difficult text, I want to suggest that this frequently scorned position makes far more sense if we take the inclusive view of perception that I have just outlined, according to which it has emotional and imaginative, as well as intellectual, components. The agent who is swayed by pleasure does not have to be dislodged from factual knowledge of his or her situation, that is, that this is a case of infidelity or overeating. There is a sense in which she can be said to know this throughout: for, as Aristotle in the same context says explicitly, she may say all the right things when questioned, and offer factually correct descriptions. She may, he adds, even correctly perform means–end deliberations in connection with her akratic action, which presumably she could not if she did not in a certain sense grasp, by intellect, its character.[47] She is, however, evasive. She is not fully confronting or acknowledging the situation to herself, allowing herself to see vividly its implications for her life and the lives of others, and to have the responses that are appropriate to that vision. Her interest in short-term pleasure causes her to insulate herself from these responses and from the knowledge they help to constitute. So her intellectual grasp doesn't amount to perception, or to a real grasp and use of the minor premise. Even though she has the facts right, there is a perfectly good, though quite non-Socratic, sense in which she doesn't know what she is doing.

This reading offers a new insight into the phenomenon of *akrasia,* one that places the Aristotelian view in an illuminating relation both to its own tradition and to ours. Our Anglo-American tradition tends, like Plato, to think of *akrasia* as a problem of passion, whose solution lies either in some rational modification of the troublesome passions or in some technique of mastery and control. Like Plato again, we tend (influenced, certainly, by the modern moral theories I have mentioned) to think of the passions as dangerously selfish and self-indulgent items that will, given any latitude, swell up and lead us away from the good. On the Socratic view, it is ethical knowledge that stops *akrasia,* by transforming the beliefs on which complex passions are based; on the mature Platonic view, knowledge must be combined with suppression and "starvation." But the cause of the problem, in all these cases, is found in the so-called irrational part of the soul.

If I am right, the Aristotelian account quietly turns this picture on its head, pointing out that *akrasia* is frequently (though not always) caused by an excess of

---

47. *EN,* 1142b18,20; see also 1147a18–24, where Aristotle compares the intellectual grasp of the akratic agent to the grasp of a principle that a student has when he or she is first learning it: "That they [sc. akratics] make the statements of a knowing person is no sign of anything. For people affected in this way can also recite demonstrations and quote the verses of Empedocles. And students who are learning something for the first time string statements together, but they don't yet understand; for the statements have to grow to be a part of them *(sumphuēnai),* and this requires time. So we should suppose that akratics speak in about the way that actors do." Both the student and the actor comparison bear out my point. What the akratic has is factual (intellectual) knowledge; what she lacks is real recognition or understanding, the kind of grasp of what is really at stake that comes from somewhere deep within her, from something that is part of her. The comparison to the actor makes it especially likely that deficiency of genuine feeling is in question, at least some of the time.

theory and a deficiency in passional response. The person who acts akratically against his or her knowledge of the good is frequently quite capable of performing correctly in all the intellectual ways; what she lacks is the heart's confrontation with concrete ethical reality. We could express this by saying that knowledge needs responsiveness to be effective in action; we could also say that in the absence of correct response there is no, or no full, practical knowledge. The Aristotelian account, putting things in the second way, urges us to think of real practical insight and understanding as a complex matter involving the whole soul. The opposite of Platonic knowledge is ignorance; the opposite of Aristotelian perception can, in some cases, be ignorance; but it can also, in other cases, be denial or self-deceptive rationalization.

We can go further. Frequently a reliance on the powers of the intellect can actually become an impediment to true ethical perception, by impeding or undermining these responses. It frequently happens that theoretical people, proud of their intellectual abilities and confident in their possession of techniques for the solution of practical problems, are led by their theoretical commitments to become inattentive to the concrete responses of emotion and imagination that would be essential constituents of correct perception. It is a familiar problem. Sophocles' Creon, fascinated by his theoretical effort to define all human concerns in terms of their productivity of civic well-being, does not even perceive what at some level he knows, namely that Haemon is his son. He mouths the words; but he does not really acknowledge the tie—until the pain of loss reveals it to him. Proust's narrator, after a systematic study of his heart using the methods of precise empirical psychology, concludes that he does not love Albertine. This false conclusion (which, again, he soon acknowledges as false in and through responses of suffering) is reached not in spite of the intellect, but in a way because of it; because he was encouraging it to go off "itself by itself," without the necessary companionship of response and feelings. Henry James's *The Sacred Fount* is a fascinating account of what the world looks like to a man who carries this separation all the way, allowing theoretical intellect to determine his relation to all concrete phenomena, refusing himself any other human relation to them, and yet at the same time priding himself on the fineness of his perception. What we discover as we read is that such a person cannot have *any* knowledge of the people and events around him. His sort of incomplete perception can never reach the subject matter or engage with it in a significant way. So the Aristotelian position does not simply inform us that theorizing needs to be completed with intuitive and emotional responses; it warns us of the ways in which theorizing can impede vision. The intellect is not only not all-sufficient, it is a dangerous master. Because of its overreaching, knowledge can be "dragged around like a slave."[48]

All this, once again, has clear implications for the contemporary theory of choice. Many contemporary theories of rationality, as taught and practiced in the academy and in public life, share the goals and the policies of Mr. Gradgrind. That is, they make every attempt to cultivate calculative intellect and none at all to cultivate "fancy" and emotion. They do not concern themselves with the books

---

48. On all these issues, see *Fragility,* especially chap. 3, Interlude 2. [Also, in this volume, "Fictions" and "Love's Knowledge."]

(especially works of literature) that would cultivate those responses; indeed they implicitly deny their relevance to rationality. Aristotle tells us in no uncertain terms that people of practical wisdom, both in public and in private life, will cultivate emotion and imagination in themselves and in others, and will be very careful not to rely too heavily on a technical or purely intellectual theory that might stifle or impede these responses. They will promote an education that cultivates fancy and feeling through works of literature and history, teaching appropriate occasions for and degrees of response. They will consider it childish and immature *not* to cry or be angry or otherwise to experience and display passion where the situation calls for it. In looking for private models and public leaders, we should desire to be assured of their sensitivity and emotional depth, as well as of their intellectual competence.

IV. The Three Elements Together

We have now identified three different parts of Aristotle's picture of perception and practical knowing. All of them appear to form part of his attack on the notion that practical reason is a form of scientific understanding, a view that is defended prominently by Plato. Plato's conception (at least at some periods) insists on the qualitative homogeneity of the values; it argues that practical knowledge is completely summarized in a system of (timeless) highly general universals; it also insists that intellect is both necessary and sufficient for correct choice. Plato is certainly not the only thinker in history who has linked these three ideas together. In this sense, Aristotle's conception already looks unified, as being directed against different elements of a single coherent position. But it is possible to say more about the internal coherence of this picture of perception; for its various elements support one another in more than a polemical way.

Noncommensurability, as we have said, is not sufficient for the priority of particular to universal. But commensurability in the strong form of Singleness is certainly sufficient for the priority of both the general and the universal to the particular: for the single measure will have to be some sort of highly general universal, that is, one thing that turns up in qualitatively the same way in many different things. Even the limited commensurability of Metricity is sufficient for the rejection of unique nonrepeatable properties from practical salience. And we can see that the general spirit of Aristotle's noncommensurability leads directly to and supports his account of the priority of particulars. For his noncommensurability says, Look and see how rich and diverse the ultimate values in the world are. Do not fail to investigate each valuable item, cherishing it for its own specific nature and not reducing it to something else. These injunctions lead in the direction of a long and open-ended list—for we would not want to rule out beforehand the possibility that some new item will turn up whose own separate nature is irreducibly distinct from those we have previously recognized. In the context of friendship and love, especially, these injunctions are virtually certain to guarantee that the list of ultimate values will include some nonrepeatable particular items: for each friend is to be cherished for his or her own sake, not simply as an instantiation of the universal value, friendship. And it appears that this will include not only character, but also a shared history of mutuality. In this way, although Aristotle does have independent arguments for the priority of particulars (those having to do with indefiniteness and mutability), the first two elements certainly support each other well.

The account of emotion and imagination gives further support to and is supported by both elements. For it is in the nature of imagination, as we have said, to recognize highly concrete and, frequently, uniquely particular objects. And the objects to which we are most strongly attached by our passions are frequently like this as well. In the *Politics,* arguing against Plato, Aristotle says that the two things that above all make people love and care for something are the thought that it is all their own and the thought that it's the only one they have (1262b22–3); so our most intense feelings of love and fear and grief are likely to be directed at objects and persons who are seen as irreducibly particular in their nature and in their relationship to us. To argue that emotion and imagination are essential components of practical knowing and judging is to suggest very strongly that good judging will at least in part be a matter of focusing on the concrete and even the particular, which will be seen as incommensurate with other things. And in *EN* X.9 he indeed explicitly connects the loving relation between parent and child with an ethical knowledge that is superior to that of the public educator in its concrete particularity (1180b7–13). On the other hand, to defend noncommensurability is to reopen the space in which the emotions and imagination operate and have their force. A Platonist ethical position, Aristotle plausibly argues, undermines the strength of the emotions (Pol. 1262b23–4); and Plato himself would concede that belief in commensurability and universality at least cuts away many of the most common emotional reactions, since he, too, grants that these are based on perceptions of specialness. Again, to defend the priority of particulars is to inform us that imagination can play a role in deliberation that cannot be altogether replaced by the functioning of abstract thought. It would be possible to defend a flexible context-oriented perception of particulars without giving a prominent role to emotion and imagination; for one might try to describe a purely intellectual faculty that would by itself be adequate for seizing the relevant features. There is some precedent for this in some pre-Aristotelian Greek accounts of practical wisdom, which defend an improvisatory contextual use of reason that looks very cool, wily, and self-controlled.[49] Aristotle would feel, I think, that this sort of reason was insufficient for the sensitive task of deliberating about ends, though it might be all right for technical means–end reasoning. Here he is in agreement with an important tradition in Athenian political thought. For although Thucydides, as we have mentioned, praises the resourceful improvisational ability of Themistocles without mention of emotions, the funeral oration of Pericles makes it abundantly clear that full political rationality requires passion, and the sort of judgment that is made with and through love and vision. Athenians are to cultivate the ability to conceive in imagination of their city's greatness and still greater promise; and they are to "fall in love" with her when they see this greatness (II.43.1). He would probably conclude, not implausibly, that a citizen who did not feel this love had in a certain way failed to perceive both Athens and his own place in her.

One final connection between this feature and the other two: if one believes,

---

49. See M. Detienne and J. P. Vernant, *Les ruses de l'intelligence: la mètis des grecs* (Paris, 1974), discussed in *Fragility,* esp. chaps. 1, 7.

with Plato, that the strong emotions are sources of unbearable tension and strain in a human life, one will have good reason to cultivate a way of seeing and judging that limits and reduces their power. Both commensurability and universality do this, as Plato argues. Because the Aristotelian position accepts emotional attachment as an intrinsically valuable source of richness and goodness in human life, it lacks one of Plato's most prominent motivations for the transformations involved in the first two features.

The three elements fit together, then, to form a coherent picture of practical choice. I see no significant tensions among them, and numerous reasons why the defender of one will wish to defend the others as well. They seem to articulate different aspects of a single idea. We might characterize this central idea, borrowing a phrase from Henry James, as one of becoming "finely aware and richly responsible"; of being a person on whom nothing is lost."[50] Being responsibly commited to the world of value before her, the perceiving agent can be counted on to investigate and scrutinize the nature of each item and each situation, to respond to what is there before her with full sensitivity and imaginative vigor, not to fall short of what is there to be seen and felt because of evasiveness, scientific abstractness, or a love of simplification. The Aristotelian agent is a person whom we could trust to describe a complex situation with full concreteness of detail and emotional shading, missing nothing of practical relevance. As James writes, "The person capable of feeling in the given case more than another of what is to be felt for it, and so serving in the highest degree to record it dramatically and objectively, is the only sort of person on whom we can count not to betray, to cheapen, or, as we say, give away the value and beauty of the thing."[51] But this means that the person of practical wisdom lies surprisingly close to the artist and/or the perceiver of art, not in the sense that this conception reduces moral value to aesthetic value or makes moral judgment a matter of taste, but in the sense that we are asked to see morality as a high type of vision of and response to the particular, an ability that we seek and value in our greatest artists, and especially our novelists, whose value for us is above all practical and never detached from our questions about how to live. Fine conduct requires above all correct description; such description is itself a form of morally assessible conduct. "To 'put' things is very exactly and responsibly and interminably to do them." The novelist is a moral agent; and the moral agent, to the extent to which she is good, shares in the abilities of the novelist.[52]

V. Yearnings of Thought, Excursions of Sympathy

Let us examine this conception further, then, by turning to a novel. The believer in a general system of rules or a general decision procedure could at this point go on to enumerate those rules or to describe that procedure. The Aristotelian tells us that we must instead look for instruction to exemplary, experienced models of

50. H. James, *The Princess Casamassima* (New York, 1907–9) I. 169.

51. Ibid., preface, I. xiii.

52. *Golden Bowl,* Preface; see "'Finely Aware,'" this volume.

practical wisdom. The commitment of Aristotelian practical wisdom to rich descriptions of qualitative heterogeneity, to context-sensitive perceiving, and to emotional and imaginative activity has already suggested to us that certain sorts of novels would be good places to see the good of this conception fittingly expressed. And, as I have already suggested, I believe that the novels of Henry James are such novels: that if we want to know more about the content of the Aristotelian way of choosing, and why it is good, we cannot do better than to turn to one of them. I can also think of no better way to indicate the distance between this picture and the picture of choice present in decision theories of many kinds than to show and comment upon the kind of prose in which the Aristotelian view is appropriately embodied.

To juxtapose Aristotle and James is not to deny that in many salient features their conceptions of reasoning are not identical. They have relevantly different conceptions of consciousness, of the nature and taxonomy of the emotions; and all of this should be borne in mind. And yet the convergence of sympathies is more striking than these differences; nor is the convergence purely fortuitous. For one thing, numerous lines of influence connect James with Aristotle—from his own direct reading to indirect philosophical and literary influences of many kinds. But it is more important still to point out that if in fact, as I have suggested, this conception truly answers to deep human intuitions about practical reason, intuitions that recur in much, though not exactly, the same form across differences of time and place, then it is no surprise that two perceptive writers about practical reason should independently converge upon them. The problems of choosing well have a remarkable persistence; convergence on a good response requires less explanation than convergence in error.

It may appear peculiar to place such a long and mysterious piece of prose at the heart of an article. It is intended to appear so; and the reader should reflect on the difference, asking what is missing in moral philosophies that deny themselves resources of this sort.

Here, then, from the final pages of Henry James's *The Golden Bowl,* is a part of Maggie Verver's deliberation:

'Well—?' Mrs. Assingham urged.

'Well, I hope—!'

'Hope he'll see her?'

Maggie hesitated, however; she made no direct reply. 'It's useless hoping,' she presently said. 'She won't. But he ought to.' Her friend's expression of a moment before, which had been apologised for as vulgar, prolonged its sharpness to her ear—that of an electric bell under continued pressure. Stated so simply, what was it but dreadful, truly, that the feasibility of Charlotte's 'getting at' the man who for so long had loved her should now be in question? Strangest of all things doubtless this care of Maggie's as to what might make for it or make against it; stranger still her fairly lapsing at moments into a vague calculation of the conceivability, on her own part, with her husband, of some direct sounding of the subject. Would it be too monstrous, her suddenly breaking out to him as in alarm at the lapse of the weeks: 'Wouldn't it really seem that you're bound in honour to do something for her privately before they go?' Maggie was capable of weighing the risk of this adventure for her own spirit, capable of sinking to intense little absences, even while conversing as now with the person who had most of her confidence, during which she followed up the possibilities. It was true that Mrs Assingham could at such times somewhat restore the balance by not wholly failing to guess her thought. Her thought however just at present had more than one face—had a series that it successively presented. These were indeed the possibilities involved in the adventure of her concerning herself for the quantity of compensation Mrs Verver might still look to. There was always the possibility that she *was* after all sufficiently to get at him—there was in fact that of her having again and again done so. Against this stood nothing but Fanny Assingham's apparent belief in her privation—more mercilessly imposed or more hopelessly felt in the actual relation of the parties; over and beyond everything that from more than three months back of course had fostered in the Princess a like conviction. These assumptions might certainly be baseless—inasmuch as there were hours and hours of Amerigo's time that there was no habit, no pretence of his accounting for; inasmuch too as Charlotte, inevitably, had had more than once, to the undisguised knowledge of the pair in Portland Place, been obliged to come up to Eaton Square, whence so many of her personal possessions were in course of removal. She didn't come to Portland Place—didn't even come to ask for luncheon on two separate occasions when it reached the consciousness of the household there that she was spending the day in London. Maggie hated, she scorned, to compare hours and appearances, to weigh the idea of whether there hadn't been moments during these days when an assignation in easy conditions, a snatched interview in an air the season had so cleared of prying eyes, mightn't perfectly work. But the very reason of this was partly that, haunted with the vision of the poor woman carrying off with such bravery as she found to her hand the secret of her not being appeased, she was conscious of scant room for any alternative image. The alternative image would have been that the secret covered up was the secret of appeasement somehow obtained, somehow extorted and cherished; and the difference between the two kinds of hiding was too great to permit of a mistake. Charlotte was hiding neither pride nor joy–she was hiding humiliation; and here it was that the Princess's passion, so powerless for vindictive fights, most inveterately bruised its tenderness against the hard glass of her question.

Behind the glass lurked the *whole* history of the relation she had so fairly flattened her nose against it to penetrate—the glass Mrs Verver might at this stage have been frantically tapping from within by way of supreme irrepressible entreaty. Maggie had said to herself complacently after that last passage with her stepmother in the garden of Fawns that there was nothing left for her to do and that she could thereupon fold her hands. But why wasn't it still left to push further and, from the point of view of personal pride, grovel lower?—why wasn't it still left to offer herself as the bearer of a message reporting to him their friend's anguish and convincing him of her need? She could thus have translated Mrs Verver's tap against the glass, as I have called it, into fifty forms; could perhaps have translated it most into the form of a reminder that would pierce deep. 'You don't know what it is to have been loved and broken with. You haven't been broken with, because in *your* relation what can there have been worth speaking of to break? Ours was everything a relation could be, filled to the brim with the wine of consciousness; and if it was to have no meaning, no better meaning than that such a creature as you could breathe upon it, at your hour, for blight, why was I myself dealt with all for deception? why condemned after a couple of short years to find the golden flame—oh the golden flame!—a mere handful of black ashes?' Our young woman so yielded at moments to what was insidious in these foredoomed ingenuities of her pity that for minutes together sometimes the weight of a new duty seemed to rest upon her—the duty of speaking before separation should constitute its chasm, of pleading for some benefit that might be carried away into exile like the last saved object of price of the *émigré,* the jewel wrapped in a piece of old silk and negotiable some day in the market of misery.

This imagined service to the woman who could no longer help herself was one of the traps set for Maggie's spirit at every turn of the road; the click of which, catching and holding the divine faculty fast, was followed inevitably by a flutter, by a struggle of wings and even, as we may say, by a scattering of fine feathers. For they promptly enough felt, these yearnings of thought and excursions of sympathy, the concussion that couldn't bring them down—the arrest produced by the so remarkably distinct figure that, at Fawns, for the previous weeks, was constantly crossing, in its regular revolution, the further end of any watched perspective. Whoever knew, or whoever didn't, whether or to what extent Charlotte, with natural business in Eaton Square, had shuffled other opportunities under that cloak, it was all matter for the kind of quiet ponderation the little man who so kept his wandering way had made his own. It was part of the very inveteracy of his straw hat and his white waistcoat, of the trick of his hands in his pockets, of the detachment of the attention he fixed on his slow steps from behind his secure pince-nez. The thing that never failed now as an item in the picture was that gleam of the silken noose, his wife's immaterial tether, so marked to Maggie's sense during her last month in the country. Mrs Verver's straight neck had certainly not slipped it; nor had the other end of the long cord—oh quite conveniently long!—disengaged its smaller loop from the hooked thumb that, with his fingers closed upon it, her husband kept out of sight. To have recognised, for all its tenuity, the play of this gathered lasso might inevitably be to wonder with what magic it was twisted, to what tension subjected, but could never be to doubt either of its adequacy to its office or its perfect durability. These reminded states for the Princess were in fact states of renewed gaping. So many things her father knew that she even yet didn't!

All this at present with Mrs Assingham passed through her in quick vibrations. She had expressed while the revolution of her thought was incomplete the idea of what Amerigo 'ought' on his side, in the premises, to be capable of, and then had felt her companion's answering stare. But she insisted on what she had meant. 'He ought to wish to see her—and I mean in some protected and independent way, as he used to—in case of her being herself able to manage it. That,' said Maggie with the courage of her conviction, 'he ought to be ready, he ought to be happy, he ought to feel himself sworn—little as it is for the end of such a history!—to take from her. It's as if he wished to get off without taking anything.'

The first thing we notice, as we read through these pages, is that, by comparison with our standing toward an example of formal decision theory, and even toward a well developed nontechnical philosopher's example, we are at sea here. If we do not have some familiarity with the novel as a whole, it is very difficult to figure out what is being deliberated about and decided, much less what the meaning and weight of each of the factors is. In consequence of this, it is also hugely difficult to determine whether Maggie's thought and response here is rational and praiseworthy, or the opposite. To decide this would require us to know a great deal about her story as a whole; it would seem hasty and arbitrary to form any such judgment in advance of the fullest possible scrutiny of the entire novel. (More than this: this novel, by emphasizing the fact that it is written from several among many possible points of view, reminds us again and again that the whole of the relevant reality is more complex yet than the text, that many potentially relevant insights are being denied us.) These very facts make the passage a good example of Aristotelianism. The rich contextuality of good choice, and its attentiveness to particulars in all their contextual embeddedness, imply that we should not expect to be able to plunge in so near the end of a complex story and comprehend or assess everything. As a good doctor will neither prescribe in advance of a full scrutiny of this patient's history nor assess the work of a fellow doctor without making herself master of all the contextual material this doctor used in arriving at her choice, so we cannot really expect that Maggie's reasons will be perspicuous to and assessible by us unless we immerse ourselves in her story. The fact that this example is really not excerptable is its virtue, and Maggie's. If everything she treats as relevant to her choice at the end of the passage *were* capable of being adequately summarized for us in these few paragraphs, her choice would almost certainly be irrational and bad. We would be highly suspicious of any real person who did choose with so little contextual baggage, in the way that philosophical examples all too often indicate. This means that we should really have quoted the whole novel as our example. It also means that in real life the models that will be most helpfully exemplary for us as Aristotelians will be those whose stories are known in sufficient detail that the meaning and richness of particular deliberations is comprehensible— namely, the lives of friends, and of characters in novels insofar as we allow these to become our friends. I have felt free to use the example only because I feel that by now I stand to the novel in the appropriate relation of friendship, a relation that, like deliberation itself, is affective as well as intellectual.[53]

As soon as we notice that we are lost without the fuller context, we also discover that the style of this example sounds like something that does not belong in philosophy at all. To contrast it with the prose of an example in a theoretical work of decision theory would be too comic. But even the less scientific prose of a typical philosopher's example is simplicity itself next to this complex and mysterious construction, full of indefiniteness and obliquity, periphrasis and indirection, conveying the core of its meaning in metaphors and pictures rather than in logical formulae or in universal propositions. This is, I believe, the prose of Aristotelian perception, expressing the "yearnings of thought and excursions of sympathy" that the person of practical wisdom will perform. This prose expresses the commitment of the agent to confront all the complexities of the situation head on, in all their indeterminacy and particularity, and to regard the act of deliberation as an adventure of the personality as a whole. It depicts in its cadences the moral effort of straining to see correctly and to come up with the appropriate picture or description; its tensions, obliquities, and circumnavigations express the sheer difficulty of finding the right description or picture for what is there before one. If, as James says, to "put" is to "do," showing this is showing moral activity of a valuable kind.

As we examine further the content of this deliberation, we notice that each of the major features of Aristotelian deliberation is present, and in a way that ought

53. See Introduction, "Flawed Crystals," and "'Finely Aware,'" this volume.

to convince us that *this,* and not some simpler or neater thing, is what rationality requires. Noncommensurability is an interesting case in point. Earlier in the novel, Maggie has made a great point of conceiving of all the claims upon her as homogeneous along a single quantitative scale. Financial imagery for ethical values has been prominent, expressing this reductive strategy. Even when she is not using this imagery, she is continually showing, in a number of ways, her determination not to acknowledge conflicting obligations, not to waver from "that ideal consistency on which her moral comfort almost at any time depended." This involves her, repeatedly, in one or another sort of reinterpretation of the values with which she is concerned, so as to ensure that they harmonize with one another, are "round" rather than angular. A claim will be acknowledged only to the extent to which it consents to fit in with other claims that are held fixed; but this involves Maggie in considerable neglect of the separate nature of each distinct claim. For separate natures are rough-edged angular items that cannot always be easily slipped into a preexisting structure. Her architectural imagery, like the financial imagery of commensurability, expresses a denial of separate natures. The structure of the moral life is compared to solid, simple, clean-lined buildings, the pure white classical houses and the manicured gardens of Eaton Square rather than the ambiguous grays and complex shapes of Portland Place.[54]

In this scene, as in much of the novel's second part, Maggie shows her recognition that commensurability in particular, consistent harmony in general, are not good aims for the rational deliberation of an adult woman. She allows herself to explore fully the separate nature of each pertinent claim, entering into it, wondering about what it is, attempting to do justice to it in feeling as well as thought. "Her thought . . . had more than one face—had a series that it successively presented." First she considers the situation of her husband and Charlotte, asking herself what account of their current relationship is the most probable. She then turns from this consideration of probabilities to a deeper inspection of Charlotte's character and the character of their love, attempting to understand it and its implications for her choice, allowing herself vividly to picture and imagine the suffering of her friend, in a way that brings home to her the moral difficulty of her own project, which is the cause of this suffering. Then, while she is nearly overwhelmed by pity, her "yearnings of thought and excursions of sympathy" are brought up short, as if by a collision, by the equally vivid picture of her father, who appears as it were before her as a "so remarkably distinct figure," forcing consideration of his claims. She used to see her father as the source of all moral claims, an authority with which nothing could be allowed to be in conflict. Now she sees him "contrasted and opposed, in short, objectively presented": that is, she sees *him,* in his own distinct nature, just because she now sees the particular way in which his needs and wishes are in tension with other claims. She has a vivid sense of his separateness and also of his qualitative individuality, just because of the "concussion" with which his interests oppose her sympathy for Charlotte. She sees him as the cause of Charlotte's captivity and pain, and sees therefore that any attempt to do justice to his needs must end by wronging and further paining her; on the other hand pity, and this project of being truthful, must threaten his control and his

54. For fuller development of these points, see "Flawed Crystals," this volume.

dignity.[55] As we follow all this we sense that this way of looking into the distinctness of separate and heterogeneous items is not *less* rational than her old adherence to commensurability or to weaker related principles. It is a way of growing up morally, of reasoning like a mature woman rather than a fearful child.

This case is also a very good place to understand what the Aristotelian means by insisting that the particular is prior to the general. It is not that Maggie drops, in the event, all her guiding principles, giving them up to some rudderless intuition about the irreducibly particular. Much of her deliberation is firmly historical, asking how past commitments undertaken and past actions performed bear on the situation at hand. It is seen as fully continuous with and falling under the influence of that past. Furthermore, we cannot understand the force that many of these commitments have for her if we do not use general terms. She expresses concern for such general and universalizable principles as promise-keeping, duties of gratitude to a friend who has given help and encouragement, duties of a child to a parent. If we described the particulars on which her thought dwells using proper names only, avoiding such general terms as "father," "husband," and "friend," we would not properly capture the meaning they have for her. She does not simply think of Adam as a radically unique item generating claims that are sui generis. And even where the terms of her reflection are highly *concrete*—for example, when she thinks of what she owes to a friend with whom she has a certain sort of concrete history—much of her thought is universalizable, carrying with it the implication that if exactly similar circumstances arose in any time and place, the same choice would again be right. All of this is consistent with Aristotelianism, which lays great stress on good habits and on a commitment to the general definitions of the virtues.[56]

Moreover, in her willingness to admit a conflict of duties and commitments, Maggie is even more true to her antecedent general principles than would be an agent who simply denied that there could be a real conflict of duties, or one who viewed the conflict in terms of greater and lesser amounts of one and the same thing. For the fact that the world produces a tragic conflict of "oughts" does not cause her either to judge that one of the conflicting principles no longer binds her or to rewrite the nature of the conflict so that it no longer presents the same tragic aspect. Far from being more rootless and ad hoc, Aristotelian deliberation is in this way more faithful to its past than many other types that have been proposed.[57]

But at the same time there are several ways in which the concrete particularity of Maggie's situation is prior to general guidelines. First, she is prepared to recognize non-repeatable and unique items as morally relevant alongside the universalizable. "Father" does not exhaustively describe the morally salient features of her situation with Adam, nor is the "so remarkably distinct figure" who appears before her an abstract Parent. The general and universal description must be completed by attention to his personal qualities and to their unique personal history—

55. See the interpretation of her earlier encounter with her father in "'Finely Aware,'" this volume.

56. See Introduction and Note to "'Finely Aware,'" this volume.

57. See, for the charge to which this is a reply, Hilary Putnam, "Taking Rules Seriously: A Response to Martha Nussbaum," *New Literary History* 15 (1983) 193–200; and also my reply in the same issue.

just as her concern for the relation of "best friend" must be completed by thought and feeling about who Charlotte individually is. Some of this will be universalizable, though not in the least general; some of it will not be universalizable. But if we rewrote the passage so as to leave in the repeatable features and omit the vivid and specific pictures and the nonrepeatable memories, we would have lost a lot of its moral richness, and the deliberation would seem bizarrely irrational.

Then too, Maggie sees, as an Aristotelian ought to, how the contextual inter-weaving of the various items in the scene shades their moral meaning. She must consider not simply what, in a general way, her duties to her friend Charlotte are. She must think what they are given Charlotte's concrete situation, on which she focuses in agonizing detail. In order to judge what to urge, even in order to say what each one of her possibly conflicting obligations requires, she must imagine what Charlotte's current situation is, what she is likely to be feeling and desiring. A beneficent action that did not fit itself to the concrete requirements of that silent suffering and that concealed humiliation would not be morally correct, any more than a move in navigation that was all right by the book but chosen without regard to the concrete circumstances of the navigator would be the correct navigational choice. We can say more. It is not simply that the action, to be correct, must be "tuned" to its context. We can also see that there is no way of describing the chosen action itself without reference to features of context that are far too concrete to figure in a usefully action-guiding principle, and in many cases not altogether universalizable. Maggie's choice is not to urge a last confrontation in order to permit a result that protects the dignity of the family; it is to favor a certain way of dealing with Charlotte's particular pain in the circumstances, in order to protect the dignity of a very particular father. The tonality of the action (or non-action) itself is particular and enmeshed, and can hardly be well described (if we want to capture its *rightness*) without the subtleties of the novelist.

Finally, the particular is prior in the sense that Maggie persistently permits dis-covery and surprise, even a surprise that might cause serious reversal in her entire ethical conception. The first half of the novel shows her approaching other people as if they were sculptures or paintings, situations as if they were all episodes of contemplation of one's collection of such objects. The objects do not act or move; they lack the power to behave in unpredictable and alarming ways; the whole moral scene has about it an atmosphere of cool contemplative control. The second half shows her thinking instead in the imagery of theatrical improvisation. She has become an actress who suddenly discovers that her script is not written in advance and she must "quite heroically" improvise her role. "Preparation and practice had come but a short way; her part opened out, and she invented from moment to moment what to say and to do." I postpone a full discussion of this revealing metaphor to the next section; but clearly it indicates a keen sense of responsibility to the moment and an openness to such surprises as it may contain.

Maggie's deliberation shows us quite clearly what it means to say that imagi-nation and emotional response have a guiding role to play in perception and that they are partly constitutive of moral knowledge. Had she approached the situation of Charlotte and Amerigo and Adam with the intellect alone, it is very doubtful that she could have seen in it all that she is able to see. The images of Charlotte tapping on the glass, of Adam walking along holding Charlotte as in an invisible halter, have an ability to communicate to her and to express the precise ethical significance of Charlotte's predicament; this ability would, we feel, be absent from any confrontation with Charlotte that avoided the use of images. And we see, too, how closely intertwined this imaginative function is with the work of the emotions. Maggie's pictures are suffused with feeling; indeed, we sometimes see that the picture is suggested or engendered by an emotion. Her thoughts are brought up short by a *concussion,* which then finds its expression in the picture of her father walking. The emotional shock or surge of concern for Adam is the source of the way in which she then pictures him. And emotion seems to be an indefeasible element *in* the picture. She imagines Adam as a beloved father; her image is itself loving. (We could as well say that it is a characteristic of her vivid and highly responsive emotional life to use images. We could not give a good account of her emotions without mentioning how she sees the objects of her loves and anxieties.) And all of this fused and highly complex material appears to be essential in leading her to a correct ethical perception of each of the claims upon her. If she had not permitted herself to see Adam in that sort of detail, to be "brought up short" by that concussive picture, she would not have understood what she owed him in that circumstance. Emotions can be excessive and misleading, as we see from the moment in which her comprehensive effort to do justice to the entire situation almost founders in the surge of her pity for Charlotte. But correction comes, when it comes, not in the form of a cool intellectual judgment, but in the form of the self-critical feeling-infused picture of the bird in the cage, which then makes room for the complex image of Adam, beloved and fearful, strolling across the forefront of her mind with the silken noose between his fingers.

And once again, I think we want to insist that these excursions of imagination and yearnings of sympathy do not serve as means only, to an intellectual knowledge that is in principle (though not perhaps in fact) separable from them. We see no such knowing here. The intent focusing on the concrete, an activity in which all of her personality is actively involved, looks like an end in itself. Suppose we rewrite the scene, adding on, after the Adam picture, several sentences of the type, "From this she inferred that her duty to her father was. . . ." Would we be convinced that this further stage represented real progress in moral knowing? Does it add anything to the "quick vibrations" of her perception? The Aristotelian claims that it does not—except, perhaps, in the sense that it fossilizes or preserves the work of perception in a form in which it could be tapped on another occasion as a guide, or a substitute should there be no time for full perception. On the contrary, the Aristotelian will insist that the intellectual conclusion may well even be a regression or falling off from the fullest knowing or acknowledging of the situation, defensible in the way I have indicated, but also dangerous, since fossilized partial knowing can too easily become a form of denial unless it is continually awakened into perception.

Finally, we are told by the Aristotelian view that the exercise of practical wisdom is itself a human excellence, an activity of intrinsic value apart from its tendency to produce virtuous actions. Our case gives us a vivid sense of what this position comes to. Both before and after the pages of thought that are quoted here, Maggie speaks and acts in more or less the same way. She does not change her mind, or speak and act differently. James draws our attention to this by the sentence, "But she insisted on what she had meant," and by ascribing to her, before and after, almost identical words. But he also insists that before the thoughts recorded, "the revolution of her thought was incomplete." If this deliberation has a moral value, it seems not to lie in its productivity of overt activities. But we are convinced that it does have a moral value.[58] Something significant has been added by her faithful confrontation with all of the factors, even if the decision itself remains unchanged. The silent inner work of perception is shown here as a praiseworthy case of human excellence in its own right. This means that its constituent parts are constituent parts, as well, of the good life for this human being.

VI. An Empty Situation Morality?

This ethical norm will be charged with being empty of content. In one sense this charge is correct. Because of the priority of the particular, we can give no general account of deliberative priorities, and also no general account of the techniques and procedures of good deliberation, that would suffice to discriminate good from defective choice in advance of a confrontation with the matter of the case. A general account may give us necessary conditions for choosing well; it cannot by itself give sufficient conditions. Aristotle says this plainly: just as the agent's own decision rests with perception, so too does our decision as to whether he or she has chosen well. The demand to set up exhaustive general criteria for correct perception should be resisted (*EN* 1126b2–4). In Aristotle's city the people of practical wisdom do not go about with placards on their backs, so that all we need to do is to follow them. Nor can we ever in life have a complete water-tight guarantee that perception has in a particular case been correctly exercised. There are no sufficient conditions: our own decision rests with perception.

But the charge of emptiness has been made in a stronger and more troubling form. Hilary Putnam, commenting on a previous attempt of mine to elicit an Aristotelian picture of choice from *The Golden Bowl,* suggested that this view is in danger of collapsing into "an empty situation morality" in which everything is "a matter of trade-offs."[59] I take it that this amounts to the charge that the agent who puts so much weight on the concrete choice situation and judges primarily with a view to the demands of the situation will be deficient in ethical continuity and commitment over time, lacking in firm principles and in a reliable general conception of the good life. So long as the agent agonizes enough over the material of the case, she can do anything she likes.

We have begun to answer this charge already, by insisting on the role that general principles play as guides inside Maggie Verver's deliberation. We have also pointed out that the ability of the Aristotelian conception to recognize conflicts of duties permits a deeper sort of fidelity to principles than we get in many ethical

---

58. See "'Finely Aware,'" this volume, and Iris Murdoch, *The Sovereignty of Good* (London, 1970).

59. Putnam, "Taking Rules Seriously."

conceptions. But we now need to go further to answer Putnam: for this will permit us to give a richer account than we have so far of the interplay of the general and the particular in Aristotelian choice.

We can begin by returning to the metaphor of theatrical improvisation, which is a favorite Jamesian as well as Aristotelian image for the activity of practical wisdom. Maggie Verver is an actress who has prepared and practiced, and now discovers that she must "quite heroically," "from moment to moment," improvise her role. Does she, in learning to improvise, adopt a way of choosing in which there are no principles and everything is ad hoc? (Perhaps: in which everything is permitted)? The image of the actress suggests how inaccurate such an inference would be. The salient difference between acting from a script and improvising is that one has to be not less but far *more* keenly attentive to what is given by the other actors and by the situation. You cannot get away with doing anything by rote; you must be actively aware and responsive at every moment, ready for surprises, so as not to let the others down. An improvising actress, if she is improvising well, does not feel that she can say just anything at all. She must suit her choice to the evolving story, which has its own form and continuity. Above all, she must preserve the commitments of her character to the other characters (of herself as actress to the other actors). More, not less, attentive fidelity is required.

Consider the analogous contrast between a symphony player and a jazz musician. For the former, commitments and continuities are external, coming from the score and the conductor. Her job is to interpret those signals. The jazz player, actively forging continuity, must choose in full awareness of and responsibility to the historical traditions of the form, and actively honor at every moment her commitments to her fellow musicians, whom she had better know as well as possible as unique individuals. She will be more responsible than the score-reader, not less, to the unfolding continuities and structures of the work. (We can also say that as the classical player ascends the scale of musical excellence, so to speak, becoming not simply a rote reader of the score but an active thinking interpreter who freshly realizes the work at each performance, she resembles more and more the jazz musician in the nature of her attention.)

These two cases indicate to us, then, that the perceiver who improvises morally is doubly responsible: responsible to the history of commitment and to the ongoing structures that go to constitute her context; and especially responsible to these, in that her commitments are forged freshly on each occasion, in an active and intelligent confrontation between her own history and the requirements of the occasion.

In ethical terms, what this means is that the perceiver brings to the new situation a history of general conceptions and commitments, and a host of past obligations and affiliations (some general, some particular), all of which contribute to and help to constitute her evolving conception of good living. The organized internalization of these commitments constitutes her character. She will see the situation as made up, in good part, out of general items; her moral description of it will use (as we saw) terms such as "father" and "friend." It will also acknowlege obligations, both general and particular, that bear upon her responsibility in this situation. This will be so, as we said, even where to do so brings the pain of conflict; for this is a part of acknowledging this concrete situation for the situation it is.

Perception, we might say, is a process of loving conversation between rules and concrete responses, general conceptions and unique cases, in which the general articulates the particular and is in turn further articulated by it. The particular is constituted out of features both repeatable and nonrepeatable; it is outlined by the structure of general terms, and it also contains the unique images of those we love.[60] The general is dark, uncommunicative, if it is not realized in a concrete image; but a concrete image or description would be inarticulate, in fact mad, if it contained no general terms. The particular is prior for the reasons and in the ways that we have said; there are relevant nonrepeatable properties, there is some revisability. In the end the general is only as good as its role in the correct artic-ulation of the concrete. But particular human contexts are never, if seen well, sui generis in all of their elements, nor divorced from a past full of obligations. And fidelity to those, as a mark of humanity, is one of the most essential values of perception.[61]

And we now see another way in which novels can play an important role in the articulation of an Aristotelian morality. For novels, as a genre, direct us to attend to the concrete; they display before us a wealth of richly realized detail, presented as relevant for choice. And yet they speak to us: they ask us to imagine possible relations between our own situations and those of the protagonists, to identify with the characters and/or the situation, thereby perceiving those similarities and differences. In this way their structure suggests, as well, that much of moral rele-vance is universalizable: learning about Maggie Verver's situation helps us under-stand our own.

One more point can be added: that Aristotelian deliberation, as I conceive of it, is concerned very deeply with one general notion above all: the notion of the human being. The starting point of an Aristotelian inquiry in ethics is the ques-tion, "How should a human being live?" (see Introduction). And the general answer to this question suggested by Aristotle himself is, "In accordance with all the forms of good functioning that make up a complete human life." The notion of good human functioning steers and guides the inquiry at a deep level, focusing attention on certain features of situations rather than others. The agent brings to the situation of choice her evolving picture of the good or complete human life. She views the situation as one in which good human functioning will or will not be realized; and the concept "human being" is one of the very most central ones she uses to demarcate it, in thinking about others and about herself. She views the good particular judgment as a further articulation of this evolving conception of the human good—or as a revision of it, if it should seem defective. Nothing is unrevisable; but the guidance of the tentative conception is very important in her thought about what occasions the situation creates for functioning of various kinds. Furthermore, as "Transcending" argues, this concept is not optional. Any choice that will be a good choice *for her* must be a good choice for her *as a human being.* This contributes in no small measure to our feeling that the Aristotelian

---

60. "'Finely Aware'" shows that things are slightly more complicated: in some cases general terms cannot even *outline* the particular, in that the distinction between general good and bad rests in getting the particulars right.

61. See Introduction, and endnote to "'Finely Aware,'" this volume.

conception is not at all rootless (far less so, for example, than deliberation schemes based upon one's preferences of the moment), and to our feeling that it does give the agent good guidance as to the direction her thought might take.

This is a large issue; and its further implications cannot be pursued here. I have studied them elsewhere.[62] But one especially important point should be mentioned: the Aristotelian view does not imply subjectivism, or even relativism. The insistence that deliberation must take contextual features into account does not imply that the deliberated choice is correct only relative to local norms. Aristotelian particularism is fully compatible with the view that what perception aims to see is (in some sense) the way things are; it requires further argument to decide on the best interpretation of the position here. And surely the use of the concept "human being" will play an important role in suiting the conception to make cross-cultural judgments and to ground a cross-cultural debate.[63] So if Putnam's worry is partly on this score, I think there is little basis for it.

And here, we should add, novels once again prove appropriate vehicles for the Aristotelian conception. For while they do speak concretely about human beings in their varied social contexts, and see the social context in each case as relevant to choice, they also have built into their very structure a sense of our common humanity. They speak to human beings about human beings, and the sense of a common human form of life, characterized by certain possibilities and certain sorts of finitude, is a powerful link among them, and between each of them and its readers. The concrete is seen as a scene for human functioning, and the reader is invited to assess it accordingly. Thus, while it is extremely difficult, and frequently impossible, to assess intuitively, as a possibility for oneself, an ethical or religious treatise from an extremely different cultural tradition, novels cross these boundaries far more vigorously, engaging the reader in emotions of compassion and love that make the reader herself a participant in the society in question, and an assessor of what it offers as material for human life in the world. Thus in their very structure they contain the interplay between the evolving general conception and the rich perception of the particular; and they teach the reader to navigate resourcefully between those two levels.

VII. Improvising When to Improvise

Sometimes the perceiver holds to a standing commitment; sometimes the new situation causes her to revise her scheme of ends. Sometimes she recognizes an irresolvable conflict of values; sometimes she decides that one or more of the values does not in fact apply in this particular case. Sometimes she attends more to the general features of her situation and sometimes to the unique or the new. How can we tell when to do each of these things? How can we be sure to improvise at

---

62. On this point see "Nature, Function, and Capability," "Non-Relative Virtues"; also "Aristotle on Human Nature and the Foundations of Ethics" (n. 19). See also Wiggins, "Deliberation."

63. "Non-Relative Virtues" and "Aristotle on Human Nature" provide further arguments on this point.

the right and not the wrong time, with the right and not the wrong sort and amount of flexibility?"[64]

The answer shows another dimension of the priority of the particular in good deliberation. For it must be: there is no general rule for this, the discrimination rests with perception. The experienced navigator will sense when to follow the rule book and when to leave it aside. The "right rule" in such matters is simply: do it the way an experienced navigator would do it. There is no safe guarantee at all, no formula, and no shortcut. And yet this absence of formula does not mean that we have laissez-faire, or that any choice one makes is all right. There are many ways of wrecking a ship in a storm, and very few ways of sailing it well. As Aristotle says, "There are many ways of missing the target . . . and only one way of hitting it; so one is easy and the other is hard" (1106b28–32).[65] Nor does it mean that we have no place to turn for guidance. We turn to stories of practical wisdom, both for representations of fine attention, and in order to be formed ourselves, as readers, into just such attentive and discriminating beings.

Has anything been said here? Does all this have any content? This question keeps on returning. For there is a tendency, both in philosophy and in life, to seek out theories that fix things in advance. It seems both shameful and dangerous to have accomplished so little and to have left so much to the occasions of life. The answer is: just as much content as the truth.

VIII. Public and Private: The Perceiver as Leader

We have spoken primarily about individual and private choice. We have given as our example a woman agonizing in a solitary way over what to do. And there is reason for this. For in the discrimination of perception the emphasis is on the private and separate work of each individual judge, who must greet each new situation with responsive flexibility. Rules are in the public domain; we can imagine them being followed by a community as a whole. In the same way, a general maximizing technique can obviously be applied to the situation of a large group, taken as a whole. In Aristotelian perception, things look otherwise. The emphasis on the inner work of imagination and emotion, the value ascribed to improvisational resourcefulness, the claim that the "matter of the practical" has an indefiniteness that is hard to put into words at all—all this leads us naturally to think of the view as a model for personal choice that has little applicability to the public sphere. And often in contemporary ethical theory those who are sympathetic to an Aristotelian morality for personal choice make at the same time a strong distinction

64. This is isomorphic to, though not the same question as, the question about when to maintain a balanced vision of the good of all and when to take up the exclusive attention characteristic of love as that question is raised in "Flawed Crystals," "Perceptive Equilibrium," and "Steerforth's Arm," this volume.

65. Here we should probably see a difference between the case of improvisatory ethics and the case of theatrical or musical improvisation: in the latter, there is an indefinite plurality of ways of making a right choice. This is connected with the fact that in ethics the agent is more deeply bound to past obligations, or bound in a different way: see "'Finely Aware,'" this volume.

between public and private, insisting that public procedures should be more explicit and codified than the Aristotelian procedure would recommend.[66]

Aristotle did not share this view. In fact, it is evident that in many of the passages we have discussed he is above all concerned with the conduct of public life. Passages attacking commensurability, and some of those indicating the limits of general rules, are found in his discussions of law and political systems. The virtue of equity and the use of the flexible ruler are properties of a good political judge. Aristotle's ideal person of practical wisdom is no solitary Jamesian heroine, but a politically active citizen of Athens; Pericles is an example. Indeed, even when we read those parts of his discussion that appear to be about personal choice, we must remember that there is no strong distinction between the public and the private in Aristotle's ethical conception. The good human life is a life with and toward others; membership in a *polis* is an important part of one's other-directed activity. And each of the virtues is said to have a social aspect:[67] this is what it means to say that in a way justice is the entirety of human excellence. Even the idea that correct emotional response is part and parcel of virtue, even the idea that literature and poetry can teach this element of the virtues—these are for Aristotle thoroughly public ideas. Athenian males did not reserve expression of love, grief, and anger for the privacy of the home. The public sphere was suffused with the emotional and imaginative energy that we sometimes associate, instead, with the private sphere, just as the sphere of the household was itself suffused with public concern. Dramatic poetry was a central part of a major public festival; Aristotelian philosophy presents itself as valuable for public practice.

In insisting that perception is the norm for political rationality, Aristotle is not innovating, though he is taking sides in a controversy of long standing. For his picture has, as we have suggested, strong links with the ideals of Periclean Athens; and his criticisms of general rules are at the same time criticisms of some of the political ideals of Sparta. As Thucydides represents the contrast, Spartan morality taught that civic strength and courage can best be promoted by a system of inflexible rules, to which all citizens are to regard themselves as thoroughly subservient. Spartans are characterized as cautious, slow, heavy. They are taught not even to think of improvising on their own, not to think their own intelligence more reliable than the law's guidance. ("We are educated to be too unlearned to look down on the law with contempt," I.84.) Nor are they to attend, in decision making, to the particularities of individuals and situations: for their king Archidamus reminds them that individuals do not differ very much—and he seems to connect this reminder with the injunction to trust the rule as a sufficient guide.[68] Both qualitative heterogeneity and the separateness of each individual chooser are denied in Spartan morality, as is, apparently, the value of personal emotional and imaginative engagement.

Athenian political morality, by contrast, elevates concrete perceptions above rule-following and makes public policy a matter of creative improvisation. The highest virtue of a leader is Themistocles' ability "to improvise on his own what

66. See, for one prominent example, S. Hampshire, *Morality and Conflict.*
67. For the interpretation of this claim, see *Fragility,* chap. 12.
68. See Thuc. I. 84.

the concrete situation requires" *(autoschediazein ta deonta)*. Athenian political life is characterized by intense attention to the particularities of individuals and situations. Its education teaches young citizens to "use their judgment as most intimately their own" (I.70); and self-directed judgment (educated in part by the love of art and music, whereas Spartan education is constituted by laborious drill) learns to value the distinctive qualities of each person and situation. Athenian political life is characterized as innovative, daring, mobile, "many-colored." And it is also full of feeling. Pericles is explicit on this point, as we have seen (see p. 83). He wants neither subservient followers nor calculating technocrats; he wants improvisers whose creativity is animated by passion.[69]

Aristotelian perception is, then, a style of public rationality. Can we take it seriously in this role? We need to ask, first, whether we want leaders and policy-makers who reason in the Aristotelian way. Then we will go on to ask what form of government might support the Aristotelian abilities.

First, then, do we, and should we, demand that our public leaders reason as Aristotle recommends? In assessing their behavior do we, and should we, look for the improvisatory imagination and the rich responsiveness that characterizes Aristotle's good and equitable judge? Hampshire has objected that Aristotelian perception is not explicit, not codified enough for public life. It is sometimes rather difficult to tell whether the claim is that Aristotle's is not a good ideal, or that, though a good ideal, it will not work in practice in many cases. The second claim is insisted on by Aristotle himself. For he insists, as we have said, that we need formal procedures and codified rules in the public sphere for a number of reasons: to speed up the working-through of complex material that could not be surveyed by perception in the available time; to guard against corruption in situations where bias could easily distort judgment; and, in general, to provide a context of choice for those whose reasoning we do not really trust.[70] The rule of law is defended and given a place of honor in Aristotelian politics.

And yet Aristotle made a distinction. He concedes repeatedly that rules *must* frequently be used in public life, and that this is better than any available alternative. He denies, however, that they are the norm toward which the public domain should strive. Can we make sense of this distinction and accept this point? Or do we believe that the judgment of the person of practical wisdom is a norm *in principle* unsuitable for the public sphere? And to what in our institutions might the recognition of such an ideal correspond?

Aristotle speaks of the equity of the flexible ruler as the virtue of a good judge. And his idea is that a judge of practical wisdom, rather than being unreflectively subservient to law, will apply it in accordance with his very own ethical judgment, looking attentively at the history and the circumstances of his city as he does so. He believes that including this element of flexible ethical judgment in the institutions of the city gives it a moral reach and vision that it would not otherwise have. Legislators, too, should show practical wisdom and vision; but it is striking that Aristotle singles out the judicial context as one in which equitable response is most especially required.

69. See Thuc. II. 37ff.
70. See *Aristotle's De Motu,* Essay 4.

Aristotle's demand corresponds closely to a prominent strand in our American tradition of legal and judicial reasoning. The dialogue between rule and perception in Aristotelian morality has a close and interesting relationship to the procedures of a good judge, who must bring to bear, in the concrete situation, her knowledge of law, the history of precedent, her own sense of the moral convictions embodied in the law, and her understanding of the case before her. Although there are, in the American legal debate, conflicting understandings of what a judge should be doing, several contending theories agree in rejecting, as normative in the process of judicial reasoning, the marks of "scientific" reasoning that Aristotle attacks. Few would urge legal reasoning to reduce qualitative distinctions to quantitative distinctions. And most insist on the centrality of the confrontation with the complexities of particular cases, seen as parts of a concrete history, evolving through precedent. Most insist (though in various different ways) on the complex interaction of principle, precedent, and new perception. (Evidence that Robert Bork rejected this complex conception and the role it ascribes to historical precedent, preferring a more dogmatic and noncontextualized conception of judgment, was a great part of what led to his rejection as nominee to the United States Supreme Court.) As for the emotions, although their contribution is sometimes denigrated here as elsewhere, they too have been prominently recognized as of value in steering or guiding the best legal reasoning. Sometimes this argument is made by legal relativists who view all legal judgment as expressive of "ideology," and who deny that there is any normative distinction to be made between power and persuasion, any room for a substantial conception of objectivity in legal judgment. But the point has also been made by legal thinkers whose views lie closer to Aristotle's— who do defend a substantial conception of practical wisdom, and simply insist that in the process of wise judgment rich emotional response is a mark not of irrationality but of rich or complete rationality. Prominent in this latter group is the constitutional lawyer Paul Gewirtz, who has argued that, although the passions *can* delude, they "can also open, clarify, and enrich understanding," and that "the values and achievements of a legal system—and of lawyers, judges, and citizens involved with a legal system—are shaped by what the emotions yield."[71]

In short: good legal judgment is increasingly being seen as Aristotle sees it—as the wise supplementing of the generalities of written law by a judge who imagines what a person of practical wisdom *would* say in the situation,[72] bringing to the business of judging the resources of a rich and responsive personality. It is not surprising that such reflections have recently led lawyers to take a keen interest in

71. For a discussion of recent work connecting law with literature, and speaking of the role of emotion and imagination in legal reasoning, see my "Introduction," n. 76, where this passage from Gewirtz is quoted in full, with references and bibliography; the passage quoted here is from the same paragraph.

72. Aristotle's requirement could be interpreted to mean "say what the *original* legislator would say," and thus to give support to the idea that constitutional interpretation attempts to seek out the intent of the founders. But it is better read as instructing the judge to imagine what a *wise* legislator would say, and thus to give judges the latitude to put together precedent, principle, and perception in their own way.

literature and to claim that works of literature offer insight into norms of legal judgment. For the account of judgment that Gewirtz and others provide has a natural link with the activity of the reader (or spectator) implied within many literary (and dramatic) texts. Thus Gewirtz's reflections about perception and emotion lead him to speak of "the special place literature can have in developing the legal mind to its fullest richness and complexity."

Within American ideals of legal judgment, then, the Aristotelian ideal is already recognized; and it will be important to develop these arguments further, both theoretically and historically, explaining what was good in court decisions of the past. But we notice that the ideal of the good judge is closely connected (in Gewirtz's thought and in the tradition on which he comments) to a more general political norm. The good judge is also a model citizen; and in Aristotle's view he will ask himself, as well, what a wise legislator would say. For although, as Aristotle would grant, formal and rule-governed procedures of many kinds have an invaluable role to play at many levels of the decision-making process, what is above all demanded of a good leader, and what we ought to demand of ourselves as citizens, is a different, and more Aristotelian kind of reasoning. We do not usually believe that training in quantitative social science techniques is essential for being a good representative, though we do need such experts around. We do insist, appropriately, and should insist more, on the development of the imagination, on a vigorous sense of concrete human reality, and even on a rather Athenian level of passionate engagement with life. The dangers of not insisting on this, and of giving way, instead, before the seductive lure of the technical intellect, are clear. We will have, as we have already had in the policy making that conducted the Vietnam war, impoverished models of humanity before our leaders' eyes—numbers and dots, taking the place of women and men. And when one's deliberation fails to endow human beings with their full and complex humanity, it becomes very much easier to contemplate doing terrible things toward them. We want leaders whose hearts and imaginations acknowledge the humanity in human beings. Walt Whitman's portrait of Abraham Lincoln's "large, sweet soul" is a portrait of such an Aristotelian leader, visionary in love, resourceful in imagining. And such images can still be found in American political life, though not often enough.

IX. A Society of Perceivers

I have suggested that Aristotelian norms are already a part of our political and legal traditions; so I have implied that they are not, as such, foreign to democracy, or biased in the direction of aristocracy. And Aristotle himself introduced the norms in connection with the ideal of a society of "free and equal citizens, ruling and being ruled in turn." But it has often been suspected that Aristotle's norm is not, in fact, compatible with a democratic way of life. This question needs our scrutiny. For even if we are satisfied that the Aristotelian virtues are valuable in both leaders and citizens, we might decide to pursue a different norm, if we were convinced that they could be cultivated only by abandoning institutions that we regard, for independent reasons, as best and most just.

I have written elsewhere about the general form of Aristotle's political conception; and I have described the form of democracy that is demanded by his ideal.[73] So here I shall be brief, focusing on the abilities of perception, and their material and institutional conditions.

First, it must be conceded that Aristotle's demand for leaders of equity and practical wisdom can frequently best be realized through the inclusion in a political system of certain institutions that are not directly democratic in character. Aristotle himself was divided about this—both praising Pericles in his role as "first citizen" and insisting on the ideal of "ruling and being ruled in turn." For the contemporary student of Aristotle, it will seem likely that a non–directly democratic institution such as the United States Supreme Court has an essential role to play in keeping perception at the heart of politcial life. On the other hand, it is also very important that this body be responsive, at some level, to the perceptions of citizens and to their sense of their traditions. In the defeat of the nomination of Robert Bork to the Supreme Court, a surprising consensus of citizen perceptions defeated the claims of a putative expert; and this possibility, too, seems in line with Aristotelian demands.

Second, if the form of government in an Aristotelian city is to be democratic, giving to all citizens the two forms of participation, judicial and legislative, that Aristotle demands, it is essential that government should concern itself with the provision of education. Aristotle argues that to be a citizen perceiver requires freedom from manual labor. He argues this on the grounds that, as he sees it, a life of such labor makes it impossible to get the rich and full education required to cultivate the various abilities involved in perception. He believes the provision of such an education to be the "first and most essential" task of government, and he frequently reproves actual governments for their neglect in this regard.

On the point about labor, we might well wish to moderate Aristotle's requirement of lifelong freedom from manual tasks. For the point of his requirement is above all, as we have said, a point about the provision of both basic and what we might call higher education. And although in the ancient Greek context it might well have seemed impossible to combine this rich or full education with a subsequent life in the laboring class, our own possibilities are more numerous. It seems altogether reasonable to make universal access to higher education a goal of a modern democracy, and to insist on its importance for citizenship much as Aristotle does, while reaching out further than Aristotle was able to do, to include a larger group within this citizen body. Thus the provision of adequate resources for education, including higher education, becomes one of the very most essential tasks of a government based on perception. Treating higher education not as a luxury for the privileged few, but as a necessity for a fully human development of the faculties of citizen perception, government would then be committed to ensuring that no citizen, however poor, would be cut off from the opportunity to receive such an education because of poverty and the need to hold a job. This does not mean that we will neglect the larger question about the relationships between forms of labor in later life and a fully human use of one's faculties. Aristotelian

---

73. See "Nature, Function, and Capability." Also, "Aristotelian Social Democracy," *in Liberalism and the Good,* ed. G. Mara and H. Richardson (New York, 1990).

politics is also profoundly interested in such possible tensions, since it is committed to making sure that all citizens have the necessary conditions for fully good human functioning. But education is seen as modifying all of subsequent life and making it more humane. So questions about education would be the first and most crucial questions.

In short, there is a strong element of perfectionism in the Aristotelian theory, which insists that rather demanding material and institutional conditions must be met if people are to realize their full humanity. This is not aristocracy in the hereditary or nature-based sense. As I have argued elsewhere, it has more in common with modern forms of social democracy that are based upon a substantial notion of the human good and good human functioning.

Aristotelian education is aimed at producing citizens who are perceivers. It begins with the confident belief that each member of the heterogeneous citizenry is a potential person of practical wisdom, with the basic (that is, as yet undeveloped) ability to cultivate practical perception and to use it on behalf of the entire group.[74] It aims at bringing these basic abilities to full actuality. As both Aristotle and Periclean Athens insist, the core of this education will be found in the studies that we now call "the humanities"—in the qualitatively rich study of human life through works of art and literature, through the study of history, and through humanistic forms of social inquiry. (It would also prominently include teaching in the understanding of nature embodied in mathematics and the natural sciences, though it would be careful not to confuse these studies with the humanistic studies.) Technical and quantitative analyses of social reality will be presented as tools, frequently very valuable, but incomplete in themselves, incomplete without the richer study of human ends that they cannot themselves perform. This would mean, for example, a public educational policy that moves in a direction roughly opposite to that now being taken by the Thatcher government in Britain, where humanistic studies (and also basic scientific inquiry) are being demoted and squeezed in favor of the development of technical and entrepreneurial abilities. This impoverished and impoverishing conception will not, the Aristotelian claims, prove able to sustain a democratic citizenry. Perception is fully compatible with democracy. But it does have material and institutional necessary conditions; and it is the responsibility of legislators to put these in place.

Where the teaching of moral reasoning itself is concerned, the Aristotelian conception will strongly endorse recent American efforts to make this a central part of education in medicine, law, business, and in undergraduate education more generally. But here again distinctions need to be made. The sort of moral reasoning course recommended by the Aristotelian will be clear, well argued, theoretically rich. But it will also make large demands upon the imagination and the emotions. It will be very far from a course in formal decision theory, or in the principles of economic rationality (as these are most often portrayed). It will at all times encourage the student to attend closely to the heterogeneity of life. And course materials will include works of literature that enrich and develop the sense of life, expressing, in their own attention to particularity and their richness of feeling, elements of the Aristotelian conception. It will include as well the deep and

74. See "Nature, Function, and Capability."

rigorous study of alternative moral conceptions, in order to give the student a clearer sense of the available choices. All this will be in the service of promoting the student's ability to choose a general conception of the good life, and to perceive, in practice, what this conception requires. At every stage in the process, the student would continue to refine her abilities to reflect and perceive in and about concrete cases, perhaps again through continued contact with works of literature and history.[75]

In short: the acceptance of an Aristotelian conception should lead to the recognition that the humanities are the core of our public culture, and that other techniques of reasoning are tools whose place is to assist them in their task of revealing and enacting a full and rich sense of human life and its public requirements. We do not have far to go to reach Walt Whitman's idea (contained in our epigraph here) that in a society based upon perception the poets (and philosophers who think like poets or welcome the insights of literature into their philosophy) are models of teaching and judgment. For they above all are devoted to finding precisely the right way of rendering the concrete, putting all the variety, messiness, and indefiniteness of the "matter of the practical" into words that will not debase its value, or simplify its mystery.[76]

Endnote

This essay has been published in a shorter version, but this is the first complete publication. All sections have been rewritten for this occasion. It is a continuation of some of the work on Aristotelian practical reasoning that was done in Chapter 10 of *The Fragility of Goodness* and resembles that chapter in its general argument. But this presentation of the Aristotelian position is more complete in its coverage of issues and more explicit in its contrasts between Aristotle's position and several of its rivals. It is philosophically central to this collection, since (along with the Introduction) it brings forward the philosophical conception of the ethical life and ethical reasoning in connection with which, as these papers argue, the works of literature discussed have an essential role to play in ethical inquiry. Of course, in the overall pursuit of the "how to live" question (see Introduction, "Perceptive Equilibrium"), this Aristotelian conception is only one of a number of alternatives to be fully investigated. This essay does not claim to have provided

75. See the Introduction, and also "Perceptive Equilibrium," this volume, on the distinction between the Aristotelian framing method, which considers all the alternative theories of the good human life, and the Aristotelian ethical conception, one particular conception that is considered by the framing method. As my discussions there indicate, the distinction between these two levels is not always easy to draw, since the methods recommended by the framing method include the use of some faculties that are especially valued by the Aristotelian conception, and less so by the other conceptions. However, the claim is that by being more inclusive, by including faculties that other architectonic methods omit, the Aristotelian framing method can claim to be fair to all the alternatives.

76. For comments that have helped me in my work on these ideas I am very grateful to Lawrence Blum, Dan Brock, and Henry Richardson.

that full investigation, and thus not a full defense of the Aristotelian position. It aims only at describing sympathetically the salient elements of the Aristotelian conception and at showing how, within and from its own point of view, it defends itself against several rivals. A full defense would require a far more systematic and sympathetic investigation of the rivals.

It is important to be clear about the relationship between this ethical conception and the role I claim for literature. My claim is that without *concluding* the investigation proposed by the overall ethical question, without, therefore, establishing any more than that the Aristotelian conception is a serious ethical alternative, we can still conclude that literature (of the sort and in the ways described) has an invaluable role to play inside moral philosophy, as expressive of that conception (or those conceptions, since I claim that it is a family of related views).

This essay shows the essential importance of the philosophical commentary on literature that I discuss in the Introduction, section F (see also "Love's Knowledge"). It is itself an example of such an Aristotelian commentary.

The claims about the political implications of the Aristotelian position are further developed in "Perception and Revolution" (and its endnote). The claims about the priority of the particular and the contrast between general and universal are further developed in the Introduction, and in "'Finely Aware'" (with endnote), which develops further the metaphor of improvisation.

Plato on Commensurability and Desire

And look: I gave them numbering, chief of all the strategems.
Prometheus, in Aeschylus, Prometheus Bound

Every circumstance by which the condition of an individual can be influenced, being remarked and inventoried, nothing ... [is] left to chance, caprice, or unguided discretion, everything being surveyed and set down in dimension, number, weight, and measure.
Jeremy Bentham, Pauper Management Improved

If ethical values are all commensurable, differing from one another only in quantity, what difference does this make?[1] Plato gives us a stark and simple answer. The adoption of an ethical "science of measurement," at the heart of which is the belief in commensurability, is both necessary and sufficient for "saving our lives," that is, for giving human beings a life that will be free of certain intolerable pains and confusions. Here I propose to examine one aspect of Plato's "life-saving" project, namely, some alleged connections between the belief in the commensurability of value and the nature of the human emotions. It is Plato's idea, I shall argue, that the belief in commensurability cuts very deep: taken seriously, it will transform our passions as well as our decision making, giving emotions such as love, fear, grief, and hence the ethical problems that are connected with them, an alto-

1. This paper is closely related to *Fragility,* chaps. 4 and 6; the manner of presentation is different, and some of the arguments, especially in sect. IV, do not appear in the book at all. The interpretative issues are more fully defended in the book, with much reference to and discussion of the secondary literature. I therefore confine myself here to acknowledgment of the sources that have been most important for my work. For the *Protagoras* these are C.C.W. Taylor's excellent commentary in the Clarendon Plato Series (Oxford, 1976), and T. H. Irwin, *Plato's Moral Theory* (Oxford, 1977). David Wiggins's "Weakness of Will, Commensurability, and the Objects of Deliberation and Desire," *Proceedings of the Aristotelian Society* 79 (1978–9) 251–77 has several points of intersection with this essay. I first read an earlier draft of it in 1974, long before I began developing these views, and returned to the published piece only at the stage of final revision of this article. I am not aware of a direct influence; but there may have been some. In any case, conversations with Wiggins on this and related topics over the years have been an invaluable source of encouragement and illumination.

gether different character. We shall begin with the *Protagoras,* investigating the connection between the adoption of a quantitative measure of value and the elimination of the problem of akrasia. Next, turning to the *Symposium* and *Republic,* we shall see how commensurability reforms several of the most vexing emotions, especially passionate love and grief. To pursue Plato's arguments will yield two philosophical dividends. It will enrich our discussion of the connections between emotion and belief, typically focused upon the beliefs that are closely associated with each particular emotion, by showing how a certain background belief functions as a necessary condition of much of our ordinary emotional life. And it will remind us that certain proposals in ethics and especially in economic theory that present themselves as innocuous extensions of ordinary belief and practice could actually lead, followed and lived with severity and rigor, to the end of human life as we currently know it.

I

The stage was set, historically, for Plato's attempt.[2] The fifth century had seen considerable discussion of what was required for the establishment of a successful *technē,* that is, of an orderly systematization of practice in some area that would yield increased control over the ungoverned aspects of human existence. In this debate the role of commensurability as criterion of rationality and index of progress was great. The medical writers, for example, are on the defensive, feeling the need to argue that their science is a real science *(technē)* and can really make progress beyond ordinary belief *in spite of* its lack of a quantitative measure. And in general the connection between number and order, between the ability to count or measure and the ability to grasp, comprehend, or control, runs very deep in Greek thought about human understanding. It pervades literature from Homer on; it lies at the heart of Pythagorean epistemology, of which Plato was probably a serious student. An examination of fifth- and early fourth-century uses of words associated with measure and commensurability reveals that they come freighted with heavy evaluative associations. What is measurable or commensurable is graspable, in order, good; what is without measure is boundless, elusive, chaotic, threatening, bad. The tremendous anxiety brought about by the discovery of incommensurability (and therefore "irrationality") in the subject matter of mathematics, the clearest of the sciences, testifies to the power and pervasiveness of such beliefs. Given this situation, it is hardly surprising that someone who wanted to claim that he had developed a rational *technē* making progress in some area would feel obliged to answer questions about the measurability of the subject matter. And it would be natural that, confronted with a subject matter as confusing in its variety and indeterminacy as human valuation and choice, a thinker with an interest in order and progress should ask himself whether this area of our lives could be, or become, a science of measurement.

2. This is a condensation of a detailed historical discussion of *technē* from *Fragility,* chap. 4, where there are extensive references to other Platonic passages, to many other ancient authors, and to the literature. See also the related discussion in my "Eleatic Conventionalism and Philolaus on the Conditions of Thought," *Harvard Studies in Classical Philology* 83 (1979) 63–108, esp. 89–91.

II

The subject of the *Protagoras* is the establishment of a *technē* of practical reasoning. Each of the two protagonists has an interest in such a science. Protagoras claims that he teaches it; Socrates claims at least to know what it would be like to have and to teach it. Each has quite a different conception of what such a science would be like and how it would speak to our ethical difficulties. Protagoras' *technē* seems to involve little more than a reflective elaboration of the ethical status quo; it leaves intact and tries to show the point of the plurality of (apparently incommensurable) values recognized in ordinary belief. Socrates evidently believes that this is insufficient: the urgency of our ethical difficulties requires the life-saving power of a *technē* of measurement. The relevance of a science of measurement to the resolutions of ethical disagreements and uncertainities is evident; the analogy was pressed in this connection already in the *Euthyphro* (7B–D), and it is more than an analogy here. But a surprising further dividend promised by the *Protagoras* Socrates is the removal of a further deep ethical problem, the problem of akrasia. To see how the resolution of this problem is connected with Socrates' interest in measurement we must look closely at the argument in which Socrates purports to show us that this problem does not, as described, occur: scientific knowledge of the good is sufficient for correct choice.

Much has been written about this argument, whose structure now seems to be well understood.[3] But before we can probe into the issue of commensurability, we need to say, briefly, what the net result of these discussions has been. The argument falls into three stages: first, a description of the problem; second, an argument that this problem does not really arise; third, an alternative diagnosis of practical error. The problem is a familiar one. A can do either x or y. A knows that x is better (overall), but chooses y, because she is overcome by pleasure. (The first statement of the problem adds, as alternatives, pain, love, and fear—but Socrates, quite reasonably in light of the hedonist agreement, speaks only of quantities of pleasure in what follows. This is important.) Knowledge, then, is "dragged around like a slave."

Protagoras and Socrates have explicitly agreed, from the outset, on two crucial premises:

> H: Pleasure is identical with the good.
> H_1:   A believes pleasure to be identical with the good.

It is quite clear that this premise is seriously endorsed by Socrates, regarded by all as a serious proposal of Socrates', and absolutely crucial to the validity of the argument for the conclusion, an important Socratic doctrine.[4] And yet, the absence of any sustained examination of the nature of pleasure and its intuitive credentials makes us suspect that pleasure is introduced less for its intrinsic appeal than for its promising status as single measure of value.[5] The conclusion of the argument

---

3. See especially Irwin, to whose formulation mine will be close; and Taylor, who links the analysis of the argument to an illuminating discussion of measurement.

4. See 351C, 357A; there is a full discussion of texts and critics in *Fragility,* chap. 4.

5. My position is close to that of I. M. Crombie, *An Examination of Plato's Doctrines* (London, 1962) I.232ff.

is that we desperately need a science that weighs and measures using a single standard.[6] Such a science needs a measure of value that will be single, ubiquitous, and relevant to the choices in question. Pleasure is as good as anything might be for such a measure. The post-Socratic history of the ethical measuring science shows that its appeal as standard of choice is deep, even among thinkers not otherwise hedonistically inclined (Mill, Sidgwick).[7] We have reason, then, to suspect that Plato's choice of pleasure is motivated first and foremost by his commitment to commensurability; the elaboration and defense of the particular choice of a standard is posterior and not really attempted here. If we find it odd that Socrates can feel confident about the *form* that an ethical science will take before establishing that there *is* a candidate for the standard that is unitary and omnipresent in the requisite way, we might begin to reflect that perhaps Socrates (like Bentham and Sidgwick) is less interested in our current intuitions about ends than he is in giving us a gift that will save our lives. Zeus (in Protagoras' story) did not require that justice be already a central human concern when he decided to make the attachment to justice a linchpin of his saving *technē*.

Now, in the crucial second phase of the argument, Socrates uses these premises, substituting "good" for "pleasant" to produce an absurdity in the description of what allegedly happens: A knows *x* is more good than *y;* A chooses *y,* because she is overcome by (desire for) the good in *y.* "What ridiculous nonsense," Socrates now remarks, "for a person to do the bad, knowing it is bad [i.e., inferior], and that he ought not to do it, because he was overcome by good."

At first we do not see what the absurdity is: for isn't this, in a way, just what happens in akrasia? This other good over here exerts a special kind of pull that draws us to it, so that we neglect our commitment to the good that is better overall. But we must look at how Socrates himself explains the absurdity, showing us what he means by "overcome." Is the good in *y,* he now asks, *a match for* the badness involved in missing out on *x?* No: for this would contradict the description of the case, according to which there is, and is known to be, *more* good in *x* than in *y.* But then if *y* really offers a smaller *amount* of good, an amount that is not *a match for* the good in *x,* then what A is doing is choosing a smaller package of pleasures and giving up a larger package. But how absurd that A should, with full knowledge, give up the larger package because she was overwhelmed by the smaller amount in the smaller package. It is like saying, "A, offered the choice between $50 and $200, chose the $50, because she was overcome by the quantity of the $50." And that does seem absurd. In short, notions of *amount* and of qualitative homogeneity seem to be doing some work here in producing the absurd result. We shall shortly see just how central their place is.

How could such an absurd mistake occur? Socrates can explain it only as the result of a mistaken judgment about the size of the packages. Just as adverse physical conditions sometimes give rise to false beliefs about size, nearer items appearing taller or larger, so nearer pleasures, too, can strike us as bigger and more important than they are on account of their nearness. The closeness of the present

6. 356DE: the *metrētikē technē* is, apparently, both necessary and sufficient for saving our lives *(sōtēria tou biou)*.

7. See the discussion of pleasure as standard of choice in John Rawls, *A Theory of Justice* (Cambridge, Mass., 1971), 554–60.

pleasure produces a false belief about size that temporarily displaces the agent's background knowledge about the real sizes involved. It is clear that, with pleasure as with size, a science of measurement would suffice to put an end to our errors.

Our attention must now be drawn to Socrates' premises in the second, absurdity-producing part of the argument. For the explicit hedonistic assumptions are clearly not enough to get Socrates to his conclusion. He is making tacit use of at least two further assumptions:

> M: Whenever A chooses between x and y, she weighs and measures by a single quantitative standard of value.
>
> C: A chooses x rather than y if and only if she believes x to be more valuable than y.[8]

M gives us the use of a quantitative standard in each particular case. H_1 gives us the singleness of the standard across all cases. C gives us the reliable connection between the beliefs that are the outcome of the weighing and the agent's actual choices. Together they yield the conclusion Socrates wants: if A's choice is not the result of a correct weighing, and is not made under duress (ruled out in the description of the case), then it must result from an incorrect weighing. For this is the only reason why someone who could have more would choose to have a smaller quantity of the same thing.

Each of these premises has a certain plausibility as an account of our deliberative procedure *some* of the time. Yet anyone who accepts the initial description of the case as the account of an actual human occurrence should take issue with them. For together they succeed in telling us that a problem by which we are intuitively gripped and troubled does not exist. Akrasia was supposed to be a case where ordinary deliberative rationality breaks down. What Socrates has done is not so much to prove that there can never be such breakdowns as to clarify the relationship between a certain sort of deliberative rationality and the akrasia problem. If we believe in a single end or good, varying only in quantity, and always deliberate by weighing or measuring quantitatively by a single standard, *and* always choose to act in accordance with our beliefs about the greater overall quantity of good, then akrasia will not happen. So, we are tempted to say: as long as rationality works it doesn't break down. We didn't need Socrates to tell us that.

At this point, many interpreters dismiss the entire argument. Seeing that the premises are not empirically acceptable as accounts of what we do in *all* cases (after all, their failure to hold was just what our ordinary belief in akrasia articulated), then it looks as if Socrates had better do some more looking at the ways people actually live and think.[9] Socrates' conclusion, however, should make us suspect that something more is going on here. What he told us, and Protagoras agreed, is that only an ethical science of measurement will *save our lives*. If we accept his diagnosis of our problems and their urgency, and agree that we want to save our lives, it may occur to us that we are given, in Socrates' argument, an advertisement, as it were, for its premises. The argument need not rely on the

---

8. See 358D; my formulation here is indebted to Irwin's.
9. For this criticism, see Aristotle, *EN* 1145b25ff.

common-sense intuitive acceptability of the premises. (Socrates stresses in this dialogue his disdain for the confused intuitions of the ordinary human being.) It shows us a connection between these premises and the disappearance of a problem—indeed, of more than one problem. An agent who thinks the way these premises describe has no confusion about choice, no disagreements with others about choice, *and,* it is claimed, no problem of *akrasia.* The whole thing, premises and all, appears to be the Socratic *technē* of practical reasoning, the life-saving art. The most astonishing claim implied by this argument is that the acceptance of the qualitative singleness and homogeneity of all the values actually modifies the passions, removing the motivations we now have for certain sorts of irrational behavior. Akrasia becomes absurd—not a dangerous temptation, but something that would never happen. To see how this is supposed to be so, we need to return to Socrates' talk of packages and amounts and to enter more deeply into the life and world view of his hypothetical agent.

An ordinary case of akrasia looks like this. Phaedra knows that if she eats a bagel just before she goes running she will get a cramp and cut down the distance she can complete. She will be angry with herself later and she will find her health less good than it would have been had she run further and eaten less. She knows, then, let us say, that it is better, all things considered, not to eat the bagel now, but instead to go running directly. But she is very hungry, and the bagel looks so very appealing, sitting there hot and buttered on its plate. Its appeal to her is quite distinct and special; it does not look like a little bit of exercise or a small package of health. It looks exactly like a buttered bagel. And so (swayed by the desires it arouses) she eats it.[10]

Contrast the following case. Phaedra's rational principle, for some reason, is to maximize her bagel-eating. Standing in the middle of the room, she sees on a table on one side a plate containing two fresh bagels, toasted and buttered. On the other side of the room, on a similar table, is a plate containing one toasted buttered bagel. The bagels are the same variety, equally fresh, equally hot, buttered in the same way. She can go for either one plate or the other, but (for some reason) not both. She knows that, given her rational principle, she ought to eat the two bagels. But, overcome by desire, she eats the one. Now this does seem highly peculiar, in a way that our first case did not. We must comprehend that there is *no* respect in which the single-bagel plate differs from the two-bagel plate, except in the number of bagels it contains. The bagels are in no way qualitatively different. Nor is the arrangement of bagels on plate or plate on table somehow more aesthetically appealing. The single-bagel plate is not even nearer, it is the same distance away. What could make Phaedra's choice anything but absurd, given that she really has the principle we say she has? I find myself imagining, as I try to understand her action, that there must after all be *some* distinguishing quality to that single bagel. It looked so cute, with its little burned spot on the crust. Or: it was from New York, and the other two were not. Or: she remembers eating bagels with her lover at *this* table, and not at that one. Or: she is a mathematician and she thinks that

---

10. Notice how close this looks to a case of contingent value conflict (on which see *Fragility,* chaps. 2 and 3); this closeness is remarked by D. Davidson, in "How Is Weakness of Will Possible?" in *Moral Concepts,* ed. J. Feinberg (Oxford, 1969), 93–113.

the single bagel in the middle of its plate exhibits a more pleasing geometrical arrangement. Or: it is so funny to see a bagel sitting on an elegant Lenox plate (the others being on a plain kitchen plate): it reminds her of the contradictions of existence. We could go on this way. But I mean to rule out every one of these sources of qualitative specialness in the description of the case. I insist on absolute qualitative homogeneity: the alternatives seem to her to differ in quantity only. And then, I believe, we do get the result Socrates wants. It is absurd. It would never happen; the motivating desires would never arise; nobody who really saw the choice that way would choose that way.[11]

What Socrates gets us to see, if we dig deep enough, is the connection between our akrasia problem and the way we ordinarily see things—the enabling role played by our belief in an incommensurable plurality of values in getting the problem going. Akrasia as we know and live it seems to depend upon the belief that goods are incommensurable and special: that this bagel, this person, this activity, though in some sense less good over all than its rival, has nonetheless a special *kind* of goodness that pulls us to it, a goodness that we could not get in just the same way by going in the other direction. It's one thing to be unfaithful through passionate desire for a lover whom one sees as a special and distinct individual. But suppose him to be a clone of your present lover, differing qualitatively in no feature (and let us suppose not even in history—as would be true of lovers in Plato's ideal city), and the whole thing somehow loses its appeal.

We might say, then, returning to the premises, that if we really have H_1 and M, C falls out as a natural consequence (with a couple of residual exceptions that we shall take up later). C is not true as an empirical description of the workings of desire. It does, however, appear plausible as a description of the desires of agents who really believe to the bottom of their souls in the qualitative homogeneity of all of their alternatives. (For our case is, after all, only the shallowest beginning: what we ultimately must get ourselves to imagine is that Phaedra sees *every one* of her choices this way, *and* that in every choice it is one and the same measure of value that she recognizes. There is no heterogeneity at all, even across cases.) The recognition of heterogeneity, the dialogue tells us, is a necessary condition for the development of irrational motivations; in its absence, they will simply not develop; or, if once developed, will wither away.

In short, I claim that Socrates offers us, in the guise of empirical description, a radical proposal for the transformation of our lives. He compares himself to the Prometheus of Protagoras' myth. Like the other gifts mentioned by Protagoras, this science of measurement will enter into and reshape the nature and attachments of the being who receives it. It is now not surprising that he tells us little about the intuitive acceptability of his proposed end: for it may not be something that can be properly assessed from our ordinary viewpoint. From our ordinary viewpoint, things do indeed, as Protagoras insisted, look plural and incommensurable. But our ordinary viewpoint leaves us in confusion: we want, and know we need, to assume the viewpoint of science. The founder of a science is not obliged to show that the science recapitulates the structure of ordinary belief in every way: for it would be surprising if any science worthy of the name were so

11. See Wiggins, "Weakness of Will," Sect. VIII.

conservative; and if it were it would not make a positive difference to our lives. This point is very well put by Sidgwick, after he has observed that the motivation for hedonism comes from the intractability of problems of choice, rather than from the common-sense plausibility of this choice of an end:

> But it must be borne in mind that Utilitarianism is not concerned to prove the absolute concidence in results of the Intuitional and Utilitarian methods. Indeed, if it could succeed in proving as much as this, its success would be almost fatal to its practical claims; as the adoption of the Utilitarian principle would then become a matter of complete indifference. Utilitarians are rather called upon to show a natural transition from the Morality of Common Sense to Utilitarianism, somewhat like the transition in special branches of practice from trained instinct and empirical rules to the technical method that embodies and applies the conclusions of science; so that Utilitarianism may be presented as the scientifically complete and systematically reflective form of that regulation of conduct, which through the whole course of human history has always tended substantially in the same direction.[12]

So too for Socrates. Measurement is continuous with ordinary belief in that it fulfills an ideal of rationality embodied in ordinary belief: thus there is a natural transition from ordinary belief to scientific practice. To make this transition, clearly, science's choice of an end must also have *some* continuity with ordinary beliefs about ends: this is why pleasure is plausible as a candidate, while other conceivable choices, for example weight or length, would clearly be absurd. But the worth of the science as science is connected with its willingness to go beyond the ordinary and to transform it.

III

Plato never again puts forward this very same proposal for the ethical science. Pleasure proves unsalvageable as single standard, once examined further; and the qualitative homogeneity of all the different virtues is never again defended in exactly this way.[13] But we should not conclude from this that Plato loses interest in commensurability and its power to transform desire and motivation. The best part of the soul, in the middle dialogues, the one translators christen "rational," is usually called by Plato the "calculative," or even "the one that has confidence in calculation and measurement" (*Rep.* 603A). *Republic* VII insists that any science *(technē)* or (scientific) understanding *(epistēmē),* insofar as it is that, must deal in numbering and measuring (522Bff). A fortiori this will be true of the ethical science of the philosopher rulers. And in fact, in the middle dialogues we find commensurability subtly present as a tool of ethical progress. Indeed we find even more explicit consideration of the issue of most interest to us, the way in which a belief in commensurability allegedly alters motivating desires and emotions—particularly, here, the emotions of love and grief.

12. *The Methods of Ethics,* 7th ed. (London, 1907), 425; Crombie makes a similar point about Plato.
13. On this see *Fragility,* chap. 4 and Interlude 2; also Irwin, *Plato's Moral Theory.*

The *Symposium* recognizes, and shows, that human beings often lead disorderly and unsatisfactory lives because of the extent to which they are motivated by passionate love. The lives are unsatisfactory both because of akrasia and related problems and because of the vulnerability of the lover to accidents of loss, departure, betrayal. Diotima offers qualitative homogeneity as a remedy for both of these problems. I have analyzed her proposal at length in an article; but I shall recapitulate the main points before pursuing our question further.[14]

First of all, we can observe that Socrates' preliminary argument with Agathon is valid only on the assumption that the *kalon* is all qualitatively homogeneous, beauties being distinct only in quantity and in spatiotemporal location. (It is a complicated matter to show this, and I shall not repeat myself here; but it is evidently true.)[15] This argument, however, which turns our attention to commensurability as an issue, does not yet tell us what ethical work that idea is going to do. Diotima does tell us. In her account of the soul's development toward understanding and happy life, the idea of homogeneity plays, explicitly, a crucial role. We begin with a young person whose life is both unstable and unhappy, a person who is frequently led astray from other worthwhile pursuits by the lure of passion, and who is "enslaved" to the unique objects of those passions, who are not always available to be happily loved. (The young Socrates, she tells us, was such a person [212C].) We now entrust this person to a "correct" guide who will undertake to make his life "livable" by offering a particular kind of teaching about the objects of love.

This person will begin by loving a single beautiful body—or, more precisely, the beauty and value (the *kalon,* a notion much broader than "beauty") of a single body. "Then he must see that the *kalon* in any one body is closely related *(adelphon)* to the *kalon* in another body; and that if he must pursue the *kalon* of form, it is great mindlessness not to consider the *kalon* of all bodies to be one and the same" (210A5). First, then, he sees only the beauty or value of his loved one's body. Then he is asked to notice a *similarity* or family-related *closeness* between that value and other comparable values. Then—and this is the crucial step—he *decides* that it is *prudent* to consider these related beauties to be "one and the same," that is, not just qualitatively close, but qualitatively homogeneous, interchangeable instances of some one inclusive value. He then sees that he "must set himself up as the lover of all *kalon* bodies, and relax his excessively intense passion for one body, looking down on that and thinking it of small importance" (210B). In other words, the consideration motivating the move to commensurability is

14. "The Speech of Alcibiades: A Reading of Plato's *Symposium,*" *Philosophy and Literature* 3 (1979) 131–72; a revised version appeared as chapter 6 of *Fragility.* The analysis brings together the many ways in which Plato draws our attention to these problems and urges us to think that a life with them is not "livable for a human being."

15. 199E–201B; see "The Speech" and *Fragility,* chap. 6. The main point is that from the assumptions (1) that a lover loves that which is *kalon* and (2) a lover lacks that which she loves one cannot infer that the lover lacks the *kalon* altogether—without making two further assumptions: (a) that the object of the lover's love is the *kalon* of the person, and not the whole person who has the property of being *kalon;* and (b) that all manifestations of the *kalon* are sufficiently like one another in quality that if a person lacks one sort it is possible to conclude that she lacks the *kalon* altogether.

one of *prudence,* and the benefit of the move is a welcome change in the nature and intensity of the passion of love. It is mindless not to take the step from closeness to homogeneity because this step is so helpful to the personality, relaxing tensions that have become difficult to bear.

At each subsequent stage, the aspiring lover learns to consider apparently heterogeneous values to be comparable and intersubstitutable, differing only in quantity. We hear talk about comparisons of *size* between one sort of value and another (210B6, 210C5), of a "vast amount" of value (210D1). (Later Socrates will ascribe to Alcibiades the desire to "make an exchange of *kalon* for *kalon*" (218E)—and, since Socrates' *kalon* is "entirely surpassing," Alcibiades stands accused of *pleonexia,* a greedy desire for *more.*)[16] First the value of bodies is compared against the value of souls and found "small"; then vision is broadened to take in the value of laws, institutions, and sciences. At last the lover, his vision "turned round" by education (cf. *Rep.* VII), is able to conceive of the whole of the *kalon* as a vast ocean, whose components are, like droplets, qualitatively indistinguishable:

> And looking towards the great extent of the *kalon,* he will no longer, like some servant, loving the *kalon* of a particular boy or a particular man or of one set of customs, and being the slave of this, remain contemptible and of no account. But turned towards the wide sea of the *kalon* and contemplating, he gives birth to many *kalon* and grand speeches and reasonings in his abundant love of wisdom. (210C7–D6)

Diotima's speech is much more explicit than the *Protagoras* about the transformations of vision involved in learning commensurability, the extent to which this vision of the "sea" is the achievement of a complex therapeutic process that takes the pupil, by gradual steps, far away from ordinary intuitive beliefs about love. (If we doubt this, Alcibiades, the unregenerate lover, shortly brings it home to us.) She is more explicit, too, about the commitments involved in the teaching: we are now told that we must see the beauty or value of bodies, souls, laws, institutions, and sciences, as *all* qualitatively homogeneous and intersubstitutable, differing only in quantity. Finally, she is explicit concerning the human results of the teaching. There will be a deep transformation of the emotional structure of love, so that it is no longer a source of distraction, disorder, and painful vulnerability. She connects the love of nonhomogeneous particulars with tension, excess, and servitude, the love of the uniform "sea" with health, freedom, and creativity. The lover who has achieved this unifying vision has a life that is "livable," whereas before it was wretched and slavish (cf. 211DE).[17]

It is difficult to get clear about the relationship of this proposal to the *Protagoras*

---

16. Two passages are less clearly quantitative: "more honorable" at 210B7 and "gold for bronze" at 219A1. But both are compatible with a quantitative reading (gold is *worth more* on the single scale of financial measure; and it is just what is at issue whether differences in honorableness are qualitative or only quantitative). So neither passage cuts against the preponderant evidence for a single quantitative scale.

17. Here I do not discuss the transition from the "wide sea" to the unitary form; see *Fragility,* chap. 6.

science, since it remains unclear how far the *kalon* in this dialogue is a unifying general notion of value. At the very least, we are being asked to see different instantiations of one very important value as all qualitatively homogeneous; but since *"kalon"* is used as interchangeable with *"agathon"* (201C2 states that all *agatha* are *kala,* and the biconditional is required for the argument at 201C4–5), there may actually be a single unifying value in terms of which we are ultimately to see the special values such as justice and wisdom. But whatever is true on that issue, it is clear that the *kalon* is supposed to include everything that is relevant to the experience of passionate love—everything, then, that human beings find lovable in the world. And it is clear that a belief in the homogeneity of the *kalon,* like the *Protagoras* science, profoundly alters our emotional and motivational relationship to the world. The aspiring lover is not assuming a fashionable ethical decision strategy as a theoretical posture that leaves the important things of daily life essentially unchanged. Diotima demands more than lip service; she wants the belief in homogeneity to penetrate to the bottom of the soul, transforming the whole vision of the world.

It is a startling and powerful vision. Just try to think it seriously: this body of this wonderful beloved person is *exactly* the same in quality as that person's mind and inner life. Both, in turn, the same in quality as the value of Athenian democracy; of Pythagorean geometry; of Eudoxan astronomy. What would it be like to look at a body and to see in it exactly the same shade and tone of goodness and beauty as in a mathematical proof—*exactly* the same, differing only in amount and in location, so that the choice between making love with that person and contemplating that proof presented itself as a choice between having n measures of water and having $n + 100$? Again, what would it be like to see in the mind and soul of Socrates nothing else but (a smaller amount of) the quality that one also sees in a good system of laws, so that the choice between conversing with Socrates and administering those laws was, in the same way, a matter of qualitative indifference? What would it be, finally, to see not just each single choice, but all choices (or at least all choices involving love and deep attachment) as similarly unvariegated? These proposals are so bold as to be pretty well incomprehensible, from the ordinary point of view. We can perhaps, though with difficulty, get ourselves, in imagination, into the posture of seeing bodies as qualitatively interchangeable with one another—because we have, or can imagine having, relevant experiences of promiscuity or of nonparticularized sexual desire. (Indeed, we might even say that nonparticularized sexual desire will be the only experience most of us unregenerate cave-dwellers have of what Diotima wants, namely, a powerful longing that treats all of the individualizing traits of the object as irrelevant. So, ironically, loveless sex could be a useful form of training for Platonic love.[18]) We might even imagine the interchangeability of souls, helped by a religious heritage according to which we are all equally, and centrally, children of God. We might even try putting these two together, to get a thoroughgoing interchangeability of persons; and we can see how that sort of replaceability would indeed subvert motivations

18. I owe this observation to Joel Feinberg. I make a related point about *Republic* VIII and the first two speeches of the *Phaedrus* in *Fragility,* chap. 7.

for certain troublesome and disorder-producing acts. (Think of Epictetus' profound observation that if Menelaus had been able to think of Helen as just another woman, "gone would have been the *Iliad,* and the *Odyssey* as well.")

But the wide sea of the *kalon* is beyond us. We sense only that to see in this way, if one could do it, would indeed change the world. We can comprehend the extent to which it would erode the motivation for running after Alcibiades, for devoting oneself to a particular beloved person, even for loving one city above all other things. The lover, seeing a flat uniform landscape of value, with no jagged promontories or deep valleys, will have few motivations for moving here rather than there on that landscape. Even if we allow the argument to stop short of the unitary form, we can see how likely it is that some form of contemplative life would be preferred over more concrete practical engagements. And we can certainly see how any life that was selected from that point of view would be both calmer (less prone to akratic disruption) and more secure than our empirical lives: for the departure of one droplet matters far less to the lover of the ocean than the loss of a lover to the unregenerate.

We can see, furthermore, how not only passionate love but also other emotions, such as grief and fear, would be affected, for what reasons for grief will such a person have in a death or a loss? And if love is not unstable, and there are no reasons for grief, what bad things are there to fear? Plato insists on this in the *Republic:* the proper attitude toward the world removes reasons for both grief and fear. The literature of the ideal city will not be permitted to depict Achilles mourning the death of Patroclus, or any other case of a good person feeling personal grief; it will leave such retrograde emotions, and their expression, to "women, and not very good women at that." Plato sees clearly how thoroughly our stories rest on beliefs about specialness that threaten the wise person's emotional equanimity; and his purge of literature is deeply bound up with his desire to reform these emotions.[19]

IV

We now see something of the emotional transformation that commensurability brings about. And we are clear by now that this transformation is no mere incidental consequence of its adoption, but one of the most important motivations for going beyond our ordinary beliefs in this way.[20] Now we must begin to ask questions. They will be of three types. Is Plato's idea logically/metaphysically coherent? Is it psychologically plausible? And is it ethically desirable?

Coherence first. We must take very seriously the fact that *every* property of objects relevant to practical motivation will be homogenized qualitatively with every other. (The *Protagoras* recognizes only one ethically salient property; in the *Symposium* only one is relevant to love, and this, as we said, comes to much the

19. These issues are further discussed in *Fragility,* chap. 6, and especially Interludes 1 and 2, where I discuss Plato's criticism of literary art and Aristotle's reply (with special reference to fear and pity). Now see also "The Stoics on the Extirpation of the Passions," *Apeiron* 1987.

20. One very important motivation for following his suggestion is surely the example of Socrates, whose life and character exemplify the benefits of ascent.

same thing.)[21] Now the question is, what is left of objects and persons in this scheme? Everything about an object or person that *counts* for desire and action is flattened out into the "wide sea." So what is left for the body or person to *be?* What individuates it, enables us to refer to it, trace it through time, identify and reidentify it? Our Phaedra example clearly did not go far enough, for it allowed bagels to be different from plates and persons, for example, and from laws and proofs, in all sorts of individuating and potentially significant ways. In reality, what the good agent will see is just a map on which the value areas are colored a uniform shade of blue, and marked off only from parts of the world's landscape in which none of the valuable is to be found. A body, a person, will seem to be nothing but a pure container or location for a certain quantity of value. To see it as *being* more is to introduce, potentially, the motivational complications that this scheme wishes to avoid. But is this enough to give us a definite object to love, to speak about? Is it even enough for us to continue regarding ourselves as definite subjects? Plato is notoriously evasive about what Aristotle would call the issue of the substrate; it is no surprise to find him less than clear about the definite this-ness of persons or bodies, about what they in their nature *are* and continue being, as they go on through time and change, as opposed to the properties they merely *have.* Indeed it is notorious that his use of neuter expressions such as *"to kalon,"* in the *Symposium* and elsewhere, is often ambiguous between the property of some object and the object itself, characterized as having that property. We can now see, however, one ethical route that may have led Plato into this thicket. For under a radical and thoroughgoing belief in commensurability it is not evident that a metaphysically serviceable distinction between substrate and property will be forthcoming. For if we reserve some items to *be* (the essential nature of) the object in question, as distinct from the value properties that it *has,* and if these items are in any way thick or interesting enough to provide an adequate founda-tion for practices of individuating and identifying, then we will run the risk of finding them practically relevant or salient in a way that sets the object off from the homogeneous value that objects have; but this contradicts the description of the world embodied in the doctrine of commensurability. For example, suppose we say that what Alcibiades *is,* as opposed to the value of body/soul that he *has,* is the functional organization of a living body. Then the measuring scientist will immediately want to know, is functional organization itself potentially a lovable or valuable or practically interesting thing, a thing that could ever be more than a matter of indifference? If the answer is "yes" (and it must surely be yes), then it turns out that we will not be permitted to distinguish it from the value properties that he *has,* after all: it must be homogeneous with that value. But anything for which the answer will truly be "no" (his bare location at *t?* his moment of birth?)

21. It is much less clear what the situation is in the *Republic;* a good answer would require an account of the Form of the Good, which I shall not attempt here. The *kalon* in that dialogue is sometimes discussed as one value among others; but there is also great stress on numbering and calculating as hallmarks of practical *epistēmē.* (Plato's word for the best part of the soul is *to logistikon,* "the calculative element.") At any rate, it is clear (see below) that persons are supposed to be interchangeable with one another in their value: all citizens are "alike and friends," and mourning for the death of a particular loved one will be unknown.

is likely to be too thin to carry the metaphysical weight of being (to use Aristotelian language) "exactly what Alcibiades is."

All this is not yet a knock-down argument against commensurability. It does warn us, however, that commensurability had better work on this problem, especially if it wants to claim to bring benefits to persons. And it prepares us to find that the world as seen in the metaphysics of commensurability may not look like the ordinary world of distinct objects and relatively enduring continuants. We must be prepared to find that the adoption of this belief might bring results so radical that they would alter our whole view of what a thing is, of what we are; and we should demand of any social theorist who professes this belief an account of how these transformations are going to go and what coherent world order will result. Quite a few contemporary theorists have not yet undertaken this challenge.

Now for plausibility. Is it even remotely likely that any agent will ever live in the world who thinks and acts like this? There are at least two questions here. First, is it possible to bring up an agent for whom the belief in commensurability is deep and thoroughgoing enough to satisfy Plato? And, second, are there some desires in the human being that are not responsive to belief at all? Concerning the first question, we wonder whether the earliest experiences of human children in the world don't teach them that some objects are special and specially lovable. A child nurses at the mother's breast. Later, it finds itself surrounded with special objects that form the context of its life and are cherished as its own. It learns to single out its own parents, friends, home, clothing, city, from all other similar items. It is exposed to literary works that reinforce these perceptions. Once development has proceeded along these lines, it will not be possible, perhaps, for the Platonic philosopher to come along and teach commensurability. Or if the teaching is successful it will be so only at a much more superficial level, as it is for many modern utilitarians: it will be a formal way of speaking that will not very much alter the nature of daily perceptions.

The *Protagoras* has nothing to say about these problems. The *Symposium* does indicate that the training involved in the ascent takes considerable time and effort; but it proceeds as if one could take an adult citizen trained in the ordinary way and, over time, produce Diotima's result. But the *Republic* shows us that Plato has not neglected our issue. In order that the citizens of the ideal city should regard themselves, their friends, and their property as all interchangeable and not special, Plato sees that there must be a profound restructuring of early human experience, beginning, in fact, with the experience of the breast. Babies are farmed out to nurses and denied the opportunity to form a special bond with the mother as nurturer, the father as authority. (Only worries about incest prevent the commensurability of persons from being total: they do learn to single out that *generation* for special treatment.) As they grow they will not have or see private property; nor will they know of works of literature that teach the specialness of persons, the irreplaceability of loved objects. We can hardly say whether these psychological devices would succeed, since they have never been practised; and even in fiction they have (outside the *Republic*) been imagined only in a relatively crude and biased manner. But we can say at least that Plato saw the depth of the problem and with powerful imagination pursued his idea through in rich detail. He saw, too, an obstacle to full success: in the unregenerate privacy of the body, the fact that, no matter how interchangeable everything else becomes there still remains the fact that the sensations of this piece of flesh have a connection with me that is altogether different from the connection I have with this other piece of flesh over there. The *Laws* tells us that the teachers of the young will do whatever lies in their power to undermine this special love of something irreducibly one's own:

> The notion of the private will have been by hook or by crook completely elimi-
> nated from life. Everything possible will have been done to make common in
> some way even what is by nature private, like eyes and hands, in the sense that
> they seem to see and hear and act in common. (739CD)

It is a formidable problem.

With this mention of the body's recalcitrance we come to our second question. Are there some human desires that are not responsive to belief, so that they will continue to assert themselves despite the best education in commensurability? Plato is convincing when he claims that emotions such as love, grief, and fear have a deep connection with and reliance upon belief, such that a change in belief about what is valuable, lovable, or interesting will effect a transformation of those atti- tudes. But is the same thing true of hunger and thirst? The view of the *Protagoras* suggests that it is. Once I come to regard my eating and drinking as forming part of a unified calculus of goodness with, for example, just and courageous action, I will be stopped from the special sort of attitude toward food and drink that makes akrasia possible. The *Republic* appears to modify this view. The appetite for food and drink is held in Book IV to be an "unqualified desire," that is, one unrespon- sive to teaching concerning the good; it must, then, be trained not just by the general scheme of education, but by specifically nonrational techniques of sup- pression.[22] It is likely that a belief in the thoroughgoing commensurability of value would not, in fact, leave our behavior with respect to food and drink unaffected. For to change the evaluative component of these practices (the element of taste and selectivity, the search for novelty and specialness) is surely to diminish their power to disturb a life. The number of people who eat and drink akratically merely in order to pile in an increased quantity of food and drink is far smaller than the number of those who are akratic with respect to food and drink. Glaucon was surely right when he connected disorderly appetitive behavior with the search for luxury and specialness; in the "city of pigs" (in a community of animals) there is no akrasia, despite the existence of the bodily appetites.[23] Plato, then, seems right to acknowledge, as he does in *Republic* IV, that the bodily appetites do differ in structure from the emotions and may continue to be problematic even when the emotions are under control. But he also seems right in thinking that commen- surability makes the problem far less disturbing, and hardly grave at all.

22. See Irwin, *Plato's Moral Theory;* and G. Watson, "Free Agency," *Journal of Philosophy* 72 (1975) 205–20.

23. Compare Epicurus' diagnosis of unruly appetitive behavior as the result of false beliefs about value and need. Natural appetitive need is moderate, easily satisfied with whatever is at hand. See my "Therapeutic Arguments: Epicurus and Aristotle," in *The Norms of Nature,* ed. M. Schofield and G. Striker (Cambridge, 1986), 31–74.

Plato's attitude to the sexual appetite is more complicated. At times he does indeed treat it as one more bodily appetite, which will exert its pull regardless of our beliefs about objects.[24] But he recognizes and stresses the extent to which our beliefs and perceptions concerning objects alter the workings of this appetite. Sex is not a moral problem for the good pupil of Diotima: his appetites themselves appear to be affected by his new view of the bodies and souls of others. The same appetitive energy that once led Socrates toward young boys now goes into "intercourse" with the form.[25] Alcibiades does not arouse him. At the first stage of the ascent, his desire for all attractive bodies will, we said, be something like ordinary nonparticularized sexual longing. But once intellectual objects are seen to be possessed of the same thing that bodies have, only more so, the natural result is that most of his *eros* will channel itself in this new direction, leaving very little for the bodies that were once prized. The residue will not be enough to be disturbing. Indeed, it is a little hard to know how the guardian class would reproduce itself, except by acquiring the ability that Augustine, in the *City of God,* ascribes to our first parent before the fall (XIV.24). This one appetite, then, seems thoroughly educable; and it is clearly this appetite that Plato believes to pose the greatest problem for human good living.

There is one more irrational desire that Plato never considers. He never entertains the thought that there may be in human beings a desire simply to act in a perverse and irrational way. For in describing Phaedra's situation we have ignored the possibility that she will eat the single bagel just in order to go against good reasons, to show that she is not bound by reasons, or goodness, or anything else. In *Notes from Underground* Dostoyevsky suggests that one of the great defects of a Socratic picture of akrasia is its neglect of this desire, in which he sees the basis for human freedom.[26] We cannot go into this deeply here; but we can say that it is deeply questionable whether an agent who really had the thoroughgoing Platonic belief in commensurability could have, at the same time, the basis for this desire. For it seems to require a conception of the specialness of the self, and its radical separateness from its surrounding world, that would be unavailable to such a Platonic agent. What may have been a good argument against Russian consequentialists seems less appropriate against Plato's more radical and thoroughgoing proposal.

We can conclude that Plato's account of the psychology of commensurability is complex and deep; if he leaves many questions open, at least he presses all the right questions. And if we are not convinced that a total change in human psychology can be brought about by the teaching he describes, still he shows that it

24. This seems to be true in the *Republic* and in Socrates' first speech in the *Phaedrus;* the *Symposium* and *Philebus* give more complex accounts. On Socrates' second speech in the *Phaedrus,* see below.

25. See Diotima's use of *suneinai* for the love of boys at 211D6, for intercourse with the form at 212A2; at 211D she suggests that Socrates will find himself inflamed with longing not for boys and clothing and money, but for his intellectual object.

26. This passage was very well discussed, in connection with both Plato and Aristotle, in a Ph.D. thesis by the late Eunice Belgum, Harvard 1976. See also Julia Annas, "Action and Character in Dostoyevsky's *Notes From Underground,"* *Philosophy and Literature* 1 (1976–77), 257–75.

could effect some remarkable alterations. Now we might wonder about the positive motivational question: in getting rid of so much, what motivations has Plato left us with to propel our ethical lives? Aristotle contends in the *Politics* that Plato's denial of qualitative specialness to persons and objects has undermined the strongest sources of human motivation to choose good and virtuous action: "There are two things that above all make human beings care and love, the thought that something is your own and the thought that it is the only one you have; neither of which will be present in the citizens of that city" (1262 b22–4). Plato's image is of a stream of motivational energy flowing forth from the soul that will remain unchanged in quantity and intensity, and will just be spread around differently over the available objects. Aristotle answers that to take away the specialness of close personal attachment makes all attachment and all motivation weak and diffuse. We will have agents who are impotent in more than the sexual sense. This seems to be a strong objection to Plato; and it is one that Plato himself takes to heart. I believe, and argue elsewhere, that in the *Phaedrus* Plato concedes this point, granting that intense erotic love of a particular person, seen as that and not as a replaceable piece of the *kalon,* plays a central role in motivating us to grow ethically and to pursue our search for true beauty and goodness—not only at a stage, but throughout our lives. Indeed I believe he goes further still: he allows that this specialness of response to a beloved person is of *cognitive* value as well, giving us information about the nature of true beauty and about excellences of character, information that we could not have gotten without this sort of intimacy and its associated beliefs.

Finally, we must ask about the goal of all of this. Is the condition of self-sufficiency and stability that Plato achieves by his stratagem a valuable condition of the person, and is the life of such a person a good and valuable human life? A life embracing everything of true intrinsic value? Plato's own ambivalence on this question expresses itself in the structure of the *Symposium* itself, where, as I have argued elsewhere, the speech of Alcibiades, with its portrayal of a uniquely personal love, at once motivates the ascent and calls it into question. And I believe that the *Phaedrus* also defends the intrinsic value of personal love, defending both qualitative specialness and inviolable personal separateness in a way that is foreign to, and expresses a criticism of, Diotima's teaching. Plato's use of the plant as the central metaphor for the aspiring person's soul suggests that he now believes that there are certain sorts of beauty and value that are inseparable from vulnerability to loss, and that self-sufficiency is not an appropriate end for an ethical theory to aim at. Grief and passionate love return in their humanly recognizable form, and the best human life becomes one that is not free of certain ordinary tensions and risks.

But the appeal of commensurability is very deep; and therefore the end that it promises needs continued probing. It is important for our contemporary ethical inquiries to do this probing. A brief consultation with untutored intuition is hardly enough to satisfy Plato's demands. For it seems implausible that any such procedure could be fair to a proposal of this radical nature. It is hard to know what else to do. It raises profound questions of ethical method. But Plato has, I believe, shown us the way. To show us the benefits of his science, one of his strategies is to show us how it takes us beyond certain miseries depicted in literature.

To ask our questions about his picture of value, we might, then, try to continue this line of imagining, conducting our own Platonic examination of cherished literary works of our day, asking how much of what makes them compelling to us as depictions of human value would survive in the world of the commensurable, and how they would have to be reformed to be admitted into a curriculum that trained pupils for this world. I attempted this, in fact, with a section of Henry James. The results were interesting, and fully justified my belief that the novel is profoundly committed to an anti-Platonic view. (Plato is surely right when he holds that a change in view about value requires a change not only in the *content* of literature, but also in its *style*.)

A second and equally important strategy suggested in Plato is the detailed fictional imagining of lives lived both outside and inside of the science of measurement. When, in the *Symposium,* he follows Diotima's speech with the speech of Alcibiades; when, in the *Republic,* he describes every minute circumstance of the new lives he envisages; when, in the *Phaedrus,* he vividly describes the lives and feelings of rather different people, showing us the value of *that*—in all these cases Plato seems to me to be doing the sort of tough work of imagination that is required for anyone who is going to make an informed choice in this matter. We need to follow his lead. We need not just philosophical examples (which contain only a few features that the philosopher has decided are of greatest relevance to his argument); we also need novels about the whole way of life of people who really think and live the life of commensurability; about how they got there and how they now deal both with others and with themselves.[27] We need to allow these works, and other works about people who live and value differently, to address us not just in and through the intellect, but by evoking nonintellectual responses that have their own kind of selectivity and veracity. Any social theory that recommends or uses a quantitative measure of value without first exercising imagination along these lines seems to me to be thoroughly irresponsible. In the *Laws,* the Stranger tells us that one of the greatest obstacles to good political practice is that many people lightly believe different things to be commensurable when they really are not so. This lack of seriousness about the issue of commensurability he calls "a condition not human but more appropriate to certain swinish creatures," concerning which he declares himself "ashamed not only on my own behalf, but also on behalf of all Greeks" (819D). The condition may be more widespread than his remark suggests.

Endnote

This essay is closely linked to the arguments of *Fragility,* chaps. 4 and 6; but its focus and organization are different (see n. 1). It is reprinted here because of its close thematic connections with several of the other essays, especially "Discern-

---

27. Of course we also need—before we begin this part of the job—to compare the different types of commensurability invoked in contemporary theory with Plato's various proposals. I am obviously not attempting that here.

ment" and "Narrative Emotions." Its arguments about the connection between emotion and belief or judgment receive further development in "Narrative Emotions," and are a major theme in my current work on ancient Greek philosophy. (See, for example, "The Stoics on the Extirpation of the Passions," *Apeiron* 1987; "Beyond Obsession and Disgust: Lucretius on the Therapy of Love," *Apeiron* 1989.)

The relationship between philosophy and literature is an important, if ancillary, theme of the essay. For its last section argues that one good way to get really clear philosophically about what acceptance of a belief in the commensurability of values would really mean in a human life is to turn to the literary imagination, asking for stories of people who really live this belief, stories that would show us with a concreteness and reach that are frequently absent in abstract philosophical reflections on the topic, just what the world would look like to such people. This is, obviously, not the same claim as that made for literature in most of these essays, and in the Introduction. For, on the one hand, it is a *broader* claim for the role of the literary: a certain sort of more or less literary imagining is here said to play a role in the adequate assessment of many ethical views (not just the Aristotelian view) as possible ways of life. On the other hand, this broader claim is not, and should not be, understood as an argument for turning to novels such as those of James and Proust in connection with the investigation of these non-Aristotelian views. The "literary works" projected here should not have a narrative structure and form that itself expresses and states elements of the Aristotelian conception, if it is going to investigate fairly the way of life proposed by the Utilitarian or Kantian conceptions. This may mean that we will not have characters and incident of the type we have come to expect from the novel, and that the work in question would fall into no very recognizable literary genre. And yet it does seem a fair demand to make of the alternative conceptions that they should be realizable in *some* sort of narrative of a human life, that there should be stories we can tell ourselves of what it is like to live the life recommended in the conception. (One such story is begun at the end of *Fragility,* chap. 4, in connection with the life of commensurability; and one thing that emerges is that the people who live that life have no interest in or understanding of literary works of the familiar sort, e.g., Greek tragedies.)

The Plato described here is just one aspect of that philosopher, whose views on these topics I believe to be both complex and temporally evolving. *Fragility,* chaps. 4, 6, and 7, discusses some of these tensions.

4

Flawed Crystals:
James's *The Golden Bowl* and
Literature as Moral Philosophy

At the centre, the bed of crystalline Love was dedicated to her name most fittingly. The man who had cut the crystal for her couch and her observance had divined her nature unerringly: Love *should* be of crystal—transparent and translucent.... Its roundness inside betokens Love's Simplicity: Simplicity is most fitting for love, which must have no corners, that is, no Cunning or Treachery.

Gottfried von Strassburg, Tristan

No dogs, bicycles, or tricycles allowed in this garden at any time *by order.* The gardeners are required to conduct from the garden anyone infringing these rules.

Sign in the garden of Cadogan Square, London, 1980

I

She wants, this woman, to have a flawless life. She says to her good friend Fanny Assingham, "I want a happiness without a hole in it big enough for you to poke in your finger.... The golden bowl as it *was* to have been.... The bowl with all our happiness in it. The bowl without the crack" (II.216–17)[1]—signaling in this way to us, who know the properties of this remarkable flawed object, that she wishes her life to be (unlike the bowl) a pure and perfect crystal, completely without crack or seam, both precious and safely hard.

Two features of Maggie Verver's moral life, in the first half of this novel, strike us as salient. One is this assiduous aspiration to perfection, especially moral perfection. The other is the exclusive intensity of her love for her father, the oddness

---

1. All page numbers are cited from *The Golden Bowl,* New York Edition (New York: Charles Scribner's Sons, 1909). Prefaces to other works are cited from James, *The Art of the Novel* (New York, 1970), hereafter *AN.* On the fact that this passage comes from the end rather than the beginning of the novel, see p. 134 below.

of her marriage to the Prince, which, far from effecting the usual reordering of the commitments and obligations of childhood, has permitted her to gratify, to an extraordinary degree, her "wish to remain, intensely, the same passionate little daughter she had always been" (I.395). This wish to be without flaw and this desire to remain her father's daughter—we suspect that they must be somehow connected. And yet the nature of the connection is not altogether obvious, especially since it is far from obvious that this refusal to move from father to husband is a perfect way of living for an adult woman. But I believe that a connection, and a deep one, will emerge if we scrutinize more closely the particular nature of Maggie's moral aspiration. This will be a route into the novel, by which we can begin to appreciate the ways in which James is working here with questions about moral ambition, moralism, and the nature of our worldly relation to value. (Since it is in connection with its exploration of these elements of experience that I wish to make, on behalf of this novel, the claim that it is philosophical or makes an important contribution to moral philosophy, it will serve at the same time to broach these further questions.)

Maggie, then, wants to be as good as possible; and when she says this, it is evidently moral goodness that is uppermost in her thoughts. If we ask more closely about what, for her, constitutes moral perfection, we find that the central idea is one of never doing a wrong, never breaking a rule, never hurting. "Maggie had never in her life," her father reflects, "been wrong for more than three minutes" (I.236). The "note of the felt need of not working harm" (II.64), the "superstition of not 'hurting'" (I.160)—these are the concerns pressed urgently by her "quite heroic little sense of justice" (I.395) in every situation of choice. It does not surprise us that her husband should compare her, in thought, to a Roman *matrona,* bearing "the transmitted images of rather neutral and negative propriety that made up, in his long line, the average of wifehood and motherhood" (I.322). What sharply sets her apart from this sternly upright figure is, above all, the intensity, the note of real fear, with which she insists on the claims of guiltlessness. In a revealing moment, she compares the requirements of morality (and especially its prohibition of certain bad acts) to the "water-tight" insides of an ocean liner: "Water-tight—the biggest compartment of all? Why it's the best cabin and the main deck and the engine-room and the steward's pantry! It's the ship itself—it's the whole line. It's the captain's table and all one's luggage—one's reading for the trip" (I.15). Morality and its rules of not hurting constitute for her a safe world in which to live and voyage, protected against nameless dangers. If ever a breach were made in the walls of that vessel, if even one seam should give way—but she does not dare to imagine that. She avoids it. She sits in the liner (perhaps the same vessel that Fanny refers to later as "Mr. Verver's boat" [I.267]) and reads only what the captain, or father, has provided for the trip.

So, surrounded by her innocence, she goes about straining to keep herself right, to make her life a flawless crystal bowl holding, as far as pleasures go, "nothing, one was obliged to recognize, but innocent pleasures, pleasures without penalties" (I.11). The novel is dense with images for this splendid aspiration: images of crystal, of roundness, of childhood—and above all, references to the happy innocence which was, as the Prince says, "the state of our primitive parents before the Fall"

(I.335).[2] As innocent as these of any knowledge of evil, either for doing or for seeing, they live, she and her father Adam, sheltered by the immaculate white walls and the placid gardens of "monotonous Eaton Square" (I.333), a place which is the appropriate embodiment of Maggie's Edenic longing:[3] "They knew, it might have appeared in these lights, absolutely nothing on earth worth speaking of—whether beautifully or cynically; and they would perhaps sometimes be a little less trying if they would only once for all peacefully admit that knowledge wasn't one of their needs and that they were in fact constitutionally inaccessible to it. They were good children, bless their hearts, and the children of good children" (I.333–34). In this passage, as in Maggie's speech about the steamer, we have a sense that bulwarks of ignorance are being erected against some threat that presses in from the world; that knowledge of some truth is not simply absent, but is being actively refused for the sake of beautitude. (For Adam's *daughter* was not born in Eden; and the "children of good children" must have, in virtue of being this, some connection with original sin.)

Maggie has reached a time in her life at which we might expect her to notice a difficulty attaching to her ideal. She has, specifically, married. She has undertaken to become a woman and to move from her father's home into a husband's. This time might be expected to be a time of conflicting obligations. For the daughter of so exacting a father, a daughter who, moreover, has served for most of her childhood and adolescence as her father's sole traveling companion, friend, and partner, it might be expected to be a time of a painful breaking away from past attachments and commitments. To become a separate woman in her own right and the Prince's wife, this woman, it is clear, will have to give pain. Even if, as Fanny says, natural attachments "may be intense and yet not prevent other intensities" (I.395), the nature of this particular blood relation, as deep as any marriage, surely makes claims that would block other, complicating loves.[4] But Maggie's conscience so shrinks from the guilt of rendered pain that she cannot bear at all

2. The Prince is here referring to the anomalous innocence to which he and Charlotte are forced to pretend because of the innocence of the other pair. References to the Edenic condition of the Ververs are striking throughout, and too frequent to enumerate. (For only a few examples, in addition to I.335 and II.367, discussed in the text, see I.78, 187, 309, 385, 393–95.)

3. Eaton Square, structurally solid, immaculately white, and "synonymous for respectability" even before James's time (Susan Jenkins, *Landlords of London* [London, 1975] 82), represents, for the pair, a retreat from worldly complication: "The 'world', by still another beautiful perversity of their chance, included Portland Place without including to anything like the same extent Eaton Square" (I.320). It should be noticed, too, that Maggie at first attempts, by interior decoration, to make Portland Place as well embody her moral ambition: "she stood there circled about and furnished forth, as always, in a manner that testified to her perfect little personal processes. It had ever been her sign that she was for all occasions *found* ready, without loose ends or exposed accessories or unremoved superfluities; a suggestion of the swept and garnished, in her whole splendid yet thereby more or less encumbered and embroidered setting that reflected her small still passion for order and symmetry, for objects with their backs to the walls, and spoke even of some probable reference in her American blood to dusting and polishing New England grandmothers" (II.152).

4. Compare Sigmund Freud, *Three Essays on Sexuality* (1905), *Standard Edition of the Complete Psychological Works of Sigmund Freud,* trans. and ed. J. Strachey (London, 1953–72) VII, 207–43.

to embark on this job of separation. Her resourceful imagination therefore discovers that in every conflict of loves or of values, one can, by the right sort of effort, reach an allegedly guiltless consistency and harmony—even "that ideal consistency on which her moral comfort almost at any time depended." What is this strategy? "To remain consistent," we are told, "she had always been capable of cutting down more or less her prior term" (II.6). This image from syllogistic logic means, I suppose, that a promising way to resolve a conflict of obligations is always to rewrite the major premise of the practical syllogism so that the prior term no longer covers the entire extension of the middle term. Instead of "all B are A," we will now have, at most, "some B are A." By this device Maggie can cause a potentially troublesome value term no longer to apply in the given situation. She preserves her comfort by preserving her consistency; she preserves her consistency by "simplifying" her world and even her character, as the Prince observes (I.322). In the case at hand, she solves the apparent conflict of marital love with filial duty by "cutting back" the claims of marriage, marrying in such a way that she can still remain her father's, "undivided" (I.323).

So in a funny way, what began as the noble idea of failing in no duty and cherishing every value ends, consistently pushed through, in an enterprise that cuts back, cuts down, alters values to fit the claims of consistency. Any claim that seems capable of conflicting with her primary duty to her father—a duty which to this good daughter looks identical with morality itself—can be allowed to have validity only insofar as it accords with his requirements, consents, as she and her father say, to be "round" rather than angular, harmonious rather than discordant.[5] She and her father are, she imagines, in a boat together, sailing away from "luxuriant complications" (II.255).

Maggie's attachment to moral simplicity brings with it some disturbing consequences. The first is, plainly, an avoidance or suppression of her own adult sexuality. If she allows herself to mature and to experience marriage fully, then she opens herself immediately to complication and to the possibility of a break. She and her father will no longer be "undivided." Therefore Maggie, as she ostensibly matures, has cultivated, increasingly, an androgynous and even an ascetic persona. "Extraordinarily *clear* . . . in her prettiness" (I.9), she is even described as "prim." Her father recalls that "when once she had been told before him, familiarly, that she resembled a nun, she had replied that she was delighted to hear it and would certainly try to" (I.188). Later she is compared to "some holy image in a procession"; her character is said by Fanny to be like "that little silver cross you once showed me, blest by the Holy Father, that you always wear, out of sight, next your skin" (II.112). This deliberate suppression of her womanliness is evidently promoted by her father, who associates womanliness with weakness, the absence of judgment, and the inability to give genuine companionship, and who, on the other hand, thinks of his daughter as his first companion in his spiritual

5. See I.135–38, especially: "No visibility of transition showed, no violence of accommodation, in retrospect, emerged" (I.135); "'Oh if he *had* been angular!—who could say what might *then* have happened'" (I.137). Adam associates the Prince's "roundness" with the claim that "for living with, you're a pure and perfect crystal" (I.138).

adventures. He is an intellectual and artistic pioneer, a Cortez discovering a new world. When he asks himself whether his wife might have accompanied him in this adventure, he comes quickly to a conclusion that rules out the womanly (or at least women of his own class) altogether: "No companion of Cortez had presumably been a real lady: Mr. Verver allowed that historic fact to determine his inference" (I.143).

To become a "real lady" is, then, to abandon her father, to wound him by ceasing to be his companion in all things. It is, I think, this moral claim, and not merely some vague girlish fear, that leads Maggie, even in marriage with a man to whom she is deeply attracted, so to repress her womanly responses that Fanny can confidently and, we feel, correctly assert that she has never really "had" the Prince (I.384).[6] This link is confirmed by James's subtle use of water imagery in connection with both sexual passion and moral conflict or complication—frequently the two of these together. We have already noticed Maggie's "water-tight" steamer, secured against a harm or a violation, and Mr. Verver's boat, which sails safely away from complication. What we can now point out is that the first image is closely joined by Maggie herself to an admission that she does not respond to her husband's "particular self"; in the second case, the complications from which Maggie imagines father and daughter sailing away are "husbands and wives" who had "made the air too tropical" (II.255). Maggie even asks herself at this point, "Why . . . couldn't they always live, so far as they lived together, in a boat? She felt in her face with the question the breath of a possibility that soothed her; they needed only *know* each other henceforth in the unmarried relation." Sexuality is seen and feared as a ground of conflict, a threat against the moral safety of not harming. Maggie's fear of water expresses the link between these two refusals—just as, in the passage in which the Prince and Charlotte renew their relationship, imagery of flooding (linked with a picture of breaking through or out of a perfect circle) indicates at once both their mutual sexual response and their acceptance of moral guilt: "Then of a sudden, through this tightened circle, as at the issue of a narrow strait into the sea beyond, everything broke up, broke down, gave way, melted and mingled. Their lips sought their lips, their pressure their response and their response their pressure; with a violence that had sighed itself the next moment to the longest and deepest of stillnesses, they passionately sealed their pledge" (I.312).[7] This willingness to burst out of the tight circle of harmony, to risk the ocean, is what we know Maggie has so far lacked. In the case of her father's parallel avoidance both of moral guilt and of a full sexual life, we are told in no

6. See I.398, where Fanny says of Adam, "'But the whole point is just that two years of Charlotte are what he hasn't really—or what you may call undividedly—had,'" and Bob responds, "'Any more than Maggie by your theory, eh, has "really or undividedly," had four of the Prince? It takes all she hasn't had . . . to account for the innocence that in her too so leaves us in admiration.'"

7. Both Leon Edel in his biography (*The Master* [New York, 1971], 222–23) and Stephen Spender in his essay on the novel have suggested that this passage indicates a new acceptance, on the part of James himself, of the fact of physical intimacy. Spender writes that we see in the author "a person who, profoundly with his whole being, after overcoming great inhibition, has accepted the *idea* of people loving" (quoted in Edel, pp. 222–23).

uncertain terms that the consequence has been physical impotence with his new wife.[8] With Maggie this is less clear and perhaps less important; whatever takes place physically, we are clear that there is a failure, on the level of imagination and emotion, to respond as a separate adult woman to her husband's own separate sexual presence. She is still intact in her innocence; nothing is damaged. "She had been able to marry without breaking, as she liked to put it, with her past" (II.5).[9]

Another consequence of Maggie's innocence is, plainly, an inability in any area of her life to see values, including persons, emerge as distinct ends in their own right. In every case they are rounded, accommodated, not recognized insofar as their claims collide with other claims. But this is plainly a way of viewing persons—those recalcitrant, inveterately "angular" objects—that leads to a certain neglect. First, there is the neglect of what Maggie calls her husband's "unknown quantity, [his] particular self" (I.9). She even tells him, "You're not perhaps absolutely unique" (I.12). And in the famous image of the pagoda at the beginning of Part II she betrays for the first time a curiosity about her situation, of which the Prince is so prominent a part. She desires for the first time to peer inside this odd, towerlike object which for so long has oddly occupied a place at the center of her garden, and into which "no door appeared to give access from her convenient garden-level" (II.4). It is no wonder that at this point she begins to see, too, that her moral imagination is rather like an unsorted storeroom, full of "confused objects," "a mess of vain things, congruous, incongruous," tossed in, in a heap, and shut behind a locked door. "So it was that she had been getting things out of the way" (II.14).

And it is not only personal qualitative uniqueness that goes into Maggie's store-room; it is also, we need to add, personal *separateness,* the value of each person and each end as a distinct item generating its own claims. In the romance of Tristan, whose praise of love's crystalline simplicity James very likely had in view,[10] the lovers' cultivation of simplicity makes them blind to the way in which each commitment and each value is separate from and liable to conflict with each

8. See I.307, where Charlotte says that she knows now that she and Adam never will have any children and asserts positively that it is not her fault. (I assume that she could be so positive at this date only if impotence or unwillingness on his part, and not sterility, were the reason.)

9. Compare Freud, *Three Essays,* 227: "At every stage in the course of development through which all human beings ought by rights to pass, a certain number are held back; so there are some who have never got over their parents' authority and have withdrawn their affection from either very incompletely or not at all. They are mostly girls, who, to the delight of their parents, have persisted in all their childish love far beyond puberty. It is most instructive to find that it is precisely these girls who in their later marriage lack the capacity to give their husbands what is due to them; they make cold wives and remain sexually anaesthetic."

10. The golden bowl itself recalls a bowl given by George I to a newborn child of the Lamb family, which much impressed James on a visit to Sussex in 1902 (see Edel, p. 209). There are also, doubtless, allusions to Ecclesiastes 12:6–7 ("or ever the silver cord be loosed, or the golden bowl be broken, ... then shall the dust return to the earth as it was: and the spirit shall return unto God who gave it"), and the Blake's "Can wisdom be kept in a silver rod,/ Or love in a golden bowl?" But the fact that the bowl is a flawed crystal, and the repeated allusions to the perfect simplicity of crystal elsewhere, are not explained by any of these allusions, and we may very well have an allusion to the well-known symbolism of this great love legend. (For other aspects of the bowl's complex symbolism, see Quentin Anderson's *The American Henry James* [New Brunswick, N.J., 1957].)

other; in the same way, Maggie sees only roundness where in real life there is angularity, and therefore misses the distinct claims of each particular value. This is, strikingly, true even of her love for her father, as we see from a brief, proleptic scene early in the novel. Returning from church, Maggie finds her father besieged by Mrs. Rance, an irritating woman who wants to marry him. For the first time Maggie perceives that her own marriage *has* begun to entail for Adam the pain of abandonment and of harassment from would-be companions. And strangely, this idea suddenly gives her, also for the first time, a sense of her father as a separate person: "He was on her mind, he was even in a manner on her hands—as a distinct thing, that is, from being, where he had always been, merely deep in her heart and in her life; too deep down, as it were, to be disengaged, contrasted or opposed; in short objectively presented" (I.155). Moral objectivity about the value of a person (or, presumably, any other source of moral claims) requires, evidently, the ability to see that item as distinct from other items; this in turn requires the ability to see it not as a deep part of an innocent harmony but as a value that can be contrasted or opposed to others, whose demands can potentially conflict with other demands. In making her father's law normative for a world of harmlessness, Maggie has, ironically, failed to see *him*. It is not until much later that she really takes this in; her next move here is to resolve the conflict and restore the "harmony" by giving him Charlotte as a wife. But because of this scene, *we* are aware of her maneuvers as self-deceptive and false. Knowledge of a good, that is to say a value, in the world requires, we see, knowledge of evil, that is to say of the possibility of conflict, disorder, the contingent necessity of breaking or harming. Without eating this fruit she is just a child, ignorant of the value of the good as well.

We are now in a position to appreciate one of the oddest and most striking features of James's portrait of this idealistic pair of Americans: the inveterate tendency of both father and daughter to assimilate people, in their imagination and deliberation, to fine *objets d'art*. This matter is given considerable emphasis in James's design. One of the most striking incursions of the authorial voice into a narrative told, for the most part, through the consciousness of one or another of its characters begins, "Nothing perhaps might affect us as queerer, had we time to look into it, than this application of the same measure of value to such different pieces of property as old Persian carpets, say, and new human acquisitions" (I.196). And such a strange way of valuing is present too in our very first glimpse of Maggie, where she speaks of her husband as "a rarity, an object of beauty, an object of price. . . . You're what they call a *morceau de musée*" (I.12). We are, of course, invited to take the time ourselves to look into this odd matter.

We soon realize that this propensity for the aestheticization of persons does not precisely indicate that the Ververs neglect the moral, or reduce the moral to the aesthetic. Indeed, it is agreed all around that they are distinguished for their keen *moral* sense, even for their strict moralism. It is rather that the peculiar nature of their moral aim, with its extreme emphasis on flawless living and, because of this, on consistency and harmony, is best supported by a view of persons that tends to assimilate their properties to certain salient properties of works of art. Works of art are precious objects, object of high value. And yet it is a remarkable feature of our attention to works of art that it appears to spread itself round smoothly and harmoniously. I can, visiting a museum, survey many fine objects with appropriate awe and tenderness. I can devote myself now to one, now to another, without the sense that the objects make conflicting claims against my love and care. If one day I spend my entire museum visit gazing at Turners, I have not incurred a guilt against the Blakes in the next room; nor have I failed in a duty toward Bartok by my loving attention to Hindemith. To live with works of art is to live in a world enormously rich in value, without a deep risk of infidelity, disloyalty, or any conflict which might lead to these. It is the Ververs' brilliantly resourceful idea that the moral life, too, can be flawless and innocent of violation, while remaining full of value, if only persons can be made to resemble aesthetic objects, things to be displayed in a gallery for innocent attention. Closely linked with Mr. Verver's aestheticization of Charlotte is a wish "for some idea, lurking in the vast freshness of the night, at the breath of which disparities would submit to fusion" (I.205–6). This idea—that he should marry Charlotte so as to restore the general harmony—comes to him during the very moment at which he sees the precious Damascene tiles "successively, and oh so tenderly, unmuffled and revealed," until they "lay there at last in their full harmony and their venerable splendor" (I.215). It is surely the splendid order and harmony of these aesthetic objects (each tile lies uncompetitively side by side with its neighbors; the demands of tender attention to all can be faithfully met) which Mr. Verver covets for his human life; and coveting it, he turns Charlotte, by marriage, into the finest piece of all. For Maggie as well, the wonderful idea is that a husband who resembles a "fine piece" can be packed and unpacked, stored and brought out for show—or, if he should become too "big," be sent to American City to be "buried" (I.14); in none of these circumstances will its presence place a strain on the deliberation of the collector or spoil the harmony of the museum, or life, which testifies to his rare powers of perception.[11]

In short, then, we have begun with a noble and venerable moral ideal—not just the fancy of a childish girl, but a picture of personal conduct and personal rightness that has very deep roots in the moral tradition of our entire culture. (It is not fortuitous that this combination of moralism and excessive simplicity is attributed to the American characters in this novel—nor that these Americans should be as resourceful in technical deliberation as they are naive in emotional response.) We are shown that this ideal, followed out to its strictest conclusion, generates an extraordinary blindness to value and ends by subordinating the particular claim of each commitment and love to the claims of harmony. And that *is,* we see, the fancy of a childish girl. It does not work on its own terms, since it does wrong to persons and commits acts of blindness and cruelty. (It is not inappropriate that Maggie and her father, as well as the other pair, are, in effect, charged with disloyalty and adultery [see I.304]—for each has been unfaithful to the commitments involved in making a marriage just because of this childlike unwillingness to break away or to experience guilt.) And it is morally objectionable in that it commits the holder to a systematic neglect of certain features of persons—namely, both

---

11. It is instructive to examine the many places in the novel where a person is praised with the aesthetically linked word "splendid." It usually emerges that to call a human being that is to refuse that person a properly human tenderness and care.

their separateness and their qualitative uniqueness—on which their specific personal value might be thought to rest. The richness of the novel's moral vision lies in the way in which it both shows us the splendor of a rigorous moralism (for this simple vision attracts not only the Americans but to some extent every major character in the novel) and at the same time erodes our confidence in this ideal by displaying the guilt involved in such innocence. There is, as Maggie later says, an "awful mixture in things" (II.292).

The world of *The Golden Bowl* is a fallen world—a world, that is, in which innocence cannot be and is not safely preserved, a world where values and loves are so pervasively in tension one with another that there is no safe human expectation of a perfect fidelity to all throughout a life. (This novel works out this idea in the sphere of human personal love, but *The Princess Casamassima* shows us that James is ready to extend it more broadly to include nonpersonal commitments and values.) In this world our first choice as adults is the choice to pursue our personal goals at the expense of a separation from and a break with the parent. And we cannot ever count on the fact that our love of a husband will not require the spiritual death of a best friend and mentor, that fidelity to a wife will not require cruelty to a former lover. There are better and worse choices, naturally, within this tangled world; but it is childlike to refuse to see that it *is* in this way tangled, for this is a feature of our situation as creatures with values operating in the world of nature. As James wrote in the preface to *What Maisie Knew:* "No themes are so human as those that reflect for us, out of the confusion of life, the close connexion of bliss and bale, of the things that help with the things that hurt, so dangling before us for ever that bright hard metal, of so strange an alloy, one face of which is somebody's right and ease and the other somebody's pain and wrong" (*AN* 143).

I am claiming, then, that this novel works out a secular analogue of the idea of original sin by showing a human being's relation to value in the world to be, fundamentally and of contingent necessity, one of imperfect fidelity and therefore of guilt; by showing us ourselves as precious, valuing beings who, under the strains imposed by the intertwining of our routes to value in the world, become cracked and flawed. Guilt toward value is here, if not literally a priori, still a feature of our humanness which attaches to us as a structural feature of our situation in nature and in the family,[12] prior to the specific choices and failures that we enter upon in a particular life. The Prince says about crystal, "Its beauty is its *being* crystal. But its hardness is certainly its safety." On this analogy, human beings, like the golden bowl, are beautiful but not safe: they have ideals, but they split. Charlotte's question about the bowl was, "If it's so precious, how comes it to be cheap?" The answer to this question is the story of four human lives.

This novel, I have indicated, is about the development of a woman. To be a

---

12. One might ask whether to show that certain strains inhere in the structure of the family as we know it is in any way to show that they are an essential feature of human life. This question is nowhere more courageously pressed than in the *Republic,* where it is indeed argued that the most troublesome and pervasive of our moral conflicts have their roots in the family and could be eliminated by eliminating the family. But Plato is also aware that this would involve making human beings, especially with respect to their attachments and emotions, radically different from anything that we have known.

woman, to give herself to her husband, Maggie will need to come to see herself as something cracked, imperfect, unsafe, a vessel with a hole through which water may pass, a steamer compartment no longer tightly sealed. Later, as her perception is shifting, she will in fact see herself as a house not perfectly closed against the elements: "She saw round about her, through the chinks of the shutters, the hard glare of nature" (II.303). And in the world of nature, what Maggie sees is the suffering of Charlotte, caused by her act. Her guilt has entered her vision.

The second half of the novel is the story of Maggie's initiation into knowledge of her fallen world. Beginning to *live* (see I.385–6) is, for her, beginning to see that meaningful commitment to a love in the world can require the sacrifice of one's own moral purity. To regain her husband she must damage Charlotte. We are fully aware, as is she, that her cruelty and dishonesty to Charlotte are in no way purified or effaced by the fact of Charlotte's own offense. Her love, unlike the ideal of the Tristanic lover, must live on cunning and treachery; it requires the breaking of moral rules and a departure from the comfortable garden.

It would be an important and fascinating task to trace the details of this development: the way, for example, in which exposure to conflict and a womanly exposure to sexuality are linked, here as before, in the imagery of water, as Maggie the passenger becomes a swimmer;[13] the way she comes to see that the value of persons and of objects is partially constituted by the risk they bring of pain and opposition—that "any deep-seated passion has its pangs as well as its joys, and that we are made by its aches and anxieties most richly conscious of it" (II.7); the way in which the departure from Eden brings with it the possibility of certain moral emotions which were unknown in that garden—among them shame, jealousy, tenderness, and respect; the way in which, from having seen only clear, splendid objects, Maggie learns, inhabiting a human world, to be a "mistress of shades" (II.142), a reader of nuance and complexity. (There are no books in Eden.)[14]

But although we do not have space to go into all of this, what we now must notice is that these new dimensions of perception and response begin to amount, strangely, for us and for Maggie, as things go on, not so much to a way of living with imperfection as to a new way of getting at perfection. Maggie, still as exigent and idealistic as ever, discovers a way of remaining a splendidly pure and safe object *within* this fallen world, "as hard . . . as a little pointed diamond" (II.145). (The alert reader will have noticed that the quotation with which this paper began came not from the novel's early chapters or later reflections on them, but from a very late point, at which Maggie is already deliberating in the newer and riskier way.) We might describe the new ideal this way: See clearly and with high intelligence. Respond with the vibrant sympathy of a vividly active imagination. If there are conflicts, face them squarely and with keen perception. Choose as well

---

13. See, for example, II.42–43, II.263; compare the descriptions of Fanny at I.365–79. It is worth noting that during the period in which Maggie is "beginning to live" in the human world, her images for herself are frequently these images, linked as they are with birth or the wish to be born. See Freud, *The Interpretation of Dreams* (1900), *Standard Edition* V, chap. 6, sect. E.

14. I have found illuminating, in this connection, the reading of the first chapters of Genesis given in Andrew Martin, "The Genesis of Ignorance: Nescience and Omniscience in the Garden of Eden," *Philosophy and Literature* 5 (1981) 3–20.

as you can for overt action, but at every moment remember the more comprehensive duties of the imagination and emotions. If love of your husband requires hurting and lying to Charlotte, then do these cruel things, making the better choice. But never cease, all the while, to be richly conscious of Charlotte's pain and to bear, in imagination and feeling, the full burden of your guilt as the cause of that pain. If life is a tragedy (see II.311–12), see that; respond to that fact with pity for others and fear for yourself. Never for a moment close your eyes or dull your feelings. The ideal is summarized by James in his preface to *The Princess Casamassima* as one of "being finely aware and richly responsible"; it is nowhere more fittingly and fully embodied than in the long passage of deliberation in which Maggie, picturing vividly Charlotte's silent suffering, decides to urge her husband to speak to Charlotte once more before her departure (II.327–31). Here we feel that Maggie's keen sensitivity to the values of love and friendship, which she herself is violating, redeems and transfigures the cruelty of her act. If she acts badly of necessity, at least she takes upon herself the conscious guilt for that badness and, by her sense of guilt, shows herself as a person to whom badness is odious. It is not surprising that Maggie repeatedly imagines herself as a sacrificial figure who bears the pain and guilt of the situation through the fine responsibility of her consciousness. This idea of bearing guilt for love's sake is evidently the source of the comparisons of Maggie to the scapegoat of ancient Greek religion, who saves the community by bearing its pollution (II.234), and also to Christ, who took upon himself the sins of the world (II.112). The difference in her case is that she assumes this world's burden of sin not by going into exile or dying but by sinning, and by seeing that she is sinning, and by bearing, for love, her own imperfection.

But as the end approaches, we are troubled by our sense that this is, after all, a new way of being innocent. We are troubled by Maggie's comparison of herself to a diamond, more angular than the original crystal, but even more safely hard.[15] We note that she is still fond of the language of moral absolutes: "'consummate' was [a] term she privately applied" (II.359). She has not so much altered her moral categories as rearranged the items to which she attaches these favored terms; not so much accepted evil in herself as seen a new way to be (internally) safely innocent. We have been put on our guard against projects of safety and projects of perfection, so we wonder whether Maggie's new ideal has itself a crack in it.

And now, as we reflect in this way, it should strike us that in fact, according to the last scene of the novel, Maggie has not yet, as she approaches the final parting with Charlotte and her father and the final confrontation with Amerigo, eaten the fruit of the tree of knowledge of good and evil. It is still hanging before her, just before the end, "the golden fruit that had shone from afar" (II.367). So the new moral ideal cannot really have been the fruit of that eating, and Maggie, until the very end, is still in some significant sense an innocent, though more responsive and more womanly than before.

15. Compare Adam's use of the diamond as an image of the angularity which Amerigo allegedly lacks: "I can see them all from here—each of them sticking out by itself—all the architectural cut diamonds that would have scratched one's softer sides. One would have been scratched by diamonds—doubtless the neatest way if one was to be scratched at all—but one would have been reduced to a hash" (I.138).

What is, then, Maggie's innocent failure of recognition, and what can we discover in the final scene that will explain to us why here, and only here, James presents her as falling from purity? We notice, in her last encounter with Adam and Charlotte, some significant signals. Aesthetic images for persons reappear and multiply. There is talk of the "human furniture required aesthetically by such a scene" (II.360); there is talk of the emptiness of a house with "half of its best things removed" (II.362). There is, above all, a marked aestheticization of Charlotte as "incomparable," "too splendid." We are forced to ask why, at this point of triumph for Maggie's new ideal rightness, she should reimport the techniques of the old innocence—why, after so deeply responding to Charlotte's solitude and pain, and after urging Amerigo to do the same, she should suddenly retreat behind these old refusals. An answer begins to emerge along with the question; we begin to sense the discovery for which James is preparing us.

Amerigo has refused Charlotte not only his love, but also his response and his vision. He refuses to see her pain; he allows it to remain at a distance, receiving her as "Royalty" rather than as a woman who has arranged her life around her passion for him. What we now begin to see is that Maggie was wrong to think that it could, should be otherwise. The demands of his love for Maggie will not, in fact, allow the moral luxury of clear sight and generous response. To love one woman adequately he cannot always be tormented by a consciousness of the other. He must, then, of necessity banish the other, wronging her not only, like Maggie, in act, but also in the depths of his imagination and his vision. The demands of the new ideal of seeing are not always compatible with an adequate fulfillment of each of our commitments, for some loves are exclusive and demand a blindness in other quarters. Instead of being "finely aware and richly responsible" we may, in fact, have to become, as lovers, grossly insensitive and careless with respect to other, incompatible claims. The mere fact of being deeply engaged forces a blindness. The moment at which Maggie finally tastes the "golden fruit" is such a moment: on both sides, obtuseness feeds the triumph of love.

> "Isn't she too splendid?" she simply said, offering it to explain and to finish.
> "Oh, splendid!" With which he came over to her.
> "That's our help, you see," she added—to point further her moral.
> It kept him before her therefore, taking in—or trying to—what she so wonderfully gave. He tried, too clearly, to please her—to meet her in her own way; but with the result only that, close to her, her face kept before him, his hands holding her shoulders, his whole act enclosing her, he presently echoed: "'See'? I see nothing but *you*." And the truth of it had, with this force, after a moment, so strangely lighted his eyes that as for pity and dread of them she buried her own in his breast. (II.368–69)

The Prince, then, sees nothing but Maggie. And Maggie, seeing this singleness of vision, reacts to her sight of Amerigo as to a tragedy—with "pity and dread." For she sees, in truth, that he *does* see only her, that she and he together have brought about, within his imagination, an extinction of vision and a failure of response; and that this has happened of tragic necessity because of the requirements of his commitment to her. Long ago, Maggie did not see that choice among competing values could ever be tragic. Then she saw that it could be tragic, but thought that a heroine of tragedy could still avoid tragedy inwardly by being richly responsible to everything in intellect and feeling. Now she sees in her husband the genuine, unredeemed article, a "hero" violating love for the sake of love, purified by no inner sympathy, no note of higher consciousness.

But at this moment, with the "golden fruit" of knowledge hanging there before her, she discovers, too, that she cannot gaze on this tragedy like the perfectly responsive and responsible spectator, seeing and feeling for everyone, and still have the knowledge of love for which she has sacrificed. Aristotle argued that tragedy brings illumination concerning values: through the "pity and dread" inspired by tragic events, we learn about what matters to us, and we are clarified. Maggie, in the last sentence of the novel, recognizes that the keen vision and acknowledgment of the good tragic spectator are themselves values which can, in the world of nature, collide with other values. To see all, to be present to all, requires of the spectator a narrowness of love; to surrender to love requires an infidelity of the soul's eyes. To look will be to judge him; to judge him is to fall short of the fullness of his passion. "'Thank goodness, then,' said Charlotte, 'that if there *be* a crack we know it!'" (I.119). Here Maggie sees beyond her, seeing that the gifts of love require a gentleness that goes beyond, and covers, knowledge.

So she makes for him the last and greatest sacrifice of all. She gives him her purity of vision, her diamond hardness—as he had given up, for her, his vision of Charlotte's humanity. Once he had, long before, asked Fanny Assingham to give him her eyes, meaning to lend him the higher keenness of her American moral sense (I.30). Now his American wife gives him her eyes in fact, burying her own vision, therefore her perfect rightness, in his body.[16]

And does one, as Charlotte asked, make a present of an object which contains, to one's knowledge, a flaw? To that Maggie herself has had, in the deeper moments of her connoisseurship, an answer: "The infirmity of art was the candour of affection, the grossness of pedigree the refinement of sympathy; the ugliest objects in fact as a general thing were the bravest, the tenderest mementos, and, as such, figured in glass cases apart, worthy doubtless of the home, but not worthy of the temple—dedicated to the grimacing, not to the clear-faced, gods" (II.156).

What are we to say about this? Is there, then, a moral ideal in this novel, or isn't there? Do the insights of the prefaces and of Part II stand or fall? I want to say that they stand, that there is an ideal here. It is not altogether undermined; it is still precious. It is only shown to be, like everything human, imperfect. (And perhaps, as the passage just mentioned suggests, this flaw in it is partly constitutive of its specifically human value and beauty.) The end of the novel does not tell us that it is pointless to become "finely aware and richly responsible"; it only warns

---

16. The moment is prepared earlier by another refusal of vision that is, like this one, an expression of gentleness that opens the way for love: "She sank to her knees with her arm on the ledge of her window-seat, where she blinded her eyes from the full glare of seeing that his idea could only be to wait, whatever might come, at her side. It was to her buried face that she thus, for a long time, felt him draw nearest" (II.294).

us against turning this norm into a new form of watertight purity by showing us
that a deep love may sometimes require an infidelity against even this adult spiritual standard.

Well, how do we know? When are we to pursue this ideal and when to let it go?
How much is a deep love worth, and under what circumstances is it worth a blinding? What boundaries are we to draw? What priorities can we fix? These, I take
it, are the little girl's questions, resurfacing now, again, at yet another level—as
they will resurface so long as the nature of little girls is still the same. She wants
to be told ahead of time exactly what's right and when. She wants to know exactly
how much she loves this person, and exactly what choices this entails. To counter
her insistent demand, James repeatedly, in the second half of the novel, holds up
to us a different picture: that of an actress who finds, suddenly, that her script is
not written in advance and that she must "quite heroically" improvise her role.
"Preparation and practice had come but a short way; her part opened out, and
she invented from moment to moment what to say and to do" (II.33). The final
understanding to which his criticism of little girls transports us is that *this* is what
adult deliberation is and should be. And there's no safety in that, no safety at all.

II

Suppose that this novel does explore, as I claim, significant aspects of human
moral experience. Why, it may still be asked, do we need a text like this one for
our work on these issues? Why, as people with an interest in understanding and
self-understanding, couldn't we derive everything we require from a text that
stated and argued for these conclusions about human beings plainly and simply,
without the complications of character and conversation, without the stylistic and
structural complexities of the literary—not to mention the particular obliquities,
ambiguities, and parentheses of this particular literary text? Why do I wish to enter
on behalf of this text the claim that it is philosophical? And even should this claim
be granted, why should we believe it to be a major or irreplaceable work of moral
philosophy, whose place could not be fully filled by texts which we are accustomed
to call philosophical?

There are really two questions here. One is a particular question about the claim
of this particular novel; another is a more general question about the philosophical
importance of literary works generally—that is, of works which share with this
work certain general features by virtue of which they are commonly classified and
studied apart from admitted philosophical works. I shall not really attempt to
answer the second question here, insofar as it ranges beyond the first. Among the
particular features of this text on which I shall stake its claim to philosophical
importance, some are, indeed, shared with other related novels and with tragic
dramas; others are peculiarly its own, or belong to it in a particularly high degree.
I therefore shall speak only about *The Golden Bowl* and James's later style; I leave
to the reader the job of exploring the wider consequences of what I shall say for
our conventional distinction between philosophy and literature.

First, to prevent confusion, we must have some rough story about what moral
philosophy and the job of moral philosophy are—for on some accounts of these

things, particularly the Kantian account, this text obviously falls entirely outside of moral philosophy in virtue of the empirical and contingent character of its content. We would like to find some way of characterizing the aims of moral philosophy that would be generally enough agreed not to prejudice the answer to our question about this text, and yet specific enough to give us some purchase on our question. I propose, therefore, that we begin with the very simple Aristotelian idea that ethics is the search for a specification of the good life for a human being. This is a study whose aim, as Aristotle insists, is not just theoretical understanding but also practice. (We study not just for the sake of learning but also to see our "target" and ourselves more clearly, so that we can ourselves live and act better.) Nor can the theoretical aims of this study be accomplished in isolation from the practical aspect, for the working-through of the alternative theoretical conceptions is itself a Socratic process, which demands the active engagement of the interlocutor's own moral intuitions and responses.[17] The aim of the study will be to produce an intelligent ordering of the "appearances"—the experiences and sayings of human agents and choosers. It cannot, then, in any way be cut off from the study of the empirical and social conditions of human life; indeed, ethics, in Aristotle's conception, is a part of the social study of human beings.

I choose this conception of moral inquiry not only because I find it appealing and broadly correct, not only because I hope that it will be sufficiently inclusive to command wide agreement, but also because James describes his conception of his own authorial task in language which brings him into intimate connection with the Aristotelian enterprise. In the preface to *The Princess Casamassima,* he describes his end as the production of an "intelligent report" of human experience, that is, of "our apprehension and our measure of what happens to us as social creatures" (*AN* 64-5). We can then hope to be assessing James's text against the background of a conception of moral writing that is at once powerful and one to which he himself lays claim.

I can here do no more than to sketch out the very general lines along which I would like to argue the case for *The Golden Bowl,* but I hope that the programmatic character of these remarks will prove suggestive rather than frustrating. The first claim concerns the moral content of this text, as I have elucidated it in Part I; the second centers on the nature of the moral abilities involved in reading and interpreting it. (This does not, as I hope will soon become evident, really amount to any claim that one can sever this novel's form from its content.)

First, then, the claims of this text concerning value and imperfection are views whose plausibility and importance are difficult to assess without the sustained exploration of particular lives that a text such as this one makes possible. The claim that our loves and commitments are so related that infidelity and failure of response are more or less inevitable features even of the best examples of loving

---

17. Compare the remarks about the Socratic nature of moral theory in John Rawls, *A Theory of Justice* (Cambridge, Mass., 1971), 46–53. Rawls traces elements of this view back through Sidgwick to Aristotle. I have discussed Aristotle's view in "Saving Aristotle's Appearances," in *Language and Logos,* ed. M. Schofield and M. Nussbaum (Cambridge, 1982); *Fragility,* chap. 8; and also in *Fragility,* chap. 1, "Perceptive Equilibrium," and "Introduction," this volume.

is a claim for which a philosophical text would have a hard time mounting direct argument. It is only when, as here, we study the loves and attentions of a finely responsive mind such as Maggie's, through all the contingent complexities of a tangled human life, that the force of these ideas begins to make itself felt. When we have before us a consciousness who responds well and keenly, and when we see that even for such a consciousness the golden bowl is broken—then we have something like a persuasive argument that these features hold of human life in general. It is not only, then, the novel's capacity to explore the length and breadth of a life, but the combination of this exploratory power with the presence of a character who will count as a high case of the human response to value, that creates the telling argument. James tells us emphatically that the moral claims of his texts depend centrally on the presence inside them of such high characters, both agents and interpreters of their own lives, whose readings of life we will count as high exemplars of our own. In the preface to *The Princess Casamassima,* he writes of his choice of a hero: "The person capable of feeling in the given case more than another of what is to be felt for it, and so serving in the highest degree to *record* it dramatically and objectively, is the only sort of person on whom we can count not to betray, to cheapen or, as we say, give away the value and beauty of the thing. By so much as the affair matters *for* some such individual, by so much do we get the best there is of it" (*AN* 67).

Here we see James deftly, as often, drawing together the good person with the good character, the good reader in life with the good reader inside a text; and both of these in turn suggest parallel norms of response and vision for the reader *of* this character and this text, who must be a moral being of the appropriate sort or else he (or she) will clearly cheapen the value of the text. Last of all in this assembled group of consciousnesses, and behind them all, stands, James makes clear, the author, whose responsibility it all ultimately is, and whose conscious testimony will either reveal the value of life or by neglect cheapen it. The author's struggle to express life's value and also its mystery is, in this preface, closely coupled with and likened to the task of the character who must respond to the confusions of his world; and the author, of course, is the one from whom the character's struggle and sense of life must flow. Of the author he now goes on to write: "If you haven't, for fiction, the root of the matter in you, haven't the sense of life and the penetrating imagination, you are a fool in the very presence of the revealed and assured; but . . . if you *are* so armed you are not really helpless, not without your resource, even before mysteries abysmal" (*AN* 78). Similarly, at the end of the preface to *The Golden Bowl,* he speaks of the author as striving toward a high sort of moral responsibility for the works which are his "acts," striving with "his active sense of life" (I.xvii), which is "the silver clue to the whole labyrinth of his consciousness," so to express the "general adventure" of that intelligence that a new reading, a renewed confrontation with the completed act or text, will leave no room for "mere gaping contrition" (I.xxv).

We appear to have moved by now far beyond our immediate point and into the labyrinth of James's complex conception of his authorial task. But it is, in fact, not possible to speak about the moral view revealed within this text without speaking at the same time of the created text, which exemplifies and expresses the responses of an imagination that means to care for and to put itself there for us. "Art," James writes, "is nothing if not exemplary," "care . . . nothing if not active" (I.xxv), and the "example" in *The Golden Bowl* is, of course, not merely the adventures of the consciousness of one or another character, as our emphasis heretofore may have suggested. It is the entire text, revealed as the imaginative effort of a human character who displays himself here as the sort of character who reads lives and texts so as not to cheapen their value. I claim that the views uncovered in this text derive their power from the way in which they emerge as the ruminations of such a high and fine mind concerning the tangled mysteries of these imaginary lives. And we could hardly begin to see whether such views were or were not exemplary for us if this mind simply stated its conclusions flatly, if it did not unfold before us the richness of its reflection, allowing us to follow and to share its adventures.

It is a further fact about the views of this text that they are views very seldom put forward and seriously examined in works of moral philosophy. And this, I claim, is no accident. Any view of deliberation that holds that it is, first and foremost, a matter of intuitive perception and improvisatory response, where a fixed antecedent ordering or ranking among values is to be taken as a sign of immaturity rather than of excellence; any view that holds that it is the job of the adult agent to approach a complex situation responsively, with keen vision and alert feelings, prepared, if need be, to alter his or her prima facie conception of the good in the light of the new experience, is likely to clash with certain classical aims and assertions of moral philosophy, which has usually claimed to make progress on our behalf precisely by extricating us from this bewilderment in the face of the present moment, and by setting us up in a watertight system of rules or a watertight procedure of calculation which will be able to settle troublesome cases, in effect, before the fact. Philosophers who have defended the primacy of intuitive perception are few. And when they have appeared, they have naturally also concluded—as does, for example, Aristotle—that moral theory cannot be a form of scientific knowledge that orders the "matter of the practical" into an elegant antecedent system; and they have also naturally turned to works of literature, as Aristotle turns to tragic drama, for illumination concerning practical excellence. In fact, Aristotle makes it very clear that his own writing provides at most a "sketch" or "outline" of the good life, whose content must be given by experience, and whose central claims can be clarified only by appeal to life and to works of literature.[18]

To show forth the force and truth of the Aristotelian claim that "the decision rests with perception," we need, then—either side by side with a philosophical "outline" or inside it—texts which display to us the complexity, the indeterminacy, the sheer *difficulty* of moral choice, and which show us, as this text does

18. On the "sketch" and its relation to particular intuitive judgments, see "Discernment," *Fragility,* chaps. 8 and 10. For some further remarks about literary storytelling as an expansion of experience, see *Fragility,* chap. 6. A picture of deliberation closely related to the one sketched here is developed in David Wiggins, "Deliberation and Practical Reason," *Proceedings of the Aristotelian Society* NS 76 (1975–76) 29–51.

concerning Maggie Verver, the childishness, the refusal of life involved in fixing everything in advance according to some system of inviolable rules. This task cannot be easily accomplished by texts which speak in universal terms—for one of the difficulties of deliberation stressed by this view is that of grasping the uniqueness of the new particular. Nor can it easily be done by texts which speak with the hardness or plainness which moral philosophy has traditionally chosen for its style—for how can this style at all convey the way in which the "matter of the practical" appears before the agent in all of its bewildering complexity, without its morally salient features stamped on its face? And how, without conveying this, can it convey the active adventure of the deliberative intelligence, the "yearnings of thought and excursions of sympathy" (II.330) that make up much of our actual moral life?[19]

Finally, without a presentation of the mystery, conflict, and riskiness of the lived deliberative situation, it will be hard for philosophy to convey the peculiar value and beauty of choosing humanly well—for we have suggested that the flawed and unclear object has its own, and not simply a lower, sort of beauty. James himself expresses this point, again in the preface to *The Princess Casamassima:* "It seems probable that if we were never bewildered there would never be a story to tell about us; we should partake of the superior nature of the all-knowing immortals whose annals are dreadfully dull so long as flurried humans are not, for the positive relief of bored Olympians, mixed up with them" (*AN* 63–4). It is this idea that human deliberation is constantly an *adventure* of the personality, undertaken against terrific odds and among frightening mysteries, *and* that this is, in fact, the source of much of its beauty and richness, that texts written in a traditional philosophical style have the most insuperable difficulty conveying to us. If our moral lives are "stories" in which mystery and risk play a central and a valuable role, then it may well seem that the "intelligent report" of those lives requires the abilities and techniques of the teller of stories. (And in this way we might come to see James not so much as a novelist-by-profession who, because that was his profession, expressed in that form his moral vision, as an intelligent maker of a moral vision who embodied it in novels because only in that form could he fully and fittingly express it.)

These remarks suggest, then, that there are candidates for moral truth which the plainness of traditional moral philosophy lacks the power to express, and which *The Golden Bowl* expresses wonderfully. Insofar as the goal of moral philosophy is to give us understanding of the human good through a scrutiny of alternative conceptions of the good, this text and others like it would then appear to be important parts of this philosophy. But we said at the beginning of this section that the aim of moral philosophy was not simply theoretical understanding, but also something connected with practice—meaning by this that the philosophical study of the human good is inseparable from, cannot be conducted in isolation from, a Socratic working-through of the interlocutor's or reader's own moral intuitions

---

19. There are obvious connections between these thoughts and the line of argument pursued in Iris Murdoch's *The Sovereignty of Good* (London, 1970), whose view of the moral importance of imaginative work I discuss in *Fragility,* chap. 2.

that will leave this person clearer about his or her own moral aims.[20] What we must now take into account, then, is the activity and response of the reader of this text—an activity to which James makes frequent and emphatic reference, both by direct remarks about what "we," or some concerned observer, or someone whose attention to the character qualifies the character's isolation (I.125) might find to say and to feel about these happenings; and also by the inclusion within the text of two characters, the Assinghams (Fanny alone among the characters is referred to as "our friend" [II.162]), whose function, like that of the Greek tragic chorus, seems to be that of concerned interpretation of the events to which they bear witness. (The connection between this imaginary reader and the imagination of the responsible author is suggested at several points and brought out most strikingly in the preface, whose main theme is the author's rereading of his own created text.) Our question must be, What sort of activity on the reader's part will best fulfill the aims of the Socratic assessment process?

What I now want to suggest is that the adventure of the reader of this novel, like the adventure of the intelligent characters inside it, involves valuable aspects of human moral experience that are not tapped by traditional books of moral philosophy; in this way as well it would be necessary for the completion of the enterprise of working through all of our moral intuitions. For this novel calls upon and also develops our ability to confront mystery with the cognitive engagement of both thought and feeling. To work through these sentences and these chapters is to become involved in an activity of exploration and unraveling that uses abilities, especially abilities of emotion and imagination, rarely tapped by philosophical texts.[21] But these abilities have, at the very least, a good claim to be regarded as important parts of the moral assessment process. In his preface James speaks of a reading of his novel as "the very record and mirror of the general adventure of one's intelligence" (I.xix). If traditional philosophical texts do not record this whole adventure, call upon all of the abilities that are engaged in it, this would be a good reason to think that a Socratic enterprise requires texts like this one for its completion.

We have spoken so far as if the ideal reader of this text were like the "ideal" Maggie Verver of the novel's second part. He or she would, then, be someone keenly alive in thought and feeling to every nuance of the situation, actively seeing and caring for all the parties concerned—and therefore safely right in the perfection of his or her attention. But we know already that this "ideal" is not the work's

20. If one is persuaded that a sharp distinction is to be made between moral theory and moral education, the following remarks can be taken as remarks about the importance of this text for moral education. Since, however, the conception of moral philosophy with which I am working makes philosophy's specification of the good an outgrowth of an educational, Socratic interchange between text and reader, who actively judges how well the text accounts for his or her ethical experience, I shall speak as though the activity of the reader is pertinent to moral philosophy. On "moral" versus "ethical," and on "philosophy" versus "theory," see "Perceptive Equilibrium," n. 2, this volume.

21. The interpenetration of imagination, reflection, and feeling in deliberation is revealingly characterized (and called upon) throughout the novel; this, on further examination, emerges as one of its most fascinating contributions. I discuss these issues further, with reference to Proust, in "Fictions of the Soul."

entire story about human practical wisdom. We know that where there is great love in one direction there may also be, in another direction, a tragically necessary blindness. We now want to know whether this feature of our moral life also finds its place in the author's way of being responsible to his created story and in the reader's way of responding to his text. In other words, does the text itself acknowledge the flawed nature of the consciousness that produced it and elicit from us in turn, as readers, an acknowledgment of our own imperfection?

I want to claim that it does, in two ways. First, with this text, as perhaps with few others in English literature, we are struck at every point by the incompleteness and inadequacy of our own attention. We notice the way we are inclined to miss things, to pass over things, to leave out certain interpretative possibilities while pursuing others. This consciousness of our own flaws and blind spots (created in the first place by the sheer difficulty of James's later style) is heightened by Fanny's regular self-criticism, her ongoing revision of her previous, defective "readings." It is nourished, too, by the frequent reminders of the author-reader's "we" that our concern has its limits. Phrases such as "at the moment we are concerned with him" (I.3), "at the particular instant of our being again concerned with her" (I.245), "had we time to look into it," "which we have just found in our path" (I.163) recall to us the fact that our path is only one path and that we cannot humanly follow all paths through these tangled lives at all times. The authorial voice also reminds us that, even when we do attend, our attention, like all human attention, is interested and interpretative. We are told that such-and-such is "the main interest . . . for us" (I.326) in these events, and we work through an account of "these gropings and fittings of his conscience and his experience, that we have attempted to set in order here" (I.319). In all these moments, the author places himself humanly within the world of his text and links us to himself as limited and human adventurers.

It is the explicit design of this novel that this should be so. For James tells us in his preface that he has elected to avoid "the mere muffled majesty of irresponsible 'authorship'" and to become a responsible (and, we suspect, therefore guilty) agent in the midst of his work. "It's not," he continues, "that the muffled majesty of authorship doesn't here *ostensibly* reign; but I catch myself again shaking it off and disavowing the pretence of it while I get down into the arena and do my best to live and breathe and rub shoulders and converse with the persons engaged in the struggle" (I.vi)—persons whom he soon describes as "the more or less bleeding participants." James here implicitly criticizes a tradition in the English novel for having created, in the authorial voice, a persona who is not humanly finite and who therefore does not show us a way to the understanding of our own finitude.[22] *The Golden Bowl* looks, then, like an attempt to move the novel itself out of the Eden of pure intelligent responsibility.

Central to this task, and of at least as much importance for it as the scattered first-person remarks, is the fact that the intelligence animating this text, in virtue of its choice to engage itself with and, we might say, to care for one or another of the characters, has left beyond itself and, therefore, us certain deep mysteries into which our adventuring consciousness has no access. As we carefully follow and

---

22. It is plain from other writings of James that George Eliot is a primary target.

respond to Maggie, seeing this world through her intelligent eyes, we hardly notice that we ourselves are rapidly becoming as distant from Charlotte, and as blind to the inner life of her pain, as Maggie herself. It is sometimes said by critics that the second part of this novel shows Charlotte to be a morally superficial character with an impoverished inner life. It would be more accurate, and more in keeping with the announced spirit of James's design, to say that it is not so much Charlotte who is revealed as superficial; it is Maggie, and therefore we, who are revealed as superficial and impoverished with respect to Charlotte. Charlotte and her pain are, at the end, not revealed but hidden.[23] Our active care for Maggie and our acceptance of the invitation to see as Maggie sees have brought upon us (upon the "we" composed of author and reader) a blindness with respect to this part of the moral world. (The second and last time we do get a direct feeling for the inner life of this woman, James stresses the oddness of the event by calling this "the particular instant of our being again concerned with her" [I.245].) James tells us that our responsive attention, when we choose to bestow it, "qualifies" the "isolation" of his characters (I.125)—much as in life, our solitary separateness is qualified, though never removed, by the fact of another person's care. Charlotte, lost to our attention, becomes at the end our pagoda: a "splendid" object with its "affirmed presence" (II.356), "throned" in our midst (II.358)—and here James significantly adds, "as who should say." As who, indeed, should say. For into that isolation and pain and silence our intelligent conversation and response do not enter. No door appears to give access from the convenient garden level. The "great decorated surface" remains "consistently impenetrable and inscrutable" (II.4).

So, as readers, with the author as our guide and accomplice, we eat the golden fruit. With pity and dread we bury our eyes.[24]

Endnote

This essay was the first piece of writing I did in this literary/philosophical project (apart from its development in my work on ancient Greek philosophy). It was

23. James's notebooks show that the novel was begun with the tentative title *Charlotte* (see Edel, p. 572). This essay was also begun, long ago, as an essay about Charlotte. It appears to be a confirmation of the claims advanced here that the paper's original aim of focusing attention on Charlotte was frustrated by the ubiquity of the author/reader's care and concern for Maggie, who more or less inevitably "took over." Could this have been James's experience with his own creation? Or did he think of giving a title that would point us to the central importance of the novel's silences, just as its actual title points us to the flaws in human response that produce these silences?

24. I owe thanks to Daniel Brudney, Stanley Cavell, Arnold Davidson, Guy Sircello, and Susan Wolf for their valuable criticisms of an earlier draft of this paper; and especially to Richard Wollheim and Patrick Gardiner, who commented on the paper at the American Philosophical Association, Pacific Division, and the Oxford Philosophical Society, respectively. I am especially grateful to David Wiggins for showing me the parts of London in which this novel is set, helping me to learn something about their history, and, in general, for giving me a sense of "the fashion after which the prodigious city . . . does on occasion meet half-way those forms of intelligence of it that *it* recognizes" (*The Golden Bowl,* I.xii).

written in the middle of the drafting of *Fragility,* and constituted my first attempt to state the questions of this book in a general way for a general philosophical audience. It is no accident that this general questioning began out of a longstanding love for a particular novel and its characters.

On its presentation at the American Philosophical Association, the paper received comments from Richard Wollheim; Patrick Gardiner was the commentator at a similar occasion in Oxford. The paper and these two sets of comments were then printed in *New Literary History,* together with further comments by Hilary Putnam and Cora Diamond. I replied to these comments in a separate piece in the journal. This piece is not reprinted in the volume, since it depends on the texts of these other papers. Several of the most important points they raised have since, in various ways, been incorporated into my thinking about the subject. Wollheim's point about the importance of philosophical commentary (described in "Love's Knowledge" and the Introduction) is now central to my own view. His account of the ways in which the novel leads the reader outside of morality is also, I now think, of central importance (see Introduction, "Perceptive Equilibrium," and "Steerforth's Arm"). Putnam's criticisms of the morality of perception have been with me ever since and have provoked a good deal of my further clarification of the Jamesian/Aristotelian position: they are explicitly discussed in "Discernment," "'Finely Aware,'" and "Perception and Revolution." Diamond's valuable paper provoked some of the further reflection on the "framing method" (see Introduction and "Perceptive Equilibrium").

It remains, then, to describe here a valuable point made by Patrick Gardiner about my reading of the novel and its use of aesthetic imagery. This point is alluded to briefly in "'Finely Aware,'" but its importance demands a fuller discussion. Taking up my question about the function of aesthetic imagery for persons in the ethical reflection of the Ververs, Gardiner argued that in the second half of the novel this aestheticizing is not altogether repudiated, but comes to be used in a new way, showing us a fruitful link between aesthetic activity and the moral point of view. Specifically, the comparison of our relations with a person to our relations with a work of art show us a way in which ethical attention might have fine-tuned perception and responsive feeling, while remaining free of the personal resentment, rage, and jealousy that too frequently characterize our personal dealings. Thus, Maggie's earlier attitude has, despite its deficiencies, positive elements that promote her later growth.

Gardiner makes this point using one striking example: the scene in which Maggie, just before she is confronted by Charlotte, looks through a window at the assembled group of people in the manner of someone who is looking at a painting:

> She continued to walk and continued to pause; she stopped afresh for the look into the smoking-room, and by this time—it was as if the recognition had of itself arrested her—she saw as in a picture, with the temptation she had fled from quite extinct, why it was she had been able to give herself so little, from the first, to the vulgar heat of her wrong. She might fairly, as she watched them, have missed it as a lost thing; have yearned for it, for the straight vindictive view, the rights of resentment, the rages of jealousy, the protests of passion, as for something she had been cheated of not least. . . . The sight, from the window, of the group so con-

stituted, *told* her why, told her how, named to her, as with hard lips, named straight *at* her, so that she must take it full in the face, that other possible relation to the whole fact which alone would bear upon her irresistibly. It was extraordinary: they positively brought home to her that to feel about them in any of the immediate, inevitable, assuaging ways, the ways usually open to innocence outraged and generosity betrayed, would have been to give them up, and that giving them up was, marvellously, not to be thought of.

He points to the significant contrast between this scene and the one immediately preceding, in which Maggie, seated *among* the people in the room, does indeed think of giving them up and indulging her jealousy. The experience of quasi-aesthetic distancing, here, is associated with a move away from these more selfish and blinding emotions to a balanced and active general sympathy.

I think this is right and extremely perceptive. It shows us something valuable about James's conception of the moral, something that comes up for us in other novels as well (see "Perceptive Equilibrium" and "Perception and Revolution") and that marks James as very different from Proust in his sense of which emotions we should trust (see "Love's Knowledge" and "Steerforth's Arm"). We should add, however, I think, that there are crucial differences between this new and right aesthetic attitude and Maggie's earlier use of aesthetic imagery. Her earlier aestheticizing denies the living humanity of the people so regarded; it is an aestheticism divorced from active love and a sense of obligation. This new aestheticizing, by contrast, never fails to conceive of its objects as alive, as in need, as having claims to press. The painting is more a theater piece than a painting (theatrical imagery is prominently used earlier in the chapter); the group of people is seen as speaking to her, naming, insistently bringing home to her the fact of their need and her responsibility. Aestheticizing, then, can be divorced from ethical concern and from love; by itself it is no guarantee of rightness. But it seems likely that, for James, such an aestheticism is not a full or complete love of art either—as his portrait of Gilbert Osmond suggests. Certainly such a nonmoral and nonloving aesthetic attitude would not, for James, be a complete or completely right way of relating to a novel such as this one, which contains, as he often tells us, a "projected morality."

The new expanded version of "Discernment" says much more about the rightness of Maggie's new way of deliberating in the second half of the novel, connecting this analysis with the account of the Aristotelian ethical view.

"Finely Aware and Richly Responsible": Literature and the Moral Imagination

"The effort really to see and really to represent is no idle business in face of the constant force that makes for muddlement."[1] So Henry James on the task of the moral imagination. We live amid bewildering complexities. Obtuseness and refusal of vision are our besetting vices. Responsible lucidity can be wrested from that darkness only by painful, vigilant effort, the intense scrutiny of particulars. Our highest and hardest task is to make ourselves people "on whom nothing is lost."[2]

This is a claim about our ethical task, as people who are trying to live well. In its context it is at the same time a claim about the task of the literary artist. James often stresses this analogy: the work of the moral imagination is in some manner like the work of the creative imagination, especially that of the novelist. I want to study this analogy and to see how it is more than analogy: why this conception of moral attention and moral vision finds in novels its most appropriate articulation. More: why, according to this conception, the novel is itself a moral achievement, and the well-lived life is a work of literary art.

Although the moral conception according to which James's novels have this value will be elicited here from James's work, my aim is to commend it as of more than parochial interest—as, in fact, the best account I know of these matters. But if I succeed only in establishing the weaker claim that it is a major candidate for truth, deserving of our most serious scrutiny when we do moral philosophy, this will be reason enough to include inside moral philosophy those texts in which it receives its most appropriate presentation. I shall argue that James's novels are such texts. So I shall provide further support for my contention that certain novels are, irreplaceably, works of moral philosophy. But I shall go further. I shall try to articulate and define the claim that the novel can be a paradigm of moral activity. I confine myself to *The Golden Bowl*,[3] so as to build on my previous interpretation.[4]

1. Henry James, *The Art of the Novel* (New York, 1907) 149. In the citations that follow, individual preface titles will not be given. The title quotation is from *AN* 62.
2. Henry James, *The Princess Casamassima* (New York Edition) I.
3. All page references to *The Golden Bowl* (*GB*) are to the New York Edition (New York, 1909).
4. See "Flawed Crystals."

I begin by examining the nature of moral attention and insight in one episode, in which two people perform acts of altruism without reliance on rules of duty, improvising what is required. This leads to some reflection about the interaction of rules and perceptions in moral judging and learning: about the value of "plainness," about the "mystic lake" of perceptual bewilderment, about "getting the tip" and finding a "basis." Finally I probe James's analogy (and more) between moral attention and our attention to works of art. In short: I begin assessing the moral contribution of texts that narrate the experiences of beings committed to value, using that "immense array of terms, perceptional and expressional, that . . . in sentence, passage and page, simply looked over the heads of the standing terms— or perhaps rather, like alert winged creatures, perched on those diminished summits and aspired to a clearer air" (*GB,* pref., I. xvi–xvii).

I

How can we hope to confront these characters and their predicament, if not in these words and sentences, whose very ellipses and circumnavigations rightly convey the lucidity of their bewilderment, the precision of their indefiniteness? Any pretense that we could paraphrase this scene without losing its moral quality would belie the argument that I am about to make. I presuppose, then, the quotation of Book Fifth, Chapter III of *The Golden Bowl.* Indeed, honoring its "chains of relation and responsibility," I presuppose the quotation of the entire novel. What follows is a commentary.

This daughter and this father must give one another up. Before this "they *had,* after all, whatever happened, always and ever each other . . . to do exactly what they would with: a provision full of possibilities" (II.255). But not all possibilities are, in fact, compatible with this provision. He must let her go, loving her, so that she can live with her husband as a real wife; loving him, she must discover a way to let him go as a "great and deep and high" man and not a failure, his dignity intact. In the "golden air" of these "massed Kentish woods" (II.256) they "beat against the wind" and "cross the bar" (II.264): they reach, through a mutual and sustained moral effort, a resolution and an end. It is, moreover (in this Tennysonian image), their confrontation with death: her acceptance of the death of her own childhood and an all-enveloping love (her movement out of Eden into the place of birth and death); his acceptance of a life that will be from now on, without her, a place of death. She, bearing the guilt that her birth as a woman has killed him; he, "*offering* himself, pressing himself upon her, as a sacrifice—he had read his way so into her best possibility" (II.269). It is a reasonable place for us to begin our investigation; for the acts to be recorded can be said to be paradigmatic of the moral: his sacrifice, her preservation of his dignity, his recognition of her separate and autonomous life.

The scene begins with evasion, a flight from dilemma into the lost innocence of childhood. For "it was wonderfully like their having got together into some boat and paddled off from the shore where husbands and wives, luxuriant complications, made the air too tropical" (II.255). They "slope" off together as "of old" (II.253); they rest "on a sequestered bench," far from the "strain long felt but never named" (II.254), the conflicts imposed by other relations. They might have been again the only man and woman in the garden. They immerse themselves in "the inward felicity of their being once more, perhaps only for half an hour, simply daughter and father" (254–55). Their task will be to depart from this felicity without altogether defiling its beauty.

The difficulty is real enough. Could it be anything but a matter of the most serious pain, and guilt, for her to give up, even for a man whom she loves passionately, this father who has raised her, protected her, loved her, enveloped her, who really does love only her and who depends on her for help of future happiness? In these circumstances she cannot love her husband except by banishing her father. But if she banishes her father he will live unhappy and die alone. (And won't she, as well, have to see him as a failure, his life as debased, as well as empty?) It is no wonder, then, that Maggie finds herself wishing "to keep him with her for remounting the stream of time and dipping again, for the softness of the water, into the contracted basin of the past" (II.258). To dare to be and do what she passionately desires appears, and is, too monstrous, a cruel refusal of loyalty. And what has her whole world been built on, if not on loyalty and the keen image of his greatness? It is no wonder that the feeling of desire for her husband is, in this crisis, felt as a numbing chill, and she accuses it: "I'm at this very moment . . . frozen stiff with selfishness" (II.265).

This is moral anguish, not simply girlish fear. Keeping down her old childish sense of his omnipotence exacerbates and does not remove her problem; for seeing him as limited and merely human (as Adam, not the creator) she sees, too, all the things he cannot have without her. And in her anguish she has serious thought of regression and return: "Why . . . couldn't they always live, so far as they lived together, in a boat?" (II.255). In pursuit of that idea she calls upon her ability to speak in universal terms, about what "one must always do." The narrator says of this "sententious(ness)" that it "was doubtless too often even now her danger" (II.258)—linking the propensity for abstractness and the use of "standing terms" with her past and present refusals to confront the unique and conflict-engendering nature of her own particular context.

I say this to show the moral difficulty of what is going on here, the remarkable moral achievement, therefore, in his act of sacrifice which resolves it. The general sacrificial idea—that he will go off to America with Charlotte—is in itself no solution. For it to become a solution it has to be offered in the right way at the right time in the right tone, in such a way that she can take it; offered without pressing any of the hidden springs of guilt and loyalty in her that he knows so clearly how to press; offered so that he gives her up with greatness, with beauty, in a way that she can love and find wonderful. To give her up he must, then, really give her up; he must wholeheartedly *wish* to give her up, so that she sees that he *has* "read his way so into her best possibility."

Maggie has spoken of her passion for Amerigo, saying that when you love in the deepest way you are beyond jealousy—"You're beyond everything, and nothing can pull you down" (II.262). What happens next is that her father perceives her in a certain way:

> The mere fine pulse of passion in it, the suggestion as of a creature consciously floating and shining in a warm summer sea, some element of dazzling sapphire

and silver, a creature cradled upon depths, buoyant among dangers, in which fear or folly or sinking otherwise than in play was impossible—something of all this might have been making once more present to him, with his discreet, his half shy assent to it, her probable enjoyment of a rapture that he, in his day, had presumably convinced no great number of persons either of his giving or of his receiving. He sat awhile as if he knew himself hushed, almost admonished, and not for the first time; yet it was an effect that might have brought before him rather what she had gained than what he had missed . . . It could pass further for knowing—for knowing that without him nothing might have been: which would have been missing least of all. "I guess I've never been jealous," he finally remarked.

And she takes it: "Oh it's you, father, who are what I call beyond everything. Nothing can pull *you* down." (II.263–64).

This passage records a moral achievement of deep significance. Adam acknowledges, in an image of delicate beauty and lyricism, his daughter's sexuality and free maturity. More: he wishes that she be free, that the suggestion of passion in her voice be translated into, fulfilled in a life of sparkling playfulness. He assents to her pleasure and wishes to be its approving spectator, not its impediment. He renounces, at the same time, his own personal gain—renounces even the putting of the question as to what he might or might not gain. (For even the presence of a jealous or anxious question would produce a sinking otherwise than in play.) The significance of his image resonates the more for us if we recall that he used to see Maggie (and wish her to be) like "some slight, slim draped 'antique' of Vatican or Capitoline hills, late and refined, rare as a note and immortal as a link, . . . keeping still the quality, the perfect felicity, of the statue" (I.187). That image denied (with her evident collusion) her active womanliness; it also denied her status as a separate, autonomous center of choice. It expressed the wish to collect and keep her always, keep her far from the dangers so often expressed, in the thought of these characters, by the imagery of water and its motion. Now he wishes her moving and alive, swimming freely in the sea—not even confined to his boat, or to the past's "contracted basin." Not "frozen stiff" with guilt, either.

We can say several things about the moral significance of this picture. First, that, as a picture, it *is* significant—not only in its causal relation to his subsequent speeches and acts, but as a moral achievement in its own right. It is, of course, of enormous causal significance; his speeches and acts, here and later, flow forth from it and take from it the rightness of their tone. But suppose that we rewrote the scene so as to give him the same speeches and acts (even, *per impossibile,* their exact tonal rightness), with a different image—perhaps one expressing conflict, or a wish to swim alongside her, or even a wish for her drowning—in any of these cases, our assessment of him would be altered.[5] Furthermore, the picture has a pivotal role in his moral activity here that would not be captured by regarding it as a mere precondition for action. We want to say, *here* is where his sacrifice, his essential moral choice, takes place. Here, in his ability to picture her as a sea creature, is the act of renunciation that moves us to pain and admiration. "He had read his way so into her best possibility"—here James tells us that sacrifice *is* an

5. See Iris Murdoch, *The Sovereignty of Good* (London, 1970).

act of imaginative interpretation; it is a perception of her situation as that of a free woman who is not bound by his wish. As such it is of a piece with the character of his overt speech, which succeeds as it does because of his rare power to take the sense and nuance of her speeches and "read himself into" them in the highest way.

The image is, then, morally salient. I need to say more about what is salient in it. What strikes us about it first is its sheer gleaming beauty. Adam sees his daughter's sexuality in a way that can be captured linguistically only in language of lyrical splendor. This tells us a great deal about the quality of his moral imagination—that it is subtle and high rather than simple and coarse; precise rather than gross; richly colored rather than monochromatic; exuberant rather than reluctant; generous rather than stingy; suffused with loving emotion rather than mired in depression. To this moral assessment the full specificity of the image is relevant. If we had read, "He thought of her as an autonomous being," or "He acknowledged his daughter's mature sexuality," or even "He thought of his daughter as a sea creature dipping in the sea," we would miss the sense of lucidity, expressive feeling, and generous lyricism that so move us here. It is relevant that his image was not a flat thing but a fine work of art; that it had all the detail, tone, and color that James captures in these words. It could not be captured in any paraphrase that was not itself a work of art.

The passage suggests something further. "It could pass, further, for knowing—for knowing that without him nothing might have been." To perceive her as a sea creature, in just this way, is precisely, to know her, to know their situation, not to miss anything in it—to be, in short, "a person on whom nothing is lost." Moral knowledge, James suggests, is not simply intellectual grasp of propositions; it is not even simply intellectual grasp of particular facts; it is perception.[6] It is seeing a complex, concrete reality in a highly lucid and richly responsive way; it is taking in what is there, with imagination and feeling. To know Maggie is to see and feel her separateness, her felicity; to recognize all this is to miss least of all. If he had grasped the same general facts without these responses and these images, in all their specificity, he would not really have known her.

Her moral achievement, later, is parallel to his. She holds herself in a terrible tension, close to the complexities of his need, anxiously protecting the "thin wall" (II.267) of silence that stands between them both and the words of explicit disclosure that would have destroyed his dignity and blocked their "best possibility." Her vigilance, her silent attention, the intensity of her regard, are put before us as moral acts: "She might have been for the time, in all her conscious person, the very form of the equilibrium they were, in their different ways, equally trying to save " (II.268). She measures her moral adequacy by the fullness and richness of her imaginings: "So much was crowded into so short a space that she knew already she was keeping her head" (II.268). And her imagination, like his, achieves its moral goal in the finding of the right way of seeing. Like an artist whose labor produces, at last, a wonderful achieved form, she finds, "as the result, for the present occasion, of an admirable traceable effort" (II.273), a thought of her father "that placed him in her eyes as no precious work of art probably had ever been placed in his own" (II.273). To see Adam as a being more precious than his precious works of art becomes, for her, after a moment, to see him as "a great and

6. On Aristotle's similar view, see *Fragility,* chap. 10, and "Discernment."

deep and high little man" (II.274)—as great *in,* not in spite of, his difficulty and his limitation and his effort, great because he is Adam, a little man, and not the omnipotent father. In short, it is to see that "to love him with tenderness was not to be distinguished a whit, from loving him with pride" (II.274). Pride in, belief in the dignity of, another human being is not opposed to tenderness toward human limits. By finding a way to perceive him, to imagine him not as father and law and world but as a finite human being whose dignity is in and not opposed to his finitude, Maggie achieves an adult love for him and a basis of equality. "His strength was her strength, her pride was his, and they were decent and competent together" (II.274–75). Her perceptions are necessary to her effort to give him up and to preserve his dignity. They are also moral achievements in their own right: expressions of love, protections of the loved, creations of a new and richer bond between them.

Moral communication, too, both here and later in the scene, is not simply a matter of the uttering and receiving of general propositional judgments. Nor is it any sort of purely intellectual activity. It partakes both of the specificity and of the emotional and imaginative richness of their individual moral effort. We see them drawing close in understanding by seeing where they come to share the same pictures. When we hear of "the act of their crossing the bar" and their "having had to beat against the wind" (II.264), we discover all at once that we cannot say whose image for their situation this is. We can only say that it belongs to both of them: each inhabits, from his or her own point of view, the world of the same picture. "It was as if she had gotten over first and were pausing for her consort to follow." The paragraph melds their two consciousnesses and two viewpoints—not by confounding their separateness, for they see each other, within the picture, as distinct individuals, but by showing the extent to which fine attention to another can make two separate people inhabit the same created world—until, at the end, they even share descriptive language: "At the end of another minute, he found their word." And: "she helped him out with it" (II.265). Together they give birth, in love and pain, to a lucid description of the moral reality before them. Father and mother both, he carries and nurtures it; she assists in the delivery. The true judgment is the child of their responsive interaction. In the chapter's final moments we hear talk of "their transmuted union" (II. 274). Their moral likemindedness is neither, on the one hand, merely a shared relation to something external (a rule, a proposition), nor, on the other, something internal in such a way that awareness is fused and separateness lost. It is the delicate communication of alert beings who always stand separated as by "an exquisite tissue" (II.267), through which they alertly hear each other breathing.

The final moment of the scene describes the act that is the fruit of this communicating. I have said that these picturings, describings, feelings, and communications—actions in their own right—have a moral value that is not reducible to that of the overt acts they engender.[7] I have begun, on this basis, to build a case for saying that the morally valuable aspects of this exchange could not be captured

---

7. See also *AN* 65, where James attacks "the unreality of the sharp distinction . . . between doing and feeling . . . I then see their 'doing' . . . as, immensely, their feeling, their feeling as their doing" (from the preface to *The Princess Casamassima;* for further comment on this passage, see "Perception and Revolution").

in a summary or paraphrase. Now I shall begin to close the gap between action
and description from the other side, showing a responsible action, as James conceives it, is a highly context-specific and nuanced and responsive thing whose
rightness could not be captured in a description that fell short of the artistic.
Again, I quote the passage:

> "I believe in you more than anyone."
> "Than anyone at all?"
> She hesitated for all it might mean; but there was—oh a thousand times!—no
> doubt of it. "Than anyone at all." She kept nothing of it back now, met his eyes
> over it, let him have the whole of it; after which she went on: "And that's the way,
> I think, you believe in me."
> He looked at her a minute longer, but his tone at last was right. "About the
> way—yes."
> "Well, then—?" She spoke as for the end and for other matters—for anything,
> everything else there might be. They would never return to it.
> "Well then—!" His hands came out, and while her own took them he drew her
> to his breast and held her. He held her hard and kept her long, and she let herself
> go; but it was an embrace that, august and almost stern, produced for its intimacy
> no revulsion and broke into no inconsequence of tears. (II.275)

We know, again, that the overt items, the speeches and the embrace, are not the
only morally relevant exchange. There are, we are told, thoughts and responses
behind her "Well then"—thoughts of ending, feelings of immeasurable love, without which the brief utterance would be empty of moral meaning. But we can now
also see that even where the overt items are concerned, nuance and fine detail of
tone are everything. "His tone at last was right": that is, if he had said the same
words in a different tone of voice, less controlled, more stricken, less accepting,
the whole rightness of the act, of his entire pattern of action here, would have been
undone. He would not have loved her as well had he not spoken so well, with
these words at this time and in this tone of voice. (His very tentativeness and his
silences are a part of his achievement.) Again, what makes their embrace a wonderful achievement of love and mutual altruism is not the bare fact that it is an
embrace; it is the precise tonality and quality of that embrace: that it is hard and
long, expressive of deep passion on his side, yielding acceptance of that love on
hers; yet dignified and austere, refusing the easy yielding to tears that might have
cheapened it.

We can say, first, that no description less specific than this could convey the
rightness of this action; second, that any change in the description, even at the
same level of specificity, seems to risk producing a different act—or at least
requires us to question the sameness of the act. (For example, my substitution of
"austere" for "august" arguably changes things for the worse, suggesting inhibition of deep feeling rather than fullness of dignity.) Furthermore, a paraphrase
such as the one I have produced, even when reasonably accurate, does not ever
succeed in displacing the original prose; for it is, not being a high work of literary
art, devoid of a richness of feeling and a rightness of tone and rhythm that characterize the orginal, whose cadences stamp themselves inexorably on the heart. A
good action is not flat and toneless and lifeless like my paraphrase—whose use of

the "standing terms" of moral discourse, words like "mutual sacrifice," makes it too blunt for the highest value. It is an "alert winged creature," soaring above these terms in flexibliity and lucidity of vision. The only way to paraphrase this passage without loss of value would be to write another work of art.

II

In all their fine-tuned perceiving, these two are responsible to standing obligations, some particular and some general. Perceptions "perch on the heads of" the standing terms: they do not displace them. This needs to be emphasized, since it can easily be thought that the morality of these hypersensitive beings is an artwork embroidered for its own intrinsic aesthetic character, without regard to principle and commitment.[8] James, indeed, sees this as its besetting danger; in the characters of Bob and Fanny Assingham, he shows us how perception without responsibility is dangerously free-floating, even as duty without perception is blunt and blind. The right "basis" for action is found in the loving dialogue of the two. Here, Maggie's standing obligations to Adam (and also those of a daughter in general to fathers in general) pull her (in thought and feeling both) toward the right perception, helping to articulate the scene, constraining the responses she can make. Her sense of a profound obligation to respect his dignity is crucial in causing her to reject other possible images and to search until she finds the image of the work of art with which she ends (II.273). Adam's image of the sea creature, too, satisfies, is right, in part because it fulfills his sense of what a father owes an adult daughter.

So, if we think of the perception as a created work of art, we must at the same time remember that artists, as James sees it, are not free simply to create anything they like. Their obligation is to render reality, precisely and faithfully; in this task they are very much assisted by general principles and by the habits and attachments that are their internalization. (In this sense the image of a perception as a child is better, showing that you can have the right sort of creativity only within the constraints of natural reality.) If their sense of the occasion is, as often in James, one of improvisation, if Maggie sees herself as an actress improvising her role, we must remember, too, that the actress who improvises well is *not* free to do anything at all. She must at every moment—far more than one who goes by an external script—be responsively alive and committed to the other actors, to the evolving narrative, to the laws and constraints of the genre and its history. Consider the analogous contrast between the symphony player and the jazz musician. For the former, all commitments and continuities are external; they come from the score and from the conductor. The player reads them off like anyone else. The jazz player, actively forging continuity, must choose in full awareness of and responsibility to the historical traditions of the form, and must actively honor at every moment his commitments to his fellow musicians, whom he had better know as well as possible as unique individuals. He should be more responsible than the score reader, and not less, to the unfolding continuities and structures of the work. These two cases indicate to us that a perceiver who improvises is doubly

---

8. For the objection, see Hilary Putnam, "Taking Rules Seriously: A Response to Martha Nussbaum," *New Literary History* 15 (1983) 193–200.

responsible: responsible to the history of commitment and to the ongoing structures that go to constitute her context; and especially responsible to these, in that her commitments are internalized, assimilated, perceived, rather than read off from an external script or score.

Furthermore, the case of moral improvisation shows an even deeper role for obligation and rule than do these artistic cases. For a jazz musician, to depart from tradition in a sudden and radical way can be disconcerting, sometimes self-indulgent or irresponsible; but it can equally well be a creative breakthrough before which the sense of obligation to the past simply vanishes. In Jamesian morality this is not, I think, the case. There will be times when a confrontation with a new situation may lead the perceiver to revise her standing conception of value, deciding that certain prima facie obligations are not really binding here. But this never takes the form of leaping above or simply sailing around the standing commitments. And if the perceiver, examining these commitments, decides that they do in fact bind her, then no free departures will be permitted, and the effort of perception will be an effort of fidelity to all elements of the situation, a tense and labored effort not to let anyone down. It is not open to Maggie, as perceiver, to turn her back upon her father, not open to him to depart from her. The task of "the whole process of their mutual vigilance" (II.267) is to know "that their thin wall might be pierced by the lightest wrong touch" (II.267); good improvisation preserves, and does not rend, that "exquisite tissue."

How, then, are concrete perceptions prior? (In what sense are the descriptions of the novelist higher, more alert, than the standing terms?) We can see, first, that without the ability to respond to and resourcefully interpret the concrete particulars of their context, Maggie and Adam could not begin to figure out which rules and standing commitments are operative here. Situations are all highly concrete, and they do not present themselves with duty labels on them. Without the abilities of perception, duty is blind and therefore powerless. (Bob Assingham has no connection with the moral realities about him until he seeks the help of his wife's too fanciful but indispensable eyes.)

Second, a person armed only with the standing terms—armed only with general principles and rules—would, even if she managed to apply them to the concrete case, be insufficiently equipped by them to act rightly in it. It is not just that the standing terms need to be rendered more precise in their application to a concrete text. It is that, all by themselves, they might get it all wrong; they do not suffice to make the difference between right and wrong. Here, to sacrifice in the wrong words with the wrong tone of voice at the wrong time would be worse, perhaps, than not sacrificing at all. And I do not mean wrong as judged by some fortuitous and unforeseeable consequences for which we could not hold Adam responsible. I mean wrong in itself, wrong of him. He is responsible here for getting the detail of his context for the context it is, for making sure that nothing is lost on him, for feeling fully, for getting the tone right. Obtuseness is a moral failing; its opposite can be cultivated. By themselves, trusted for and in themselves, the standing terms are a recipe for obtuseness. To respond "at the right times, with reference to the right objects, towards the right people, with the right aim, and in the right way, is what is appropriate and best, and this is characteristic of excellence" (Aristotle *EN* 1106b21–23).

Finally, there are elements in their good action that cannot even in principle be captured in antecedent "standing" formulations, however right and precise—either because they are surprising and new, or because they are irreducibly particular. The fine Jamesian perceiver employs general terms and conceptions in an open-ended, evolving way, prepared to see and respond to any new feature that the scene brings forward. Maggie sees the way Adam is transforming their relationship and responds to it as the heroic piece of moral creation it is—like an improvising actress taking what the other actor gives and going with it. All this she could not have done had she viewed the new situation simply as the scene for the application of antecedent rules. Nor can we omit the fact that the particularity of this pair and their history enter into their thought as of the highest moral relevance. We could not rewrite the scene, omitting the particularity of Maggie and Adam, without finding ourselves (appropriately) at sea as to who should do what. Again, to confine ourselves to the universal is a recipe for obtuseness. (Even the good use of rules themselves cannot be seen in isolation from their relation to perceptions.)

If this view of morality is taken seriously and if we wish to have texts that represent it at its best (in order to anticipate or supplement experience or to assess this norm against others), it seems difficult not to conclude that we will need to turn to texts no less elaborate, no less linguistically fine-tuned, concrete, and intensely focused, no less metaphorically resourceful, than this novel.[9]

III

The dialogue between perception and rule is evidently a subject to which James devoted much thought in designing *The Golden Bowl*. For he places between us and "the deeply involved and immersed and more or less bleeding participants" (I.vi) two characters who perform the function, more or less, of a Greek tragic chorus. "Participators by a fond attention" (*AN* 62) just as we are (Fanny alone of all the characters is referred to as "our friend" (II.162)), they perform, together, an activity of attending and judging and interpreting that is parallel to ours, if even more deeply immersed and implicated. James has selected for his "chorus" neither a large group nor a solitary consciousness but a married couple, profoundly different in their approaches to ethical problems but joined by affection into a common effort of vision. In his depiction of their effort to see truly, he allows us to see more deeply into the relationship between the fine-tuned perception of particulars and a rule-governed concern for general obligations: how each, taken by itself, is insufficient for moral accuracy; how (and why) the particular, if insufficient, is nonetheless prior; and how a dialogue between the two, prepared by love, can find a common "basis" for moral judgment.

Bob Assingham is a man devoted to rules and to general conceptions. He permits himself neither surprise nor bewilderment—in large part because he does not permit himself to see particularity:

9. For related arguments, see "Flawed Crystals," *Fragility,* chaps. 1, 2, 6, 10; and "Discernment," this volume.

His wife accused him of a want alike of moral and intellectual reaction, or rather indeed of a complete incapacity for either. . . . The infirmities, the predicaments of men neither surprised nor shocked him, and indeed—which was perhaps his only real loss in a thrifty career—scarce even amused; he took them for granted without horror, classifying them after their kind and calculating results and chances. (I.67)

Because he allows himself to see only what can be classified beforehand under a general term, he cannot have any moral responsibilities—including amusement—that require recognition of nuance and idiosyncrasy. (By presenting him for *our* amusement, as a character idiosyncratic and unique, James reminds us of the difference between the novelist's sense of life and his.)

Fanny, on the other hand, takes fine-tuned perception to a dangerously rootless extreme. She refuses to such an extent the guidance of general rules that she is able to regard the complicated people and predicaments of her world with an aestheticizing love, as "her finest flower-beds"—across which he is, to her displeasure, always taking "short cuts" (I.367). She delights in the complexity of these particulars for its own sake, without sufficiently feeling the pull of a moral obligation to any. And because she denies herself the general classifications that are the whole of his vision, she lacks his straight guidance from the past. Her imagination too freely strays, embroiders, embellishes. By showing us these two characters and the different inadequacies of their attempts to see and judge what stands before them, James asks hard questions about his own idea of fine awareness. He shows how, pressed in the wrong way, it can lead to self-indulgent fantasy; he acknowledges, in Bob, "the truth of his plain vision, the very plainness of which was its value" (I.284). So he suggests to us (what we also see in his protagonists, though less distinctly) that perception is not a self-sufficient form of practical reasoning, set above others by its style alone. Its moral value is not independent of its content, which should accurately connect itself with the agent's moral and social education. This content is frequently well preserved, at least in general outline, in the plain man's attachment to common-sense moral values, which will often thus give reasonable guidance as to where we might start looking for the right particular choice.

And in a scene of confrontation between Bob and Fanny, James shows us how a shared moral "basis," a responsible vision, can be constructed through the dialogue of perception and rule. Fanny has been led to the edge of realization that she has been willfully blind to the real relationship between Charlotte and the Prince. In this chapter (Book Third, Chapter X) she and her husband will acknowledge together what has happened and accept responsibility for nourishing the intrigue by their blindness. This preparation for real dialogue is announced by the contiguity of the metaphors in which they represent themselves to themselves. She, brooding, becomes a "speechless Sphinx"; he is "some old pilgrim of the desert camping at the foot of that monument" (I.364–5). As he stands waiting before her, we begin to sense "a suspension of their old custom of divergent discussion, that intercourse by misunderstanding which had grown so clumsy now" (I.365). She begins to perceive in him a "finer sense" of her moral pain (I.365); and this very sense of her trouble is, on his side, fostered by his old characteristic sense of duty. He imagines her as dangerously voyaging in a fragile boat; and

he responds to this picture, true to his plain, blunt sense of an old soldier's requirement, with the thought that he must then wait for her on "the shore of the
mystic lake; he had . . . stationed himself where she could signal to him at need"
(I.366).

As the scene progresses, this very sense of duty brings him to a gradual acknowledgment of her risk and her trouble—and these elements of his old moral view
combine with anxious love of her to keep him on the scene of her moral effort,
working at a richer and more concrete attention. His sternness, on the other hand,
prevents her from finding an evasive or self-deceptive reading of the situation, an
easy exit; his questions keep her perceptions honest. Bob, while becoming more
"finely aware," never ceases to be himself. Still the duty-bound plain man, but
loving his wife concretely and therefore perceiving one particular troubled spot in
the moral landscape, he begins to attend more lucidly to all of it; for only in this
way (only by being willing to see the surprising and the new) can he love and help
her: "he had spoken before in this light of a plain man's vision, but he must be
something more than plain man now" (I.375)—Something *more,* and not something *other:* for it is also true that he can help her in *her* effort to perceive well
only by remaining true to the plainness of his vision. Because he sees himself as
on the shore to help her, she cannot evade her presentiment of moral danger. He
keeps her before the general issues, and thus before her own responsibility.

As they move thus toward each other, they begin to share each other's sentences, to fill, by an effort of imagination, each other's gaps (I.368). And they move
from contiguity in images to the inhabiting of a shared picture that expresses a
mutual involvement in moral confrontation and improvisation: they are now
"worldly adventurers, driven for relief under sudden stress to some grim midnight
reckoning in an odd corner" (I.371). A short time later she presents him with a
picture into which he "could enter" (I.374). At the climactic moment, Fanny feels
(as the result of *his* effort) a sharp pain of realized guilt; and Bob, responding with
tenderness to her pain, opens himself fully to her moral adventure, to the concrete
perception of their shared situation. She cries, and he embraces her,

> all with a patience that presently stilled her. Yet the effect of this small crisis, oddly
> enough, was not to close their colloquy, with the natural result of sending them
> to bed: what was between them had opened out further, had somehow, through
> the sharp show of her feeling, taken a positive stride, had entered, as it were, with-
> out more words, the region of the understood, shutting the door after it and bring-
> ing them so still more nearly face to face. They remained for some minutes look-
> ing at it through the dim window which opened upon the world of human trouble
> in general and which let the vague light play here and there upon gilt and crystal
> and colour, the florid features, looming dimly, of Fanny's drawing-room. And the
> beauty of what thus passed between them, passed with her cry of pain, with her
> burst of tears, with his wonderment and his kindness and his comfort, with the
> moments of their silence, above all, which might have represented their sinking
> together, hand in hand, for a time, into the mystic lake where he had begun, as
> we have hinted, by seeing her paddle alone—the beauty of it was that they now
> could really talk better than before, because the basis had at last once for all
> defined itself. . . . He conveyed to her now, at all events, by refusing her no gen-
> tleness, that he had sufficiently got the tip and that the tip was all he had wanted.
> (I.378–79).

Both plainness and perception, both sternness and bewilderment, contribute to the found "basis." Perception is still, however, prior. They are, at the end, in the "mystic lake" together, not upon the dry shore. To bring himself to her he has had to immerse himself, to feel the mystery of the particular, leaving off his antecedent "classifying" and "editing." The "basis" itself is not a rule but a concrete way of seeing a concrete case. He could see nothing in this case until he learned her abilities; and he was able to learn them only because there was already something in him that went beyond the universal, namely, a loving, and therefore particular, vision of her. The dialogue between his rules and her perceptions is motivated and sustained by a love that is itself in the sphere of perception, that antecedes any moral agreement. James suggests that if, as members of moral communities, we are to achieve shared perceptions of the actual, we had better love one another first, in all our disagreements and our qualitative differences. Like Aristotle, he seems to say that civic love comes before, and nourishes, civic justice. And he reminds us, too, of Aristotle's idea that a child who is going to develop into a person capable of perception must begin life with a loving perception of its individual parents, and by receiving their highly individualized love. Perception seems to be prior even in time; it motivates and sustains the whole enterprise of living by a shared general picture.

Finally, James's talk (or Bob's talk) of "getting the tip" shows us what moral exchange and moral learning can be, inside a morality based on perception. Progress comes not from the teaching of an abstract law but by leading the friend, or child, or loved one—by a word, by a story, by an image—to see some new aspect of the concrete case at hand, to see it as this or that. Giving a "tip" is to give a gentle hint about how one might see. The "tip," here, is given not in words at all but in a sudden show of feeling. It is concrete, and it prompts the recognition of the concrete.[10]

I have already argued that Jamesian perceiving and correct acting require James's artful prose for their expression. Now I can go further, claiming that the moral role of rules themselves, in this conception, can only be shown inside a story that situates rules in their appropriate place vis-à-vis perceptions. If we are to assess the claim that correct judgment is the outcome of a dialogue between antecedent principle and new vision, we need to see the view embodied in prose that does not take away the very complexity and indeterminacy of choice that gives substance to the view. The moral work involved in giving and getting "the tip" could hardly be shown us in a work of formal decision theory; it could not be shown in any abstract philosophical prose, since it is so much a matter of learning the right sort of vision of the concrete. It could not be shown well even in a phi-

10. Compare Ludwig Wittgenstein, *Philosophical Investigations,* trans. G.E.M. Anscombe (New York, 1968) Part II, Sect. 11, 227e:

Correcter prognoses will generally issue from the judgments of those with better knowledge of mankind.

Can one learn this knowledge? Yes; some can. Not, however, by taking a course in it, but through *"experience."* —Can someone else be a man's teacher in this? Certainly. From time to time he gives him the right *tip.* —This is what "learning" and "teaching" are like here. —What one acquires here is not a technique; one learns correct judgments. There are also rules, but they do not form a system, and only experienced people can apply them right. Unlike calculating-rules.

What is most difficult here is to put this indefiniteness, correctly and unfalsified, into words.

losopher's example, inasmuch as an example would lack the full specificity, and also the indeterminacy, of the literary case, its rich metaphors and pictures, its ways of telling us how characters come to see one another as this or that and come to attend to new aspects of their situation. In the preface to this novel, James speaks of the "duty" of "responsible prose" to be, "while placed before us, good enough, interesting enough and, if the question be of picture, pictorial enough, above all *in itself*" (I.ix–x). The prose of *The Golden Bowl* fulfills this duty.

I say that this prose itself displays a view of moral attention. It is natural, then, to inquire about the status of my commentary, which supplements the text and claims to say why the text is philosophically important. Could I, in fact, have stopped with the quotation of these chapters, or the whole novel, dropping my commentary on it? Or: is there any room left here for a philosophical criticism of literature?

The text itself displays, and is, a high kind of moral activity. But, I think, it does not itself, self-sufficiently, set itself beside other conceptions of moral attention and explain its differences from them, explaining, for example, why a course in "moral reasoning" that relied only on abstract or technical materials, omitting texts like this one, would be missing a great part of our moral adventure. The philosophical explanation acts, here, as the ally of the literary text, sketching out its relation to other forms of moral writing. I find that the critical and distinction-making skills usually associated (not inaccurately) with philosophy do have a substantial role to play here—if they are willing to assume a posture of sufficient humility. As Aristotle tells us, a philosophical account that gives such importance to concrete particulars must be humble about itself, claiming only to offer an "outline" or a "sketch" that directs us to salient features of our moral life. The real content of that life is not found in that outline, except insofar as it quotes from or attentively reconstructs the literary text. And even to be the ally of literature—not to negate the very view of the moral life for which it is arguing—the philosopher's prose may have to diverge from some traditional philosophical styles, toward greater suggestiveness. And yet, so long as the temptation to avoid the insights of *The Golden Bowl* is with us—and it will, no doubt, be with us so long as we long for an end to surprise and bewilderment, for a life that is safer and simpler than life is—we will, I think, need to have such "outlines," which, by their greater explicitness, return us to our wonder before the complexities of the novel, and before our own active sense of life.[11]

IV

We must now investigate more closely James's analogy between morality and art and its further implications for the moral status of this text. I speak first of the relationship between moral attention and attention to a work of art; then of the relationship between artistic creation and moral achievement.

Maggie begins, as I argued elsewhere, by viewing people as fine art objects in a way that distances her conveniently from their human and frequently conflicting demands. As she matures, however, she makes a more mature use of the analogy;

11. I develop this point further in "Love's Knowledge," in this volume.

she does not drop it.[12] At the novel's end, her ability to view the other people as composing a kind of living, breathing painting, her attention to them as a response to this work (cf. II.236–38), expresses her commitment to several features of James's moral ideal which are by now familiar to us: a respect for the irreducibly particular character of a concrete moral context and the agents who are its components; a determination to scrutinize all aspects of this particular with intensely focused perception; a determination to care for it as a whole. We see, too, her determination to be guided by the tender and gentle emotions, rather than the blinding, blunt, and coarse—by impartial love for them all and not by "the vulgar heat of her wrong" (236).

But this conception of moral attention implies that the moral/aesthetic analogy is also more than analogy. For (as James frequently reminds us by his use of the author/reader "we") our own attention to his characters will itself, if we read well, be a high case of moral attention. "Participators by a fond attention" (AN 62) in the lives and dilemmas of his participants, we engage with them in a loving scrutiny of appearances. We actively care for their particularity, and we strain to be people on whom none of their subtleties are lost, in intellect and feeling. So if James is right about what moral attention is, then he can fairly claim that a novel such as this one not only shows it better than an abstract treatise, it also elicits it. It calls forth our "active sense of life," which is our moral faculty. The characters' "emotions, their stirred intelligence, their moral consciousness, become thus, by sufficiently charmed perusal, our own very adventure" (AN 70). By identifying with them and allowing ourselves to be surprised (an attitude of mind that storytelling fosters and develops), we become more responsive to our own life's adventure, more willing to see and to be touched by life.

But surely, we object, a person who is obtuse in life will also be an obtuse reader of James's text. How can literature show us or train us in anything, when, as we have said, the very moral abilities that make for good reading are the ones that are allegedly in need of development? James's artistic analogy has already, I think, shown us an answer to this question. When we examine our own lives, we have so many obstacles to correct vision, so many motives to blindness and stupidity. The"vulgar heat" of jealousy and personal interest comes between us and the loving perception of each particular. A novel, just because it is not our life, places us in a moral position that is favorable for perception and it shows us what it would be like to take up that position in life. We find here love without possessiveness, attention without bias, involvement without panic. Our moral abilities must be developed to a certain degree, certainly, before we can approach this novel at all and see anything in it. But it does not seem far-fetched to claim that most of us can read James better than we can read ourselves.

The creation side of the analogy is succinctly expressed in James's claim that "to 'put' things is very exactly and responsibly and interminably to do them" (I.xxiv). The claim has, in turn, two aspects. First, it is a claim about the moral responsibility of the novelist, who is bound, drawing on his sense of life, to render

---

12. For development of this point, see Patrick Gardiner's reply to "Flawed Crystals," *New Literary History* 15 (1983) 179–84; the main points of my reply to him (*NLH* 201–8) are summarized in the endnote to "Flawed Crystals."

the world of value with lucidity, alert and winged. To "put" things is to do an assessible action. The author's conduct is *like* moral conduct at its best, as we have begun to see. But it is more than like it. The artist's task *is* a moral task. By so much as the world is rendered well by some such artist, by so much do we "get the best there is of it, and by so much as it falls within the scope of a denser and duller, a more vulgar and more shallow capacity, do we get a picture dim and meagre" (*AN* 67).[13] The whole moral content of the work expresses the artist's sense of life; and for the excellence of this the novelist is, in James's view, rightly held (morally) accountable:

> The question comes back thus, obviously, to the kind and the degree of the artist's prime sensibility, which is the soil out of which his subject springs. The quality and capacity of that soil, its ability to "grow" with due freshness and straightness any vision of life, represents, strongly or weakly, the projected morality. (*AN* 45)

On the other side, the most exact and responsible way of doing is, in fact, a "putting": an achievement of the precisely right description, the correct nuance of tone. Moral experience is an interpretation of the seen, "our apprehension and our measure of what happens to us as social creatures" (*AN* 64–65). Good moral experience is a lucid apprehension. Like the imaginings and doings of Maggie and Adam it has precision rather than flatness, sharpness rather than vagueness. It is "the union of whatever fulness with whatever clearness" (*AN* 240). Not that indeterminacy and mystery are not also there, when the context presents them, as so often in human life it does. But then the thing is to respond to that with the right "*quality* of bewilderment" (*AN* 66), intense and striving.

Again we can see that there is more than analogy here. Our whole moral task, whether it issues in the words of *The Golden Bowl* or in Maisie's less verbally articulated but no less responsive and intense imaginings, is to make a fine artistic creation. James does not give linguistic representation pride of place: he insists that there is something fine that Maisie's imagination creatively does, which is rightly rendered in his words, even though Maisie herself could not have found those words. Perceptions need not be verbal (*AN* 145). But he does insist that our whole conduct is *some* form of artistic "putting" and that its assessible virtues are also those for which we look to the novelist.

Two clarifications are in order. First, this is not an aestheticization of the moral; for the creative artist's task is, for James, above all moral, "the expression, the literal squeezing out of value" (*AN* 312). Second, to call conduct a creation in no way points toward a rootless relativism. For James's idea of creation (like Aristotle's idea of improvisation) is that it is thoroughly committed to the real. "Art deals with what we see . . . it plucks its material in the garden of life "(*AN* 312). The Jamesian artist does not feel free to create just anything at all: he imagines himself as straining to get it right, not to miss anything, to be keen rather than obtuse. He approaches the material of life armed with the moral and expressive skills that will allow him to "squeeze out" the value that is there.

---

13. This claim, in context, is actually about the novel's hero or heroine. But it is applied elsewhere to the author: see "Flawed Crystals," this volume.

This ideal makes room, then, for a norm or norms of rightness and for a substantial account of ethical objectivity. The objectivity in question is "internal" and human. It does not even attempt to approach the world as it might be in itself, uninterpreted, unhumanized. Its raw material is the history of human social experience, which is already an interpretation and a measure. But it is objectivity all the same. And that is what makes the person who does the artist's task well so important for others. In the war against moral obtuseness, the artist is our fellow fighter, frequently our guide. We can develop, here, the analogy with our sensory powers that the term *perception* already suggests. In seeing and hearing we are, I believe, seeing not the world as it is in itself, apart from human beings and human conceptual schemes, but a world already interpreted and humanized by our faculties and our concepts. And yet, who could deny that there are some among us whose visual or auditory acuity is greater than that of others; some who have developed their faculties more finely, who can make discriminations of color and shape (of pitch and timbre) that are unavailable to the rest of us? who miss less, therefore, of what is to be heard or seen in a landscape, a symphony, a painting? Jamesian moral perception is, I think, like this: a fine development of our human capabilities to see and feel and judge; an ability to miss less, to be responsible to more.[14]

V

Is this norm practical? Is there any sense to claiming that the consciousness of a Maggie Verver or a Strether can be paradigmatic of our own responsible conduct? In short (James reports a critic's question), "Where on earth, where roundabout us at this hour," has he found such "supersubtle fry" (*AN* 221)? And if they are not found, but "squeezed out" from coarser matter by the pressure of the artist's hand, how can they be exemplary for us? James's answer is complex. He grants, first, that he cannot easily cite such examples from daily life (*AN* 222). He insists, on the other hand, that these characters do not go so far beyond actual life that their lucidity makes them "spoiled for us," "knowing too much and feeling too much ... for their remaining 'natural' and typical, for their having the needful communities with our own precious liability to fall into traps and be bewildered" (*AN* 63). Like Aristotle's tragic heroes,[15] they are high but possible and available, so much so that they can be said to be "in *essence* an observed reality" (*AN* 223). And if the life around us today does not show us an abundance of such examples, "then so much the worse for that life" (222).

Here the opponent responds that it surely seems odd and oddly arrogant to suggest that the entire nation is dense and dull and that only Henry James and his characters are finely sensible enough to show us the way. Surely patterns for public life must be nearer to home, straightforwardly descriptive of something that is readily found. James has moved too far away; his sense of life has lost its connec-

14. This view has strong similarities with the view developed in Nelson Goodman's *Ways of Worldmaking* (Indianapolis, Ind., 1978). I am grateful to Goodman for helpful comments on an earlier version.

15. On the Aristotelian hero, see *Fragility,* Interlude 2.

tion with real life. James's answer is that there is no better way to show one's commitment to the fine possibilities of the actual than (in protest "against the rule of the cheap and easy") to create, in imagination, their actualization:

> to *create* the record, in default of any other enjoyment of it: to imagine, in a word, the honourable, the producible case. What better example than this of the high and the helpful public and, as it were, civic use of the imagination? . . . Where is the work of the intelligent painter of life if not precisely in some such aid given to true meanings to be born? He must bear up as he can if it be in consequence laid to him that the flat grows salient and the tangled clear, the common—worst of all!—even amusingly rare, by passing through his hands. (*AN* 223–24)

If he has done this—and I think he has—then these alert winged books are not just irreplaceable fine representations of moral achievement, they are moral achievements on behalf of our community. Like Adam Verver's sacrifice: altruism in the right way at the right time in the right images and the right tone, with the right precision of bewilderment.[16]

Endnote

This essay, taken together with "Discernment" and "Perceptive Equilibrium," provides the collection's argument for holding that, in good deliberation and judgment, the particular is in some sense prior to general rules and principles. "Discernment" (and see also Introduction) distinguishes several different aspects of this Aristotelian thesis; both the present essay and "Perceptive Equilibrium" argue that an approach to ethical judgment that omits awareness of and response to these particular contextual features is deficient. Both this essay and "Discernment," however, insist that an Aristotelian defense of the priority of the particular does not mean discarding the guidance of general principles. Indeed, such rules frequently provide an invaluable sort of steering, without which perception would be dangerously free-floating. This essay's account of Bob and Fanny Assingham shows what I do and do not claim on this point. Nonetheless, the way in which an Aristotelian perception-based morality uses the general is very different from the way of much contemporary moral theory, as the essay tries to show.

It is very important here to distiguish the *general* from the *universal*—see also "Discernment" and Introduction in the section on "The Aristotelian Ethical View." The argument of this essay is directed primarily against the claim of *general* descriptions, and supports the novelist's finely tuned and highly concrete descriptions as providing more of what is morally relevant to the case. To some

16. A shorter version of this article was published under the title, "'Finely Aware and Richly Responsible': Moral Attention and the Moral Task of Literature." *Journal of Philosophy* 82 (1985) 516–29, and presented in an American Philosophical Association Symposium on Morality in Literature, December 29, 1985. On that occasion my commentator was Cora Diamond whose excellent paper, entitled "Missing the Adventure" (abstracted *JPhil* 530ff), has contributed in several ways to the development of my views in the present version.

extent, the ethical rightness of the characters' deliberations here is universalizable, and could be captured by a set of extremely concrete and fine-tuned universal principles, such as those recommended by R. M. Hare. (For references, see Introduction and "Discernment.") In this connection, Hare remarked to me in conversation, "What are novels anyway but universal prescriptions?" And although the remark shocks, and was evidently meant to, one should grant that it has force, in four different ways. First, the novel, insofar as it presents, as Henry James claims, a moral "record" and "projection," presents its particular characters and events as samples of something that *might happen* in a human life (see Aristotle, *Poetics,* chap. 9). Thus, their concrete doings and imaginings take on, through James's conception of the novelist's task, a universal significance. (Proust makes the same claim, much more explicitly.) Second, the moral activity of the reader, as we have described it, involves not only a friendly participation in the adventures of the concrete characters, but also an attempt to see the novel as a paradigm of something that might happen in his or her own life. (For Proust, this involves the suggestion that the reader should "mine" his or her experience for similar material.) Thus, the universalizing tendency of the moral imagination is encouraged by the very activity of novel-reading itself, with its alternations between identification and sympathy.

Third, in our very articulation of what is right in Maggie's and Adam's responses we have strongly implied that two people who had a situation with all the same contextual features, in all of their historical specificity, ought to act, in many cases at least, in the same way. Our judgment that what has gone on is right and justified was a judgment that it was an appropriate response to those described features; and this judgment surely involves some such element of universalizing.

Fourth, we must grant that the language of the novelist is, as Nietzsche too pejoratively puts it, "herd language": that is, even the "alert winged creatures" are public and shared items, common to all who read the language. Thus, one might worry that in the end there is a level and kind of particularity that even this language cannot express. The novel, as "Narrative Emotions" and "Steerforth's Arm" argue, is a cultural construct that itself helps to constitute its readers as social beings. It uses the language of community, and joins readers with both characters and author (and with one another) in bonds of community. This observation will trouble us—make us feel that there is something profound that the novel cannot capture—only if, with Beckett's characters, we believe that what is most personal and most fundamental about each human life is not shared and sharable. The novel takes its stand with Aristotle, that human beings are fundamentally social; I believe this, and it is one of the origins of my own interest in the novel. We should grant that the recognition of this lends support to Hare's claim.

On the other side, however, we must enter several qualifications. First, it is extremely important to insist, once again, that the universalizing we do when we read a novel like this one involves very little generalizing. The person who, reading this scene, concluded from it that "All daughters should treat their fathers as Maggie treats Adam here," would have shown herself a blunt reader indeed. The reading I have presented suggests, instead, that "any daughter with Maggie's history and character who has a father with Adam's history and character (where this would be filled in by a very long and probably open-ended set of descriptions), should, if placed in a situation exactly like this one, respond as Maggie responds here." It also suggests, more pertinently, "All daughters should treat their fathers with the same level of sensitivity to the father's concrete character and situation, and to the particularities of their histories, that Maggie displays here." The universalizing, in the latter case, provided not a principle, but a direction of thought and imagination.

Second, we must point out that beyond a certain point the recognition of the moral relevance of so many concrete features makes the whole idea of universalizing seem peculiar. At the very least, the "principles" that such universalizing generates are not likely to provide the sort of fixity, uniformity, and before-the-fact guidance that defenders of the universal have usually sought. But we can also say that some of the morally relevant descriptions the novelist gives, especially descriptions of features of personal character and history, seem so essential to the individual person depicted that the idea of imagining *another* person like that begins to lose its coherence. The defender of the universal in such cases needs a theory of personal identity to support his or her claim that this thought experiment is coherent; and it seems to me that the best theory we could find might well not be one that would support Hare's project here.

We can also add that where love is concerned, the attachment to the particular seems to contain, as an essential element, the thought that this person is not replaceable, is the only one who will occupy exactly this relation. (See also Introduction and "Discernment.") Would, or should, Maggie accept as a replacement for her father a substitute who had all the same descriptive features? Surely not without the same history. But even a person who shared, descriptively, the same history (let us say, with a daughter in a twin world who shared all of Maggie's descriptive features) should not, one feels, be acceptable to her as a substitute for Adam, and an object of the very same judgment. It is this very one, the very one she has lived with and loves, and no other, that she wants; and it is this one and no other about whom she judges. Hare's view, though far more sensitive to this sort of concern than most Kantian and utilitarian views, does not, it seems to me, accommodate this intuition, and is required to reject it as unethical and perhaps even irrational. I don't think it is. The novelist's vision, on the other hand, endorses it as an essential part of complete rationality in such situations. Human life is lived only once, in a single direction; and some love is the love of something that is essentially, ineliminably, and rationally seen as unique.

Perceptive Equilibrium:
Literary Theory and Ethical Theory

Mrs. Newsome's dress was never in any degree 'cut down', and she never wore round her throat a broad red velvet band: if she had, moreover, would it ever have served so to carry on and complicate, as he now almost felt, his vision?[1]

Henry James, *The Ambassadors*

Speaking to Little Bilham about Chad Newsome's surprising development, Strether describes his own viewpoint and his interest:

I'm speaking—in connexion with her—of his manners and morals, his character and life. I'm speaking of him as a person to deal with and talk with and live with—speaking of him as a social animal. (I.283)

The speech of literary theory, especially in recent years, has not often shared Strether's concerns and connections. I believe that it has an impoverished future without them. I imagine, instead, a future in which our talk about literature will return, increasingly, to a concern with the practical—to the ethical and social questions that give literature its high importance in our lives. A future in which these interests, like Strether's here, will find themselves connected to an interest in Mme. de Vionnet—in, that is, those emotions and desires that do not reside harmoniously within the domain of ethical judgment. In which a literary–philosophical inquiry, with something like Strether's "candour of fancy" (I.52) and his "conscientious wonder" (I.49), will ask what literary works express about these matters—express in virtue of their "content," but also, and inseparably, in virtue of their forms and structures, their ways of describing, since those ways are "at all times" (as Strether "philosophized") "the very conditions of perception, the terms of thought" (II.49). In short, a future in which literary theory (while not forgetting its many other pursuits) will also join with ethical theory in pursuit of the question, "How should one live?"

1. Henry James, *The Ambassadors,* New York Edition (New York: Charles Scribner's Sons, 1907–9), Vol. I.50. All page references will be to this (two-volume) edition.

Join, I mean, not as didactic moralist but as both devious ally and subversive critic. For we notice that Strether's answer contrasts his own fuller perception of Chad with the narrow moralizing vision of Woollett, Massachusetts. And before the assault of Strether's crowded perceptions those of us who are drawn to systematic ethical theorizing will be likely to feel, as he does, that "an inexorable tide of light seems to have floated us into our perhaps still queerer knowledge" (II.201).

The Absence of the Ethical

Recent literary theory has taken a keen interest in philosophy. In fact, it is hard to distinguish it from philosophy, either by the nature of its questions or by the names to which it turns for illumination. Questions about realism, relativism, and subjectivism; about skepticism and justification; about the nature of language—these are now common ground between the two professions. And in pursuit of these questions literary theory discusses and teaches not only the work of philosophers who write directly about literary matters (e.g., Nietzsche, Heidegger, Hans-Georg Gadamer, Stanley Cavell, Nelson Goodman, Hilary Putnam), but also the ideas of many (e.g., W.V.O. Quine, Paul Feyerabend, S. A. Kripke, Thomas Kuhn, Jürgen Habermas) who do not. (These lists, intentionally eclectic, show, too, the diversity of the philosophical styles and methods that have influenced the current literary scene.) Indeed, with several prominent contemporary figures—above all Jacques Derrida and Richard Rorty—there is no clear answer to the question, to which profession do they belong? The question, indeed, loses its interest, since the professions share so many issues, and since differences about method are internal to each group, rather than divided simply along disciplinary lines.

But when we turn from epistemology to ethics, the situation is very different. This is a rich and wonderful time in moral philosophy.[2] One cannot find for generations—since the time of John Stuart Mill, if not earlier—an era in which there has been so much excellent, adventurous, and varied work on the central ethical and political questions of human life. Questions about justice, about well-being and social distribution, about moral realism and relativism, about the nature of rationality, about the concept of the person, about the emotions and desires, about

2. Throughout this essay, I tend to use the term "ethical theory" rather than "moral theory," since the former does not suggest a divison of human values into two distinct groups, the moral and the nonmoral. On this division and some reasons for questioning it, see B. Williams, *Ethics and the Limits of Philosophy* (Cambridge, Mass., 1985), and Nussbaum, *Fragility,* chaps. 1 and 2. I use the term "moral philosophy" here simply because no corresponding term "ethical philosophy" is in use (as both ethical theory and moral theory are). My use of the distinction between ethical theory and moral philosophy is closely related to Rawls's use of a distinction between moral theory and moral philosophy: see J. Rawls, *A Theory of Justice* (Cambridge, Mass., 1971) 46ff. Moral philosophy is a general and inclusive rubric covering, in principle, many different types of ethical investigations, of which one sort is the theoretical study of substantive ethical positions, or ethical (moral) theory. A consequence of this distinction for my project is that an ethical investigation that is not systematic and theoretical, and therefore not ethical theory, might still lie within moral philosophy. It was with this broad understanding of moral philosophy that I argued, in "Flawed Crystals," that certain works of literature are part of moral philosophy. See also the Introduction in this volume.

the role of luck in human life—all these and others are debated from many sides with considerable excitement and even urgency. These philosophical debates have frequently become interdisciplinary, touching as they do on human issues that are central to more than one field of study. On the emotions, for example, moral philosophers have a lively dialogue with psychologists; on moral relativism, with cultural anthropologists; on rationality and well-being, with economists. One would certainly expect that literature and theory about literature would play a role in these debates. For literature offers us insight on all of these questions, and in a way that is inextricable from literary forms. So one would expect that the people whose profession it is to think in general about literature and its forms would speak to these issues and join in these public debates.

This, we know, has not happened. Literary criticism dealing with particular texts and authors continues, of course, to speak about the ethical and social concerns that are central to those authors. But even this sort of concern has been constrained by pressure of the current thought that to discuss a text's ethical or social content is somehow to neglect "textuality," the complex relationships of that text with other texts; and of the related, though more extreme, thought that texts do not refer to human life at all, but only to other texts and to themselves.[3] And if one turns from criticism to more general and theoretical writing about literature, the ethical vanishes more or less altogether. One way we perceive this is by considering the philosophical references. Philosophers' names constantly appear. But the names of the leading moral and political philosophers of our day—of John Rawls, Bernard Williams, Thomas Nagel, Derek Parfit, Judith Jarvis Thomson, and many others—and also the names of the great moral philosophers of the past—of Mill, Bentham, Henry Sidgwick, Rousseau, of the ethical sides of Plato, Aristotle, Hume, and Kant—do not appear, more or less, at all. (This is strikingly true even of those recent moral philosophers, such as Bernard Williams, Hilary Putnam, and Iris Murdoch, who have criticized systematic ethical theory in ways that lead them to ally themselves with literature.) These writers about ethics are not studied in literary theory programs, as their epistemological and metaphysical companions are; those among them (past and present) who write on both ethics and epistemology are studied one-sidedly. In short, these diverse and excellent analyses of human social experience are usually not taken to have any interesting bearing on the activity of the theorist.

Literary theory could neglect moral philosophy and still show a keen interest in the ethical—though I shall later offer, tentatively, some reasons why a turn to philosophy can offer valuable illumination here. But in the midst of all this busy concern with other types of philosophy, the absence of moral philosophy seems a significant sign. And in fact it signals a further striking absence: the absence, from literary theory, of the organizing questions of moral philosophy, and of moral philosophy's sense of urgency about these questions. The sense that we are social beings puzzling out, in times of great moral difficulty, what might be, for us, the best way to live—this sense of practical importance, which animates contemporary ethical theory and has always animated much of great literature, is absent

---

3. See Arthur Danto, "Philosophy As/And/Of Literature," *Proceedings and Addresses of the American Philosophical Association* 58 (1984) 5–20.

from the writings of many of our leading literary theorists. One can have no clearer single measure of this absence than to have the experience of reading Jacques Derrida's *Éperons*[4] after reading Nietzsche. Once one has worked through and been suitably (I think) impressed by Derrida's perceptive and witty analysis of Nietzsche's style, one feels, at the end of all the urbanity, an empty longing amounting to a hunger, a longing for the sense of difficulty and risk and practical urgency that are inseparable from Zarathustra's dance. A longing for some acknowledgment of the fact that Nietzsche saw a crisis at hand for Europe, for all of human life; that he thought it mattered deeply whether one lived as a Christian or in some other as yet unspecified way; and that he dedicated his career to imagining that way. Nietzsche's work is profoundly critical of existing ethical theory, clearly; but it is, inter alia, a response to the original Socratic question, "How should one live?" Derrida does not touch on that question. "Of all that is written," says Zarathustra, "I love only what a man has written with his blood."[5] After reading Derrida, and not Derrida alone, I feel a certain hunger for blood; for, that is, writing about literature that talks of human lives and choices as if they matter to us all.[6]

This is, after all, the spirit in which much of great literature has been and is written and read. We do approach literature for play and for delight, for the exhilaration of following the dance of form and unraveling webs of textual connection. (Though even here I would not be quick to grant that there is any coherence to an account of aesthetic pleasure that abstracts altogether from our practical human interests and desires.) But one of the things that makes literature something deeper and more central for us than a complex game, deeper even than those games, for example chess and tennis, that move us to wonder by their complex beauty, is that it speaks like Strether. It speaks *about us,* about our lives and choices and emotions, about our social existence and the totality of our connections.[7] As Aristotle observed, it is deep, and conducive to our inquiry about how to live, because it does not simply (as history does) record that this or that event happened; it searches for patterns of possibility—of choice, and circumstance, and the interaction between choice and circumstance—that turn up in human lives with such a persistence that they must be regarded as *our* possibilities. And so our interest in literature becomes (like Strether's in Chad) cognitive: an interest in finding out (by seeing and feeling the otherwise perceiving) what possibilities (and tragic impossibilities) life offers to us, what hopes and fears for ourselves it underwrites or subverts.[8]

To explain how literary theory lost this practical dimension would be a long story. This story would include the influence of Kant's aesthetics; of early twen-

---

4. Jacques Derrida, *Spurs: Nietzsche's Styles,* trans. B. Harlow (Chicago, 1979).

5. F. Nietzsche, *Thus Spoke Zarathustra,* trans. W. Kaufmann (New York, 1966), Part I, "On Reading and Writing."

6. Clearly, feminist criticism and Marxist criticism are major exceptions to the situation described here. But they are, in their difference from and frequent opposition to what surrounds them, exceptions that prove the rule.

7. See Danto, "Philosophy."

8. See *Fragility,* Interlude 2; also H. Putnam, "Literature, Science, and Reflection," in *Meaning and the Moral Sciences* (London, 1979) 83-96.

tieth-century formalism; of the New Criticism. It would include the influence of several prevailing trends in ethical theory as well—above all that of Kantianism and of Utilitarianism, ethical views that in their different ways were so inhospitable to any possible relation with imaginative literature that dialogue was cut off from the side of ethics as well.[9] It would include, too, a critical look at some writing about literature that did, during this long period, keep ethical concerns in view. For much of this writing has understandably given ethical writing about literature a bad name, by its neglect of literary form and its reductive moralizing manner. It has been easy enough to feel that ethical writing must do violence to the literary work. Of course it should have been obvious that to concentrate on form to the neglect of the work's sense of life and choice is not a solution, only violence of a different sort. It should have been recognized that neither sort of violence is required: that we grasp the practical content of a literary text adequately only when we attentively study the forms in which it is embodied and expressed; and that, in turn, we have not correctly described the literary form of, say, a James novel if we have not asked what sense of life it expresses. But, with certain striking exceptions,[10] this was on the whole not acknowledged; and we can see the historical reasons why.

One important task for a future literary theory, as I see it, will be to write out this history in detail. I shall not attempt that task here. I shall instead begin on a different part of the enterprise that I imagine. By bringing one example forward in a certain amount of detail, I shall try to illustrate this idea of a literary theory that works together with ethical theory, sketching out some of the concerns this theory might have; and I shall suggest ways in which a dialogue with moral philosophers might help us develop them. It will be no surprise by this point in the argument that I shall talk about James's *The Ambassadors,* which I take to be a major work in moral philosophy—talking about what it is to be assailed by a perception, about how the character of Mrs. Newsome's gown points to a deficiency in some accounts of ethical rationality that even now influence our daily lives.

Reflective Equilibrium

But before we can begin to talk of Strether we need some story, however sketchy and incomplete, about the enterprise in which I propose to join literary theory with ethical theory.[11] For some enterprises, and some descriptions of this one, will demote one or the other party to the partnership. The very difficulty of discovering a nonprejudicial description of the task of ethical inquiry will itself illuminate our problem; and the concealed prejudices in some prominent contemporary philo-

---

9. On this see "Discernment," in this volume.

10. I think, first, of F. R. Leavis and Lionel Trilling (see nn. 42 and 43); see also, more recently, Peter Brooks, *Reading for the Plot* (New York, 1984), Martin Price, *Forms of Life: Character and the Moral Imagination in the Novel* (New Haven, Conn., 1983); and especially Wayne Booth, *The Company We Keep: An Ethics of Fiction* (Berkeley, 1988).

11. Compare my sketch of an ethical inquiry in "Flawed Crystals," and also *Fragility,* chaps. 1 and 8; and see also Introduction. A related picture is developed, with greater skepticism, in Cora Diamond, "Having a Rough Story About What Moral Philosophy Is," *New Literary History* 15 (1983) 155–70.

sophical descriptions of the task will begin to show us what moral philosophy has lost through the absence of dialogue with literary thought.

I have said that the question with which my projected literary–ethical inquiry begins is the question, "How should one live?"[12] This choice of starting point is significant. This question does not (like the Kantian question, "What is my moral duty?") assume that there is a sphere of "moral" values that can be separated off from all the other practical values that figure in a human life. Nor does it assume, as does the utilitarian's focus on the question, "How shall I maximize utility?" that the value of all choices and actions is to be assessed in terms of a certain sort of consequence that they tend to promote. It does not assume the denial of these claims either. So far it is neutral, leaving them for investigation inside the inquiry. The point is to state the opening question in a general and inclusive way, excluding at the start no major story about the good life for human beings.

The inquiry asks, then, what it is for a human being to live well. This investigation as I imagine it, is both empirical and practical. Empirical in that it is based on and responsible to actual human experience; it aims to elicit an "intelligent report," as James puts it, of that experience—that is, of "our apprehension and our measure of what happens to us as social beings."[13] (It is not, as Kant thought, a priori.) Practical in that it is conducted by people who are themselves involved in acting and choosing and who see the inquiry as having a bearing on their own practical ends. They do not inquire in a "pure" or detached manner, asking what the truth about ethical value might be as if they were asking for a description of some separately existing Platonic reality. They are looking for something in human life, something, in fact, that they themselves are going to try to bring about in their lives. What they are asking is not what is the good "out there," but what can we best live by, and live together as social beings? Their results are constrained, and appropriately constrained, by their hopes and fears for themselves, their sense of value, what they think they can live with. This does not mean that inquiry cannot substantially modify their antecedent conception of their "target," specifying goals that were vague before and even convincing them to revise in substantial ways their conception of their goal. But their end is practice, not just theory. And inquiry is valuable because it contributes to practice in two ways: by promoting individual clarification and self-understanding, and by moving individuals toward communal attunement.[14] By now this view of procedure should be recognizable as Aristotle's; it has been endorsed and used by later thinkers, such as Henry Sidgwick and, recently and influentially, by John Rawls, in *A Theory of Justice*.[15] It has a good deal in common with Henry James's remarks about his purpose as a novelist.

The central procedural idea is that we work through the major alternative views

12. On this question and its relation to the moral/nonmoral distinction, see Williams, *Ethics,* and Nussbaum, *Fragility,* chap. 1.

13. H. James, Preface to *The Princess Casamassima*—see "Flawed Crystals" and "Perception and Revolution," this volume.

14. I discuss this further in "Therapeutic Arguments: Epicurus and Aristotle," in *The Norms of Nature,* ed. M. Schofield and G. Striker (Cambridge, 1986) 31–74; and also in *The Therapy of Desire,* forthcoming.

15. Rawls, *A Theory,* 46ff. Rawls's discussion refers both to Aristotle and to Henry Sidgwick's *The Methods of Ethics,* 7th ed. (London, 1907).

about the good life, holding them up, in each case, against our own experience and our intuitions. The first step will be to get a perspicuous description of these alternatives (though we should bear in mind that these descriptions will already contain an element of evaluation and response). Prominent among these views will be views embodied in texts of many kinds, both recent and older. Next we notice and clearly describe the conflicts and tensions among the views that we find. Where there is inconsistency or irreconcilable tension—and where this tension corresponds to something that we notice in our own experience and thought (individually or communally)—we aim to revise the overall picture so as to bring it into harmony with itself, preserving, as Aristotle says, "the greatest number and the most basic" of the original judgments and perceptions. There is no rule about how to do this.[16] Individuals simply ask what looks deepest, what they can least live without—guided by their sense of life, and by their standing interest in consistency and in community. That is, they want to arrive at a view that is internally coherent, and also at one that is broadly shared and sharable. (Thus frequently they will move away from a personal claim, even when narrow consistency does not require it, in order to find one on which more of them can agree.) Nothing else is non-negotiable, not even the precise interpretation of these regulative principles themselves. The procedure is holistic:[17] it holds nothing unrevisable, but seeks for coherence and "fit" in the system as a whole.

So far, notice, we have said nothing about what faculties of the person (intellect, imagination, emotion) we trust, or trust most, inside the procedure; nothing, again, about which judgments we would tend to trust more than others; and nothing very concrete about how, and in what result, the procedure comes to an end. This is appropriate, since norms of good (or rational) judgment and appropriate sorting—of the intelligent "reading" of life—are themselves up for debate inside the procedure. But in preparing the way for Henry James's contribution (which I believe to be closely related to Aristotle's), I want to describe a prominent and influential version of the Aristotelian procedure that does add at this point some further (and very un-Aristotelian) specifications. What is interesting for us is that these are added as if they were about as noncontroversial as anything could possibly be; and indeed, within the tradition of modern moral philosophy, this is pretty well true. In *A Theory of Justice*, then, describing the task of moral theory, John Rawls adopts a procedure that he traces explicitly to Aristotle; but he makes three significant additions to the general outline I have reported.[18] First, Rawls gives a name to the desired end of the procedure: it is "reflective equilibrium." This is the condition at which we arrive when we have gone through the procedure; the name suggests balance, an absence of inconsistency or tension, and the dominance of intellectual judgment. Second, he provides an account of "considered judgment" that tells us which judgments to trust and mistrust during the procedure. (He seems to assume from the start that we are using only standing judgments of varying degrees of concreteness, and not immersed situational per-

16. See *Fragility*, chap. 8 and "Discernment"; also Rawls, *A Theory*, 46ff.

17. See Rawls; also the excellent discussion of Rawls's method in Henry Richardson, *Deliberation Is of Ends*, Ph.D. thesis, Harvard University, 1986.

18. Pages 46–53 and 130–35; see also Rawls's Dewey Lectures, "Kantian Constructivism in Ethical Theory," *Journal of Philosophy* 77(1980).

ceptions.)[19] Mistrusted will be "those judgments made with hesitation, or in which we have little confidence. Similarly, those given when we are upset or frightened, or when we stand to gain one way or another can be left aside."[20] This is taken to give us the conditions "in which our moral capacities are most likely to be displayed without distortion."[21] Finally, Rawls later adds five constraints that must be met by any ethical theory that will even be seriously considered during the procedure of scrutiny. These conditions are that its principles should be *general* in form and *universal* in application; that they should be *public* and available to all; that they should impose a general ordering on conflicting claims; and that these principles should be regarded as final and conclusive—"the final court of appeal in practical reasoning." In short, "if we think in terms of the fully general theory which has principles for all the virtues, then such a theory specifies the totality of relevant considerations and their appropriate weights, and its requirements are decisive."[22]

I have said that Rawls regards these requirements, including the final five, as relatively uncontroversial. And so, indeed, they have been, in contemporary debates about his (otherwise controversial) theory. Strether's relation to them is no simple one, as we shall see; much of our work on his story will consist in articulating this (sometimes tragic) relation. And in general we might expect that ethical thought that begins from literature—which, if it shares anything at all, would seem to share a commitment to the ethical relevance of particularity and to the epistemological value of feeling—would not find these limits at all trivial or uncontroversial. Should we indeed aim at a condition of balance or equilibrium? Should this equilibrium indeed be "reflective"—that is, presumably (as Rawls uses the word), a condition that is detached from powerful feeling and from particular situational immersion? Should we in fact exclude our bewilderment and our hesitation from the deliberative process? Should we automatically mistrust the information given us by our fear, or grief, or love? (For being in love would surely count as a case of "being upset.") Should we in fact go for theories that embody generality and universality—rather than saying, with Aristotle, that "the discrimination lies in perception"?[23] Do we believe that a general (rather than a particular) ordering *can* be imposed, and imposed in advance, upon conflicting claims?

19. This is not explicitly stated by Rawls, but is implied in his discussion; it is argued convincingly by Richardson, in a way that seems to have met with Rawls's agreement.

20. Rawls, *A Theory,* 47.

21. Ibid., 47–48.

22. Ibid., p. 135. Since this discussion is not part of the discussion of reflective equilibrium, there is some unclarity as to whether it is supposed to be a part of the general method that we use to consider all theories or is to be understood as a part of the specific account of the moral point of view that is contained in the (Kantian) original position. But since its restrictions are said to "hold for the choice of all ethical principles and not only for those of justice" (p.130), and since they govern the choice of the theories that the parties are even permitted to consider, it seems likely that Rawls regards them as reasonable moral constraints to impose on all practical reasoning, not only the reasoning of the specifically Kantian conception. There is, in any case, some difficulty in disentangling these two levels of Rawls's project, since even the account of "considered judgments" that is explicitly made a part of the general method that we use to consider all alternative conceptions—that that should therefore be fair not only to the Kantian conception but to its rivals as well—has strong affinities with Kantianism. This problem is further discussed in the Dewey Lectures, with no definitive resolution.

23. *Nicomachean Ethics* 1109b18–23 and 1126b2–4; see also "Discernment."

Above all, do we feel that a general system of principles can and should be a court of last appeal in practical reasoning, determining standards all in advance of life itself? In these conditions we begin to sense the austere presence of Mrs. Newsome, "all fine cold thought," impervious to surprise, idealistic and exceptionless in her justice.

Straightness and Surprise

"That's just her difficulty—that she doesn't admit surprises. It's a fact that, I think, describes and represents her; and it falls in with what I tell you—that she's all, as I've called it, fine cold thought. She had, to her own mind, worked the whole thing out in advance, and worked it out for me as well as for herself. Whenever she has done that, you see, there's no room left; no margin, as it were, for any alteration. She's filled as full, packed as tight, as she'll hold, and if you wish to get anything more or different either out or in—"

"You've got to make over altogether the woman herself?"

"What it comes to," said Strether, "is that you've got morally and intellectually to get rid of her." (II.239)

Jame's richly comic portrait of Mrs. Newsome lies at the center of his story of Strether's adventure. Present vividly in her absence, she articulates, by contrast, Strether's moral movement. He begins as her ambassador, the agent of her antecedently fixed moral purpose; he ends as a child "toddling" alone, a diver in depths, a hearer of strange and crowded voices, a floater upon inexorable tides of light. To understand Strether's struggle we must understand *her*—and with a certain sympathy: asking how, for example, her refusal of surprise "falls in" with the fact that she is all fine cold thought; asking, too, why her vision of life appeals to our friend and stirs, as it continually does, his moral imagination.

We notice first and most obviously her moralism, her preoccupation with questions of moral right and wrong, with criticism of offense, with judgment upon vice. "Essentially all moral pressure" (II.198), as Strether describes her, she motivates his own obsession with discipline and punishment, his determination "always, where Lambert Strether was concerned, to know the worst" (II.69). Indeed he is attracted to her, perhaps, just because of "his old tradition, the one he had been brought up on and which even so many years of life had but little worn away; the notion that the state of the wrongdoer, or at least this person's happiness, presented some special difficulty" (II.272). It is no accident that her principles are, for him, embodied in the dream figure of a judging mother who "loom(s) at him larger than life" until "he already felt her come down on him, already burned, under her reprobation, with the blush of guilt. . . . He saw himself, under her direction, recommitted to Woollett as juvenile offenders are committed to reformatories" (II.61).[24] To her obsession with the priority of moral right, which fills, it seems, the entirety of her exalted consciousness (the presence of moral pressure is "almost identical with her own presence" [II.198]), we may add rigorism in her

24. The figure in the dream is actually identified as Sarah Pocock, but she figures here as Mrs. Newsome's ambassador.

conception of principles. Everything in her world must be "straight" (Strether, later, calls her "the whole moral and intellectual being or block"); and her rules of right admit of no softening in the light of the present circumstance, the individual case. "She was the only woman he had known, even at Woollett, as to whom his conviction was positive that to lie was beyond her art": she "refused to human commerce that mitigation of rigor" (I.95). Strether links his thought of her with the idea of an exceptionless justice that dwells outside "in the hard light" (II.5). This moral rigorism, together with the ubiquity of moral assessment, permits her two attitudes only, when confronted with a new occurrence: approval or disapproval. "From the moment they're not delighted," Strether says of her and her new Ambassador Sarah, "they can only be—well what I admit she was" (II.218).

If universal and general principles of right take precedence over (and indeed swallow up) all other elements of life, there are three aspects of human experience that Mrs. Newsome especially dislikes and avoids: emotion, passivity, and the perception of particularity. These items are connected in an interesting and, in a certain sense, profoundly appealing way. Strether describes her as a person who "won't be touched" (II.239); when he imagines her his eyes "might have been fixing some particularly large iceberg in a cool blue northern sea" (II.240); and, as we have seen, he refers to her, in her "tightly packed" fullness, as a "block." Her emotional coldness is seen by him, in these images, as an aspect of her larger impassivity, her resistance to any modification by worldly circumstance. This is why her being all "fine cold thought" "falls in" so well with her resistance to surprises. Solid and purely active as she is (essentially all *pressure* without response), life cannot leave a mark on her. It is not *permitted* to enter in, or to pull anything out. She is, Strether muses, the sort of meal that can be "served cold" (represented by an ambassador) "without its really losing anything" (II.237) of its essential flavor—so little does its character consist in responsiveness to what is at hand.

This connection between absence of emotion and absence of passivity is made long before on behalf of Woollett as a whole, when Strether tells Maria Gostrey, "Woollett isn't sure it ought to enjoy. If it were, it would" (I.16). The first half of this remark is frequently quoted by critics; the second is, I think, even more significant. For it informs us that Woollett conceives of everything valuable in life as activity that can be morally willed. If it *were* sure that enjoyment was its duty, it would set itself to do that duty, it would simply will itself to enjoy. The oddness of this idea reminds us that some of the valuable things in life have more to do with passivity and responsiveness than with active willing; and their connection with "ought" is therefore to be viewed with deep suspicion.

What all this comes to is that the people of Woollett cannot, will not, live in the present moment, confronting the things that life brings their way in all their newness and particularity. They come to a situation determined that it should not touch them, holding their general and rather abstract principles fixed and firm. These principles, the court of last appeal in practical reason, even govern what they may *see* and consider relevant in the new. Particularity of vision brings surprise, surprise passivity and a loss of moral control. Chad is therefore "the youth," Mme. de Vionnet "the Person"; it is already clear beforehand what principles will govern Woollett's dealings with them. Any more personal encounter is made impossible by the nature of the view itself. It comes to what Strether, speaking for the Woollett in himself, calls "the obsession of the other thing": "I'm always considering something else; something else, I mean, than the thing of the moment" (I.19). And this tendency, which strikes Strether with perplexity and even with "terror," is Mrs. Newsome's fineness and her exaltation.

For Mrs. Newsome is "exalted." Behind her coldness and her blocklike hardness, Strether permits us to understand the deep sense of dignity that motivates her assault on life. "Pure and by the vulgar estimate 'cold,'" she is not, he reflects, coarse or hard, but, rather, "deep devoted delicate sensitive noble" (II.47). We see her underlying motivation nowhere more revealingly than in the one verbatim quotation we are given:

> Sarah's answer came so straight, so 'pat', as might have been said, that he felt on the instant its origin. 'She has confided to my judgment and my tenderness the expression of her personal sense of everything, and the assertion of her personal dignity.'
> They were the very words of the lady of Woollett—he would have known them in a thousand; her parting charge to her child. (II.203)

This surprises us at first; for we may have been encouraged by some of Strether's remarks to think of this woman as a hard insensitive being, whose utterances would be icy imperatives. Her words, which we are told to see as exemplary, suggest, I think, a more complex understanding. We have here the expression of a keen sense of human dignity—of an idea of our worth as agents that is the basis of Kantian morality (and through this of Rawls's Kantianism). It is the idea that we do not need to go through the world as the plaything of its forces, living "from hand to mouth," merely "floating" with its currents. We are dignified moral beings; and it is in virtue of our moral powers of will and judgment that we can *be* dignified, making rather than being made, agents rather than victims or dependents. Strether recognizes Mrs. Newsome by the assertion of her dignity; and he knows that what the vulgar see as coldness is really a kind of nobility. What this comes to, I think, is that he sees her moralism as based on an idea of the dignity of agency. To the noble and autonomous moral agent, nature has, and should have, no power to jolt or to surprise, and also no power to inspire delight and passionate wonder. Such an agent will seem cold to the vulgar; but any other relation to the world surrenders dignity, inviting violation or at least seduction.

Such an agent will treat others with an equal respect, attending to their own dignity as moral beings. For Mrs. Newsome, we remember, would never wear her dress cut down, encouraging Strether to perceive her as a surprisingly particular physical being and so to surrender his own dignity before her. (In her actual black ruched dress she reminds him of Queen Elizabeth, virginal out of a commitment to autonomy, preserver of the dignity of a nation [I.51].) What seems like insensibility in the women of Woollett is, from their point of view, the high determination to treat each other person as an autonomous moral will, relating to them through the moral faculties and judging them with a stringency that shows respect for their freedom. Any note of tenderness would compromise this moral relation. When Strether yields to the gentle voice of Marie de Vionnet, the Woollett in him observes, "She really had tones to make justice weep" (I.275).

It is because Mrs. Newsome is no mere caricature, but a brilliantly comic rendering of some of the deepest and most appealing features of Kantian morality, that the novel has the balance and power that it does. We see the Kantian attitude as one that gives us a special dignity and exaltation; we see it, too, as a deep part of our culture. We see that the women of Woollett, unlike Marie de Vionnet in her love of an irreplaceable particular person, are able to triumph over life and to avoid becoming its victims. But that's just it: they triumph over life, they don't *live*. What is absent from the speech of the lady of Woollett? Particularity; the names of Chad and of Strether; the injunction to look and see; a sense of personal vulnerability; a fear of loss. Strether says that no trivial alteration will make this woman admit surprises, and we feel that he is correct. But is there another way to be rational and moral, a way that is more hospitable to life?

Strether begins the novel with a question. (The first sentence is: "Strether's first question, when he reached the hotel, was about his friend" [I.3].) That's already a departure. From the beginning we sense in him a curiosity about the actual situation before him, an openness and a lack of self-sufficiency, that make him a dubious ambassador of Mrs. Newsome's will. In the style of Woollett, the interrogative, we feel, must play a small role. Strether is still closely linked, at this point, to his past, but: "He was burdened, poor Strether—it had better be confessed at the outset—with the oddity of a double consciousness. There was detachment in his zeal and curiosity in his indifference" (I.5). In his moral purpose as ambassador is an independence of purpose; in his lack of interested engagement with the new is an eager desire to *see* it. His initial steps into the new world that confronts him are marked by a child's fresh delight in seeing and an undirected openness to the new concrete thing. He has "the idlest eye" (I.36) for the sights and sounds of the garden; the "smallest things so arrested and amused him" (I.39). He finds himself "given over to uncontrolled perceptions"—among them the perception of Maria Gostrey's complicating neckband; and he takes this surprising piece of red velvet as "a starting-point for fresh backward, fresh forward, fresh lateral flights" (I.51). His relation to his situation is dominated, above all, by the sense of freshness and susceptibility to adventure; and he sees this susceptibility as connected with a new sharpness of perception:

> Nothing could have been odder than Strether's sense of himself as at that moment launched in something of which the sense would be quite disconnected from the sense of his past and which was literally beginning there and then. It had begun in fact already, . . . begun with a sharper survey of the elements of Appearance than he had for a long time been moved to make. (I.9)

This sense that life is an adventure, and that part of its joy precisely is the confrontation with the new—this is a sense of life already far removed from that of Woollett, where dignity is preserved by keeping down the new, acknowledging it only insofar as it exemplifies some law whose sense is already understood. Mrs. Newsome is about as far removed from the childlike as a human being can be. (In comparing her to Queen Elizabeth—who never even mothered children and seems to the reader of history to have been always adult, always self-sufficient—Strether depicts her as heroically untouched by any horrible or wonderful aspect of life.) But Strether, as he embarks on his adventure, becomes no longer a controlling adult; he is a child learning to "toddle" (II.48), eyes wide open, vulnerable, wondering at each new thing.

In his growing awareness of the world we discover the three elements of judgment that Mrs. Newsome above all avoids, significantly linked in his affirmation as they were in her denial. Most emphasized in the text is Strether's willingness to be passive, surrendering the invulnerable agency of the Kantian self. He speaks of "letting go" (II.64), of "taking things as they come" (I.83), of living "from hand to mouth" (II.3); perceptions bear in or "press" (I.276) upon him, acting on him rather than being made or impressed upon the world. He even feels himself to be like a person who has "been tripped up and had a fall" (I.276), so sharply does life make itself felt. But passivity is more often joyous. A sharp "assault of images," in Gloriani's garden, makes him have "the consciousness of opening . . . for the happy instant, all the windows of his mind, of letting this rather grey interior drink in for once the sun of a clime not marked in his old geography" (I.196–97). In the novel's continual emphasis on this feature, we are made to feel that it is somehow a key to all the rest: that a willingness to surrender invulnerability, to take up a posture of agency that is porous and susceptible of influence, is of the highest importance in getting an accurate perception of particular things in the world.

For Strether's vision of particularity involves a willingness to be incomplete, to be surprised by the new, to see that and how our "actual adventure" (I.176) transcends our "personal experience." And so, by being able to grant the incompleteness of past experience, which he calls "this last queer quantity" (I.176), Strether allows himself to emerge as (in Maria's words) a person for whom "nothing . . . will ever come to the same thing as anything else" (I.70). Part of this vision of the particular lies in his sharp concrete perceptions of particular objects and people; part, too, in a new willingness to see a composite situation as so connected together, so complex in its relations, that as a whole it is like no other. Just as Maria's neckband is permitted to complicate his vision, so in general new elements constitute new relations. "All voices had grown thicker and meant more things; they crowded on him as he moved about—it was the way they sounded together that wouldn't let him be still" (II.210).

And this vision of particularity is shaped (as Woollett's view could not be) by the responsive activity of the emotions and the imagination, working closely together. From the beginning, Strether is surprised by "how much there had been in him of response" (I.6); and Maria correctly observes, "No one feels so much as you. No—not any one" (II.126).

All of this comes together in the sense of happy though perplexed immersion in the adventure of living[25] that makes it possible for Strether to make such simple statements as, "The Sunday of the new week was a wonderful day" (I.193)—a chapter opening that could never have been written by the lady of Woollett; in the way, too, that he is with people, "looking kindly from one to the other and

25. See "'Finely Aware,'" in this volume. At the original American Philosophical Association symposium where I presented that paper, I had the benefit of excellent comments by Cora Diamond, entitled "Missing the Adventure," and abstracted in *Journal of Philosophy* 82 (1985) 529ff; these have shaped my views on these questions.

wondering at many things" (I.222); in the hesitation with which he searches for names (I.49), gropes after the right description for the strange things that confront him. Hesitation and bewilderment are a part of his sense of life, *and* part of its accuracy:

> 'It isn't playing the game to turn on the uncanny. All one's energy goes to facing it, to tracking it. One wants, confound it, don't you see?' he confessed with a queer face—'one wants to enjoy anything so rare. Call it then life'—he puzzled it out—'call it poor dear old life simply that springs the surprise. Nothing alters the fact that the surprise is paralyzing, or at any rate engrossing—all, practically, hang it, that one sees, that one *can* see.' (I.167–68)

The life of perception feels perplexed, difficult, unsafe. (Strether's sentences here have the awkwardness and riskiness of which he speaks.) But this life also seems to Strether—and to us—to be richer, fuller of enjoyment, fuller too of whatever is worth calling knowledge of the world. In one of the novel's most famous passages, he connects immersion in impressions with being really alive, having one's life; and he passionately urges Little Bilham not to miss that adventure:

> 'Live all you can; it's a mistake not to. It doesn't so much matter what you do in particular, so long as you have your life. If you haven't had that what *have* you had? This place and these impressions—mild as you may find them to wind a man up so; all my impressions of Chad and of people I've seen at *his* place—well, have had their abundant message for me, have just dropped *that* into my mind. I see it now. I haven't done so enough before—and now I'm old; too old at any rate for what I see. Oh, I *do* see, at least; and more than you'd believe or I can express. . . . Don't at any rate miss things out of stupidity. . . . Live! (I.217–18)

(And we notice, once again, that the novel connects this new sense of life with a certain literary style: for Strether delivers this speech "slowly and sociably, with full pauses and straight dashes" (I.218), writing his own response to life in the style of a Henry James novel.)

Strether's consciousness finds vivid metaphors to express this new moral attitude—images of improvisatory game-playing; of complex connectedness and the absence of Woollett "straightness"; of childhood, of flying; above all, images of water, and of water and light together—signaling that illumination is now seen as inseparable from a risky passivity before the physical being of things. (To Sarah's protest against his new view, he replies that he can hardly help the way he has come to see: "an inexorable tide of light seems to have floated us into our perhaps still queerer knowledge" [II.201].) We notice, too, how he and Maria Gostrey, in conversation about what they have seen, will arrive at a new perception and, struck by it as if by finding themselves suddenly in a place where they have never been and to which they have not realized they were going, exclaim, "So there we are,"—or, "Then there we are" (II.138, 143, 327). (The novel, which began with a question, ends on just such a moment of surprised arrival.)

In the new norm of perception, unlike the norm of Woollett, there is a bewildering problem about authority. For if the ethical norm consists not in obeying certain antecedently established general rules, but in improvising resourcefully in response to the new perceived thing, then it is always going to remain unclear, in the case of any particular choice or vision, whether it is or is not correctly done. This does not mean that there are no criteria and anything goes. But it does mean that the standard will ultimately be nothing harder or clearer than the conformity of this choice or description to those of agents on whom we can rely for competent judgment—just as, in Aristotle's very similar view, the norm of good perception is the judgment of a certain type of person, the person of practical wisdom.[26] In this very way, when Strether wonders whether he has not "only been silly," his recourse can only be to think of the company he keeps:

> He glanced at such a contingency, but it failed to hold him long when once he had reflected that he would have been silly, in this case, with Maria Gostrey and Little Bilham, with Madame de Vionnet and little Jeanne, with Lambert Strether, in fine, and above all with Chad Newsome himself. Wouldn't it be found to have made more for reality to be silly with these persons than sane with Sarah and Jim? (II.81)

And we ourselves, in asking how right Strether is, can only do the same—wondering, for example about whether Chad Newsome's judgment is, after all, such a very fine thing, and wondering about the part of Lambert Strether's imagination that holds Chad in such great esteem. There is no sure guarantee, either for the judge or for our judgment about him. As Aristotle says in just this context, "The discrimination lies in perception."

This is an ethical norm to rival the norms of Woollett.[27] It deserves to be taken seriously as a picture of rationality and correct choice. And insofar as it captures our imagination and answers to our sense of life, it calls into question those elements of the pictures of judgment and agency in our moral theories that are motivated by the concerns of Woollett and resemble Woollett in their structure. Holding Strether up against Rawls's idea of considered judgment and his constraints upon admissible theories, we want to object that emotions may after all in many cases be an invaluable guide to correct judgment; that general and universal formulations may be inadequate to the complexity of particular situations; that immersed particular judgments may have a moral value that reflective and general judgments cannot capture. We want to suggest that bewilderment and hesitation may actually be marks of fine attention. As Strether summarizes the matter, "There's all the indescribable—what one gets only on the spot" (II.126)—and all of this appears to be omitted from the data that lead to reflective equilibrium. Indeed, his experience suggests a rival story about the end of the ethical process itself. There is still a search for equilibrium here, as Strether tries to make it all "hang beautifully together" (II.172). But his equilibrium, dealing, as it does, with impressions, emotions, and, in general, with particulars, had better be called by a different name. We would do better, perhaps, to call it "perceptive equilibrium":

26. The charge that the view has no standards was forcefully made (against the Jamesian view of "Flawed Crystals") by Hilary Putnam, in "Taking Rules Seriously: A Response to Martha Nussbaum," *New Literary History* 15 (1983) 193–200. For my reply, see "Discernment," "'Finely Aware,'" "Perception and Revolution," and "Introduction," in this volume.
27. See "Discernment" and "'Finely Aware,'" this volume.

an equilibrium in which concrete perceptions "hang beautifully together," both with one another and with the agent's general principles; an equilibrium that is always ready to reconstitute itself in response to the new.

Can we view this new norm as simply an extension of the old one—so that we *supplement* Rawls's general theories with the immersed judgments of experience? This idea has been persuasively argued, with reference to Aristotle and Rawls's Aristotelianism, in some very interesting recent writing by Henry Richardson, who coins the name "extended reflective equilibrium" to designate the end of an ethical procedure that takes in all of this.[28] Strether had, we recall, a different view about Mrs. Newsome—that one cannot touch her, put any of life into her, fully packed as she is; that it's fundamental to her entire being and her basic motivation not to *be* touched by the immersed perceptions of life. (We supported this in our analysis of her Kantian conception of agency; for we said that it was fundamental to her whole project not to be passive toward the world.) So what one must do, if one chooses to value perceiving, is to get rid of "the whole moral and intellectual being or block." (To put it differently, you cannot add Maria Gostrey's red velvet band to Mrs. Newsome's ruche: she would not wear such a garment, she would view it as a desecration of her dignity.) This does not mean that the way of perceiving cannot make use of rules and universal principles; plainly it does, and it would be an important part of an extended inquiry into Strether's standards to ask how and when.[29] But it cannot use them in the way and for the reasons that Mrs. Newsome would recommend; and it must give a central place to elements of judgment that she would, for consistency and dignity, insist on leaving out.

What prepares Strether to see this way? Why, among all those who come out from America to Paris, does he alone "come out" in fact,[30] opening himself to the influences of perception? We are given several clues. One, certainly, is his low sense of his own dignity. So far is he from asserting it that he permits himself to be treated, persistently, as an agent of the purposes of others. His name (in the Woollett Revue) is "on the green cover, where he had put it for Mrs. Newsome" (I.84); and his willingness to serve as her ambassador shows a not altogether robust sense of Kantian autonomy. It is an unsettling thought, and one on which James insists,[31] that this very weakness in him (from the point of view of our interest in our dignity) may be a necessary preparation for this other sort of strength.

But James points even more insistently to another sort of preparation. For from the beginning Strether has a deep connection with literature. An editor and writer himself, he has a serious love of all the arts, but especially of the literary art, and the novel above all. The imagination of the reader and the writer are shown as abilities that have prepared him to see and to respond in a non-Kantian way. His concern with novels is an old one; and Paris recalls it to him, reminding him of the "lemon-colored volumes" he brought back from Europe and of "the sharp

28. Richardson, "Deliberation." I am very grateful to Richardson for discussion of these issues. A new paper of his, "The Emotions of Reflective Equilibrium," carries the issue further, in a manner that is close to the argument of this essay, and especially close to the argument of "Steerforth's Arm."

29. See "Discernment," this volume.

30. Compare *The Ambassadors,* I.200, 209, 213, etc.

31. See I.209: "Our poor friend, conscious and passive . . ."

initiation they represnted" (I.86–7). These volumes have been sitting "stale," "soiled," even unbound, in Woollett—but their memory "throbs again" for him in Paris until his conscience reacts with alarm, "amusing itself for the forty-eight hours by forbidding him the purchase of a book" (I.87).

It does no good: for the early love of stories floods back, animating his desire to wait and see, his tendency to attend to new people and events with the novelist's "vision kindly adjusted,"[32] a loving nonjudgmental attention to their particularity. References to his favorite authors grow increasingly dense until, floating finally in the current of new sights and sounds, he notices that "it was the way of nine tenths of his current impressions to act as recalls of things imagined—of some fine firm concentrated heroine of an old story, something he had heard, read, something that, had he a hand for drama, he might himself have written" (II.6–7). And writing too (narrative, however, and not dramatic)[33] expresses increasingly his determination not to fall short, not to miss anything that is there to be seen and cared for: "When anything new struck him as coming up, or anything already noted as reappearing, he always immediately wrote, as if for fear that if he didn't he would miss something" (I.257). It is the narrative character of his letters (quite different, we must suppose, from her own) that so alarms Mrs. Newsome. Writing this way, seeing this way, he is no longer her ambassador. His style gives him away.

Here James shows us that there is a complicity between the consciousness of the reader (and the writer) of stories and the consciousness, the morality, of perception. For stories cultivate our ability to see and care for particulars, not as representatives of a law, but as what they themselves are: to respond vigorously with senses and emotions before the new; to care deeply about chance happenings in the world, rather than to fortify ourselves against them; to wait for the outcome, and to be bewildered—to wait and float and be actively passive. We are so accustomed to the novel that we tend to forget how morally controversial a form it has been in the eyes of various sorts of religious and secular moralisms. (Even as I write this, fundamentalist parents in the state of Tennessee are seeking a ban on stories that freely exercise the imagination, holding that the law laid down in the Bible is truth enough.) Questionable with very good reason: for the novel acknowledges a wonder before worldly sensuous particulars that Mrs. Newsome would never feel or approve; and they attach a dangerous importance to outcomes that lie beyond the control of the moral will. By showing us the novel's world (more or less) through Strether's eyes, indeed by making it next to impossible to distinguish those eyes from the author's eyes—and by showing us at the same time how different the story would look (or the events and people would, as a nonstory, look) to the women of Woollett—by letting us know enough of what they see to discover that they do not perceive and could not describe the same reality—James makes a case for the moral significance of the novelist's (and the reader's) "sense of life," for the vigilant and responsive imagination that cares for everyone in the situation and refuses the injunction of Woollett to "simplify" for the sake of purity and safety. The very sentences are Strether's, straining toward perceptual rightness

32. I.8; the description of Strether that follows is a result of this vision.
33. The negative reference to dramatic writing encourages, clearly, our connection of Strether with Henry James himself.

in the midst of wonderful puzzling mysteries.[34] The sentences of Woollett are crisp, "straight," and, as Strether says, "pat." And the fullness, the density, of the narrative style is itself the fitting expression of a certain sort of moral imagination. Indeed, James recalls to us that even the novel, with all its richness, can actually express but a fraction of the crowded consciousness of someone who is really making an effort to *see*. For at one point he remarks, "If we should go into all that occupied our friend in the watches of the night we should have to mend our pen; but an instance or two may mark for us the vividness with which he could remember" (I.139). The novel has its own simplifications—but it is the genre, among the available forms of writing—that most appropriately exemplifies what James calls the "projected morality."[35]

Perception and Method

We begin to see two opposing conceptions of practical reason, together with some of the motivations for and consequences of each. The morality of perception is put before us in a textual form that fittingly expresses its claim on our imaginations. What now would be the next step in the proposed interchange between literary and ethical theory? Here nothing can be said in depth; but I can sketch out some of the pieces that I think this larger project might include.

First, I believe, we would need, in pursuing our goals of understanding and attunement, to get a much richer and deeper understanding of the Kantian conception and of its modern continuations (Rawls's above all). This novel is Strether's story. Mrs. Newsome does not do full justice to the power of Kant's arguments in the way that Strether does justice to his own way (and to Aristotle's related conception). If we are correct about the close relationship between content and form this is no accident. No narrative dealing in empirical particulars *could* see Kant's conception in a fully sympathetic way. This does not mean that there isn't a special interest, too, in seeing just what sort of character in a story (in our lives) a thoroughgoing Kantian would be: for this certainly helps us see how Kant matches (or fails to) our own active sense of life. But we would want to look at the arguments of Kantian philosophers directly and seriously in their own right; otherwise this inquiry could too easily get corrupted, get used to treat complex philosophical positions as straw men. The same applies to other leading ethical conceptions with which Strether's perception might fruitfully be contrasted—above all, the morality of classical Utilitarianism.[36]

Having started on this sort of investigation, we would now, I think, want to look very carefully at the different elements of Strether's conception (and their relatives

---

34. There is a fine account of the novel's style in Ian Watt, "The First Paragraph of *The Ambassadors:* An Explication," in *Essays in Criticism* 10 (1960) 254–68; a revised version appears in A. E. Stone, Jr., ed., *Twentieth-Century Interpretations of the Ambassadors* (Englewood Cliffs, N.J., 1969), 75–87.

35. The phrase is used by James in the Preface to *Portrait of a Lady;* see James, *The Art of the Novel* (New York, 1907), 45.

36. For some elements in that contrast, see "Discernment" and "Plato on Commensurability," this volume.

in the contrasting conceptions) asking how they are connected and interrelated, how each one is supported and defended. How the perception of particularity is connected with an openness to surprise; how both are connected with a commitment to the cognitive guidance of emotion. Of particular importance here will be to ask what role rules and universal principles *can* and should play inside the morality of perception, and in general what sort of systematic theoretical approach to practice would be compatible with Strether's insights. This needs to be carefully considered, if we want to defend this conception as normative, especially for our public life. I imagine that by confronting Strether (and his philosophical relatives) with challenges from the Kantian and Utilitarian positions, we will arrive at a deeper understanding of this position and of the connection all the positions have with our own sympathies.

At this point many fruitful and interesting projects suggest themselves. We need to pursue in much greater depth and detail the stylistic portion of my argument, saying a great deal more, in connection with many more authors and many different genres and styles, about the practical and human expressive content of structural choices at all levels of specificity. And we would want to look at philosophical authors as makers of stylistic choices, asking what ethical commitments their own literary choices express. (I suspect that we will often discover that some of these choices are not supported by the argument in the "content" of the work, and that some may even be in tension with the content—as when an article about the crucial cognitive role of the emotions is written in a style that seems to assume that the intellect is the only part of the reader worth addressing. It is not clear that there are no good reasons for this discrepancy; but we need to ask hard questions about it.).

We would also want to turn to our own lives, both private and public, examining the conceptions of rationality (of the person, etc.) that we discover there, and asking how all this fits with what we have so far puzzled out. It would be an especially useful exercise, for example, to work through the contemporary economic literature on rationality, in which there is much pertinent debate about commensurability, about ordering, about universality, and to see what elements of Strether's "position" are incorporated in these debates; to ask, too, what workable social science could be built on what Strether offers us. Many other related projects can be imagined.

Throughout this open-ended inquiry, we will need to maintain as much self-consciousness as possible about our own methods and our implicit ends, asking what evaluative content they themselves express. Perceptive equilibrium is not the same end as reflective equilibrium; it does not use the same judgments or the same faculties. This does not mean that there can be no objectivity in the ethical inquiry; it does not mean that all choices of method are subjective.[37] But it does mean that procedures themselves are value-laden, and thus part and parcel of the holistic enterprise they organize; replaceable, like any other part, to the end of deeper and more inclusive attunement. So we must examine them at each stage, asking whether they are capable of doing full justice to everything that our sense of life wants to include.

37. On this, see "Therapeutic Arguments," above, n. 14.

Perception and Love

At this point, however, we are brought back again to *The Ambassadors.* For we
have given, so far, too simple a story about Strether's imagination.[38] And part of
the longer story of perceptive equilibrium is surely to discover the ways in which
James's novel itself complicates our admiration for Strether, causing us to see that
the perception of life may not have, in the end, an equilibrium—that the keen
sight of the writer and reader of life is in a standing tension with the "sight" of
passion. We have thought of Strether as yielding to the impressions of life as they
unfold themselves before him—as allowing himself to be seduced. We must now
think, also, of his inability to see, and later to accept, the sexual love of Chad and
Marie de Vionnet; his inability to see Maria Gostrey's deepening feeling for him;
his failure to examine and to acknowledge his own complicated feelings for Marie
de Vionnet, and his jealousy of Chad. We must think of his blush of shame, when
he realizes how he had concealed from himself their intimacy, "dressed the possibility in vagueness, as a little girl might have dressed her doll" (II.266). He too
has simplified life; and by refusing himself feelings and ways of living that he could
not reconcile with his personal demand for perceptual clarity and unselfish general
concern, he has prevented himself, in the end, from perceiving a crucial fact about
the situation around him. ("'It's beautiful,' he said to Miss Barrace, 'the way you
all can simplify when you will.' But she gave it to him back. 'It's nothing to the
way *you* will when you must'" [II.180].) When he does confront Marie de Vionnet
in his newly gained knowledge, he cannot achieve, in this one case, a particular
perception; she becomes, distanced by his own inner refusal of passion, a mere
abstraction. "It was actually moreover as if he didn't think of her at all, as if he
could think of nothing but the passion, mature, abysmal, pitiful, she represented,
and the possiblities she betrayed" (II.286). From her wonderful variegated self she
becomes, for him, merely "a creature so exploited," "a maid servant crying for
her young man." Distant watcher, pitying judge, he is in the end, in his way, the
ambassador of Woollett; for his sharp eye will not turn aside in tenderness before
the intimacy of others, and his spirit will not moderate its ubiquitous demand for
rightness and for judgment. He too resists; he too refuses to allow his vision to be
complicated by the band of broad red velvet.

And now we see, too, that the earlier remark about Strether's "double consciousness" can have another reading. There *is* a curious "detachment in his
zeal"—in his zeal to see there is a detachment from strong emotion. And in his
"indifference"—his perceiver's impartiality, the equipoise of the body drawn
strongly to no extreme—there is an almost voyeuristic "curiosity," the curiosity
of the uninvolved gaze.

And this incompleteness in Strether is unmistakably linked to his interest in
literature: for we are shown repeatedly that the stance of the reader and writer of
life is a stance that achieves a certain clarity of vision at the expense of a certain
emotional depth; one that forgoes, or even scorns, immersion in the darker, messier passions, one that "reduces" them all to a simplified generic story, read with

---

38. These aspects of the novel are well discussed by Philip Weinstein in *Henry James and the
Requirements of the Imagination* (Cambridge, Mass., 1971), 121–64.

only a reader's interest (to what Strether calls "the convenient terms of Victor Hugo" [II.7]). The outing during which Strether makes his upsetting discovery has been seen by him, up until that moment, as if it were the exploration of a Lambinet painting that he remembers: his life, to that point, "continued in the picture . . . and had meanwhile not once overstepped the oblong gilt frame" (II.251–2). Even the loving couple in their boat can be held in the "picture" (or the story, since the picture has, for Strether, a marked narrative quality)—so long as he doesn't have to acknowledge them as the very individuals he cares about and has to deal with in his own personal life, so long as he doesn't have to acknowledge his own personal feelings of jealousy and longing. Then the story is no longer just a story, then it is threat to equilibrium.

James reminds us here that before a work of art we are detached perceivers, free to explore all fine perceptions, but liberated (or cut off) from the tumultuous perceptions of personal passion, freed also—as we enjoy its delicious half-expected surprises—from the hard jolting shocks of the real surprises that mark our actual personal relations. Reading is a preparation for a life that is lived at one remove from life, a life that gains fineness and clarity by warding off certain risks and dangers. Is this good, or is it bad? When Strether sits, later, in Maria Gostrey's dining room, he reflects: "To sit there was, as he had told his hostess before, to see life reflected for the time in ideally kept pewter; which was somehow becoming, improving to life, so that one's eyes were held and comforted" (II.319).[39] Art does not simply perceive life; it also comforts us by keeping us at a distance from life's violence and arbitrariness. (For even when its content deals with violent passion, our own relation to it is not violent; the terms of Victor Hugo are indeed so much more "convenient" than those of our own loves and jealousies and fears and angers.) The novelist stands apart from some of the confusing complexity of the human scene; he owes his clarity to that "improving" absence of immersion. And yet, doesn't this make him, as a human being, somehow incomplete, somehow lacking in humanity? Reassuring Strether, who fears that Waymarsh may talk about him behind his back, Maria says, "'For what do you take people, that they're able to say words about anything, able remorselessly to analyze? There are not many like you and me'" (I.44). The novelist is a third; as reader we follow. Is this, in fact, a good or full way to live?

Do we put such problems down to Strether's own idiosyncrasy, and to his regretful sense that he is too old for what he sees, or are they the faults of the morality of perception? One of his reflections is, I think, significant. What he dislikes about the revealed intimacy is that it was, before, concealed: it went on between two people apart from perception and description. "Intimacy, at such a point, was *like* that—and what in the world else would one have wished it to be like? It was all very well for him to feel the pity of its being so much like lying" (II.266). What Strether senses is that what he calls the "deep deep truth" of sexual love is at odds with the morality of perception, in two ways. It asks for the privacy, for others to avert their gaze; and on the inside it asks that focus be averted from

39. This passage and others using the word "life" are well discussed in Joan Bennett, "The Art of Henry James: *The Ambassadors*," *Chicago Review* 9 (1956) 16–26, reprinted in *Twentieth-Century Interpretations*, 57–65.

all else that is outside. Lovers see, at such times, only one another; and it is not really deep if they *can* carefully see around and about them. That vision excludes general attention and care, at least at that moment. And this intimacy is a part of the world that demands *not* to be in the eyes of the perceiving, recording novelist—at least not in all of its particularity. But to the person who is dedicated to perceiving (to novel-writing), that looks like a bad way to be; bad both because it impedes the subject's moral vision of the whole and because it asks not to be included as an object in that vision. To be sure, these ruminations emerge from Strether's loneliness. But he is convinced that loneliness is the condition of luminous perception; and his fear of intimacy is at the same time a fear for his moral being.

We need to take this seriously. Perception as a morality enjoins trust in responsive feeling; but its feelings are the feelings of the friend. (Strether's first question was about his friend; and the novelist's vision of him is a vision "*kindly* adjusted.") There is reason to suppose that the exclusivity and intensity of personal love would in fact impede the just and general responsiveness that these gentler feelings assist. And if they impede that, they impede the perceiver's contribution to our moral project, to our communal effort to arrive at perceptive equilibrium. But the recognition that there is a view of the world from passion's point of view, and that this view is closed to the perceiver, shows us that perception is, even by its own lights, incomplete. The perceiver as perceiver cannot see it all; to get the whole he must at times stop being the sort of person who cares for wholeness. As a perceiver he is morally admirable, both wonderful and quite lovable. Yet just that commitment that Maria loves (not just admires, but loves) in Strether, just that is the reason why he not only cannot love her, but cannot in any way understand or see her love or any love. She "can't resist" him when he tells her the reasons for his refusal; this is their comedy and their tragedy. Maria's "all comically, all tragically" (II.327) is a response to the moral impossibility of human love. For so long as our eyes are open, we are wonderful and lovable and finely responsive; but when we immerse ourselves in the most powerful responses, entering silence, closing our eyes, are we then capable at all of asking questions about our friends, of thinking of the good of the community? And if we are not capable of this, are we worthy of the deepest feelings and commitments of others? James once wrote about his mother that, swallowed up in her intense love of her husband and family, she had nothing "acutely to offer."[40] Does any lover do better? Without this depth life seems incomplete and perception itself seems blind; but it cannot itself be ordered inside the equilibrium of perception or seen by its fine-tuned vision of the complete life.

This complicates still further our idea of what might be the practical goal of ethical inquiry. It would be simple if Strether's perceptive equilibrium were simply undercut, shown not to be a high human goal. But perceptive equilibrium is loved and affirmed, "all comically, all tragically," at the novel's end. It is what makes him fine and lovable, even while it is what makes him incapable of love. It would be simple, again, if we were shown a way in which Strether's incompleteness could be completed and filled up, by love, in some harmonious manner. (A way in

---

40. From a letter quoted in L. Edel, *Henry James: The Untried Years* (New York, 1953), 49.

which the novelist could have an intimate personal life and still see for us all.)
Neither of these easy exits is offered us. And if there is for us any prospect held
out for a life that combines fine perception with the silence and the hidden vision
of love, it would only be in a condition that is not itself "equilibrium" at all, but
an unsteady oscillation between blindness and openness, exclusivity and general
concern, fine reading of life and the immersion of love.

Here we find another way in which the novel can make a contribution to ethical
theory. So far it has (or this one novel has) shown the way from a narrow Kantian
understanding of the question, "How should one live?" to a wider and richer
understanding. Now it asks us to see the limits of that ethical question itself. It
gestures toward the limits of ethical consciousness, making us aware of the deep
elements in our ethical life that in their violence or intensity lead us outside of the
ethical attitude altogether, outside of the quest for balanced vision and perfect
rightness. It can include, or at least indicate, the silence into which its own responsive prose has no entry.

Literary Theory and Ethical Theory

I have imagined a literary theory that works in conversation with ethical theory.
I have imagined this partnership as a practical one, in which we search for images
of life by which we might possibly live together, and ask what conceptions and
images best match the full range of our perceptions and convictions, as we work
toward "perceptive equilibrium." (And now we have, too, the thought that the
goal might not be equilibrium at all, but a dynamic tension between two possible
irreconcilable visions.) I have imagined that literary theory will make a creative
and rather radical contribution to this enterprise—as we see from the fact that the
very end and methods of the enterprise have been called into question by Strether's achievement, and his tragedy.

Why, however, *should* literary theory engage itself with ethical theory here? For
we might acknowledge the practical dimension of literature and insist on restoring
that dimension to theoretical writing, without taking the further step proposed
here. Why can't the literary theorist simply say about Henry James what it is lucid
and helpful to say, without studying and teaching Kant and Aristotle, Bentham
and Rawls, and drawing these figures into the account he or she gives of James's
novels? This question arises all the more since major figures of past theory with
whom I implicitly link my proposal—F. R. Leavis, say, and Lionel Trilling—seem
to have been perfectly able to speak of the ethical content of literature and the
ethical expressiveness of literary forms without bringing moral philosophy into the
picture.

The explicit and deep study of ethical theory will, first of all, clarify to us just
what it is that works of literature offer to our sense of life. We grasp by contrasting;
we sense what something *is* by bounding it off against something different. If it
should prove true that novels share certain ethical commitments (to particularity,
to the moral relevance of surprise) just in virtue of their form, we will grasp these
shared commitments better by seeing on what grounds some philosophers have
denied or refused them. We grasp the force of James's account of perception more
clearly when we see how it goes against norms of considered judgment that prevail

in almost all of the Western ethical tradition. And we have to do this by reading the philosophers in a serious way, not, as I say, by using them polemically, as straw men. Our understanding is enhanced in a different way when we encounter inside philosophy several friends of perception and of literary insight, whose explicit arguments against much of the prevailing tradition clarify for us the elements of Strether's accomplishment. (I think here, in different ways, of Aristotle, of Iris Murdoch, of Bernard Williams—and, also, of William James.)[41] And if we look more closely now at the examples of Leavis and Trilling, I think we will discover that they do not go against these claims. For Leavis's denigration of the late novels of James[42] is, I believe, surperficial in a way that most of his work is not, precisely *because* he does not make these reflective philosophical contrasts and so demarcate for himself what it is that James is opposing and putting forward. Trilling's wide and deep knowledge of political and ethical and psychological thought, though displayed with understated grace and elegance, does, I think, consistently inform his most memorable and characteristic writings—not least his writing on James in *The Liberal Tradition*.[43]

Then, too, ethical theory, just because of its systematic and inclusive disciplinary character, can contribute to our understanding of a literary work by raising questions that this work may or may not explicitly ask itself concerning the relationship of its ethical views to other issues on which we have to make up our mind—issues about social structure, about economic distribution, about the self and personal identity. My imagined theoretical dialogue will, for example, lead us to ask what political structures are compatible with Strether's moral norm, whether in opting for that norm we would have to forgo some or all of our democratic traditions. We will have understood James more deeply if we can answer this question. And the answer will emerge not only out of a deeper reflection about novels such as *The Ambassadors* and *The Princess Casamassima,* but also out of a more general reflection about the connections between a conception of personal rationality and a political conception.

These are some reasons why literary theory needs ethical theory. (And this close connection with theory would be one way of distinguishing literary theory, should we want to, from good criticism—to which it should always remain almost inseparably close.) On the other side a similar and equally strong argument can be made. It is reasonably clear by now what that argument is: that literary theory can improve the self-understanding of ethical theory by confronting it with a distinctive conception or conceptions of various aspects of human ethical life, realized in a form that is the most appropriate one for their expression. Insofar as great literature has moved and engaged the hearts and minds of its readers, it has established already its claim to be taken seriously when we work through the alternative conceptions.

These alternatives could be described and investigated by the ethical theorist;

---

41. I am thinking particularly of the essay "The Moral Philosopher and the Moral Life," in William James, *Essays on Faith and Morals* (New York, 1962), 184–215.

42. F. R. Leavis, *The Great Tradition* (London, 1948), 154–72.

43. Lionel Trilling, *The Liberal Imagination: Essays on Literature and Society* (New York, 1950), especially the essays *"The Princess Casamassima,"* "Manners, Morals, and the Novel," and "The Meaning of a Literary Idea."

sometimes they are. But this too often results in a criticism that simply mines the work for a set of propositional claims—rather than what I am calling for, an investigation of that which is expressed and "claimed" by the shape of the sentences themselves, by images and cadences and pauses themselves, by the forms of the traditional genres, by narrativity, themselves. It seems unlikely that this richer ethical task can be carried out by someone who is not in the habit of attending to these things.

But why should we *care* about describing literary alternatives to ethical theory? Suppose there is a task in (or side by side of) ethical theory that literary people are best equipped to perform: why should anyone want to take on that task, rather than some other one of the many interesting tasks that literary theory might and does perform? If moral philosophers (or political theorists or economists) have gotten themselves into difficulty, why should we bail them out? Here I come back to my idea of the practical goal of ethical inquiry—which involves self-understanding and communal attunement. These goals matter. Each of us is not only a professional, but a human being who is trying to live well; and not simply a human being, but also a citizen of some town, some country, above all a world of human beings, in which attunement and understanding are extremely urgent matters. Now certainly we can promote these goals in indefinitely many ways, apart from our professional lives: by raising children, by engaging in some form of political action, by using our money generously, by seeing and conversing and feeling. And yet, when a person happens to have a professional activity that is or becomes relevant to major ends of human life—how exhilarating that activity then is, and how deep, I think, the obligations it then imposes.

All around us other intellectual disciplines are shaping the private and public life of our culture, telling us how to imagine or think about ourselves. Economic theory forges conceptions of human rationality that govern public policy decisions, decisions about the distribution of food, about social well-being. Legal theorists and jurists search for understanding of basic rights (for example, the right to privacy) and the role that they play in our lives with one another. Psychology and anthropology describe our emotional lives, our experience of gender, our forms of communal interaction. Moral philosophy attempts to arbitrate disputes concerning medical care, abortion, basic freedoms. Literary theory has been too silent too long in these debates. And yet it has a distinctive speaking role to play— a first part of which might be to confront reigning models of political and economic rationality with the consciousness of Strether. Silence, in these matters, is a kind of capitulation. If these alternatives are not brought forward and described, we will go on being governed from day to day by conceptions of rationality that seem impoverished next to the ones we know well and care about in novels that we love. Worse, most people will not perceive, and therefore not really have, the choice among conceptions. The hungry will be fed (or not fed) according to some idea of the person; patients will be treated; laws and policies will be made—all according to some conception or conceptions of human personhood and human rationality. If we do not take a hand in these choices, they will be made by default without us.

I propose an apparently thankless task. Is there any reason at all to suppose that entrenched conceptions (of rationality, of value) that currently govern our daily lives through their reception in economic theory and public policy will be modified by contact with Lambert Strether, or that the holders of these conceptions will pay any attention at all to Henry James and related authors at any time? Can any possible practicable goal be achieved by subtle precise writing about books that most people in public life do not read anyway? Those of us who are Americans might also ask: can *any* writing that is Strether's, that is responsive and delicate and committed to perception, impose itself upon the form of our American culture, concerning which we sometimes have good reason to think (as Strether of Mrs. Newsome) that it "won't *be* touched," that it can only come to a question of dislodging "the whole moral and intellectual being or block" that looms up before us, with its strange combination of Utilitarianism and religious moralism, like some particularly large blue iceberg in a cool blue northern sea. (The same question may of course be asked about the practical value of ethical theory itself, with whose collaboration we proposed to "touch" her—though theory's colder hand may less quickly be felt as a threatening assault.)

Well, what can we do but try? Some major choices affecting our lives—say, Supreme Court decisions—made in effect by one or two complex reflective processes in the minds of one or two reading, thinking, feeling beings. An eloquent piece of writing (say, about James on the moral value of privacy) might possibly alter the course of that reflection. Do we know such things before attempting? James once wrote that the task of the literary imagination, face to face with social obtuseness and general failure of perception, would be:

> to *create* the record, in default of any other enjoyment of it; to imagine, in a word, the honourable, the producible case. What better example than this of the high and the helpful public and, as it were, civic use of the imagination?[44]

We could aim, for a future, at that degree of love. (Though bewildered, increasingly, about the nature of that love and its relation to other loves, to life itself.) His plain gravestone, in the Cambridge Cemetery, on an open bright hill (where one can sit and read all morning alone in the still sun, vaguely hearing children's voices reflected up, as it were, from the school below) bears the inscription: "Henry James, novelist, citizen of two countries, interpreter of his generation on both sides of the sea." So—as Strether observes—there we are.[45]

Endnote

This essay was written for a volume exploring *The Future of Literary Theory.* Unlike many of the essays here, it attempts to show not only why moral philosophy needs literature, but also why literature needs moral philosophy. It argues

---

44. James, *The Art of the Novel,* 223–24.
45. This paper was first read at the conference on Virtue and Agency at Santa Clara University, February 1987. I am grateful to David Fisher for his stimulating comments delivered on the occasion. I am also grateful to Paul Seabright and Amartya Sen, whose questions and comments led to numerous revisions, and to audiences at Oxford University, the University of York, Yale University, the University of London, Harvard University, and the Rhode Island Humanities Forum.

that contemporary theoretical writing about literature, while not forgetting its many other concerns, should concern itself, as well, with the ways in which works of literature address themselves to the readers' questions about how one should live. In keeping with its explicit account of the starting point and the overall dialectical method of such a literary–philosophical inquiry, it insists that the imagined project needs not only those forms of philosophy that sympathize with the perceptions contained in the novels, but also forms of philosophy that powerfully argue for a different view of the right way to live—Kantianism and Utilitarianism above all. This article displays Strether's view of life as a view in many ways deeply appealing; but it argues that to understand our own relation to it—even to understand it fully—we need to set it beside alternative conceptions. On the other hand, the adherents of the rival conceptions, if they share this commitment to the scrutiny of major alternatives, ought to agree that their own overall project requires texts like this novel for its completion.

This essay shows clearly the difficulty of characterizing the overall project in a way that does not exclude major candidates from the start. The difficulties this raises for my enterprise, and my response to them, are discussed in the Introduction.

The essay, dwelling on this particular novel, links the stance of the novelist with a refusal of passionate erotic love. The picture is complicated, where James is concerned, by the accounts of *The Golden Bowl* given in "Flawed Crystals" and "'Finely Aware.'" And the whole issue is discussed much further in the Introduction and in "Steerforth's Arm."

7

Perception and Revolution:
The Princess Casamassima
and the Political Imagination

I

'She told me you've changed—you've no more the same opinions.'

'The same opinions?'

'About the arrangement of society. You desire no more the assassination of the rich.'

'I never desired any such thing!' said Hyacinth indignantly.

'Oh if you've changed you can confess,' his friend declared in an encouraging tone. 'It's very good for some people to be rich. It wouldn't be right for all to be poor.'

'It would be pleasant if all could be rich,' Hyacinth more mildly suggested.

'Yes, but not by stealing and shooting.'

'No, not by stealing and shooting. I never desired that.'

'Ah no doubt she was mistaken. But today you think we must have patience?' the Prince went on as if greatly hoping Hyacinth would allow this valuable conviction to be attributed to him. 'That's also my view.'

'Oh yes, we must have patience,' said his companion, who was now smiling to himself in the dark. (II.319)

Only months before, Hyacinth Robinson had viewed the workers' revolution and the utopian future it projected as goals to be approached with passionate optimism and a violent desire for confrontation. Now we find him in at least verbal agreement with one of the more obtuse and decadent members of the aristocracy: speaking of progress in a mild voice in which we hear no accent of blood, approving of patience and gentleness toward political change, even when this coincides (both comically and tragically) with the exploiter's fondest wish. His smile in the dark acknowledges, wryly, the incongruity. What has happened? And what is it, what can it ever be, this politics of patience, based, as it seems, on gentleness to human life, on the love of beauty, on the fine-tuned perception of particular things and people, the responsive and responsible activity of feeling?

When I first saw Hilary Putnam, back in that long summer of 1970, he was standing on a platform in Zion, Illinois, calling for the workers' revolution in a voice of infinite gentleness, mildly assenting to killings of the innocent and guilty. That summer the urgency of human need seemed to many to leave no place for any patience; and the violence of the war, which saturated all of life with its ugliness and baseness, seemed to convict any slow liberal response of naïveté at best— at worst, of collaboration with evil. One saw then, too, before one, the shining image of the Marxian "Kingdom of Freedom" on the far side of the cleansing struggle, the rectification on this earth of all crimes that had ever been committed against human dignity, the new world in which all alike, liberated from constraints of class and from alienating labor, would achieve, in peace and leisure, their full humanity. And that image, resonating that night through Putnam's speech, became a part of the call for violence, making the projected war a holy war and sluggishness a sin. Later that night in Zion, we watched the film *The Battle of Algiers,* with its compassionate killings, its blood-thirst for the kingdom.

I wondered then, as I now wonder, about the strange juxtaposition, in Putnam's politics at that period, of gentleness with violence, of the loving perception of concrete human lives with the call for abstract killing. In one way these elements seemed to imply one another: for a keen response to suffering seemed then to call forth a rapid and a radical solution. But in another way they seemed, quite obviously, to point in different political directions. Most people who made such revolutionary statements left out the gentleness; and their discourse had a correspondingly greater unity of tone. What was, and is, after all, then, the place of the gentle perceiving heart in the political life? Is the sensibility of a Hyacinth Robinson anything but a liability, when the task is to help?

In recent years Hilary Putnam has criticized the utopian politics of the form of Marxism he formerly endorsed, characterizing it as "a politics which combines hatred with exaggerated optimism."[1] He has also written that "the central *long run* philosophical problem facing people generally is how to maintain a belief in progress without a belief in Utopia."[2] Like Hyacinth Robinson, he has claimed that any viable conception of progress must insist upon the continuity of culture, and on a careful patient conservatism toward the social traditions and the works of art through which human beings express and identify themselves. He has, like Hyacinth again, spoken of works of art as essential sources of insight and illumination, which could not be taken from human societies without robbing us of a central element in our moral life.[3] He has described a "model for a political stance" that contains three elements: "*socialism* as the guiding principle in the economy; *liberalism* as the guiding principle in politics; *conservatism* as the guiding principle in culture"[4]—all of which would find, as we shall see, many echoes in Hyacinth's own reflections. So I have decided, in honoring this extraordinary philosopher and wonderful friend, whose compassion for suffering humanity has been, throughout, a mainspring of his thought and action, to turn to the one novel in which Henry James, that apostle of a fine-tuned awareness of particulars, asks about the relationship between that ideal and his own compassion for suffering

---

1. Hilary Putnam, "A Note on Progress," Erkenntnis" 11 (1977), 1–4, on p. 1.
2. Ibid.
3. Putnam, "Literature, Science, and Reflection," in his *Meaning and the Moral Sciences* (London, 1979), 83–96; also "A Note," 3–4.
4. Putnam, "A Note," 4.

humanity. I shall turn, then, to *The Princess Casamassima,* asking what its idea of progress might be, and what role the perceiving imagination plays in it; what relationship there might be between Hyacinth's views about culture and his belief in patience, between his being a person "on whom nothing is lost" and his inability to stick with the optimism of revolutionary socialism. Asking, above all, the novel's tragic and comic question: how can one in fact be a person of compassion and either kill, or, after all, not kill, the enemies of the people?

II

My project faces opposition, from two related sources. For it has been influentially claimed by Irving Howe, in *Politics and the Novel,* that *The Princess Casamassima* cannot be mined, as I wish to mine it, for political thought, since it actually shows Henry James's complete indifference to, and incapacity for, political thought.[5] Howe assumes that a certain propensity for abstraction and a fondness for general statement are hallmarks of the real political thinker; and, furthermore, that the proper subject matter of political thought is "a collective mode of action": a way of seeing action that is not reducible to, or properly approached in terms of, the actions and desires of particular human beings. He then observes that in James's novel we notice an "aversion" to generalizing that amounts to "a deep distrust, indeed a professional refusal." We find what Howe calls a "trained inexperience in abstract thought." And, finally, we find the absence of any sense of a "larger view of politics as a collective mode of action"—the attention of the novelist being, instead, all turned toward the doings and sufferings of particular human beings.[6] All this seems, in a sense, accurate enough as description of the novel. But we might still hold out some hope for our political interest in James if we consider that perhaps this refusal of the abstract and the general might spring from a deeper source in James's thought than the habits of the novelist's trade; that the inability to see events in collective, rather than personal, terms might spring from a deep sense of what morality actually requires, and that the propensity to generalize (present in the novel, as we shall see, in the discourse of more than one of its socialist characters) might seem from this viewpoint to be a moral and also a political deficiency; that (as I have elsewhere argued) the best way to regard James might be not so much the way Howe regards him, as a novelist by trade who, because that was his trade, expressed in that form (with whatever its limitations) his moral vision, but as a thinker about human social life whose thought about life found in the novel its necessary form and fitting expression.

Putnam himself, however, has expressed, concerning Henry James, a reservation that, while related to Howe's, is both more fundamental and more carefully expressed.[7] Unlike Howe, Putnam acknowledges that it is essential to James's moral vision that the perception of particulars is in a sense prior to general moral rules and principles—that in this sense the fine-tuned nonabstractness of these

5. Irving Howe, *Politics and the Novel* (New York, 1957). The chapter on James is reprinted in *Henry James: A Collection of Critical Essays,* ed. L. Edel (Englewood Cliffs, N.J., 1963), 156–71. Page numbers are cited from that edition.

6. Howe, 165–67.

7. Putnam, "Taking Rules Seriously: A Response to Martha Nussbaum, *New Literary History* 15 (1983), 193–200; the article was a response to "Flawed Crystals."

novels appropriately expresses something that was important to James's conception of what human life should be. But Putnam expresses doubts about the value of this idea as a model, even for the personal life. He charges that this morality of perceptions, which is also a morality of tender attention towards particulars, is dangerously lacking in general rule-guided toughness. A person who deliberates in the way that James recommends might be all too free from binding obligations, all too capable of any trade-offs. I have more than once tried to answer this charge where personal morality is concerned, and to spell out carefully the dialogue between rules and perceptions that we actually find in James's morality.[8] But even if we can defend James in that context, we might still feel that the objection has some force in the political life, where even moral thinkers who advocate particularism in personal choice still sometimes claim that we need to be guided by firm and general rules.[9] Putnam has not connected his own political interest in art and literature (and in the related new model of progress, conservative with respect to culture) with these criticisms of James's conception of morality. But the juxtaposition of Putnam's anti-utopian "Note on Progress," so apparently close to the thought of Hyacinth Robinson, with "Taking Rules Seriously," so skeptical of James's heroes and heroines, forces *us* to inquire about the moral and, in this case, political viability of the Jamesian conception.

It is evident that James himself was prepared to defend his moral ideal as appropriate for the public as well as the private realm. He repeatedly speaks of the author's task as not only moral, but also political. And he once says, concerning the author's work in creating heroes and heroines of a certain sort, that the goal is

> to *create* the record, in default of any other enjoyment of it: to imagine, in a word, the honourable, the producible case. What better example than this of the high and helpful public and as it were, civic use of the imagination?—a faculty for the possible fine employment of which in the interest of morality my esteem grows every hour I live.[10]

So a central task of our reading of *The Princess Casamassima,* the most overtly public and civic among his many public and civic writings, must be to ask how a James character can (*pace* Howe) express political thought, and also how (*pace* Putnam) we might defend this thought as valuable in our actual political lives.

III

This novel places before us a consciousness of a certain sort, even as it also demands that we be, as readers, just such actively responding consciousnesses. In its intricate sentences and paragraphs it creates the record of such a mind, and it

8. In "Reply to Richard Wollheim, Patrick Gardiner, and Hilary Putnam," *NLH* 15 (1983) 201–8, in "Discernment" and in "'Finely Aware.'" The most important points from the reply are raised in this volume in the Introduction and in the endnote to "Flawed Crystals."

9. On this see "Discernment," this volume.

10. H. James, Preface to "The Lesson of the Master," in James, *The Art of the Novel* (New York, 1907), 222–23. See also the discussion of this passage in "'Finely Aware,'" this volume.

bids us, as we follow their complicated windings, to be ourselves the complexity it shows. This aspect of the novel is given tremendous emphasis, both within its design and in the remarkable Preface, one of James's most extended and justly famous accounts of the role of a certain sort of hero in his conception of the novelist's function. Hyacinth Robinson is a person "on whom nothing was lost" (I.169).[11] James has endowed him, he tells us in the Preface, with a fine sensitive intelligence, with the power to feel intensely everything that befalls him, with, in short, "the power to be finely aware and richly responsible" (I.viii). In contrast to the "coarse and the blind" (viii), for whom what befalls has little import, Robinson will be among "the more deeply wondering, . . . the really sentient" (viii). James stresses that while "the imputing of intelligence" is here the "very essence" (ix) of the novelist's work, by intelligence he means not simply intellectual keenness, but, rather more, an ability to perceive and also to feel the practical significance of each particular event and person and perplexity. Indeed, the distinction between responding and acting loses its sharpness in the life of such characters, since a great part of what they morally and significantly and assessibly *do* will consist in fitting response to the seen. "I then see their 'doing,' that of the persons just mentioned, as, immensely, their feeling, their feeling as their doing" (I.xi), he concludes. And the political scene of the novel will, crucially, be displayed to us through "a consciousness (on the part of the moved and moving creature) subject to fine intensification and wide enlargement" (xii), a consciousness many of whose most appropriate acts are just such feelings and perceptions. It is made clear that this is not simply a useful device for conveying to the reader a rich sense of what happens; it is a device with a distinct moral dimension, through which we get "the value and beauty of the thing" (xiii); we can count on Hyacinth Robinson not only as our storyteller, but also, in some sense, as a fine moral touchstone and guide.

I have written elsewhere about James's moral ideal and the role it plays in his claim that the work of the author and the reader is an exemplary kind of moral conduct.[12] I shall return later to some of the particular features of Hyacinth's moral imagination. But if we are to take James's heroes seriously as models for the political, as well as for the moral life, we must confront, clearly, a number of troublesome questions. First, we will be asked what political conception this moral norm implies. If it is best for human beings to be "finely aware and richly responsible," doesn't this imply that the best political structure is some sort of aristocracy or oligarchy? (And if it does, might this not give us reason to be skeptical of the moral norm itself?) This question is implicitly raised by many of James's novels, with their concentration on the vibrant sentience of people who just happen also to be leisured gentlemen and ladies, with these novels' suggestion that the essence of the moral life resides in the sort of exchange that might take place at a house party. *The Princess Casamassima* shows us that James does not shirk this ques-

---

11. All page references to the novel are to *The Novels and Tales of Henry James: New York Edition* (New York, 1907–9.) Volumes 5 and 6 of the edition are *The Princess Casamassima,* volumes I and II. The Preface to *The Princess Casamassima* will be cited in that pagination, and not as it appears in *The Art of the Novel.*
12. In "'Finely Aware,'" this volume.

tion, but anxiously confronts it. So one primary task of any reading of this novel would be to see what comes of that confrontation.

Next, we will have to turn from the question of political structure to the question of the political imagination and to the question raised by Putnam and Howe. To cast it in political terms, doesn't all this agonized feeling and subtle perceiving have both too much complexity and nuance and also too little rule-governed toughness? Don't we need something straighter, harder, more direct, more general, when it is social choice that is in question? Again, this is a question that James by no means shirks;[13] and he gives us an interesting array of political actors against whom, by contrast, the claims of Hyacinth's imagination can be assessed. As we consider them, we will also need to consider the political significance of Hyacinth's attachment to art and to the continuity of culture; for these attachments are presented as essential elements in his moral outlook, integrally connected to his way of seeing and feeling. And they have, clearly, political consequences of a problematic kind. Do we, then, want political actors who share those attachments?

Finally, we cannot avoid confronting the most intractable question, the question that bears in upon us with embarrassing force from the moment that we hear his name: Isn't such a character really too gentle for this world? Too soft, too little, too like a flower, too naturally incapable of violence and of crudely vigorous response, to engage in the political life, which seems much of the time to be nothing if not crude and violent? Isn't such a character, dedicated to tender care for the particulars, just the wrong sort of person for, and rather ludicrous in, that dark and corrupt environment? The delicacy that in the personal life, that in the work of the novelist, may be an asset looks in politics like a fatal liability. Such a person can do no good for anyone; he can only be crushed, or bent to the will of the oppressor. James will not permit us not to confront this question. From the names alone, we know that Hyacinth is a delicate plant to Paul Muniment's fortified stronghold. Is not a politics of perception, then, nothing more than a weak or foolish politics?

IV

If we take our moral norm from the movements of thought and feeling represented, and created in us, by James's sentences, must we then be aristocrats? It could seem so. For if that sort of finely responsive thinking has, as the novels frequently suggest, certain necessary conditions, such as the absence of mindless grinding labor, a certain level of education, and perhaps a certain amount of leisure, and if this sort of thinking is really the only sort we can trust for good decision making, then it might seem that we will be urged to leave decision making to a privileged few, and to let them take care, Platonically, of the interests of those who are too dull to see clearly on their own. In many of James's novels, this issue is simply not addressed; for we see there only the upper-middle and upper classes,

---

13. Compare the question of the imaginary interlocutor in the preface to "The Lesson of the Master": "Where on earth, where round about us at this hour," has James found "such super subtle fry?" (*Art of the Novel*, p. 221).

usually in conditions removed from work, even when we know (as in the case of Adam Verver, Lambert Strether, Mervyn Densher) that work has been a substantial part of their existence. But the issue is confronted head on in *The Princess Casamassima,* with its working class hero.

In order to see how James confronts the issue we must first distinguish, as many who depict James as an aristocratic conservative do not, between two sorts of defenses of aristocracy—or, better put, between a defense of aristocracy and a defense of a general political perfectionism. On the one hand, there is the traditional aristocratic view, of which James sometimes stands accused: the view that only the members of a certain class have, by nature, the refinement of mind that is essential to good governing, and that they, therefore, should govern for everyone. On the other hand, we have a perfectionist view that insists that not all human lives are equally complete, equally flourishing—even where moral development itself is concerned—and that this is so, in great part, because the central human capabilities have, for their development, material and educational necessary conditions that are not, as things are in most actual societies, available to all. The latter (Aristotelian) view is not a conservative view.[14] If we combine it, as Aristotle does, with the claim that it is the essential task of politics to make people, everyone in the city, capable of living well in the most important human ways, it generates a radical demand for social and educational change, with the aim of bringing to all human beings[15] the conditions of *eudaimonia* and practical wisdom. *The Princess Casamassima,* I believe, shows us that James's view is the Aristotelian view, and not the conservative/aristocratic view.

The novel shows to us clearly, recommends to us as an important social insight, that thinking, imagining, and even desiring are very much affected by the material circumstances of life—by nutrition, by the squalor or spaciousness, the beauty or ugliness, of one's surroundings, by education, by the stability and quality of one's family ties. The worst things about poverty and squalor, as this book presents them, is that they corrupt the capabilities of thinking, feeling, and desiring. Hyacinth tells the Princess that "centuries of poverty, of ill-paid toil, of bad insufficient food and wretched housing hadn't a favourable effect on the higher faculties. . . . In his own low walk of life, people had really not the faculty of thought; their minds had been simplified—reduced to two or three elements" (I.245–46).

This sentiment is, of course, not one that is easy for compassionate, privileged, somewhat radical people to swallow. We are, as readers expected to share the Princess's discomfort, as "she turned about, she twisted herself vaguely as if she wished to protest" (I.246). And yet the novel makes perfectly clear how far removed its own position is from the endorsement of hereditary aristocracy, by insisting repeatedly that it is material conditions, conditions that can be changed, that make the difference in thought. Once Hyacinth almost forgets this; but he is

14. See Nussbaum, "Nature, Function, and Capability: Aristotle on Political Distribution," *Oxford Studies in Ancient Philosophy,* Supplementary Volume 1988.

15. On the question of exactly who is included in Aristotle's own distributive project, see "Nature, Function, and Capability." For a discussion of the contemporary implications of Aristotle's view, see Nussbaum, "Aristotelian Social Democracy," in *Liberalism and the Good,* ed. G. Mara and H. Richardson (New York, 1990).

brought up short by Muniment who, for all his moral defectiveness when it comes to perceiving and feeling, still is permitted here to state the truth as the novel presents it:

'The low tone of our fellow mortals is a result of bad conditions; it's the conditions I want to alter. When those who have no start to speak of have a good one it's fair to infer they'll go further. I want to try them, you know.' (II.216)

Hyacinth assents to the diagnosis. And when, later, he finally ventures out, curious Princess on his arm, to confront for the first time the most squalid conditions in the London slums, he understands that even the desire for amelioration can be undercut by misery:

He was aware the people were direfully wretched—more aware, it often seemed to him, than they themselves were; so frequently was he struck with their brutal insensibility, a grossness proof against the taste of better things and against any desire for them. (II.262)

One may not like this. I find that my privileged students, at this point, wishing to be, as they take it, more compassionate, tend to protest, saying, for example, "But what about Tolstoy's peasants?" But the view that goodness and fine thought have no material conditions is a view inseparable, in Tolstoy, from a Christian conception of the soul as both impervious to material conditions and awaiting another world's reward. The novel does not endorse that conception of the soul. Indeed the otherworldly promises of Christianity are unambiguously portrayed, in James's novel, as accomplices of a callous and repressive aristocracy. (The Prince says that the absence in England of "the true faith" is what explains the excessive demands of the English poor for social change: with faith, one is willing to wait longer [II.312].) James would presumably claim that Tolstoy's sentimentalizing account of the poor is both false about the relation between the spirit and its material conditions and itself an obstacle to social progress. The more truly compassionate view, he could plausibly claim, is the one that shows the full ugliness of poverty without shrinking, and shows its cost not only to the body, but also to the soul. The humanistic writings of the young Marx about what full human functioning requires, and about the worker's alienation from all but the most animal use of his human faculties, correspond in their harshness to the perceptions of Hyacinth Robinson.[16] And the aim of those writings—as, I claim, of

16. See, for example, the following passage from *Economic and Philosophical Manuscripts of 1944*, written in response to Marx's reading of Aristotle:
It is obvious that the *human* eye gratifies itself in a way different from the crude, non-human eye; the human *ear* from the crude ear, etc. . . . The *sense* caught up in crude practical need has only a restricted sense. For the starving man, it is not the human form of food that exists, but only its abstract being as food; it could just as well be there in its crudest form, and it would be impossible to say wherein this feeding-activity differs from that of *animals*.
Trans. M. Milligan, in *The Marx-Engels Reader,* ed. Robert C. Tucker (New York, 1978), 88–89.

this one—was surely to arouse a less self-serving and a more radical kind of compassion toward workers, by measuring clearly the distance between their current lives and the full flourishing of which we think human beings capable.

The novel shows us as the most miserable in soul those whose physical conditions are horrendous. But it does not stop, clearly, at this point. It shows even the life of skilled laborers like Hyacinth to be, in part, a life inimical to the full exercise of practical reason. Here labor itself does not seem to be at fault: the trade of the bookbinders is shown, in the novel, as one in which much high humanity can be lovingly expressed. The workers at the bindery, and also the other skilled laborers who frequent the political meetings at the Sun and Moon café, are shown as decent fellows, capable of discontent, capable of vision, of friendship, of political deliberation. But they lack education; and their minds have not been influenced by the experience of high complex creation, either artistic or intellectual. Because nobody led them to read or otherwise perceive works in which thought is rigorous and sentiment refined, their own political discourse is usually muddy and gross. They strive for the good "blindly, obstructedly, in a kind of eternal dirty intellectual fog" (I.340). They continually repeat themselves; they substitute "iterations" for arguments. One of them "had always the same refrain: 'Well now are we just starving or ain't we just starving? I should like the v'ice of the company on that question.'" Others "remarked to satiety that if it was not done today it would have to be done tomorrow" (I.339). It comes as no surprise to the reader of James that there is in this novel no sentimentalizing of simplicity. Life, both personal and political, is a tough, complex business, requiring, at its best, much refinement of feeling and much clarity of thought. There is no use pretending that this thought and feeling spring up spontaneously, without education, or that political discourse without it is discourse at its best and most human.

Again, I think James is right here, both right and more truly compassionate than an author who would sentimentalize simplicity, or pretend that complexity has no requirements. James's view is as far from Tolstoy's as a social view can be, both on the issue of simplicity of soul and concerning the art we need to shape the soul. It is, however, very close, here again, to the views of the young Marx, who imagines that the worker's new-found leisure will be used for the full education of the mind, by contact with great works of art and literature.

How has Hyacinth escaped? For if we can understand how, in spite of these facts, a working class man can be a hero of a Henry James novel, we will have more insight into the background conditions for James's norm. Clearly Hyacinth has been brought up in conditions that meet adequate minimum standards of nutrition and health care. He is healthy and strong; and though Lomax Place is drab, it is not squalid, as we clearly see from his horrified reactions elsewhere. The availability of decent medical care is something James goes out of his way to document. When Pinnie is ill, Hyacinth calls in a famous expensive doctor, only to be told by this doctor that the treatment their usual local doctor had already given has been admirable. We also learn that Hyacinth has been raised stably and with love, by both Pinnie and Vetch; this, again, is given emphasis by juxtaposition to the casual domestic violence and drunkenness of the Henning establishment. (In that case, we are given some clear hints about a set of social problems that are often connected to poverty and that demand urgent attention.)

Hyacinth's work, furthermore, is not alienating work, work to which the worker feels external. He affirms himself in his bookbinding, identifies himself with what he produces, takes pride in his creations as expressions of his thought and feeling. And his work leaves him enough leisure to pursue social relations and entertainment. (Much of the novel's activity takes place on Sundays.)

And Hyacinth has been educated. Pinnie and Vetch have given every encouragement to his desire for learning, so that, in spite of class barriers, his resourceful mind has managed to go through quite a lot of great literature (we hear casual allusions to Dumas, Balzac, Musset, Tennyson), to attend the theater frequently, to listen to music, at least of the theatrical sort, to master French and some Italian, and to learn enough about the history of art so that he knows how to situate and appreciate what he sees when he later sees it. It is clear that Hyacinth is a remarkably well-motivated and able pupil. We are not led to believe that everyone could be a successful autodidact in this way. But Vetch, too, is one, and wiser than any aristocrat. And we feel that being brought up with a sense that this is what is absolutely expected of one's dignity has done far more than has native energy, important as that is, to propel Hyacinth on his way. So we are left with the thought that if education were not only demanded of all, but also held out to all (by the family, by society generally) as their appropriate birthright and the appropriate completion of the humanity they each have, an essential first step would have been taken. It's hardly a sufficient step; Sholto is educated without being intelligent, and the Princess' idle desire for new emotional intensities leads her to abuse the educated intelligence she possesses. But it is, in this world, something.

And this brings me to one last feature in Hyacinth's biography. His most unusual feature, if we contrast him with the novel's other working-class characters, is that he has been brought up to believe that he is really a gentleman—therefore, one of whom clarity of thought and refinement of sentiment are demanded, one of the ones about whom great works of art are written, one for whom there is no excuse if he does not live up to the standard held out in those works. Both the responsibilities and the opportunities of being a certain sort of human being are vividly conveyed to him in the myth of his origin on which he is lovingly brought up. And allegiance to a high image of himself is, throughout, an essential part of what keeps him straining to miss nothing, to be just and fine and gentle and lucid. By contrast, the other workers expect little of themselves, seeing their possibilities always in the images of members of their class held out to them by the disdainful aristocrats who control their cultural life. (Only Millicent Henning, with her boundless energy and her "large, free nature," manages to escape self-stereotyping and to live out her own unique part with a joyful exuberance that is no less wonderful, in its own way, than Hyacinth's subtle responsiveness.)

In this way James shows us another invidious feature of English class distinctions: that they cripple people's sense of the possible by tying images of high humanity to images of class membership. The life of Rosy Muniment is twisted by her inability to imagine beauty in other than an aristocratic garb; even the loving Pinnie associates freedom and nobility with images of aristocracy. And Hyacinth, too, is, finally, caught. He cannot imagine a constructive political solution because he thinks of the moral goal, always, in connection with the idea of becoming like one of the privileged ones. This is perhaps why, before the poor, his thought yields to "a sense of the inevitable and insurmountable" (II.262). James, however, shows us—through the limitations of his characters, Hyacinth among them—that what would be absolutely essential to any "ameliorating influence" (II.170) in education would be images of high humanity with which the pupil of whatever class might identify. It is one of his great achievements here to show us how Hyacinth both does and does not escape the traps set by a class-divided society for the thought and desire of a person of his class: escapes, to the extent that he finds ways of believing in his own dignity and projecting it into society, trusting the resources of his imagination; does not escape, to the extent that his image of himself as dignified is so closely linked to his fantasy of himself as a nobleman's child. Certain parts of French literature give Hyacinth a start beyond this point. For in Paris he proves able to imagine his proletarian revolutionary grandfather speaking to him, as in a novel of his own creation, with "a gaiety which even political madness could never quench", and with a French prose "delightful and sociable in accent and phrase" (II.122). This "vague yet vivid personage" (II.122) is the projected hero of a new literature for humanity. Hyacinth himself is, for us, another.

What, politically, does this give us? Seeing, as we must, through Hyacinth's eyes, we can see this none too clearly. But insofar as we are invited to think critically about him, we are invited also to imagine for ourselves the possibilities. We seem, in fact, to have a case made out for all three elements in Putnam's "model for a political stance." First, for socialism in the economy: for we are clearly shown that the provision to all of basic needs of life, including food, housing, recreational space, decent health care, and education, is an essential part of any society that would have any chance of transcending the wrongs with which this novel confronts us.

"Liberalism as the guiding principle in politics": this too is, I believe, in the novel. For James shows us a conception of the human being according to which our essential dignity resides in the free and responsive activity of thought and the free creative use of language. And he displays revolutionary socialism, insofar as it impinges on the liberties of thought and speech, as a prison for the spirit as pernicious as the prison of poverty. The frequency of images of the prison, and the denial of freedom, in connection with both socialism and the repressed condition of the poor, leaves no doubt of this intent. The novel's strong claims for the moral value of the literary imagination are inseparable from a demand for the artist's freedom of expression, for freedom of expression generally. The tyrannical attitude of the revolutionary leader Hoffendahl, who "treated all things, persons, institutions, ideas, as so many notes in his great symphonic massacre" (II.55) is contrasted throughout with the humanity of the artist's loving perception, an "ameliorating influence" (II.170) that could not survive under that sort of socialism. The contrast indicates that the latter had better not be put under the direction of the former.

The novel advocates liberalism, too, in its mistrust of revolutionary violence and its preference for patient slow change; this theme we shall examine shortly. It advocates liberalism, finally, in that, while it certainly does insist that not all ways of life are equally valuable, it insists as well that we do not want a politics that coerces diverse individuals into identical paths, or prevents their diverse self-expression in choices of profession, friends, entertainments. With Vetch we see as remarkably dreary the socialistic vision of Poupin,"where the human family would sit in groups at little tables, according to affinities, drinking coffee (not tea, *par exemple!*) and listening to the music of the spheres. Mr. Vetch neither prefigured nor desired this organized beatitude; he was fond of his cup of tea" (I.96). Here James confronts us with a telling point about many socialist (and many conservative) visions of the good: that they consist, all too often, of the enforcement as a general law for everyone of some elite's arbitrary preference. Because the Frenchman Poupin prefers coffee, everyone will have to have coffee. Vetch, wisely, wants to protect, albeit within a general vision of good human functioning, a substantial amount of space for the freedom of private choice.

"Conservatism as the guiding principle in culture." James suggests, as we have seen, the importance of creating new heroes, new identifications, of criticizing the old. He does not recommend nostalgic traditionalism, clearly. He also causes us to think about the need to devise ways of public access to the finest works of art, to humanistic education generally. But preservation, for all, of cultural traditions is, with these qualifications, a central emphasis of the novel. We shall shortly return to those arguments as we ask what sort of political agent a Henry James hero can be.

In short, there is, it seems to me, a political program, or at least a political stance, in this novel, and one that the Britain of the pre-Thatcher years was going a long way toward executing, with its combination of socialist economic policies in health and nutrition with the protection of liberal freedoms, with its policies of free public access to museums and galleries, with its public parks and musical performances, with its schemes, however vexed with difficulty, of public education.

V

We still have not answered Howe and Putnam. We still have not shown that the sort of consciousness James puts before us as exemplary *is* actually exemplary in the political life. Isn't a Henry James hero after all, as Putnam suggests, *too much* concerned with particulars and not enough with principle? Too much with the finely concrete and not enough with moral abstractions? To answer Howe we need to ask the same question. For what we want to show is that the absence of generality of thought and expression in Hyacinth Robinson—and in the novelist's consciousness as well—is not neglect or incapacity, but the deliberate creation of a different, and plausible, norm.

We have begun to say something of what, as an actor on the political scene, "our hero" is. (And since I have elsewhere discussed in detail the moral approach of Hyacinth's close relatives in *The Golden Bowl* and *The Ambassadors*,[17] I shall be brief.) Above all, Hyacinth is "a youth on whom nothing was lost." The "stage of his inner consciousness" (I.169–70) is peopled with rich impressions, as, "pre-

17. See "Flawed Crystals," "'Finely Aware,'" and "Perceptive Equilibrium," in this volume.

cociously attentive" (I.19) and "all-observant" (I.76), he responds, almost without conscious effort, to all that presents itself to his faculties, "seeing indescribable differences" (I.167) in things:

> For this unfortunate but remarkably-organized youth every displeasure or grati-
> fication of the visual sense coloured his whole mind, and . . . nothing in life had
> such an interest or such a price for him as his impressions and reflections. They
> came from everything he touched, they made him vibrate, kept him thrilled and
> throbbing, for most of his waking consciousness, and they constituted as yet the
> principal events and stages of his career. . . . Everything in the field of observation
> suggested this or that; everything struck him, penetrated, stirred; he had in a word
> more news of life, as he might have called it, than he knew what to do with—felt
> sometimes as he could have imagined an overwhelmed man of business to whom
> the post brought too many letters. The man of business indeed could keep a sec-
> retary, but what secretary could have cleared up for Hyacinth some of the strange
> communications of life? (I.159)

We see, here as elsewhere, not only a lively responsiveness of the physical senses, we see also that he *reflects* and *feels* intensely; reflects intensely even when reflec-tion leads to bewilderment, and feels intensely even when feeling has its "price." This combination of a capacity to be bewildered, *not* to simplify, with a willing-ness to be "penetrated" emotionally—all this, James makes clear, both in the text and in the Preface, is what makes him, in fact, a perceiver, on whom nothing is lost. For if you are going to see life as it is, you have to be willing to be perplexed, to see its mystery and complexity; consoling simplification brings dullness of vision. And, as Godfrey Sholto tells the Princess, "There are mysteries you can't see into unless you happen to have a little decent human feeling"—so if he is going to see he will have to "vibrate," in his heart, for what he sees. His feelings, as the Preface insists, are a large part of his morally assessible "doings," and in Hyacinth's relation to the world around him we "have then at once a case of feel-ing, of ever so many possible feelings, stretched across the scene like an attached thread on which the pearls of interest are strung"(I.xii).

James makes it very clear that Hyacinth's perceiving is inseparable from a keen sense of ethical value, and from an active love of human beings. The Preface tells us that his responsiveness is a responsiveness to value. And from the beginning of the novel Hyacinth "wants to be very good" (I.52); he "strove to cultivate justice in his own conduct," "catching every aspect and feeling every value" (II.7). The values he feels include, primarily, ethical values. And this means that his encoun-ter with human misery brings him torment (I.viii): his ability was "fairly founded on" the "knowledge of suffering." It is made clear that the ability to perceive par-ticular lives and contexts with clarity, and to imagine, as he constantly does, the motivations and experiences of others is combined with a general desire for good-ness and justice; and that it is this combination that makes Hyacinth a fine ethical and political agent.

But the nature of his fineness can even more clearly be seen from the novel's contrasts, as Hyacinth's richly peopled and concrete mind is set up against minds whose moral grossness is the consequence of an obtuseness of vision, a refusal to see and feel concretely any particular unique life. And it is James's contention, in the peopling of this novel, that most actual political thought and agency suffer from this obtuseness. Eustache Poupin is an honest, well-intentioned man, apparently generous and benign. And yet, from the moment when we are told of the coarse, flat sentimentality of his socialist image of utopia, in which "all the nations of the earth would abolish their frontiers and armies and custom-houses, and embrace on both cheeks and cover the earth with boulevards"—we know that the mind that is hooked on this image of "organized beatitude" has a dull eye for the actual lives of individuals. His eventual betrayal of Hyacinth is, from that moment, prepared. The grander direction of the revolutionary movement is shown as even more coarsely lacking in the ability to see and feel for people one by one—as the brief account of the mind of the revered leader Hoffendahl scathingly shows:

> Humanity, in his scheme, was classified and subdivided with a truly German thoroughness and altogether of course from the point of view of the revolution. . . . He treated all things, persons, institutions, ideas, as so many notes in his great symphonic massacre. (II.55)

But it is in the brilliant portrait of Paul Muniment, charismatic future leader of the socialist bureaucracy, that James gives us his most penetrating indictment of political generalizing. For Muniment's relation to Hyacinth is, or so it seems, a relation of personal friendship. To Hyacinth, this relation requires trying to see the good in Muniment's thoughts and actions, even when they seem impossibly remote from his own responses; and for Muniment, this *should* mean, or so we with Hyacinth expect, the effort, at least in this one case, to achieve an emotionally rich particular response and vision. Through the narrative of the failure of their friendship, in tragic bewilderment on one side and a high obtuseness on the other, James most pointedly shows us his case for a political discourse based on perception, and his indictment of the abstracting tendency.

From the beginning, we know that Muniment is coarse: "a delicate tact was not his main characteristic" (I.124), and his face "offered our quick youth the image of a rank of bristling bayonets." And Hyacinth finds for Muniment's remoteness from concrete human life images such that, if we are familiar with James's iconography of guilty innocence (of the kind of remoteness from the real that allows one to do terrible things with a sublime sense of one's own purity), we sufficiently get the tip: images of loftiness, of "singleness of vision" (II.218), description of a "touch of a hand at once very firm and very soft yet strangely cold" (II.212). Determined to love him still, and, loving him, to see the good in his betrayal, Hyacinth gets himself for a moment to carry, in his imagination, the "weight" of

> the sense of such a sublime consistency. Hyacinth felt that he himself could never have risen so high. He was competent to take the stiff engagement to Hoffendahl and was equally competent to keep it; but he couldn't have had the same fortitude for another, couldn't have detached himself from personal prejudice so effectually as to put forward in that manner for the terrible 'job' a little chap he to all appearances really liked. (II.136)

And shortly after this we understand how Muniment had risen so high. For we are permitted—perhaps through Hyacinth's empathetic efforts to understand him—a glimpse of the way the world looks through Muniment's eyes:

On behalf of others he never sounded the pathetic note—he thought that sort of thing unbusinesslike; and the most that he did in the way of expatiation on the woes of humanity was occasionally to allude to certain statistics, certain 'returns', in regard to the remuneration of industries, applications for employment and the discharge of hands. In such matters as these he was deeply versed, moving ever in a dry statistical and scientific air in which it cost Hyacinth an effort of respiration to accompany him. (II.137)

Above all, we learn, as we go on, of Muniment's "absence of passion, his fresh-coloured coolness, his easy exact knowledge, the way he kept himself clean (save for fine chemical stains on his hands) in circumstances of foul contact" (II.137). And emotionless and dedicated to having "as little" emotion "as possible" (II.291), he keeps himself clean to the end, but for the fine stain of his friend's life (scientifically and chemically recorded) upon his efficient hands.

This is political discourse. We cannot deny (thinking back, once again to the revolutionary parties of the sixties) that we recognize its note and know the people. We can't deny either that in a certain conventional sense Hyacinth's contrasted discourse and thought are personal and not political. He can't rise that high, breathe in that air. He cannot help seeing each individual person in all his or her individuality, in all his or her tangled web of relations to others and to himself, in all of his or her history; and his imagination, holding him close to the tangled world, will not permit him the lofty cleanliness of mathematical abstraction. But it's James's point that this commitment to the personal *is* political; that it is in rising so high that politics becomes capable of atrocity, ceases to breathe the human air. That the stance of the perceiver is superior not only on account of what it *can* see, be touched by, and therefore do (all the things to which Muniment is blind and which he therefore cannot include in any vision for a nation), but also on account of what it *cannot* do, is prevented from doing. James connects the delicate emotion-laden perception of particulars (Hyacinth's sort, infused with ethical aspiration and the desire for human justice) with gentleness and kindness, the ability to cut off emotion and to rise high above the people with the possibility of terrible acts. The claim seems to be that if you really vividly experience a concrete human life, imagine what it's like to live that life, and at the same time permit yourself the full range of emotional responses to that concrete life, you will (if you have at all a good moral start) be unable to do certain things to that person. Vividness leads to tenderness, imagination to compassion. The patient effort to see moderates the coarseness of which political horror is made. (We recall, in this connection, the tendency of Nazi functionaries to speak of Jews as "cargo," or as certain quantities of merchandise, to be packed, transported, quantified. Allowing themselves the sight of a particular human being was for them, as for Muniment here, a jeopardy.)

One scene in the novel makes this point with particular clarity. Hyacinth and Lady Aurora Langrish meet after both have been abandoned by the Princess. They sit "looking at each other in an odd, an occult community of suffering" (II.354). It now would be very natural that they might get angry together, express rage or hatred, even wish or plan some revenge. But this is not what happens:

> A tacit confession passed and repassed, and each understood the situation of the other. They wouldn't speak of it—it was very definite they would never do that; for there was something in their common consciousness that was inconsistent with the grossness of accusation. (II.354)

Here, as so often in James's novels, we find a refusal to retaliate, a refusal to hate, linked with the perceiver's fine consciousness of the particulars of the situation. The connection is made by responsiveness, by love. Hyacinth and Aurora love the Princess, love her in a perceiving way, seeing her in all her tangled complexity. To complain about her would be, then, too blindly self-proclaiming, too crudely unloving and self-absorbed. Focusing on *her,* they lay down their revenge. (The most persistent complainer and accuser in the novel is Rosy Muniment, wrapped in a fog of envy, unable to see beyond her own injured condition. And the socialists too are, all to frequently, as Hyacinth sees, motivated by the spirit of envy, which takes them away from the vision of what is before them.) Clarity leads, it seems, to gentleness. To see as the novelist sees is to see more humanely.

If this is plausible, then Howe's criticism misses the mark: for instead of showing himself incapable of political thought, James is offering us a searching critique of most actual political thought, and arguing that the sort of thought we usually call personal promises a politics richer in humanity. Lionel Trilling, whom Howe dismissively criticizes, saw all of this more deeply.[18] And as for Putnam's worry that the perceiver will be capable of anything, we see here, I think, a convincing argument that it is rather the person who goes by the general that we should worry about; that the perceiver (if adequately steered by an education that includes, we insist again, moral vision and good moral principles) will be most deeply and firmly bound to human values in choosing political action.

But we still have not described the whole of James's case for the politics of perception. For we still have not discussed one of this novel's central political insights, namely, the tension between the love of art and high culture and the politics of the workers' revolution. As Trilling has movingly shown,[19] Hyacinth's growing disenchantment with the motivations and goals of the revolution is closely linked to his love for art and culture, his desire to conserve this "fabric of beauty and power" (II.125) that he sees and, seeing, loves. Architecture, literature, and painting are for him "the richest expression of the life of man" (II.265), "splendours" that "took the form sometimes, to his imagination, of a vast vague dazzling presence, an irradiation of light from objects undefined" (II.217). This love of art, seen as a beauty and a mystery, is a great part of Hyacinth's tragedy, since it is his (true) belief that the revolution intends to destroy the continuity of culture, that Hoffendahl would with equanimity "cut the ceilings of the Veronese

---

18. Lionel Trilling, *"The Princess Casamassima,"* in *The Liberal Imagination* (New York, 1950), 58–92.

19. Trilling, ibid.

into strips" (II.146) that precipitates his abandonment of revolutionary goals. But what *are,* more specifically, the motivations and the political consequences of this desire to conserve?

In the first place, we have to say that Hyacinth's love of art is a natural consequence of his perceiver's approach to the world, and one that reinforces, in him, that approach. Hyacinth learned his habits of vision from books; and these habits make him, in turn, a better lover of books and other artworks. To love high art, literary or visual, one must stay close to the sensuous and the concrete; and if one combines Hyacinth's closeness with his dedication to the seeing of value, a deep response to great works of art is, James suggests, the natural result. Loving art, furthermore, makes him love more intensely, and with a generous love, the world and its concrete inhabitants, including, indeed, himself. As he walks along the Seine,

> a sudden sense overtook him, making his heart falter to anguish—a sense of everything that might hold one to the world, of the sweetness of not dying, the fascination of great cities, the charm of travel and discovery, the generosity of admiration. (II.141)

And, seeing in himself this connection between art and a generous love of the world, he comes to believe, as well, that art must be kept because it is, for all human beings, an incentive to life and to good life:

> 'I think there can't be too many pictures and statues and works of art,' Hyacinth broke out. 'The more the better, whether people are hungry or not. In the way of ameliorating influences are not those the most definite?' 'A piece of bread and butter's more to the purpose, if your stomach's empty,' the Princess declared. (II.170)

This is a difficult exchange for us, with our political interests and our sympathy with some aspects of Marx's vision. It might be taken to suggest, on James's part, a lack of concern with hunger and a callous preference for elite values. It also might be taken to negate the insight we earlier found in the novel: that perception and responsiveness have material necessary conditions. Both, I think, would be mistaken readings. What is being said is that politics must not address the problems of human life entirely from the bottom up, so to speak, thinking of the spirit only at a time when the needs of the body have been completely satisfied. The revolution wishes to destroy the treasures of art in order to get everyone materially satisfied. Hyacinth's argument is that any real solution to the problems of hunger and misery must take place in the context of an ongoing sense of life's richness and value and full humanity. That food has point only as food for something, and if the sense of this something is lost, feeding will be a feeding of animals. If, in the process of concerning ourselves for hunger, we allow life to be emptied of that which holds people to the world, that which inspires love of life and of humanity itself, then we will have, in the end, at best well fed pigs. James is clearly opposed to the role played by organized religion in getting people to place a certain sort of spiritual promise ahead of their material needs. His placement of those arguments in the Prince's mouth discredits them utterly. We should not accept a promise of comfort in the next world as a substitute for social change in this one. But James does hold that a more worldly development of spirit is an essential part of giving life, including material life, a human meaning, and that art, and what we might call a general education in the humanities, are an essential part of that development.

A further argument for Hyacinth's cultural view is found in his reflection about the connection between cultural continuity and a population's sense of its own identities, individual as well as collective. The revolution seems sometimes to him like a flood that will "ris(e) over the world" and "sweep all the traditions of the past before it" (II.262). This means pulling down "things with which the yearnings and tears of generations have been mixed" (II.146–46). It is clear that for Hyacinth it is not only the beauty and humane value of art, it is, as well, its historical depth as record of what has given a people its identity that makes him so fear its desecration. And his fear that under the revolution his trade of bookbinding will no longer win esteem (II.263) is a fear not only for the loss of beauty, but also for the loss of history and the historically constituted self. Once again, this is not an uncritical defense of tradition, nor is it the restriction of humanistic education to works drawn from the history of one's own culture. We are already aware of Hyacinth's keen interest in a new literature of the working class; and his imagination is stirred by many different images of humanity, distant as well as near. But he reminds us, simply, that *one* important function of humanistic education is to learn about one's own history, and that this historical understanding is essential to self-understanding.

There is a further point in Hyacinth's concern with culture that helps us, beyond what we have said already, to understand his new respect for patience in the political life. This is, that fine works of art, loved and studied, show, both in their content and in the facts of their production, some of the deeply rooted conflicts and tragic tensions out of which human history is woven: the connection of beauty with ugliness, of a high goal with someone's suffering and misery, of good with evil intentions. Hyacinth sees that the treasures he admires are "rescued" and "redeemed" from the people's misery and toil; that they issue from a civilization that supported this misery. His attention to them is full of critical reflection; in no sense is this a nostalgic traditionalism. (Indeed, it seems wrong to use Putnam's language of cultural *conservatism,* and I have not used it here.) And the art itself, he sees, expresses "yearnings and tears": in its very content it shows him (as this novel shows us) the complex tangle of human motivations, the frequent connection, as James wrote in another preface, of "bliss and bale, of the things that help with the things that hurt," of "somebody's right and ease" with "somebody's pain and wrong,"[20]—in short, the pervasiveness of tensions among the goods that, with imperfect attention and defective circumstances, human agents pursue.

James frequently insists that a central function of literary art is to show us the tensions that make us flawed objects with respect to our highest aims, the tragic tensions in our love and attention, as well, to the objects that claim us. And he reminds us that a knowledge of these flaws is an essential prerequisite of any gen-

---

20. Preface to *What Maisie Knew,* in *The Art of the Novel,* 143.

uine altruism—for, as Charlotte Stant says, "If we may perish by cracks in things we don't know, we can never then give each other anything." Denial of these difficulties breeds an innocence that is, in its exaggerated optimism, frequently intolerant and even cruel to what actually exists. Knowledge of difficulty breeds a tenderness to the flawed object, toward also oneself, seen as flawed.

Here James makes the point a political one. Great art plays a central role in our political lives because, showing us the tangled nature of our loves and commitments, showing us ourselves as flawed crystals, it moderates the optimistic hatred of the actual that makes for a great deal of political violence, moderates the ferocious hopefulness that simply marches over the complicated delicacies of the human heart. As Putnam writes, politics needs, what Marxism as he sees it lacks, a realistic moral psychology, an understanding of the humanly possible. It needs, too, an understanding of the plurality of human values and the often tragic tensions among them.

With this understanding goes a political attitude that is not more *tolerant* of evils, but is, perhaps, more inclined to mercy, less to anger, seeing how pervasive the obstacles to goodness are, how deeply rooted, how much a part of oneself as well as others. This politics tends to diverge from the strict and merited punishment toward humane patience, from cruel retaliation toward a slow gentle fostering of what good there may be. It is a politics of patient consistent labor for hardwon slow progress, a politics aimed (as Seneca once wrote, reproving political anger) "not at ending evils, but at preventing their victory" (*De Ira* II.10). We need art to keep difficulties before us, keeping us from excessive crudeness of hope.

The Princess Casamassima is itself just such a reminder of the difficult. For in its tragic conclusion, Hyacinth's sense of obligation to his promise (and to the cause of the workers, which he has agreed to represent) and his newer obligation to perception of the fine collide, leaving him, as he sees it, no exit but a bullet through the heart. His new awareness of art makes him more, not less, responsive to the workers' misery; he can abandon neither side.[21] Muniment's "sublime consistency" will, we know, always keep him safe from tragedy, enabling him to deny any claim that would be too difficult to see and to feel. The Princess, too, will in her way survive, for "the Princess Casamassima had a clear faculty of completely ignoring things of which she wished to take no account; it was not in the least the air of contempt, but thoughtful, tranquil, convenient absence, after which she came back to the point where she wished to be" (I.211). The high view of difficulty brings with it a terrible vulnerability, both to Hyacinth and to us, since his "emotions, [his] stirred intelligence, [his] moral consciousness, become thus, by sufficiently charmed perusal, our very own adventure" (I.xv). Seeing and feeling his tragedy, keeping his difficulty all before us, we see something that is true, for us, of the condition of goodness in the world.

Visiting Cambridge, Massachusetts, in 1941, W. H. Auden wrote a poem of reflection about the relationship between the political attitude that makes and is made by war and the habits of mind that are encouraged by the novels of Henry James, at whose grave the poet/speaker stands. This is a part of that reflection:

---

21. See the fine discussion of this in Trilling.

Now more than ever, when torches and snare-drum
Excite the squat women of the saurian brain
    Till a milling mob of fears
Breaks in insultingly on anywhere, when in our dreams
Pigs play on the organs and the blue sky runs shrieking
    As the Crack of Doom appears,

Are the good ghosts needed with the white magic
Of their subtle loves. War has no ambiguities
    Like a marriage; the result
Required of its *affaire fatale* is simple and sad,
The physical removal of all human objects
    That conceal the Difficult.

Then remember me that I may remember
The test we have to learn to shudder for is not
    An historical event,
That neither the low democracy of a nightmare nor
An army's primitive tidiness may deceive me
    About our predicament,

That catastrophic situation which neither
Victory nor defeat can annul; to be
    Deaf yet determined to sing,
To be lame and blind yet burning for the Great Good Place,
To be radically corrupt yet mournfully attracted
    By the real Distinguished Thing.

And shall I not specially bless you as, vexed with
My little inferior questions, today I stand
    Beside the bed where you rest
Who opened such passionate arms to your *Bon* when It ran
Towards you with Its overwhelming reasons pleading
    All beautifully in Its breast?[22]

In certain ways, I believe, Auden distorts James's moral vision—in particular, by placing the accent on a "radical corruption" of the heart, rather than, what James more often emphasizes, the difficulty of doing justice, in a tangled world, to all our loves and commitments, the difficulty even of seeing truly all we ought to see, feeling all that we ought to feel. But the essential point is wonderfully made: that war is, from the Jamesian viewpoint, the easy crude cowardly way with the problems of the moral and political life, whereas a patient lucid confrontation with difficulty is the way of true courage. War doesn't confront, doesn't *see,* our humanity, it simply breaks in on it. It appears to be strong, vigorous, passionate; but it avoids passionate engagement with the reality, the complexity of each thing. The James novel, on the other hand, confronts those complexities and ambiguities, opening its arms, passionately and tenderly, to humanity's hopes and conflicts as to a child, with all the love, patience, and gentle interest in the difficult that this parental relation entails.

22. W. H. Auden, "At the Grave of Henry James," in *Collected Poems* (London, 1979).

Now we see more fully why Hyacinth smiles when the Prince attributes to him a sentiment that agrees, verbally, with the Prince's own: "We must have patience." (Or, as the Prince earlier expresses it more freely in Italian, *"Che vuole? Ci vuol' pazienza."* ["What do you want? These things require patience."]) The Prince means by this that the poor should stop making trouble, should go get involved in otherworldly religion, should await the discretion and the almsgiving charity of their betters. Hyacinth does not mean this. He remains committed to the people to the end, though unable in his tragic situation to undertake a practicable strategy for their material and spiritual betterment. He does not want the people to depend upon characters like the Prince. And yet, he says, "We must have patience." For tragically, and with bewilderment, smiling in the dark, he is groping toward the thought that a genuine and lasting political solution must be achieved by a non-violent patient effort to change hearts and minds—an effort of the imagination, of persuasion, an effort, we might say, of writing and reading. This is not to say that such a politics would never find revolutionary strategies justified, for we know that Hyacinth admires the French Revolution. But such strategies will always be subordinated to the deeper and larger end of changing the heart; and all too often they do not serve, but actually impede, such changes. The revolution projected in the novel, for example, simply covers the depth of the problem. Hyacinth smiles, in the dark, at the irony and the difficulty of his verbal coincidence with the forces of reaction; at the difficulty of getting respectable lovers of the people to take this seriously as a response; the difficulty of convincing sensitive readers of life that what looks like a capitulation is actually the truest courage. And perhaps this smile in the dark is also the novelist's smile at the fact that intelligent readers will no doubt mistake his own advocacy of patience for reaction, his defense of perception for an aversion to political ideas.

VII

But still, isn't he simply too weak? James repeatedly brings us back to his littleness, his physical fragility, his delicacy, his vulnerability. How can "our little hero" (II.155), "our slight hero" (I.261) survive, after all, in politics? Isn't he bound to be simply walked over, even wiped out, by the "superior brutality" (I.338) of the Muniments of this world? Auden's poem, too, draws attention to this question; for its portrait of James embracing his vision of humanity is almost pathetic in the exposed and childlike character of the love it describes, pathetic by contrast to the violence that will, we feel, surely prove able to eclipse it. Isn't there in this novel a recipe for the impotence and even for the suicide of good?

James does not make this issue easy; for in many ways he does invite us to criticize Hyacinth Robinson. This imperfection in his hero (even beyond the general imperfection of human life) is an important part, we have suggested, of his design. For if he showed Hyacinth as escaping altogether through effort and imagination the constraints of his class-divided society he would undercut the case he makes for the link between perception and social conditions. Thus Hyacinth has the fault that comes of having, as images of dignity and worth, only images of aristocracy: he is far too trusting when it comes to the Princess, far too ready, generally, to see in the elegant a nonexistent moral worth. His failure to find a viable course of action is to some extent explained by these failings. And James complicates our question still further by placing together with Hyacinth, at the heart of the novel, a character altogether different, healthier, stronger, less refined, less credulous, but nonetheless still generous and compassionate and loving. Millicent Henning is, we might say, to Hyacinth what Bob Assingham is to Fanny: her simple rule-governed morality and her genuine kindness of heart sustain him in a very essential way. We are led to think that a healthy political community would be made up not only of Hyacinths, but, perhaps, from an affectionate partnership between these two sorts of spirits.[23]

But in the end we are brought back to "our hero," whom we love with all his difficulties. And here we must once again reply that it is not in the least evident that Hyacinth is, in the novel, a weak character. To say that he is weak is not to take seriously the inversion that James proposes in our usual judgments of weakness and of strength. We are asked to recognize that in patient lucidity and nonviolent slow effort are more strength altogether than in bristling bayonets, a courage to and for humanity rather than a flight from it into the sublime air. As Hyacinth turns the saying on its head, "One might as well perish for a lamb as for a sheep" (I.145)—for in being a lamb one exposes oneself for the sake of others, and shows in this a superior courage of imagination. Things that at first naturally strike us as ridiculous—for example, the name "Hyacinth Robinson," which would not get many votes in an election ("Muniment" perhaps would, suggesting a tough defense policy)—are, at the novel's end, to strike us as not only finer but also as braver than the tough things, just as it is braver to be a plant, as a man, than a fortification. For a real man *not* to dare to be a flower: *that,* we must see, is the cowardly thing. Lady Aurora Langrish, who patiently helps people one by one, is, in this same way, seen to be a far more courageous revolutionary than the radicals, who play games of violence without looking any one human life in the face.[24]

VIII

There is, then, a revolution called for in this novel. Not the revolution its characters envisage at the start, but one both more achievable and more radical. Not the revolution that consists in hating and then in killing, but the revolution in the heart that consists in learning to see and to love, without disgust, imperfect human beings. It is the demand that we not rest content, as social beings, with half-baked abstract discourse and crude perceptions, with what James elsewhere calls "the rule of the cheap and easy"; but that, in public and in private, we create our lives with one another with as much subtlety, responsiveness, delicacy, and imagination as are involved in the creation of a work of literary art, dismantling our anger, fostering our gentleness. That, as a politics of perception requires, we work with patient commitment to bring to human beings the material conditions of this life of the spirit, and, at the same time, the spiritual and educational conditions of a

---

23. See my discussion of the Assinghams in "'Finely Aware.'"

24. See the related reflections in Isaiah Berlin, "On the Pursuit of the Ideal," *New York Review of Books,* March 17, 1988.

loving relation to the world and to one another. Novels like this one create that revolution as a record, and also generate it, as an act, in the hearts of its readers, who exemplify for some brief hours the record and who may come to feel, thereafter, a marked discontent with the crudeness of everyday discourse and action and feeling, a marked desire for the finer, the more truly compassionate, thing. As James said: "What better use than this of the high and helpful public and, as it were, civic use of the imagination?"

"And suppose the readers don't feel this. That nothing happens and it all goes its way as before."

"What do you want? These things need patience."

(Smiling, perhaps, in our darkness.)

Endnote

The Introduction and several of the essays (especially "'Finely Aware'" and "Perceptive Equilibrium") have spoken of an Aristotelian philosophy whose investigations are affectionate conversations among friends. This essay provides an example of that sort of investigation. For it shows a part of an ongoing exchange of perceptions within a friendship that has supported my reflections on the issues of this book for twenty years. It was written for a volume in honor of the sixtieth birthday of Hilary Putnam, Walter Beverly Pearson Professor of Modern Mathematics and Mathematical Logic at Harvard University. To philosophers reading this volume, Putnam needs no introduction. But since many readers of the essays may not know his work, I have a welcome excuse for introducing him.

Putnam is among the very finest living American philosophers, one of a small number whose work towers above the profession in scope, power, and depth of insight. He has made outstanding contributions in almost every major area: logic, philosophy of mathematics, philosophy of physics, general philosophy of science, metaphysics, epistemology, philosophy of language, philosophy of mind, moral and political philosophy, philosophy of literature. His work is Aristotelian in its ability to range over many areas, bringing insights developed in one area to bear on problems in another; Aristotelian, too, in its combination of rigor with generosity of human concern. Among the major Anglo-American philosophers of his generation, Putnam has been virtually unique in his respect for the great works of the history of philosophy and in his enthusiastic use of history to illuminate current concerns. Equally unusual has been his respect and love for literature, his interest in developing an ethical view that will make room for the insights embodied in literature. He is well known for pursuing the truth wherever it leads, even if this means rejecting an earlier position; thus, his philosophical opinions have frequently changed over time. The reference to a change of opinion also alludes to the fact that we have coauthored a paper, entitled "Changing Aristotle's Mind" (forthcoming in a volume of essays on Aristotle's *De Anima,* ed. M. Nussbaum and A. Rorty), whose subject is the need to revise certain current views of Aristotle's position on the mind–body problem; we also describe changes in our own position regarding the correct reading of Aristotle.

Putnam was a leader of antiwar activity on the Harvard campus during the Vietnam War. Having at first been a liberal opponent of the war, he then moved to the left and joined the Progressive Labor Party wing of the SDS. For several years he was deeply involved in political activity. When I first met him (the event described in the paper), he was a guest speaker at a conference for new recipients of Danforth Graduate Fellowships; I was a first-year graduate student helping to organize the conference for that year's newly elected fellows. (My own political position was that of a supporter of Eugene McCarthy and the liberal opposition to the war.) Putnam left PL a couple of years later; he now holds the positions described in the article. Like Hyacinth Robinson he is a person "on whom nothing is lost"; like Robinson, a person of deep loyalty, generosity, and courage.

This essay relies on a previous sympathetic assessment of Aristotelianism in personal ethical reasoning, and thus on the arguments of "Discernment," "Flawed Crystals," and "'Finely Aware.'" Like "Discernment," it attempts to extend those conclusions into the area of political reasoning. In the process it attempts to confront two charges against the Aristotelian/Jamesian view that in my experience have been especially pervasive: (1) the claim that the position that there is an objective answer to the "how should one live" question is bound to be an elitist and reactionary position; and (2) the claim that James's emphasis on the individuality of perception and imagination is in itself bourgeois and reactionary. These claims are often made with a certain vagueness; so before one answers them one must state them more precisely. This the article tries to do. The first claim is heard especially often in recent literary theory, where defenses of objective truth (even sophisticated ones, involving notions like Putnam's "internal realism") are all too quickly branded as reactionary and even "fascistic" (see "Sophistry"). In responding to this it is important to recall the many ways in which relativist appeals to local tradition and denials of objectivity have been invoked to support reactionary and even totalitarian views in politics; it is equally important to note what James keenly notices, how corruptible desire and perception are as witnesses to the good. The second claim I discuss at length in the article. It is wonderfully explored, with reference to contemporary left-wing politics, in Doris Lessing's *The Golden Notebook*.

In a series of interrelated papers not included in this volume, I develop the Aristotelian political view further:

"Nature, Function, and Capability: Aristotle on the Basis of Political Distribution," *Oxford Studies in Ancient Philosophy,* Supplement Volume 1988.

"Non-Relative Virtues: an Aristotelian Approach," in *Midwest Studies in Philosophy* 1988, and forthcoming in a slightly different form in M. Nussbaum and A. Sen, eds., *The Quality of Life,* Oxford University Press.

"Aristotle on Human Nature and the Foundations of Ethics," forthcoming in a volume on the philosophy of Bernard Williams, ed. R. Harrison and J. Altham, Cambridge University Press.

"Aristotelian Social Democracy," in *Liberalism and the Good,* ed. G. Mara and H. Richardson (New York, 1990).

Since questions about the role of "great books" in education have recently played an important role in American political debates, it is important to say what I believe this novel, and my reading of it, imply for issues of a curricular nature.

(Here I make no claim on behalf of Putnam, whose "cultural conservatism" may be a different position from my own.) The novel insists that the humanities, including the study of excellent works of literature and art, are a central and ineliminable part of a good education. They cannot and should not be *replaced* by books of a more technical or social–scientific sort, though such books may have their own usefulness. This is the central curricular idea that I see the novel as putting forward; and I support it. (See also "Discernment.")

But questions will be raised about *what* books the novel urges us to place at the center; and the suggestion may be made that Hyacinth's clear preference for recognized classics of the Western tradition is the novel's own recommendation. I believe that things are more complicated. Hyacinth has, as we have seen, three arguments for the importance of literature and art in education. One concerns the role of art in realizing people's fullest capabilities as feeling and reasoning beings; one concerns history and the historically constituted sense of identity; one concerns the importance of understanding difficulties and tensions one is likely to encounter in trying to live well. The first and third arguments require works of depth and excellence; they do not require works from one tradition rather than another. And indeed the novel's complex ruminations on the first argument suggest that people will do best, educationally, when they interact with works that include and validate their own origins and promote their self-respect. (Such novels would also be valuable for nondeprived people, in learning to respect them.) Hyacinth has therefore had to invent a working-class hero; and James has, of course, done the same. The curricular implication of this, where our own society is concerned, seems to be that we should choose excellent works from a variety of perspectives, including underclass and minority perspectives. And if we add to these concerns another that James himself does not make central here, but does in other novels—the concern for respect and understanding *across* cultures—this gives us further reason to choose a diversity of origins in our selection of excellent works.

The second argument does underline the importance of understanding one's own tradition and history. But, first, it understands that project to require studying the history of exclusions from high culture (the people's misery and toil) as well as the history of high culture itself; and, second, it in no way militates against a diversification of the curriculum, as long as one's own tradition is *among* the topics to be studied.

Sophistry About Conventions

> We'll let Teisias and Gorgias continue sleeping. For they noticed that
> plausible stories win more public honor than the truth. And so they
> make trivial things seem important and important things trivial
> through the power of their discourse, and they dress up new views in
> old language and old views in new language, and they have discovered
> how to speak about any subject both concisely and at interminable
> length.
>
> Plato, *Phaedrus* 267a6

The sophists are once again among us. Like Socrates, we need a "true rhetoric."
That is, we need a form of discourse about literature that concerns itself with real
things of serious human importance and that reveres, in so doing, the recently
despised notions of truth, objectivity, even of validity in argument, clarity in definition. For if we are talking about real things, it does matter, and matter deeply,
whether we say this or that, since human life, much though we may regret the
fact, is not simply a matter of free play and unconstrained making. And if it matters, it is worth taking the pains to do years of undramatic, possibly tedious, rigorous work to get it right.

That is my initial unsorted reaction to Stanley Fish's paper, much of which I
found alarming. It will be evident that I am expressing two related worries—one
about the content of some of the views expressed, the other about a way of proceeding in giving them expression. One about a loose and not fully earned extreme
relativism and even subjectivism, the other about a disdain for rigor, patience, and
clarity in some of the discourse articulating this subjectivism or relativism. For a
number of contemporary literary theorists, as for the Greek sophists, these two
items, content and form, are not accidentally connected. For if one really believes
that each person (or group) is the criterion of truth and/or that there is no salient
distinction between rational persuasion and causal manipulation, one is not likely
to have much respect for traditional philosophical ways of attending to validity
and clarity. One will tend to regard those who go on about such things as reac-
tionaries who have failed to see something. (The terms *left* and *right* were freely,
and astonishingly, used in Fish's paper to make this point, lambasting the unfash-
ionable truthseekers among us. I am not sure what political position in America
does have a deep commitment to open public dialectic governed by traditional

220

norms of rational argument and fair procedure, but I believe that it is not the right. I have a suspicion that it just might be that equally maligned and allegedly old-fashioned character, the liberal.)[1] At the same time, if one secretly, or openly, despises rational argument and wishes, like Gorgias, to win fame and fortune by some other means, what more convenient doctrine to espouse in the process than the Gorgianic view that there is no truth anyway and it's all a matter of manipulation, more or less like drugging? Then one's failures to exhibit the traditional rational virtues will look like daring rather than sloppiness.

I have mentioned sophists. And in fact I want now to talk about the Greeks. For the history of relativism and its interaction with dialectic in Greek philosophy contains clearly many moves that are being made in current literary debates about truth. We can perhaps see the illegitimate transitions more clearly, and understand what motivates them better, when the object of our scrutiny is further from ourselves.

Greek philosophy, in both science and ethics, began, it appears, by being naively realistic. Alternative scientific views were put forward without any hesitation as candidates for the way things really were in the universe. Even ethical norms were taken to be given for all time by the gods, independently of culture or history. During the fifth century, a variety of factors caused thinkers to focus on the presence of an irreducible human element in the purported eternal truths, an element of interpretation or conceptualization that seemed to entail that our theories do not passively receive and record a prearticulated given. (Among the factors that led to this emphasis were: the discovery of quite different human communities that lived by quite different beliefs; a new interest in the way our perceptual apparatus shapes what it receives; the presence of radical or skeptical views that forced the recognition that for us to think and speak at all, certain things must be accepted as true—for example, the world must contain plurality and change, and so forth.) It seemed to some no longer possible to reassert the old story of the received and altogether uninterpreted given.

At this point, the field was open for a variety of responses. One fashionable one was the view that came to be called Protagorean subjectivism, though it is unlikely that Protagoras himself held it. This is the view that, given the variety and non-homogeneity of the deliverances of perception, and given the apparent absence of any "harder" criterion of adjudication, each person must be regarded as the criterion of truth. If the wind feels hot to A, it just is hot for A; if it feels cold to B, it just is cold to B; and nothing more can legitimately be said. A more radical version dropped the qualifications "for A" and "for B"; its holders were thus forced to suspend the Principle of Noncontradiction. The wind is at one and the same time both hot and cold, just in case we can find two people to say so. (The view was not confined to cases like heat and cold, where its appeal is at least comprehensible; it was a quite general view about all assertions.)

---

1. All this talk of "left" and "right" in connection with professionalism and antiprofessionalism seems to do little more than reopen the old question whether there is any substantial difference between authoritarianism and totalitarianism; and it is far less interesting than that debate, since the metaphorical use of terms here is so vague. (Is the profession as described by Fish a military junta or a party? Does it matter?)

This doctrine leads naturally to a question about what discourse and teaching can be. Since each citizen or each critic is the arbiter of how things are, how can the Protagorean attract pupils? This was a troublesome question. The Protagorean position implies that argument is not really argument; it removes the idea of a common truth concerning which we are striving to come into agreement. In its mild form it tells us that there are no arguments, only assertions of one's views and perceptions. In its radical form it knocks a vital prop out from under all argument by doing away with noncontradiction. What, then, is going on when people purport to argue and to instruct? And why should we listen to a professional instructor? Gorgias provided one famous answer. What discourse really is, is a kind of drug, a tool for the causal manipulation of behavior. Like Stanley Fish, he (or his spokesperson Helen of Troy) asserts that there is no distinction between persuasion and force. It is all manipulation, and the ability to manipulate can be taught. The influence of this position produced, as one might expect, a serious crisis of confidence in the political arena. As one of Thucydides' speakers puts it, "A state of affairs has been reached where a good proposal honestly put forward is just as suspect as something thoroughly bad." (This state of affairs seems to me to be the logical conclusion of Fish's way of talking and the climate of discussion that it naturally engenders.)

Now the thing that is likely to strike us as we examine these developments is that they are not rational. The discovery that there is not a divine code fixed eternally independently of our existence and thought, the discovery that truth is to some extent or in some manner human and historical, certainly does not warrant the conclusion that every human truth is as good as every other and that such time-honored institutions as the search for truth and the rational criticism of arguments have no further role to play. We wonder, then, what would motivate people to make this inference, and what would lead others to applaud them when they made it.

Aristophanes, wise here as in so many things, provides a revealing example. A young man comes home from a day of sophistical education. He says to his father, "Dad, I can prove to you that sons ought to beat their fathers." The father exclaims, "But that's not the convention anywhere." He has said the magic fashionable word, and now the son's fatal "proof" follows directly. If these beliefs are really only conventions, then, says the son, it was a human being who made them, a human being just like you and me; and he imposed them on others by force of persuasion. So then I, being a human being, can perfectly well make my own new convention, that sons should beat their fathers in return for the beatings they received as children. What is most amazing of all, the father, "persuaded," bends over and takes his beating. Now in this farrago of Protagorean my-law-is-as-good-as-his and Gorgianic let's-impose-our-law-by-any-means-we-can, there is an important truth lurking—namely, that this son *wants* to beat his father. The argument appeals not because it is a good argument, which it plainly is not (for there are all sorts of good human grounds for preferring the old set of human institutions to this one), but because it is a handy, elegant justification for what this son want to do anyway. He doesn't want truth, he wants power. This shows us something about him, not something about truth. It does not show us that truth is power, or that there is no such thing as the search for truth as distinct from the search for power. The father's acquiescence is no mystery either, if we read the rest of the play and understand its warnings about the extent to which simple people who try to emulate the intelligentsia can be led by the nose out of sheer guilt over their own rusticity.[2]

In this situation, with sophists getting richer and truth in disrepute, many lovers of the search for truth gave up in exhaustion and despair. Both Plato and Aristotle record this problem, as they grapple with the challenge of defining a true and honest rhetoric—or, as Aristotle puts it, a dialectic that is distinct from mere eristic.[3] But so as not to set that sort of negative example for one's students, it is important, they both agree, to get into the arena and grapple with these famous people, unravel their arguments, and show them that there is profound incoherence in their own position.[4] Not all will in fact be persuaded by such attempts, for "some need persuasion, and others need violence," Aristotle wryly remarks, recording his belief in the importance of this difference.[5] His attempt to restore the search for truth (in all areas) to its place of honor is a good one for us to examine, since (as I have argued elsewhere)[6] it relies on no idea of a reality "as it is," given to us independently of all conceptualization; and yet it argues that within the "appearances," that is, the world as perceived and interpreted by human beings, we can find all the truth we need, and much more than the sophists believe.

At the rock-bottom level, there will be at least one principle—the Principle of Noncontradiction—to which any thinking, speaking being is committed just in virtue of being that. As Aristotle argues in chapters of *Metaphysics* 4 concerned with the Protagorean opponent, we can show the attacker of this principle that any discourse in which he engages, even in articulating his attack, depends on this principle. He has only two choices: either he will say something or he will remain silent. If he remains silent, we no longer have to deal with him. "It is comical to

2. The scene in question is Aristophanes *Clouds,* 1399ff. It should be noted that the father is brought to his senses by the son's suggestion that he will beat his mother as well. I have discussed this scene and related questions about convention and truth in "Aristophanes and Socrates on Learning Practical Wisdom," *Yale Classical Studies* 26 (1980), 43–97, and in "Eleatic Conventionalism and Philolaus on the Conditions of Thought," *Harvard Studies in Classical Philology* 83 (1979), 63–108.
3. On the distinction, see G.E.L. Owen's fundamental paper, "Dialectic and Eristic in the Treatment of the Forms," in Owen's *Logic, Science, and Dialectic: Collected Papers in Greek Philosophy* (London and Ithaca, N.Y., 1986), 221–38.
4. The possibility of discouragement is described this way by Aristotle, in connection with his criticism of Protagorean subjectivism: "And it is at this point that the most unfortunate consequence arises; for if those who have observed the available truths most closely—and they are those who have sought hardest for them and cared most about them—if they hold opinions of this kind and make these pronouncements about truth, will not those endeavouring to philosophize legitimately lose heart. The quest for truth would be a wild goose-chase" (*Metaphysics* 1009b33–1010a1, trans. Kirwan).
5. Aristotle, *Metaphysics* 1009a16ff. The passage continues: "If they have this belief (sc. that the Principle of Non-Contradiction is false) as a result of perplexity, their mistake is easy to remedy, for the difficulty is not with their statement but in their thinking. But if they state it for the sake of stating it, the remedy is to refute the statement which is in their speech and in their words."
6. M. Nussbaum, "Saving Aristotle's Appearances," in *Languages and Logos,* ed. M. Schofield and M. Nussbaum (Cambridge, 1982), 267–93; a revised and expanded version of this paper appears as chapter 8 of *Fragility.* The following paragraph condenses portions of that discussion.

look for something to say to someone who won't say anything. A person like that insofar as he is like that, is pretty well like a vegetable" (1006a13–15). But if he does say something, and something definite, then you can go on to show him that in so doing he is in fact believing and making use of the very principle he attacks. For in order to be saying something definite he has to be ruling out something else as incompatible—at the very least, the contradictory of what he has asserted. Very near this bottom level will be certain other beliefs—for example the belief that change and plurality exist—that also seem to be so deeply embedded in all thought and discourse that we suspend them on pain of incoherence. At the "top," on the other hand, will be various beliefs and principles that seem purely arbitrary, that we could alter readily without changing much of serious importance. (As examples of such items Aristotle mentions certain superficial religious beliefs and conventions, for example, regarding the proper dates of festivals.) Most of the interesting cases are in the middle somewhere: it would be possible to continue to live and to speak without these principles, and what we need to do in assessing the depth of our commitment to any one of them is to ask what the cost of doing without it would be, what other beliefs, practices, attitudes would have to be given up. For example, suppose we were to believe that luck, and not our own effort, has the decisive role in making our lives valuable. Aristotle says that if we imagine taking that belief to heart, we will see that it would make our lives so flat and meaningless that we would not want to live. Philosophy justifies a belief like this by perspicuously showing its depth and centrality in our lives.

This is only the beginning of a sketch of what is involved in the Aristotelian reply to the sophists. I believe that it offers a basis for a coherent, non-naive, "internal" realism, though I have obviously not begun here to work out the position in the detail that would be required to show this. The view has close affinities with the antirelativism of Putnam's paper and with the internal realism of his *Reason, Truth and History.* Indeed, the Aristotelian argument about noncontradiction is accepted and developed by Putnam (for a somewhat weaker principle, the Minimal Principle of Contradiction) in a previous article whose argument Putnam still endorsed at this conference when dissociating himself from Mary Hesse's claim that everything is revisable.[7]

Now to draw some further parallels between my Greek story and the material of the conference. In Fish's paper and the discussion that surrounded it,[8] I notice two different sorts of language used of our relation to our beliefs and principles. On the one hand, we have the language of optionality—words as "stipulate," "construct," "judge," "decide," "convention," "useful"—all of which imply that the beliefs in question are items that we can exchange, take up, put down at will and/or because it is advantageous to do so. This is the language we noticed in connection with the Aristophanic son, who moves from the humanness and contingency of certain principles directly to an assertion of their optionality. If a

7. Hilary Putnam, *Reason, Truth and History* (Cambridge, 1981), and his "There Is at Least One *a priori* Truth," Erkenntnis 13 (1978) 153–70, reprinted in Putnam, *Realism and Reason: Philosophical Papers, Vol. III* (Cambridge, 1983), 98–114.

8. I am thinking also of the use of these two sorts of language in Richard Rorty, "Texts and Lumps," *New Literary History* 17 (1985) (i.e., the issue in which this essay was originally published).

human being made it, I can make a new one right now. On the other hand, we also find the language of depth: there is talk of the beliefs of the community being compelling, of principles informing and shaping us, even of the notion that the individual is constituted by his or her communal heritage. Fish mixes the two sorts of language in his paper. He asserts in debate that the latter is the more fundamental, and that insofar as his use of words like "stipulate" seems to imply that we are free to select our beliefs and values, those words do not truly express his position. I believe, however, that in his rejection of the distinction between persuasion and force and his defense of the idea that the profession is the criterion of truth, we find an Aristophanic son lurking behind the evident Gorgianic surface. For if the profession is not free to decide between *p* and not-*p*, if the matter is too deep to be a matter for professional optionality to alter it, then there is after all a place from which the community is entitled to criticize the profession, and it will often make perfect sense to say that the profession is flying in the face of some deep truths that any thinking being must hold. So I think that he cannot have the power and sheer arbitrary freedom he wants for the profession without endorsing conventionalism in a more radical form than he officially does. And if we look beyond the conference to the writings of numerous contemporary theorists, we will again find these two forms of expression used, sometimes separately, sometimes in combination, often without much concern for their relation to one another. (Derrida, for example, seems to speak like Protagoras/Aristophanes at the conclusion of *Éperons:* if there's no way of eliminating the possibility of alternative interpretation, then each critic becomes the arbiter of truth and criticism appears to become free play;[9] though at other times he certainly prefers the language of depth and constraint.)

What the Greek story shows, I claim, is that the two sorts of language do not go together. To the extent to which it is appropriate to say of a principle or belief that it is optional for us, to that extent it is not deep in our lives. To the extent to which it is constitutive of our procedures of life and thought, to that extent it is not optional at all. Aristotle was, I believe, correct in thinking that among the primary jobs of philosophy, if not the primary one, is the sorting out of our beliefs and principles to see where they fall along this spectrum. And he was also correct in thinking that once this painstaking task was underway, we would discover that we get back just what the Protagorean and the Gorgian want to deny us, namely, full-blown notions of public truth, of rational justification, of objectivity. When we are confronted with a contradiction between two principles, we do not say, well then, since there's no uninterpreted given, it's all free play and any story has as good a claim as any other if it can be made persuasive. We try to resolve the contradiction first, of course. But if we cannot, we recall the very basic commitment we have to the Principle of Noncontradiction as necessary for all thought and discourse. Using this, then, as a regulative principle (refusing to assert the contradiction), we set ourselves to adjudicate between the competing principles, asking in each case what the cost would be of giving each up. And we opt for the one that "saves the greatest number and the most basic," as Aristotle puts it, of our other beliefs.

---

9. For a related discussion of skepticism, see "Love's Knowledge," this volume.

Let me take an example from contemporary ethical theory. John Rawls has advanced various arguments against Utilitarianism and in favor of his own principles of justice. One of them goes, roughly, like this. (I hope that I shall be forgiven for the oversimple and schematic character of this summary.)[10] We first show that Utilitarianism is committed to a picture of the aggregation of desires that neglects or treats as ethically irrelevant the boundaries between separate persons. We show that the principles of justice do not neglect the separateness of persons. We then ask the Utilitarian whether he or she does not share with us a conception of the person that makes these boundaries highly relevant, indeed fundamental. If the Utilitarian agrees with our diagnosis, she agrees that there is an internal inconsistency in her position, which can be resolved by her giving up whichever of the conflicting principles (either the conception of the person or the Utilitarian principle) appears less deep or fundamental. Rawls bets that most Utilitarians will find the conception of the person to be more fundamental and thus that the two of them will decide to agree on the principles of justice.

Here is an example of rational argument, of rational justification, that in no way relies on an uninterpreted given; it can be said to yield, in a perfectly recognizable sense, ethical truth. It is altogether different from mere rhetorical manipulation because it proceeds by the patient clarification of alternatives and by the detection of incoherence and contradiction. And it allows ample room for a reasonable antiprofessionalism. For with such arguments Rawls can go before the profession of economics, for example, and convince it of the shallowness and incoherence of some of its reasoning, showing that certain economists have not properly articulated some beliefs about persons that they themselves hold, and have not noticed their relation to their own other beliefs. Rawls's ability to offer a justification of the principles of justice against the Utilitarian economist does not depend on his being well trained in economics (although he is so, and although *in practice* his ability to convince actual economists is certainly helped by this). It depends on his caring about human matters that are common ground between him and the profession, and caring about coherence and rational persuasion. They may or may not in fact be convinced; that is not the point. The point is that we can recognize this as the sort of argument that ought to convince anyone who proceeds rationally and who does not find fault with its premises.

Fish will be quick to reply (as he did at the conference) that my critical remarks about arguments do not really go against his thesis, since insofar as they criticize the conduct of the profession they become a part of it. By this means he can of course serenely swallow up just about anything. But I assert that I am not a part of the professional activity he describes, in two ways. First, I hold that there is a strong distinction between persuasion and manipulation; I claim to be trying to play by the rules of the former. I couldn't care less whether I in fact persuade Fish

10. Rawls first develops this argument in *A Theory of Justice* (Cambridge, Mass., 1971), 189ff. The role of the conception of the person in the argument for the principles of justice, and associated remarks about justification and objectivity, are also developed in his "Kantian Constructivism in Moral Theory: The Dewey Lectures 1980," *Journal of Philosophy* 77 (1980), 515–72. For further discussion of this sort of argument, see my "Aristotle on Human Nature and the Foundations of Ethics," in a volume of essays on the work of Bernard Williams, ed. J. Altham and R. Harrison (Cambridge, 1991).

or anyone else in the profession, so long as I offer an argument that, were they following certain rational procedures, they would accept. Insofar as the profession is playing the other game that Fish describes, I am not, then, a part of it. Second, there is in general, as the Rawls case shows, an important distinction to be drawn between having views about an institution or profession and leading the way of life characteristic of that institution—between, for example, being a doctor and having some views about how doctors should behave, between being married and having views about the institution of marriage. It is a complex and delicate matter to say how much inner sense of the way of life characteristic of the institution one needs to have in order to make pertinent criticisms; or, on the other hand, how much detachment and externality might in fact be valuable in getting a good critical perspective. What is clear is that it is sophistry to pretend that my advisory role at the Hastings Center qualifies me to practice medicine, that my attacks on the commensurability of values qualify me to teach Economics 10, that my views about marriage determine my marital status. Fish cannot co-opt the opposition by such stratagems. He will do so anyway, and, being a very engaging and articulate man, he will frequently succeed. But that's the distinction between persuasion and manipulation. In persuasion some things don't wash, no matter how charming you are.

Two thoughts more about the connection of all this with the relationship between philosophy and literature. First, I think that it is only because we have for a long time, through the dominance of various brands of formalism, lost the sense that literature deals with human matters of great importance that the Gorgianic turn could flourish as it does. For I have enough respect for Fish as a human being to conjecture (in ignorance) that in anything that really matters to him— politics, personal friendship and love, the rearing of children—he believes that there is a very important distinction between persuasion and force. (When Derrida was in jail in Czechoslovakia it was evident to all members of the profession what that distinction was.) Nor, I bet, does he think that in matters of child rearing the latest deliverances of pediatricians and child psychologists are criterial of truth and exempt from rational criticism; that in matters of love and sex the latest fads of sociology and sexology are criterial of correctness; and so on. Why is the literary profession and its subject matter treated so lightly, as if it were the one place where we could play around with these differences? Isn't it, too, about something real and really important?[11]

Second, the activity of justification I have described shows, I believe, one very important link between philosophy and literature. As we ask, concerning any belief, what its depth is for us (let us say, the belief in the incommensurability of ethical values, or the beliefs about persons mentioned above), we need to be imagining vividly what a life would look like both with and without that belief, allowing ourselves, in imagination and emotion, to get a sense of what the cost for us would be if we gave it up. To get that kind of understanding of possibilities, an understanding that is both emotional and intellectual, we need literature in philosophy; for literature can show us in rich detail, as formal abstract argument can-

---

11. For related remarks see Arthur Danto, "Philosophy As/And/Of Literature," *Proceedings and Addresses of the American Philosophical Association* 58 (1984) 5–20.

not, what it is like to live a certain way.[12] In this sense literature, and our discourse about literature, can be, and is, philosophical: it plays a part in our search for truth and for a good life. On the other side, philosophy must engage the help of literature and our discourse about it, or risk being empty about matters of greatest importance.

In short, the right way for literary discourse to be philosophical is to be more, not less, in love with truth. The right way for philosophy to be literary is to become more immersed in the complexities of human life as literature depicts them, not to emulate the playfulness of Gorgianic arguments.

Endnote

This essay was originally published as a part of the proceedings of a conference on Philosophy of Science and Literary Theory held at the University of Virginia. (These proceedings took up the entire volume of *New Literary History* in which the article appeared.) The aim of the conference, organized by E. D. Hirsch, Jr., and Richard Rorty, was to examine debates—especially the realism/antirealism debate—that take place in related ways in the two fields, and to urge a greater awareness of the arguments and results of the philosophical debate on the part of literary theorists. My comments are addressed to what seemed to me to be some general problems with the arguments concerning truth and convention that were used at the conference—but especially to Stanley Fish's arguments in his paper, entitled "Anti-Professionalism." Fish argues that the only criterion of truth we have for judgments made in a given profession is the prevailing (currently dominant) view of things among practicing members of the profession. "Prevailing" is explicitly denied all normative epistemological content: it is a descriptive term having to do with such things as power, prestige, and income. According to Fish, there is, in any case, no significant distinction to be found between persuasion and manipulation, or even violence.

Those who wish to see whether I have been fair to Fish's arguments will have to consult the journal (where they will also find an excellent paper by Hilary Putnam with whose views I am in substantial agreement). I reprint the essay not so much for its polemical or ad hominem value, but as a commentary on a tendency that has been pervasive in some recent work in literary theory. This is the tendency to respond to the putative collapse of unqualified metaphysical realism (the view that we have truth only when we have a completely unmediated and non-interpretative access to the structure of reality as it is in itself) by espousing some form of radical subjectivism, relativism, or skepticism—for example, Fish's position here, according to which statements cannot be assessed as to their rational justifiability but only as to the power of their maker. Usually these moves are made rather rapidly, without investigating the claims of more moderate antireal-

---

12. A similar point is made by Putnam in "Literature, Science, and Reflection," in *Meaning and the Moral Sciences* (London, 1978), 83–94. See also "Flawed Crystals" and "Plato on Commensurability," this volume.

isms: for example, the position of Kant's First Critique; or Hilary Putnam's (very Kantian) "internal realism"; or Nelson Goodman's pluralism, according to which there are many acceptable versions of the world, but also strict criteria of rightness that we can use to rule out a far larger number as unacceptable.

The literary world's lack of interest in such alternatives frequently seems to betray an excessive attachment to metaphysical realism itself. Just as, in Nietzsche's account, the news of god's death reduces modern human beings to nihilism, that is, to the view that all preferring and valuing are altogether groundless and anything goes, so for numerous contemporary theorists the collapse of the hope that we could walk out to the world and see it in all its unmediated presentness, as it truly is in itself, has left only the thought that no descriptions can be defended as superior to any others. But in Nietzsche's story people react this way only because they are hooked on the idea that they are nowhere without god, that their own interpretations of the world are worthless. So, too, one suspects that the retreat to subjectivism or skepticism betrays a residual commitment to metaphysical realism as the only form of truth worth having: failing that, we do not seem to have anything worth preferring to anything else. Such views are frequently not sustained by powerful philosophical arguments; in this sense the absence of engagement with Kant and with the best in contemporary thought on realism (Quine, Goodman, Putnam, Kripke, Lewis) has done real damage. But the views are so common and so influential that they require comment in a project of this sort, since this project views literature as a source of a human sort of truth.

Reading for Life

Beaten by his stepfather, cut off from the love and care of his mother, David Copperfield turns for companionship to a company of friends whom the gloomy Murdstones have not had the forethought to suppress:

> My father had left a small collection of books in a little room upstairs, to which I had access (for it adjoined my own) and which nobody else in our house ever troubled. From that blessed little room, Roderick Random, Peregrine Pickle, Humphrey Clinker, Tom Jones, the Vicar of Wakefield, Don Quixote, Gil Blas, and Robinson Crusoe, came out, a glorious host, to keep me company. They kept alive my fancy, and my hope of something beyond that place and time—they, and the *Arabian Nights,* and the *Tales of the Genii,*—and did me no harm. . . . This was my only and my constant comfort. When I think of it, the picture always rises in my mind, of a summer evening, the boys at play in the churchyard, and I sitting on my bed, reading as if for life. . . . The reader now understands, as well as I do, what I was when I came to that point of my youthful history to which I am now coming again.

In this wonderful passage (which is even more wonderful read in full), David, the mature author of his own life story, reminds his readers of the power of the art of fiction to create a relationship between book and reader and to make the reader, for the duration of that relationship, into a certain sort of friend. Novels are David's closest associates; he remains with them for hours in an intense, intimate, and loving relationship. As he imagines, dreams, and desires in their company, he becomes a certain sort of person. In fact, the narrator clearly wishes us to see that the influence of David's early reading has been profound in making him the character we come to know, with his fresh childlike wonder before the world of particulars, his generous, mobile, and susceptible heart. And the novel as a whole, in its many self-referential reflections, calls readers to ask themselves, as well, what is happening to them as they read: to notice, for example, that they are sometimes too full of love for certain morally defective characters to be capable of rigorous judgment; that they are perceiving the social world around them with a new freshness of sympathy; in short, that they are taking on increasingly, in the very shape of their desire and wonder, the view of David's father—that "a loving heart is better and stronger than wisdom."

People care for the books they read; and they are changed by what they care for—both during the time of reading and in countless later ways more difficult to discern. But if this is so, and if the reader is a reflective person who wishes to ask (on behalf of herself and/or her community) what might be good ways to live, then it becomes not only reasonable, but also urgent to ask: What is the character of these literary friendships in which I and others find ourselves? What are they doing to me? To others? To my society? In whose company are we choosing to spend our time?

These questions are obvious enough. We ask them all the time, in many contexts: when we draw up reading lists for our students, when we recommend novels to our friends, when we guide our children's reading. But recent literary theory, on the whole, has either avoided or actively scorned these issues. This resistance has several distinct sources. One is the belief that ethical criticism of literature is bound to be dogmatic and simplistic, measuring the literary work by a rigid normative yardstick which ignores the complexities of the literary form. And, in fact, the suspicion has some justification; a great deal of ethical criticism has been like this. Another source of resistance is the well-entrenched philosophical idea that aesthetic interest is fundamentally distinct from practical interest, an idea according to which ethical assessment of an aesthetic work would be a crude error, betraying the assessor's failure to understand the nature of the practice of aesthetic assessment. A closely related source of resistance is the fashionable recent dogma that literary texts refer only to other texts and not to the world—an idea implying, once again, that it is a naive error to ask how literature speaks to and about us. The old formalism and the new defense of "textuality" are distinct in terminology, but they have many links of motivation and argument. Still a further obstacle to ethical evaluation is the view, also fashionable, that all ethical evaluation is irretrievably subjective. This is sometimes expressed, in the literary world, by saying that all reason-giving is a kind of power-seeking, all argument the expression of "ideology." And finally, we must mention disaffection and loss of love. Professional writers about literature too often end up losing contact with the love of books, with the fresh delight that led David Copperfield to his friendship with the "glorious host." But once that delight is lost, little remains for evaluation, and it is easy to see why the whole idea loses its allure.

In this fine, rich book,[1] Wayne Booth takes on all of these opponents, including the last, and makes out a compelling case for the coherence and importance of ethical criticism. He does this with a vigor and openness of engagement that remind us of our own experiences of literary absorption and delight. (Booth does not discuss *David Copperfield* or the passage I have quoted, but his entire book could be seen as a commentary on it.) According to Booth's guiding metaphor, a relationship with a literary work (and he explicitly includes his own book here), is a kind of friendship; and a good friendship, he says, is something voluntary. It is, then, a little difficult to know how, in light of this metaphor, we might think about that strange kind of enforced intimacy, the relationship of reviewer to book reviewed. So I wish to begin this review by saying that this book is one that I shall

1. *The Company We Keep: An Ethics of Fiction* (Berkeley: University of California Press, 1988).

willingly read again and reread—for the range and detail of its arguments, for the vigor of its concrete readings of texts, for the importance of its questions, for its humor and clarity and generous humanity. It is to be recommended warmly to anyone with a concern for the role played by the humanities, and by the interpretation of texts, in our public culture.

Relocating Ethical Criticism

Booth tells us that he began his career as a defender, like so many others, of "happy abstract formalism" (p. 5), believing that political and ethical questions, asked of a literary work, were "blatantly non-literary" (p. 5). One day, he and other like-minded humanities teachers at the University of Chicago were discussing the freshman reading list, which had for years included Twain's *Huckleberry Finn*. Paul Moses, a young black assistant professor, "committed what in that context seemed an outrage: an overt, serious, uncompromising act of ethical criticism" (p. 3). Moses told the other instructors that the book made him angry and he could not teach it again. Its assumptions about the proper relations of liberated slaves toward whites and its distorted portrayals of blacks seemed to him "just bad education." The other instructors (all white) were both embarrassed and offended. This was no way to talk about a great work of art. "I can remember lamenting the shoddy education that had left poor Paul Moses unable to recognize a great classic when he met one" (p. 3). Poor Moses was too angry, clearly, to take up the proper aesthetic attitude.

The Company We Keep, dedicated to the memory of Paul Moses (who died at the age of thirty-seven, only four years after this event) is the record of Booth's gradual realization that this response to Moses will not do; that Moses was exactly right to ask these questions about literature, right to regard our relations with literary works as important elements in the building of character, right, therefore, to feel that critical ethical discourse about these relationships is not only legitimate, but actually essential to a just and rational society. "To me," Booth concludes, "the most important of all critical tasks is to participate in—and thus to reinforce—a critical culture, a vigorous conversation" (p. 136). This book, then, provides not only a theory of ethical criticism, but many concrete examples, as Booth describes his gradual evolution from the smug and condescending formalist of the Moses anecdote to the passionate defender of the continuity between art and life seen here; and therefore, also, from a somewhat uncritical admirer of "great art" to a person who asks and ponders many difficult questions about the ways in which great literature has portrayed women, minorities, and, in general, our political and social relations.

There have been many forms of ethical criticism of literature, some of them extremely crude and unappealing. Booth therefore spends a good deal of time in Part I of this book (entitled "Relocating Ethical Criticism") distinguishing his own proposal from its relatives. The account is complex, but four distinctions emerge as especially important. First, "ethical," as Booth uses it, is a very broad and inclusive term. It covers everything that pertains to asking and answering the question, "How should one live?" Enjoyment, distraction, even contemplation of form, are all aspects of the ethical as Booth understands it—so long as they are seen as forming part of a human life, and are assessed accordingly. The question he asks of a literary work is nothing so narrow as, "What does it show me about my moral duty?" It is, rather, "What relationship does my engagement with it have to my general aim to live well?"—and to live, we should add, as a member of a society, since Booth insists that human beings are social and political beings.

Second, Booth does not practice ethical criticism by judging particular sentences, or even particular characters, removed from their context in the work as a whole. Practiced in this way, ethical criticism is clearly vulnerable to the charge of neglecting the work's literary structure. Booth's general question is, instead, "What sense of life is expressed in this work as a whole?"—in its design, the shape of its sentences, the interrelationships of its parts. To practice ethical criticism in this way, the critic *must* be sensitive to literary form. And Booth gives us a great deal of help here, introducing a complex framework of useful analytic conceptions that he has also defended in other writings. In particular, he urges readers, as they ask questions about a literary work, to distinguish three voices that are too frequently run together: the *narrator* (the character who tells the story); the *implied author* (the sense of life or the outlook that reveals itself in the structure of the text taken as a whole); and the *writer* (the real-life person, with all her or his lapses of attention, trivial daily pursuits, and so forth). Although Booth has interesting things to say about the reader's relationship to all of these figures, ethical criticism is concerned, above all, with the relationship between the reader and the implied author. Good ethical criticism, then, does not preclude formal analysis, but actually requires it. Style itself shapes the mind; and these are the effects that a good ethical critic discerns.

Third, ethical criticism, as Booth intends it, does not have a single dogmatic theory of what literature should be or do: for example, that it should reinforce a certain definite moral code, or should put the reader in contact with "otherness." Avoiding what he calls "loaded labels and crude slogans" (p. 7), Booth sensibly insists that there are many good things for literature to do and be—just as many as there are good things in human lives. And he insists on the Aristotelian point that what is good also may be, to some extent, a function of the reader's own particular needs, background, and context. On the other hand, there are also some things *against* which ethical criticism can perfectly reasonably take its stand. We can stand against sadism, racism, sexism; and, also, apart from morality more narrowly construed, we can stand against what Henry James once called "the rule of the cheap and easy"—against, then, sloppiness, vulgarity, and the trivialization of important things.

Fourth, Booth's main concern is not with the *consequences* of reading after the fact. He does consider this an important topic; but the interactions of reading with other elements of life are so complex that relatively little, he thinks, can be said about consequences in a general way. He therefore focuses on a more tractable question: what becomes of readers *as* they read? How do works of various kinds shape their desires and imaginations, fostering, during the time spent reading, a life that is either rich or impoverished, complexly attentive or neglectful, shaped or shapeless, loving or cold—and so forth?

In all these ways Booth's ethical criticism avoids pitfalls that have plagued much of the ethical criticism of the past, and made it easy to dismiss. His subtle analyses of what sentences of certain sorts do to desire and thought convince the reader, again and again, that ethical criticism need not be preachy or formally insensitive. The balance of Part I is spent in a discussion of the logic and argumentative structure of evaluative criticism, and in arguing against skeptical opponents who hold that all evaluation is hopelessly subjective. The two arguments go together, since Booth contends that the skeptic's fall into skepticism can be traced to overly simple assumptions about the form of rational evaluative argument. Identifying all rational argument with deductive argument that proceeds from premises that are necessarily true, the critic finds that no such argument seems to be available in literary evaluation (or, one might add, in ethics more generally). Seeing this, the skeptic concludes that all argument is expression of feeling, or an attempt to gain power; there is no distinction between persuasion and manipulation. Booth responds by describing, defending, and repeatedly exemplifying a form of non-deductive, yet genuinely rational, argument that he calls "coduction": a cooperative argument not so much *ad hominem* as *inter homines,* in which principle, concrete experience, and advice from one's friends interact over time to produce and revise judgments. Since this account of practical reasoning is one of the book's most interesting contributions, I shall return to it at greater length.

Part II develops Booth's central metaphor: a literary work is like a friend, and we can assess our literary relationships in much the same way that we assess our friendships, realizing that we are judged by the company we keep. He derives his account of friendship from Aristotle, holding that it is a relationship based on trust and affection, in which we pursue our ends in a social way, sharing, to a large extent, the friend's activities, desires, and values. Evidently, then, the friends we choose are of great significance for the quality of our lives. Aristotle held that there are three different bases or grounds for friendship: pleasure, usefulness, and good character. Booth argues that all three elements, in different combinations, inform our choices of reading. And he argues that it would be difficult to explain why we would choose to spend hours in such intimacy with the mind of an (implied) author unless one or more of these three were the basis. Like Aristotle, he holds that a friendship based on character and aspiration is the best and richest, though all three types have their place in a good life. This ranking, he argues, is a good starting point for the evaluation of literary experiences, seen as component parts of a life. Especially bad will be experiences in which we are in the company of an implied author with a bad character, forming desires and projects that are sadistic, brutal, unjust, or merely wanton and sloppy. But relationships that offer, let us say, only some useful information or some momentary relief are less valuable than those that enrich our lives in some more substantial way.

Booth next proposes a set of more concrete questions that we may ask of a text as we begin our evaluation of its character and of the relationship it offers us. He tries out these questions on several texts, asking in each case how our desire and thought are shaped as we read. Peter Benchley's *Jaws* is a negative case in point. Booth deftly shows how narrow the range of our sentiments and conceptions becomes as we read it, what a "loss of life is involved in deciding to spend several hours that way."

The story tries to mold me into its limited shape, giving me practice, as it were, in wanting and fearing certain minimal qualities and ignoring all others. I am to become, if I enter that world, *that kind of desirer,* with precisely the kinds of strengths and weaknesses that the author has built into his structure. (p. 204)

Other modern examples—from Norman Mailer, Anne Tyler, W. B. Yeats, James Joyce, e.e., cummings—give rise to a variety of more complex analyses. Booth ends the chapter by praising the contributions of an open-ended list of works (by, among others, Shakespeare, Jane Austen, Cervantes, Dickens, Tolstoy) on the grounds that these works enable readers "to live during these moments a richer and fuller life than they could manage on their own" (p. 223). Part II concludes with an analysis of the ways in which literary metaphor, in particular, shapes the thought of the reader.

Part III is devoted to extended critical analyses of four writers who have recently been the targets of ethical criticism because of their political or social views. This is an especially fascinating part of the book, since we see plainly Booth's love of good writing, and the reluctance with which he is persuaded, in some cases, to the negative ethical conclusion. Booth is no rigid ideologue. He comes across as a rather cautious man, but one who cares about social justice and is committed to rational argument. His examples of his own changes of mind thus have much conviction as examples of practical reason in a democratic culture. All four analyses show him changing his judgment over time, as new advice, rereading, and experience combine with general moral principle to generate fresh evaluations.

A long, complex analysis of feminist criticisms of Rabelais ends with victory for the feminists. Booth, however hard he tries on behalf of an author he likes, cannot, once he goes into the matter thoroughly, avoid being convinced that the text as a whole has an offensive view of women. His esteem for Rabelais is consequently diminished.

An analysis of related criticisms of the ending of Jane Austen's *Emma* comes to a far more complex conclusion. Austen, Booth argues, is clearly not the dupe of a naive myth that women find happiness through the protection of beneficent father figures. She gives evidence throughout her novels of a far more skeptical and critical view of romance, and of women's possibilities. And yet, in the case of *Emma,* the structure of the ending does seduce us into loving the very outcome she elsewhere criticizes. Booth concludes that the form of the romantic novel imposes its own norms of desire and longing, even in an author as critical and independent as Austen. Undertaking to write in that form, she encounters, so to speak, a tension between its expectations and her own.

An impressive chapter on D. H. Lawrence narrates and justifies Booth's movement from disdain for Lawrence to enthusiasm. In this case, where the conclusion is somewhat less popular in liberal circles than Booth's other judgments, I think the reader is particularly likely to feel the force of the process of coduction at work, as she sees how an argument of the detailed and patient type Booth envisages (and makes) can actually lead to the revision of a once firmly held judgment.

Booth ends the book where it began: with the history of his own changes of view concerning *Huckleberry Finn,* presented now as detailed readings and re-readings of the text. Booth has not only come to agree with Moses about ethical assessment in general, he has also come round to Moses's view of the novel, noticing paternalism and condescension where he once saw only the touching portrayal of black nobility. Here we have an especially clear case of the way in which some ongoing moral principles (especially a respect for human equality) guide interpretation, in the light of new experiences and consultations with others. The revised judgment is convincing as one that embodies a more complete human understanding. The reader is likely to be persuaded that it is a rational judgment, and not merely a product of a shift in fashion or the expression of an ideology—in part because Booth carefully gives evidence for his position, but also because one senses that the story of change could not be told in the other direction. Once certain things have been noticed in a text, and connected, as here, to reflective perceptions of actual human societies, one cannot go back, choosing the ignorance that allowed an untroubled enjoyment of the novel.

This is, evidently, a large and a rich book, about which much will be written. None of its central themes can be given full critical examination in a review, even one of this length. But there are three topics on which I would like to say more and to raise some questions: the boundaries of the literary, the metaphor of friendship, and the analysis of practical reasoning in terms of "coduction" and "pluralism."

Philosophy and Literature

Booth's subtitle is *An Ethics of Fiction,* and many of his examples, including all the ones in Part III, are novels. But his analysis is actually far more wide-ranging. It includes examples from lyric poetry and also from works of philosophy. (Burke is a central example in one section, Kant in another; the section on metaphor discusses many acounts of the cosmos, both religious and philosophical.) There is, of course, absolutely no reason why Booth's analysis cannot be extended in this way. And yet one regrets that Booth focuses so little on the distinctive qualities of our relationships with *literary* works—never asking at length, for example, how the friendship one can have with a novel differs from the friendship promised by a philosophical treatise; how it differs, as well, from the relationship one is able to form with a lyric poem. The absence of sustained analysis along these lines does not undercut anything that he *does* say. But since Booth has such an enthusiasm for the works he loves, and for novels above all, one feels a disappointment that he says so little about what kind of "people," as friends, novels are.

One does not want facile generalizing here, clearly. One has to begin with particular cases and work outwards. And yet, if we think of David Copperfield's "reading for life," we become aware that a claim is being made, in Dickens, on behalf of novels more generally: a claim that they offer a distinctive patterning of desire and thought, in virtue of the ways in which they ask readers to care about particulars, and to feel for those particulars a distinctive combination of sympathy and excitement. The gloomy religion of the Murdstones would have none of Peregrine Pickle—and for good reasons, from its own viewpoint.

Dickens is well aware that novels like his cultivate desire and imagination in a way that is morally suspect—not only for the Murdstones but for ethical and philosophical positions of many different kinds, some of them very respectable. Think, for example, of Mr. Gradgrind's school in *Hard Times,* where "fancy" is forbidden. The consistent Utilitarian, in Dickens's view, must have a deep mistrust of the literary imagination, since it binds the mind to particulars that lie close to the self, discouraging that impartial concern with all humanity that is the core of utilitarian rationality. (Concerning his daughter, Louisa, Mr. Gradgrind reflects, with satisfaction, "Would have been self-willed, but for her bringing up.")

Novels, then, as a form of writing, have a distinctive, and a controversial ethical content. Even David Copperfield cannot claim that they have made him more consistent and more steady in his judgment. For he clearly connects his early love of stories with his love for his cohort in storytelling, James Steerforth—a character dashing, erotic, and amoral—and with his later willingness to judge Steerforth from the moral point of view. He also makes it clear to his readers that Agnes Wickfield, emblem of religious morality, is no novel-reader herself. Dickens's case for the novel, in the light of such challenges, is inseparable from David's claim that the fresh imagination of particularity is an essential moral faculty, and that the tender susceptible heart is morally finer than a firm one.

Such claims, and many others related to them, deserve full scrutiny within the enterprise of ethical criticism. I hope that Booth will at some point write on this subject, saying more about the complex connections between what one wishes to say and the selection of a genre or structure in which to say it.

Friendship, Seduction, and a School for the Moral Sentiments

This brings me directly to my second set of questions, about the metaphor of friendship as Booth develops it. It is a marvelously rich and illuminating metaphor, but some of its aspects remain, so far, incompletely explored. First, there is an unresolved tension, in Booth's text, between two ways of characterizing these friendships. The main line of Booth's argument speaks of the literary relation as a friendship, and refers to Aristotle for elucidation. But in Aristotle's account, though friends share one another's ends and are deeply influenced by one another, each retains independence and critical autonomy. Booth, however, also describes the reader's relation to a literary work in a different way, invoking the language of erotic seduction. He talks frequently of "succumbing," of "that primary act of *assent* that occurs when we surrender to a story" (pp. 32, 140). This language is important to his argument. For the fact that we surrender trustingly to the forms of desire in the text, allowing it, so to speak, to have its way with us, is crucial to his case for saying that ethical assessment is urgently required.

Here, I believe, we see an area in which distinctions among literary genres, and, in particular, a distinction between novels and many traditional forms of philosophical writing, would have been especially fruitful. Booth makes his claims in a very general way, as if they applied without distinction to all texts. But philosophical texts, on the whole, do not invite the reader to fall in love. Indeed, they repudiate that aim. They ask the reader to be wary and skeptical, examining each move and premise. Mistrust, rather than trust, is the professional norm since Socrates, if not earlier.

Texts built along these lines embody a distinctive view of what is important in communication and of how one ought to treat another human being—a view in which erotic love plays little part. Indeed, in very many philosophical works affection and friendship do not play a part either: the text repudiates the idea that any relationship at all is under way between vulnerable, incomplete, desiring human beings. On the other hand, certain other philosophical texts—I think especially of Aristotle—do invite the reader into friendship, a friendship in which the claims of each ethical belief and each passion and experience will be taken seriously and respectfully examined.

Novels, however, are in many cases both friendly and erotic. They both enlist the reader as a participant by sympathy and compassion, and also lure her with more mysterious and romantic charms. They ask the reader to join in a public moral world and also, at times, lure her away from that world into a more shadowy passionate world, asking her to assent, to succumb. Allowing oneself to be in some sense passive and malleable, open to new and sometimes mysterious influences, is a part of the transaction and a part of its value. Reading novels, as David Copperfield learned, is a practice for falling in love. And it is in part because novels prepare the reader for love that they make the valuable contribution they do to society and to moral development.

There is much more to be said here. For most of the great ethical novelists have approached the novel's seductive power as both a resource and a problem. Jane Austen, as Booth perceptively says, skirmishes against some of the genre's erotic structures with her skeptical good sense, both inviting the reader's trust and warning that all may not be as it seems. Dickens, in our example, wrestles with the problem of combining Agnes's moral judgment with Steerforth's romantic onward movement; and both the "good angel" and the "bad angel" dictate the shape of the text. About Henry James, Tolstoy, Proust—there would be, on this score, fascinating inquiries to be made.

To pursue such an inquiry well we would need to investigate, as well, the various forms of philosophical writing, and their seductions. For philosophy, too, has its seductive power, its power to lure the reader away from the richly textured world of particulars to the lofty heights of abstraction. It, too, can promise escape—from the messy and difficult world we live in to a world made more simple and schematic. This sort of seduction can frequently be pernicious in human life. On the other hand, the seductions of literature can frequently return us to a richer and more complex world; and the very enchantments of the novel can lead the reader past her tendencies to deny complexity, to evade the messiness of feeling.

It seems to me, however, that certain forms of moral philosophy—above all Aristotle's—are equipped to form a friendship with the reader that avoids such philosophical seductions and illuminates the contributions of literature. For Aristotelian moral philosophy remains close to the world of particulars, directing the reader's attention to these and to experience—including the emotions of experience—as the sources of ethical insight. At the same time, this sort of moral philosophy has the dialectical power to compare alternative conceptions perspicuously, contrasting their salient features. For this reason it can be an important ally of the literary work, explaining what its contributions are and how they differ from those of abstract moral philosophy. It can do this because of the distinctive type of friendship it forms with its reader, affectionate yet critical, attentive and responsive to particularity while committed to explanation.

In pursuing these and related questions, we might arrive at a new account of the role of ethical criticism. Booth's book does not seduce its reader. It forms, instead, a friendship in which sympathy is linked with concern for the perspicuous dialectical exploration of alternatives. It shows respect for the deep emotions, and it investigates their claims; but its concern with critical rationality leads it to set these claims side by side with other claims. It speaks, then, far more like an Aristotelian philosopher than like either a novelist or an abstract and schematic philosopher, inviting readers to inspect the argument, and to clarify their own relation to it by comparing it with their own experience. This level of reflection and self-examination seems essential, in fact, to the establishment of the critical culture Booth describes. A novel by itself would not have compared itself to the views of readers in many parts of the world at many times. And we know from Booth's account that such comparisons were essential not only in forming his views about the world, but also in leading him to a deeper and more adequate understanding of some of the novels. In short: Booth plausibly suggests that it is only by both succumbing and also asking ourselves why we succumbed, and what relation our experience has to the experience of others, that we respond to literature in the most fully human and social way. So by pursuing the idea of an Aristotelian philosophical criticism and its associated conception of friendship, Booth could show more clearly than he has so far what the contribution of his own project can be expected to be, even toward showing the importance and the philosophical contribution of literature.

To be the ally of literature, and to show what is philosophically important about it, philosophical criticism will need to think carefully about its own style and the statements its style makes. It will need to be, itself, less abstract and schematic, more respectful of the claims of the emotions and imagination, more tentative and improvisatory, than philosophy has frequently been. It will need, in short, to choose for itself a style that reveals, and does not negate, the insights of literature. To describe such a philosophy and its relationship both to literature and to other sorts of philosophy seems to me to be a very important task. I hope that Booth will undertake it.[2]

We now need to discuss one further point about literary friendships. It is an obvious point, so obvious that Booth does not explore it: When one reads a novel one is alone. No other live person is there responding. Therefore there can be, except in fantasy, no interchange of the sort we associate with love and friendship. This point does not undercut Booth's metaphor as he uses it—but it prompts several ethical reflections that do not come up until one states the obvious.

First, one has to say that books are not sufficient for good human living. Although, as David Copperfield's story shows, the fantasy interactions promoted

---

2. I discuss this more fully in "Love's Knowledge." See also my Introduction.

by reading are a valuable preparation for loving relationships in life, books may also promote self-absorption and hinder mutuality. One needs real people too, however correct Booth may be when he says that relations with books are sometimes richer than those with people. On the other hand, the lack of realness in a book also has a salutary side, which is brought out very well, in different ways, by both Henry James and Proust: towards novels it is not possible to feel certain bad emotions of the real personal life, such as jealousy and the desire for revenge. It is, on the other hand, perfectly possible to feel sympathy and love. So in this way novels can be a school for the moral sentiments, distancing us from blinding personal passions and cultivating those that are more conducive to community. Proust goes so far as to say that the relation we have with a literary work is the only human relation characterized by genuine altruism, and also the only one in which, not caught up in the "vertiginous kaleidoscope" of jealousy, the reader can truly know the mind of another person. I would not go that far, but there is a real issue here, and I do not think we can fully understand the ethical contribution of the novel without pursuing it.

There is one last point of a different sort that needs to be borne in mind here. I can treat a book as I would never think it right to treat a real live person. Sometimes people feel the need for complete numbing distraction, distraction so complete that it simply blots out all stress and worry. Consider, now, two people in search of such undemanding release. The one hires a prostitute and indulges in an evening of casual sex. The other buys a Dick Francis novel and lies on the couch all evening reading. There must be, I think, a huge moral difference between these people, a difference that Booth's insistence on the friendship metaphor fails to bring out. (I say this as someone who reads in just this way whenever I finish writing a paper, and I am attempting to defend myself from Booth's harsh assessment.) The person who hires a prostitute is seeking relief by using another human being; he or she engages in a transaction that exploits and debases both a person and an intimate activity. The person who reads Dick Francis is not, I believe, doing any harm to anyone. Surely she is not exploiting the *writer:* indeed, she is treating Francis exactly as he would wish, in a not undignified business transaction. Is she exploiting the implied author by hiring him for her pleasure? I find this a peculiar question; and I think the answer must be, she is doing nothing morally wrong in relieving her stress this way. I think this contrast needs to figure somehow in Booth's account, and it might moderate slightly his harshness toward the uses of popular fiction.

Practical Reason and Pluralism

This brings me to the aspect of the book that will be of most interest to legal scholars: Booth's defense of the objectivity of practical reason in the interpretation and evaluation of texts. Booth explicitly appeals to legal reasoning as a model for his own view (pp. 72–73); and the Aristotelian view of judgment he develops, both in his explicit theoretical account (pp. 70–77) and in his practice, is indeed one that has interesting links with views of legal judgment. Yet there are some obscurities in Booth's position that may limit its usefulness in this sphere.

Booth calls the evaluative judgments he recommends "coductions." (The "co" indicates both that such judgments are made socially, in conversation with others, and that they have an implicitly comparative element.) In coduction, unlike deductive demonstration, we do not begin from premises that are known, prior, and held absolutely firm throughout. We begin, instead, from our own complex history as beings with principles, with historical memory, with "untraceably complex experiences of other stories and persons" (p. 71). The initial evaluation of a new literary experience is always implicitly comparative: the text is evaluated against that complex background.

This initial impression can then be transformed in several ways, as I compare my impressions with those of others. It can become more conscious and explicit; it can become grounded in the experience of others as well as in my own; and it can be held up against background principles and norms. "Every appraisal of a narrative is implicitly a comparison between the always complex experience we have had in its presence and what we have known before" (p. 71). At this point, Booth cites Samuel Johnson on the contrast between deduction and such experience-based judgments:[3]

Demonstration [of the sort possible in scientific matters] immediately displays its power, and has nothing to hope or fear from the flux of years; but works tentative and experimental [that is, works that depend on experience] must be estimated by their proportion to the general and collective ability of man, as it is discovered in a long succession of endeavors. [Explanatory supplements supplied by Booth.]

It is a major aim of the book to show that such judgments are not just expressions of subjective whim or political ideology; they can be rational. The model of practical reason is indeed a promising one, though I think more could have been done to give it a detailed philosophical grounding. It has a great deal in common with Aristotle's account of practical wisdom, and also, more recently, with some impressive work on practical reasoning by Charles Taylor.[4] Since Booth is not a philosopher, he might have done well to supplement his own discussion with some extended description of related philosophical discussions.

But the account remains attractive; and Booth does convince the reader that skeptics about evaluation are skeptics because they are looking for the wrong sort of argument—failing to find it, they are led to give up on reason altogether. (This is a point on whch Taylor has written eloquently.[5]) We begin to have real trouble, however, when we try to connect the account of coduction with Booth's frequent claims that his view of ethical criticism is "pluralistic." Here I think the absence of explicit philosophy does real damage. For Booth's references to his "pluralism" seem to specify several distinct views, not all consistent with one another, and

3. Samuel Johnson, Preface to *The Plays of William Shakespeare* (1765), vol. 7 of The Yale Edition of *The Works of Samuel Johnson* (New Haven, 1968), 60.
4. Charles Taylor, *Philosophy and the Human Sciences,* vol. 2 of *Philosophical Papers* (Cambridge, 1986). See also Taylor, "Explanation and Practical Reason," forthcoming in *The Quality of Life,* ed. M. Nussbaum and A. Sen (Oxford, 1991).
5. See Taylor, "Explanation and Practical Reason."

some of them at odds with the claims he makes for coduction. We need to sort these views out and to ask which one (or ones) his argument actually requires.

We find at least the following positions in the text:

1. *Pluralism as multiplicity of component goods.* Frequently Booth uses the word "pluralism" in connection with the view that there are many distinct and nonhomogeneous valuable things, and, therefore, many good roles for literature to play in life. This position is fully compatible, clearly, with his claims for the nonsubjectivity of evaluation; and it is an important claim, on which much of his argument relies.

1a. *Pluralism as multiplicity with conflict.* Sometimes this multiplicity of goods generates a tragic tension—as when Booth's love for the warmth and humor of Twain's novel conflicts with his aversion to its paternalism. Here we do get some true statements of the form "X is both good and bad"—but without logical problem, since the good and bad features of the object are distinct, though contingently impossible to separate. Again, there is no threat to objectivity here.

2. *Pluralism as Contextualism.* Sometimes when referring to pluralism, Booth makes statements of the form, "X is both good and bad," in connection with what we might call an Aristotelian contextualism: what is good for you in your circumstances is not necessarily good for me in mine. As Aristotle said, the diet that is good for Milo the wrestler would be ruinous for you and me; or, as Booth observes, it would be good for a moral subjectivist to read and reflect about *The Old Curiosity Shop,* though the same experience might not be so good for someone excessively inclined to dogmatism (p. 68). Again, such claims are an important part of Booth's argument. And again they are not in tension with his claims for the nonsubjectivity of evaluation. Judgments must always be sensitive to concrete circumstances; but, given this, there is no reason why we cannot say that this, and not that, is ethically good.

3. *Pluralism as Multiple Specification of the Good.* This position notes that important ethical principles frequency operate at a rather high level of generality, and are susceptible of many concrete specifications, not all of them simultaneously instantiable and each adequate for realizing that principle in practice. Suppose, for example, that one decides that a good human life should make room for friendship, and that what is essential in good friendship is reciprocity and the effort to love and benefit the other for the other's own sake (as in Aristotle's account). One may then notice that a variety of relationships, concretely very different in kind (in different social traditions, for example), all exhibit those morally valuable characteristics. One cannot have all those forms of friendship together, and perhaps not even in a single society. But they are all similar in their morally relevant characteristics. Pluralism here would consist in saying that all of them are good, though they are in many ways noncompatible. This position is harder to pin down in Booth's book, but I think it is present often enough in many of his tolerant and democratic statements. Here, again, pluralism does not in any way compromise ethical objectivity.

At some points in his argument, however, Booth has a tendency to assert two stronger and more problematic positions. (This happens especially when he is trying to convince the reader that he is no dogmatist.)

4. *Plural world-versions without contradiction.* In the section of the book dealing with cosmological myth, Booth seems to express a view that bears a close relationship to Nelson Goodman's pluralism of world-versions,[6] though Booth does not link his view with Goodman's. This view claims that there are many alternative versions of the world that have value and validity. (It appears that these versions, as Booth describes them, are incommensurable, and thus not in contradiction with one another.) There are standards of rightness by which we can narrow the group of acceptable versions, but we cannot rationally opt for any of the acceptable ones over any other. It is very hard to assess the relationship of this view to the first three uses of pluralism and to the defense of coduction, since it is philosophically underdeveloped in Booth's text and is never applied to ethics. Such a view need not lead in the direction of ethical relativism or subjectivism, if the many versions are all mutually consistent (or at least not inconsistent), and are simply used for different purposes or in different contexts. On the other hand, some of Booth's examples from religion lead me to suspect that the claim is actually more relativistic than that, and thus more problematic for coduction.

5. *Plural versions with contradiction.* Finally, there are several places where Booth simply asserts, as an example of his open-minded pluralism, contradictions that I see no way of resolving. Early in the book, he appears to say that he holds both Aristotle's view of friendship and the Christian account (p. 173)—although in many essential respects the two are in direct contradiction (over the worth of the person, the proper basis for love, and so forth). This is a pluralism that leads to ethical confusion. On page 348, Booth explicitly urges the reader to take in, and to believe, a collection of cosmic myths that is "to some degree incoherent and self-contradictory." On page 351, he appears to sympathize with skeptical attacks on logic; and frequently in the last part of the book, he refers to his own ethical convictions (for example, his antiracism) as "my ideology." Wanting to accept and believe all candidates for truth, he reaches the verge of giving up on reason-based ethical judgment.

This more sweeping and problematic pluralism does not seem to be an easily eliminable feature in the book, since Booth makes such assertions often, as if they had some importance. But it should be eliminated, since it is a feature that undermines the book's central argument, and threatens to give the field back to the very opponents—subjectivists and skeptics of many sorts—whom Booth has so ably criticized in the book's earlier parts. I think Booth is, at this point, bending over backwards to answer his real or imagined critics in the literary world, hastening to reassure them that he is no dogmatist, no stuffy defender of logic. He should not bend over so far. First of all, it will not work. Many people will hate this book and will call Booth a reactionary; that is the price he will pay for his defense of reason. Second, it sells out his position. Antiracism, by Booth's own account, is not just his "ideology." It is an ethical position both defensible and defended by rational argument.

Booth should, I think, retain pluralism as multiplicity, as contextualism, and as multiple specification. He might combine this with some version of Goodman's

6. Nelson Goodman, *Ways of Worldmaking* (Indianapolis, 1978).

plural world-versions, if he could spell out the constraints carefully enough. But to tolerate contradiction within practical reason cuts the heart out of the process of coduction, which moves forward by noticing a tension between one claim and another. Booth should hold his head high and ignore the people in the literary world who scoff at nonsubjectivism. His books will be around a long time after those fashions have been forgotten.

Friends of books like this one, neither succumbing nor even assenting, argue a lot. The vigor of the criticism this book provokes is a clear sign of its value. Its strength and perceptiveness will enhance the public debate about these urgent questions. That, as Aristotle would say, is civic friendship, and this book is a civic friend.

Endnote

This review article was written at the same time as "Steerforth's Arm," and has close connections with it. Its account of practical reasoning has a close connection with the account of Aristotelian dialectic in the Introduction, and also in "Sophistry About Conventions." The article has been revised for the present volume.

Fictions of the Soul

Gertrude says, "O Hamlet speak no more. / Thou turnst mine eyes into my very soul." He made her see her soul, then, with a speech. And many types of speeches try to do what Hamlet did here. They present us with accounts or pictures of ourselves, attempting to communicate to us some truth about what we really are—or (to use what is already a certain sort of picture) to show us the insides of our human souls. These truths about ourselves are delivered in many different styles and forms: some through structured argument, some through more devious or more violent strategies. One distinguished thinker compares his discourse about the nature of the soul to dry translucent shafts of sunlight that disperse the dark shadows of false belief. Another represents the recipient of a true account of the inside of her soul as crying out in pain: "These words like daggers enter in my ears."

Clearly there ought to be connections between the way a thinker or writer conceives of the soul and the way he or she constructs a discourse to convey important truths to such a soul—including, and especially, the truth about the nature of the soul. Whether we are to be approached with sunbeams or with daggers, whether we need light or violent motion to show us what we are: this seems to depend upon what, in fact, we are. On the answer to questions such as: Are our souls transparent? opaque? open? thick-skinned? And: is getting in touch with a human soul like shining light through a diamond? Like embracing a friend? Like drawing blood? To speak more prosaically, on the answers to questions such as: How does a soul arrive at truth? What elements does it have that promote and impede understanding? What is the subject matter or content of the most important truths about it? And in what sort of activity does knowing it consist? A story or account of the soul is, then, told. The telling, if the story is a good one, is not accidentally connected with the content of the told. And this ought to be so whether the teller is a literary artist, whom we suppose always to be conscious of the nature of the stylistic choices, or a philosopher, whom we often think of as avoiding or eschewing style altogether. No stylistic choice can be presumed to be neutral—not even the choice to write in a flat or neutral style.

My aim in this essay is to begin working on the complicated connections between a view of what a human soul is and a view about how to address that sort of soul in writing, in the communication of the view.[1] I have chosen two very different views, associated with two extremely different styles. One will be an intellectualistic view of the person, expressed in a style commonly associated with philosophical writing; the other, expressed in a literary narrative, will be severely critical of intellectualism. The philosophical view is associated with a harsh criticism of literary art, the literary view with an equally harsh criticism of philosophical investigation. In each case, I want to ask how the story that is told engages, in the telling, with the reader's soul, and how the telling and the told are matched. I have chosen two extremes not because I wish to suggest that these positions somehow express the essence of the philosophical or the literary, but because they speak to and criticize one another in an illuminating way. By seeing their opposing elements starkly and schematically set out, we will be in a better position, should we wish to, to imagine an alternative that lies somewhere between them. My philosophical protagonist will be Plato—or certain aspects of Plato; the literary opponent will be Proust.

I shall, in fact, begin by introducing a particular example of psychological investigation from Proust's novel, in which the narrator advances an important claim about the structure of the soul, a claim which, as he later asserts, could be truthfully presented in no other style. I shall then turn to Plato, schematically introducing the features of the intellectualistic view of the soul that prove important in his condemnation of literary art. I shall contrast Proust's narrative investigation into the soul with an analogous inquiry in a hypothetical philosophical text that conforms to the strictures of the Platonic view. I shall ask of each of them what it is about their view that leads their texts to assume a certain shape, and how each could argue that the other's way of writing could not tell us the truth of what we are.

I

I begin, then, with a moment at the end of *Sodome et Gomorrhe,* where Proust's narrator begins to explore for his readers a central truth about the human soul. He has been riding with Albertine on the little seaside railway that passes through the resort towns near Balbec. He feels bored with Albertine; he has more or less decided to leave her. Just before they reach the stop that is her destination, Albertine boasts of her friendship with the daughter of the composer Vinteuil—whom Marcel knows to be a committed lesbian. Albertine's remark, by awakening his jealousy, shows him the depth of his love for her. As Albertine walks toward the door of the train, something odd and significant takes place:

> But this movement which she thus made to get off the train tore my heart unendurably, just as if, contrary to the position independent of my body which Albertine's seemed to be occupying a yard away from it, this separation in space, which

---

1. Aspects of this question are also discussed in "Flawed Crystals"; in *Fragility,* chaps. 1, 6, and 7 and Interlude 2; and in this volume as a whole.

an accurate draughtsman would have been obliged to indicate between us, was only apparent, and anyone who wishes to make a fresh drawing of things as they really were would now have had to place Albertine, not at a certain distance from me, but inside me. (II.1153–54)[2]

Shortly afterward, the narrator converts this experience into a general reflection about the structure of the human soul:

> What a deceptive sense sight is! A human body, even a beloved one, as Albertine's was, seems to us, from a few yards, from a few inches away, remote from us. And similarly with the soul that inhabits it. But if something brings about a violent change in the position of that soul in relation to us, shows us that it is in love with others and not with us, then by the beating of our shattered heart we feel that it is not a few feet away from us but within us that the beloved creature was. . . . The words: "That friend is Mlle Vinteuil" had been the *Open sesame,* which I should have been incapable of discovering by myself, that had made Albertine penetrate to the depths of my lacerated heart. And I might search for a hundred years without discovering how to open the door that had closed behind her. (II.1165–66)

This claim that the human soul contains loved persons as internal objects is an important theme in the novel from this point on. (It is given a lengthy general development, for example, in *La Prisonnière,* where the narrator shows how this conception of the loved one can explain the profound influence of all the loved one's actions on the lover; in *Albertine disparue* the inquiry into the reality of those actions brings the narrator the pain of exploratory heart surgery.) It is plainly one of the discoveries about human psychology to which the narrator attaches most importance. On almost the final page of the entire novel, he speaks of his project of representing certain "characters as existing not outside, but within ourselves, where their slightest action can bring fatal disturbances in its train"; and he then observes, "My love affair with Albertine was sufficient proof to me that any other kind of representation must be artificial and untruthful" (III.1104). So this seems to be a good example with which to begin an investigation of the methods by which Proust's narrative tells us who we are, and of the claim made in the narrative that only a narrative can truthfully present to us certain features of ourselves.

Now, however, we must introduce our other protagonist, Plato. As is appropriate, we begin, in this case, not with an example or with a concrete part of a story, but with the abstract and schematic characterization of a position. In the *Republic* and other related dialogues of the middle period of his writing, Plato describes a certain standpoint or perspective from which true accounts and correct judgments can be reached.[3] This standpoint, which he characterizes as the standpoint of the

---

2. All references to Proust are to the translation by C. K. Scott Moncrieff and A. Mayor, as revised by Terence Kilmartin (New York, 1981).

"real above" in nature, is contrasted with the standpoint from which most people, and all literary artists, make their characterizations of reality. The standpoint of the ordinary human being is one that is shaped and structured by the needs and interests of an imperfect and limited being. Its characterization of what truth and value are is distorted by the pressure of bodily need, emotional turmoil, and the other constraining and limiting features of our bodily humanity. It is possible to show convincingly that in dialogues such as the *Phaedo* and the *Republic,* Plato's arguments rely centrally on the notion that appetitive and emotional needs and desires are potent forces of both distortion and distraction, and that clear and adequate judgments concerning value can be made only by getting the intellect free and clear of their influence altogether, allowing it to go off "itself by itself." The standpoint of the "real above" in nature is the standpoint of such a separated intellect. When Plato asks what the truth is concerning anything of value, he does so by asking what such an unconstrained and unlimited intellectual being would select. For just one illustration of this epistemology of value, one might consider the passage from *Republic* IX about dreaming. Here we are told that dreams can give the dreamer access to truth *only* if the dreamer can contrive to make them the work of the intellectual element *alone.* Before going to sleep, he or she must lull the other parts, appetites and emotions, into inactivity so that they "may not disturb the better part by pleasure and pain, but may suffer that in isolated purity to examine and reach out towards and apprehend some of the things unknown to it, past, present, or future" (571D–572B). Again, in the *Phaedo,* he tells us that truth is best apprehended by the soul when it gets itself as free as possible from bodily influence and goes off, alone, to approach the pure objects of knowledge to which it bears, in its undivided purity, a close relation (65A–D).[4]

Plato, then, develops a picture of the soul according to which it is, in its truest nature, a pure noncomposite intellectual substance, capable of access to full and perfect truth insofar as it can separate itself from or protect itself against the impeding influence of the emotional and appetitive elements with which it is only contingently bound up. But it is, of course, those elements of our human nature with which literary art, as Plato knows it, is most deeply involved. A text that would promote genuine access to truth would have to promote intellectual separateness. But both in its selection of content and in its way of presenting that content, tragic poetry (the central example in *Republic* X) traffics in the irrational. In *Republic* Book X Plato claims that a tragedy representing the deliberations of calm, cool practical wisdom could not possibly hold an audience; without taking for its content the intense emotions, for example anger and passionate love, it would lose the power for which it is currently prized (604E–605A). But, Plato

3. I discuss this in *Fragility,* chap. 5; chaps. 4 and 5 and Interlude 1 also contain reflection on the relationship between this view and Plato's stylistic choices. The discussions of *Symposium* and *Phaedrus* in chaps. 6 and 7 make matters far more complex; and even where *Phaedo* and *Republic* are concerned, it is very important to bear in mind the distinction between speech to citizens of the ideal city, whose souls have never been shaped by inappropriate beliefs and emotions, and the "therapeutic" speech that would be appropriate to Plato's actual audience. Plato does not write as he urges writers in the ideal city to write; but there are good and obvious reasons for this.

4. A full account of his arguments on this point is in *Fragility,* chap. 5.

further argues, works that represent intense irrationality not only represent and give emphasis to a false scheme of values (for passionate love, for example, requires the false belief that instances of beauty are qualitatively unique and irreplaceable); it also serves to arouse our own irrational nature as we watch. Our way of coming to understand a representation of intense emotion will itself involve emotional activity. Whether we watch empathetically, assuming the emotional range of one or more of the characters, or whether, as Plato more often seems to suppose, we react to the characters' predicaments with sympathetic emotions such as pity, in either case we are emotionally active. And this means, says Plato, that this poetry is giving nourishment and strength to our emotions and appetites, "watering" just those elements of the personality which, according to his view of the soul, we "ought to dry up" (606B). The poet, then, by the nature of his art, promotes the very elements that make ordinary human life deficient in understanding and access to truth; he impedes the separation of the intellect and its ascent to the good perspective of the "real above in nature," from which really true accounts are produced.

II

With this background too briefly set in place, let us now try to imagine how a text that genuinely promoted intellectual separateness might look, as it explored the essential nature of some phenomenon. What would be the proper Platonic bedtime story to bring true dreams, and how would it differ from Proust's story in its content and its methods? (Note that I am not asking here what Plato's own texts in fact look like, since, as I would argue, Plato, writing for people whose early education has, in his view, been very deficient, has on his mind complex problems of attention and motivation that would not trouble a composer of discourses within his ideal city.) We can schematically set out several features of such a discourse, against which we can then assess our Proust passage about the internal person.

1. *Vehicle of communication.* The philosophical bedtime story would aim at Plato's ideal of communication: the conversation of one pure separated intellect with another. Its own speech would therefore be lucid, spare, and pure, unmixed with expressions of emotionality or passionate desire. It would strive to activate the *intellect* of the reader or hearer, while discouraging the engagement of appetite and emotion. This means, in Plato's view, forgoing stimulating stylistic devices, such as stirringly rhythmic language; avoiding the use of pictorial or sensuous language that would tend to activate the feelings and the imagination; and, above all, eschewing the representation of intense emotionality, or of anything that would be likely to set off a train of associations or memories leading the reader into something disturbing or arousing in his own experience. It would, then, be likely to concern itself with rigorous argumentation purified of all these distracting elements.

2. *Point of view.* What I have called the philosophical bedtime story would, for reasons closely connected with the preceding point, not really be a *story*. That is, its inquiry into the essential nature of the soul (for example) would be dissociated as much as possible from the concrete features of any ordinary human sort of life.

It would not present its general reflections as having their source or their justification in concrete human experience or in the point of view of that experience. Plato tells us repeatedly that "nothing imperfect is ever good measure of anything" (*Rep* 504A); therefore if discourse is to measure the world correctly, it will have to issue from the point of view of a being who is not humanly imperfect, who is, in fact, unlimited and unconstrained. Such discourse would exhibit souls as they appeared from there, the place that Plato calls the real above. But this is, we see, a perspective from which there are no narratives or stories to tell; for to an unlimited and eternal being nothing ever really *happens*—or no happening really *matters*. As the passage about the ascent of love in the *Symposium* makes clear, the discourse produced from the above holds contingent particulars—and, for example, such facts about the soul as the love of one such particular for another—to be of minimal importance and minimal value.[5]

3. *Subject matter: formal features.* We have said something about what elements the intellect will wish to discourage; and this has led already to some restrictions upon the content of its representation. But we can now add to this the specification of four formal characteristics of its treatment of any content whatever.

a. *Consistency.* The intellect will first and foremost present a picture of the soul (or whatever its subject matter is) that obeys the most fundamental law of the intellect, the principle of noncontradiction. It will not say *p* and then again not-*p*, exemplifying confusion and producing bewilderment in the reader. However complex its discourse becomes, all of its parts will cohere together in a self-consistent system.

b. *Generality.* What this intellect, from its high perspective, will be most likely to stress concerning the soul (or any other subject) will be the unifying general structure of all souls and the general principles of their activity—not, as we have already suggested, the vicissitudes and idiosyncrasies of individual souls. For example, as the *Symposium* shows us, such a text, instead of attending to the allegedly unique features of a single soul, will speak of the "wide sea of beauty" and strive to give a general account of beauty's essential nature in the universe as a whole.

c. *Precision.* In eliciting the truth about the structure of some matter of importance, the intellect will try, as far as possible, to give a precise set of conditions or criteria for a being's having or sharing in that value. This is a prominent feature of Platonic inquiry that I have not previously mentioned. But I hope it will be readily agreed that for Plato an intellect has grasped or understands the general nature of some item F only if it can give an account that will be sufficient to demarcate F's clearly and unequivocally from non-F's, and therefore to settle any disagreements we might have about problem cases. Our inability to draw such hard and clear boundaries arises, Plato argues, from our human cognitive limitations; the perfected philosopher's account will be free of any such failings because all of the impediments to perfect cognition will have been removed. In the case of the soul, we will have a precise set of necessary and sufficient conditions for something's being or having a soul, or having certain more concrete psychological elements; and so on for each aspect of the psychological inquiry.

5. See *Fragility,* chap. 6.

d. *Explanation.* One more feature of the Platonic discourse deserves emphasis. This is its interest in explanation. A good Platonic account of something, such as the soul, will not simply give a list of its properties; it will seek to tell us something that adequately explains these properties and how they cohere together.[6] We look, Plato emphasizes, for ever more powerful and more inclusive general theoretical hypotheses that will systematically organize our knowledge, and from which everything that we want to say will follow. This is, so far, vague. But we will return to the point later.

These are some salient features of a good Platonic text. I hope that it will be clear that this hypothetical text is no mere fantasy of mine and of Plato's, but a picture of philosophical writing that has had a deep influence upon our entire tradition. Locke, to take only one example, compares the rhetorical and emotive elements of a written text to the wiles of a seductive woman—attractive to someone in search of diversion or even pleasure, but clearly of negative value to someone actively engaged in the search for truth:

> But yet, if we would speak of things as they are, we must allow that all . . . the artificial and figurative application of words eloquence hath invented, are for nothing else but to insinuate wrong *ideas,* move the passions, and thereby mislead the judgment, and so indeed are perfect cheat; and therefore . . . they are certainly, in all discourses that pretend to inform or instruct, wholly to be avoided and, where truth and knowledge are concerned, cannot but be thought a great fault either of the language or person that makes use of them. (*Essay,* Book 3, chap. 10)[7]

If we wish a more contemporary voice, we can do no better than to turn to Iris Murdoch, one of the few philosophers writing in English who is also a prominent literary artist: "Of course philosophers vary, and some are more 'literary' than others, but I am tempted to say that there is an ideal philosphical style which has a special unambiguous plainness and hardness about it, an austere unselfish candid style. . . . When the philosopher is as it were in the front line in relation to his problem I think he speaks with a certain cold clear recognizable voice."[8] These passages show to what extent our philosophical tradition has taken over Plato's picture of philosophical style. What is extraordinary is how little they bother to engage themselves with Plato's arguments for the selection of that style. They appear to treat that style as something altogether neutral among conceptions of the person and of learning, suitable for the pursuit of truth no matter what truth is or how we are equipped to grasp it. Plato, by contrast, saw clearly that the philosopher was an artist who created, in his view of the soul, a certain picture of the truth, and whose commitment to that creation led to the selection of a style that would be its fitting embodiment.

---

6. See especially *Euthyphro,* 10–11.

7. This passage is discussed by Paul de Man in "The Epistemology of Metaphor," *Critical Inquiry* 5 (1978) 13–30.

8. Iris Murdoch, in "Philosophy and Literature," an interview with Brian Magee printed in the volume *Men of Ideas* (New York, 1979), 262–85. The relationship of these statements to Murdoch's own complex stylistic practice as novelist and philosopher seems to me difficult to ascertain.

Now we turn to Proust's narrator, as Albertine opens the door of the little train and at the same time walks down into his heart. What sort of story of and for the human soul is this story? By what means does it address us, what parts of our souls does it render active, and what sort of knowledge could we be said to derive from it? To describe what is going on here, it will be useful to deal first with "point of view" and then to ask about the parts of the soul that the story represents and addresses.

Point of view. This narrative, clearly, never moves away from the specific circumstances and conditions of human life. Its general inquiry into the nature of the soul is thoroughly rooted in the distinctive features of the human point of view: its characteristic temporality, its patterns of need, desire, and repletion. What is more, even these general features of human life are explored from the viewpoint of one particular human life. Such generalizable content as its truths have emerges as truth about and within a particular human story; and the truths are themselves presented as parts of the story. We are, for example, carefully told what particular perceptions and responses led Marcel to his general reflection. What is more, the moment he has briefly formulated a general psychological principle he moves back to dwell upon his own case, to the particular words of Albertine that opened his heart. General reflection and particular experience illuminate each other as they do in a life; and we are confronted with truth only insofar as it figures in a life, in a story in which accidents matter at least as much as truths, in which happening upon a truth has itself the nature of an accident.

How, then, do we read this story? What is our activity and our point of view as we assess its claims? We are certainly called upon to picture the scene as we read. And since the world of the scene is given us from the point of view of a single character, we are asked to enter, in our imagining, into that point of view, taking on the activities and responses of Marcel. This means that when the central psychological truth it contains is presented to us, conveyed in the odd spatial metaphor, we explore it and assess it, first of all, from the point of view of Marcel: that is, we are led up to it by assuming his experiences and responses. We are led to feel and see that picture by the very processes that led him. Our situation, however, is still more complex than this. For the narrative presents us not only with the Marcel to whom this picture occurred, but also with the older Marcel, the author of the narrative, who renders the spatial picture explicit and assesses its importance as a general truth. So we are asked to alternate between assuming Marcel's original perspective, and with this his ways of feeling and seeing, and assuming a perspective that remembers his experience now from within and now from without, examining and reexperiencing his psychology, reliving and responding to his experience. So we also feel what it is to have that experience return through memory to exercise its influence on the same person at another time. What is more, we are no doubt alternating, as we read, between assuming these two perspectives from within and responding sympathetically to the story from the point of view of a spectator, who is not identical to the spectator aspect of the later Marcel because he or she will not have the same relation to those memories.

And finally, as Proust repeatedly insists, we are at the same time to be "mining" our own experience for analogous material. So in the midst of all this other complicated and shifting activity we will also be following the associations awakened by this story in our own memories. When we are told that certain experiences put a person into our insides, we follow this up by recalling our own analogous experience of love and the fear of loss, and ask ourselves whether it felt like that— whether the loved person's deep influence upon all our thoughts and actions, his or her power to disturb through separateness, felt like, was well captured by, this picture of the person opening the door of our heart and entering in as a disturbing and ungovernable guest. This pursuit of memory will involve taking on again the thoughts and feelings of our past self; and as we do so we will stand to the influence of memory as Proust's narrator stands to the memory of his own earlier self.[9]

In short, instead of Plato's decentered beam of intellectual light we have an elusive, rapidly shifting and volatile activity of imagination and feeling, slipping with great flexibility from one viewpoint to another, from one time to another, from one person's experience to another's. And it is no surprise that this should be the experience engineered by Proust's way of writing, given the view, within the novel, of what human truth comes to. For the novel repeatedly claims that there are no truths that can be detached from the perspective of a human life and its concrete experiences, from the experience of the peculiar sort of fragmentation and of unity that constitutes a human life in its characteristic relation to time and change. Indeed, the choice of the novel as a vehicle of psychological investigation is defended, in the general reflections in its last volume, by arguments about the perspectival and contextual nature of psychological truth. Through art, it is argued, we can at any rate expand our own particular understanding by being led to assume the perspective, to enter the world, of another concrete human being; this sort of concrete attention and response provides, the narrator claims, the *only* route by which we can emerge from ourselves and have access to other "land-scapes." And in this process we also come upon a knowledge of ourselves that could be gained in no other way. So we begin to see some of the force of the claim that any other form of representation would be artificial and untruthful: style and the claims of style are intimately connected with a view of what psychological truth is like and how it can be reached.

But to go further with this we must now say more about the parts of Marcel's soul, and our souls, that are active here. And as we do so we must begin to talk about one of Proust's great themes: the importance of suffering for psychological knowledge.

Parts of the soul. Well, clearly the intellect is active here. Marcel is thinking, comparing, later generalizing. In following his story we do so too. But the intellect in its activity is not at all isolated from other elements of our personality. We have already spoken of the activity of imagination here. What we now must acknowledge is the obvious fact that this passage both represents emotional activity and calls forth this activity in us. And not just emotional activity, but violent and painful emotions. Suffering is the content of this story that claims to tell a human truth: violent suffering, in fact, the "tearing" of a human heart. And it shows the central psychological truth being grasped not through calm cogitation but by and in the suffering itself. (We shall shortly ask more about what "by and in" comes to.) To get the truth it conveys, as we perform the activity of imagination we have

9. I am indebted to valuable reflection on these issues in Richard Wollheim's third William James Lecture; see now *The Thread of Life* (Cambridge, Mass., 1984).

described, we will ourselves not only be responding to Marcel's suffering with a spectator's pity (and even this Plato expressly forbade); we will also be taking up, within Marcel's viewpoint, his violent pain, following the path by which pain shows him something about his soul. And, as we are brought into intimate relation with our own most painful memories, we will, if we do what Proust requires, suffer violently as we suffered in some past, and feel, from the present, the power of the past upon us. This part of our psychological inquiry arrives at truth, if it does so, not by straightforwardly intellectual paths, but by way of a violent surge of recognition, in which what will be in our imaginations and hearts will be not a piece of knowledge, but the face and body of some particular recollected internal person; and we will feel anew our deep emotions concerning that person. It would not be surprising if the surge of affect awakened by this procedure proved so powerful that it temporarily interrupted the act of reading itself.

We must pause here and examine this notion that human learning proceeds through suffering. For it is without doubt one of the oldest and most celebrated claims made by literary works on their own behalf and in defense of their claim to teach the human truth; to attack it is a correspondingly central part of Plato's attack upon literature. The view about human learning that gets expressed inside Proust's novel by the narrator suits his stylistic procedure; for it makes suffering and sudden strong emotional response of enormous cognitive importance. Why should this be so? In the opening pages of *Albertine disparue,* Proust's narrator seems to argue in something like the following way.

To have an understanding of human psychology, it is necessary first to investigate oneself and to come to know the elements of one's own soul. But in order for this search to be successful, the searcher must get past certain powerful obstacles. First there is habit, which both dulls our sensibilities generally and conceals from our notice, or belies the true importance of, many areas of commitment and concern. Marcel's habit of living with Albertine makes her seem dispensable and conceals from him the extent to which he needs and longs for her. Second, there are more specific defenses that we erect against truths about our condition that would be hard to live with, were they to surface. Marcel, for example, imagines that he desires affairs with other women, concealing from himself in this way the depth of his need for Albertine, therefore his own enormous incompleteness and passivity and vulnerability. Finally, there is the obstacle erected by rationalization—an activity of self-explication engaged in at a superficial and intellectual level which, by giving us the confidence that we have accomplished a scientific analysis and arrived at exact truth, deters us from a deeper or fuller inquiry. Before he hears of Albertine's departure, Marcel is engaged in such a process, full of confidence about the scientific correctness of his self-analysis: "I believed that I had, like a precise analyst, left nothing out. I believed that I knew the very bottom of my heart." To remove these obstacles, we need, as Marcel puts it, an instrument that is "subtle and powerful and appropriate for seizing truth." This instrument is given us in suffering. "How much further suffering goes in psychology," he exclaims, "than psychology itself." Smug and self-assured, he hears the sudden words, "Mademoiselle Albertine has gone." Immediately the pseudotruths that he had concocted in rationalization are simply knocked out by the power of his pain, through and in which he acknowledges his love. The failure of intellect to grasp this truth about him was not caused, he tells us, by any abuse of intellect; it was caused by limitations intrinsic to intellectual thought itself. He uses the analogy of a chemical reaction: suffering is the catalyst that precipitates out the elements that, a moment before, could not have been discerned by the clearest vision.

We had better stop here and ask some questions of this picture, since it is capable of being understood in more than one way. On one story, the claim that suffering is necessary to the grasping of certain psychological truths means that suffering is instrumental to a grasp of some truths, some pieces of knowledge, that are there to be grasped apart from the suffering and could, in principle (though not necessarily in fact), be obtained in other ways. Take Hamlet's mother: the "black and grained spots" upon her soul are there. They are there for God to see directly at any time, entirely apart from suffering or any other human emotion. Suffering is necessary for Gertrude to see them in this scene; but that is because of her own particular deficiencies and limitations, not because of anything about the nature of the knowledge. Suppose we adopt this picture on Proust's behalf. Then Proust will be agreeing with Plato that there is such a thing, in principle, as pure knowledge of the soul as it is, apart from human psychological activity and response. Knowledge of the soul need not involve the emotions; it is not in the very intrinsic nature of the knowledge itself that it involves suffering. Proust will be disagreeing with Plato only concerning the best route by which people with certain deficiences and limitations can acquire knowledge.

But there is another possibility. Here we would see the knowing of love, for example, as very different from a grasping of some independent fact about the world; as something that is in part constituted by the experience of responding to a loss with need and pain. Love is grasped *in* the experience of loving and suffering. That pain is not some separate thing that instrumentally gives us access to the love; it is constitutive of loving itself. Love is not a thing in the heart to be observed, the way God can see the blemishes on Gertrude's soul; it is embodied in, constituted by, experiences of loving, which prominently include experiences of suffering. The catalyst does not just reveal compounds that were there all along, it brings about a chemical reaction; in the same way, Albertine's words about Mlle. Vinteuil do not reveal to Marcel the fact that she was in his heart all along; they put her, insert her, into his heart. The response to those words, the surge of pain and fear of loss, is what his love is.

What are we saying, then, and finding in Proust, is that suffering is not just one route to the same kind of knowing that Plato talks about. It is part and parcel of, constitutive of, completely intrinsic to, a different sort of knowing and self-knowing.[10] A god who lacked our impediments and also lacked our emotional responses could not, in this view, know some parts of our souls. What happens to Marcel when his rationalization is disrupted by the shock of Albertine's departure is not that some set of curtains are drawn back and he sees clearly, with the same scientific sort of vision, what he had been trying to see in that way before without

10. On all of this, see Stanley Cavell's *The Claim of Reason* (New York, 1979), and the earlier article "Knowing and Acknowledging," in *Must We Mean What We Say?* (New York, 1969; repr. Cambridge, 1976), 238–66.

success. It is that for the scientist's knowing is substituted something quite other, something deeper.

Instead of trying to know himself by grasping in the scientific way, he acknowledges *in* his suffering and *in* his complex responses, who and what he his. At one level, something is there that was not there in the same way before: the love of Albertine. But at the same time it is still appropriate to speak of discovery here; for in acknowledging his love for Albertine, Marcel is brought into contact with a permanent underlying feature of his condition, namely his neediness, his radical incompleteness and hungriness, his inordinate longing to possess and control, his pain at the undefeatable separateness from him of all that is lovable in the world. So the particular suffering, which is the knowing of the particular love, also counts as an acknowledgment of something that underlies and runs through all his particular loves. And this something, we might say, is the condition of incompleteness, which is pain itself. This pain of incompleteness gives knowledge to the underlying condition because it is a case of that condition; and so in allowing himself to experience it he acknowledges, allows himself to experience, himself. There is, then, a kind of knowing that works through suffering because suffering is thoroughly intrinsic to both the knowing and the known. From this point of view, Marcel's attempt to grasp his soul by a scientific kind of knowing, to treat his experiences as somehow extrinsic or external to himself, is a form of self-avoidance. To try to grasp love by the Platonic kind of knowing is a way of avoiding loving. To try to *see* suffering is a way of *not* suffering. What would the person be like who treated thoughts, feelings, suffering as somehow external to himself, as things to be grasped and studied apart from the experience of thinking, feeling, suffering? Proust's novel indicates to us that this would be a person in flight from self-knowledge, that is from the admission of his or her own neediness and incompleteness. The novel shows many forms of this avoidance; it shows us that many of the forms of social life are just that—as, for example, in the memorable scene in which the Duchesse de Guermantes, unable to receive the knowledge of Swann's fatal illness, and through this of human mortality and fragility, accuses him of teasing her and goes to her room to get her red slippers. And in showing us these forms of avoidance, it shows us at the same time more than one form of recognition: for there is recognition in humor and the sense of the grotesque, as well as in deep personal pain. The comic and satirical elements of the novel work toward human truth, just as its tragic parts do. But what is clear in all of this is that these recognitions and responses, these surges of laughter and of tears, are not merely routes to Platonic knowing; they are parts of knowing itself.

This has important implications for the issues at stake between Proust and Plato. For if this is so, the issue is not simply one about the most efficient route to the same epistemic goal, but one about the nature of the goal. The claim that only a novel can convey psychological truth is not just the claim that it can get around certain impediments more cleverly than a philosophical text; it is the claim that there is at least some knowledge, some important human knowledge, that it provides just in virtue of its being a novel, that is to say a work that leads its reader into laughter and into suffering, that cannot even in principle be provided in another more intellectual way. The pictorial representation of Albertine's descent into the soul could not be replaced by a paraphrase, because this enormously vivid and powerful spatial picture is what sets up in the reader the activity of knowing. Now we need to deal, much more briefly, with our other points of comparison.

a. *Consistency.* Proust's narrative appears to contain unresolved contradictions. If we set this general psychological claim side by side with other claims, we would have a hard time figuring out how to understand their connections. Our passage, for example, does not tell us how to understand its own connection with other apparently conflicting observations made by the narrator about the very same relationship—for example, with the observation that Albertine is hopelessly and unknowably external to him, that she inhabits vast regions of external space into which he can never penetrate. It does not relativize its claims to the particular, saying only "This is true for Marcel at time *t*." But it does not care to show how apparent inconsistencies can be seen as a part of a unitary true picture. This is not surprising, if we are right that there is at work here a different picture of grasping truth; and the relation of this picture to the demand for consistency needs much more examination.

b. *Generality.* It goes with the preceding that the sort of generality aspired to by this text is not the sort sought by Plato's philosophical story. It does indeed claim to contain general truths about matters of importance. Proust's narrator, in the last volume, speaks of his interest in "general essences common to a number of things," saying that to a spirit like his, these essences are "its nourishment and joy" (III.905). We are invited to find the truths of the text applicable to our human lives. But these are at most contextual truths, true for human beings and at certain times in their lives; that would hardly be enough generality for Plato. Furthermore, the general truths vigorously assert the importance and uniqueness of contingent particulars. The internal object who causes Marcel such distress is not a general form of human being, but a particular woman with big round cheeks, a woman who said, "That friend is Mlle. Vinteuil." The text is general in that it asks us to see as similar certain experiences of our own. But in so doing we will not simply strike out Albertine's round cheeks and think an abstract form. We will, if we generalize appropriately, substitute some other deeply loved individuating features of some internal person of our own. We never *ascend,* as the Platonist does, from particulars to a universal that is higher, from which we disdain or neglect them.

c. *Precision* It is obvious that this passage, which does, in a way, present a paradigm case of a certain sort of human relationship, does not provide us with any set of necessary and sufficient conditions for this relationship, with reference to which we could judge whether a love of our own was or was not of this sort. Its claim to truth does not appear to depend on its presenting a clear, sharply demarcated and unitary picture of deep love. Nor does it seem likely, to say the least, that its truths could be preserved in any account that had the form, "A human relationship is deep love if and only if . . ." The picture of the internal person has a power that is neither dependent upon nor exhausted by any such definitional formulation; it also has a mysteriousness and indeterminacy that resist such formulations, which the narrator would clearly brand as "artificial and untruthful," and with good reason. In short, it has its own sort of non-scientific precision.

d. *Explanation.* In a sense this novel has a deep interest in explanation. That is, it clearly aims at bringing forward for assessment some psychological truths that are supposed to explain features of our own experience, of human experience in general. It speaks of getting at and revealing the essences that underlie and explain the many particulars. But this interest in explanation is limited by the limits of its regard for generality and for consistency: we are told nothing systematic or overarching about the way the laws fit together, or even about whether they do fit together. We do not have a hierarchical deductive system of the sort Plato would have wanted; we do not even have a more modest and open-ended framework. And it seems to be part of the truth conveyed by the novel that this should be so. What human life, as this novel shows it, is, is a series of happenings, some more, some less, mysterious. But to dispel their mystery altogether would be to control them; and this we can never, to this extent, do. Moreover, even the aim to explain the whole world, to put it all into a systematic order, may be, in the novel's terms, an inappropriate relation for a human being to have to this world in which he lives, an aim that involves him, as Marcel's scientific project of self-analysis involved him, in denial of incompleteness and vulnerability. It would be a denial of something true about the world to represent all its darkness as illuminated or even illuminable, all of its indeterminacies sorted and categorized. In a later statement of our psychological truth, the narrator refers to Albertine as a person who "as a result of an error in localisation consequent upon certain accidents but nevertheless tenacious, has lodged herself in one's own body to the point where wondering retrospectively whether or not she looked at a woman on a particular day in the corridor of a little seaside railway-train causes one the same pain as would a surgeon probing for a bullet in one's heart" (III.507). Here we see very clearly the idea that even the operation of this central psychological "law" depends to a great extent on idiosyncratic accident, and that the circumstances of love's operation here will remain to some significant extent inaccessible to psychological investigation. (We notice, for example, that even the telling of the facts of the story has shifted, and it is left unclear whether it was a word or a look from Albertine that precipitated the experience of love.) The novel's procedures do not bring everything about the soul into a perspicuous ordering; but this is part and parcel of its view that not everything about the human soul *is* perspicuous, that the deepest depths are dark and shifting and elusive. A form of representation that implied otherwise would be artificial and untruthful. Nor, in our own assessment or criticism of the view, should *we* claim to make everything perspicuous. If we did, we should be playing false the human mysteries to which it is our business to respond. The picture of the internal person cannot be paraphrased in the neutral language of the critic, dissected, explained. It must be responded to in all of its painful violent mystery.

III

We can now draw some provisional conclusions. Plato and Proust both share a certain vague conception of their task or aim. They view themselves as using speech in order to tell truth about the human soul to human souls. But they clearly have enormously different ways of engaging the reader in the search for truth. What we now begin to see is that these ways are hardly arbitrary. They are closely bound up with conceptions of human psychology, of teaching and of knowing, of the grasping of truth and the content of truth, that belong also to the content of the views that the styles express. Some of their differences are just differences about the instrumental means to truth and knowledge: having a certain picture of how human beings come upon truth and what experiences bring knowledge influences the way the author of the picture will address his reader, a potential knower. Other differences, however, go deeper: they are differences that spring from different conceptions of how we are to specify further the nature of this aim itself, this thing called knowledge of the truth about the soul. From, that is, different conceptions of what the subject matter of the truth is and of what knowing here comes to. With respect to both of these differences, and especially to differences of the second sort, the so-called literary and rhetorical elements are not mere decoration or distraction, but intrinsic to the conception of the soul. The old quarrel between philosophy and literature is, as Plato clearly saw, not just a quarrel about ornamentation, but a quarrel about who we are and what we aspire to become. Each view can appropriately claim that other styles *lie* about persons and misrepresent them; each can claim that its own mode of conversation is the *truthful* type. To see that there is a genuine opposition here, not only of conceptions but in fact also of styles, is the first step toward serious work on these questions, so long obscured by an assumption that there is a neutral contentless way of conversing. As Proust's narrator appropriately writes, "Style for the writer, no less than color for the painter, is a question of vision: it is the revelation, which by direct and conscious methods would be impossible, of the qualitative difference, the uniqueness of the fashion in which the world appears to each one of us." To choose a style is to tell a story about the soul.

What vision then does (should) this writing here express? What style could it be in which one could work at assessing fairly two such radically different styles and views? In which one could bring these two stories into some sort of conversation with one another? These are tough and long questions; space prevents me from entering into them. But their answer, I am sure, would require us to turn again to the issue of explanation, asking how far we can speak of a mystery without violating it. Somewhere in the course of this inquiry we would come upon the question, "Is a philosophical criticism of literature possible?" Or rather—to help myself to a familiar style of philosophical optimism—"*How* is a philosophical criticism of literature possible?"[11]

Endnote

This essay, written shortly after "Flawed Crystals" and thus one of the earliest in the collection, is somewhat too compressed and schematic to do full justice to its complex questions concerning form and content. (One might view the Introduc-

11. Some of the material in this article was first presented in a reply to Mary Rawlinson's paper, "The Old Quarrel Between Art and Philosophy: Reading Proust," at the Eastern Division of the American Philosophical Association, December 1981. I am grateful to Rawlinson for stimulating some of these reflections; a later version of her paper has appeared as "Art and Truth: Reading Proust," in *Philosophy and Literature* 6 (1982) 1–16. I also owe thanks to Thomas Pavel for providing a stimulating occasion for presentation and discussion of this paper at the conference on Styles of Fictionality; and especially to Richard Wollheim and Ronald Dworkin, discussions with whom very much helped me as I was writing it.

tion in this volume as a longer and fuller version of the same project.) But its central contrast, though stark, still seems to me to focus the issue in a useful way; and the categories of analysis begin to offer directions for inquiry, mapping out an elusive and largely uncharted set of issues for further work.

The reader of the Introduction will notice that several of the categories set out here have, in the later piece, been altered and rearranged. In particular, the single category "point of view" becomes the two categories "voice" and "point of view." One and the same speaker can address the reader from various different viewpoints, even with respect to the same subject matter. Proust's narrative is an obvious case of this. Again, the same sort of viewpoint, toward certain events, can be occupied by a variety of different personalities, with different voices. In any case, the categories suggested in both pieces should not be treated as exhaustively prescriptive or rigid; they simply suggest a useful set of questions that might help one get started on the analysis of texts of various sorts.

It is important here to notice the distinction between the parts of the personality involved in the represented action and the parts of the personality involved in the text's transactions with its reader. The two questions are rather closely related: for the representation (for example) of certain strong emotions frequently arouses related emotions in the reader, all the more since the beliefs communicated by the text have close links with the emotions involved. The representation of complex intellectual activity—as, for example, in a treatise on logic—tends, in a similar way, to arouse such activity in its reader. But this connection may also be broken, particularly if we are discouraged from identifying with the characters or believing what they say. Stoic tragedies, for example, represent characters in the grip of intense emotion, but in such a way as to distance the spectator from emotion. And James and Proust both suggest that our inability to share the erotic love, the rage, and the jealousy of the characters is an essential element in the novel's moral function (see "Perceptive Equilibrium," "'Finely Aware,'" and, for a different view, "Steerforth's Arm").

The Plato and Proust depicted here are simplified in obvious ways. For more complex portrayals, see "Love's Knowledge" on Proust, *Fragility,* chaps. 4–7 on Plato.

Love's Knowledge

And if a cataleptic impression does not exist, neither will there be any assent to it, and thus there will not be any certainty either. And if there is no certainty, neither will there be a system of certainties, that is to say a science. From which it follows that there will be no science of life either.

Sextus Empiricus, Adversus Mathematicos vii, 182

As we examine this view closely, it looks to us more like a prayer than like the truth.

Sextus, Adversus Mathematicos xi, 401

Françoise brings him the news: "Mademoiselle Albertine has gone." Only a moment before, he believed with confidence that he did not love her any longer. Now the news of her departure brings a reaction so powerful, an anguish so overwhelming, that this view of his condition simply vanishes, Marcel knows, and knows with certainty, without the least room for doubt, that he loves Albertine.[1]

We deceive ourselves about love—about who; and how; and when; and whether. We also discover and correct our self-deceptions. The forces making for both deception and unmasking here are various and powerful: the unsurpassed danger, the urgent need for protection and self-sufficiency, the opposite and equal need for joy and communication and connection. Any of these can serve either truth or falsity, as the occasion demands. The difficulty then becomes: how in the midst of this confusion (and delight and pain) do we know what view of ourselves, what parts of ourselves, to trust? Which stories about the condition of the heart are the reliable ones and which the self-deceiving fictions? We find ourselves asking where, in this plurality of discordant voices with which we address ourselves on this topic of perennial self-interest, is the criterion of truth? (And what does it mean to look for a criterion here? Could that demand itself be a tool of self-deception?)

Proust tells us that the sort of knowledge of the heart we need in this case cannot be given us by the science of psychology, or, indeed, by any sort of scientific use

---

1. I have discussed this passage and its view of knowledge in "Fictions." The present discussion modifies many of the views expressed in that article, and expands on others.

of intellect. Knowledge of the heart must come from the heart—from and in its pains and longings, its emotional responses. I examine this part of Proust's view, and its relation to the "scientific" opposition. The view raises a number of troubling questions, which are only partially answered by the more elaborate account of emotion's interaction with reflection that Proust develops in his final volume. I then examine an alternative view of knowledge of love, one that opposes the scientific account in a more radical way. I find this view in a short story by Ann Beattie. Finally, I ask about the relationship between these views of love's knowledge and the styles in which they are expressed, and make some remarks about a philosophical criticism of literature.

Knowledge of the Heart by Intellectual Scrutiny

We need to begin with a picture of the view that Proust is opposing when he offers his account of how we come to know our own love. It is important to recognize from the beginning that this is not simply a rival alternative account of the matter, incompatible with Proust's as one belief is incompatible with another. It is also, according to Proust, a form of activity that we engage in, a commitment we make, when we wish to avoid or block the sort of knowledge that he will describe. It is a practical barrier to this knowledge as well as a theoretical rival. To believe in the theoretical rival and live accordingly is not just to be in error; it is to engage in a fundamental form of self-deception.

The rival view is this. Knowledge of whether one loves someone—knowledge of the condition of one's heart where love is concerned—can best be attained by a detached, unemotional, exact intellectual scrutiny of one's condition, conducted in the way a scientist would conduct a piece of research. We attend carefully, with subtle intellectual precision, to the vicissitudes of our passion, sorting, analyzing, classifying. This sort of scrutiny is both necessary and sufficient for the requisite self-knowledge.[2] Proust's Marcel is deeply attached to this view. Just before he receives the news of Albertine's departure, he has, accordingly, been surveying the contents of his heart in the scientific manner: "I had believed that I was leaving nothing out of account, like a rigorous analyst; I had believed that I knew the state of my own heart" (III.426).[3] This inspection convinces him that no love for Albertine is present. He is tired of her. He desires other women.

This view of knowledge has, it hardly needs to be said, powerful roots in our entire intellectual tradition, and especially our philosophical tradition. It is also a view on which much of the thought about method and about writing in that tradition relies. The view (as it is defended by thinkers otherwise as diverse as Plato and Locke)[4] holds that our passions and our feelings are unnecessary to the search

2. On this point there is a longer discussion in "Fictions," with reference to Plato.

3. My references to Marcel Proust's *Remembrance of Things Past* will be to the volumes and pages of the translation by C. K. Scott Moncrieff and A. Mayor, as revised by Terence Kilmartin (New York, 1981). In several cases I have retranslated the French myself, in order to bring out more clearly some aspect of the original, but I still give the pages of the Kilmartin edition.

4. On this comparison and related issues, see my "Fictions" and *Fragility,* especially chap. 1, Interlude 1; on Plato see chaps. 5–7

for truth about any matter whatever. What is more, feelings can easily impede that search, either by distracting the searching intellect or, still worse, by distorting its view of the world. Desire, as Plato puts it in the *Phaedo,* binds the soul to its bodily prison house and forces it to view everything from within that distorting enclosure. The result is that intellect is "bewitched," distorted in its function; a captive, it "collaborates in its own imprisonment." In short, self-deception about our condition, when it occurs, is the result of the corruption of reason by feeling and desire. Intellect "itself by itself" is never self-deceptive. Though of course it may fail to reach its goal for some external reason, it never presents a biased or one-sided view of truth. It is never internally corrupt or corrupting. Nor does it require supplementation from any other source. "Itself by itself" it reaches the truth.

This view has implications for questions of method and style. Locke has, of course, an altogether different view from Plato's about the relationship between intellect and bodily sense-perception, but he is no more charitable to the passions and their role in the search for truth. His attack on rhetorical and emotive features of style (which I have discussed further elsewhere) presupposes that the passions are never necessary to the grasp of truth, and are usually pernicious. I quote it as typical of a prejudice that runs through much of our philosophical tradition:

> But yet, if we would speak of things as they are, we must allow that all . . . the artificial and figurative application of words eloquence hath invented, are for nothing else but to insinuate wrong *ideas,* move the passions, and thereby mislead the judgment, and so indeed are perfect cheat; and therefore . . . they are certainly, in all discourses that pretend to inform or instruct, wholly to be avoided, and, where truth and knowledge are concerned, cannot but be thought a great fault either of the language or person that makes use of them. (*Essay,* bk. 3, chap. 10)[5]

Notice especially the inference: "move the passions and *thereby* mislead the judgment"; notice also the explicit claims that that emotive elements in style have no good or necessary function and that they can and should be altogether dropped. Intellect is a sufficient criterion of truth; we have no other veridical elements. Therefore a discourse that claims to search for truth and impart knowledge must speak in the language of the intellect, addressing itself to (and, as Plato might say, encouraging the separation of) the reader's own intellect. Using this view of knowledge and of discourse as our (somewhat simplified) target, we can now proceed to explore Proust's counterproposal.

The Cataleptic Impression: Knowledge in Suffering

Self-assured and complacent, carrying out his analytical scrutiny of the heart, Marcel hears the words, "Mademoiselle Albertine has gone." Immediately the anguish occasioned by these words cuts aways the pseudotruths of the intellect,

5. On this passage, see also Paul de Man, "The Epistemology of Metaphor," *Critical Inquiry* 5 (1978), 13–30.

revealing the truth of his love. "How much further does anguish penetrate in psychology," he observes, "than psychology itself" (III.425). The shock of loss and the attendant welling up of pain show him that his theories were forms of self-deceptive rationalization—not only *false* about his condition but also manifestations and accomplices of a reflex to deny and close off one's vulnerabilities that Proust finds to be very deep in all of human life. The primary and most ubiquitous form of this reflex is seen in the operations of habit, which makes the pain of our vulnerability tolerable to us by concealing need, concealing particularity (hence vulnerability to loss), concealing all the pain-inflicting features of the world—simply making us used to them, dead to their assaults. When we are used to them we do not feel them or long for them in the same way; we are no longer so painfully afflicted by our failure to control and possess them. Marcel has been able to conclude that he is not in love with Albertine, in part because he is used to her. His calm, methodical intellectual scrutiny is powerless to dislodge this "dread deity, so riveted to one's being, its insignificant face so incrusted in one's heart" (III.426). Indeed, it fails altogether to discern the all-important distinction between the face of habit and the true face of the heart.

In various ways, indeed, intellect actively aids and abets habit, concealing that true face. First, the guided tour of the heart conducted by intellect treats all landmarks as on a par, pointing out as salient and interesting many desires that are actually trivial and superficial. Like the account of social life offered in the parody journal of the Frères Goncourt (in which the color of the border on a dinner plate has the same importance as the expression in someone's eyes), intellect's account of psychology lacks all sense of proportion, of depth and importance. Accordingly, it is inclined to reckon up everything in terms of the numbers, "comparing the mediocrity of the pleasures that Albertine afforded me with the richness of the desires which she prevented me from realizing" (III.425). This cost–benefit analysis of the heart—the only comparative assessment of which intellect, by itself, is capable—is bound, Proust suggests, to miss differences of depth. Not only to miss them, but to impede their recognition. Cost–benefit analysis is a way of comforting oneself, of putting oneself in control by pretending that all losses can be made up by sufficient quantities of something else. This stratagem opposes the recognition of love—and, indeed, love itself.[6] Furthermore, we can see that not only the content of the intellectual account but the very fact of engaging in intellectual self-scrutiny is, here, a distorting source of comfort and distance. The very feeling that he is being subtle and profound, that he is "leaving nothing out of account, like a rigorous analyst," leads Marcel into complacency, deterring him from a richer or deeper inquiry, making him less likely to attend to the promptings of his own heart.

What is the antidote to these stratagems? To remove such powerful obstacles to truth, we require the instrument that is "the subtlest, most powerful, most appropriate for grasping the truth." This instrument is given to us in suffering.

6. On these issues, see the further discussion in *Fragility,* chap. 10. On the modification of our emotional life by a belief in commensurability, see chap. 4, and "Plato on Commensurability". In "Discernment" I discuss the relationship between Aristotle's attack on commensurability and some models of rationality in contemporary economic theory.

Our intelligence, however lucid, cannot perceive the elements that compose it and remain unsuspected so long as, from the volatile state in which they generally exist, a phenomenon capable of isolating them has not subjected them to the first stages of solidification. I had been mistaken in thinking that I could see clearly into my own heart. But this knowledge, which the shrewdest perceptions of the mind would not have given me, had now been brought to me, hard, glittering, strange, like a crystallised salt, by the abrupt reaction of pain. (III.426)

The Stoic philosopher Zeno argued that all our knowledge of the external world is built upon the foundation of certain special perceptual impressions: those which, by their own internal character, their own experienced quality, certify their own veracity.[7] From (or in) assent to such impressions, we get the cataleptic condition, a condition of certainty and confidence from which nothing can dislodge us. On the basis of such certainties is built all science, natural and ethical. (Science is defined as a system of *katalēpseis*.) The cataleptic impression is said to have the power, just through its own felt quality, to drag us to assent, to convince us that things could not be otherwise. It is defined as a mark or impress in the soul, "one that is imprinted and stamped upon us by reality itself and in accordance with reality, one that could not possibly come from what is not that reality."[8] The expe-

---

7. The cataleptic impression is an enormously complex historical issue. For the main ancient sources, see J. von Arnim. *Stoicorum Veterum Fragmenta* 1 (Stuttgart, 1905), 52–73, and II (1903), 52–70. The most important texts are Diogenes Laertius, *Lives of the Philosophers* VII (Zeno), 46–46, 50–54; Sextus Empiricus, *Adversus Mathematicos* (hereafter *M*), VII.227ff, 236ff, 248ff, 426; Cicero, *Academica Priora* II. 18, 77, 144; and Cicero, *Academica Posteriora* I.41. The view I articulate here—that the impression itself compels assent by its own intrinsic character— is the view most commonly taken by the ancient expositors (two of whom, however, are quite hostile to the view). This is surely the idea that Marcel, as a reader of Sextus and of Cicero, would have absorbed. Modern commentators have tried to find in the evidence a more complex and sophisticated position, and it has at least become clear that later Stoics modified the original simple Zenonian view. For discussions of all the evidence, see: J. Annas, "Truth and Reality," in *Doubt and Dogmatism,* ed. J. Barnes et al. (Oxford, 1980), 84–104; M. Frede, "Stoics and Skeptics on Clear and Distinct Impressions," in *The Skeptical Tradition,* ed. M. Burnyeat (Berkeley, 1983), 65–94; J. Rist, *Stoic Philosophy* (Cambridge, 1969), chap. 8; and F. Sandbach, *"Phantasia Katalēptikē,"* in *Problems in Stoicism,* ed. A. A. Long (London, 1971), 9–21.

"Cataleptic" is the Greek *katalēptikē,* an adjective from the verb *katalambanein,* "apprehend," "grasp," "firmly grasp." It is probably active rather than passive: "apprehensive," "firmly grasping (reality)." In the epigraphs I have translated the associated noun *katalēpsis* (the condition of the person who has such an impression) as "certainty." This seems to me appropriate: it brings out the essential point that this person now has an absolutely indubitable and unshakable grasp of some part of reality, a grasp that could not have been produced by nonreality. However, it is important to note that only an orderly system *(sustēma)* of such *katalēpseis* will constitute scientific understanding or *epistēmē.*

One further point about these impressions should be borne in mind as we consider Proust's analogue: they can be, and very frequently are, propositional—that is, impressions *that* such-and-such is the case.

8. For the definition, see Sextus, *M* VII.248, 426; Sextus, *Outlines of Pyrrhonism* II.4; Diogenes, *Lives* VII.50; and Cicero, *Acad. Pr.* II.18, 77. The point of the last clause seems to be not only that the impression couldn't come from what is altogether unreal or nonexistent but also that it couldn't come from anything else but the very reality that it claims to represent. For the definition of science *(technē)* as a "system of *katalēpseis* ordered together for some useful practical purpose," see reference in von Arnim, *SVF* I.73.

rience of having one is compared to a balance scale being weighed down by a very heavy weight—you just have to go along with it; it compels assent.[9] Again, Zeno compares its closure and certainty to a closed fist: it's that firm; there's no room for opposition.[10] It seems to me that Marcel—who elsewhere reveals his serious interest in the Hellenistic philosophers[11]—is working out a (highly non-Stoic)[12] analogue to Zeno's view for our knowledge of the inner world. Knowlege of our heart's condition is given to us in and through certain powerful impressions, impressions that come from the reality itself of our condition and could not possibly come from anything else but that reality. Indeed he uses explicitly Zenonian language of the way in which we gain self-knowledge through these experiences. He tells us that the impression is "the only criterion of truth" (III.914); that all our understanding of our life is built up on the basis of the text "that reality has dictated to us, whose impression in us has been made by reality itself" (III.914). The cataleptic impressions in this case, however, are emotional impressions—specifically, impressions of anguish.

What is it about the impressions of suffering that makes them cataleptic? Why do they convince Marcel that truth is *here,* rather than in the deliverances of intellect? We are conscious, first of all, of their sheer *power.* The suffering is "hard, glittering, strange"; "an anguish such that I felt I could not endure it much longer" (III.425); an "immense new jolt" (429); a "physical blow . . . to the heart" (431); "like . . . a thunderbolt" (431); it makes "an open wound" (425). The power of this impression simply overwhelms every other impression. The superficial impressions of the intellect "could no longer even begin to compete . . . , had vanished instantaneously" (425).

These passages show us that, in addition to sheer force, there are also surprise

---

9. See Cicero, *Acad. Pr.* II.38; Sextus, *M* VII.405.

10. Cicero, *Acad. Post.* I.41 and *Acad. Pr.* II.144. (*Technē* itself is like a hand grasping the closed fist.)

11. See Proust, *Remembrance,* especially I.768, where the anxiety aroused in Marcel by the sight of a beautiful girl prompts the following remark:

and I found a certain wisdom in the philosophers who recommend us to set a limit to our desires (if, that is, they refer to our desire for people, for that is the only kind that leads to anxiety, having for its object something unknown but conscious. To suppose that philosophy could be referring to the desire for wealth would be too absurd.)

The connection between setting a limit to desire and the avoidance of anxiety is an individuating feature, prominently stressed, in Hellenistic ethical thought (both Epicurean and Stoic), and in Skepticism as well, with slight variation. (It should also be borne in mind that the Hellenistic philosophers were central in Marcel's curriculum in a way that they are not for us; Cicero, Plutarch, and Seneca were read more widely than Aristotle, and the Skeptics too enjoyed continuous prominence.) Only a short time after this interesting remark, Marcel meets Albertine.

12. The true Stoic could never countenance an emotional cataleptic impression. This would come close to being a contradiction in terms, since the Stoics argued that emotions are forms of false judgment. However, as one looks into this more closely, the difference grows narrower. The false judgments with which emotions are identical for the Stoic are judgments about the value of external uncontrolled objects: thus love—*if* we understand by this an emotion involving a high valuation of the loved one, seen as a separate being—is a false emotion in their terms. But it is not at all clear that Marcel's conception of love would be objectionable to the Stoic in this way (see below). See my "The Stoics on the Extirpation of the Passions," *Apeiron* (1987), 129–77.

and passivity. The impression comes upon Marcel unbidden, unannounced, uncontrolled. Because he neither predicts nor governs it, because it simply gets stamped on him, it seems natural to conclude that it is authentic and not a stratagem devised by self-assuaging reason. Just as the Stoic perceptual impressions drag the perceiving agent to assent not only by their vividness but also by their unbidden and external character—they seem such as could not have been made up; they must have come from reality itself—so too with these emotional impressions. For Proust it is especially significant that surprise, vivid particularity, and extreme qualitative intensity are all characteristics that are systematically concealed by the workings of habit, the primary form of self-deception and self-concealment. What has these features must have escaped the workings of self-deception, must have come from reality itself.

We notice, finally, that the very painfulness of these impressions is essential to their cataleptic character. Our primary aim is to comfort ourselves, to assuage pain, to cover our wounds. Then what has the character of pain must have escaped these mechanisms of comfort and concealment; must, then, have come from the true unconcealed nature of our condition.

We now confront an ambiguity in Marcel's account.[13] He has told us that certain self-impressions are criterial of psychological truth about ourselves. But this picture can be understood in more than one way. On one interpretation, the impression gives us access to truths that could *in principle* (even if not in fact) be grasped in other ways, for example, by intellect. We, perhaps, cannot so grasp them because of certain obstacles in human psychology. But they exist in the heart, apart from the suffering, available for knowledge. Marcel's love is the sort of thing that some superior being—say, a god—could see and know without pain. Pure intellectual knowledge of the heart as it is in itself is possible in principle, apart from emotion; it is not in the very nature of the knowledge itself that it involves suffering. On this reading, Marcel will be taking issue with the intellectualist only about the instrumental means to knowing; also, in some cases, about the content of the knowledge gained. But he will not be taking issue in a fundamental way about what knowing *is,* what activity or passivity of the person constitutes it.

There is, however, another possibility. For the Stoic the cataleptic impression is not simply a route to knowing; it *is* knowing. It doesn't point beyond itself *to* knowledge; it goes to constitute knowledge. (Science is a system *made up of katalēpseis.*) If we follow the analogy strictly, then, we find that knowledge of our love is not the fruit of the impression of suffering, a fruit that might in principle have been had apart from the suffering. The suffering itself is a piece of self-knowing. *In* responding to a loss with anguish, we are grasping our love. The love is not some separate fact about us that is signaled by the impression; the impression reveals the love by constituting it. Love is not a structure in the heart waiting to

13. This discussion closely follows the treatment of this contrast in "Fictions," but with some significant changes, especially concerning the relationship between creation and discovery. I now say that there are both creation and discovery on both the particular and general levels, whereas before I said that the particular love was created, the general discovered.

be discovered; it is embodied in, made up out of, experiences of suffering. It is "produced" in Marcel's heart by Françoise's words (III.425).

This reading is borne out by Marcel's chemical analogy. A catalyst does not reveal chemical compounds that were there all along. It brings about a chemical reaction. It precipitates out the salt. The salt was not there before, or not in that state or form. The words, like the catalyst, both reveal a chemical structure and create something that was not there in the same way. Françoise's words are like the catalyst. They do not simply remove impediments to scientific knowledge, as if some curtains were pulled back and Marcel could now see exactly what he could have seen before had the curtains not been there. They bring about a change, which *is* the suffering; and this suffering is not so much an object of scientific knowing as an alternative to that knowing. In place of scientific knowing is substituted something that *counts as* knowing himself in a way that the scientific sort of grasping didn't—because it is not a stratagem for mastery of anything, but simply a naked case of his human incompleteness and neediness. Its relation to self-deception is not that of a rival and more accurate account of standing structures in the heart. It *is* the thing from which the deception was protecting him, namely, the love, the needy, painful reaching out that is not only a specific condition of his heart now toward Albertine but also a fundamental condition of the human soul.

Marcel is brought, then, by and in the cataleptic impression, to an acknowledgment of his love. There are elements of both discovery and creation here, at both the particular and general levels. Love of Albertine is both discovered and created. It is discovered, in that habit and intellect were masking from Marcel a psychological condition that was ready for suffering, and that, like the chemicals, needed only to be affected slightly by the catalyst in order to turn itself into love. It is created, because love denied and successfully repressed is not exactly love. While he was busily denying that he loved her, he simply was not loving her. At the general level, again, Marcel both discovers and enacts a permanent underlying feature of his condition, namely, his neediness, his hunger for possession and completeness. That too was there in a sense before the loss, because that's what human life is made of. But in denying and repressing it, Marcel became temporarily self-sufficient, closed, and estranged from his humanity. The pain he feels for Albertine gives him access to his permanent underlying condition by being a case of that condition, and no such case was present a moment before. Before the suffering he was indeed self-deceived—both because he was denying a general structural feature of his humanity and because he was denying the particular readiness of his soul to feel hopeless love for Albertine. He was on the verge of a precipice and thought he was safely immured in his own rationality. But his case shows us as well how the successful denial of love is the (temporary) extinction and death of love, how self-deception can aim at and nearly achieve self-change.

We now see exactly how and why Marcel's account of self-knowledge is no simple rival to the intellectual account. It tells us that the intellectual account was wrong: wrong about the content of the truth about Marcel, wrong about the methods appropriate for gaining this knowledge, wrong as well about what sort of experience in and of the person knowing is. And it tells us that to try to grasp love intellectually is a way of not suffering, not loving—a practical rival, a stratagem of flight.

Cataleptic Impressions and the Science of Life

Marcel's cataleptic view is a powerful alternative to its theoretical and practical rival. And most of us have had such experiences, in which the self-protective tissue of rationalization is in a moment cut through, as by a surgeon's knife. Zeno's picture seems more compelling, in fact, as a story about emotional knowing than as an account of perceptual knowledge, its intended function. And yet, as we reflect on Marcel's story, mining, as Proust urges, our own experience for similar material, we begin to feel a certain discontent.

This blind, unbidden surge of painful affect: is it really the "subtle and powerful" instrument Marcel believes it is? Can't it, too, be deceptive—occasioned, for example, by egocentric needs and frustrations that have little to do with love? Isn't it, moreover, in its very violence and rage—qualities that were important to its cataleptic status—a rather coarse and blunt instrument, lacking in responsiveness and discrimination?

There are several different worries here; we need to disentangle them. They fall into two groups; worries that Marcel has picked the wrong impressions to be the cataleptic ones, and more general worries about the whole cataleptic idea. First, then: if there are cataleptic feelings where love is concerned, why must they be feelings of suffering? We understand why Marcel thinks this: these are the only ones we would never fake. But still, as I consider my own experiences here, I find myself asking, Why not feelings of joy? Or some gentler passions, such as the feeling of tender concern? Why not, indeed, experiences that are more essentially relational in nature—experiences of the exchange of feeling, the mutual communication of emotion; experiences that cannot be characterized without mention of the other person's awareness and activity? If we accept Marcel's claim that our natural psychological tendency is always toward self-insulation and the blunting of intrusive stimuli, then it does seem reasonable to suppose that a feeling of intense suffering wouldn't be there if it weren't in some sense true, an emanation from depths that we usually conceal. But should we accept this story? And even if we do, does it give us reason to think that other feelings could not also have depth?

We notice, further, that if suffering is the only reliable impression where the heart is concerned, and if suffering *is* love, then the only reliable answer to the question "Do I love?" must always be "yes." We can see why Proust wishes to say this, but it seems peculiar nonetheless. Aren't there possibilities of self-deception on both sides?

This brings us to our second group of questions. Can any feeling, taken in isolation from its context, its history, its relationship to other feelings and actions, really be cataleptic? Can't we be wrong about it and what it signifies? Emotions are not, nor does Proust believe they are, simply raw feelings, individuated by their felt quality alone. Then to be sure that this pain is love—and not, for example, fear or grief or envy—we need to scrutinize the beliefs and the circumstances that go with it, and their relation to our other beliefs and circumstances. Perhaps this scrutiny will disclose that Marcel was simply ill or lacking sleep; perhaps he is really feeling discouragement about his literary career, or a fear of death—and not love at all. The impression does not seem to come reliably labeled with the name of the emotion it is. And even if it is love, can one impression inform him, beyond doubt, that it is a love of Albertine (and not longing for his grandmother, or some more general desire for comfort and attention)? Impressions, in short, require interpretation. And reliable interpretation may well be impossible if we are given only a single experience in isolation. Even an extended pattern might be wrongly understood. But to concede this much is to give up cataleptic impressions.

All this leads us to ask whether Marcel has not been too hasty in (apparently) dismissing intellect and its scrutiny from the enterprise of self-knowing. He may perhaps have shown that it is not sufficient for knowledge of love; he has not shown that it is not necessary. We shall shortly see that Proust later concedes this point—in a limited way.

But now we come upon a deeper criticism, which we borrow from Sextus Empiricus' attack on the Stoic cataleptic impression. This is that Marcel's whole project has about it an odd air of circularity. How do we know love? By a cataleptic impression. But what is this thing, love, that gets known? It is understood to be, is more or less defined as, the very thing that is revealed to us in cataleptic impressions. We privilege the impression of suffering as the criterion, and then we adopt an account of love (hardly the only possible account) according to which love is exactly what this criterion reveals to us. We suspect that Marcel will not allow love to be something that cannot be cataleptically conveyed, something toward which we cannot have the certainty of the single and solitary impression. We suspect that at the root of his emphatic rejection from the account of love of many aspects of what we usually call love—say, mutuality, laughter, well-wishing, tenderness—is the thought that there is, for these things, no catalepsis. Even so, the Stoic defines the cataleptic impression as "that which is imprinted and impressed by what is real," and so forth, and then defines "what is real" as "that which produces a cataleptic impression."[14] In this way, the science of life is established on a sure foundation.

Marcel's relation to the science of self-knowledge now begins to look more complex than we had suspected. We said that the attempt to grasp love intellectually was a way of avoiding loving. We said that in the cataleptic impression there is acknowledgment of one's own vulnerability and incompleteness, an end to our flight from ourselves. But isn't the whole idea of basing love and its knowledge on cataleptic impressions itself a form of flight—from openness to the other, from all those things in love for which there is in fact no certain criterion? Isn't his whole enterprise just a new and more subtle expression of the rage for control, and need for possession and certainty, the denial of incompleteness and neediness that characterized the intellectual project? Isn't he still hungry for a science of life?

---

14. See Sextus, *M* VII.426. A different and extremely interesting account of Marcel's error is in Richard Wollheim, *The Thread of Life* (Cambridge, Mass., 1984), 191ff.

For consider a remarkable consequence of the project. Proustian catalepsis is a solitary event. This is emphasized in the narrative, where true knowledge of love arrives in Albertine's absence, indeed at a time when, although he doesn't know it, Marcel will never see her again. The experience does not require Albertine's participation or even awareness; it has no element of mutuality or exchange. And it certainly does not presuppose any knowledge of or trust in the feelings of the other. It coexists here with the belief that he does not and cannot know whether she loves him. In fact, the cataleptic experience seems to possess even object-directed intentionality only in a very minimal way. What Marcel feels is a gap or lack in himself, an open wound, a blow to the heart, a hell inside himself. Is all of this really love of Albertine? And isn't it clear that the determination to have cataleptic certainty, together with the recognition that the separateness and independence of the other gives no purchase in the other for such certainty, is what has led him to portray the nature of love in this highly peculiar manner?

The result is actually more disturbing still. We said that the cataleptic impression can coexist with skepticism about the feelings of the other. In fact, it implies this skepticism. For on the cataleptic view an emotion can be known if and only if it can be vividly experienced. What you can't have you can't know. But the other's will, thoughts, and feelings are, for Marcel, paradigmatic of that which cannot be had. They beckon to him out of Albertine's defiant, silent eyes at Balbec, a secret world closed to his will, a vast space his ambitious thoughts can never cover.[15] His projects of possession, doomed before they begin, satisfied only in their own self-undercutting—as when he guards a sleeping Albertine, who at that moment no longer eludes him, but who, in having become merely "a being that breathes," does not inspire love either—teach him that the heart and mind of another are unknowable, even unapproachable, except in fantasies and projections that are really elements of the knower's own life, not the other's. "The human being is the being who cannot depart from himself, who knows others only in himself, and, if he says the contrary, lies." Albertine can never be for him anything more than "the generating center of an immense construction that rose above the plane of my heart" (III.445). In short: "I understood that my love was less a love for her than a love in me. . . . It is the misfortune of beings to be for us nothing else but useful showcases for the contents of our own minds" (III.568).[16]

This condition is their misfortune; in a sense it is also ours. But skepticism is not just an incidental and unfortunate consequence of Marcel's epistemology. It is at the same time its underlying motivation. It is because this is a suspicious man who can be content with nothing less than full control, who cannot tolerate the other's separate life, that he demands cataleptic impressions and a certainty that the other can never give him. It is because he wishes not to be tormented by the ungovernable inner life of the other that he adopts a position that allows him to conclude that the other's inner life is nothing more than the constructive workings of his own mind. The skeptical conclusion consoles far more than it agonizes. It

---

15. See Proust, *Remembrance* I.847ff.

16. There are many other similar statements; for only a few examples, see Proust, *Remembrance* III.656, 908–9, 950.

means that he is alone and self-sufficient in the world of knowledge. That love is not a source of dangerous openness, but a rather interesting relation with oneself.

Catalepsis Ordered by Reflection: Proust's Final View

Before we turn away from Proust, we should recognize that this is not Marcel's final word on the knowledge of love. The position he articulates in the novel's last volume complicates the cataleptic view, apparently in response to some of our criticisms. I think we shall see, however, that our deepest worries remain unaddressed.

Intellect, Marcel still insists, must begin its work from unbidden nonintellectual truths, "those which life communicates to us against our will in an impression which is material because it enters through the senses but yet has a spiritual meaning which it is possible for us to extract" (III.912). Intellect, using cataleptic impressions, and above all impressions of suffering, as its basic material, extracts from them the general "laws and ideas" to which they point. We *think* what we had "merely felt" before. Reflection achieves this generality by drawing on a number of impressions and linking them together in an artistic way. "It is our passions which draw the outlines of our books, the ensuing intervals of repose that write them" (III.945).

What truths about love does reflection deliver that would not have been perspicuous in and through feeling alone? First of all, the general form and pattern of one's loves:

> A work, even one that is directly autobiographical, is at the very least put together out of several interrelated episodes in the life of the author—earlier episodes which have inspired the work and later ones which resemble it just as much, the later loves being traced after the pattern of the earlier. For to the woman whom we have loved most in our life we are not so faithful as we are to ourself, and sooner or later we forget her in order—since this is one of the characteristics of that self—to be able to begin to love again. At most our faculty of loving has received from this woman whom we so loved a particular stamp, which will cause us to be faithful to her even in our infidelity. We shall need, with the woman who succeeds her, those same morning walks or the same practice of taking her home every evening or giving her a hundred times too much money. . . . These substitutions add then to our work something that is disinterested and more general. (III.145–46)

But this generalizing power does more: it shows us that love is not simply a repeated experience; it is a permanent structural feature of our soul. "If our love is not only love of a Gilberte (the one who is causing us so much suffering), it is not because it is also love of an Albertine, but because it is a portion of our soul . . . which must . . . detach itself from beings to restore its generality"(III.933). At this level of depth, love unites in itself and shows us the unity in different disappointments and sufferings that we might previously not have called forms of love at all. In reflection we see that the suffering of love and the suffering of travel "were not different disappointments at all but the varied aspects which are assumed, according to the particular circumstances which bring it into play, by our inherent powerlessness to realize ourselves in material enjoyment or in effective action" (III.911). In other words, we know this love for Albertine as an instance of our loving, and our loving as the general form of our permanent finitude and incompleteness—in this way deriving a far more complete and correct understanding of love than we could have had in the impression alone.

Finally, reflection shows us "the intermittences of the heart"—the alternations between love and its denial, suffering and denial of suffering, that constitute the most essential and ubiquitous structural feature of the human heart. In suffering we know only suffering. We call our rationalizations false and delusive, and we do not see to what extent they express a mechanism that is regular and deep in our lives. But this means that in love itself we do not yet have full knowledge of love—for we do not grasp its limits and boundaries. Sea creatures cannot be said to know the sea in the way that a creature does who can survey and dwell in both sea and land, noticing how they bound and limit one another.[17]

This reformulation of the cataleptic view appears to answer some of our worries, for reflection permits the critical assessment of impressions, their linking into an overall pattern, their classification and reclassification. Proust now concedes that about certain impressions we can be wrong: we do not notice that the pain of travel and the pain of love are one and the same emotion. Interpretation begins to play the role we sought for it. But caution is needed here. First, we still cannot be wrong about *love*. We go wrong only in failing to pick out as love another pain that is really love. The revision that takes place consists in noticing love's ubiquity as *the* basic form of desire, not in becoming more subtle and selective concerning which experiences to count as love. Second, it is essential to notice that the cataleptic impressions of love are still the unchallenged foundations of all knowledge. Reflection and art may fill in the outline; they can never challenge or revise it. "The impression is the only criterion of truth," therefore the only source for truths of reflection (III.914). The emotional impression is to the artist, Marcel continues here, what observational data are to a Baconian scientist: although in some sense the data are not really and fully known until they are integrated into a theory, still the scientist starts from them alone, and relies on them implicitly. Thus the revised view does not really answer our questions about suffering—whether it is the best guide, whether any solitary impression is really evidence of *love*.

And it has a further consequence. The connection between self-knowledge and skepticism about the other is actually reinforced in the complex view. Built upon cataleptic data and trusting these alone, reflection can never penetrate to the thoughts and feelings of the other. And, being reflection, it turns this fact into a theoretical conclusion, an "austere lesson." The greatest courage of the artist, Marcel announces, lies in his or her willingness to acknowledge the truth of skepticism, "abrogating his most cherished illusions, ceasing to believe in the objectivity of that which one has oneself created, and, instead of cradling oneself for the

---

17. Here I am responding to criticisms of my account of Proust in "Fictions" made at the time of its first presentation, in different ways, by Peter Brooks and Richard Wollheim.

hundredth time with the words, 'She was very sweet,' reading *through* them, 'I enjoyed kissing her'" (III.932). Belief in the other is a weakness, a form of consoling self-deception.

And yet, we can hardly help feeling that there is something more consoling still in the austere lesson of solipsism, certified and pinned down and made scientific by the operations of thought. Sextus seems to be right: this view looks more like a wish or a prayer for something than like a statement of truth. And isn't it perhaps a wish for the very thing the intellectualist sought: freedom from disturbance and pain?[18]

Learning to Fall

I turn now to a view that share Proust's criticisms of intellectualism but locates love's knowledge in an altogether different place. It says, in effect, that knowing love is knowing how to go beyond Proustian skepticism and solitude. And how is skepticism to be overcome here? By love.

Unlike Proust's view, this view does not simply subtitute for the activity of the knowing intellect some other single and simple inner attitude or state of the person, holding that knowledge consists in this. It insists that knowledge of love is not a state or function of the solitary person at all, but a complex way of being, feeling, and interacting with another person. To know one's own love is to trust it, to allow oneself to be exposed. It is, above all, to trust the other person, suspending Proustian doubts. Such knowledge is not independent of evidence. Typically it is built upon a good deal of attention over time, attention that delivers a lot of evidence about the other person, about oneself, about patterns of interaction between the two. Nor is it independent of powerful feelings that have real evidential value. But it goes beyond the evidence, and it ventures outside of the inner world.

It is in the nature of this view that it is difficult to say much about it in the abstract. Its message is that there are no necessary and sufficient conditions, that knowledge of love is a love story. The best way to explore it seems to be to turn to stories ourselves. We could find it in many places (I think above all of Henry James and Virginia Woolf). But I have chosen instead a contemporary example that exemplifies the view with a remarkable compression and intensity of focus. This is Ann Beattie's story "Learning to Fall."[19] As its title announces, it is the

18. Here I am obviously not pursuing all the relevant aspects of Proust's account of our knowledge of others. Above all, I am not pursuing the claim of the last volume that we *can* have knowledge of the mind of another in one case: we can know the mind of the artist through reading a work of literary art. I therefore ascribe both the simple and the complex cataleptic views to the character Marcel without drawing any official conclusions about Proust's overall view, even of our knowledge of those we love. But I do think it fair to say that the novel as a whole discourages optimism about knowledge of another within personal love and appears to endorse Marcel's solipsistic conclusion, by showing all apparently more hopeful cases of loving to be based upon some kind of self-deception.

19. Ann Beattie, "Learning to Fall," in *The Burning House* (New York, 1979), 3–14.

story of a woman who learns to know her own love and not to fear her own vulnerability. I want to let this woman's voice, whose shifting rhythms are themselves part of her emerging knowledge, tell the story as far as possible. So I shall sketch the "plot" crudely, then comment on three passages.

The narrator is a woman in her thirties, a Connecticut housewife, unhappily married to a dry and successful professional man. She had a lover named Ray, in New York. She broke up with him some time before, "when I decided that loving Ray made me as confused as disliking Arthur, and that he had too much power over me and that I could not be his lover anymore" (p. 12). Now when she goes into the city, she avoids Ray by taking with her the son of her best friend, Ruth. The boy is a lonely, slightly brain-damaged third grader with a drooping mouth and unusual capacities of perception. This day she takes him to various places in the city, all the while thinking about Ray but not calling him. Then, discovering that she has (perhaps intentionally) made them late for the train back to Connecticut, she does call. He joins them for coffee. The end of this story I shall discuss in detail, but first we need the beginning.

> Ruth's house, early morning: a bowl of apples on the kitchen table, crumbs on the checkered tablecloth. "I love you," she says to Andrew. "Did you guess that I loved you?" "I know it," he says. He's annoyed that his mother is being mushy in front of me. He is eager to seem independent, and cranky because he just woke up. I'm cranky too, even after the drive to Ruth's in the cold. I'm drinking coffee to wake up. If someone said that he loved me at this moment, I'd never believe him; I can't think straight so early in the morning, hate to make conversation, am angry at the long, cold winter. (p. 3)

Ruth is the trusting and trusted, the one most capable of love, the one whose poor messy warm house is for the narrator the antithesis of the opulent sterility of her own marriage. ("She earns hardly any money at the community college, but her half-gallons of wine taste better than the expensive bottles Arthur's friends uncork. She will reach out and touch you to let you know she is listening when you talk, instead of suggesting that you go out to see some movie for amusement" [p. 8].) We begin in Ruth's house, situated as by a stage direction, surrounded by her presence. For Ruth, asking a question about love is—can only be—a loving game, a way of saying I love you gently and playfully. "Did you guess," she can ask, because their whole life is so far beyond guessing. (The boy's father left her abruptly, shortly before the birth, and has had no contact with them since. Even at that, she's "not bitter," just "angry at myself. I don't often misjudge people that way" [p. 9].) The little boy has never thought of asking a real skeptical question. To him all the question means is that his mother's being mushy. "I know it" is the reply the game demands; but for him as for her, it has nothing to do with really seeking for knowledge. He isn't examining his (or his mother's) psychology; he isn't looking for or experiencing any cataleptic anything. He's just eating his breakfast, saying the usual things. Knowledge of love is his whole way of life with his mother. We see that he isn't sure he likes this knowledge. He wants to separate himself, learn not to say those words. He may already think of male adulthood as requiring that repudiation.[20] To repudiate it, however, would not be to discover some new facts about her heart or his. It would be simply to stop playing that game, living that life.

The narrator is a skeptic. She wouldn't believe a claim of love. She wouldn't believe it because she is angry, confused, sleepy, ill-at-ease with conversation. She doesn't have Ruth's grace at touching and being touched. She holds herself to one side, aloof, wondering. She drinks coffee a lot, and Andrew knows she doesn't eat "during the day" (p. 4). She has to control everything, her thinness, her lover, the time. Always early, hurrying for the train, fascinated with the food she refuses.

This brings me to her watch.

> I look at my watch. The watch was a Christmas present from Arthur. It's almost touching that he isn't embarrassed to give me such impersonal presents as eggcups and digital watches. To see the time, you have to push in the tiny button on the side. As long as you hold it, the time stays lit, changes. Take away your hand and the watch turns clear red again. (p. 7)

The watch is impersonal time, time scrutinized, controlled, and intellectualized: the time of the skeptic. (Ruth just takes the time, feeling there's "plenty of" it, hand on your back, not on her watch.) Hand always on the time, she won't let the things happen that take time. It took eight years, she remembers, for Andrew to trust someone other than his mother.[21] Only with Andrew—because she has fun with him, because she "know[s] him so well," because he is not alarming and she pities him—does she take her hands off the watch sometimes. "I almost love him." Her whimsical fantasy of Superman launching himself from the Superman patch on Andrew's knee and flying a foot above the ground, disconcerting the passers by (p. 4)—this has a charm, an unguarded quality of enjoyment and humor, that we haven't seen in this woman before. It's possibly the first time she hasn't had a thought for herself.

It's after she has been walking down the street with Andrew, swinging hands, that she realizes that they are late. The watch is wrong and she knew it. (It wasn't

20. It is perhaps worth mentioning that discussion with Brown University undergraduates (taking my course on Philosophy and the Novel) showed that male students overwhelmingly sympathized with the cataleptic view, while female students stressed the importance of time and a pattern of interaction. (Were they talking about the same phenomenon? Were they, like Marcel, shaping the definiendum in accordance with epistemological convictions? Does the gap between the two groups pose new epistemological problems of its own?) I do not believe at all that one view is in any deep or necessary way a male view and the other a female view. But it may be that the emphasis on autonomy and control in the education of males in this culture leads many of them in the direction of a view of love that promises such self-sufficiency. This is borne out by the portrait of Andrew here. Also see the related observations of Carol Gilligan, *In a Different Voice* (Cambridge, Mass., 1982).

21. The story depicts love of a lover as continuous with, and yet infinitely more difficult and risky than, love of the parent. Andrew's difficulty in turning from the safe reliability of home to the outer world of children and strangers is extreme, born of his handicap. But his self-consciousness, unusual for a child, is here an image of what the narrator takes to be true for adult love in general—the difficulty of allowing oneself to be exposed, the fear of being criticized, deceived, and mocked. She doesn't feel any more at home in her body than Andrew does in his, and she, too, is afraid of being rejected. Also, she is more afraid of being accepted.

even good at its impersonal job.) Andrew "thinks what I think—that if I had meant to, we could have caught the train" (p. 11). While she was relying on it to distance her from love, to keep her from that knowledge by precise knowledge, another part of her was using its untrustworthiness to work toward trust of another sort. She goes to a pay phone in Grand Central and calls Ray.

For the intellectualist view, knowledge of love is measured by the clock like everything else. It is in measured time, and it is itself a measuring, assessing activity, very like the measuring of the watch. (It weighed and measured one pleasure against another, counting costs and benefits.) Proust shows us how the temporality of the heart breaks with the rhythms of measuring devices. The full story of love—its intermittences, its rhythms of pain and avoidance—can be comprehended only by a reflection that observes the specifically human temporality of desire and habit, which proceeds by its own laws of felt duration. And the blinding moment of cataleptic knowledge, like any other break in the walls of habit, has the feeling of eternity, of the whole of a life: mysterious and momentary, instantaneous yet forever, "hard, glittering, strange," with the precipitous finality of death. It is not a progress or a sequence; it is not a relation evolving over time. In fact, it's because it is not a relation at all—it has really nothing to do with the other, it's a chemical reaction in oneself—that it can have this instantaneous character. Proust moves us from clock time to human time, but to a human time that will not take time for things to happen—because they might happen, and then one would perhaps not be alone. Beattie's narrator turns from her digital watch to a different sort of human time—to a trust that evolves over time, that is learned, that must be permitted, in time, through missing a train and taking the time, to happen.[22]

What do we know about this man? More, I find, in the story's ten pages than about Albertine in three thousand. That's already a sign of something. He makes himself felt from the first, long before we see him, as an intrusive, confusing presence—with his soft voice, his laconic speech, his boots, his joy in physical objects, his beautiful hands, and his patience. His sexual power, intense yet gentle, is everywhere she goes—the Guggenheim, the loft in Soho, the station phone booth. From the beginning this is a story about two people, the story of a knowledge that resides in the other and in the space between them. "I used to sleep with him and then hold his head as if I believed in phrenology. He used to hold my hands as I held his head. Ray has the most beautiful hands I have ever seen." She's using the present tense, watching them. "Want to stay in town?" he says (p. 12).

The moment that's comparable to and so different from Proust's is precipitated

---

22. On the importance of time for the trust required in love and friendship, see Aristotle, *Nicomachean Ethics* 1156b25ff. See also Stanley Cavell's reading of *It Happened One Night* in *Pursuits of Happiness* (Cambridge, Mass., 1982) chap. 2. Several motifs in Cavell's discussion of this film intersect with the reading of Beattie here: see particulary the discussion of eating. Diogenes tells us that Zeno, famed in general for iron self-control, didn't like to be publicly associated with the humbler bodily functions. To cure him of this shame, the Cynic philosopher Crates
    gave him a potful of lentil-soup to carry through the Ceramicus; and when he saw that he was ashamed and tried to keep it out of sight, with a blow of his staff he broke the pot. As Zeno took to flight with the lentil-soup flowing down his legs, Crates said, 'Why run away, my little Phoenician? Nothing terrible has befallen you.'" (*Lives* VII.3 trans. Hicks, with my revisions)
Diogenes also reports that at parties Zeno liked to sit at the far end of the couch, so as not to be too near others. (VII.14).

by the boy, catalyst with a Superman patch on his knee—omnipotence, a foot above the ground. They are sitting in a restaurant booth. Andrew is eating as always, drinking a milkshake. More coffee for her. Ray wanted a drink, but he has to put up with coffee. The story ends this way:

> Andrew shifts in the booth, looks at me as if he wants to say something. I lean my head toward him. "What?" I say softly. He starts a rush of whispering.
> "His mother is learning to fall." I say.
> "What does that mean?" Ray says.
> "In her dance class," Andrew says. He looks at me again, shy. "Tell him."
> "I've never seen her do it," I say. "She told me about it—it's an exercise or something. She's learning to fall."
> Ray nods. He looks like a professor being patient with a student who has just reached an obvious conclusion. You know when Ray isn't interested. He holds his head very straight and looks you right in the eye, as though he is.
> "Does she just go plop?" he says to Andrew.
> "Not really," Andrew says, more to me than to Ray. "It's kind of slow."
> I imagine Ruth bringing her arms in front of her, head bent, an almost penitential position, and then a loosening in the knees, a slow folding downward.
> Ray reaches across the table and pulls my arms away from the front of my body, and his touch startles me so that I jump, almost upsetting my coffee.
> "Let's take a walk," he says. "Come on. You've got time."
> He puts two dollars down and pushes the money and the check to the back of the table. I hold Andrew's parka for him and he backs into it. Ray adjusts it on his shoulders. Ray bends over and feels in Andrew's pockets.
> "What are you doing?" Andrew says.
> "Sometimes disappearing mittens have a way of reappearing," Ray says. "I guess not."
> Ray zips his own green jacket and pulls on his hat. I walk out of the restaurant beside him, and Andrew follows.
> "I'm not going far," Andrew says. "It's cold."
> I clutch the envelope. Ray looks at me and smiles, it's so obvious that I'm holding the envelope with both hands so I don't have to hold his hand. He moves in close and puts his hand around my shoulder. No hand-swinging like children— the proper gentleman and the lady out for a stroll. What Ruth has known all along: what will happen can't be stopped. Aim for grace. (pp. 13–14)

She knows what Ruth knew all along: what will happen can't be stopped. But what this means is that she lets herself not stop it, she decides to stop stopping it. She discovers what will happen by letting it happen. Like Ruth, slowly falling in the class exercise that teaches and manifests trust, she learns to fall. As Andrew says, she doesn't just go plop (as Marcel did, abruptly plunging); she gently, slowly yields to her own slow folding, to the folding of his arm around her. She lets that touch not startle her. Like Ruth's bodily fall and, as she see, like prayer, its's something done yet, once you do it, fundamentally uncontrolled; no accident, yet a yielding; an aiming, but for grace. You can't aim for grace really. It has so little connection, if any, with your efforts and actions. Yet what else can you do? How else are you supposed to pray? You open yourself to the possibility.

Is this discovery or creation? Both, we have to say. A pattern is there already; it vibrates through the story. The final moment has the conviction, the power, the crazy joy it does because it is the emerging of something that has been there all along and has been repressed. We can talk of self-deception here just as we could in Marcel's case, because she has been denying the power Ray continuously exerts over her imaginings and her actions. Andrew knew about her what she denied to herself. But of course she is loving Ray now as she didn't before. Love feared and avoided is not just sitting there beneath the skin waiting to be laid bare, any more than Ruth's slow fall Platonically inhabits the narrator's stiff, thin, coffee-drinking body. It has to be created. The removal of self-deception is also a change in the self. Both discovery and creation are present on the general level too, as she both finds a vulnerable and passionate side of herself that had been denied and makes herself evolve into a more trusting woman. She decides to let those elements flourish, be actualized.[23]

The cataleptic view has its role to play inside these experiences. There's no doubt that she was missing him, that she missed the train because she was missing him. There's no doubt either of the power of her arousal, and also her fear, when he reaches across the table and takes her hand. All this has some role in her knowledge of love, and the power of those impressions is a part of what prepares her love. But that's the point: they prepare it, they aren't it. The knowing itself is a relation, a dizzy elated falling. There are powerful feelings here—sexual feelings, feelings, I think, of profound joy and nakedness and giddiness and freedom: the feelings of falling. But he's too intrinsic to it all for us to say that those feelings just *are* the falling, the loving. The loving is about him, an opening toward him, as prayer in her image, would be an opening toward God. She could also say that faith is a certain strong feeling in the region of the heart. Proust's prayer, the cataleptic prayer, is that this should be all there is to say.

Knowledge of her own condition and knowledge of him are inextricable here. Not in the sense that she has succeeded in doing phrenology, in getting a scientific account of his head that's beyond doubt. Not in the sense that she possesses his experiences or feels them herself. She could be wrong, that's clear. Evidence is not for nothing, either in her view or in ours about her. It's not for nothing that she has this history with him, that she knows how he makes jokes, that he has waited so patiently for her. But none of this puts her, or us, beyond doubt of him. Ruth misjudged someone and was betrayed. Faith is never beyond doubt; grace can never be assured. The enterprise of proving God's existence has little to do with it. You aim for it by not asking to prove it. What puts her beyond doubt is the absence of the demand for proof, the simple fact that she allows his arm to stay around her back. (We must add: in this she allows herself to be tender and attentive toward him, to notice and respond to what he is doing, in a way that she hadn't before, caught up as she was in her own anxiety.)

I find myself returning again, as I consider this pair, to their jokes, to the entire role of jokes and humor in separating this view of love from Proust's. Ray thinks it is very important to make this woman laugh. "You know what, lady?" he says,

---

23. I have been asked whether this story and the view I find in it depend on Ray's being this sort of secure, strong, (apparently) nonneurotic person, toward whom she can safely quite simply fall. Could we talk of falling, and so forth, if he was as complex and neurotic as she? The answer, I believe, is yes; we could in that case speak of learning to fall on both sides. But then it would have to be a much longer story.

after his first success; "I do better amusing you over the phone than in person" (p. 12). He knows, as we do when she laughed then (for the first time in the story), that her laughter is a yielding, a surrender of that tight control. And at the end her yielding comes in a smile, responding to his smile. She shares with him the joke of her own tightness as she holds the envelope so she doesn't have to hold his hand. The "proper gentleman and the lady out for a stroll" are, I imagine, laughing together (as that phrase indicates, so comically inappropriate for an improper, adulterous woman and her lover with his black boots and his language so unlike Arthur's—yet so appropriate, too, to their gentleness with one another, to their relationship that goes so far beyond eggcups and digital watches)—laughing at the comedy of control and uncontrol, self-sufficiency and yielding. Laughter is something social and relational, something involving a context of trust, in a way that suffering is not. It requires exchange and conversation; it requires a real live other person—whereas Marcel's agonies go on in a lonely room and distract him from all outward attentions. To imagine love as a form of mourning is already to court solipsism; to imagine it as a form of laughter (of smiling conversation) is to insist that it presupposes, or is, a transcendence of solipsism, the achievement of community.[24] It is worth adding here: we imagine that this pair have a happy sexual life together, whereas Marcel's view implies that there is really nothing but masturbation. "The beings whom we love . . . are nothing but a vast vague space where we can externalize our own desires" (III.505). As Cary Grant once said, "Why that's no good. That's not even conversation."

And why do we trust Ray, and not wonder who he is really, with his boots and his ballet tickets, what his intentions really are? Because we follow her. For that matter, why do we trust her? Why do we suppose without doubt that she is telling us the truth? Because, like her, we have learned to fall. Reading a story is like that. Like her love, it takes time; you learn it from childhood. And if your mother asked you, "Did you guess that that character was really feeling what I said she was?" you'd be as amused, or mystified, or annoyed, or embarrassed as Andrew at the breakfast table.

Forms of Discourse and Arts of Life

What, then, do we make of the fact that we are dealing here with a story? Proust argues that a work that is going to represent knowledge of love must be a work capable of representing cataleptic suffering. Furthermore, if it is to convey this knowledge, not merely to represent it, it must be capable of eliciting responses of suffering in the reader. The reader of Proust's novel comes to know his or her own love by way of a very complex activity, one that involves empathetic involvement with Marcel's suffering, sympathetic responses to his suffering, and the concomitant "mining" of his or her own life experience for analogous loves. In the process of suffering, the reader is brought into contact with the reality of his or her own condition. The final Proustian view adds to this picture the activity of reflection.

24. See Cavell, *Pursuits,* esp. chap. 2, 80ff, and also the chapter on *The Philadelphia Story,* from which film the remark at the end of this paragraph is quoted.

For even as Marcel, creating his literary work, discerns and articulates the pattern of his loves, making perspicuous the structure of their intermittence, even so the reader, comprehending the overall pattern of Proust's work (and setting her own life before her in a similarly perspicuous structure) is delivered, like Marcel, from bondage to the present experience and takes possession of the entirety of her love. The only text that could promote this sort of knowing would be a text that had the requisite combination of emotive material with reflection—that is to say, a text like the sui generis hybrid that is Proust's novel. His view concerning the truth of the human heart—what its content is and through what activities of knowing it is grasped—determines his view concerning what text or texts can serve as vehicles and sources for knowing.[25]

If we turn now to Beattie, something analogous is borne in upon us—and with even greater force. For if it is not possible to grasp the truth of the cataleptic view in isolation from texts that both show and give us cataleptic experiences, it is surely more difficult by far to show in a non-narrative text the view of love and its knowledge that I have ascribed to Beattie.[26] This knowledge is "kind of slow"; it unfolds, evolves, in human time. It is no one thing at all, but a complex way of being with another person, a deliberate yielding to uncontrollable external influences. There are no necessary and sufficient conditions, and no certainty. To show these ideas adequately in a text, we seem to require a text that shows a temporal sequence of events (that has a plot), that can represent the complexities of a concrete human relationship, that can show both denial and yielding; that gives no definitions and allows the mysterious to remain so.[27] Could any non-narrative text do all this? We can barely imagine how we (or Zeno) might describe and defend the cataleptic view of love in an article without reference to any whole literary work—using, perhaps, schematic examples. We can imagine this because the experience in question is fundamentally self-contained and isolated. And it announces a set of necessary and sufficient conditions; it tells us what love *is*. With Beattie's view, a treatment even by schematic examples is bound to seem empty, lacking in the richness of texture that displays knowledge of love here. We seem to require no unit shorter than this actual story, with all its open-endedness. The view says that we cannot love if we try to have a science of life; its embodiment must be a text that departs, itself, from the scientific.

If we now consider *our* relation *to* the literary work, the case for its inelimina-

---

25. On this, see the longer discussion in my "Fictions." On the general issue, see *Fragility*, esp. chaps. 1 and 7, and Interludes 1 and 2. For further pertinent discussion of Proust's view of art, see Mary Rawlinson, "Art and Truth: Reading Proust," *Philosophy and Literature* 6 (1982), 1–16, and the very illuminating discussion of Proust's narrative technique in Gerard Genette's *Narrative Discourse*, trans. Jane E. Lewin (Oxford and Ithaca, N.Y., 1980).

26. This difficulty is beautifully confronted in part IV of Stanley Cavell's *The Claim of Reason*, where Cavell, in order to tell the story of our acknowledgment and avoidance of others and ourselves, tells stories, moves in and out of complex examples, takes time to let them unfold, and ends with a reading of Shakespeare's *Othello*. One difficulty that philosophers have sometimes had with this book is that there is no one place in it where Cavell gives a concise definition of acknowledgement, with necessary and sufficient conditions. But this does not mean that he has not given a philosophical account of the sort the subject matter requires.

27. On the depth of our interest in plot and the connections between structures of plot and forms of human desire, see Peter Brooks, *Reading for the Plot* (New York, 1984).

bility becomes still stronger. For, as I suggested, this story not only describes falling and learning to fall; it also enlists us in just such a trusting and loving activity. We read it suspending skepticism; we allow ourselves to be touched by the text, by the characters as they converse with us over time. We could be wrong, but we allow ourselves to believe. The attitude we have before a philosophical text can look, by contrast, retentive and unloving—asking for reasons, questioning and scrutinizing each claim, wresting clarity from the obscure. Beattie knows what she's doing when she links love's knowledge with faith and not with philosophical argument (when she represents Ruth as a teacher of literature, reading the Russian novelists, and not a teacher of philosophy, reading Kant). We aren't very loving creatures, apparently, when we philosophize. "The unexamined life is not worth living"—not, perhaps, the saying of an altogether trusting man. "Did you guess that I love you?" "You use this word love all the time, Mother, applying it to many different things. But could you possibly tell me, please, what the *one* thing is that you are speaking of whenever you use that word? For I feel I lack an understanding of what these things all share, and you surely must know this, Mother, since you speak of love so often." He won't be answered. And, speaking this way, he's not her child any longer.

Before a literary work (like this story) we are humble, open, active yet porous. Before a philosophical work, in its working through, we are active, controlling, aiming to leave no flank undefended and no mystery undispelled. This is too simple and schematic, clearly; but it says something. It's not just emotion that's lacking, although that's part of it. It's also passivity; it's trust, the acceptance of incompleteness.

But this sounds very fishy, coming at the end of a discussion like this one. For what could I mean by saying that Ann Beattie's story gives us all the knowledge we need, when I am here very obviously composing a paper *about* that story and about its relation to two other stories? Is Beattie's story really sufficient by itself to give an account of the knowledge of love and to convey this knowledge to us? Could I have ended by quoting the story and dropping my commentary on it?[28] Indeed, do we need the framework of the paper at all? Couldn't we just have the story alone, perhaps along with Proust's novel? Is there anything about the knowledge I'm describing that is essentially philosophical? Or with regard to which philosophy is not only not an adversary, but actually a friend?

Here, as often, I find myself saying Aristotelian things.[29] I believe that we have made progress in understanding when we have set these three opposed views of love and its knowledge beside one another, examining their relationships both to one another and to our experiences. In a certain sense there is nothing in this paper that is not already in the stories and in whatever it is about our experience that makes us take an interest in these stories. But it is philosophy, or philosophical criticism, that has set up the confrontation, clarified the oppositions, moved us from an unarticulated sympathy with this or that story to a reflective grasp of

28. Richard Wollheim made this point in response to "Flawed Crystals," *New Literary History* 15 (1983), 185–91. I am now closer to Wollheim's position than I was in that reply: see Introduction, in this volume.

29. See my "Saving Aristotle's Appearances," in *Language and Logos,* ed. M. Schofield and M. Nussbaum (Cambridge, 1982), 267–93; a longer version, with reference to Wittgenstein, is chap. 8 of *Fragility.*

our own sympathies. We see more clearly what our relation to Marcel's story is when we see in what way it entails solipsism—and how that solipsism is overcome, in the opposing story, not by any trick of the intellect but by love itself. We contrasted the skeptical and mistrustful demeanor of the reader of philosophy with the openness of the reader of stories. This is in a sense correct. But we must now also acknowledge that it was philosophy, and not the story, that showed us the boundaries and limits of the stories—that returned us to Beattie's story and, so to speak, permitted us to trust it, by clarifying its relation to Proust's cataleptic solipsism. Again, it was philosophy and not a surge of emotion that articulated for us the idea that knowledge might *be* something other than intellectual grasping—might be an emotional response, or even a complex form of life. And although it is true that we must at some level have known that already, our understanding, after the reflective examination, is of a firmer order; we are less likely to be derailed from it or led into mistrusting it by the claim of specious theory. Philosophy can itself be specious theory. There is no doubt of that. But the very probing and questioning that seemed, in philosophy, unloving, can also express, properly and patiently applied, the most tender and protective care for the "appearances"—for our experiences of love and our love stories.

There is another aspect to this point. We suggested that theories about love, especially philosophical theories, fall short of what we discovered in the story because they are too simple. They want to find just one thing that love is in the soul, just one thing that its knowledge is, instead of looking to see what is there. The story could show us a complexity, a many-sidedness, a temporally evolving plurality that was not present in the explicit theories, even Proust's. We said that it was very difficult indeed to speak about this view philosophically precisely because of this complexity. All right. But, here again, wasn't it philosophy that said, "Look and see?" That wouldn't let us stop with some excessively simple idea, say Proust's? Wasn't it philosophy that directed us to the story and showed us why it was important? This is going to seem hopelessly arrogant and chauvinistic, and someone will surely say, "No no, it was the human heart itself; it was love itself. We don't need a professor of philosophy to tell us this." In one sense, the reply is just. But sometimes, I think, the human heart needs reflection as an ally. Sometimes we need explicit philosophy to return us to the truths of the heart and to permit us to trust that multiplicity, that bewildering indefiniteness. To direct us *to* the "appearances," rather than to somewhere "out there" or *beneath* or *behind* them.

What are those times? Times, perhaps, when someone is feeling the need for a science of life. And since, as Proust and Beattie in their different ways show, this need is as deep and persistent as our need for self-sufficiency and our fear of exposure, and is in fact a form of that need, this would mean that a therapeutic philosophy will always have a job to do: exposing these various self-deceptive projects, showing their underlying kinship and their strange consequences, and pointing to the parts of life that they cover or deny. A moment ago we depicted the philosopher as a skeptical and untrusting character, a character whose Socratic refusal of the unexamined brings him clsoe to the searchers for the cataleptic. This is true of some philosophers and in some contexts. But we must also acknowledge that in certain contexts this skeptical uneasiness can lead back to and express a respect for the multiplicity of the everyday. In certain contexts it is above all the philosopher who does in fact say, "Look and see; observe the many-sidedness; observe that here there is no cataleptic certainty." Who, dismantling simplifications, knocking down certainties, clears a space in which love stories can exist and have their force.[30]

To make room for love stories, philosophy must be more literary, more closely allied to stories, and more respectful of mystery and open-endedness than it frequently is. It must draw very close to the best and most truly reasonable of non-philosophical writing. I find this conception of a human philosophy beautifully articulated in William James's "The Moral Philosopher and the Moral Life":

> In all this the philosopher is just like the rest of us non-philosophers, so far as we are just and sympathetic instinctively, and so far as we are open to the voice of complaint. His function is in fact indistinguishable from that of the best kind of statesman at the present day. His books upon ethics, therefore, so far as they truly touch the moral life, must more and more ally themselves with a literature which is confessedly tentative and suggestive rather than dogmatic,—I mean with novels and dramas of the deeper sort, with sermons, with books on statecraft and philanthropy and social and economical reform. Treated in this way ethical treatises may be voluminous and luminous as well; but they never can be *final*, except in their abstractest and vaguest features; and they must more and more abandon the old-fashioned, clear-cut, and would-be 'scientific' form.[31]

But, I think, the philosopher would be neither fully just nor fully luminous if she or he simply left the field to these other forms of writing. James asks for alliance, not surrender. It is evident that not just any type of philosophy could be the ally of literature; to be an ally it must adopt forms and procedures that do not negate the insights of literature. But our picture of an Aristotelian philosophy has indicated why it should still retain a separate critical identity—why an alliance of still separate spheres may be necessary for the justice and luminosity of both.

No form of discourse is cataleptic. None contains in its very style and methods a sure and certain criterion of truth. None is incapable of being used for self-deceptive ends. But perhaps in the attentive—or I might even (too naively?) say loving—conversation of philosophy and literature with one another we could hope to find, occasionally, mysterious and incomplete, in some moments not governed by the watch, some analogue of the deliberate fall, the aim for grace.[32]

30. On this image and Wittgenstein's use of it, see *Fragility,* chap. 8. A similar account of philosophy in its relation to literature is developed in Cora Diamond's "Having a Rough Story about What Moral Philosophy Is," *New Literary History* 15 (1983), 155–69.

31. William James, "The Moral Philosopher and the Moral Life," reprinted in James, *Essays on Faith and Morals,* ed. Ralph Barton Perry (New York, 1962), 184–215; quotation from p. 210.

32. I am grateful to Jeffrey Cobb, who, in conversation as we taught Proust together in the fall of 1984, asked questions that provoked some of the central points of this paper. An invitation to present the paper to a philosophy department colloquium at the State University of New York at Stony Brook was a source of valuable discussion, and I am especially grateful to Mary Rawlinson, Eva Kittay, and Patricia Athay for their questions. Others who generously helped me with written comments include Sissela Bok, Arthur Danto, Cynthia Freeland, David Halperin, Brian McLaughlin, Henry Richardson, Amélie Rorty, and Gregory Vlastos. I know that I have not adequately responded to all the points they raised.

Endnote

This essay provides a fuller and more balanced account of Proust's project than "Fictions of the Soul"—with which it is not, however, incompatible. In particular, it provides an account of the way in which the knowledge conveyed in emotional impressions must be systematized and pinned down by the activity of reflection. This essay is also more critical, clearly, of Proust's conception of emotional knowing and its motivations. To be complete as an account of Proust's position on these issues, it would need to include discussion of several further elements: above all, of the reader's relationship to the literary work of art itself, which is held to be one human relationship that is both intimate and free from jealousy—and which can therefore yield, as "real-life" relationships do not, genuine knowledge of another particular mind.

Proust's text, combining as it does narrative concreteness with explanatory philosophical reflection, might seem to be an example of the combination of narratives with philosophical explanation that I have called for in this essay and in the Introduction. But there is need for caution, as the paper's criticism of cataleptic impressions makes clear. For Proust's reflection takes the impressions of suffering as its cataleptic data, and trusts them completely in the reflection that follows. The Aristotelian method recommended in my concluding section here is (as the methodological remarks in "Perceptive Equilibrium" and the Introduction also make clear) committed to regarding nothing as unrevisable and above (or beneath) criticism. It seeks for coherence and fit in the system as a whole; this means that it will frequently scrutinize emotions—as this paper scrutinizes Marcel's (see also "Narrative Emotions").

One sees here, again, the difficulty of characterizing the debate between the literary works and standard philosophy in any way that will yield a shared account of the goal. Self-knowledge is understood so differently by these three different conceptions—both with respect to the *content* of the knowledge gained and to the understanding of what knowing *is*—that we have difficulty saying what the debate is about without using terms peculiar to one or another party. Yet I think we also have the sense that there *is* a genuine debate here, the sense that self-knowledge, even if vaguely specified, is a goal with real content and real importance, capable of organizing further inquiry. In this way it resembles the ancient Greek concept *eudaimonia* ("human flourishing," "the good human life"), concerning the further specification of which there was little agreement, but which, as a concept, still served to organize ethical debate for centuries.

For a wonderful recent treatment of these same issues, with discussion of related issues of philosophical method and style, see Bas van Fraassen, "The Peculiar Effects of Love and Desire," in *Perspectives on Self-Deception,* ed. B. McLaughlin and A. Rorty (Berkeley, 1988).

Narrative Emotions:
Beckett's Genealogy of Love

I

Two voices, immobilized by life, go on telling their stories about emotion. One voice has no name. It says:

> They love each other, marry, in order to love each other better, more conveniently, he goes to the wars, he dies at the wars, she weeps, with emotion, at having loved him, at having lost him, yep, marries again, in order to love again, more conveniently again, they love each other, you love as many times as necessary, as necessary in order to be happy, he comes back, the other comes back, from the wars, he didn't die at the wars after all, she goes to the station, to meet him, he dies in the train, of emotion, at the thought of seeing her again, having her again, she weeps, weeps again, with emotion again, at having lost him again, yep, goes back to the house, he's dead, the other is dead, the mother-in-law takes him down, he hanged himself, with emotion, at the thought of losing her, she weeps, weeps louder, at having loved him, at having lost him, there's a story for you, that was to teach me the nature of emotion, that's called emotion, what emotion can do, given favourable conditions, what love can do, well well, so that's emotion, that's love.[1]

The other voice calls itself Malone. It tells a story about one Macmann, who himself tells stories to himself, lying cheek to the ground, soaked by the "heavy, cold, and perpendicular rain":

> The idea of punishment came to his mind, addicted it is true to that chimera and probably impressed by the posture of the body and the fingers clenched as though in torment. And without knowing exactly what his sin was he felt full well that living was not a sufficient atonement for it or that this atonement was in itself a sin, calling for more atonement, and so on, as if there could be anything but life, for the living. And no doubt he would have wondered if it was really necessary to

1. Samuel Beckett, *Molloy, Malone Dies, The Unnamable* (New York, 1955), 406. All references to the trilogy are to this edition, in which the translations of the second and third novels are by the author and that of the first by the author in collaboration with Patrick Bowles. Page numbers will be given in parentheses in the text.

be guilty in order to be punished but for the memory, more and more galling, of his having consented to live in his mother, then to leave her. And this again he could not see as his true sin, but as yet another atonement which had miscarried and, far from cleansing him of his sin, plunged him in it deeper than before. And truth to tell the ideas of guilt and punishment were confused together in his mind, as those of cause and effect so often are in the minds of those who continue to think. And it was often in fear and trembling that he suffered, saying, This will cost me dear. But not knowing how to go about it, in order to think and feel correctly, he would suddenly begin to smile for no reason ... to smile and give thanks for the teeming rain and the promise it contained of stars a little later, to light his way and enable him to get his bearings, should he wish to do so. (pp. 239–40)

(And that story is a love story too, don't think that it isn't).

Beckett's voices, here and elsewhere in the *Molloy* trilogy, share an attitude toward emotions like love, fear, guilt, disgust, hope—and to the complex intersection of all of these that is aroused, for the second voice, by the thought of mother's body. It is that emotions are not feelings that well up in some natural and untutored way from our natural selves, that they are, in fact, not personal or natural at all, that they are, instead, contrivances, social constructs. We learn how to feel, and we learn our emotional repertoire. We learn emotions in the same way that we learn our beliefs—from our society. But emotions, unlike many of our beliefs, are not taught to us directly through propositional claims about the world, either abstract or concrete. They are taught, above all, through stories. Stories express their structure and teach us their dynamics. These stories are constructed by others and, then, taught and learned. But once internalized, they shape the way life feels and looks. In the first passage, the meaning of love is given in paradigm stories of longing, fear, loss, conflict, despair. In the second, the complex scenario that describes Macmann's efforts to reenact a cultural paradigm of guilt, fear, and longing serves the narrating voice, at the same time, as its own paradigm story of the complex interrelationships among all these. Society has given Macmann a story about his guilt and the guiltiness of his very efforts to atone; it has given him, too, standards of "correctness" for his longing for salvation. This complex story, accepted, shapes and constitutes his experience of feeling; and his story in turn shapes and expresses the emotional world of the narrating voice. Indeed, it seems right to say, along with the nameless voice, not only that a certain sort of story shows or represents emotion but also that emotion itself is the acceptance of, the assent to live according to, a certain sort of story. Stories, in short, contain and teach forms of feeling, forms of life.

These voices express isolation and despair. They connect their predicament in no uncertain way with the fearful, disgusted, and guilty love that is, because of the stories, the only love they know. So at the same time that they ask us to see the origins of feeling, they invite us to consider critically these contingent structures and the narratives that are their vehicle. Indeed, they themselves make increasingly radical attempts to put an end to the entire project of storytelling and to the forms of life that this practice supports. They ask us to see their forms of feeling as a pattern that can be unraveled, a writing that can be unwritten, a story that can be ended—not by bringing it to the usual happy or unhappy ending but by ending the storytelling life. If stories are learned, they can be unlearned. If emotions are constructs, they can be dismantled. And perhaps the silence onto which this deconstructive project opens is an opening or clearing in which human beings and animals can recognize one another without and apart from the stories and their guilt. And perhaps, too, the longing for that silence is itself an emotion of and inside the stories. Perhaps the negative project is a happy-ending story trapped, itself, inside the very thing that it opposes.

These disturbing thoughts are among the obsessions of Beckett's trilogy, as of much of his work. They are thoughts that need to be confronted by anyone who thinks about the relationship between narrative and human self-understanding or who approaches narrative searching for an understanding of human life and its prospects. But they are especially subversive, dangerous, and necessary for anyone who wishes to claim that fictional narratives play a central and, so to speak, a positive role in self-understanding, a role that is not as adequately played by texts that lack narrative form. There is, in particular, a project that Beckett's voices seem to call into question. This project involves supplementing abstract philosophical attempts at self-understanding with concrete narrative fictions, which are argued by the proponents of the project to contain more of what is relevant to our attempts to imagine and assess possibilities for ourselves, to ask how we might choose to live.

Since this is a project that I believe to be both valuable and viable—not only for professional philosophers but for people who are, in their lives, pursuing questions about life—and since Beckett's voices have been for some time audible to me in the background of this work, speaking their subversive claims, audible even as Henry James praises the moral role of the novelist or as Proust argues for the epistemological value of narrative form, I want to let them speak and to see how much of this work they really do call into question, how their insights about the narrative forms of human desire and emotion would cause us to revise it—or perhaps, even, to end it. In short (using already their words), I want to judge this work with the judgment of Molloy when he writes, "It is in the tranquillity of decomposition that I remember the long confused emotion which was my life, and that I judge it, as it is said that God will judge me, and with no less impertinence" (p. 25). (And perhaps that, and this, act of judgment is itself inside the stories and, therefore, doomed to affirm the stories even as it calls them into question.)

The assessment must begin with a description of the project—just as Moran's search begins with the story of its "quarry" (p. 110). Next we need to describe in more detail the view about emotions that we have heard in Beckett's voices. We shall find that it is not a view peculiar to the voices but one that has a long philosophical–literary history, and one that is recently reemerging as the dominant view of emotion in philosophy and in social anthropology. This means that we cannot evade its challenge by saying to ourselves that Beckett and his voices have a rather peculiar view of life—which, I think, is the way that Beckett is read and refused, more often than not. Then we shall turn again to the *Molloy* trilogy, looking closely at Beckett's particular stories of narrative emotion; not in the trilogy as a whole, which would be too vast a task, but in its first section, *Molloy,* and especially at that novel's stories of love, guilt, and their relatives hope and fear, and the source of all these in a socially taught religious view of life. Moran writes a story whose aim is, increasingly, the frustration of the reader's emotion, the dismantling of narrative structures that both represent emotions and evoke them. We will consider next this project of ending, asking about its relationship to its own critique. And we can then compare this genealogical critique of stories with two other related philosophical enterprises (those of Lucretius and of Nietzsche) and judge its relevance for our own.

II

I shall speak here of "the project"; and I shall refer to an explicitly organized and theoretically justified enterprise that goes on the borderline (or by refusing to acknowledge that there is one) between philosophy and literature.[2] Nonetheless, I do not mean to say that it is only a specific form of more or less philosophical writing that is called into question here. For the project describes itself as an explicit extension of activities that are implicit in the activity of reading and of thinking reflectively about reading. It claims to be a description of a function (not the only function, but an important one) that narrative fiction has traditionally had in human lives, a function that needs to be mentioned in any explanation of the great human importance we ascribe to narrative fiction.[3] The project stands to this human activity as a descriptive grammar to the use of a native speaker.

The project, even in its explicit form, is not new; in its essentials it is as old, even explicitly, as the debate between the Greek tragic poets and their opponent Plato.[4] It is the project of a dialogue between philosophy and literary analysis in pursuit of the human question, "How should one live?" It takes its bearings from Henry James's claim that the novelist's art performs a practical task, the task of assisting us in our pursuit of that question by expressing a "projected morality" and an active "sense of life," and also from Proust's claim that it is only in a text having narrative form that certain essential truths about human life can be appropriately expressed and examined.[5] At its core is the claim that literary form and human content are inseparable: that forms themselves express a content and that

2. My own work in this area can be found in the other papers in this volume: especially "Flawed Crystals," "'Finely Aware,'" "Perceptive Equilibrium," "Love's Knowledge," "Love and the Individual," and "Steerforth's Arm." See also my *The Fragility of Goodness* (Cambridge, 1986). Other recent work in this area to which my own thought is especially indebted includes work of Hilary Putnam, especially *Meaning and the Moral Sciences* (London, 1979), 83–96 and "Taking Rules Seriously: A Response to Martha Nussbaum," *New Literary History* 15 (1983) 193–200; of Stanley Cavell, especially *The Claim of Reason* (Oxford, 1979); of Cora Diamond, especially "Missing the Adventure," abstracted in *Journal of Philosophy* 82 (1985) 529ff; and of Arthur Danto, especially "Philosophy As/And/Of Literature," *Proceedings and Addresses of the American Philosophical Association* 58 (1984) 5–20.

3. For further remarks on this point, see "Perceptive Equilibrium," and Danto (see n. 2). The linguistic analogy is first used (to my knowledge) by Plato's character Protagoras in the dialogue of that name.

4. See *Fragility* and "Perceptive Equilibrium."

5. For further discussion of James's conception of the novelist's task, see "'Finely Aware.'" For discussion of Proust on the task of literary art, see "Fictions" and "Love's Knowledge," this volume.

the content cannot be prized loose, without change, from the form in which it is expressed. The project joins to this claim another: that literary forms call forth certain specific sorts of practical activity in the reader that can be evoked in no other way; that, as Proust insists, a certain sort of self-scrutiny requires a certain sort of text, namely, a narrative text, for its evocation; or, as Henry James would insist, that we need a story of a certain kind, with characters of a certain type in it, if our own sense of life and of value is to be called forth in the way most appropriate for practical reflection.

The project moves on from these claims to a number of more concrete investigations into the relationship between literary form and practical content. One of its primary aims is to criticize some contemporary work in moral philosophy, on the grounds that this work claims, on the one hand, to assess all of the major available conceptions of human personal and social life, while, on the other hand, it confines itself entirely to forms of writing which, in their abstract and emotionless character, are far better suited to investigating some practical conceptions than others and which call up a correspondingly narrow range of responses and activities in the reader. Nor does this work present arguments justifying its implicit assumption that these responses are the only ones relevant to the task of practical assessment.[6] This critical part of the project is especially (or, one might say, obsessively) interested in a certain sort of practical conception: one that, taking its bearings from Aristotle's norm of practical "perception," emphasizes the human importance of a fine-tuned responsiveness to complex particular cases and of a willingness to see them *as* particular and irreducible to general rules. This conception urges a flexible immersion in the "adventure" of living and a process of practical choice based upon perception and improvisation. It insists, as well, that the correct perception of a practical situation requires emotional as well as intellectual activity, that the emotions have a valuable informational role to play within the ethical life as forms of recognition.[7] The project now argues that for several reasons this practical conception is most adequately expressed—and, therefore, can be most appropriately scrutinized—in texts that have a complex narrative structure; and that those narratives are also the texts best suited to evoke in the reader the moral activities associated with this conception, in particular emotional activities to which the conception ascribes both cognitive and intrinsic ethical value. The argument is that if moral philosophers (and, in general, people pursuing "wisdom" about the practical) wish to assess fairly and duly this and related conceptions of human life, they will need to include in their study texts that have the appropriate form. If philosophy is a search for wisdom about ourselves, philosophy needs to turn to literature.

The project does not wish to claim that this is the only inquiry into narrative that is of literary interest—or, indeed, the only literary inquiry into narrative that is of human interest. But it does urge vigorously the thought that literary study has too frequently failed to speak about the connectedness of narrative to forms

---

6. These criticisms of contemporary moral philosophy are developed in *Fragility*, chap. 1, in "Perceptive Equilibrium," and in "Discernment."

7. See *Fragility*, chap. 10, and "Discernment."

of human emotion and human choice.[8] By insisting that narratives embody forms of human life and desire, and by insisting that certain types of human understanding are irreducibly narrative in form, it calls for a literary discourse that studies the connections between narrative forms and forms of life and also between narrative movement and the desiring activity of the reader of narrative. In this way it links itself to various other postformalist currents in the contemporary study of narrative that are urging us once again to regard narrative as a human structure.[9] This does not mean a return to a simple-minded moralizing criticism of literature that extracts a useful practical content while neglecting subtleties of literary form.[10] For the proposed study of content insists on content's inseparability from form. And the project claims, in fact, that a study of literature that attends to form alone, without asking what human content (what desires, projects, choices) the forms themselves express is, while not without great interest, seriously incomplete.

III

The project has spoken about emotions and emotional activity. It has praised the novel for representing emotional responses as valuable sources of information about the practical and as of high practical value themselves, even apart from this informational role. It has also insisted on the ability of narrative to evoke emotional activity in the reader; and it has spoken as if this is an activity valuable, again, both for itself and for its epistemological role. In speaking this way, the project has used, and also argued for,[11] a conception of the major human emotions according to which they are not simply blind surges of affect, stirrings or sensations that arise from our animal nature and are identified (and distinguished from one another) by their felt quality alone. Instead, they themselves have a cognitive content; they are intimately related to beliefs or judgments about the world in such a way that the removal of the relevant belief will remove not only the reason for the emotion but also the emotion itself. The belief is the necessary basis and "ground" of the emotion. It might even be said to be a constituent part of the emotion itself. Anger, for example, is defined by Aristotle, the first great proponent of this view, as a composite of painful feeling with the belief that I have been wronged. This implies (as seems correct) that if I discover that my belief is false— that the apparent wrong did not in fact take place—I will, discarding my false belief, cease to be angry. If some residual painful feeling does persist, it will not

---

8. A similar argument is made by Danto.

9. For example, Peter Brooks, *Reading for the Plot: Design and Intention in Narrative* (New York, 1984); Martin Price, *Forms of Life: Character and the Moral Imagination in the Novel* (New Haven, Conn., 1983). In "Perceptive Equilibrium" I discuss, in this connection, work of Lionel Trilling and F. R. Leavis.

10. See especially "Perceptive Equilibrium," this volume.

11. Especially in *Fragility,* chap. 10 and Interlude 2, and in "Discernment." This conception is developed in more detail in my *The Therapy of Desire,* Martin Classical Lectures, in preparation; relevant portions have appeared as "The Stoics on the Extirpation of the Passions," *Apeiron* 1987, and "Beyond Obsession and Disgust: Lucretius on the Therapy of Love," *Apeiron* 1989.

be considered anger any longer but, rather, as residual irrational irritation or excitation.[12]

Within this general cognitive picture of emotion, several different accounts are given about the precise relationship between emotion and belief. Some versions make the belief a necessary cause of the emotion but no part of what the emotion is. Some, for example Aristotle's, make the belief one component part of the emotion but hold that it is not, by itself, sufficient for the emotion. (I can believe that I am wronged and yet not be angry.) Some hold that the belief is (whether as external cause or as component part) sufficient for the emotion: if I do not get angry, then I do not really truly accept or believe that I have been wronged. Some, in particular the view of the great Greek Stoic philosopher Chrysippus, who is in my view the most profound thinker on emotion in the entire philosophical tradition, insist that the emotion is itself identical with the full acceptance of, or recognition of, a belief. I myself defend this last and strongest cognitive view.[13] But since it is at first sight a rather strange view, it takes detailed argument—in particular, it requires careful unpacking of Chrysippus's notions of recognition and acceptance, or "assent" to a belief, to make it plausible. So I shall not insist upon it here.

What we find in this entire family of cognitive conceptions, however, is a common idea: the idea of the criticism and assessment of emotion. If emotions are not natural stirrings but constructs, if they rest upon beliefs, then they can be modified by a modification of belief. And they can be assessed in the way that beliefs are assessed—as rational or irrational (in respect of their manner of acquisition), as helpful and noxious, even as true and false. If I hastily and uncritically believe a false story that I have been wronged, my anger may be criticized as both irrational and false. And argument can change it, by removing the belief that was both false and irrationally formed.[14]

This idea can be applied at several different levels of specificity: for I might hold on to the very general belief that there are some wrongs that I can suffer through another's agency that would, if they did occur, be grounds for anger, while criticizing particular cases in which my beliefs about wrongs had been false: X did not, in fact, wrong me in that way just now. Moving toward a more general criticism, I might judge that a whole range of cases that I had previously taken to be serious wrongs, and therefore grounds for anger, were not of serious importance after all. For example, by changing my views about the importance of public reputation, I would alter my experience of anger with respect to that class of situations involving slights to reputation. Finally, at a still higher level of generality, I might decide that the whole structure of belief that made that emotion possible was false and/or irrational: for example, I might come to feel that there are in fact no damages that anyone could do to me that would be sufficiently important to be grounds for anger. And the claim of the cognitive view is that if I really truly believe that, I will no longer be angry.

---

12. See *Fragility,* Interlude 2, and *The Therapy of Desire* for discussion of this passage.
13. "The Stoics on the Extirpation of the Passions."
14. This is the central theme of *The Therapy of Desire,* developed in connection with Epicurean, Skeptic, and Stoic therapies.

What this picture is claiming is, then, not only an intimate connection between emotion and belief but also, in particular, a connection between the emotions and a certain *sort* of belief, namely, beliefs about what is valuable and important.[15] Anger requires the thought that I have suffered not trivial but important damages at another's hand. Fear requires the thought that I may possibly suffer serious damages in ways that lie beyond my control. Love requires a high evaluation of its object, grief the thought that what is lost is of serious value. And, we notice, these emotions all require not only beliefs about value but also beliefs about a certain sort of thing: beliefs that things outside of us, things not fully under our own control, have value or importance. Thus if we imagine a person who cares nothing at all for the world outside of him or her, who attaches no importance at all to that which he or she does not fully control, we see that nothing that happens to that person could ever have the power to grieve, or to anger, or to frighten, or to delight. And here we arrive at the most general level of emotion criticism. For now we see that if we really get someone to hold the Stoic belief that no external or uncontrolled item was of any value at all, that person would have (as, indeed, the Stoics insisted) no emotional life at all. We would not want to teach a person this if we think their emotion beliefs are either true or helpful. But if we should believe, with the Stoics, that they are both false and in other ways pernicious, if we believe that a life with emotion beliefs in it is bound to be in certain specifiable ways a life in which we both suffer agony ourselves and do harm to others, then we would have good reason to set about undoing those beliefs. This project of undoing would take different forms in different societies, for each society structures emotion beliefs in certain highly specific ways, and the undoing will have to be correspondingly specific in order to counter the very thoughts that grip us. It is my suggestion that Beckett's voices are engaged in one form of this project of radical undoing.

The criticism of emotion cannot proceed in the same way in which the criticism of, for example, scientific or mathematical beliefs proceeds—by giving the person a logical argument, or fresh perceptual evidence. For the evaluative beliefs that ground our emotional life are not learned in logical arguments either. They are learned through exposure—usually very early and very habitual—to complex social forms of life, in which these beliefs and the related emotions are housed, so to speak, and by which, for the individuals who learn them, they are constructed. A child does not learn its society's conception of love, or of anger, by sitting in an ethics class. It learns them long before any classes, in complex interactions with parents and society. These interactions provide paradigms of emotion and teach the cognitive categories that underlie the experience of emotion. And, since we are all tellers of stories, and since one of the child's most pervasive and powerful ways of learning its society's values and structures is through the stories it hears and learns to tell, stories will be a major source of any culture's emotional life. What fear, or love, *is* will be, for a child—as for Beckett's voices—a construct out of stories, the intersection, the somewhat confused amalgam of those stories. Sto-

---

15. See *Fragility,* Interlude 2, and "The Stoics on the Extirpation of the Passions." This aspect of the cognitive conception of emotion is not, as far as I know, stressed in any of the modern defenses of it.

ries first construct and then evoke (and strengthen) the experience of feeling. So a criticism of emotion must be, prominently, an unwriting of stories.

So much, roughly speaking, is common ground among the major cognitive theories of emotion, from the ancient Greek thinkers through to today's philosophy of psychology and cognitive psychology, the more cognitive parts of psychoanalytic thought, and the various forms of "social construction" theory about emotion that prevail in social anthropology and also in radical social history.[16] (In the case of the last group I am thinking of Foucault, but also of more objectively critical historians of desire, who write, frequently, from a left-wing perspective and stress the possibility of criticism and change in our socially taught distinctions of feeling.)[17] Views vary at this point in many ways: in the degree to which they find the origin of the emotions in early infancy and in the family, as opposed to later social interactions; in the degree to which they find a common cognitive structure across societies or, on the other hand, stress the relativity of emotion to particular social forms; and, finally, in the degree to which they hold that there is available any possibility of change in the structures with which our past has presented us. (For the cognitive conception makes change a logical possibility; but the real availability of change depends on further beliefs about how structures of this sort can be challenged.)

There is a great deal of territory here that needs further exploration; and it is unfortunate that there is very little contact among the different groups who hold views of this type, therefore little synthetic working out of these issues. I cannot even begin to sort them out here in an adequate way, so I shall simply assert what I myself take the status of the current debate (and nondebate) to be, what I myself would be prepared to argue for. It is that emotions are taught to us by our culture from early infancy, in patterns of interaction between the child and others, prominently including parents, and later including the wider community. (But parents, as psychoanalytic thought too frequently forgets, already embody and teach the social conception of which they are a part.)[18] This teaching takes highly specific forms in specific cultures. Prominent among the structures that embody and teach

16. For examples of these different approaches, with extensive bibliography, see A. Rorty, ed., *Explaining Emotions* (Berkeley, 1980). For an excellent recent collection of articles on anthropological social construction views, see R. Harré, ed., *The Social Construction of Emotion* (Oxford, 1986), especially the articles by Harré, Armon-Jones, and Averill; see also Catherine Lutz, *Unnatural Emotions* (Chicago, 1988). In psychoanalytic thought I have been particularly influenced by work of Melanie Klein: see especially *Love, Guilt, and Reparation and Other Works, 1921–1945* (London, 1985).

17. M. Foucault, *Histoire de la sexualité*, vols. 2 and 3 (Paris, 1984). For an especially lucid presentation of the latter group of views I am indebted to Henry Abelove, "Is Gay History Possible?" (paper delivered at the Brown University conference on Homosexuality in History and Culture, February 1987); but there are numerous other historians of desire writing from a similar perspective: e.g., Jeffrey Weeks, *Sex, Politics, and Society: The Regulation of Sexuality since 1800* (London and New York, 1987).

18. But as Melanie Klein insists, anthropologists too frequently ignore similarities in the structure of infantile object-relations across societies (see "Postscript" to her "Our Adult World and Its Roots in Infancy," in *Envy, Gratitude, and Other Works, 1946–1963* [London, 1984], 247–63).

these specific forms are a culture's stories. There will be many family resemblances among cultures, since most societies teach schemes of value that support some form of anger, fear, love, grief, and so on by supporting the beliefs about importance, on which, as we argued, these emotions depend. But the ways in which emotions are demarcated, related to one another, and connected with other aspects of life will vary greatly among societies, as will, then, the narrative structures in which they are housed. This concrete social shaping is an essential part of what it is to have an emotion in each case. We could not sufficiently define the emotion in terms of the acceptance of a certain sort of abstract proposition. And if stories are, as Beckett's voices claim, primary vehicles of emotion teaching, then we might say that to have an emotion will be (or centrally involve) the acceptance of a certain sort of story. This implies that to grasp the full story of the emotional life of an individual or group will require examining the stories it tells itself and the connections among these: understanding, for example, why love, in our first story, is connected in that particular way with frantic anxiety and with the expectation of death; why, in the second, love of a mother is associated with guilt, with a need for atonement that is unsatisfiable, with a feeling of sinfulness and a fear of judgment, with, finally, a certain sort of impossible hope. And if it should be seen that this complex emotional fabric is, in its specific cultural manifestation, in some ways an obstacle to human life, then its criticism will require the criticism not only of abstract propositions but also, above all, of stories (including those stories that dwell in us at an unconscious level), and also of our love of stories, of the patterns of desire, hope, and expectation that are formed and called forth by our experience of reading.

Acceptance of a social constructionist account of the origins and the nature of emotion does not seem to me to imply that we are simply stuck with what we have got, with no possibility for active criticism and change. The depth at which these stories dwell in us is sufficiently great that change is going to be a matter of prolonged therapy, not of one-shot argument. But I see no reason to suppose that we cannot devise therapies capable of altering us, even at the unconscious level. Nor does the view imply that there is no account of human flourishing available to us, as we ask the question how we ought to live, with reference to which we may appropriately criticize our own social stories. Although this is not often seen by proponents of social construction views (especially in anthropology), the diversity of cultural emotion stories in no way implies a complete cultural relativism about the normative values involved in the emotions, any more than in any other case a conflict of beliefs implies the subjectivity of belief. Social construction theory makes us face the question of relativism; it does not, by itself, answer it. I think it is plain that individuals are critical and active, as well as passive, in the process of social construction and that frequently they criticize and act out of a view about what is good for the flourishing of human life—either a view that they have found within that society itself narrowly understood, or one that they have discovered elsewhere and made comprehensible to themselves. Marxist versions of social construction theory insist that we must conduct a criticism of desire with reference to some such notion of human flourishing. I see no reason to suppose that this general approach is doomed and that all such critical projects are merely uncomprehending intrusions upon each culture's own autonomous self-constructive activity.[19]

IV

In one way, the acceptance of this view of emotion gives great support to the philosophical/literary project we have described. For the view makes clear exactly why, and on what basis, we wish to say that the emotions are cognitive and that a process of practical deliberation that omits them leaves out material of rich informational value. It shows us, too, a deeper reason than the project has so far given why *narratives* are essential to the process of practical reflection: not just because they happen to represent and also evoke emotional activity, but also because their very forms are themselves the sources of emotional structure, the paradigms of what, for us, emotion *is*. This gives us additional reason to say that we could not acquire the rich information we seek by simply adding to abstract theoretical treatises a few examples of emotion and a few emotive appeals: for the whole story of an emotion, in its connections with other emotions and forms of life, requires narrative form for its full development.

But in another evident way the acceptance of this view of emotion calls the project into question. For the project has in common with a good deal of work in contemporary moral philosophy a reliance on intuitive responses to the concrete, prominently including emotional responses, as data of special importance and, so to speak, veracity in giving us a sense of life.[20] It insists with Aristotle that "the discrimination rests with perception" and that "among statements about conduct, those that are universal are more general, but the particular ones are more true— for action is concerned with particulars, and statements must harmonize with these."[21] Its case for the practical ineliminability of stories rests on an idea that the concrete judgments and responses embodied in stories are less likely to lead us astray, in the sense that they will contain what is deepest for us, most truly expressive of our moral sense, and most pertinent to action, by comparison with the abstractness of theory. But once we are reminded that intuitions do not come from nature, or indeed from any special part of ourselves that is more "pure" and more accurate than the place from which our theories and principles emerge, that, indeed, they are learned in a society in much the same way as our other beliefs, we can no longer leave the intuitions, emotions, and stories unsuspected and unquestioned.[22] And indeed, when we reflect that we learn emotion stories when

19. The issue of the rational "internal" criticism of a culture is discussed in M. Nussbaum and A. K. Sen, "Internal Criticism and Indian Rationalist Traditions," in *Relativism,* ed. M. Krausz (Notre Dame, 1989).

20. See especially Thomas Nagel, *Mortal Questions* (Cambridge, 1979), and Bernard Williams, *Problems of the Self* (Cambridge, 1973) and *Moral Luck* (Cambridge, 1981).

21. Aristotle, *Nicomachean Ethics,* 1107a29-32.

22. Nagel's criticism of Epicurus' position on death seems to me to miss this dimension of Epicurus' critical argument, simply assuming that we can use uncriticized intuitions to object to Epicurus' position: see "Death," in *Mortal Questions;* see also the intelligent criticism of Nagel in S. Rosenbaum, "How to Be Dead and Not Care: A Defense of Epicurus," *American Philo-*

we are less critical and less rationally adept, on the whole, than when we learn our theories, when we reflect that these stories from then on constrain, in many ways of which we are not even aware, our new perceptions and responses—then we see that it would be foolhardy indeed to rely uncritically on the data drawn from our experience of stories and, also, that it will be extremely difficult to find a criticism that is not itself shaped by and expressed in terms of the structures that it purports to criticize. This does not exactly undermine the project, as we shall see, but it tells us not to expect to find in stories a golden age of unsullied ethical purity.

V

"It is in the tranquillity of decomposition that I recall the long confused emotion which was my life, and that I judge it, as it is said that God will judge me, and with no less impertinence" (p. 25). Molloy suggests that the emotions are not a discrete episode inside his life story but, rather, the living out of a story that has a certain shape. And in fact his story shares with the story of his double Moran a complex emotional structure in which guilt, fear, disgust, hope, and love do not pop up in isolation from one another, identifiable separately and singly defined. Instead, they emerge as interwoven aspects of a single narrative. The two passages with which we began, and especially the second, give a part of the recipe for this emotional concoction, showing that love does not occur without guilt, the fear of judgment, and the longing for reparation and salvation—and that all attempts to love are watched and judged, as Molloy now judges himself, as God will judge him.

The life story that is Molloy's "long confused emotion" is the story of two journeys: of Molloy's journey back from the outer world to the inside of his mother's room and of agent and detective Moran's journey to find and judge Molloy. Both are stories of progressive disintegration, as the crisp orderly Moran becomes indistinguishable from the prey he quarries and as the bodies of both give way, increasingly, to ludicrous and somewhat revolting weaknesses. This search, which Moran explicitly describes as a search for and through his own insides (p. 113), so that it is more than usually apparent that the story of this novel is the story of emotions, has a geography that informs us about the structure of those insides. Molloy's native country is called Bally. It is the hub of the region of Ballyba (p. 134). Moran, on the other hand, is a native of Turdy, home of the Turdy Madonna, goddess of pregnant married women (p. 173). Another town in the vicinity is Hole. And Moran's son "was capable of hanging about Hole, under God knows what conditions" (p. 143). So Moran travels from Turdy to Ballyba (he never quite reaches Bally) and camps out in the vicinity of Hole. And Molloy, having departed from Bally, ends up inside his mother's room (p. 7)—"her who brought me into the world, through the hole in her arse if my memory is correct. First taste of the shit" (p. 15). So the basic fact in this world, the fact that structures all of its geography, is the fact of the filthiness of conception, the fact that the pregnant married woman is by her act wrapped in shit, and that the new baby, even before it acts or feels, is born into the world through the shit. His entire life is lived, from then on, in shameful proximity to vagina, anus, and balls. Inasmuch as the child is a child born of a woman, he is covered in her filth. Inasmuch as he is a man who feels sexual desire (a resident of Bally), he compounds the transgression. His desire is filthy because of the original filth and also because it is a desire for the mother, who is already seen as covered, herself, in filth. The journey back to the mother's room or womb, which might in one way be a project of atonement, an attempt to cancel the sin of his birth by returning to a fetal condition, is, in the light of the sexual desire that motivates it, a guilty desire for filthy penetration and a compounding of original guilt ("that this atonement was in itself a sin, calling for more atonement, and so on, as if there could be anything else but life for the living"). "What business has innocence here?" asks Molloy as he sets out. "What relation to the innumerable spirits of darkness?" (p. 10). Guiltily placed between balls and hole, born through the anus and doomed to return through it, sinning further.

And there is one further fact about the geography of this place. It is all watched—watched by the chief of a vast organization, whose home is at a distance but who gives all journeys their purpose and meaning and who judges them all with an arbitrary and unpredictable (p. 115) combination of paternal care, anger, and furious judgment (p. 162). He likes to use the "prophetic present" tense of actions that the beings under his command will perform (e.g., "Your son goes with you"). And his name is just such a prophetic present: "Youdi," or "You die." Mortality is the punishment meted out for universal original transgression. Youdi has a messenger named Gaber (a relative of angel Gabriel), who visits Youdi's "agents" to convey his commands; and even this messenger is watched, not permitted to perform a sexual act without disturbance (p. 94). Youdi's role of judge and assessor is imitated by his agents in their own lives, as they play the role of judge to their women, their children, their own guilty thoughts and desires. The paradigm of Youdi infuses their journeys with purpose; and through membership in the Youdi organization all their movements and actions take on a significance beyond themselves.

We could summarize the emotion story that is Molloy's life by saying that it is the story of original sin, of the fear of God's judgment, and of the vain longing for salvation.[23] This would begin to show us how these voices' experience of fear and love differs from the experience of those emotions in a non-Christian culture; but it would not, being a summary, contain the particular and highly specific learned tonality that makes the Christian world of these people a world of highly concrete and distinct form and feeling, in which the ubiquity of guilt and an anal form of disgust (and humor) color every emotion and perception. We want not only to say that these people feel guilt at original sin; we want to say also that it is guilt at a parental sexual act that is seen as immersing the mother in excrement and causing the birth of the child through excrement. Not only that they feel dis-

---

23. A marvelous discussion of these aspects of Beckett's work is in Stanley Cavell, "Ending the Waiting Game," in his *Must We Mean What We Say?* (New York, 1969; repr. Cambridge, 1976).

gust and loathing, but also that their disgust has as its object, above all, the female body—and their own bodies seen in the aspect of virility and desire, seen, by extension, as mortal, since mortality is seen itself as the punishment for sexual guilt. Not only that they feel fear, but that it is a fear of being punished by a supreme being who watches their every feeling, and a punishment that they more than deserve simply in virtue of existing. Not only that they feel hope, but that it is hope for "succour" (p. 71) and for a merciful waiving of just punishment (p. 162). And even this is so far too abstract. What they feel is best given in the concreteness of the sentences of the story.

And love? We cannot tell the story of their love without making all of these connections and still others. For erotic love, here, lived around the paradigm scenario of the child's reparative but guilty attempt to enter his mother's womb, becomes a peculiar, highly specific mixture of longing for bliss with loathing and disgust, both toward the object and toward oneself, suffused, always, with the premonition of disaster. When Molloy recalls his experience of "true love," he thinks first, guiltily, of his mother: "Could a woman have stopped me as I swept towards mother? Probably . . . Now men, I have rubbed up against a few men in my time, but women? Oh well, I may as well confess it now, yes, I once rubbed up against one. I don't mean my mother, I did more than rub up against her" (p. 56). The woman met him, he goes on, in a rubbish dump, as he was "limply poking about in the garbage saying probably, for at that age I must still have been capable of general ideas, This is life" (p. 57). Her invitation to him to "know what love was" (p. 57) is greeted with eagerness, as a salvation. She even at first appears to have an aperture for lovemaking that is "not the bunghole I had always imagined, but a slit." But after the act—made pleasureless (or remembered as pleasureless) on account of her ugliness and the "doglike" position she assumed, Molloy is not certain after all that their intercourse was not anal: "Perhaps after all she put me in her rectum. A matter of complete indifference to me, I needn't tell you" (p. 57). It is of indifference because genitality is covered in shit, and the vagina, as birth canal, just is a rectum.

All of this, and more, is a view of love, a view taught by a certain concrete society at a certain point in history. The view forms a seamless unity with the society's other views or stories of emotion, with its cosmology, its shared forms of life. Molloy feels always, in this world, that he dwells in an "atmosphere of finality without end" (p. 111) and that he is a "contrivance" of this world, a role-player "playing my parts through the bitter end" (pp. 114, 122). The substitution of "through the bitter end" for the expected "through to the bitter end" expresses his sense that all social parts are played out through filth. All utterance, like birth, is anal.

We have said that this story is a structure of feeling. But we could equally well say that these forms of feeling act themselves out in forms of life, as the characters play out with doomed repetitiveness the paradigm scenarios their culture and its stories have taught them. The central drama of these two narratives (interweaving with the dream of the search for mother's room) is the plot of the hunt for the guilty one, who is at the same time oneself. For the human being internalizes, as we said, the role of judge and punisher, even as he is aware that his own desires are the object of the punishment. Moran, agent of Youdi, imagines his task:

There somewhere man is too, vast conglomerate of nature's kingdoms, as lonely and as bound. And in that block the prey is lodged and thinks himself a being apart. Anyone would serve. But I am paid to seek. I arrive, he comes away. His life has been nothing but a waiting for this, to see himself preferred, to fancy himself damned, blessed, to fancy himself everyman, above all others. (pp. 110–11)

This drama, a detective–adventure story in which the guilty party is "man" and any individual man would do as well as any other, displays the strange mingling of damnation and salvation, fear and hope, that are intrinsic to Moran's story.[24] The story is an expressive structure and, at the same time, a source or paradigm for emotions. And it shows us how our most loved story patterns, prominently including the detective story, express and further nourish the emotions of this world, teaching us to imagine ourselves as hunters after guilt and to long for a final judgment.

In other parts of life the same story is played. "I knew how difficult it was not to do again what you have done before," says Molloy (p. 85). And both he and Moran reenact, compulsively, their cultural habits, in every relationship. It should be no surprise by now that all relations with women are colored by the longing and loathing that makes Molloy add to the syllable "Ma" the phoneme "-g":

because for me, without my knowing why, the letter g abolished the syllable Ma, and as it were spat on it, better than any other letter would have done. And at the same time I satisfied a deep and doubtless unacknowledged need, the need to have a Ma, that is a mother, and to proclaim it, audibly. For before you say mag you say ma, inevitably. . . . Besides for me the question did not arise, at the period I'm worming into now, I mean the question of whether to call her Ma, Mag or the Countess Caca. (p. 17)

Nor should it be a surprise that Moran is reminded, in his journey, of "the old joke about the female soul. Question, Have women a soul? Answer, Yes. Question, Why? Answer, In order that they may be damned" (p. 137). Nor is it surprising that the world of nature is itself, in many perceptions, infused with Christian significances: that plants offer Moran "a superfetatory proof of the existence of God" (p. 99), that the earth, in his eyes, is "the earth that lifts itself up, to be approved, before it sets out" (p. 140).

But it is in the most fully developed fictional relationship in the trilogy that the consequences of these repetitions are most vividly seen—namely in Moran's relationship with his son. We first meet the boy as he passes by, "caught up," his father hypothesizes, "in I know not what fantasy of flight and pursuit. I called to him not to dirty himself" (p. 93). From this point on, the relationship plays out the Youdi roles: parental punishment strangely mixed with paternal care, love blocked by the need to discipline. Moran's own feeling that "I myself had never been sufficiently chastened" causes him to "go too far when I reprimanded my son, who was consequently a little afraid of me" (p. 95). In consequence, each instinct of affection must be checked by guilty moral resolve: "This sight went straight to my heart, but nevertheless I did my duty" (p. 109; cf. p. 121). Moran's

24. On the plot of the detective story, see Brooks.

conception of the proper job of father is that it requires, above all, teaching the young human a proper degree of guilt: "I inclined his young mind towards that most fruitful of dispositions, horror of the body and its functions" (p. 118); "I brought him unerringly to a proper sense of his iniquities" (p. 160). And it requires, as well, a vivid disgust at the child, seen as a being similar to oneself: "Did he love me then as much as I loved him? You could never be sure with that little hypocrite" (p. 120). The human communication of the pair is never personal, never direct or directly tender, mediated as it always is by the structures of religion: "And the only walk we regularly took together was that which led us, every Sunday, from home to church and, mass over, from church to home. Caught up in the slow tide of the faithful my son was not alone with me. But he was part of that docile herd going yet again to thank God for his goodness and to implore his mercy and forgiveness, and then returning, their souls made easy, to other gratifications" (p. 129). That's parental love, and the narrative language it uses, reproducing itself from generation to generation.

VI

Moran's journey is a journey of disintegration and of ending. The Molloy who was seen as a quarry outside him proves to be the disorder and unseemliness within (pp. 113, 115). And his "pilgrimage," which takes him out as far as Ballyba (though not to Bally itself, nor yet to Hole)[25] proves to be, finally, a journey back home to Turdy—a pilgrimage, as he lies, to the Turdy Madonna, goddess of pregnant married women (p. 173). In short, it becomes, increasingly, indistinguishable from Molloy's journey to his own mother's room or womb, his desirous and therefore guilty attempt to preexist the sin of his own conception. From the straight, crisp, orderly life that was his at the story's opening, Moran moves increasingly into Molloy's life of inertia and decomposition. He speaks of the "change" from what he was, of a "crumbling, a frenzied collapsing of all that had always protected me from all I was always condemned to be" (p. 148), of his "growing resignation to being dispossessed of self" (p. 149).

In one way, this journey is simply a discovery, within him, of the other side of the social emotions that Moran already inhabited and a working out of their inner logic. For wherever there is a hunter there is a prey. And if the hunter is born and dwells in Turdy he must himself be at the same time the prey; and Youdi's purpose must surely be to judge and punish him (cf. pp. 154, 162) as he judges and punishes the prey; and so, inasmuch as he imitates Youdi's judging activity, this must be his own purpose toward hmself. And so the discovery of self as prey and filth and disorder is simply the discovery of self as "man." But man is what he always was, so guilt and fear and the role of prey were always his also.

There is, however, another and more radical collapsing in this story. It appears to be the collapsing of the emotional structure itself, as Moran increasingly distances himself from the entire armature of love, disgust, guilt, and longing, by distancing himself from the religious meanings that have constituted them and the stories that are their primary vehicle. At first the "crumbling" looks just like

25. This may suggest that he is impotent as well as guilty.

the reverse side of the earlier judging and seeking. But as Moran goes further on, his project of ending seems to become the project of ending the whole game, of cutting himself off from both of its sides, even at the cost of losing the order on which he has based his life and a great part of himself.[26] When he finds in his thought the "hopes that spring eternal, childish hopes"—hopes of a reconciliation with his son, of a reconciliation with Molloy in the role of father, of a reconciliation, at last, with a Youdi who ceases to be angry and to punish—he does not indulge or nourish the hopes but rejects them in an attempt to empty out his entire spiritual being, cleansing it of these conceptions: "Yes, I let them spring within me and grow in strength, brighten and charm me with a thousand fancies, and then I swept them away, with a great disgusted sweep of all my being, I swept myself clean of them and surveyed with satisfaction the void they polluted" (p. 162). And now, thinking of his possible punishment at Youdi's hands, Moran simply laughs, shakes with "a mighty fit of laughter" (p. 162).

It is at this point that Moran hears the report of Youdi's words to Gaber, that life is "a thing of beauty . . . and a joy forever" (p. 164); and instead of embracing the sentiment with longing and desire, he asks, with what seems to be a new detachment, a skeptical question: "Do you think he meant human life? . . . Perhaps he didn't mean human life" (p. 165). It is at this point, too, that he speaks a few words to himself "to prepare my soul to make an end" (p. 166). These words include sixteen absurd and abstruse theological questions, whose grim and outrageous humor serves to distance us (Moran and the reader both) from the serious life of the religious view. (Christ never laughed [p. 101].) They also include a prayer that displays, even more vividly, Moran's new distance from religious emotions: "And I recited the pretty quietist Pater, Our Father who art no more in heaven than on earth or in hell, I neither want nor desire that thy name be hallowed, thou knowest best what suits thee. Etc. The middle and the end are very pretty" (p. 167). The narrative is progressing in the direction not of any conventional happy or unhappy ending but of a more radical breaking down of religious significances and religious desire.

Increasingly at this period Moran's thoughts turn to his bees, as to creatures whose lives are not "polluted" by religious meanings. Their dances seem to him to display a "different way" from human communication, for they have a complex and discernible form, they can be studied, and yet (unlike human agency under God's eye) they have no significance—or, if a significance, then an alien one, "too noble ever to be sullied by the cogitations of a man like me, exiled in his manhood" (p. 169). He considers the life of the bees to be a life apart from the life of emotions and his own relation to the bees to be the one relation in his life that is not mediated by emotion and the other infirmities of the flesh: "And I would never do my bees the wrong I had done my God, to whom I had been taught to ascribe my angers, fears, desires, and even my body" (p. 169).

And increasingly Moran gives indications that this new and radical attitude to religious emotion requires a new attitude to literature and the writing of literature and a new attitude to the relationship between writer and reader. We might say that in the old narratorial relationship the writer is, for the reader, God the father:

26. See Cavell, "Ending the Waiting Game."

the one who makes things mean, the one who makes the world, the one who evokes and structures the reader's emotions of delight and longing and guilt and fear. In Moran's detective story, the writer is the one who manipulates the reader's desire to seek and condemn, to track and judge the guilty prey. So increasingly, as he distances himself from Youdi and from that fear and longing, Moran refuses the task of the narrator and refuses us the emotions of the reader. He calls his life an "inennarable contraption" (p. 114), reminding us of the simplifications and refusals imposed by narration. Shortly after this, he identifies himself as the author of this entire novel and of Beckett's other novels—but he tells us that, this time, novel writing will not take place: "Oh the stories I could tell you, if I were easy. What a rabble in my head, what a gallery of moribunds. Murphy, Watt, Yerk, Mercier and all the others. . . . Stories, stories. I have not been able to tell them. I shall not be able to tell this one" (p. 137). In such moments he seems to echo Molloy's expression of frustration with the ongoing and unending character of the stories: "For if you set out to mention everything you would never be done, and that's what counts, to be done, to have done" (p. 41). But whereas Molloy considered that goal unachievable and hoped, at most, for a "change of muck, to move from one heap to another a little further on" (p. 41), Moran seems to believe that narration will not take place any more, that it is all ending, that he is ending it all.

And often he finds himself on the verge of the old literary games, writing so as to arouse our narratological desire—and he turns away from that activity with firm resolve. "I'll tell you. No, I'll tell you nothing. Nothing" (p. 134). Introducing a new character, he balks at the narrator's task of rich description, one of the primary strategies used by an author to summon up our interest in a character who will then hunt, or be hunted, or love, or be filthy, or all of these. "I shall have to describe him briefly, though such a thing is contrary to my princples" (p. 150). Twice he politely refuses us what we would have wanted from his story, as if literature would be his, and our, weakness, and the time is now too late for backward movement: "I am sorry I cannot indicate more clearly how this result was obtained, it would have been something worth reading. But it is not at this late stage of my relation that I intend to give way to literature" (p. 151). "I would have described them once, not now, I am sorry, it would have been worth reading" (p. 166). And even as he frustrates and destructures our desire, he achieves an ending to his own narrative longing. Refusing the opportunity to tell of adventures (obstacles, fiends, misdemeanors, disintegrations) on the road to Ballyba, he comments: "It was my intention, almost my desire, to tell of all these things, I rejoiced at the thought that the moment would come when I might do so. Now the intention is dead, the moment is come and the desire is gone" (p. 159). He even wonders whether he is beyond thinking and conceiving altogether (p. 165). But whatever awaits him, what is "certain" is that it will not "be known," will not be in any story (p. 172). His talk of preparing his "soul to make an end" (p. 166) and his announcement, "Now I may make an end" (p. 174) refer, perhaps, to the end of this written story. But, beyond this, they point to the end of storying, the end of the forms of life taught and lived in stories.

Moran's narrative ends where it began, in the garden of his home. But this ending seems to confirm our view that a great change has taken place and that a new life is beginning:

My birds had not been killed. They were wild birds. And yet quite trusting. I recognized them and they seemed to recognize me. But one never knows. Some were missing and some were new. I tried to understand their language better. Without having recourse to mine. They were the longest, loveliest days of all the year. I lived in the garden. I have spoken of a voice telling me things. I was getting to know it better now, to understand what it wanted. It did not use the words that Moran had been taught when he was little and that he in his turn had taught to his little one. So that at first I did not know what it wanted. But in the end I understood this language. I understood it, I understood it, all wrong perhaps. That is not what matters. It told me to write the report. Does this mean I am freer now than I was? I do not know. I shall learn. Then I went back into the house and wrote, It is midnight. The rain is beating on the windows. It was not midnight. It was not raining. (pp. 175–76)

We seem to see here a clearing beyond disgust and guilt, an acceptance of nature and body that does not ask them to be redeemed by any beyond, a relation with living beings that no longer requires to be mediated by religious emotions or even by the language in which they are constructed. With the refusal of human language we seem to have broken the chain by which the "long confused emotion" perpetuates itself, father to son. Even Moran's indifference to questions of meaning and understanding seems to be the happy discovery that the world does not need to be interpreted, it can simply be lived in, accepted, trusted as the birds trust. He lives in the garden, a part of nature, no longer hunting, no longer hunted.

Beckett alludes, in this ending, to two powerful stories of antireligious salvation; and these allusions strengthen our conviction that the constraints of religious emotion really have been transcended. The ending in the garden refers, most obviously, to the conclusion of Voltaire's *Candide,* in which the return home to one's own and the choice *cultiver son jardin* represents the overthrow of the Leibnizian search for a religious meaning in all events, and a decision to live in the world as in a chancy arbitrary place made partially habitable by the decency of friendship. But Beckett's and Voltaire's gardens have, as well, an earlier reference: to the Garden of Epicurus, in which pupils learned, by a patient therapeutic criticism of the emotions that society had taught them, to live a life free from religious fear and longing, and the love that is based upon these.[27] Epicurus's doctrine that the root cause of human unhappiness lies in our desires and emotions and that these bad desires are "empty" social constructs, erected by convention and capable of being dismantled by opposite habits, is the doctrine about emotion that is being worked out in this book as a whole; so it is not really surprising that the ending to Moran's story should have this Epicurean setting. Even Beckett's interest in animals parallels that of Epicurus (and Lucretius): animals have forms of life apart from the pollution of religion; they show us what it could be to be alive without hope or fear or disgust or even love.

But for Epicurus, Lucretius, and Voltaire, the garden really is a place of happiness, an oasis of human acceptance in a casual and violent universe. Does Mor-

---

27. See *The Therapy of Desire;* an earlier version of a relevant portion has appeared as "Therapeutic Arguments: Epicurus and Aristotle," in *The Norms of Nature,* ed. M. Schofield and G. Striker (Cambridge, 1986), 31–74.

an's story have a similarly happy ending, even to this limited extent? And if it did have one, if in this way it did fulfill our readerly longing, wouldn't that itself imply that what we have just been saying about the end of storytelling has been in part false? A happy end state is precisely what the reader's old emotions deeply desire: a salvation, a redemption. So if this is what we are getting here, then, ironically, it really is not what we are getting. We can be redeemed only by ending the demand for redemption, by ceasing to use the concepts of redemption. Beckett's antinarrative is too many-sided, too ironic, to leave us with any simple comfort. He makes us call the new turn into question from its inception, making us ask ourselves whether this project of bringing hope and the other emotions to an end is not itself a project that lies securely in the grip of the old emotions, a project born of disgust, straining toward salvation. Remember that when Moran swept away his hopes, he did so "with a great disgusted sweep of all my being" (p. 162). His ensuing laughter at Youdi is indistinguishable, in its violent shaking, from fear: "strange laughter truly, and no doubt misnamed" (p. 162). The list of mocking theological questions is followed by a list of personal questions that ask about the salvation, in heaven, not only of Moran and his family but also of the author's other characters in other novels (pp. 167–68). It begins to look as if the new movement of ending is motivated, like the old, by guilt. The only difference is that previously the disgust was directed at only a certain aspect of the self—the bodily, born-of-woman aspect—whereas now it moves, so to speak, one level up and takes as its target Moran's whole being as a social "contrivance," including, and especially, his emotions of guilt and disgust. This second-order disgust, and the corresponding second-order longing (for a redemption from the longing for redemption) are the structures that organize Moran's homeward journey. Even his search for ending is a preparation of the soul (p. 166), a preparation, presumably, for final judgment.

We are forbidden by such indications to have the comfortable thought that something happy and liberating and conclusive is happening here. And when we notice that things are not happy and conclusive, we notice in ourselves yet a third level of disgust: disgust at the disgust with human disgust that motivates Moran's search for ending and keeps him always within the constraints that this search opposes. But then, of course, we are likely to notice that that reaction is, as well, a part of the same old trap: for it sets our desires rushing off to imagine what would be a *real* happy ending. And that's itself a defect calling for more judgment. "Atonement was in itself a sin, calling for more atonement, and so on, as if there could be anything but life for the living."

And Moran's writing? The fiction that he is putting an end to fictions is, we are informed in the end, an artfully constructed fiction of his own, commanded as a penance (p. 133), executed under orders from a strange voice (p. 131). So—once again—it is encased within the very structures it opposes, and it announces as much with relish, confessing, in the end, to its own fictionality and making us see that this assault on stories is just another story. Only, perhaps, one in which the prey is stories themselves and their structures of desire, the hunter our readerly judgment upon the lying character of stories, and the judgment our aggressive and disgusted lashing out at the disgust and guilt that hold us. Its acts of confessing and judging, though directed at the whole apparatus of confession and judgment, are nonetheless the same old religious acts and are no less violent, no less constraining, than the original first-order confession concerning the filth of the body. More damning, really, since we might have thought that it was the word that was going to be our salvation.

What it comes to is that you can't go beyond writing, if writing is what you are in fact doing. You are, apparently, stuck with "the convention that demands you either lie or hold your peace" (p. 88). Perhaps a bee dance, or Moran's birds, would be truly beyond disgust and guilt—*but*—that song and dance are not what we readers of literature desire, for they would not express *us,* as we have been contrived. We have learned our lesson so thoroughly that we cannot depart from it, even to end it. We go on telling stories in the only way we know; and on the other side, if anything, is only a silence. But we feel that if our death and its silence did come at last, they would probably come, like Malone's, inside a story of our own telling. And the weapon of aggression might be, indifferently, a hammer, a stick, a fist, a thought, a dream, or a pencil (p. 288).

VII

This attack on religious desire has ancestors. Two of them are Lucretius and Nietzsche. For both Epicurus's great poet–pupil and the evangelist of God's death believed that a religious view of the world had deeply poisoned human desires in their time, constructing deformed patterns of fear and longing. Both believed, too, that certain influential art forms were powerful accomplices of religious longing and that a successful attack on religion required the undoing of these forms. And yet neither ended by embracing silence. Both, indeed, imagined a fruitful life for human beings beyond religious expectation, and both constructed forms of writing that seemed to them appropriate for that more fruitful life, or at least for the movement toward it. Perhaps the pursuit of this difference of ending, so to speak, will help us to see where we have been and whether we had to go there.

Lucretius, following Epicurus's teaching, held that a great part of human desire and emotion is "empty": built upon beliefs that are both socially taught and false, beliefs that express, for the most part, the aim of a religious elite to gain power over humans by making them unhappy and disgusted with the merely human in life. Central to this religious project is a teaching about death that engenders fear and loathing, along with the passionate longing for immortal life. And it was Lucretius's view that most of our other emotions—including the anger that motivates war and the erotic love that seeks personal salvation through fusion with a "goddess"—were disguised forms of this religious fear and longing. These forms of feeling are perpetuated in poetry, especially in the poetry of mourning and in erotic love poetry. So an attack on these socially constructed emotions requires an attack on those poetic forms. In his own poetry, Lucretius pursues the attack, through satire and scathing negative argument.[28]

Yet Lucretius believed that there were many human desires and motivations that were not pernicious in this way. There were the natural desires of the body; there was a human being's natural love of the use of reason; and, finally, there

28. This account of Lucretius is developed in detail in "Beyond Obsession and Disgust."

were some learned but still fruitful desires, such as the desire for friendship and the sense of justice—all of which could be tapped in order to construct a fruitful human life on the other side of religion. He believed that one could imagine this life and even describe it in writing. And he seems to have believed that even though some of the desires that motivate writing are the same ones that his argument attacks—longing for immortality, erotic love, anger at one's finitude—still, this was not true of all writerly motivations. For example, there is a "pure" desire to give and receive pleasure that stands apart; a desire, as well, for social justice and peace, a desire for fruitfulness. So even though his writing had to attack many of the forms of writing common in his time, including most actual poetry, still it did not have to tear all writing down, and it did not need to subvert itself. There is a therapeutic discourse that can be housed in verse, albeit very unusual verse, that will give pleasure to the reader without falling under its own critique. Perhaps even on the other side of therapy—though this is less clear—there is something for writing to do and to be: a source of pleasure, a bond of friendship.

Nietzsche had a still more pessimistic view about the extent to which existing patterns of feeling in his time were the product of religious teaching. Nineteen hundred years of Christianity have, he believes, made a tremendous difference in human self-conceptions. Now the human being is so radically alienated from natural bodily humanity, so thoroughly immersed in longing for a happy ending in another world, by contrast to which this one is seen as poor and loathsome, that the removal of religious hope creates a crisis of nihilism. Religious teleological patterns of desire are so deep in us, the horror of the body is so deep in us, that it is not clear that there is any vivid life in us that is not made in religion's image, nothing, therefore, to motivate us to construct a new life after its demise.[29] The threat of nihilism is the prospect of the collapse of the will, the refusal to continue ordering and valuing.

And yet Nietzsche did hold out hope for a human life beyond nihilism. And he believed his task as a writer to be the creation of that hope as a vivid possibility. The first step in the creative task must be negative: the thorough, detailed dismantling of religious beliefs and teleological desires through the techniques of debunking genealogy, mordant satire, horrific projection. But even this negative movement in Nietzsche's writing contains, already, a positive side: images of human strength and "virtue," and, in its portrait of the ancient Greeks, the image of an entire people who lived, and felt, without fear. And beyond the "nay-saying" stage of the spirit, Nietzsche foresaw, and held out as a possibility, a joyful affirmative life for the spirit and the body together, a life truly beyond the constraining oppositions of disgust and awe, loathing and longing. And although most actual poets and artists are criticized as valets of conventional religion—even Goethe is in the end found lacking, a captive of the quest for beatitude—Nietzsche clearly believed, as well, that art, including music and dance and including as well the art of the philosopher–poet, had a central positive role to play in restoring man to himself and to the earth. This writing has to struggle against being inspired, and limited, by the desires of its own time; even Zarathustra longs for a contented end-

---

29. A fine discussion of this element in Nietzsche's thought is in Henri Birault, "Beautitude in Nietzsche," translated in *The New Nietzsche,* ed. David Allison (Cambridge, Mass., 1985).

state and yearns to throw off his burdens. But this temptation is one that the writer can overcome in himself and still find speech and creation. "Do I aspire to *happiness?*" says Zarathustra joyfully at last. "I aspire to *works.*"[30]

VIII

Beckett is a member of this therapeutic company. But his pessimism (or that of his voices) denies a possibility that they hold open. We need to understand this denial more deeply if we are to see, finally, where we are. One thing that becomes very clear, as we read these novels, is that we are hearing, in the end, but a single human voice, not the conversation of diverse human voices with diverse structures of feeling. Beckett emphasizes this fact, by identifying Moran with the author of his other novels.[31] And the solipsism of this voice's sense of life is so total that we get no sense of the distinctive shape of any other lives in this world. An implicit claim is made by these voices to be the whole world, to be telling the way the world is as they tell about themselves. But is there any reason to suppose that this one life is, in that way, representative? To speak rather bluntly, even if Christian emotion of this particularly sterile form does so deeply infuse *some* lives in some parts of the world, that for those people there is no emotion and no writing beyond it, have we any reason to think this true for us all, or an undermining of the emotional lives of us all? This question arises naturally if one reads Beckett side by side with one of his own great heroes, Proust, and even more so if one at the same time reads other great novelists whose work Beckett would, in his youth, have read, such as Henry James or Virginia Woolf. For in none of these writers does one find that religion plays a role of paramount importance; nor is religion's disgust with the body a major source of emotional life. Whatever problems they find with our emotions and their social construction, these problems do not generate Beckett's nihilism and his search for silence. Is this simply because they have failed to see something about our society that Beckett sees more clearly? Or isn't it, instead, because in the lives they depict and the sense of life they express, these problems really are not central? Not all persuasive voices speak Moran's language.

Along with an absence of human diversity, we find in Beckett, as well, an absence of human *activity* that seems foreign to our experience of emotional development, even at the cultural and social level. Beckett's people are heirs of a legacy of feeling that shapes them inexorably. They cannot help being shaped in this way, and they feel like "contrivances," like machines programmed entirely from without: "You think you are inventing, and all you do is stammer out your lesson, the remnants of a pensum one day got by heart and long forgotten" (p. 31). They are made, and the only thing they make is a child in their own image. This is not a convincing picture either of an individual child's development or of

---

30. F. Nietzsche, *Thus Spoke Zarathustra,* Part IV, "The Sign," my translation. (W. Kaufmann's version uses "work" for *Werke,* which does not adequately convey Zarathustra's emphasis on creation, falsely suggesting that the German contains the word *Arbeit:* see W. Kaufmann, ed. and trans., *The Viking Portable Nietzsche* [New York, 1966].)

31. See also p. 412, where the unnamed voice proves to be the author of all the trilogy's stories.

a society's evolution. Children actively select and interpret; and the society around them contains a plurality of active voices, striving to persuade us in new directions. And persuasion, not just manipulation, is at least a part of what explains those changes. The point about diversity and the point about activity seem connected: for it is in part because Beckett sees society as single and monolithic that he is able to omit the presence of argument, criticism, and change. In all this we sense, I believe, a deeply religious sensibility at work; for we have at all times the sense that mere human beings are powerless to make, on account of the fact that there is something very much more powerful in this universe that does all the making. We are at best its *agents;* and that is why we cannot *act.*

Beckett has shown us how the desires engendered by narrative are responses to our sense of finitude, our powerlessness. Hope, fear, passionate longing, all are bound up with our feeling that the world eludes our control and that cherished things out in the world are not governed by our will. But we could agree with this general analysis of the relationship between emotion and finitude—indeed, we did agree with this in our general account of emotion (see sec. III)—without conceding that this sense of finitude, and our emotional responses to it, are themselves necessarily suffused with a sense of *guilt* and of *disgust.* There is a peculiar movement in Beckett's talk of emotions—which we notice even in our first two passages—from a perception of human limits to a loathing of the limited, from grief to disgust and hatred, from the tragedy and comedy of the frail body to rage at the body, seen as covered in excrement. It is as if Beckett believes that the finite and frail can only inspire our disgust and loathing—that life (in the words of Youdi) can be "a thing of beauty and a joy" only if it is "forever." And this is because, as we said, mortality in Beckett's world is seen not as our neutral and natural condition but as our punishment for original sin.[32] The complete absence in this writing of any joy in the limited and finite indicates to us that the narrative as a whole is an expression of a religious view of life. Lucretius and Nietzsche stand apart from what they condemn. They have a separate and uncorrupted sense of pleasure and of value; and because of this they can see how a finite life can have its own peculiar splendor. Beckett's narrative does not see this. But then his assault on narrative does not remove from us the possibility of another sort of narrative: one whose structures express the beauty of that which is human and fragile and call forth in us a love of that beauty and the limits that constitute it.

Finally, we notice in this narrative one further religious prejudice: the prejudice against that which is made in society and in favor of the pure soul, the soul before and apart from all social constructing. For it is not only the specific forms of socially constructed desire that inspire loathing in Beckett's voices. It is also the whole idea of social construction itself, the whole idea that a group can tell me who and what I am to be and to feel. These reflections are most fully developed in *The Unnamable,* with its attacks on the "pupil Mahood," who thinks and feels as he has been taught to do and who has, therefore, only a species language, only species feelings, who can never, in virtue of this, say or even think *himself.* But

---

32. Compare the illuminating remarks about the differences between Lucretius and Dante in George Santayana, *Three Philosophical Poets* (Cambridge, Mass., 1910).

this line of reflection is present throughout the trilogy, beneath its loathing of specific social forms, and it contributes powerfully to the novels' despairing message.

But, we might ask, why is it that these voices are so intolerant of society and of shared forms of thought and feeling? Why aren't they willing to allow that the common-to-all might be and say themselves? Isn't it, really, because they are in the grip of a longing for the pure soul, hard as a diamond, individual and indivisible, coming forth from its maker's hand with its identity already stamped upon it? Don't they reject shared language because they long for a pure language of the soul itself by itself and for pure relationships among souls that will be in no way mediated by the contingent structures of human social life? Everywhere the voices turn, they find the group and its history. They cannot go beyond that. But this is a tragedy for them only because they are gripped by the conviction that nothing man-made and contingent could ever stand for them. Their very despair gives evidence of their deep religiosity. They have not been able to go far enough outside the Christian picture to see how to pose the problem of self-expression in a way that is not shaped by that picture. If they could get that far outside, they might discover that it is no disgrace to be a political animal, that the fact that human language is not available either to beasts or to gods is no point against it.

IX

The project, and related projects, have several important lessons to learn from Beckett's voices, despite these criticisms. First, it must always bear in mind that the emotions, if they are cognitive and therefore useful sources of information concerning human values, are also, by the same token, subject to social manipulation. This, as I said, does not imply a relativism in which no construct is better than any other, any more than the fact that different societies teach different beliefs implies that they are all equally true. But it does mean that the issue of social origin must be squarely faced with emotions as with beliefs, that emotions do not give us a bedrock of reliable "natural" evidence that stands apart from what society makes. It means that with emotions as well as with beliefs, the social and also psychogenetic origins must be carefully investigated, before we are entitled to draw any conclusions about their role in human life. And before any normative conclusions can be drawn about what is or is not conducive to human flourishing, the issue of relativism must be confronted. The project, in short, must look at social history, and not without a critical eye.

We need to bear in mind, as well, that narratives contain emotions in their very structure; so their form stands in need of the same sort of scrutiny that we give to emotions represented within it. Narrative is not unshaped human life; indeed, human life is not either. Narratives are constructs that respond to certain patterns of living and shape them in their turn. So we must always ask what content the literary forms themselves express, what structures of desire they represent and evoke.

This means, where the assessment of abstract principles and theories is concerned, that we must not treat the literary "evidence" as Baconian observation data that any good theory must fit. Instead, we will see both principles and stories as different sorts of theories or views about life; and in the case of a discrepancy we would not always give priority to the story and its emotions. The whole enterprise of examining our sense of life should be holistic: frequently we will reject an abstract theoretical account for being at odds with the concrete perceptions of life and feeling embodied in literary forms; but sometimes, too, we may criticize a story by setting it beside a theoretical account—if we decide that the latter includes more of what we want to preserve. There is no Archimedean point that we can occupy as we do this; and there is no hard-and-fast rule as to how this will be done.[33] But our reflection about the depth of Christian feeling in the construction of our narrative forms suggests, at the least, that we should keep strongly alive the theoretical and critical side of the enterprise and subject the emotions to rational scrutiny.

Finally, we need to consider, as Beckett forces us to consider, that the choice to write at all expresses, itself, a content, that, therefore, if we really wish to examine all the attitudes toward human life and its value, we cannot simply examine the contrasting forms of writing. We must ask as well, if we can, along with Beckett's voices, exactly what writing itself *is* in human life; how it is related to the ambition to control and order, therefore, perhaps to a certain discontent with or even a hatred of human life as it is lived; how it might displace both writer and reader from a loving acceptance of the world. We have so far spoken as if writing could express all the human forms of feeling, in its own many forms. But writing is itself a choice, an act, and not a neutral act either. It is opposed to other forms of action or passion: to listening, to waiting, to keeping silent.[34] And so its forms of feeling may be similarly confined, opposed to other forms. In *The Unnamable,* the voice perceives itself as "shut up" inside a wall of words, constrained by its own speaking. And "the silence is outside, outside . . . nothing but this voice and the silence all round." And the thought of silence is linked with the thought of freedom (p. 409); a freedom, perhaps, from both making and being made.

And even that thought, the voice realizes, is uttered in the old language, the language of stories, of progress, of hope and happy endings. It is not silent enough to accept being as it is. In the end, he imagines that he might live a different story and that words have taken him only to the "threshold of my story, before the door that opens on my story" (p. 414). And if that door opens, "it will be the silence" (p. 414), and the end of knowing and conceiving, and the end of writing and speaking; and that silence would be the only exit from a life of writing, the only story that ends stories. (And isn't that thought of ending itself an ending, in the old style?) These things, too, we must consider as we go on (as we must, as he must) using the words that are all we have to say ourselves.

And what emotion, if any, does the silence itself express? Could there be a form of love in the silence, in the act of not structuring, not writing? Or perhaps an absence of emotion, of story construction, that is itself more loving still than love

33. On this (with reference to Rawls) see "Perceptive Equilibrium," this volume.

34. It is opposed as well, of course, to speaking orally; but Beckett's voices do not seem to make a significant distinction between storytelling and story-writing. In any more extended treatment of this matter, however, the difference between writing and speaking would have to be considered.

has ever been? This, too, must be considered in any writing on this topic, although the act of writing obscures it as a possibility.

Endnote

This essay comments on the project contained in all of the others; and its comments are self-explanatory. It calls for an extensive inquiry into connections between emotion and narrative form that it begins but by no means completes. (That inquiry is pursued further in some of my current work in progress on Greek philosophy, especially "Beyond Obsession and Disgust: Lucretius on the Therapy of Love," *Apeiron* 1989. And it will be the central theme of my Gifford Lectures 1992–93.) And by showing the plausibility of the claim that we learn our emotional repertory, in part at least, from the stories we hear, it gives a reason why not only moral philosophy, but also philosophy of mind and philosophy of action, need to turn to literature to complete their own projects.

In its remarks about silence, this paper touches on some large issues that the articles, as a group, do not pursue. Human symbolic representation/interpretation of the world takes many forms: linguistic, pictorial, musical, architectural, kinetic, and so forth. In discussing the relationships among different varieties of written linguistic symbolizing, I have not inquired into the relationship between written and nonwritten verbal discourse; far less into the relationship between linguistic and nonlinguistic forms of representation or between all of these overt representations and silent waiting, thinking, or feeling. We find in both James and Proust the thought that the novelist's dedication to the articulate word, to the selection of the right word for each complexity of situation and each nuance of feeling, is connected with ideals of full awareness, responsibility, and responsiveness that are defended as good ways to live and to be. In James, the claim is that the artist's conduct is exemplary for us all: we should all write our lives more attentively. (Note, however, that he does not insist that the representation must be linguistic: see "'Finely Aware.'") Proust makes a further claim: that the artist's life, as realized in the fully achieved work of art, is the only really fully lived life, all other lives being, by contrast, routinized and incompletely sentient (see Introduction). We need to scrutinize these norms, asking to what extent the moment in which the imagination alertly, discerningly selects the right word is paradigmatic of the kind of attention that we wish to include; whether other humbler or more receptive forms of attention as well are not perhaps required to make a life really complete; and whether those forms of attention can or cannot be captured in any form of writing. "Flawed Crystals," "Perceptive Equilibrium," and "Love and the Individual" explore one aspect of this question in the context of personal love; but it clearly needs to be pursued further.

This essay calls the emotions of the reader into question. "Steerforth's Arm" both provides a very different account of the emotions of the novel-reader and defends these as central in the ethical life. The need to sort this out shows the importance of the sort of Aristotelian philosophical criticism described in the Introduction and in "Love's Knowledge." And even if one concludes that Beckett's charge against the novel misses the mark, the question he raises should always be asked: Do the emotions upon which our interest, as readers, depends themselves embody questionable beliefs, defective forms of life? Indeed, as "Transcending" argues, the question needs to be asked of philosophical writing as well, and perhaps more urgently; for much of the interest readers have had in a certain style of philosophical writing has traditionally been connected with an interest in transcending everyday humanity, an aspiration problematic at best.

Love and the Individual:
Romantic Rightness and
Platonic Aspiration

In February 1984, the Stanford Humanities Center held a conference in memory of Michelle Rosaldo, the distinguished anthropologist, who died tragically during her pioneering field work in the Philippines. Since much of her work had been devoted to the investigation of cultural differences in the understanding of the individual—especially as subject and object of various emotions—the conference organizers chose the theme: "Reconstructing Individualism." The participants were to consider aspects of traditional Western conceptions of the individual and criticisms of that tradition, asking what new conception or conceptions might emerge from that critique. Since I had recently published a paper on the individual as object of love in Plato's *Symposium*,[1] I was asked to address the topic, "Love and the Individual."

The assignment gave me some difficulty. For love is a difficult topic to think and write about at any time; and life does not always assist the investigation. Besides, I had said what I wanted to say about Plato's view already, both in the *Symposium* article and in related writing on the *Phaedrus*. And I had done a related article on Proust for the journal *Philosophy and Literature*. What form, then, should this new paper take?

While I was worrying about this problem, I was also moving most of my books and papers down to Brown, where I was scheduled to begin teaching the following fall. Since I was short of space at home, I had been allowed to store my things at Brown for the rest of the year, until my office there became available. One damp cold Saturday in late December, the movers carried my files and boxes into the Philosophy Department building, piling them up in a closet under the stairs where I had been told to leave them. There in this closet, on the floor, I noted a strange document. It was a manuscript of some thirty-eight pages, typewritten. Its title was "Love and the Individual: Romantic Rightness and Platonic Aspiration. A

1. M. Nussbaum, "The Speech of Alcibiades: A Reading of Plato's *Symposium*," *Philosophy and Literature* 3 (1979) 131–72; a revised version appears as chap. 6 of *Fragility*. See also chap. 7 of *Fragility*, for an interpretation of Plato's *Phaedrus*.

Story." Now this was a remarkable coincidence; for I had just chosen this title for my presentation at Stanford. I sat down right there in the closet, after the movers left, and read it through. It was an odd document indeed, a strange hybrid of fiction and philosophy. But it was on my topic, a topic on which I myself had found nothing at all to say. I began to consider taking it and reading parts of it at Stanford. But I could not figure out who its author was. I strongly suspected that it was a woman, and a philosopher. The setting is a real place, a philosopher's house; I've even been there. I thought immediately of my one female colleague in philosophy, Diana Ackerman. But, I reasoned, she works on completely different topics. (Now her name is Felicia Ackerman, and now I know that she does write fiction. She has recently won a major award for a short story. But it still seems to me unlikely that she can have been the author. Her style is very different, and she has no interest in Plato.) This author, I saw, is familiar with Plato and Aristotle, as well as Proust and Henry James. Her interests, in fact, lie very close to mine. What's odder still, she introduces as a sentence allegedly written by one of her characters (the one called "she") a sentence that I wrote and published in my article on the *Symposium*. Her other character (the one called "I") claims to have written my article on Henry James.[2] Well, I thought, sitting on the closet floor, whoever she is, if she can lift my words, I can lift hers. So I decided to do that at Stanford, and in the volume that followed. I reproduce this odd document again in this volume, revising this introductory account, in the hope that it will contribute to this investigation of the relationship between philosophical and literary writing.

A Story

> Or incomincian le dolenti note
> a farmisi sentire; or son venuto
> là dove molto pianto mi percuote.
>
> Now the sounds of misery have begun
> to reach my ears. Now I come to a place
> where many cries of anguish beat against me.
> Dante, *Inferno* V.25–27

Late one January night, in that winter of 1982, when it snowed all over Florida, blighting the orange crop, she found herself wide awake in Tallahassee, thinking about love. And, not surprisingly, about an individual who was the object of hers. Her guest room looked out over a white-blanketed golf course whose genteel contours, enduring with Protestant dignity the region's prospective loss of millions, offered a polite reproof to her more disorderly experience of loss. The insouciant smile of the country club moon, floating above natural disaster as clear and round and single-natured and unaffected as a Platonic form—or a resurrected orange— seemed to her to express the Platonic thought that loved individuals, like orange crops or even like oranges themselves, always came along one following the other

---

2. See "Flawed Crystals," this volume.

in due succession, essentially undistinguishable from one another in their health-bringing and energizing properties. A loss of one could be compensated fully and directly by the coming-into-being of the homogeneous next. One had only, therefore, to endure a brief interstitial period of whiteness, snow, and clear light.

Finding this hygienic Diotiman optimism impossibly at odds with her messier ruminations, finding it, indeed, not to speak genteelly, absurd as a consolation addressed to real personal loss (for it was in those days a point of honor with her to accept no replacements, to insist that any willingness to be so consoled was a falling off from grace), she rejected it and considered other possibilities. As she leaned out the window, feeling on her eyelids the unmoving starry air, she saw that the appropriate next step would be to break up that calm; to demonstrate somehow her complicity with Diotima's opponent Alcibiades and his more accurate view of love. Perhaps by going out and smashing several sacred statues; or by doing violence to the seventeenth green. But the truth was that she was a gentle character, for whom the consolation of violence was a constitutional impossibility. And besides, wasn't her own real view the view she had found and described in writing about the *Phaedrus,* namely, that personal love was not necessarily linked with disorder, but was actually constitutive of the best sort of orderly life, a life dedicated to understanding of value and goodness? That madness and sanity, personal passion and rational aspiration, were, in their highest forms, actually in harmony with or even fused with one another? That we do not really need to choose between Socrates and Alcibiades? It was just this, indeed, that she saw as her problem; for if only disorder were gone one might even contrive to be pleased.

That afternoon when she first saw him, years before, he was walking down the sun-streaked hallway, laughing and talking, his whole body fiercely illuminated from behind by the light from the door, so that he looked to her like Turner's Angel Standing in the Sun. Or, better, like some counterpart good angel, equally radiant but entirely beneficent in power. Like what the *Phaedrus* calls a "form truly expressing beauty and nobility." It is not necessary to choose between Socrates and Alcibiades. Under the right circumstances.

At odds, then, with both Diotima's order and Alcibiades' violence; feeling not like Turner's fishermen, irradiated by that angel's light; or even like the lover of the *Phaedrus,* awestruck by the splendor of some beautiful boy; feeling more like Plato's Stesichorus, blinded by the gods, groping for the verses that would restore his sight, she turned for help and light to the only help that occurred to her. Nothing dramatic, or even Platonic. Aristotelian rather. She turned into the room and began looking through the books.

There are too many individuals, and all of them are married. This is the only piece of general wisdom I have to offer on this topic about which I so rashly agreed to write. Socrates said in the *Symposium,* "I understand nothing—with the exception of love." This preposterous statement tips us off, of course, that something funny is going on. For, sure enough, it turns out that the claim to have grasped and understood the nature of love is part and parcel of an enterprise that is busy converting loved persons into instantiations of a universal, and so into proper objects of (scientific) understanding, all in order to repudiate and transcend the phenomenon of love as ordinary mortals experience it. The sight of the knowing intellect is incompatible, Diotima tells us, with the sight of the human body. Uttered about ordinary passion by an ordinary mortal, the claim to have a general understanding of love is as good an example of the self-refuting proposition as anything philosophy has to offer. More, like Socrates' claim, it is also some sort of denial or refusal of love's dangers. As Alcibiades, telling his love story, shows. ("Oh love. I know all about that." I'd say that in the same tone of voice I used for my opening "general truth." For similar reasons.) The question, then, becomes how to write about love of the individual, if one does not wish, even tacitly, to make the Socratic claim to general understanding. How to limit and undercut one's claims, making it clear that they are not guilty of Socratic "overweening." How, at the same time, to authenticate such limited statements as are made, showing where they come from and what gives them any claim to be telling human truth. Thinking of what I had written about Alcibiades, about Henry James, above all about Proust, I could not avoid the conclusion that I would only be entitled to speak about love in the form of a narrative.

This will, to be sure, be a conspicuously philosophical narrative. Most of its "plot" will be a story of thought and work. Its title sounds like the title of an article. Part of it will be an article, or a sketch for one. It will tell you at length about this lady's general reflections; how she thought and even wrote; how she interpreted the *Phaedrus;* how she marshaled objections and counterexamples. For thought is one of the things that occupies space in a life, especially this one. It is also a major device by which this life tries to keep itself in line. A love story should not fail to show this.

And her story is philosophical in yet another way—in the way in which Aristotle said poetry was philosophical and history was not. For it is, like Alcibiades' narrative, like Proust's, not simply the record of some idiosyncratic things that in fact happened. (You should doubt whether any of it happened as told.) It is, rather, a record, addressed to the reader, of "the sort of thing that might happen" in a human life. And if the reader is not determined to conceive of himself or herself as radically individual, sharing with this lady no relevant responses and possibilities, the reader can take it to be, *mutatis mutandis,* his or her own love story.

But it will be, this philosophical story, quite unlike a philosophical treatise or article on the same topic. For it will show her thoughts arising from pain, from hope, from ambition, from desperation—in short, from the confusion in which thought is born, more often than not. It will present them, these offspring, all wrinkled and naked and bloody, not washed and dressed up for the nursery photographer. You will be in no doubt as to their provenance, and also their fragility. And you will be encouraged to ask how their characteristics are explained by the particular desires and needs that engendered them. This should by no means make you dismiss the question of truth or treat them as mere subjective reportings. But when you entertain them as candidates for truth, you will be able to ask hard, suspicious questions about background conditions that might have biased the inquiry, questions about what bias is in such an inquiry, and what objectivity. While you are made suspicious, however, you are to feel in another way reassured. For seeing the blood and hearing the cries, you are to know that these babies did come out of somewhere real, that they are live, ordinary children of human life and action, not some philosophical changelings simply masquerading as children. For changelings never go so far as to masquerade the pain of being born.

I shall embark, then, on this rather confused lady's philosophical love story. I am not certain that I am entitled now to write it. It is not 1982 now. Though once again it is cold and white and silent, and oranges (grapefruits, I believe, as well) are dying all over Florida. It is not 1982; and I am not, like her, mourning. In fact, I have been happily sitting in my kitchen this afternoon drinking tea and reading Dante. Just now I was in the middle of writing a love letter to somebody else. The title "Love and the Individual" is, I now see, ambiguous. I took it as a question about the individuality of the object of love. But it also forces me to raise questions about my own individuality and continuity from one love to the next. As Wittgenstein said, the world of the happy man is different from the world of the unhappy man. Can the inhabitants of two such different worlds really be the same person?

My discontinuity from her is not, however, total. For the radio's mournful announcement, last night, of the demise of fruit, the solemnly intoned tale of moribund grapefruit and of orange juice cut off before its prime, pulled me oddly back inside her old tale of the demise of a love. And today the newspaper photograph of a young orange wrapped in a sheath of ice reminded me of a sentence she once wrote: "When the light of Socrates 'appears all at once' for Alcibiades, it is the sort of light that, radiantly poured round the aspiring body, may seal or freeze it in, like a coat of ice. That is its beauty." I don't altogether approve of that, but it moves me. Now, in spite of my lack of sympathy with her more apocalyptic and self-indulgent responses, despite my desire to treat the topic playfully and not to weep over it all, I find myself once again in her presence, seeing her and seeing the image of him that she then saw, that image more like a lightning bolt than a sun (as Alcibiades knew) in its power to strike, even as it brings illumination.

You shall have her story, then—but as I tell it. And you must, therefore, be on your guard. For you can see by now what an interest I have in making it come out one way rather than another. So that it will be both true and morally acceptable that I survived and am here cheerfully replacing. That, loving a different individual, I am myself the same one, and not too bad either. For I have an interest in being her heir and continuant, rather than a mere two-year-old. And if I shall say, further, that to survive the death of love is not just logically possible but also morally best, if I even contend that the best conception of love is one that permits some sort of replacement of individuals, you must remember that these arguments, though placed in her mouth, may be shaped by the fact that I have just been writing a love letter to somebody else. It is not only in the context of war that survivor guilt is a useful explanatory concept.

Now, guarding against her and yet pulled by the power of her love, half toughly warding her off, half longing to know her passion, in the manner of cautious Dante before the spirit of Francesca, I approach her. What can I do but what he did: call her "by the love that leads" her? And like some mad, disorderly dove, through the dark air of that malignant winter, she comes before me, "directed by desire," quite gentle in her grief. I'm not like that.

I said that her search through the books was Aristotelian. This was inexact. Augustine's *Tolle lege* was, far more, the motivating hope. She wanted to have, right then, a text that would change the course of her life from damnation to salvation, a text that would set her on the path to beatitude, lifting her above the winds of longing onto a promontory from which she could survey all the world and her own place in it. She was not quite but almost *nel mezzo dal cammin,* as they liked to conceive of it in those unhealthy times, so it seemed about right that some salvation should come her way.

But there are no sacred books in Tallahassee. So what could she do but see what was in fact in the guest room, taking a book at random and reading her fate in its pages? (And how clear it was in any case that she desired the salvation not of religion but of love.)

Her hosts had filled this particular guest room with books by and about members of the Bloomsbury group. This did not seem promising. She would have preferred Proust. She knew little about the people of Bloomsbury, but she thought they were probably well suited to their Diotiman surroundings. She knew enough, at any rate, to suspect them of excessive gentility of feeling and a strong interest in the replacement of one person by the next. It was, then, with no very high expectations that she selected from the shelf nearest the windows a large volume of Dora Carrington's letters and diaries and turned (hoping against hope, I suspect, for something tragic enough to suit her) to the end, though ignorant, as yet, of the nature of Carrington's.

There she came upon the following entry. (She memorized much of it at once involuntarily and carried it about with her for some months as a ready source of tears, but I have had to get hold of it from the library. And when I read it I find that very little of it is even familiar. This makes me wonder.)

No one will every know the special perfectness of Lytton. The jokes when he was gay. "The queen of the East has vanished." I believe you eat my nail scissors and then at lunch pretending to play a grand fugue before we got up. And the jokes about the coffee never coming because I stayed so long eating cheese. Sometimes I thought how wasteful to let these jokes fly like swallows across the sky. But one couldn't write them down. We couldn't have been happier together. For every mood of his instantly made me feel in the same mood. All gone. . . . And now there is nobody, darling Lytton, to make jokes with about Tiber and the horse of the ocean, no one to read me Pope in the evenings, no one to walk on the terrace. No one to write letters to, oh my very darling Lytton.

. . . What point is there now in what I see every day, in conversations, jokes, beautiful visions, pains, even nightmares? Who can I tell them to, who will understand? One cannot find such another character as Lytton and curious as it may seem to G. B. these friends that he talks of as consolers and substitutes for Lytton cannot be the same, and it is *exactly* what Lytton meant to me that matters.

One cannot live on memories when the point of one's whole life was the interchange of love, ideas, and conversation.

She felt that she had written this entry, so directly did it express her own mourning. She sat there, somewhat absurdly weeping into the book, and the phrase "spe-

cial perfectness" conjured up an image so concrete that she shuddered at its nearness and wept again. (I find it difficult to describe this.)

Here, she thought, was something worth reading about love. Call it the view of
Alcibiades. Call it (right now) her own. For she too knew those consolers and their
games. She knew, and all too well, that what she loved and did not have was, as
this woman said, a special perfectness, an exact, nonrepeatable thing that could
not be found again. There was a value and a knowledge that were inseparable from
this particular relation. To try to recapture or replace them would be as futile as
to go hunting for a joke after it has gone by. And she thought of their jokes.

Well, what was this individuality? In what did it consist, according to Carrington? (You now begin to see how this lady is: she goes on thinking at all times. She
won't simply cry, she will ask what crying consists in. One tear, one argument:
that's how her life goes on.) Carrington had, in this passage, several distinct,
though related, quarrels with her consolers. Three, to be exact. First, the friends
do not seem to grasp the fact that unique, nonrepeatable properties are essential
to love. They talk of others who could be substitutes. This implies that they believe
that there are certain general features of Lytton that could be instantiated in someone else—perhaps in someone with similar values and character. But Carrington
knows that, in the sense that counts for loving, there is not such another character
as Lytton. That nobody else makes those wonderful jokes or has the power to
transform the ordinary by that precise sort of magic. Sameness of species might
be good enough for Aristotle; it is not what she wants. It is that exact thing, unique
and (as she too well knows) transient. ("Death," she writes on the same page, "is
unfortunately *not* incomprehensible. It is all too easy to understand." The end of
an affair brings similar epistemic problems, with less dignity.)

Beyond this, second, she knows that some of the things she most loves in Lytton
are not in him at all; they are properties of his relation to her. There was a special
affinity of mood, a rightness of humor, a mutuality of understanding, that are
themselves nonrepeatable values, not to be searched for by any rational method,
but just found—as when one of Aristophanes' jagged people suddenly comes
upon the jagged other half that perfectly fits his or her own odd shape. Surely,
surely, part of what so moved her in Carrington's diary was that so much of it was
private and unintelligible to her; it gestured toward a density of intimate communication that no person outside the relation could altogether grasp. For she
knew, like Carrington, the dreadful isolation that comes with the knowledge that
nobody will laugh with her in just that way or respond with that special rightness
to her responses. It occurred to her to remember many things. These thoughts
took some time. She did not find it possible to include them in a numbered list
of any kind.

And beyond all this, she thought—pulling herself back to the list, for she had
said there were three items, and in her stubbornness of character she was not going
to let anything stop her before she reached three—beyond all this, there is their
history. Even if there might have been, in the first place, more than one person
who could have aroused the same dimension of love in Carrington (a fact that in
her own case she very much doubted), such another person could not possibly
step in as a substitute now. For now the relationship had been enriched by years
of intimacy, of conversation, of letters written and received. One could say that

the love is in large measure constituted out of this history, out of the habit, for example, of telling every experience and of finding a fresh joy from each experience in the telling. Their relational rightness may have been in part a matter of initial fit, but history and its intimacy is a large part of what constitutes it as this deep, this irreplaceable.

Nobody else will ever know his special perfectness. One cannot find such another character. And if I chose to describe the images that filled her as, her list of three points exhausted, she reached Carrington's uncomprising conclusion, you would perhaps understand her better, and the love that was so great a part of what she then was. I do not so choose. I plan that you shall know nothing of the concrete individuality of her beloved, of their relation, their history, the immediate reasons for her grief. There are many reasons for this. Some I won't mention; some are connected with the Aristotelian point about what makes a story philosophical. But not least among the reasons is the thought that if I allowed myself to become the full companion of her wanderings through memory and pain and wonder, if I allowed the power of that individuality to overwhelm me as it then intermittently overwhelmed her, I would not, perhaps, go on with the letter I am writing. And, equally clearly, I would not continue writing this paper or story, whichever it is. There is a price, I think, for writing about love's fragility; this is a certain refusal of a certain sort of knowledge or recognition of that fragility. Could it be that to write about love, even to write humbly and responsively, is itself a device to control the topic, to trap and bind it like an animal—so, of necessity, an unloving act? And if I could set him down in writing, every movement and look and virtue translated into words, if I could do this without in fact ceasing to write, would I not have most perfectly, most finally controlled him and so banished the power of that love? Seen this way, my inability to do so looks like an accidental grace.

What I am after, it seems, is a noncontrolling art of writing that will leave the writer more receptive to love than before. That will not be guilty of writing's usual ruthlessness toward life. For the fashionable idea that writing is a form of creative play, and that everything is, after all, writing, seems to me to ignore the plain fact that much of human life is not playful at all, or even creative. And writing's relation to that nonplayful side of life is deeply ambiguous. Writing records it, to be sure. But even as it does so it goes to work fixing, simplifying, shaping. So it seems difficult for it not to be the enemy and denier of mystery and of love. Overwhelmed by the beauty of some landscape, the power of some emotion, I run for my pad of paper; and if I can put it into words, set it down, I breathe a sigh of relief. A kind of humble passivity has been banished. Writing, then, seems not to be everything, but to be opposed to something—say, waiting. Beckett tries to find a way to use language to undo, unravel the simplifications and refusals of language, undermining stories with a story, words with words. If I were not so determined to survive, I'd try to write like that.

These are thoughts she might have had. They don't entirely suit me. She probably reads Heidegger too, heaven help her. I'm getting too close to her, like Dante. But for me, there's only one angel in the picture, and the only salvation might be to be as thoroughly damned as possible. Now, as I watch her weeping, uncontrollably at this point, into the pillow on which she has placed her book, I feel with her what it is to love an individual and to be loved, as well, by one. And for fear of saying something individual of my own—for it would describe him and thus violate the canons I have laid down—I simply say:

> Oh lasso,
> quanti dolci pensier, quanto disio
> meno costoro al doloroso passo!

> Alas,
> how many sweet thoughts, how much desire
> led them to this miserable condition.

But even as she wept, she began to wonder whether Carrington had really had the last word against her consolers. It was a terrible last word; she had read far enough to see to what conclusion it led. She wanted to know, so did it frighten her, whether Carrington had been altogether fair. (For fairness in argument seemed a possible way of evading that conclusion.) It was clear as one read on that one of the consolers' arguments did precisely address the conception of individuality relevant to her love and blamed her for in effect misunderstanding the very thing on which she herself laid most stress. She seems to find all of Lytton's individuality, all of what he really is, in the unique, the evanescent, the relational. And yet, they argue, Lytton was a person with a definite moral and intellectual character and a definite set of values, commitments, and aspirations. How could she claim to love Lytton if she did not love and see the central importance of these elements, which are a far deeper part of him than the fact that on a particular day he talked about cheese? All of this had promising implications for mourning and the continuation of life. But for now, what began to impress her was this idea that the extreme romantic view of love (or Aristophanic, since we can trace it back at least to those unique jagged other halves), this view that holds that love is above all a matter of contingent particular fit, may not contain a deep enough conception of the individual, precisely because it slights these repeatable elements.

These elements are, of course, really at the heart of Carrington's love. (So, clearly, at the heart of her own.) For consider her talk of the exchange of ideas and conversation. Or consider even her sentence "One cannot find such another character as Lytton." One does not, she thought, use such a sentence of someone whom one does not admire, and admire on account of certain virtues and values. What one means in saying it (what she herself meant when she thought it especially apt for her case) is that this person is exceptionally good in ways in which one believes it important to be good. Alcibiades said it of Socrates, not confining his love to the (repeatable) virtues, but insisting that they were a very central and essential part of what he loved when he loved Socrates. In loving he was aspiring; he was not simply seeking his other half. He could not have said the same thing of Agathon, except as a joke. How could Carrington claim to love Lytton without understanding how central it was to his being Lytton that he had and lived by certain values, that indeed he built his life around a certain picture of value?

But now something intriguing seemed to follow. For in that case, as the consolers correctly argue, there is something that has survived his death, something that she can continue to love and cherish although it is no longer realized in that particular life. Listen to how she answers them. "They say one must keep your standards and values of life alive. But how can I, when I only kept them for you? Everything was for you. I loved life, because you made it so perfect, and now there is no one left to make jokes with, or to talk about Racine and Molière and talk of plans and work and people." They ought to reply, she thought, excited, that this utterance reveals a deep confusion about love and about Lytton. For it is crucial to his being him that he is a person who does have values and standards, who loves valuable things for their own sake. How can she claim it is Lytton that she loves, if she has not tried to share the sense of what Racine means for him, if she makes of Racine just a jagged idiosyncrasy, a piece of contingent fit? These consolers, she began to think, had a point. For, clearly, she herself did not love the man she loved just as someone who was in arbitrary ways right for her, but more because he was an angel. This is to say, radiantly good and fine in ways in which it was important to her also to be good and fine. That is to say, uncompromised in his pursuit of standards to which she also aspired, loving them for their own sake. (You think you don't know anything about him. Knowing that, you could pick him out from ten million.)

She was by now not weeping but pacing about the room, excited. For it seemed to her that it would be an excellent result for her grief if a richer love of the individual, a love that was most truly a love of the individual, her love let us say, turned out to be based upon an acknowledgment that certain things have intrinsic value which, being repeatable and not idiosyncratic, will survive the death or departure of the individual. That the better one loved this individual the more one would see that there was, in fact, something to live for beyond that person, something connected with the commitments and aspirations on which the love is itself based. And this something could be sought in someone else, even pursued on its own, apart from love. (For like many a recalcitrant pupil of Diotima, this lady, who thought of herself as a hopeless romantic, and was so on Mondays, Wednesdays, and Fridays, also liked to look about for the morally acceptable ways to satisfy her longing for stability. The way of Diotima was not acceptable. But if the truest value of the unique and uniquely loved could turn out also to impart stability to the life that loved it—this would be the best conjuring trick of all. As I warned you, I'm trying a variant of that trick now; trying, by doing justice in writing to love's fragility, to make that very fragility a source of stability for myself.)

The hope of bringing off this argument against Carrington excited her beyond tears. It would require a lot of probing, of debating back and forth—since the powerful appeal of that implacable grief made her deeply suspicious of any such *consolatio philosophiae*. And to be convincing it would have to be done in writing, for she was never convinced by her own thoughts until she saw them fixed.

Where would she begin this assault on Carrington (also, as you see, an assault on the moral superiority of her own death)? She envisaged a statement of the view about value and the superiority of a love based upon repeatable features of commitment and aspiration, followed by a series of objections by Carrington and replies to those objections. For the initial statement she might have thought only of her own love, but so much was she a lover of the general that she could not even try to understand something so particular without holding it up against some philosophical account that would illuminate it, and be illuminated by it. The text that had always seemed to her to describe better than any her own views about love, the text that seemed to her to argue effectively both against Diotima's banishment of individual passion and against Aristophanes' extreme emphasis on other halves was, of course, Plato's *Phaedrus*. She got out a pen and a pad of yellow paper (with which she was always equipped, even in despair), sat down at the desk, and began to write, for herself, the following.

I feel no pity for her now. For she is a very tough lady, as she sits there writing objections and arguments. No longer a timorous dove, but a self-assured, agile professional. Far more like me.

"*A la guerre comme à la guerre,* then," I say to her, as James's Prince, so ambiguously, to Charlotte Stant. "But I am charmed by your courage and almost surprised by my own."

Loving an Individual: Romantic Rightness
and Platonic Aspiration

I. The 'Phaedrus': the best view of love bases it on a view of the individual as essentially constituted by values and aspirations.

This is not a description of what passionate love in general is like. It is a description of the best type of passion. Socrates argues that this sort of "mad" passion for another individual is an essential part of the best human life and the way that passion best figures in a good life. This is also supposed to be the best way in which love loves an individual. Against Lysias, who argues that the person in love never gets to know who the beloved really is, Socrates argues that it is in passion (not all sorts, but this high sort) that one person is most truly able to know and to love another—to love what the other most truly is.

It begins with the recognition of values. Souls are individuated by what they most deeply care about. For example, the Zeus-like type cares most about philosophy and moral value and pursues these two together. To care about these values is the essence of such a soul. We could imagine these people losing their money, their reputation, their youthfulness—and still being essentially the same. We couldn't in the same way imagine them ceasing to care about knowledge or justice. Aristotle says this succinctly: the character and value commitments (as opposed to superficial pleasantness or advantageousness) are what each person is *kath' hauto,* in virtue of himself or herself. To love a person himself or herself, and not the accidental features of a person, is to love that.

The values are recognized in a way that truly involves, even requires, passion. And being passive. The first thing that happens is that the lover is simply, mysteriously, struck by the splendor of the other, the "form truly expressing beauty and nobility." He is dazzled, aroused, illuminated. His soul is compared, in its arousal, to the gums of a teething child. He is also compared to a plant, watered and nourished by the presence of the other's beauty and excellence. What he experiences is nothing like cold respect or mere admiration. And yet, it is crucial that in the beauty that arouses him he sees a sign of the values that he cherishes and pursues. What he is always doing is "following the trace of his god." The beauty of the other is not, even in the begining, seen as mere superficial attractiveness but as the radiance of a committed soul. Awe and wonder are essential components of his love.

The point is, he wouldn't be in love really if the other didn't answer to his aspirations. Love and sexuality (at least in good people) are themselves selective and aspiring. What excites the passion, makes him shudder and tremble, is the perception of something that answers to the desires of his soul. Passion loves *that:* it demands an object that is radiant with value. What it wants from the person, ultimately, is a mutual exchange of love and ideas that will be a seamless part of each one's pursuit of their central aspiration.

Aspiration, on the other hand, becomes in this account something not detached and self-sufficient, but needy, vulnerable, bound up with motion and receptivity. They cannot pursue their values without the inspiration and nourishment of love. In order to be moved toward value, each soul must, first of all, be open and receptive. The crucial first step toward truth and knowledge comes when the stream of beauty that enters in at the eyes is allowed to moisten and melt the solid dry elements of the soul. Only then does the soul begin to have insight into itself and its aims. And as time goes on, with "unfeigned passion," both touching and conversing, they "follow up the trace," each in the other, of their own god, coming to know one another, themselves, and true value at the same time.

And where, in all this, is the individual? The essential individuality of each is to be found in the fineness of soul, the character and commitments that make each the follower of a certain god. Since these patterns of commitment are repeatable and not idiosyncratic, the account implies that there might have been, at least at the beginning, more than one person of the appropriate soul type who might have answered to the lover's inner needs. It is also plausible that a single life might (in the wake of a death or a departure) come to contain a plurality of similar loves. And yet there are limits. First, such people will not be easily found. Then, the person must also have a more mysterious attractiveness that compels and overwhelms. Next, there is, too, the evident importance of history: the deepening of the relationship over time is clearly one of the sources of its value as a source of knowledge, self-knowledge, and motivation. The accidents in this way draw close to the core. Finally, against Carrington's consolers we must notice that Plato's account does not allow the bereaved person to go on pursuing the loved one's values alone, in the total absence of love; at least, they cannot be pursued nearly as well. The bereaved person has to wait to be struck again.

Still, there is room both for personal survival and for replacement. The lover will not feel that he is nothing at all without the love, has nothing to live for, can't go on being the same person. For his love was based on things that endure—that are, we might say, "bigger than both of us." To have a new love is crucial to the continued pursuit of philosophy, or whatever, and if what the lost love loved was that, it is natural that the bereaved person should try to perpetuate and further the goals of the relationship.

She paused, relatively satisfied. Here was a challenge to Carrington subtle enough that even that hopeless romantic ought to take it seriously. But she was not really convinced, as she reread what she had written, that it did justice to the things that had moved her in Carrington's account of Lytton. For didn't this view imply, after all, that one could in principle advertise for a lover, say, in the *New York Review of Books?* (Zeus-type soul, committed to philosophical and ethical values, seeks excellent man with similar aspirations . . .) And if the list could be complete enough, and if there were in addition some reliable way of making sure that the applicant really had the virtues he purported to have, then didn't the view imply that the successful applicant would be her passionate lover? And wasn't this absurd? Plato is less crude than the advertisement on the epistemological issue, for he insists that real knowledge of habits and ways requires a context of intimacy. You cannot tell beforehand: you go by that trace; you allow yourself, in considerable ignorance, to be melted. But it looked as if the real presence of these general traits was, in his view, sufficient for passionate love and sufficiently defined love's object. And this seemed bad or absurd enough. It was not only epistemology, surely, that prevented her from taking out such an advertisement.

I tend to agree with her here. When I first said that I would write on this topic, I tried to draw up a list of the repeatable properties I admired and aspired to; I rated against this list of properties men I had loved, and also men that I plausibly might have but hadn't. Not surprisingly, the men I had seriously loved came out with the highest rating. But I knew that I had made up the list by thinking about them. Like Aristotle's flexible ruler, this list looked posterior to the perception of concrete particulars. Though it might summarize these, it "bent to the shape of the stone, and was not fixed." It was quite clear that a new lover who lacked some of the properties on this list and had others would not, just on that account, be rejected. If I loved him I'd change the list. The question then would be, was I discovering something about myself that had been true all along (a kind of Platonic inner list), or was I really changing the list? I saw no clear reason to prefer the first alternative.

Her sketch, she saw, had not gone far enough. She was left still feeling the absurdity of Platonism, the dignity and truth of Carrington's repudiation. She would have to go on with the second part of her plan: a real debate between Carrington and the *Phaedrus*. She would imagine the romantic objections one by one, giving Plato in each case the strongest possible reply. The scholastic and numerical look of what she then wrote testifies to the violence of her confusion.

(When, much later, I first felt desire for another man, she became violent in a different way. I hadn't realized she was still there; or I thought that she had by now become me. She, or the he that she carried around inside her, the internal person who had, like Proust's Albertine, walked down into her heart and taken up residence there, a jealous and disturbing guest, kept me awake all night for several days with what felt like a series of kicks to the head and stomach. It was later diagnosed as viral labyrinthitis. But I knew.)

II. Romantic objections and Platonic replies.

The romantic opponent has several different types of objections to make to Plato. Some are objections to the particular contents of a Platonic list of valuable properties; some pertain to his use or construal of that list; some, finally, are objections to the entire idea of basing love on a list of properties.

A. *Objections to the content of Plato's list.*

Objection 1. The Platonic list enumerates the individual's commitments and aspirations. But a lot of the valuable properties of an individual are not values. Intelligence, a sense of humor, warmth: these are not commitments and aspirations, and yet they are very valuable, arguably central, to the individuality of the person who has them.

Objection 2. Furthermore, the properties on the list are all high-minded moral and intellectual properties. But some of the repeatable features that will be pertinent to my loves will not be of this sort. They may be morally (aspirationally) irrelevant, such as a certain coloring, or height, or ethnic background. They may even have a negative relation to aspiration. Carrington's persistent choice of men who belittled her artistic ambitions and treated her like a child surely worked against her aspirations, and yet it is a salient pattern in her loves and an important part of the individuality of those she loves.

Objection 3. The Platonic list stresses shared aspiration and similarity of commitment. But some of the properties that will be most valued in a beloved person are properties that are not shared; often they are valued precisely because the lover lacks them. Carrington, not well educated in literary matters, values Lytton's eloquence and knowledge. A shy and nervous person, she values someone who has the ability to tell marvelous fantastic jokes.

Objection 4. There are far too few properties on Plato's list. He says that there are twelve types of souls, correlated with twelve forms of aspiration. But in fact the properties that are relevant to aspiration are much more subtly demarcated, more numerous, and susceptible of more varied combination.

Reply to Objection 1. It is indeed striking how many valuable properties do have to do with a person's values and commitments. We don't value a person's kindness, or courage, unless we believe that the person is in some sense committed to behaving in that way, values that way of behaving. If it's just accidental or sporadic, it won't be valued in the same way, and it won't enter in the same way into an account of what that person really is.

Reply to Objection 2. Plato does not want to insist that all loves fit his account. This is a normative, not a descriptive, view of human love. Of course there are people who are repeatedly attracted to some arbitrary property, or even to evil. Aristotle points out that the first is characteristic of immature people, of whatever age; the second is clearly an illness, though the Greeks have little to say about it. Furthermore, if we find a repeated feature in our loves that seems aspirationally irrelevant but is ubiquitous and rather deep, it may turn out that its deep meaning for us is, after all, not unconnected with our aspirations and values.

Reply to Objection 3. These diversities, if we press them, are rooted in a similarity. Their different careers are complementary ways of pursuing a commitment to artistic creation. Bloomsbury is nothing if not a community of aspiration based upon shared values. It would have been a different matter had the commitments been altogether unrelated, or even antithetical. Then, however, we would feel that the difference was a disadvantage to the love; we would doubt whether they could fully love one another for what each one really was. Plato's soul types are very general forms of aspiration. He nowhere rules out complementary differences of this sort, and the differences in age and experience between the lover and beloved make some such differences inevitable.

Reply to Objection 4. Here Carrington seems to have a point. Being a philosopher is, for example, far too coarse a property to explain the shape of my aspiration and therefore my aspiring love. It all depends on what kind of philosopher, and what the view of philosophy is. Furthermore, the combination of values that I will go for in making up a plan for a good life will almost surely be heterogeneous enough not to correspond to any one of Plato's types. But we should be wary of pressing this specificity too far, for one thing Plato's approach does permit is an informative account of the unity among the loves of a single person.

So far, she saw, Plato had not had to give very much ground before the objections. His essential conception remained untouched. Carrington, however, had barely begun to state her case.

B. *Objections to the use or construal of the list.*

Objection 5. The list, insofar as it suggests that I can go out into the world looking (or advertise in the *New York Review*) for someone with, for example, justice or wisdom, fails to capture the most characteristic ways in which the deeper aspiration-properties present themselves to our awareness. They do not march up to us wearing placards; they make themselves known through other related and more obvious properties, through images, masks, and disguises. Often I will know only that this person is beautiful and exhilarating in some way I cannot yet describe.

Reply to Objection 5. This point was not ignored by Plato. Indeed, he insists on it. It is in fact one of his main reasons for thinking that you can't understand values like justice or wisdom in yourself or in the world without personal love. For only personal love draws a person into the exchange of choices and thoughts that will suffice to reveal, over time, the nature of these values. Love itself begins not so much with these values, which are hard to discern, as with the experience of being struck by a mysterious kind of beauty. [She tried not to think of the way the sunlight from the doorway flamed at the edges of his shoulders and ringed his head.] Even if the values are apprehended through these indirect traces, they are still what is loved. A more serious point lurks here, however, a point about how beloved properties are really individuated and which the really relevant ones are. What's to say that looking a certain way in the sunlight is merely a mode in which brilliance and beneficence make themselves visible?

Objection 6. A list of value properties is something fixed, fixed in advance of the discovery of the loved one. I am a Zeus-like soul, and what I want is to match up with another similar soul. I may as yet not know what type I am, but according to Plato I am already one type or another. It is there for me to discover, partly by following up the traces of my god in the soul of the person I love. But in real life my aspirations and values are not this fixed. I operate with an open-ended, revisable list, and I frequently must decide to commit myself to one thing or another, to pursue one value rather than another. When I love in the aspiring way, it is as much a matter of decision as of discovery. The choice between one potential love and another can feel, and be, like a choice of a way of life, a decision to dedicate oneself to these values rather than these. The choice to devote myself to that love is a choice to love and cultivate those elements in myself.

Reply to Objection 6. This objection has force, but it is not an objection to the list per se, or even to the idea of regarding the list of value properties as normative for particular choices of lovers. It just points out that not all my norms and values are set; some are still evolving. If we think about how this evolution works, we find that it has very much the same shape as rational deliberation elsewhere in life. In neither case does the deliberation proceed in a vacuum. When I think about what, for me, will count as living well, I hold certain commitments firm in order to deliberate on others, or I hold the general conception of one element firm while I ask, more concretely, what will count as realizing that. Even so, in making choices in love I recognize and hold firm some general values while deliberating about others. So the objection does not even show that an antecedent list is a bad guide; it just warns us about holding too fixedly to it. We have, then, a friendly amendment.

She paused. Plato was enormously strong. She was surprised at the strength of the replies she was finding on his behalf.

And here she noticed, all at once, that this well-ordered scholastic questioning, this probing scrutiny of love with its numbered objections and replies, could not claim to constitute an external and neutral investigation of the phenomenon that resided in her heart (and in the obscure connections between that organ and other portions of the world distant, perhaps, in space, but dwelling in close proximity). For as she investigated, the investigation was effecting a change in her heart, was calming its grief and loosening its connections. It was opening a clear, high space over and around her ribs, a space that, being empty of the internal presence of the loved person, was filled with air and light. She thought of Proust's narrator, trembling before the equanimity of his own heart as before a deadly snake; for he knew that a life in which his love and his suffering for Albertine no longer existed would be a life in which he no longer existed. She too felt panic. Am I really myself right now? she asked herself, hoping that some tears would come to prove it.

How clear it is to me that there is no neutral posture of reflection from which one can survey and catalogue the intuitions of one's heart on the subject of love, holding up the rival views to see how well they fit the intuitions—no activity of philosophizing that does not stand in some determinate relation to the love. The relations can be of many kinds; they are not always, as here, inhibitory and consoling. For the *Phaedrus* shows, precisely, that a certain high type of philosophical activity may be called into being by, and in turn express and nourish, the energy and beneficence and subtle insight of happy love. And the insights gained in passion can best be pursued collaboratively, in the context of the love. (As in Phaedrus's fantasy, in the *Symposium,* of an army composed of pairs of lovers, a fantasy made reality in the Sacred Band. We might by analogy imagine a philosophy department similarly constructed, dedicated to the understanding of love. I wonder what the Thebans did when they broke up.) On the other hand, as in her case, the philosophy might, as here, emerge from and reinforce the desire for distancing and safety; it might effect and express a transformation of the perceptions and intuitions of love, and even of the lover, inasmuch as the relation seems to her to be partly constitutive of her identity. The object of my scrutiny, Heraclitean (or rather Cratylan even) is never the same the minute you begin to step into it, even once.

In addition to the question who shall write about love, we have still on hand our old question how. I gave you some reasons for thinking that a narrative might be truer than a treatise or article on the subject. I can add to these now the argument that narrative writing, more than standard philosophical writing, seems to express the author's own acknowledgment of the power and importance of particular love and to elicit from the reader a similar response. (My experience right now is different from hers; as she is moving further from her love through scholastic argument, I risk being quite immersed. I can't write this story, however abstract it is and however much concerned wtih thought and argument, without launching myself into those currents.)

But the point is not simple, as I see it. For stories too impose their own simplifications. They demand that something happen, that there be a plot with a beginning and a middle and an end. They demand singleness where in life there is multiplicity, statement where there is indeterminacy, description where there are indescribable, undepictable things. So they do not escape the general suspicions I have expressed about writing. In some ways philosophy might fare better; for it follows the inquiry wherever it leads, without insisting on drama, or interest, or endings. Proust's idea was that only through the focusing and sharpening power of narrative art could the messy matter of life assume a shape, become really real and true. I feel the force of that. But I see even more clearly the other side, and here I turn to Beckett: art, especially narrative art, forces life to assume a shape rather than letting it be in its formlessness; forces it to demand an ending where one way of loving might be to forbear to do that. This forces us to ask, not just who should write about love, not just how, but also whether.

As she took note of her own forgetfulness, her heart shivered. And as it shivered, it cracked like the ice on top of a stream, and the currents of her feeling, like the liquid in one of Plato's melted souls, welled up. Outside, oranges were dying, wrapped in their coats of ice. Inside, she could not find ice enough to halt her own demise. For she knew, and with certainty, that Carrington was right. There was no life for her without that love, no continuation of its meanings without that particular person, radiant and separate. Carrington's diary goes on: "Human beings seem to me divided into those who can say 'I live for myself alone' and those who know that 'without this person or thing I could not live.'" Once Plato's souls were melted, how could they help dying of a loss? She knew, and with certainty, that she was not one of the self-sufficient ones.

What do I mean by writing "She knew, and with certainty"? Not that she had come up with new and clever arguments destined to refute the skeptic on the plane of intellect. Argument, indeed, had led her to the opposite conclusion. I mean that she felt her stomach rising up into her mouth. That she felt like one of those Greek tragic unfortunates to whom someone has given a poisoned cloak that causes the wearer to sweat blood. The half of her had gone out, the next minute, into the empty space where he was and was floating around with him in the still moonlight above the golf course, lightly carried on the wind. For she saw how beautiful he was, and she did not want to be apart from him. All this is knowledge of love. And all this is happening now to me.

"Amor ch'al cor gentil ratto s'apprende," love that quickly takes hold in the gentle heart, is taking hold in mine as I watch, showing it to be more gentle than hard. I am, I tell you, the visitor and watcher of her grief, and yet as I record her knowledge I begin to have it. Francesca says:

> Amor, ch'a nullo amato amar perdona,
> mi prese del costui piacer si forte,
> che, come vedi, ancor non m'abbandona

> Love, who absolves no beloved one from loving,
> seized me with such a strong desire for him
> that, as you see, it has not left me yet.

I want only to watch. But she is seeing him. Her watcher sees him too. I can hardly distinguish the spectator I am from the one she is. She wants Carrington to win the debate now. She wants to get all the way to that conclusion, so she won't be happier than love is.

I'm very tired, and I'm shaken by all this. I haven't finished my letter. What's strangest is that I'm more worn out than she is. I'll tell you what's going to happen now. She's going to write some more. Can you believe it? She will go all the way back to her original list of three objections, calling them, now, Objections 7, 8, and 9; she writes them out, putting Carrington's case with new force. She adds two more she has just thought up to help her. One charges the Platonist list with making love seem more determinate and reason-based, less mysterious, than it is; the other with making it too active and will-governed. I don't feel like reproducing them; you know the sort of thing she will say. And I suppose you expect that now she will get exhausted and go to sleep despairing. Not this lady. Her father died putting his papers into his briefcase; shriveled by cancer to half his former weight, he never lay down once. Her father's father once served on a jury. After ten days of deliberation he came home: the jury couldn't agree; they had ordered a new trial. He walked into the house and said to his wife, "Those were eleven of the stubbornest men I have ever seen." Now you know what you're dealing with. Do you think a lady from that background—and a philosopher on top of it all—is going to give up the argument just because it is 3:00 A.M. and most of the oranges are dead? Do you suppose, furthermore, she is going to let Carrington, and death, have the last word? No, she's going to fight it out to the end, fighting against that love with Platonist replies about value, pen in her hand and a stubborn foot in his face.

This is love she's dealing with. Can't she ever stop writing?

I won't reproduce it all. I'll give you the last paragraphs. Then I'll go to sleep, or faint like Dante.

I propose, then, a new construction of the individual as object of love. We can, I think, combine the best elements of the *Phaedrus* with several concessions to the strongest romantic objections. We begin by insisting with Plato that the best kind of love, the kind that loves the individual for what he or she really is, is a love of character and values. But we make some alterations in the way the *Phaedrus* presents the search for character. To the first six objections we make the concessions already noted, concerning variety of properties and flexibility of choice. The final five require us to make a more substantial modification. We say something like this: in any love that is based upon character, the lovers will also see in one another, and truly love, many relational and nonrepeatable properties. They will not love these in a merely incidental way; they will come to see one another as wholes, not as composites of essence and accident, so that the nonrepeatable will be just as intrinsic to the love as the repeatable. The history, too will come to have more than an enabling and extrinsic value; they will love it for its own sake too, rejecting even a substitution that could *(per impossibile)* preserve the same trust and knowledge. Carrington will love Lytton's character and standards; she will also love his jokes, their letters, their years of intimacy.

We can still maintain, however, that the *Phaedrus* elements take priority, in the following way. We know that to be a good object of love, a person must have these repeatable character traits and not these—for example, be committed to justice and not injustice. We don't in the same way care which lovable accidents the person has. There have to be some; but insofar as they are morally neutral, it seems not to matter what they are (whether he makes jokes about cheese or some other jokes).

This construction permits of real mourning; for there has been a real loss of an intrinsic value that will never come again. But it also entails that not everything is lost when a particular love is lost. The *Phaedrus* elements will sustain the person and provide continuity from one love to the next. Because both lovers love the values for themselves, it will not be disloyal to engage in such a search.

This proposal has not made things altogether easier for the bereaved person. In one way, it has made them harder—by insisting on the felicitous combination of two elements that are hard enough to find singly. A few people are really good; a few are truly pleasing and "right"; very few indeed are both. The romantic can take comfort from the thought that Platonism, so modified, has actually made things worse.

Now she's going to sleep at last, feeling victorious. She's not going to die, not her. Me? As Dante says, and Virgil's Dido before him, "Conosco i segni de l'antica fiamma." "Agnosco veteris vestigia flammae." I recognize those traces.

It's morning now. When morning came in Florida, she went running on the golf course. For even when she had been thinking of death it never occurred to her not to be healthy. The cover of snow was thawing under a cheerful Florida sun. She ran, as often, to the tune of the March to the Scaffold from Berlioz's *Symphonie Fantastique,* which she could conjure up in her head when she wished to go on, but in a tragic way. She ran from one fairway to the next, aware that she did not know the way back to her hosts' house but convinced that the numbers would bring her back in safety. She noticed the opulent ugliness of the bordering houses and remembered true beauty. She did not want to go on. She went on. And as the frozen ground began to thaw beneath her feet, the Berlioz march paused briefly. A head, flaming in the doorway. The unhappy lover heard once more from a distant place, tender and absent, the music of his only beloved. It came and hovered over the guillotine, the angel standing. And then the rapid cymbal clashes came to end it. She went on, as she thought she might. Someone went on; she thought that it was her.

When I first saw him, he was walking down the sun-streaked hallway, laughing and talking, his whole body fiercely lit up from behind by the light from the door. He looked to me like Turner's Angel Standing in the Sun, or like a counterpart good angel, victorious but tender, beneficent in power. And was there, within that remarkable and dangerous radiance, a division to be found between repeatable value properties and idiosyncratic accidents? Or was it all one seamless "perfectness"? In spite of all her constructing, there still seems to me to be no clear answer to this question. So much depends on the use you intend to make of it. And now I don't want to use it to forget. I would like to want that, but I don't. "Amor, ch'a nullo amato amar perdona"—love who lets no loved one off the hook—"mi prese del constui piacer sì forte, che, come vedi, ancor non m'abbandona." I'm in the story now, floating around. "Amor condusse noi ad una morte. Caina attende chi a vita ci spense." Love brought us to one death; Caina waits for the one who took our life.

Who am I, then, truly? Am I Francesca, the dead one, carried on the winds, dead of her love and loving on in death? Or am I, as seems more likely, the one who was responsible for her death and the death of her love, for whose callousness, for whose happiness, the icy pit of traitors is the just reward? I used to be able to distinguish myself from her, my narrative voice from hers. I was the bright, wary, slightly tough, optimistic one, the one who made jokes, who was happy, who was writing a love letter, who had survived to love again through her Platonic commitment to general values. She was the fragile one, in mourning for her loss, tossed on the currents of confused desire. Then I, sympathizing, came like Dante close to her, and the intensity of her devotion put my salvation to shame. And now: haven't we changed places? There she goes, running along the melted fairway, listening to heaven knows what romantic music. But she goes quite toughly on, thinking and running. She has survived. She is well on her way to being me. I, now, am mourning, now I feel the force of the past upon me, I am no different from her; I will not finish a love letter to somebody else; I'll be the individual constituted by her love.

I refuse to be happier than love is.

I didn't expect the story to end like this. My writing didn't have the same result for me as hers did for her, clearly. Perhaps because it was a different kind of writing. There is much more to be said about the connection between these experiences and ethical objectivity. But I am too immersed to say it. I'm seeing a "form truly expressing beauty and nobility." It's like being one of those fishermen in their light-drowned boat.

Did I find what I wanted, then, the noncontrolling art of writing?

I write only what occurs to me now. It won't look this way tomorrow. Tomorrow I'll see my current lover. Who is an individual. With many repeatable (and even repeated) properties, and some that are unique. We'll have dinner in a good restaurant, and I'll tell jokes about this paper and its strange effect upon my mood. I'll say how happy I am. It will be true.

"Caina attende chi a vita ci spense."

What ending did you expect? Did you think I would collapse, or die? Remember, I'm the one who wrote this down. Remember, this is writing you're reading.

"Love, and be silent."

Endnote

The essay is an experiment. The whole-hearted pursuit of this project seemed to me to require it. The volume's persistent question about the relationship between fiction and philosophical commentary takes here a new shape. And the question that lurks in the background of several of the essays (above all "Perceptive Equilibrium," "Narrative Emotions," and "Steerforth's Arm")—the question about the ethical stance of the author, and how appropriate that stance is to the immersed perceptions of life—here becomes a central theme. Proust and James in their different ways suggest that the life of the literary artist, or rather the life that this artist sets down on the page, is life more fully lived than life not written can ever be. Beckett suggests that beyond and beneath the cultural simplifications of life embodied in literary patterns of expression is the possibility of a less controlled and perhaps more intimate relation to the world. Dickens, by contrast, suggests that the life embodied in the text is isomorphic, in its oscillation between propriety and love, to a certain sort of good and active life; thus the reading of such a text prepares the way for good life. What should we think here? The heroine attempts to wrestle with this question, considering in turn both standard philosophical writing and literary writing—with much uncertainty.

The position on love that emerges is closely related to the discussions of love and particularity in "Love's Knowledge" and "Steerforth's Arm" and to the discussions of love and reflection in "Flawed Crystals," "Perceptive Equilibrium," and "Steerforth's Arm." But, like the analysis of Plato's *Phaedrus* to which it alludes (*Fragility,* chap. 7), it places more emphasis than any of those essays does on the role of aspiration and wonder in love. Like "Flawed Crystals" and "Steerforth's Arm," however, it also insists on the importance to love of the waiving of a strict judgment of merit. The entire posture of the remembering narrator toward her lover exemplifies this feature. For the story, vague as it is, leaves room for judgment and for resentment, if that had been what she wanted to feel. But, like David before the body of Steerforth, like Maggie alone with Amerigo, she loves without asking whether there is a ground for resentment. I do not say that resentment would always be unjustified in the context of love; and sometimes it is all too inevitably a part of the experience of unhappily loving. But, even where justified and even where inevitable, I believe that resentment, directed at someone whom one has loved, is a morally ugly condition, and one incompatible with a certain sort of truthful seeing of the particular (see "Perception and Revolution"). It is also a condition of the heart that is likely to be ill-suited to storytelling. Here I agree with the suggestion of both *David Copperfield* and *The Princess Casamassima* that the novelist's loving and nonjudgmental attention to the characters is paradigmatic of an element in love toward which one should aim in life itself.

Proust's Marcel argues that all love stories should be autobiographical, meaning that they should have roots in the author's own psychology and experience of suffering. But he also advises the writer that any such narrative should be based not on a single experience alone, but on the extraction, from at least two experiences, of a general form or pattern. This essay attempts to follow that advice, as far as autobiography is concerned. This means, as well, that it is less autobiographical, given my conception of love, than Marcel's story is, given his conception. For unlike Marcel (see "Love's Knowledge"), I hold that love is in its essence a relationship with a particular person, and that the particular features of the other person are intrinsic to its being the love that it is. So no story in which no particular other person appears could really, for me, be the story of a love. This is, one might well say, a story of mourning—in which the love itself takes place in the silences beyond the boundaries of the recorded recollection.

Steerforth's Arm:
Love and the Moral Point of View

I

The summer my daughter fell in love with James Steerforth, she was fourteen and I was forty. We were traveling around England, and, in response to her Dickensian longing, we had ended up in Yarmouth, to inspect, so to speak, the scene of the crime. I had indulgence, but little sympathy, for this literary infatuation. For I felt that I had known long ago, and would have known even if I hadn't made it my business to write on ethical topics, that he was simply not worthy of a good person's love. And I suspected her, as well, of immature reading. For surely, as I remembered it, it was Dickens's intention to make the reader judge Steerforth from the moral point of view, not to encourage her, or him, to fall in love with Steerforth. Full of maternal superiority, and bored with the garish coarseness of Yarmouth—in 1987 a place of oil refineries and cheap summer holiday facilities—I undertook to reread the novel in order to establish my point.

My composure survived the first encounters, where I firmly took the side of Mr. Mell, censured Steerforth for selfishness and egotism in his relation to the other boys, even concurred with Agnes in warning innocent David against his bad angel. And then one afternoon, sitting on the Yarmouth beach in the early July sun, my back turned to the ugly casinos, the cheap hotels, the pink and blue cottages, my eyes shifting from the pages of the novel to the generous sweep of the dark blue sea that beckoned onward before me, I felt a wind in my face and an excitement in my heart, a sensuous delight in the fresh presence of each thing that seemed to be connected, somehow, with the vividness of the chapters, with the power, above all, of Steerforth's presence. I felt my heart quite suddenly take itself off, rushing happily from the firmness of judgment into the eager volatility of desire. And, as I read on, the very words made my "heart beat high" and my "blood rush to my face," until, with tears and with love, maternal authority utterly vanquished, I saw him there before me, "lying with his head upon his arm, as I had often seen him lie at school."[1]

---

1. The sections in quotation marks are taken from the novel; see below. The paragraph as a whole is in the spirit of the novel, and contains many paraphrases and allusions.

The question I want to ask in this essay is, quite simply, what has happened here? First, how is the point of view of love related to the moral point of view, and what, precisely, are the tensions between them? And also: how does novel-reading, the reading of this novel in particular, explore these tensions, constituting its readers as hybrid transmoral agents who slip dangerously back and forth from one world, one point of view, to the other?

II

The subject of romantic and erotic love is not often treated in works on moral philosophy, especially in the Anglo-American tradition. In part this has been a matter of reticence—for that philosophical tradition has lived within a conventional morality that disapproves, on the whole, of the public expression and even the public discussion of deep feelings. In part, too, it has been a matter of *style:* for the plain unadorned nonrhetorical style that the Anglo-American moral tradition both chooses and justifies as the most appropriate for moral reflection is not a style in which the topic of romantic/erotic love can be very easily or very fully discussed. (We see this, for example, in the thinness of Hume's account, which hardly compares to his analyses of pride or sympathy in persuasive and intuitive power.) The topic seems to demand for its convincing treatment a more literary style, a style that uses metaphor and narrative, that represents and also awakens powerful feelings. And all of this Anglo-American moral philosophy has usually avoided.

But these views about public expression and about style do not simply express, on the part of these philosophers, an unreflective adherence to cultural conventions. Philosophers are creatures of habit, to be sure. And one sees the effect of this traditions's habits of writing in the work of some contemporary moral philosophers who defend the moral centrality of intimate personal relationships, romantic love prominently included, but who write, nonetheless, as if philosophy would be better off not going too deeply into the texture of these relationships, not investigating too closely or too concretely the contribution they have to make to the good human life. But, as I say, habit is not all that is motivating philosophers in this tradition. There are deeper motivations too, arising from beliefs about morality and the moral point of view, beliefs that make it questionable whether romantic love could ever correctly be included inside morality, or be anything but subversive of the moral point of view.[2]

Some of these deeper reasons are, roughly speaking, Kantian. Romantic love is not something that is governed by the will. It is, instead, something with respect to which we are, at least in part, *passive.* It seems that we can't choose to fall in love with someone; it simply *happens* to us. And we can't altogether govern the way in which, or the goodness with which, it will happen. As Pindar long ago

---

2. In this essay I use the word "moral" rather than "ethical" as the generic word (see "Perceptive Equilibrium," Notes) following the usage of the moral sentiment tradition. Adam Smith's own terminology (see below) is more complex: for he describes his task as the analysis of the "moral sentiments," but frequently also uses the terminology of virtue and the virtues, probably under the influence of the Stoics.

observed, some are lifted up by "the gentle hands of necessity," but "others with other hands" (*Nemean* VIII). So if one believes that the domain of morality is the domain of the will-governed and the actively chosen, one will be likely to feel, as Kant does, that romantic/erotic love must lie outside the domain of morality.

This is the motivation for Kant's remarkable distinction, in the *Doctrine of Virtue,* between *pathological love,* his name for the romantic, non-will-governed variety, and *practical love,* an attitude of concern that one can will oneself to have toward another human being, and which is, for that reason, a part of morality.[3] If one believes, in addition, that the realm of morality is of special and perhaps of supreme importance in human life—a belief that it seems fair to attribute to Kant—one will be likely, having once made that distinction, to ascribe high *human* worth to practical love, and far less worth to the pathological variety. In fact, since the relationship between the two loves for Kant is not simply neutral, since pathological love, indulged, actually draws us away from the correct moral attitude, sapping and subverting it, and since the moral attitude, actively cultivated, on the other hand activates our wills, making them less likely to succumb to the lures of pathological love, the Kantian will be likely to ascribe to pathological love a low human value indeed, probably a disvalue.

All this would not exactly suggest that moral philosophy should not be concerned with the topic of pathological love: for one who makes the negative judgment might become preoccupied, as, for example, Spinoza is preoccupied, with showing exactly what sort of threat love is to morality, and how this threat might be headed off.[4] But the negative judgment on love does imply that a treatise written from the point of view of morality will not display the value of love as lovers see it, or investigate the experience of love with empathy, from within.

But it is not this objection to love that I want to consider in the body of this essay. The Kantian objection, based on the distinction between activity and passivity, has certainly been influential in explaining the absence of love from our moral philosophy. But the objection is, in the context of our interest in understanding the properties of *love,* too large-scale and, so to speak, unrefined an objection. It throws out too many things to show what might be morally problematic about love in particular. For it holds, if it holds, not only against (romantic) love, but also against all the other sentiments, inclinations, passions, and even perceptual states with respect to which we are, in a manner, passive. The specifically Kantian tradition on the sentiments and passions finds moral problems in pity as well as love, in friendly feeling as well as erotic passion, in anger, fear, even sympathy—all these are morally problematic insofar as they are not will-governed. It is beyond my purpose here to criticize that general line of argument against the sentiments.[5]

What is more revealing, if it is romantic love we wish to understand, is the

---

3. I. Kant, *The Doctrine of Virtue* (Part III of *The Metaphysics of Morals,* Berlin, 1797), trans. M. J. Gregor (Philadelphia, 1979), Akad. 500–1, 447ff; see also *Critique of Practical Reason* (Berlin, 1988), trans. Lewis White Beck (Indianapolis, Ind., 1956), Akad. 83ff.

4. B. Spinoza, *Ethics,* Parts III and IV, esp. "Definitions of the Emotions," df. VI.

5. An effective general criticism of the Kantian position on the emotions and the other sentiments is in Larry Blum, *Friendship, Altruism, and Morality* (London, 1980).

absence of this love from moralities based upon compassion and other sentiments. For it is plain that philosophers who argue that morality ought to be based upon sentiment and who insist that the ideal moral viewpoint is one that is rich in feeling, including a lot of what Kant would call *pathological* feeling, still find romantic love morally problematic in a special way. They still hold that it is to be left out of the moral point of view (not counted as a part of what animates someone who sees from that point of view), for reasons that have nothing to do with a general rejection of passivity. So if we want to understand what is uniquely troublesome about *love* in our moral tradition, we would do best to examine those arguments. It is also plain to me that if our interest is in the absence of love from modern writing in the Anglo-American tradition, it is this sentiment-based line of argument that explains our current situation—and our related ambivalence about the relationship between moral philosophy and the novel—to a far greater degree than does the Kantian tradition. Finally, if we need one further inducement to examine these arguments against love, I suggest that we have one in their power and cogency. I believe that they perspicuously describe a tension that really exists betweeen love and morality, and, in this way, they advance our understanding of the question: What role might romantic love play, or not play, in the good life for a human being?[6]

I shall turn first of all to a succinct philosophical statement of the argument in which I am interested, in Adam Smith's *The Theory of Moral Sentiments.*[7] Smith himself suggests that we develop our sense of the objection and its force by considering our experience as readers of works of literature or as spectators at plays; so we shall investigate the parallel. But the experience of readership has, it seems, as a moral experience, a more complicated character than Smith allows. In pursuit of this complexity, we shall return to *David Copperfield,* which I take to be one of the most profoundly interesting treatments in the English novel of the tension between the point of view of romantic love and the point of view of moral sentiments. We shall ask about the relationship between Agnes' arm, which points morally upward, and the opposing gesture of Steerforth, who lies with his head reclining easily on his arm. And this will lead us to wonder what the relation of the narrator might be to both morality and romance, and how his narrative moves, and moves both him and us, between these two opposing viewpoints.

III

In *The Theory of Moral Sentiments,* Adam Smith argues that the ideal moral point of view, the point of view of the "judicious spectator," is a viewpoint rich in feeling. Not only compassion and sympathy, but also fear, grief, anger, hope, and certain types of love are felt by this spectator, as a result of his active, concrete imagining of the circumstances and aims and feelings of others.[8] The spectator's

6. There are, of course, many varieties of love, and even of romantic love; the rubric "romantic/erotic," and the descriptions and discussions to follow, will make more concrete the type I have in mind.

7. Adam Smith, *The Theory of Moral Sentiments,* 1st ed. 1759; 6th ed., extensively rev., 1790, ed. D. D. Raphael and A. L. Macfie (Oxford, 1976). Hereafter *TMS.*

8. *TMS,* esp. Part I Sections i–ii. ". . . the spectator must . . . endeavour, as much as he can, to put himself in the situation of the other, and to bring home to himself every little circumstance

feelings are not just willed attitudes of concern, they are really passions; and Smith clearly believes that it is both possible and essential to cultivate the passions, making people not less but more responsive and, so to speak, passive, in certain ways at certain times. Correct feeling is, for Smith, both morally *useful,* in showing us what we ought to do, and also morally *valuable* in its own right, as a kind of proper recognition of the ethical character of the situation before us. For Smith, who refers back to the Greek Stoics here,[9] the passions have a cognitive dimension—they are at least partially made up out of beliefs—so that it is natural for him to think of them as both guides and as pieces of recognizing.

The link between passion and the deliberately undertaken is forged by the imagination. By cultivating our ability to see vividly another person's distress, to picture ourselves in another person's place—and this, he makes clear, is something that we *can* set ourselves deliberately to do—we make ourselves more likely to respond with the morally illuminating and appropriate sort of response. It is clear that Smith attaches considerable importance to literature as a source of this kind of moral development; and literature is also, for him, an artificial construction of ideal spectatorship, which leads us into the morally good viewpoint naturally, and offers us in that way a model we can refer to in real life. For frequently, in order to show his reader what he means by a certain claim about the ideal spectator's responses, or in order to support his assertion that the spectator in a certain case will respond this way and not this, he refers to our experience as readers of stories and watchers of plays, asking us to notice what sentiments we experience in that role.[10] He proceeds as if readership and spectatorship are more familiar to us, more securely and concretely grasped, than the moral problems of life, concerning which he wishes to persuade us. He also assumes that we will agree that literary readership is structurally isomorphic to the spectator's moral role, so that a dubious issue in the real-life moral sphere can legitimately be pinned down by appeal to literary experience. The experience of readership is a moral activity in its own right, a cultivation of imagination for moral activity in life, and a test for correctness of real-life judgment and response.

What is, however, very remarkable, in the midst of this tremendous emphasis on the cultivation of the passions, is that two types of passion that play a prominent role in our lives and (or so we might have suspected) our literary experiences are considered by Smith to be totally absent from the judicious spectator and therefore totally to be omitted when we describe the limits of moral propriety. Whereas most passions are moderated and channelled, but still assiduously cultivated within the moral point of view, these two sorts are omitted from it altogether. The two are the bodily desires, including sexual desire, and the so-called

---

of distress which can possibly occur to the sufferer. He must adopt the whole case of his companion with all its minutest incidents; and strive to render as perfect as possible, that imaginary change of situation upon which his sympathy is founded" (I.i.4.6).

9. The Stoics are referred to prominently throughout, and Part VII contains extensive discussion (and some criticism) of their views. The cognitive nature of the view of passion is made clear from the start: see I.i.1.8, and many other places. Smith is critical of the Stoics for urging the extirpation of the passions, which he regards as elements in complete virtue.

10. Literature is first mentioned very near the beginning of the argument, in I.i.1.4 ("tragedy or romance"), and these references form an important part of the account of the spectator throughout Part I.

"passions which take their origin from a particular turn or habit of the imagination." The salient example in the latter category is romantic love. If we combine the two passages, we have a sweeping rejection from morality and the moral viewpoint both of love and also of the erotic desire that is, Smith himself emphasizes, a prominent component of it. We also have, as I think we shall see, a claim in its own way as uncompromising as Kant's concerning the subversive relation between love and morality—though this claim is defended with arguments that have nothing to do with the rejection of passivity.

How does the argument work? Let us take the bodily passions first. Smith asks us, first, to imagine his judicious spectator looking on at someone else's hunger for food. The spectator, as elsewhere, is imagined as someone who is a concerned friend of the parties, emotionally involved with their good and ill, able to imagine vividly what it is like to be them. At the same time, he lives a life distinct from theirs and connects himself to theirs primarily through imagining rather than interacting. As I have said, Smith's frequent way of getting us to see what such a spectator is like and what he will feel is to ask us to think of him as like us when we read a novel or see a play, caring about the characters and vividly responding to their predicament. And seeing what this spectator will feel gives us a test to determine the proper sort and degree of feeling for us to have in our own real lives, in situations where we are not spectators but actively involved as moral agents. (For example, we will learn not to have excessive anger in a personal case of our own by reminding ourselves that the friendly spectator would feel anger for our situation only up to a certain limit.)

Smith now argues as follows. When we read a story about hungry people (in, he says, "the journal of a siege, or of a sea voyage") we can sympathize with, both respond to and assume in our empathetic imagining, their grief, fear, and "consternation" at being in such a predicament. What we can't take on as readers is the hunger itself, since that is based on a physical condition that we are not in. Therefore hunger is not, by itself, a moral response, or a part of the moral point of view.[11] We could better convey the centrality of this point of view in Smith's account of human agency by saying that hunger is not a constituent part of a fully and adequately human response to the world. This doesn't mean that we should never feel hunger, or should feel guilty about our hunger; it just means that we should not identify ourselves with it, think of it as a good human thing or any part of our true humanity.

The same, Smith now continues, is true of "the passion by which Nature unites the two sexes."[12] It is a very strong passion—in fact, "naturally the most furious of the passions." But, unlike other strong passions such as anger and grief, it proves altogether improper and extramoral, when we apply the spectator test. The claim seems to be that we do not become sexually aroused when we look, as spectators, at people who are themselves sexually excited by one another. The closest we get to their excitement in our own state is, says Smith, a spirit of "gallantry" and "sensibility" toward them. As in the food case, Smith would presumably wish to say that reading about erotic arousal does not cause us to become, ourselves, aroused—although the absence here of any explicit remark to that effect (in con-

11. *TMS* I.ii.1.1.
12. *TMS* I.ii.1.2

trast to the hunger case, where literature is prominent) may indicate that he is familiar enough with pornography to sense a difficulty in his argument at this point. In any case, the conclusion, as before, is that sexual desire is outside of the moral viewpoint on the world, and to be judged improper when we look at the world from that viewpont. "All strong expressions of it are upon every occasion indecent, even between persons in whom its most complete indulgence is acknowledged by all laws, both human and divine, to be perfectly innocent."[13]

Smith now adds a further point. The ancient philosophers, he says, hold that the reason these bodily passions are problematic is that we share them with "the brutes." Not so he replies: for we share with "the brutes" many passions:

> such as resentment, natural affection, even gratitude, which do not, upon that account, appear to be so brutal. The true cause of the peculiar disgust which we conceive for the appetites of the body when we see them in other men, is that we cannot enter into them. To the person himself who feels them, as soon as they are gratified, the object that excited them ceases to be agreeable: even its presence often becomes offensive to him; he looks round to no purpose for the charm which transported him the moment before, and he can now as little enter into his own passion as another person. When we have dined, we order the covers to be removed; and we should treat in the same manner the objects of the most ardent and passionate desires, if they were the objects of no other passions but those which take their origin from the body.[14]

In other words, there is a point of view that we are deeply committed to, which expresses something very fundamental about our humanity. And it is because the bodily passions do not appear in us, when we assume that viewpoint, that we must reject them from morality, not because they arise from some brutish element in us.

There are some problems with Smith's account of the spectator in this passage: a tendency to blur the distinction between empathy and sympathy; a tendency to confuse propriety in feeling with propriety in the public expression of feeling.[15] But we see the general shape of the argument well enough. What a concerned friend or a reader cannot respond to out of friendly concern (and I think that the point can be made without Smith's assumption that all sympathetic response involves having the *very same* feeling), what the reader can't, as a reader, be moved by, is somehow morally suspect. We turn now to the next group of banned passions: for it is here that romantic love itself gets rejected.

Among the passions derived from the imagination, Smith writes, are some that "take their origin from a peculiar turn or habit it has acquired." And these are always morally problematic:

> The imaginations of mankind, not having acquired that particular turn, cannot enter into them; and such passions, though they may be allowed to be almost

13. Ibid.
14. *TMS* I.ii.1.3.
15. See, for example, I.ii.1.2, discussed above; there are many other such passages. But perhaps this is, after all, not such a confusion, since the moral world is, for Smith, the world of the publicly expressible, and whatever cannot with decency be publicly expressed would be ipso facto suspect; see below.

unavoidable in some part of life, are always, in some measure, ridiculous. This is the case with that strong attachment which naturally grows up between two persons of different sexes, who have long fixed their thoughts upon one another. Our imagination not having run in the same channel with that of the lover, we cannot enter into the eagerness of his emotions. If our friend has been injured, we readily sympathize with his resentment, and grow angry with the very person with whom he is angry. If he has received a benefit, we readily enter into his gratitude, and have a very high sense of the merit of his benefactor. But if he is in love, though we may think his passion just as reasonable as any of the kind, yet we never think ourselves bound to conceive a passion of the same kind, and for the same person for whom he has conceived it. The passion appears to every body, but the man who feels it, entirely disproportioned to the value of the object; and love, though it is pardoned in a certain age because we know it is natural, is always laughed at, because we cannot enter into it. All serious and strong expressions of it appear ridiculous to a third person; and though a lover may be good company to his mistress, he is so to nobody else. He himself is sensible of this; and as long as he continues in his sober senses, endeavours to treat his own passion with raillery and ridicule. It is the only style in which we care to hear of it; because it is the only style in which we ourselves are disposed to talk of it. We grow weary of the grave, pedantic, and long-sentenced love of Cowley and Petrarca, who never have done with exaggerating the violence of their attachments; but the gaiety of Ovid, and the gallantry of Horace, are always agreeable.[16]

We can, he continues, enter into the lovers' hopes of happiness, or their fear of disappointment—but not into the love itself, making its seriousness real and vivid for ourselves.

Smith's point seems to be that romantic and erotic love is based upon a strong response to morally irrelevant particularities, in such a way that it can't be explained, it retains always an element of the surd, the mysterious, the impenetrably arbitrary. We can't imagine *why* it has happened between these two people in this way at this time—and so we can't see the love from the lovers' own viewpoint. This is all the more so, presumably, because this romantic love contains within it the bodily arousal that Smith's argument has already rejected, and which Smith here calls "perhaps, the foundation of love."[17]

Smith now returns to the issue of literary spectatorship. For it would appear to be a natural objection to his argument that romantic and erotic love are a staple of literature, and among the things that, in literature, most move and engage the

16. *TMS* I.ii.2.1.

17. *TMS* I.ii.2.2. Smith is here discussing the origin of our interest in pastoral poetry and other related literary works, and is arguing that we are drawn by the depiction of the lovers' wish for serenity and contentment, not by their love:

We feel how natural it is for the mind, in a certain situation, relaxed with indolence, and fatigued with the violence of desire, to long for serenity and quiet, to hope to find them in the gratification of that passion which distracts it, and to frame to itself the idea of that life of tranquillity and retirement which the elegant, the tender, and the passionate Tibullus takes so much pleasure in describing; a life . . . free from labour, and from care, and from all the turbulent passions which attend them. Even scenes of this kind interest us most, when they are painted rather as what is hoped, than as what is enjoyed. The grossness of that passion, which mixes with, and is, perhaps, the foundation of love, disappears when its gratification is far off and at a distance; but renders the whole offensive, when described as what is immediately possessed.

reader's imagination. This Smith now denies. The lovers' wish for happiness and their fear of reversal—*these* are certainly staples of literary experience; and these are the foundation of our interest, he claims, both in pastoral poetry and in "modern tragedies and romances." But the *love itself* is not the object of the reader's interest, except in the comic manner already mentioned:

> The author who should introduce two lovers, in a scene of perfect security, expressing their mutual fondness for one another, would excite laughter, and not sympathy. If a scene of this kind is ever admitted into a tragedy, it is always, in some measure, improper, and is endured, not from any sympathy with the passion that is expressed in it, but from concern for the dangers and difficulties with which the audience foresee that its gratification is likely to be attended.[18]

Smith adds that romantic love, since it is frequently mixed with "humanity, generosity, kindness, friendship, esteem," is not, despite its extravagance and its mysteriousness, found actually revolting or odious—only, perhaps, a little ridiculous.

In order to understand Smith's argument here, we must first attempt to say more plainly what romantic love *is,* as he sees it. Unlike his Stoic predecessors, unlike, as well, Descartes and Spinoza, Smith does not offer definitions of the passions; so this is a little hard to do. But I think that we can infer from his examples and descriptions in this passage that he takes romantic love to contain, as necessary ingredients, at least the following elements:

1. Mutual feelings of sexual attraction and arousal.
2. Beliefs (on both sides, presumably) about the supreme importance of the object, beliefs that go beyond any reasoned justification that the lover could articulate to others—even though they may contain, as well, some articulable element of esteem.[19]

We can add that the romantic love Smith describes appears to connect these two elements closely: sexual arousal is felt towards the person *seen as* supremely valuable and important.

3. A complex intimate way of life that involves the exchange of affectionate communications, both verbal and erotic; a way of life in which lovers are totally wrapped up in one another, attending for long periods of time to nobody else, and in which, characteristically, they take themselves off into privacy, not inviting or wanting any scrutiny or even company, seeking a "perfect security."

---

18. *TMS* I.ii.2.3.

19. Smith has spoken of the disproportion between the passion and the value of the object, as seen from the spectator's viewpoint. But this and other passages depicting the intimate habits of loving exchange and conversation indicate, I think, that the problem is not an *illusion* on the lover's part; it is, rather, a strong response to what cannot be justified as admirable in the public world—to glances, gestures, habits of intimacy. What we are dealing with is a "peculiar habit" of the lovers' imaginations, entrenched ways of seeing and valuing that are idiosyncratic and not publicly communicable. It is not that the lover makes these things up when they aren't there; rather he or she endows them with an importance that the spectator cannot find in them.

For the lovers, this life has the charms of mystery, secrecy, and intimacy; from the outside it is simply mysterious.

Once again, we can add that the third element is closely connected with the other two: sexual desire is felt toward the person seen as part of an intimate way of life, apart from others; intimacy enhances the sense of importance; and at the same time sexual desire and the belief in importance are strong motivations to undertake the way of life in the first place.

I should add that by insisting on this last, very complex, element, Smith seems to me to go beyond his philosophical predecessors on this topic, who all seem to define love as some sort of combination of feeling and belief,[20] without sufficiently taking account of the fact that love cannot exist in a single instant, but requires a pattern of exchange and mutuality, of mutual attention evolving over time. In this way he brings to the analysis of romantic and erotic love the insight first introduced in the sphere of friendly love by Aristotle:[21] love is fundamentally a relation, not something *in* a single person at all—a relation that involves the give and take, over time, of feeling, thought, benefits, conversations. Smith adds that this relation, where romantic love is concerned, evolves its own mysterious habits and delights in the charm of its secret routines, so inscrutable to the nonparticipant.

Smith's objection to this relation seems to be based, precisely, on its mysteriousness and exclusivity. We might expand his point about the spectator as follows. Lovers wrapped up in loving conversation (and it is, I think, significant that his paradigm scene of love is a scene of conversation) are not, insofar as they are lovers, also spectators. Being in love is altogether different, as a kind of attention, from being a judicious spectator; for lovers do not look around at the entirety of their world, but are exclusively wrapped up in one another. They do not enter into anyone else's predicament; their imaginations do not see out. By the same token, if we imagine the judicious spectator looking at his world, he will not be able to find in it, no matter how fine his imagination, the passion that they feel for one another. It is a mystery to him; he can't see into it. Lovers, then, neither see nor are seen with the judicious eye of sympathetic moral concern.[22]

We now must confront an ambiguity in Smith's account. For there are two ways in which the moral function of the spectator might be understood. (These two possibilities arise in interpreting most ideal-judge views, beginning with Aristotle's.[23]) On one reading, the judicious spectator is merely heuristic: moral appropriateness and propriety in passion exist independently, can in principle be specified independently of his response, and imagining his response is a useful device for us in finding out the appropriate response. On this reading, there is something inappropriate about love, something that demands apology, apart from the spec-

20. R. Descartes, *Les Passions de L'Âme,* Part II, Art. VI; Spinoza, *Ethics* "Definitions of the Passions," Def. VI. For Stoic definitions, see *Stoicorum Veterum Fragmenta,* ed. J. von Arnim, Vol. III., 397–420.

21. Aristotle, *Nicomachean Ethics* VIII–IX; cf. *Fragility,* chap. 12. For a related account of romantic love, see "Love's Knowledge."

22. Compare the discussion of Henry James's *The Ambassadors* in "Perceptive Equilibrium."

23. On Aristotle, see *Fragility,* chap. 10, pp. 311–12; there is an excellent discussion of this question in unpublished writing by Christine Korsgaard.

tator's inability to enter into it, and the spectator shows us the way to the correct conclusion. On the second, and stronger reading, however, the spectator's responses are themselves constitutive of what is and is not morally appropriate. The fact that he cannot enter into love is not a sign that points beyond itself to some independently existing inappropriateness in the relation. It is the very fact that he cannot enter in, that *makes* the passion inappropriate. It is what is deficient, or excessive, about it.

The second reading can, I believe, be strongly supported from a number of passages in the text. To confine ourselves to the sections we are discussing, we might recall Smith's vigorous insistence that the *reason for* the inappropriateness of bodily passion is not some separate brutishness in hunger and sexual desire; rather, the "true cause" of our negative view is "that we cannot enter into them." This may just be a psychological remark; but it looks like something more. Not just the cause, but the justification for our negative view, seems to be found in the fact of the spectator's incomprehension.[24]

What, in that case, is the deeper significance of the spectator's failure to enter into these passions? What is the moral significance of the spectatorial stance?[25] I think that Smith's underlying point is this. Morality essentially involves thinking of oneself as one person among others, bound by ties of friendship and sympathy to those others. These ties, in turn, involve, essentially, two further things. First, they require us to look around us, taking thought, so to speak, for all that we can see. And they involve, too, general social conversation, the giving and receiving of justifications and reasons. Therefore, they require that we permit ourselves and our actions to *be seen*. These practices both express our concern for our fellow beings and bind them to us in a network of mutual concern. The presence of these features in the spectator explains why assuming, in thought, the spectator's position can be a way of assuming the moral point of view. We have built into the account of the spectator the most essential features of our moral humanity.

And that, we may now also add, thinking of Smith's reliance on literature, is why going to plays and reading novels and stories is a valuable part of moral devel-

---

24. There are many passages that point in this direction. Consider especially I.ii.1.12, where the fact that the spectator enters little into another's bodily pain is called "the foundation of the propriety of constancy and patience in enduring it." If the spectator were merely heuristic, he would be not the "foundation" of propriety here, but only a clue as to where propriety (specified in some independent way) was to be found. Similarly, when Smith asks what we ought to feel in a case where our own response to a personal calamity is inclined to be much more violent than that which the spectator would feel, he simply answers without further remark that we should keep our feeling down to that which the spectator would experience (rather than pointing to some independent moral value that the spectator helps us discover); and he specifies the desire of the agent for "a more complete sympathy" with others as the reason why he will be right to leave aside the special involvement he has with his own case (I.i.4.7–8). The passage culminates in a praise of "society and conversation" (I.i.4.10). Similarly, in asking what we should feel for the dead, Smith grants that there is no independent thing there to inquire about—for the dead are dead; but it is the fact that the judicious spectator will grieve that makes such grief appropriate.

25. By asking for the "deeper significance" of the spectator stance I am not returning to the first (heuristic) sort of view. What I am asking is why this particular stance, described as Smith describes it, should be thought to be constitutive of moral appropriateness—why he has built up the spectator in this and not some other way.

opment: not because it points beyond itself to a separately existing moral realm, but because it is among the ways in which we constitute ourselves as moral, and thus as fully human, beings. For we find, as we read novels, that we quite naturally assume the viewpoint of an affectionate and responsive social creature, who looks at all the scene before him with fond and sympathetic attention, caring for all the people, and caring, too, for the bonds of discourse that hold them all together. Interpreting a novel or play involves one, indeed, in a kind of sympathetic reason-giving that is highly characteristic of morality; for we ask ourselves, as we try to enter into the plot, why the characters do what they do, and we are put off if our inquiries lead to nothing but mystery and arbitrariness.

But mystery is what love is all about. And the fact that we cannot, where love is concerned, enter into the essential forms of moral give and take is the very thing that makes love, as a relation, inappropriate to our highest humanity, and sub-versive of the moral community.

IV

Smith's idea about the moral stance and his connection of that stance to the experience of the reader of fiction has had a long history (whether through direct influence or through a more general cultural dissemination) in the reflections of English novelists themselves about the moral role of their craft.[26] I have argued elsewhere that Henry James takes a very similar view about the reader's activity and its moral worth.[27] And James has related worries about the role, in the moral vision that sustains his novels, of personal love, and of related emotions such as jealousy and the desire for revenge. Love, as James sees it, requires both hidden-ness and a willful self-blinding, both a turning from the good of others and a request that others turn away their eyes. For these reasons it threatens a valuable norm of moral attention. And I have suggested that it is for this reason that strong personal love, in James, occurs only, so to speak, in the margins of the novel—in the silence beyond the ending of *The Golden Bowl,* after Maggie has buried her eyes in her husband's embrace, tragically surrendering her equal vision of the claims of all; in the boat where Chad and Marie de Vionnet are sailing, *before* that boat has been recognized by the spectator Strether and become a part of his, and the reader's, vision; in the trip of Charlotte and the Prince to Gloucester, where they step out of the novel's vision into a silence prefigured by their determination to "go" for that one day, only "by" each other. As readers, we are not encouraged to fall in love with any of James's characters, nor are we at all encouraged to take up a stance toward them that would make this a possible response. We are not seduced, not led, ourselves, into their silences. In this way we are borne up mor-ally, held as "participators by a fond attention"[28] in the adventures of all the char-acters, even when we are reminded that there are silences into which the morality of fine-tuned social perception has no entry.

26. Other authors who should be considered in this connection are Jane Austen and George Eliot.
27. See "Perceptive Equilibrium," "Flawed Crystals" (with Notes), this volume.
28. Henry James, *The Art of the Novel* (New York, 1907), 62.

But Smith's nonerotic idea of readership, and James's similar but more complex idea, which complicates the austerity with erotic silences, are not all that novel-reading has morally to offer us. For if Smith's claim that we don't get seduced by fictional characters seems, up to a point, correct as an account of certain novels, for example the novels of James, we know well, also, that there are other experiences of novel reading that are, while still profoundly moral, also disturbingly erotic. And perhaps by investigating the relationship between moral community and erotic privacy in the novels that do have a seductive dimension we can better understand the tension between love and the moral viewpoint. And we might even discover, as Smith did not discover, a path between them, a way in which morality itself, most richly and generously construed, leads beyond itself into love.

I shall, then, for the balance of this essay turn to Dickens's *David Copperfield,* and to the question with which I began: Why is it that, morally attuned as the reader of this novel is made to be, the reader nonetheless falls in love, as David also falls in love, with James Steerforth? Why, and how, does this novel, which begins with an open question about who the hero of David Copperfield's life actually is, and which ends (apparently) with the upward-pointing gesture of morality, lead us, at times, outside of morality into the "shadowy world" of moonlight and love, of magic, and an arm curved along the pillow?

V

I shall begin by enumerating, simply, certain facts.[29] That David Copperfield was born with a caul—which signifies that he would never drown at sea (p. 49). That the hour of his birth, midnight on a Friday, signified that he would be unlucky in life, but be "privileged to see ghosts and spirits." That it is his persistent fantasy that he himself was born as a traveller out of that "shadowy world" (p. 60). That, in consequence of Betsey Trotwood's conjecture that he would be born a girl, he has, as well, the persistent fantasy that he has, in the spirit world, a sisterly double: "Betsey Trotwood Copperfield was for ever in the land of dreams and shadows, the tremendous region whence I had so lately travelled" (p. 60). That this shadowy world is associated with his longing for his dead father, above whose grave the light that lights such ghostly travelers shines its mysterious nocturnal light (p. 60). That David's father left David a collection of novels that he avidly read and reread, "reading as if for life" (p. 106). That Dickens, in his Preface to the novel, speaks of his own sorrow at finishing the novel, comparing the entire world of the novel to David's imagined spirit world: "An Author feels as if he were dismissing some portion of himself into the shadowy world, when a crowd of the creatures of his brain are going from him forever" (p. 45). (I regard this less as an autobiographical statement than as a part of the fiction: Dickens in this way puts himself into his own text as a character.) That David Copperfield expresses, at the novel's close (a novel he has written) a similar sorrow—"subduing my desire to linger on" he dismisses "the shadows" (p. 950) until only Agnes' solid reality remains.

---

29. All references to *David Copperfield* will be taken from the Penguin Edition, ed. Trevor Blount (Harmondsworth, 1966).

We now add to these several further facts. That David's relationship with James Steerforth casts him both as a storyteller and as the inhabitant of a world of moonlight and shadows, of enchantments and spells, in which David becomes first the Sultana Scheherazade (p. 145), who is "cherished as a kind of plaything," (p. 146) and, later on, the equally cherished character "Daisy," whose innocence is his seductive power. That Steerforth links David from the beginning with David's unborn sister, his ghostly female double:

> "You haven't got a sister, have you?" said Steerforth, yawning.
> "No," I answered.
> "That's a pity," said Steerforth. "If you had had one, I should think she would have been a pretty, timid, little, bright-eyed sort of girl. I should have liked to know her. Good night, young Copperfield." (p. 140)[30]

And Copperfield, or his shadowy sister, gazing at Steerforth as he sleeps in the mysterious moonlight, loves him from that moment:[31]

> I thought of him very much after I went to bed, and raised myself, I recollect, to look at him where he lay in the moonlight, with his handsome face turned up, and his head reclining easily on his arm. He was a person of great power in my eyes; that was, of course, the reason of my mind running on him. No veiled future dimly glanced upon him in the moonbeams. There was no shadowy picture of his footsteps, in the garden that I dreamed of walking in all night. (p. 140)

The "reason" of course is no reason; it says, in effect, that there is no reason, only a great power. He loves because he loves, and he thinks nothing, in his dreams, for morality. In the sensuous rhythm of the prose itself, we feel that he has entered the other world, the world of moonbeams and shadows, of mysterious ease and delight, the world of a particular turn of the imagination, where reasons come to an end.

Two gestures frame this novel. The first is the gesture of Steerforth's arm here, as it curves easily along the pillow, supporting his "fine face" with its "curling hair" (p. 139).[32] The second is the gesture of Agnes, on which the novel closes, as she stands by him, her arm pointing upward. The first gesture becomes Steerforth's leitmotif, just as the upward gesture is Agnes's. As his Good Angel and his other angel (for only Agnes calls Steerforth a "bad angel" (p. 426)),[33] they take up

30. There may also be a forward reference here to Steerforth's involvement with Em'ly, who is depicted as similar in age to David, and in some sense his double.

31. Strictly speaking, the love has already begun. For just before this, reflecting on the school rumor that Miss Creakle is in love with Steerforth, David remarks, "I am sure, as I sat in the dark, thinking of his nice voice, and his fine face, and his easy manner, and his curling hair, I thought it very likely" (p. 139).

32. Of Steerforth's preference for pillows, see p. 347, where he arranges for David a room with "pillows enough for six." Curling hair is also a salient trait of Steerforth elsewhere—see pp. 346 and 863. In this way, the concerned reader, staging the scene in imagination, draws in details from other parts of the novel.

33. Here David repeatedly calls Agnes a Good Angel (see p. 426), but denies that Steerforth is correctly called a bad angel: "Agnes, you wrong him very much."

their positions beside his heart, beside his bed ("You belong to my bedroom, I find" (p. 137)), contrasting guardians, beckoning to him from their different worlds. Steerforth's gesture returns at two crucial moments later in the novel, as a hauntingly concrete vision, in which sensuous perception and emotion-infused memory join together. The last time David sees Steerforth before the seduction of Emily, the last time he sees him alive and as a beloved friend, it is this gesture, once again, that arrests him:

> I was up with the dull dawn, and, having dressed as quietly as I could, looked into his room. He was fast asleep; lying, easily, with his head upon his arm, as I had often seen him lie at school.
> The time came in its season, and that was very soon, when I almost wondered that nothing troubled his repose, as I looked at him. But he slept—let me think of him so again—as I had often seen him sleep at school; and thus, in this silent hour, I left him.—Never more, oh God forgive you, Steerforth! to touch that passive hand in love and friendship. Never, never, more! (pp. 497–98)

Notice that the gesture here is made a part of the remembering novelist's present life, as his art of writing takes him again to his vision of Steerforth, and his love.

And years later, when the body of the shipwrecked sailor is washed up, dead, upon the Yarmouth shore, David recognizes it, not by its form or feature, but by that same gesture:

> The old remembrance that had been recalled to me, was in his look. I asked him, terror-stricken, leaning on the arm he held out to support me:
> "Has a body come ashore?"
> He said, "Yes."
> "Do I know it?" I asked then.
> He answered nothing.
> But, he led me to the shore. And on that part of it where she and I had looked for shells, two children—on that part of it where some lighter fragments of the old boat, blown down last night, had been scattered by the wind—among the ruins of the home he had wronged—I saw him lying with his head upon his arm, as I had often seen him lie at school.
>
> No need, O Steerforth, to have said, when we last spoke together, in that hour which I so little deemed to be our parting-hour—no need to have said, "Think of me at my best!" I had done that ever; and could I change now, looking on this sight! (p. 866)

(We have already been told that this entire episode, in addition to being a frequent dream of the narrator/novelist in later life, is seen vividly before him as he writes: "As plainly as I behold what happened, I will try to write it down. I do not recall it, but see it done; for it happens again before me" (p. 855)).

We can begin our investigation of the tension between love and morality in the novel by thinking about these two gestures. Agnes's upward-pointing gesture is clear, unambiguous, conventional, literal. What it means, it says—and in a way that anyone who sees can understand: "Strive to be more morally upright, more worthy of heaven." It is the gesture famous from Jacques-Louis David's portrait of Socrates, from, indeed, countless religious paintings and sculptures in many periods. (Agnes, in her "tranquil brightness," has already been compared by the narrator to a figure in a stained glass window [p. 280].[34]) It is the gesture of moral discourse, reason-giving, and advice: "'Everyone who knows you, consults with you, and is guided by you, Agnes. . . . You are so good, and so sweet-tempered. You have such a gentle nature, and you are always right'" (p. 333). It is a gesture that is not personal to Agnes; anyone, we feel, might use it to say the same. Nor is it personal in its directedness toward David: just as she gives advice to everyone, so she points out, for everyone alike, the moral path. It would not be stretching a point to say that it is the gesture of the sympathetic and judicious spectator, a gesture that represents, in the novel, the nonshadowy public world of morality and reason-giving moral discourse.

Steerforth's gesture, by contrast, signifies nothing publicly communicable. Its only meaning is that he is there. It is mysteriously, sensuously, his, his beyond explanations and reasons. Its power to haunt comes not from the public world of reason-giving (in fact, it distracts David from that world, making moral judgment upon Steerforth's actions impossible), but from the private world of personal emotion and personal memory. It is irreducibly particular, characteristic of him and no other. It is what David recognizes him by. And its easy charm and erotic grace are for David part of a world of shadows and moonlight, not of the world of reasons and justifications. He cannot explain its power. He can only repeat the description, in haunting and almost incantatory language, as if the description, and the gesture, were, for him, for us, a magic spell. Above all, the gesture, and the language used to describe it, are erotic. Agnes uses the bodily as an instrument of the moral; and we know that as he writes the novel David sees her with him, "journeying along the road of life" (p. 946)—a metaphor typical of Agnes in its lack of sensuous freshness—surrounded by children, emblems of a moral use of the body. In Steerforth's gesture we feel the mystery and excitement of a body animated by a unique spirit, pointing to nothing but itself and the bed on which it rests.

Agnes' gesture moves us, insofar as it does, because it reminds us of aspirations for the good life that we can articulate to ourselves and to others. Steerforth's gesture stirs us, as it hauntingly does, not because we see beyond it into something else, but because it is made, for us, a sensuous reality, because, by the spell of erotic and incantatory language we are brought, ourselves, into the charmed world of love. The emotion we feel when that language stirs us with its own magic is something akin to David's emotion. We feel toward that arm some part of the inexplicable erotic excitement, the stir of tumultuous feeling, and the sheer indefeasible devotion to a particular person that are present in David's love. And in that gesture we are led, as David is led, beyond morality. The hand curves along the pillow, fingers pointing onwards.[35]

34. See also p. 289: "I feel that there are goodness, peace, and truth, wherever Agnes is; and that the soft light of the coloured window in the church, seen long ago, falls on her always, and on me when I am near her, and on everything around."

35. For the association of Steerforth with horizontal movement "on," see pp. 488, 489, and the descriptions of him as sailor. See also p. 377: "I knew that his restless nature and bold spirits delighted to find a vent in rough toil and bad weather."

Dickens's opposition of gestures disturbs us, making us aware (as we pass from one point of view to the other) of many of the problematic features of erotic love that we have already mentioned here in reflecting on Smith. And we are all the more disturbed because we respond to the gesture against our will, so to speak, against our expectation even. Just when we thought we were most morally secure in our judgment upon Steerforth's character, there we are, watching that bed in the moonlight, ready to weep. We notice love's mysterious character of inexplicable intimacy. We notice how, caught up in that moment, we don't see out for others, and we won't be seen by them. We don't care to attend to the injustice done to poor Mr. Mell; we suspend all general sympathy. We don't even care for Ham Peggotty, since we know, with Em'ly, that he is indeed a "chuckleheaded fellow" and that we too would gladly have followed Steerforth wherever he beckoned. And we certainly won't permit Agnes to look in at us in these moments, telling us what a bad angel he is, and speaking of moral uplift. The minute we, like David, hear Steerforth's footsteps, we react as David did, when he says that they made "my heart beat high and the blood rush to my face" (p. 485). And Agnes, though we don't exactly dismiss her, is closed up for the time being in a sanctuary from which she is not permitted, so to speak, to look out or look on: As David says:

> I was never unmindful of Agnes, and she never left that sanctuary in my thoughts—if I may call it so—where I had placed her from the first. But when he entered, and stood before me with his hand out, the darkness that had fallen on him changed to light, and I felt confounded and ashamed of having doubted one I loved so heartily. I loved her none the less; I thought of her as the same benignant, gentle angel in my life; I reproached myself, not her, with having done him an injury; and I would have made him any atonement if I had known what to make, and how to make it. (p. 485)

Much of this novel takes place in the daylight world, a world of social and other-regarding concern, a world in which the good heart cares for each part of its context and strives, with active sympathy, to do good. This world is also a world in which David can explain to us *why* each thing is good or bad, a world in which his feelings are always in proportion to these reasons and play an active part, we might say, in compassionate reason-giving social discourse. But we have already been made aware, from the beginning of the novel, that there is a darker world in this book as well, a world of shadows and spirits—and that the narrator presents himself to us not only as a person who has access to that other world, but also as someone who has a female double, pretty and susceptible, dwelling in that world. He has, then, access to that double, that realm. And it is in this counterworld, set over and against, or rather around the margins of the world of sympathetic morality—that the love of Daisy and Steerforth (of the Sultan and Scheherazade) is situated.

David's love for Steerforth contains, certainly, a great deal that the spectator could see: admiration for Steerforth's strength and boldness, his courage and intelligence, his power to do almost anything without apparent effort, his outspokenness and geniality, the way he protects and cares for David. And Steerforth's love for David (for I think we may really speak of love here) can, though more obscure, be similarly understood, in part: it addresses itself to Daisy's freshness, brightness, and innocence, his trust, his intelligence, his loyalty. David often gives expression to the communicable admiring side of his love, as if he were trying to satisfy himself that it could be explained to others, that reasons could be given, bringing it out into the public world.[36] But the shortcomings of his attempts only convince us the more that it is not entirely an articulable relation.[37]

We are aware, then, from the beginning, that there is, as well, in this love, much that the spectator could not enter into—and that, insofar as we can and do, we are being led by the novel outside of the spectatorial role. The physical erotic attraction of the pair is only a part of this mysterious side. But it is stressed, in David's frequent remarks about Steerforth's good looks,[38] in his account of his physical reaction to Steerforth's presence, heart beating and blood rushing, in his jealousy of Steerforth's other friends (p. 416), in his response to the sensuous gesture of head and arm. In the punctiliousness, too, with which he informs us that he and Steerforth "parted with friendly heartiness at his door" (p. 347), slept under separate roofs at Yarmouth, and so on; in his obsessive thought of the touch of Steerforth's hand; in Steerforth's wish to be acquainted with David's shadowy sister, in the "dashing way he had of treating me like a plaything" (p. 358), in the flirtatious use of the name Daisy.

But the erotic/romantic relation goes beyond both liking and erotic flirtation. We have a sense of a secret world, dense with conversation, storytelling, ease and laughter, with magic spells and the charm of being understood and loved. From the first, Steerforth beckons to the part of David that has access to the shadowy world: "Whatever I had within me that was romantic and dreamy, was encouraged by so much story-telling in the dark." (p. 146) His first meal with Steerforth initiates him into a universe of moonlight and magic, the blue glare of the phosphorous box shedding over everything its strange alluring light:

> How well I recollect our sitting there, talking in whispers; or their talking, and my respectfully listening, I ought rather to say; the moonlight falling a little way into the room, through the window, painting a pale window on the floor, and the greater part of us in shadow, except when Steerforth dipped a match into a phosphorus-box, when he wanted to look for anything on the board, and shed a blue glare over us that was gone directly! A certain mysterious feeling, consequent on

36. See especially his praise of Steerforth to Mr. Peggotty, p. 196: praise of Steerforth is David's "favourite theme."
37. In this same scene David tells Mr. Peggotty that "it's hardly possible to give him as much praise as he deserves." And the excitement that is, he tells us, in his whole manner as he speaks of Steerforth, excites little Em'ly, who begins to fall in love from this moment.
38. On Steerforth's good looks, see for example, "very good-looking" (p. 136); "his nice voice, and his fine face, and his easy manner, and his curling hair" (p. 139); "what a noble fellow he was in appearance" (p. 151); "the clustering curls of his hair" (p. 346); "the figure of a handsome well-formed young man" (p. 345); his "handsome head" (p. 488). At p. 345, he wishes to hug Steerforth, but is held back "for very shame, and the fear that it might displease him"; instead "I grasped him by both hands and could not let them go." Here we may have a clue as to why David, in recalling his fascination with Steerforth, and in the scenes of fascination themselves, tends to focus on the *sleeping* Steerforth: shame impedes acknowledgment of his strong feelings at any other time.

the darkness, the secrecy of the revel, and the whisper in which everything was said, steals over me again, and I listen to all they tell me with a vague feeling of solemnity and awe. . . . (p. 138)

Steerforth, in this world, is the magician, shedding his strange light; and David is again in his presence, even as he brings us there. This love is at home in the night, in the bedroom; and its power of enchantment seems almost to have created around David the moonlit world. For we are made uncomfortably aware, always, of Steerforth's inexplicable power to charm:

> There was an ease in his manner—a gay and light manner it was, but not swaggering—which I still believe to have borne a kind of enchantment with it. I still believe him, in virtue of this carriage, his animal spirits, his delightful voice, his handsome face and figure, and, for aught I know, of some inborn power of attraction besides (which I think a few people possess), to have carried a spell with him to which it was a natural weakness to yield, and which not many persons could withstand. (p. 157)

It's this, of course, that Agnes finds so objectionable. The essence of this love, we have to say, is an enchantment that cannot be explained, that is too particular to be explained. The enchantment constitutes a mutual relationship of intimacy, in which David is "nearer to his heart than any other friend,"[39] and Steerforth inhibits David's dreams (p. 347).

Furthermore, we are, as readers, led by the novelist's art (by the vividness of perceptual memory that is, David tells us, at the heart of his own narratorial gift) to enter, ourselves, the shadowy world and to feel its enchantment through the enchanting power of David's poetic use of language. Led into the imaginings and habits characteristic of love, we, too, recognize the body by its posture on the beach and participate, mourning, in David's final farewell to the hand he has touched so often:

> I went through the dreary house, and darkened the windows. The windows of the chamber where he lay, I darkened last. I lifted up the leaden hand, and held it to my heart; and all the world seemed death and silence, broken only by his mother's mourning. (p. 873)

The chapter ends; the silence is also ours.

This romantic and participatory conception of readership is not only built into the structure of the novel, into the erotic ways in which it beckons to the reader. It is also explicitly described in the novel as David's own experience of readership in early life. Reading novels is his refuge from the gloomy religion of the Murdstones, and his renewal of contact with his father in the world of ghosts and spirits. His reading is passionately, generously involved, as he enacts in fantasy his favorite plots and their relations:

---

39. Strictly speaking, this records David's belief; but it seems, so far as we can tell, to be true; Steerforth values Daisy in a unique way, and blesses him.

My father had left a small collection of books in a little room upstairs, to which
I had access (for it adjoined my own) and which nobody else in our house ever
troubled. From that blessed little room, Roderick Random, Peregrine Pickle,
Humphrey Clinker, Tom Jones, the Vicar of Wakefield, Don Quixote, Gil Blas,
and Robinson Crusoe, came out, a glorious host, to keep me company. They kept
alive my fancy, and my hope of something beyond that place and time,—they,
and the *Arabian Nights,* and the *Tales of the Genii,*—and did me no harm; for
whatever harm was in some of them was not there for me; *I* knew nothing of
it. . . . It is curious to me how I could ever have consoled myself under my small
troubles (which were great troubles to me), by impersonating my favourite characters in them—as I did—and by putting Mr and Miss Murdstone into all the
bad ones—which I did too. I have been Tom Jones (a child's Tom Jones, a harmless creature) for a week together. I have sustained my own idea of Roderick Random for a month at a stretch, I verily believe. I had a greedy relish for a few
volumes of Voyages and Travels—I forget what, now—that were on those
shelves; and for days and days I can remember to have gone about my region of
our house, armed with the centre-piece out of an old set of boot-trees—the perfect
realization of Captain Somebody, of the Royal British Navy, in danger of being
beset by savages, and resolved to sell his life at a great price. The Captain never
lost dignity, from having his ears boxed with the Latin Grammar. I did; but the
Captain was a Captain and a hero, in despite of all the grammars of all the languages in the world, dead or alive.

This was my only and my constant comfort. When I think of it, the picture
always rises in my mind, of a summer evening, the boys at play in the churchyard,
and I sitting on my bed, reading as if for life. Every barn in the neighborhood,
every stone in the church, and every foot of the churchyard, had some association
of its own, in my mind, connected with these books, and stood for some locality
made famous in them. I have seen Tom Pipes go climbing up the church-steeple;
I have watched Strap, with the knapsack on his back, stopping to rest himself
upon the wicket-gate; and I *know* that Commodore Trunnion held that club with
Mr Pickle, in the parlour of our little village alehouse.

The reader now understands, as well as I do, what I was when I came to that
point of my youthful history to which I am now coming again. (pp. 105–6)

This is an important passage; for it tells us clearly how powerful novel-reading
is in and for life, how surely it forms the life of fantasy, how surely fantasy shapes,
for good or ill, the reader's relations with the world. David, as reader, is in
no sense detached or judicious, as Adam Smith seems to recommend. He is a romantic and passionate participant. He peoples the world with the characters
he loves, and puts his whole life into enacting the story. And the habits of desire
formed by the novels he reads are kinetic and erotic, conducive to falling in love
in life.

We have spoken of falling in love with Steerforth. Now we can see that this is
the sort of novel-reading David knows and cultivates. The love of a fictional character can be love because it is an active and interactive relationship that sustains
the reader for many hours of imagining, of fiction-making, beyond the time spent
with the page itself; and because, in this relation, the mysterious and ineffable
charm of interaction with a powerful presence can be experienced in much the

way it is in life; because, too, the reader is at the same time a reader of his or her own life, bringing to the imagining the hopes and loves of real life. Of course this interaction takes place in fantasy. But David insists upon the closeness of its links to love in life: its activation of the same generous, outgoing and erotic impulses, its power to transform the texture of the world. And he also indicates that the loves we find in life owe, themselves, a great deal to the storytelling imagination and to romantic projection. This does not mean that they are based upon *illusion* in any pejorative sense, as we shall see; the way one thing is associated with another, the richness of the intersection of one image with many others, all this is not mere deception, but part of the texture of life, and a part of life's excitement. Part, too, of our ability to endow a perceived form with a human life: in that sense, all sympathy, all morality, is based on a generous fantasy. Without "fancy" Mr. Gradgrind's pupils cannot see truly, cannot love.

Now, however, we are prepared to notice something further about the novel's portrayal of storytelling. Steerforth is not only a character and an episode inside this novel; not only an object of love for its readers; he is also unmistakably linked with the novelist's craft. Most obvious is the fact that, whereas Agnes is associated with school books (historical and philosophical and religious, presumably, not literary[40]), Steerforth and David meet to tell stories. It is David's ability to recreate the world of his favorite novels, to be Scheherezade, that first draws Steerforth to him. His love of Steerforth has been prepared, as we have suggested, by novel-reading; and he links Steerforth with the protective father who gave him novels to read, and who lives in the shadowy world. The onward erotic movement of storytelling is the movement of their love—whereas we associate Agnes, on the other side, with stained glass and sermons, rest and immobility.[41]

This connection is brought out very clearly when David meets Steerforth again after the years of absence. He has just seen his first professional stage production of Shakespeare, and the mystery of that event prepares him for romantic love:

> But the mingled reality and mystery of the whole show, the influence upon me of the poetry, the lights, the music, the company, the smooth stupendous changes of glittering and brilliant scenery, were so dazzling, and opened up such illimitable regions of delight, that when I came out into the rainy street, at twelve o'clock at night, I felt as if I had come from the clouds, where I had been leading a romantic life for ages, to a bawling, splashing, link-lighted, umbrella-struggling, hackney-coach-jostling, patten-clinking, muddy, miserable world. (p. 344)[42]

40. See p. 288, where she shows him how to study from his schoolbooks. Since David has to be shown how to use them, it is clear (as it is in any case, given the educational methods of the day) that they are not novels.

41. For descriptions of Agnes as "calm," "placid," "quiet," "tranquil," see pp. 279, 280, 288, 326, 430, etc.

42. The play is Julius Caesar, significant for the way in which it, too, links love and morality. And notice that David finds something altogether new and better in the historical events, when they are displayed as literature, than he found in them before from his history lessons: "To have all those noble Romans alive before me, and walking in and out for my entertainment, instead of being the stern taskmasters they had been at school, was a most novel and delightful effect."

He now sees his own past life through the play, as if it is "a shining transparency, through which I saw my earlier life moving along" (p. 345); and into this charmed picture enters "the figure of a handsome well-formed young man dressed with a tasteful easy negligence which I have reason to remember very well" (p. 345). Steerforth has returned; the mystery of literature opens onto the other mystery.

What is more, the literary association is unmistakeably linked with the generous and loving feelings that draw him to Steerforth:

> At another time I might have wanted the confidence or the decision to speak to him, and might have put it off until next day, and might have lost him. But, in the then condition of my mind, where the play was still running high, his former protection of me appeared so deserving of my gratitude, and my old love for him overflowed my breast so freshly and spontaneously, that I went up to him at once, with a fast-beating heart, and said: "Steerforth! won't you speak to me?" (p. 345)

Here David shows that love in life interacts in complicated ways with fantasy, memory, and projection. That, indeed, insofar as it involves endowing a perceived form with a mind and heart, in this way going beyond the evidence, it is always a kind of generous fiction-making. All love is, in that sense, love of fictional characters; and literature trains us for that element in love. This fiction-making, we clearly see here, need not be pernicious or self-deceptive. His fantasy has led David outside himself to see Steerforth with love and to focus generously on his actual presence. Fantasy and a genuine relatedness are mutually supportive, as the imagining of the play makes him more keenly aware of what is outside him, and prompts a generous outpouring of feeling.[43]

These are only the most obvious links between erotic/romantic love and literary narration in the novel. What we need now to record is that, through very many hints, the character and effect of Steerforth himself are linked with the novelist's task, until we cannot help asking who wrote the text we are reading, and what is happening to us as we read. Steerforth makes his first appearance in the novel as writing: "There was one boy—a certain J. Steerforth—who cut his name very deep and very often" (p. 131). Writing and an erotic romanticism are unmistakably linked; writing itself is eroticized and romanticized as bold, deep, cutting onward movement, dedicated to the particular, to a proper name. And consider the attributes of Steerforth as romantic charmer. "He is such a speaker . . . that he can win anybody over; and I don't know what you'd say if you were to hear him sing, Mr. Peggotty" (p. 196). "Steerforth could always pass from one subject to another with a carelessness and lightness that were his own" (p. 349). We know of "his natural gift of adapting himself to whomsoever he pleased, and making direct, when he cared to do it, to the main point of interest in anybody's heart" (p. 367). "How lightly and easily he carried on, until he brought us, by degrees, into a charmed circle" (p. 375). He "could become anything he liked at any moment" (p. 402). He charms even Rosa Dartle with "the fascinating influence

---

43. Compare Richard Wollheim, *The Thread of Life* (Cambridge, Mass., 1984) on projection and love. On endowing a bodily form with life, see Stanley Cavell, *The Claim of Reason* (New York, 1979), Part IV.

of his delightful art" (p. 495).[44] Aren't these all traits of a good novelist? And aren't these, as well, the arts that are being practiced on us, even as we read? The novel is written, for a great part of its length, from the moral point of view, clearly, the point of view of the compassionate spectator. But now we see, too, another art that writes it; and we are made to ask whether it isn't that art that is, somehow, more organizing, more fundamental.

One strange exchange makes the connection more complex still. Shortly before Steerforth departs for Yarmouth, he makes of his Daisy a singular request:

> "Daisy," he said, with a smile—"for though that's not the name your godfathers and godmothers gave you, it's the name I like best to call you by—and I wish, I wish, I wish, you could give it to me."
> "Why so I can, if I choose," said I. (p. 497)

This extraordinary response reminds us of the novelist's power to give names to things, to transform evil to good, guilt to innocence—or to move altogether beyond that distinction, if he so chooses. The novel can, if it chooses, fulfill our hopes for innocence and the ubiquity of morality; or, if it chooses, it can simply love Steerforth as he is and allow his charm to remain, as it does remain, untouched, at the novel's heart. David has neither changed Steerforth to Daisy nor simply condemned him; and yet he might have done either had he so chosen.

And there is something more. We are made to recall that, as so many other suggestions have indicated, Steerforth *is* in a sense the author of this novel, the creator of its erotic charm. Perhaps, then, this author has, in writing the novel, called himself David or Daisy, has separated out, given separate representation to, a strain of innocence and purity in his complex heart. Dickens's Preface, read as a part of the narrative, reminds us of the complex relation of the passionate and tumultuous Dickens character to his own many-sided creation. For he has, after all, made himself into Daisy—but into a Daisy so wrapped up in Steerforth that he sees him and loves him without condemnation, despite the allure of morality. And he has made as well, in this scene, a Steerforth who wishes to be Daisy, whose selfishness is qualified by a real love of Daisy. He has made, then, in the relation of the two, a love that lies beyond strict morality and the distinction between guilt and innocence, and yet at the same time a love that moves us as something whose

44. Rosa Dartle is the one other character in the novel who both passionately loves Steerforth and sees him as a whole. But her self-absorbed jealous vindictive love is strongly contrasted with David's nonjudgmental generosity. Like Miss Wade in *Little Dorrit,* she shows how a preoccupation with resentment and judgment undercuts the generous outward impulse to love that is for Dickens essential to the moral life. And in the scene in which Rosa harshly confronts Em'ly we are made to understand how thoroughly her stern judgmental morality, which has its origins, unmistakably, in the fantasy of persecution and injury, differs from David's morality, which has its origins in a different sort of fantasy, loving and concerned with the projection into the world of images of the figures who are most loved. Dickens clearly links the latter sort of imagination with the power to write a novel; and through Miss Wade's narrative in *Little Dorrit* he shows us that imagination of the former sort is incapable of constructing a narrative in which the reader can participate as a friend. In the present passage, in which narrative art charms even Rosa, Dickens indicates that the generous impulses involved in fiction making have the power to overcome the angry impulses connected with revenge.

human value is not to be dismissed because it cannot be seen from the spectator's viewpoint. (And if Steerforth is Daisy he cannot, as we know, be killed at sea—so the identity question raises, for us, the possibility that Steerforth in some sense lives on.) The exchange continues:

> "Daisy, if anything should ever separate us, you must think of me at my best, old boy. Come! Let us make that bargain. Think of me at my best, if circumstances should ever part us!"
> "You have no best to me, Steerforth," said I, "and no worst. You are always equally loved, and cherished in my heart." (p. 497)

He keeps the bargain, even to the end of his writing. This novel, we now begin to see, contains the writing of J. Steerforth; it contains, as well, the writing of sympathetic morality. It is written by and in the tension between these two apparently irreconcilable viewpoints. But it contains, as well, something further, something not precisely equivalent either to the charms of romantic/erotic love or to the judgments of morality—a movement of the loving heart that mediates between those two worlds, and insists on joining them in a coherently, if complexly, loving work of art. There is a profound question, in fact—the question asked in the novel's opening sentence—about who the novel's hero is, and who its author.

But before we try to answer that question, and to describe the mediating attitude, we must return to the gesture of Agnes, examining the limits of moral spectatorship as the novel presents them. The failure of Agnes to inspire love in the reader is one of the novel's most insistent problems. One tends to suppose that it is inadvertent, a defect of Dickens's craft. But Dickens has given us enough hints about the subversive and Steerforthian character of novel writing and the imagination of the writer that we are motivated to question this first judgment. The novel's final lines strike us at first as merely cloying and not terribly effective:

> O Agnes, O my soul, so may thy face be by me when I close my life indeed; so may I, when realities are melting from me, like the shadows which I now dismiss, still find thee near me, pointing upward. (p. 950)

But there is a chill behind the sweetness. And the hand that points upward is, we sense, as cold as death. For, unmistakably and quite deliberately, Dickens has made the gesture of morality equivalent to the gesture of death. In the one previous appearance of this gesture in the narrative, the one on account of which David remembers the gesture, thinks it as characteristic of Agnes, and projects it onto the Agnes who is standing at his side, it means, quite simply, that Dora, his frivolous child wife, has died. Agnes comes downstairs from her patient's bedside to David, who is staring with grief at the dead body of Jip, Dora's little dog.

> "Oh, Agnes! Look, look, here!"
> —That face, so full of pity, and of grief, that rain of tears, that awful mute appeal to me, that solemn hand upraised towards Heaven!

As Agnes displays the proper emotions of the judicious spectator, her hand points upward, both toward heaven and toward Dora, lying dead upstairs. Her gesture connects death and uplift. In the ascent to heaven we see the death of romance, of playfulness, of childhood, of trifles (and "trifles," as David has just been thinking, "make the sum of life" [p. 838]). And, since good angels make it their business to vanquish bad angels, it is the death, as well, of Steerforth, of erotic romance.

In the chapter that follows, David makes the connection between Agnes's moral role and death explicit: for he suggests to us that the figure she represents in the stained glass window of his imagination may be none other than the Angel of Death:

> And now, indeed, I began to think that in my old association of her with the stained-glass window in the church, a prophetic foreshadowing of what she would be to me, in the calamity that was to happen in the fullness of time, had found a way into my mind. In all that sorrow, from the moment, never to be forgotten, when she stood before me with her upraised hand, she was like a sacred presence in my lonely house. When the Angel of Death alighted there, my child-wife fell asleep—they told me so when I could bear to hear it—on her bosom, with a smile. (p. 839)

Here, there is a movement of thought from Agnes's upraised gesture to the idea that she is a "sacred presence"; but this figure is closely associated, more or less elided, with the thought of the Angel of Death who visits the house. And the "her" on whose bosom Dora falls asleep is, in the narrative, Agnes; but in David's sentence the pronoun most naturally refers to the Angel. In this complex and ambiguous passage, we see how closely David links Agnes with death. Furthermore, at the close of the novel, David once again, and this time explicitly, imagines Agnes presiding at a death—in this case, his own. And she presides with that same gesture, "pointing upward." The gesture represents morality, and represents it as a death in the heart, a cessation of generous outward movement.

This ambivalence toward Agnes (characterized, always, with images of composure, rest, stained glass, tranquillity, as contrasted with Steerforth's restless horizontal movement) is deliberate. And even though the internal plot of the novel ends with a moral marriage, children, and the victory of Agnes, the real plot has a more complicated ending. For it ends, we must realize, with the writing of the entire novel; with the adventures of thought, emotion, and memory that take the hero as author into the shadowy world. It ends with the victory of the novel-writing heart.

It is made abundantly clear that this heart and its activities are concerned with morality. And yet we know perfectly well that Agnes would not approve of this book, or of her husband insofar as he occupies himself as its author. For the activity of memory brings the author, once again, into the living presence of James Steerforth, as in the present tense, again and again, he relives their evening adventures in the moonlight. In those moments he does not reject Agnes; he keeps her in a sanctuary in his heart. And yet he significantly departs from her and from her judgment—and in a way, we feel, in which he does not depart from himself, from his own morality and his own heart.

For we feel that there is, somehow, morality *in* the willingness to enter into that world of love, loving Steerforth without judgment. That the book is not simply displaying to us a tension or even an oscillation between two viewpoints that it shows as irreconcilable—but that it shows us, as a coherent movement of one and the same heart David's movement from the one to the other. David is himself in all his adventures. There is romance in his morality, morality in his romance.

To get clearer about this coherence, we can return to the novel's opening, where David tells us in no uncertain terms that there is a certain cast of imagination that is characteristic of him as novelist, and that this is also a morally valuable way of confronting the world:

> . . . I believe the power of observation in numbers of very young children to be quite wonderful for its closeness and accuracy. Indeed, I think that most grown men who are remarkable in this respect, may with greater propriety be said not to have lost the faculty, than to have acquired it; the rather, as I generally observe such men to retain a certain freshness, and gentleness, and capacity of being pleased, which are also an inheritance they have preserved from their childhood. (p. 61)

David tells us that he is not like most grown men in his childlike attention to and memory for the particularities of the world, in the freshness and susceptibility with which he confronts things. Adult life is seen as blurring the sensibilities, dulling the capacity for pleasure and delight. To write this novel, David has had to escape that blurring. It is clear that this perceptual freshness and this gentleness are what has permitted him to see the entire world of the novel as he wonderfully sees it. And so in this way, insofar as the novel has, through its vividness, a moral power, this childlike imagination has shown itself to be supportive of morality and moral responsiveness. It sees all around, with an intensity that brings sympathy to our hearts.

And yet we know perfectly well that it is this same susceptibility to delight and to the sensuously vivid, this nonjudgmentally loving attitude to the world, that has permitted David to fall in love and to be led outside of morality.[45] What I believe David indicates here, and shows in the construction of the novel as a whole, is that the posture of the heart that is best for morality—most vivid, most gentle and generous, most active in sympathy—is also more susceptible and less judgmental than Agnes' heart is, and is bound, in its mobile attention to particulars, to fall in love, and to feel for the object that it loves a non-judgmental loyalty that no moral authority, however judicious, can dislodge. (Agnes, we recall, was never really a child. Substitute for her dead mother, guardian of an alcoholic father, she makes her first appearance with keys at her side, "as staid and discreet

---

45. As a child, David, we recall, played the role of Tom Jones "for a week together" (p. 106). And he has much in common with that hero, in his combination of warmth and goodness with erotic susceptibility. David is at pains to insist that he played "a child's Tom Jones, a harmless creature"; and in general that the "harm" that was in some of the books "was not there for me; I knew nothing of it." But we are encouraged by his later eroticism to be somewhat skeptical of these protestations—especially since the narrator plainly knows very well what "harm" there is in *Tom Jones.* And it would indeed be a strange reader of Fielding's novel who did not notice its physical, earthy, and erotic content. The entirety of *David Copperfield* is in many ways a continuation of *Tom Jones,* but with the more romantic understanding of love that it now recommends.

a housekeeper as the old house could have" (p. 280).[46] Love is, in a sense, outside of morality, in the sense we have described. And yet it is a natural movement of the most truly human morality, and its fitting completion.[47]

In the act of writing this book, an act of which neither Steerforth nor Agnes would have been capable, David achieves a human completeness that they both fail to attain. His moral spectatorship and his love are, though in tension, all of a piece. His love is full of sympathy and loyalty, his sympathetic spectatorship of loving susceptibility to the particular.

There is one more arm in this novel that we must now consider. And its gesture shows us, I think, how the novel understands the mediating link between the other two. For the third arm that recurs prominently in David's memory is the arm of Peggotty, who lovingly supports his dying mother's head. Peggotty foresees, long before, that she will want that arm, and at the end she takes it:

> Daybreak had come, and the sun was rising, when she said to me, how kind and considerate Mr Copperfield had always been to her, and how he had borne with her, and told her, when she doubted herself, that a loving heart was better and stronger than wisdom, and that he was a happy man in hers. "Peggotty, my dear," she said then, "put me nearer to you," for she was very weak. "Lay your good arm underneath my neck," she said, "and turn me to you, for your face is going far off, and I want it to be near." I put it as she asked; and oh Davy! the time had come when my first parting words to you were true—when she was glad to lay her poor head on her stupid cross old Peggotty's arm—and she died like a child that had gone to sleep! (p. 186)

The gesture, connected with the reflection that a loving heart is better and stronger than wisdom, is, above all, a gesture of loving attention, support, and connection. It is different from our other two gestures, in that it cannot be imagined, even as a gesture, without imagining two people; it is a relation. It is different, too, in that, rather than pointing to or standing for something—even for the presence of someone uniquely loved—it actively *does* something. Agnes' static gesture of uplift,

46. The portrait of Agnes captures in a striking manner the features of a certain sort of child of an alcoholic parent, as these are emerging in the recent clinical literature. The inability to play or to enjoy childhood, the difficulty in feeling and expressing strong emotion, a judgmental attitude to self and others, a fear of vulnerability—all are striking similarities.

In this connection, we can perhaps understand why Agnes is so drawn to David, who has an emotional robustness that she lacks and needs. And though for the most part Agnes remains in her ambivalently drawn moralizing role, the narrative permits her one expression of nonjudgmental individualized love. When she is about to confess her love for David, she repeatedly insists, "I am not myself" (pp. 934–35). And when they do embrace, there is, in Agnes' life, a moment of childhood: "And O, Agnes, even out of thy true eyes, in that same time, the spirit of my child-wife looked upon me, saying it was well." Does this single moment produce a more lasting evolution? The descriptions of Agnes at the end of the novel allow us to doubt this. And indeed, since David speaks of the fresh imagination as something *preserved* from childhood, it seems unlikely that someone who had to that extent been completely deprived of a childhood could ever securely or stably attain it.

47. Dora shows, however, that the childlike imagination is insufficient, without further development, for adult morality. Frozen in early childhood, she lacks both dimensions of David's further development: the erotic and the moral.

Steerforth's sleepy gesture of erotic presence, neither of these in itself does good for someone in this world. They are, merely, gestures. But this gesture is also an action, an action of love and unquestioning unjudgmental loyalty, of attention and responsiveness to a beloved particular. By being connected with Peggotty, the gesture is linked with the gentle childlike imagination that neither she nor David has ever lost. By being connected with the advice of David's father, it is also connected with the father's love of novels. And the fact that the gesture is a gesture of love and support toward David's mother shows us, even more fundamentally, its significance in his imagination, a way in which he understands, through that gesture, the link between his own delight in particulars and the two worlds of romance and morality.

For David's childlike imagination is not only drawn to the world by a general delight in the perception of the particular. It is drawn, from the first, by a very passionate perception of one particular above all. David's mother is the first particular thing he loves, the first object of the fresh delight, the gentleness, and the pleasure of which he tells us. And his connection to his mother combines, from the first, in a coherent way, perceptions of her beauty and kindness with incipient moral attitudes—above all tenderness, gratitude for support, and a corresponding desire to support and protect; and combines both of these, clearly, with intensely romantic feelings. (This is dramatized in many ways: in his remembrance of his mother's grace and beauty; in his jealousy of Murdstone even before his villainous character is known; in his developing fantasy of himself in the role of his mother's rescuer and true support, a fantasy deeply involved in his novel enacting—for we are told whom he casts as the villain, whom as the hero, and the identity of the heroine can hardly elude us; and finally in the extraordinary fantasy, before his mother's grave, in which he imagines (wishes) that the dead baby in her arms "was myself, as I had once been, hushed forever on her bosom" [p. 187].)

Romance, morality, and a mediating attitude of loyal support and connection are linked for him because they have been linked from the start. The pattern of all his relationships, however various, contains these basic ingredients, the ingredients that mark his earliest fantasies and encounters. And love conquers retentiveness and stern judgment in his heart because loving support, linked with novel-reading, from the first got ahead of the fear of punishment, linked for him with the Murdstones' religious moralism.[48]

David's movement from morality toward Steerforth, and his refusal to judge the person he loves, are, then, motivated not only by romantic desire, but by a complex attitude in which desire is linked with active loyalty and support, fantasy with the true perception of the particular. (Steerforth is, to be sure, a parental figure, protective and supportive; but David also, clearly, supports and protects him in his recklessness.) And this active love is linked strongly with susceptibility to romance and erotic desire, through the portrait of the childlike imagination as delighting in the sensuous world. If Agnes, in the novel, represents wisdom—as there is much reason to think she does, learned and religious as she is—David's

---

48. Dora, by contrast, is shown to lack the particular type of relationship to her parents that would promote onward movement toward adult erotic and moral attitudes. Her determination to go on playing and to refuse responsibility is encouraged by those around her.

love emerges as the love that is "better and stronger than wisdom." If Agnes is the judicious spectator, he is, as a mobile participant, stronger than the spectator. His very susceptibility to extramoral danger is part of his strength, and part of the strength of his love. Morality, at its most generous and best, is something mobile and even volatile, something actively caring and sustaining. Its gestures will be nothing more than gestures of death, if it does not retain its capability to move beyond itself into love.

In this way, the novel powerfully criticizes, as morally limited and ungenerous, an image of moral judgment dominant in the Scottish-English tradition, substituting for it a more romantic, yet, it is also suggested, also a more deeply moral norm. At the same time it continues, in its own way, the task that Smith assigned to the novel: the task of constituting its readers as moral subjects, according to this new and broader conception of morality. Only now, instead of surrendering romantic fantasy before the judgment of judicious perception, instead of dispelling the shadowy world by calling in the daylight of judicious spectatorship, the reader is encouraged to bring that fantasy and mysterious excitement into the world of reality, and to use the energy of fantasy toward a just and generous vision.[49]

The novel gives us no assurance that a single love, a single human relationship, can by itself contain and combine the sympathy of the spectator, the mystery of the erotic/romantic, and the mobile love of particulars that mediates between them. For although David's complex attitude seems to have its origin in a single relationship, he represents himself, in later life, as finding the mediation only in the act of novel-writing itself. Like other novelists with tumultuous or problematic personal lives (I think, among others, of Proust), Dickens too—insofar as he makes himself, for us, a character—represents himself as finding only in his craft the moral synthesis he imagines. But the reader is shown, nonetheless, a paradigm and a possibility. If we do not cling rigidly to the ideal of the judicious spectator, but allow ourselves a more kinetic sympathy, susceptible to the fresh perception of the particular, we may find less tension and discontinuity than Adam Smith did between the romantic/erotic and the moral. And we might even discover that in a single adult relationship all of these attitudes could be more or less coherently combined, and could even support and sustain one another, constructing among them a world in which general sympathy, erotic moonlight, and active generous loyalty live together in conversation. Something like the world of this novel.[50]

49. The novel itself represents itself as a true vision of reality propelled by fantasy of a particular sort.

50. This paper was first presented at a conference on Love at the National Humanities Center; I am grateful to Jean Hagstrum for organizing the conference and inviting the paper. At the conference it had the benefit of stimulating comments by David Halperin, whose Proustian skepticism about the romantic attitudes expressed here produced a lively discussion and provoked me to develop more fully the parts of the paper dealing with the generosity of fantasy. I am also grateful to Amelie Rorty, to Michael de Paul, to Henry Richardson, and to Christopher Rowe for helpful comments, and to audiences at the Tri-College Colloquium at Amherst College, at Randolph-Macon College (Ashland), at Furman University, at the University of Illinois at Urbana-Champaign, and at Whitman College, for their helpful remarks. Above all I am grateful to Rachel for reading the novel well and getting me to read it again.

Endnote

This essay's views about love and ethics are further discussed in the Introduction, and compared with the views expressed in some other essays in this volume.

The defense of the novel-reading heart attempted here is of special importance for the overall project of showing what the novel as genre offers to moral philosophy. For the argument vindicates as morally central some of the major structural features of the genre—its passionate onward movement, its tendency to lure the reader into a world of enchantment—that do not figure prominently in Henry James's thought, and thus not in any defense of the novel based on James. Thus, the argument enabled me to begin to move on from a defense of James to the more general defense of the novel (in connection with a particular family of ethical views) that is begun in the Introduction.

The contrast between the Dickens of this paper and the Beckett of "Narrative Emotions" is of special interest. Beckett suggests that the novel is in league with an emotion-story at the heart of which is a judging and punitive father. He suggests that the emotions of anxiety, guilt, and disgust that are generated through and represented in that story are the mainsprings of our interest in novelistic plot. Dickens, by contrast, presents a novel whose emotional structures are shown to derive from the original experience of a beautiful, loving, protective, and yet vulnerable mother. The emotions generated through fantasies issuing from this experience are love, the desire to protect and to be protected, a delight in the beauties of life. These same emotions appear to be the mainsprings of the reader's interest in the novel. And novel reading and writing in general is represented as deeply opposed to the "gloomy religion" of the Murdstones.

Transcending Humanity

Odysseus tells Calypso, once again, that he is determined to leave her. Once again, she offers him a bargain that no human being, it seems, could refuse. Stay with me on this island, she says, and you will avoid all the troubles that await you. And best of all, living here, "in calm possession of this domain," you will be "beyond the reach of death," both immortal and ageless. The love Calypso offers and has offered is, itself, endless and ageless: no fatigue, no mourning, no cessation of calm pleasure. Odysseus replies, undeflected, choosing death:

Goddess and queen, do not make this a cause of anger with me. I know the truth of everything that you say. I know that my wise Penelope, when a man looks at her, is far beneath you in form and stature; she is a mortal, you are immortal and unageing. Yet, notwithstanding, my desire and longing day by day is still to reach my own home and to see the day of my return. And if this or that divinity should shatter my craft on the wine-dark ocean, I will bear it and keep a bold heart within me. Often enough before this time have war and wave oppressed and plagued me; let new tribulations join the old.[1]

In this remarkable speech we see two elements of widely shared human belief, uneasily conjoined in Odysseus' account of his own thinking, as they are in what he implies about popular thought more generally. On the one hand, the desire to transcend the condition of humanity and to take up the life of a god with a god is, to Odysseus, a perfectly intelligible and even a highly reasonable desire. He assumes that anyone would understand it and, to some extent, share it. And he sees that from the point of view of that desire his choice to leave Calypso's island will seem perverse. On the other hand, he chooses the life of a human being, and a marriage to a woman who will both age and die, and who will either die before he does, or die after. He chooses, then, not only risk and difficulty, but the certainty of death; and not only death, but the virtual certainty that he will at some time lose what he most deeply loves, or else will cause, by his own death, great grief to her.

What, in the face of the recognized human attachment to transcendence, could justify such a choice? Odysseus has little to say. But what he does say makes it

1. Homer, *Odyssey*, V.215–24. The earlier quotes are from V.208 and V.209. I quote from the translation by W. Shewring (Oxford, 1980).

perfectly clear that the key is not any surpassing beauty in Penelope herself. He freely grants that from this point of view Calypso will be found superior. And he points to no superiority in Penelope that could counterbalance Calypso's divine excellence. So he is not, it seems, choosing a glorious prize in spite of the fact that he has to face death to get it; that is not at all how he sees the issue. He is choosing the whole human package: mortal life, dangerous voyage, imperfect mortal aging woman. He is choosing, quite simply, what is his: his own history, the form of a human life and the possibilities of excellence, love, and achievement that inhabit that form. What, then, can he say to make that choice intelligible, once the alternative of divinity and agelessness is on the scene?

And yet, to readers of the poem from ancient to modern times, Odysseus' choice *does* seem intelligible, and also admirable—the only choice we would have our hero make. In part this is because we are, as readers, already attached, before this scene unfolds, to Penelope and Telemachus; and we are not much enamored of Çalypso, who seems to be a boring monotonous character. We want Odysseus to come home and to renew his love for those two; we want him to help them out. In part, too, there is an issue of loyalty and commitment. We will think less well of Odysseus for simply abandoning his family to gratify his own desire for immortality. (Though it is perfectly clear that this issue cuts both ways, since he is in the process abandoning a woman who saved his life, gave him everything a goddess could offer, and lived with him happily for many years.)

But there is also something more elusive, both in the speech and the reactions it elicits: the feeling that the other life would just not be comprehensible as a life for a human being with human virtues and human heroism. We don't quite know what it would be for this hero, known for his courage, craft, resourcefulness, and loyal love to enter into a life in which courage would atrophy, in which cunning and resourcefulness would have little point, since the risks with which they grapple would be removed, and in which love, insofar as it appears at all, would be very different in shape from the love that connects man to wife and child in the human world of the poem. The very possibility makes one uneasy: for where, and who, in such a life, would our hero actually be? Do we wish for him a good result that involves a transformation so total that he might not remain himself? The affectionate reader's preference is likely to be for a hero who goes, so to speak, where the action is, so that he can do and achieve the things with which human heroism is usually associated. And this seems to require the context of a human life that moves, in the familiar way, from place to place and time to time, from birth to marriage and children,[2] through risks and challenges, to, at some point, death. Our preference for Odysseus' life with Penelope over his life with Calypso actually stems, I think, from this more general uneasiness about the shapelessness of the life Calypso offers: pleasure and kindliness on and on, with no risks, no possibility of sacrifice, no grief, no children. All we need to do to see this is to compare the

2. These are not the only significant elements of a hero's career; Achilles' friendship with Patroclus is stressed far more, for example, than his marriage and fatherhood. I mention these elements as the ones most significant in the *Odyssey,* and as important elements in its influence on later conceptions of the hero.

accounts of lovemaking. Odysseus and Calypso "withdrew, and in a recess of the arching cavern they took their pleasure in love, and did not leave one another's side." That's the end of that; the poet can say no more; for they have nothing to talk about, since they have done nothing and nothing has happened to them. As for the human husband and wife:

> The two in their room enjoyed the delights of love, then pleased one another with recounting what had befallen each. The queen told how much she had suffered in these halls, seeing always there the pernicious multitude of suitors who in wooing her had slaughtered so many beasts, fat sheep and oxen, and drawn so much wine from the great jars. The king told of the harm he had done to others and the misery he had endured himself. Penelope listened to him enraptured, and sleep did not fall upon her eyelids till he had told his tale to the end.[3]

It's perfectly plain that the human pair are, at least from the viewpoint of the human reader, more interesting and more erotic. A sexuality divorced from conversation, from storytelling, from risk and adventure and the sharing of risk and adventure, seems extremely boring; and we feel that it is a great tribute to the goddess's beauty that Odysseus retains his interest in her, after so much time.

And if, as readers, we begin reflecting this way about our hero and his possibilities, another fact begins to emerge as well. This is, that humanity, and the choice for humanity, is built into this story itself and into its transactions with its readers. For surely one reason why the choice for transcendence seems unappealing to the reader is that it would, quite clearly, bring the story to an end. When Calypso speaks of "calm possession of this domain," our hearts sink; for there's no story in that. When, on the other hand, she warns of troubles that await him on the sea, our mouths water, so to speak, for we know that this is how the story should go on, and, being by now lovers of stories, we want it to go on in that way. Stories have shaped and continue to shape the readers' desires, giving them a preference for onward movement over stasis, for risk over self-sufficiency, for the human form of time over divine timelessness. They play upon and nourish the emotions—fear, anticipation, grief, hope—that presuppose the form of life of a being both needy and resourceful, both active and finite—and that seem to have their point and function only within the context of such a life. What story would be left, if he made the other choice? Plato saw the answer clearly: no story at all, but only praises of the goodness of good gods and heroes. Unfortunately for Plato, readers brought up on Homer would be likely to find that prospect about as appealing as twenty-four books of description of Calypso's unchanging island. Readers, too, want to be where the action is.

---

3. *Od.* V.226–27, XXIII.300–09; see also the remarkable image at XXIII.233–40 in which the joy of the sailor who finally reaches shore begins as a simile for his joy at recovering her, and ends as an image for her joy at finding him. An excellent account of the entire passage is in J. Winkler, "Penelope's Cunning and Homer's," in his *The Constraints of Desire: The Anthropology of Sex and Gender in Ancient Greece* (New York, 1990). For my review of this impressive collection, see *Times Literary Supplement,* June 1990.

I

Human beings want to be immortal and ageless. And, perhaps even more clearly, they want the human beings they love never to age, never to die. There seems to be little doubt of this, Who, given the chance to make a spouse or child or parent or friend immortal, would not take it? (I would grab it hungrily, I confess at the outset.) And yet we don't seem to know very clearly what it is we are wishing when we wish that. And we may well suspect that there is an incoherence lurking somewhere in the wish; that what we actually love and prize would not survive such translations. That we may be doomed or fortunate to be human beings simply, beings for whom the valuable things in life don't come apart so neatly from the fearful and terrible.

In his valuable recent article on my book, *The Fragility of Goodness,* Charles Taylor asks me a tough question: what do I really think about the human aspiration to transcend humanity?[4] In the Plato section of my book, he observes, I defend the aspiration to transcend one's humanity as a coherent and valuable ethical aim for and in a human life, and the life of godlike transcendence as a beautiful and valuable ethical norm. Furthermore, I argue that the negative motivation to escape from vulnerability and pain cannot suffice to explain Plato's position: for we must also take note of the positive draw of transcendence itself, a positive draw that is, I argued, not only intelligible without reference to inadequate or obscure metaphysical conceptions, but actually a powerful part of human ethical experience. Taylor accurately reports my view, presented in a chapter on Plato's *Republic,* and endorses it, saying: "We will never understand Plato (nor I think ourselves) without coming to see the force of this aspiration. To give a reductive view of Plato in terms simply of the negative motivations ends up darkening our own self-understanding."[5]

4. Charles Taylor, Review article on M. Nussbaum, *The Fragility of Goodness: Luck and Ethics in Greek Tragedy and Philosophy,* in *Canadian Journal of Philosophy* 18 (1988), 805–14.

5. Charles Taylor, p. 813. My account of Plato is also accurately characterized, in related ways, by Jasper Griffin and Bernard Knox in their reviews (Griffin, *Times Literary Supplement,* July 4, 1986; Knox, *New York Review of Books,* December 4, 1986), which offer valuable comments on a number of issues. A peculiar misdescription on this issue damages the argument of T. Irwin's review, *Journal of Philosophy* July 1988. Irwin states, "she seems to assume (without directly facing the issue) that Platonic metaphysics and epistemology are necessary supports for Plato's belief in the invulnerability of virtue" (p. 376). This is odd in view of the fact that I devote an entire chapter (chapter 5) to arguing that Plato's ethical conclusions can be understood *without* assuming that they rely on his metaphysical conceptions, as interesting and valuable ethical positions in their own right. (Indeed, here I was criticizing the claims on that issue made in Irwin's *Plato's Moral Theory* [Oxford, 1977].) In a later chapter (chapter 6), I argue, further, that Plato's ethical conclusions provide some, though not all, of the support for his metaphysics and epistemology. This is only one of many serious misdescriptions of my theses and arguments in Irwin's review. Another one that is pertinent to my immediate concerns in this essay has to do with Aristotle. On pp. 377–78, Irwin ascribes to me an argument in five steps: from premises concerning the views of Plato and Aristotle on the value of human agreements in reaching ethical conclusions, I am alleged to infer the conclusion, "Aristotle is not a metaphysical realist about his conclusions." Irwin then goes on to criticize me for not defending all the steps in this argument— not surprising, since these steps have no resemblance to the argument I actually make. Irwin fails to mention that the book contains an entire chapter devoted to the question of Aristotle's relation to metaphysical realism (chapter 8). It reaches its conclusion (which attributes to Aristotle a posi-

On the other hand, Taylor also observes that I seem, in the Aristotle section of the book, and indeed in the book's overall conclusion, to endorse an ethical stance that defines its goal as "the human good," not the good *simpliciter.* And I suggest that a harmonious good life consisting in various forms of excellent activity and of love *(philia)* is, while still subject to impediment in various extreme circumstances, nonetheless "within the reach of any good and moderately fortunate man."[6] This fact suggests to Taylor that my version of Aristotle, and I with him, repudiate the aim to live a godlike transcendent life as an inappropriate and perhaps even incoherent aim for a human being. In other words, to use a distinction he introduces, that I interpret the Aristotelian principle, "Let's have the whole *human* good" to mean "the good consisting in all the various forms of excellent *human* activity" leaving out, even perhaps repudiating, the aspiration to transcend human life altogether; rather than, "Let's have the *whole* human good," viz., all this plus the Platonic aspiration too, and plus whatever conflicts its inclusion will bring with it.[7] (As Taylor notes, I do not deny the existence of a more Platonic side in some parts of Aristotle's writings; but he is correct in saying that I believe the passages expressive of this idea to be inconsistent with the main argument of the *Nicomachean Ethics,* on which I focus.[8]) So, Taylor wants to know, where do I myself end up? With what he calls "the inclusive view" of the good life—that is, with Aristotelian *eudaimonia* plus (and to some extent in tension with) the aspiration to transcendence? Or with what he, somewhat tendentiously I think, calls "the narrower view"—that is, just Aristotelian *eudaimonia* and nothing besides?[9]

Charles Taylor has, with characteristic insightfulness, noticed an unexplained silence in the text, on an issue of real importance. He presents an accurate account of the text, and then raises a philosophical question that eminently calls for further examination. (In fact, Taylor's article is of far more substance and interest than the usual review article, and can be warmly recommended to anyone with an interest in the issues.) And since versions of the same question have also been raised, though less extensively, by two other especially perceptive reviewers—by Christopher (C.C.W.) Taylor in *Mind* and by Stephen Halliwell in *Ancient Philosophy*[10]—it seems time for me to say more about the issue.

---

tion that I describe as a species of *realism*) from premises concerning Aristotle's views about the status of logical and scientific laws; subsequent chapters then examine the implications of this general position for ethics. Irwin's criticisms are directed at a position of his own invention. On other issues, too, the review is similarly lacking in concern for accuracy of attribution.

6. Taylor, p. 813, paraphrasing *Nicomachean Ethics* 1099b18–19 and my discussion of it, *Fragility,* chap. 11. Note that on my account bad luck damages the agent's attempt to live well primarily through impeding excellent *activity.* This is the primary emphasis in Aristotle's account and in mine of him (chap. 11); a smaller body of evidence that Aristotle may admit damage to character itself is considered in chap. 11, pp. 336–40.

7. Taylor puts the contrast this way on p. 812.

8. See *Fragility,* chap. 12, Appendix, concerned above all with *Nicomachean Ethics* X.6–8.

9. Taylor, p. 813. For my own response to Taylor's most recent book, see *The New Republic,* April 9, 1990.

10. C.C.W. Taylor, *Mind* 96 (1987), 407–14, a valuable discussion focusing on Aristotle and the question of Aristotle's Platonism; S. Halliwell, *Ancient Philosophy* 8 (1988), 313–19, an accurate and perceptive account asking some questions about the relationship between ancient tragedy and ancient religion.

My aim in this essay is, then, to begin to answer Taylor's question about where I myself do stand, philosophically, on this issue of transcendence. I shall, as I go along, make reference both to aspects of the argument in *Fragility* and to examples taken from ancient Greek thought, both popular and philosophical. But my aim will be not so much to clarify what I have said already—all of which Taylor states clearly enough—as to go beyond the book on one of its central philosophical issues.

To do this I must approach Taylor's immediate question somewhat indirectly, in order to make the relevant philosophical notions more intuitively precise. This I shall do by reflecting on Odysseus' dilemma and the questions it raises about transcendence and the godlike life. And this will lead ultimately to some related conclusions about philosophy, that peculiar activity so frequently hooked up with the aim of transcendence—about how it should speak to human beings if it is in fact the life of a human being, and not the life of transcendent gods, that it wishes to help us understand.

Two aspects of Taylor's complex challenge I shall not pursue. One is his suggestion that I might say more about my own view of Judaeo-Christian religion and about what strikes him—not without reason—as my own preference for Greek polytheism.[11] I suspect that Taylor and I do have some deep differences in this area, and that it would be interesting to investigate them. And I have certainly made no secret, in various published pieces, of my own strong objection to making the Augustinian idea of original sin the starting point for reflection about human limits and transcendence.[12] But Christianity is a protean religion; and (as Elaine Pagels has recently argued convincingly[13]) many of its forms have, in fact, begun from an idea of human helplessness that lies closer than Augustine's does to ancient Greek thought, and especially to Aristotle. So I shall defer serious engagement on that issue, and try, for the most part, to discuss the aspiration to transcendence philosophically, without assessing any particular modern religious form of that aspiration.

Nor shall I take up Taylor's historical claim concerning the consequences, within our human this-worldly life, of embracing the aspiration to transcendence as an aim of one's life as a whole. Taylor says that this aim "can turn us towards this life with a new attention and concern, as has undoubtedly been the case with the Judaeo-Christian tradition, with decisive consequences for our whole moral outlook."[14] It would be unwise to try to answer this briefly. I do, in fact, feel some skepticism about Taylor's claim. I think "undoubtedly" is certainly too strong, and I have, in fact, some sympathy with Nietzsche's analysis of the many ways in which directing our aspirations toward a "true world" has led to a denigration of our actions and relationships in this one.[15] There are related arguments in the

11. Charles Taylor, p. 813.

12. See "Narrative Emotions," this volume; "Non-Relative Virtues: An Aristotelian Approach," Midwest Studies in Philosophy 1988; Review of Alasdair MacIntyre, *Whose Justice? Which Rationality?*, New York Review of Books, December 7, 1989.

13. Elaine Pagels, *Adam, Eve, and the Serpent* (New York, 1988).

14. Taylor, p. 813.

15. See, above all, *Twilight of the Idols* ("How the True World Finally Became a Fable"), and many sections in *Zarathustra:* for example, "On the Other-Worldly," "On the Virtue that Makes Small."

ancient philosophical debate—for example in Epicurean attacks on religion.[16] But I shall not take up the whole question of consequences here, concentrating instead on the content and the coherence of the aspiration to transcendence itself.

II

A good place to begin this investigation is with a peculiar tension that one finds in the attitude of the ancient Greeks toward their gods—the tension that is present in Odysseus' speech, and in many other stories of the anthropomorphic Olympians, as these stories are told and retold, emphasizing now one aspect, now another.[17] On the one hand, then, the gods are seen as gods: beings better than us, worthy of our worship and emulation. They are better than we are, above all, because they lack certain limits and defects that characterize human life. They are immortal, *athanatoi,* while humans are mortals, *thnētoi.* They are always healthy and vigorous; we suffer disease and debilitation. They are always in their prime; we move from the impotence of childhood through a brief flourishing to the impotence of age. Their lives are stable; ours are vexed by unanticipated accidents. They have what they want without effort; our life is characterized by painful toil. Their beauty is not undermined by fatigue or illness or anxiety; ours, prone to all this, is never as good. They understand everything; we are ignorant and limited. Their loved ones will be with them forever (unless they fall in love with mortals—on which more later); our loves end in grief and mourning.

In all these ways, then, the image of divinity is an image of human self-transcendence, the image of an anthropomorphic perfection made visible by imagining the removal of constraints that make human life a brief, chancy, and in many ways miserable existence. And of course when one follows out this line of thought, the best thing to wish for, for oneself or for a loved one, seems to be a translation to that life. Thus certain Greek tales of very unusual beauty and excellence culminate in that supreme reward: Heracles made immortal for his excellence and endurance, Ganymede for his amazing erotic loveliness. Odysseus knows that his refusal of that reward goes against a deeply held view about the human good, one that he comprehends and shares with most human beings.

On the other hand, as the Greeks pursued the thought-experiment of transcendence, being both highly imaginative and unencumbered by the excessive self-hatred that belief in original sin has so frequently brought with it, they saw another way of viewing the gods' life, a way to some extent in conflict with the first, though very often mingled with it. On this way of seeing things, the gods are not so much better than us as totally, strangely different. Their form of life, lacking, as it does, the characteristic movement and structure of human life, lacking the constraints imposed by mortality, lacking vulnerabilities of many kinds, lacking the demands and the finitude of the mortal body, will of necessity lack, as well, some of the forms of life that we now find valuable and pursue as ends. This thought experiment is complex, since so much depends on which limits are imagined away and

---

16. On these arguments, see my "Mortal Immortals: Lucretius on Death and the Voice of Nature," *Philosophy and Phenomenological Research,* December 1989.

17. For a perceptive account of the Homeric gods and their relationship to human suffering, see Jasper Griffin, *Homer on Life and Death* (Oxford, 1980).

which left in place. Greek stories of the gods are not always consistent in this, and sometimes the gods appear less omnipotent and more vulnerable than at others. (We shall discuss this later.) But what does emerge clearly—especially in writers such as Homer and Sophocles,[18] with their keen interest in a specifically human heroism and its natural conditions, is that many of the activities we now prize and consider fine will not figure in a divine life, consistently imagined. In some cases, it will be only the motivation to pursue the activity that will be lacking; in other cases, we have to grant that the entire activity will lose its point, will become unintelligible.

Take first what is perhaps the simplest, clearest case: the athletic contest. The Greeks, no less than contemporary Americans, praise outstanding athletic performance as a wonderful instance of human excellence. Young people are urged to cultivate this excellence, and praised when they achieve it. But clearly, such achievement has point and value only relatively to the context of the human body, which imposes certain species-specific limits and creates certain possibilities of movement rather than others. To excel is to use those abilities especially fully, to struggle against those limits especially successfully. But if this means that even races or contests between different animal species will usually seem pointless and odd, it means all the more that there will be no athletic excellence at all, and no meaningful concept of athletic excellence, in the life of a being that is, by nature, capable of anything and physically unlimited—able, for instance, to change its shape at will and to transport itself from here to there without effort. What would such achievement be, in a being for whom it is all easy? What would be the rules of the game?

We must be careful to say what these thoughts do and do not imply. They certainly have not been taken by people over the centuries to imply that, *within* the given species and its species-specific limits, greater limitedness yields greater possibilities of excellence. The fact that I have poor coordination and little natural strength does not open to me possibilities of achievement in tennis that are denied to John McEnroe. Nor do we suppose that our athletic contests would be made better and more interesting by starving the athletes, or beating them, or denying them regular exercise. Training is encouraged to do whatever intelligent training can to push back the limits of the human body. And there is absolutely nothing inappropriate about beginning with those who have the best equipment: with seven-footers in basketball, with young flexible spines in gymnastics.

On the other hand, there is in every sport in every age, from Homer and Pindar on to our own time, a notion of the unfair or "unnatural" competitive edge—exemplified most clearly today in the controversies surrounding the use of anabolic steroids and other performance-enhancing drugs. There are certain ways athletes have of removing limits, certain ways of getting past the body's boundaries, that seem to us to remove the whole point of the activity, to make the achievement

18. On Sophocles, see Cedric Whitman, *Sophocles: A Study of Heroic Humanism* (Cambridge, Mass., 1951); Bernard Knox, *The Heroic Temper: Studies in Sophoclean Tragedy* (Berkeley, 1964); C. Segal, *Tragedy and Civilization: An Interpretation of Sophocles* (Cambridge, Mass., 1981). Related material is discussed in my "*Psuchē* in Heraclitus, II," *Phronesis* 17 (1972), 153–70.

no longer an achievement. This thought appears in its most extreme form in the picture of the Olympian gods. The gods, we might say, are like athletes with not only supersteroids, but a whole array of shape-changing and nature-altering techniques. But this means that so long as they avail themselves of that unlimitedness, they can't achieve anything in sports. The boundary seems to be set by a vague and yet powerful notion of the possibilities of the human species as such. Such possibilities, and the built-in limits that help to constitute them, are necessary conditions of that excellence. Much the same can be said for the dance, for musical performance, for many related bodily achievements. But then we can begin to see why a being who is attached to such excellences and defines his or her good life in terms of them would be puzzled by Calypso's offer. For it now begins to seem like the offer not so much of a better life, but of a different life, with different ends and excellences. And if one identifies oneself with the ends one already knows, one might well wonder whether one could in any meaningful sense survive the translation to such a life.

Now let us move to a completely different sphere, but one in which the possibilities of human beings and divinities are also very clearly distinct: the sphere of political association. Aristotle states as a truism what indeed would have seemed so to most of his audience: that the human being, as such, is divided off from both the beasts and the gods by being a political being, and one who is capable of the ethical and social virtues. A good deal of *Fragility* was spent in developing this Aristotelian idea, and I have also developed it further in a recent paper.[19] But now I want to look at its Homeric expression, which seems to me particularly clear. The Homeric gods do have some rudimentary form of political organization, to be sure: Zeus rules, the others are ruled. But this comes about, quite clearly, only on account of certain ways in which the gods are not truly godlike. They are, that is, limited by one another; and with respect to one another they have very human limits of resource and of knowledge. So politics has a role to play in regulating those interactions and dealing with those vulnerabilities—and, we must add, in keeping the whole crew safe from the Titans, who can menace them with painful, and possibly unending, punishments. On the whole, however, Aristotle is correct: beings who lack our vulnerabilities to hunger, thirst, heat, cold, and disease, beings who don't need to educate their children, to raise an army, to arrange for the fair distribution of life-supporting property and other goods, don't really have our need for politics. Politics is about using human intelligence to support human neediness; so to be truly political you have to have both elements. Beasts fail on one count, gods on the other.

It is in this area that Aristotle (as I interpreted him in *Fragility*) appears most resistant to the idea of transcending humanity as an appropriate goal for a human ethics. For at two crucial points in the *Nicomachean Ethics,* confronted by the possibility of a solitary good life that does not, *ex hypothesi,* need other humans because it does not have the forms of dependency and neediness that lead humans

---

19. See *Fragility,* esp. chaps. 1, 4, 12, 13; also "Aristotle on Human Nature and the Foundations of Ethics," forthcoming in a volume on the philosophy of Bernard Williams, ed. J. Altham and R. Harrison, Cambridge University Press. Also my introduction to a new translation of Euripides' *Bacchae* by C. K. Williams, Farrar, Strauss, and Giroux, 1990.

to reach out for others, he simply refuses to allow that such a life could count as a complete *human* life. The self-sufficiency that a human ethics appropriately seeks is defined in Book I, as a self-sufficiency achieved in company with family, loved ones, and fellow citizens, "since the human being is by nature a political being."[20] And a similar appeal to our political nature is used in Book IX to reject the suggestion that a life without political ties and ties of personal love and friendship could count as *eudaimonia*, provided all goods were at hand and all needs satisfied. He reminds his interlocutor there that we are beings who think of these ties as not just necessary but also fine; not just a resource but also an intrinsic good. A life without them will not even be worth living—far less a candidate for *eudaimonia*.[21] These goods can only be seen as goods, Aristotle freely grants, from within the human form of life with its structures of limit and finitude. He does not suppose that the gods will come searching for instruction in the political art. But he refuses to denigrate the political on that account; good activity for and to others is intrinsically fine and noble, as are the relationships of love and care that bind citizens together in families, and friendships of many kinds.

We can expand these observations by looking more concretely at the ethical virtues—which Aristotle denies to the divine life along with politics.[22] For we see, when we do so, that each of them will seem pointless, more or less unintelligible, in the god's life; and yet, each has a claim to be an end in itself for a human life. Courage is the clearest. Homeric gods usually cannot and do not have it, since there is nothing grave for them to risk. On the other hand, courageous action seems to be a fine *human* achievement.[23] (We notice that as we introduce more and more risk we get closer and closer to courage. Thus Aeschylus' Prometheus is courageous, even though immortal, on account of the way in which he faces appalling pain. His immortality does not remove courage, but actually—given the endlessness of his torture—seems to enhance it.) Moderation will go out too, since for a being who cannot get ill or become overweight or alcoholic, there is not only little motivation to moderate intake, but also little intelligibility to the entire concept. On the other hand, moderation is a challenge and a fine thing in human life: there are so many ways to go wrong here, so few ways of finding what is truly appropriate.

Justice we have already explored in discussing politics. Aristotle seems right to say that the whole notion of the gods making contracts and returning deposits is ludicrous, makes no sense at all. The same seems to be true of the distribution of scarce resources, and other elements of human justice. And here we notice that the carelessness of the gods, with regard to human standards of fairness—a carelessness inseparable from their transcendence of our whole needy way of life, and their failure, in consequence, to see what is at stake for us in that life—leads them to act in ways that are not only different from our ways, but, where we are con-

---

20. *EN* 1097b7–11, discussed in *Fragility*, chap. 12, pp. 344–45, 350ff.

21. *EN* 1169b3ff, discussed in *Fragility*, chap. 12, pp. 350–51, 365–68. Both passages are further discussed in "Aristotle on Human Nature."

22. *EN* VII, 1145a25ff; see *Politics* 1253a8ff.

23. Virtuous action, we should remember, is, in Aristotle's view, chosen for its own sake, as a constituent part of the fully good human life. In this respect he seems close to the popular beliefs of his culture.

cerned, just plain callous, lacking totally in the painstaking effort of mind and desire that is involved in human justice.[24] At the end of Sophocles' *Trachinian Women,* Hyllus reviews the terrible and painful events that have taken place; he ascribes them to the lightness, the lack of comprehension of human needs and human goods, that is Zeus and his transcendence:

> HYLLUS: Take him up, servants, showing your great fellow-thought-and-feeling *(suggnōmosunē)* with me concerning these events, and knowing the great lack-of-thought-and-feeling *(agnōmosunē)* of the gods concerning the events that have taken place—they who, having engendered us and calling themselves our fathers have overseen these sufferings. As for the future, no one can see it. What is now here is pitiable to and for us, but shameful for them; and most difficult of all for the man who bears this disaster.
>
> H. OR CHORUS:[25] Do not you, young woman, remain at home—for you have seen great recent deaths, you have seen many newly inflicted sufferings, and there is not one of these things that is not Zeus.

The human world is held together by pity and fellow-feeling. Human beings are in a sense worse off than the gods because they suffer; but they also know how to deal with suffering, and their morality is a response to the fact of suffering. The gods are better because they *can* simply overlook, look over, the sufferings of human beings, without involvement or response.[26] But precisely because they are better in this way, they simply don't fully *see* what is going on in our lives, they lack compassion, an essential ingredient of any human justice.[27] If, from our viewpoint, we prize compassion, we have to say that *in their dealings in our realm,* the gods are not just different, they are worse.

As we reflect on this point, we should notice what a profound response to this problem is embodied in Christianity. Although I promised not to get involved in that topic, on this one issue the temptation to do so is irresistible. For Christianity seems to grant that in order to imagine a god who is truly superior, truly worthy of worship, truly and fully just, we must imagine a god who is human as well as divine, a god who has actually lived out the nontranscendent life and understands it in the only way it can be understood, by suffering and death. If this is what Taylor means when he says that Christianity has turned us back to our own world with new attention and concern, I believe that he is undoubtedly pointing to

---

24. This aspect of the divine is especially prominent in the *Bacchae,* where the smiling mask of the god (referred to by the Chorus) takes on, as the drama unfolds, an increasingly sinister look. See the discussion in my Introduction (see n. 19) and see Charles Segal, *Dionysiac Poetics and Euripides' Bacchae* (Princeton, N.J., 1982), and Helene Foley, *Ritual Irony: Poetry and Sacrifice in Euripides* (Ithaca, N.Y., and London, 1985).

25. The assignment of the lines is uncertain.

26. *Ephoraō* refers frequently to the way in which the sun "oversees" the affairs of men—it looks over, looks on, without involvement or response (see LSJ, s.v.).

27. On the connection between appropriate emotional response and virtue, between both of these and practical wisdom, see *Fragility,* chap. 10, and "Discernment," "'Finely Aware,'" and "Introduction," this volume.

something important. Surely, at any rate, the universal compassion for human suffering which one associates with Christianity at its best is difficult to imagine apart from the paradigm of human suffering and sacrifice exemplified in Christ.[28]

As for that large group of the so-called "minor" excellences of daily social life, excellences such as generosity, generous hospitality, social graciousness, modesty, friendliness—all these, as Aristotle correctly suggests, are elements in our social/ political nature, and deeply rooted, therefore, in the human form of life.[29] The Olympian gods don't have them in anything like the same form, because their social life is free-floating, amorphous, uninspired by need.

Now we must return to our starting place, and to Odysseus' choices regarding love, both sexual and familial. For the implication of his statements is, first, that human love is so different from a love that gods might share that there is no straightforward ranking or comparison between the two, however much one might in some obvious ways take the god's love to be superior. He just chooses his own form of life. And his choice implies, furthermore, that insofar as a human being *can* make the comparison, there is something perfectly intelligible about preferring human love. Take, first, the love of spouse and family. Here, we have to note, first of all, that the gods have none of the motives we have for caring about their children and for preserving the structures of family life as a context of nurture and education for children. They lack our anxious relation to our own future, our desire to extend ourselves through progeny; they lack, too, the more altruistic motives, the desire to nourish and protect that which is weak and fragile, the desire to contribute to the future of the world. Divine children are not really children; divine parents are not, therefore, really parents.

Next, we notice, as well, that their limits with respect to risk limit, as well, their ability to care for one another in anything like the human way. There is no room for taking risks or making sacrifices for the person one loves; no room for loyalty so strong that it confronts death itself. In consequence of these and other light-nesses, there is a kind of playfulness and lack of depth about the loves of the gods—and one finds in fact that it looks perfectly rational for a human being to prefer the human bond, with its deeper needs and stronger intensities. (Once again, the Christian idea that god is also fully human and has actually sacrificed his life is, if it can be made coherent,[30] a most important element in the thought that god actually loves the world.)

---

28. Here Christianity is not alone: for many pagan religions contain a divinity who dies (see below on Dionysus); but it is Christianity, above all, that links this conception to a new idea of the moral example God provides to humans.

29. For further discussion along these lines, see my "Non-Relative Virtues: an Aristotelian Approach," *Midwest Studies in Philosophy* 1988; and also "Mortal Immortals" (see n. 16).

30. There is a remarkable reflection on the tensions between this idea and the idea of god's eternity and self-sufficiency in Graham Greene's *The Heart of the Matter* (1948). The hero Scobie perceives that his own profound sense of pity and responsibility toward the two women who depend on him is a moral attitude learned from his reflection on Christ's responsibility and compassion. And yet it seems to him to follow from what he has learned that he is not as responsible *to* Christ as he is to his fellow human beings, since these need him and Christ, perhaps, does not:

He was desecrating God because he loved a woman—was it even love, or was it just a feeling of pity and responsibility? He tried again to excuse himself: "You can look after yourself. You survive the cross every day. You can only suffer. You can never be lost. Admit that you must come

In sexual life these same facts have weight, as we have already suggested; and the Boucher-like dalliances of the gods seem lacking in some element of searching and striving that gives human *erōs* its characteristic beauty.[31] If we now add to this the element of conversation and communication, which we have noticed as a difference between the divine and the mortal couple, we find that it is not just brief intensities, it is the sustaining bonds of a long-term love, that will be lacking in gods—who, as Henry James noted, have nothing at all to talk about, except when, "for the positive relief of bored Olympians," perplexed, striving human beings and their fascinating stories are, or become, "mixed up with them."[32]

And here we encounter an anomalous and significant feature in the Greek portrayal of divinity. For the gods, too, really fall in love. But not with one another. When they do so with deep intensity, the objects of their loves are mortal. This fact, fundamental to the entirety of Greek mythology, is the subject of countless poems and stories. Some of these suggest a diagnosis not far from that of Henry James, which we have just mentioned: the gods are stirred by the signs of specifically mortal excellence and its propensity for adventure. They long, it seems, for that which displays effort and longing, need and striving, achievement against odds. For (in the Euripidean chorus[33]) the body of young Ganymede, sweating after a race well run. For the resourceful courage and guile of Odysseus. They attempt, these gods, to hold on to the beauty they love—and usually they fail. Odysseus chooses to leave. Ganymede, up there in heaven, carrying cups not running races, walks "softly,"[34] without effort or tension, becoming one of them. So the transcendent ones long, it seems, for a certain sort of transcendence: for transcendence of their own limit, which is to lack limit and therefore to be incapable of virtue.[35] Yet another reason to reject the aspiration to transcend humanity is here: for the life of transcendence does not contain, it now appears, all value, all excellence, all that one would long for—even from the constructed point of view of divinity itself. It comes as no surprise that Dionysus, the erotic divinity par excellence, is also the only divinity who dies, the divinity whose rhythms of birth, growth, death, rebirth inhabit the context of nature and have a close relation to human time.[36]

This line of reflection does not exalt struggle itself into an end. It does not say that human life is best when it is most fraught with difficulty, any more than it says that an athlete's life is best when he or she has the greatest handicaps. Achilles preferred a short intense life to a long one; but so far as our argument here is concerned, that choice is still open, and we insist that brevity, pain, and struggle

---

second to these others." . . . and looking up towards the cross on the altar he thought savagely: Take your sponge of gall. You made me what I am. Take the spear thrust.

31. See my Comments on David Halperin, *Proceedings of the Boston Area Colloquium for Ancient Philosophy* 5 (1989).

32. Henry James, Preface to *The Princess Casamassima*, in *The Art of the Novel* (New York, 1907), 63–64.

33. *Trojan Women*, 820ff.

34. *Habra bainōn*, 820.

35. See also "*Psuchē* in Heraclitus, II," and "Mortal Immortals."

36. See my Introduction to the *Bacchae*, with bibliography and descriptions of recent literature.

are not valuable in and of themselves.[37] The excellent activities are ends, not the struggle they involve: athletic and musical performance, just activity, courageous activity, the other virtuous actions, love—these are the things that are ends. But we are saying that in general, as in the athletic case, those ends, intrinsically valuable in a human life, are values in and for that context—which, like all contexts (including, we now see, the context of putative limitlessness) contains and is structured by limits as well as capabilities. Human limits structure the human excellences, and give excellent action its significance. The preservation of the limits in some form—and here, as in the athletic case, we can only fall back on a vague and yet not so unclear notion of the normal human life—is a necessary condition of excellent activity's excellence. And concerning excellence in the universe in general, apart from the contexts of specific forms of life, we can, as Aristotle argues well, say nothing with real content.[38]

III

What, then, becomes of transcending? And how does, how should a human life put together the two elements of the apparent contradiction that Odysseus describes and that most of us exemplify in one or another form? Which of the views that Taylor describes does this argument support? The view that our proper human goal is activity according to complete human excellence plus some form of transcending? Or the view that, in order to pursue appropriately the whole human good, we must leave aside our desire for transcendence? It may appear that I am in fact supporting, as Taylor suspected, the second view. But I believe that matters are more complex.

First of all, there are various forms of transcendence. And there is a great deal of room, within the context of a human life as this argument has characterized it, for a certain sort of aspiration to transcend our ordinary humanity. For, although I do not believe that human beings are originally evil or sinful, it is all too plain that most people are much of the time lazy, inattentive, unreflective, shallow in feeling; in short, that most human action falls well short of the fully human target of complete virtue set up by Aristotle's view as I have described it. Aristotle holds, on the one hand, that the completely virtuous life is "common to many: for it is open to anyone who is not by nature maimed with respect to excellence."[39] But he holds, as well, that acting virtuously requires not only going through the motions of correct action, but doing so with the appropriate thoughts, motives, and reactive feelings. And he holds that this is a very difficult business, requiring much experience and practice, much flexibility and refinement of thought and feeling. The point of imagining the virtuous choice as a "mean" is not to suggest

37. This is an important, if subtle point, and an important distinction between the Greek view, as I describe it, and certain romantic views; the distinction is missed in A. A. Long's review, *Classical Philology* 83 (1988), 61–69.

38. For discussion of the numerous passages in which Aristotle insists that the subject matter of ethics is the human good, see *Fragility*, chap. 10, pp. 291–94.

39. *EN* 1099b18–19; see *Fragility*, chap. 11. The discussion of "bestial vice" in Book VII seems to show that Aristotle did not think very many people were naturally so "maimed": for it focuses on very extreme cases.

that it can be mechanically plotted—not at all. It is rather to place a tremendous emphasis on the difficulty of finding the point of rightness among all the many points that would be wrong. As Aristotle himself says, "There are many ways of missing the target . . . and only one way of hitting it; so one is easy and the other is hard."[40]

This is, more or less, the view I hold of our relation to the specifically human good. In this view there is a great deal of room for transcendence of our ordinary humanity—transcendence, we might say, of an *internal* and human sort. It is for this reason, among others, that I have taken such a deep interest in the writings of Henry James and of Marcel Proust, and in their explicit claim that the artist's fine-tuned attention and responsiveness to human life is paradigmatic of a kind of precision of feeling and thought that a human being can cultivate, though most do not. Neither has the slightest interest in religious or otherworldly or even contemplative transcendence; both aim at transcendence nonetheless, and exemplify it in their writing.[41] For I believe it is no accident at all that both James and Proust, apparently independently, compare excellent literary works to angels that soar above the dullness and obtuseness of the everyday, offering their readers a glimpse of a more compassionate, subtler, more responsive, more richly human world.[42] That is a view about transcendence. And I believe that it is extremely important to make the aspiration to that sort of transcendence central to a picture of the complete human good. There is so much to do in this area of *human* transcending (which I imagine also as a transcending by *descent*, delving more deeply into oneself and one's humanity, and becoming deeper and more spacious as a result) that if one really pursued that aim well and fully I suspect that there would be little time left to look about for any other sort. And I confess that I much prefer Jamesian angels of fine-tuned perception and bewildered human grace to the angels of the religious tradition—who, as Aquinas most perceptively saw, would not be able to get around in our world at all, since they lack imagination and the ability to perceive particulars.[43]

On the other side, what my argument urges us to reject as incoherent is the aspiration to leave behind altogether the constitutive conditions of our humanity, and to seek for a life that is really the life of another sort of being—as if it were a higher and better life for *us*. It asks us to bound our aspirations by recalling that there are some very general conditions of human existence that are also necessary conditions for the values that we know, love, and appropriately pursue. It asks, further, that in the light of this fact one should at least moderate one's rage at and hatred of these limiting features, including death, which one would still appropriately fear and avoid.[44] And this would undercut, one supposes, the negative motivation to pursue various forms of alleged transcendence within human life— forms that involve withdrawing love and concern from that which cannot be sta-

40. *EN* 1106b28–32.
41. See the discussions of various aspects of their work in the essays in this volume.
42. The James passage is from the preface to *The Golden Bowl*, and is discussed in the Introduction, in the section entitled "Expressive Plants, Perceiving Angels"; the Proust passage is part of Marcel's description of the death of Bergotte.
43. Thomas Aquinas, *Summa Theologica* 1 q.89 a.1.
44. See "Mortal Immortals."

bly controlled, or admitting as valuable only that which is immune from change and alteration. (Such forms of alleged transcending were among the primary targets of critical scrutiny in *Fragility*.[45])

But the line between the appropriate (internal) sort of transcending and the other sort is not and can never be a sharp one. For human striving for excellence involves pushing, in many ways, against the limits that constrain human life. It is perfectly reasonable, within the human point of view, to want oneself and others not to be hungry, not to be ill, not to be without shelter, not to be betrayed or bereaved, not to lose any of one's faculties—and to strive as hard as one possibly can to bring all that about in life. In fact, one of the merits of focusing on the internal sort of transcendence is that it tells us that such things really matter, that these jobs are there for human beings to do, for politics to do.[46] Some forms of the aspiration to extrahuman transcendence have indeed, as Marx and Nietzsche both in different ways saw, undermined people's love of and commitment to these struggles against limit. It is also perfectly reasonable to strive to increase life expectancy, to eliminate as many categories of disease as possible, to strive to prolong any single life as best one can. And again, external transcending seems to undercut the motivation to push hard in this direction. If one thinks that the really important thing is to get over to a different sort of life altogether, then this may well make one work less hard on this one. Though I would concede to Taylor that Nietzsche made this point too simply against the Christians, it seems to me that he did have a real point.

The puzzle then is, when does the aspiration to internal transcendence become the aspiration to depart from human life altogether? There is, and should be, no clear answer to this question. Its answer can only be given in and by human history itself, as human beings look at the limits as their own struggles have constituted them. Human life now has a somewhat different shape in time because of medical and scientific progress—at least for those who are able to avail themselves of this progress. It is somewhat longer, and safer in certain ways; though other unforeseen dangers have arisen. It would be a disaster for humanity if the type of argument I am presenting were taken to imply that the desire to push our limits back further was an illegitimate desire, and that we should just live on the earth as we find it. We shouldn't, perhaps, imagine that we can coherently wish for immortality. And yet it seems reasonable to fear death, for oneself and for another, and to seek to avoid it, at any time when active living is still going on in a valuable way.[47] It is reasonable to feel that death at any time is a tragedy for the person who has died. (I have defended this at some length in discussing Epicurus' arguments, and I shall therefore not recapitulate here.) Especially tragic, perhaps, when death is, by "normal" standards, premature; but, especially since such standards are always on the move, that notion does not and should not have decisive

45. See especially chaps. 3, 4, 6.
46. See my "Nature, Function, and Capability: Aristotle on Political Distribution," *Oxford Studies in Ancient Philosophy,* Supplementary Volume 1988.
47. For some related contemporary discussions of the demented elderly, see Dan Brock, "Justice and the Severely Demented Elderly," *Journal of Medicine and Philosophy* 13 (1988), 73–99.

weight with one who is mourning another's death, or fearing her own. The larger problem has, it seems, something like the same shape as the paradox of the athlete. She shouldn't wish to be without the human body and its limits altogether, since then there is no athletic achievement and no goal; but it seems perfectly reasonable, in any particular case, to want, always, to be better, stronger, faster, to push against those limits more successfully. It is the paradox of a struggle for victory in which *complete* "victory" would be disaster and emptiness—or, at any rate, a life so different from our own that we could no longer find ourselves and our valued activities in it.

What is recommended is a delicate and always flexible balancing act between the claims of excellence, which lead us to push outward, and the necessity of the human context, which pushes us back in. It is not easy, in this picture, to say where a line is drawn. But the ancient Greek conception of *hubris* provides, perhaps, a useful guide here. There is a kind of striving that is appropriate to a human life; and there is a kind of striving that consists in trying to depart from that life to another life. This is what *hubris* is—the failure to comprehend what sort of life one has actually got, the failure to live within its limits (which are also possibilities), the failure, being mortal, to think mortal thoughts. Correctly understood, the injunction to avoid *hubris* is not a penance or denial—it is an instruction as to where the valuable things *for us* are to be found.

Does this mean that one should actually not want the people one loves to live forever? Yes, and no. One is to hate and fear the thought of their death, to try to prevent it by any means one can—and yet to know that a mortal life is the only life in which the people one loves could actually be. This tension, which is close to being a contradiction, seems to be a part of the best human life. It is difficult enough to understand it, far less to live it. In this sense, the best human life in my own conception contains more tension and conflict around this issue of transcendence than Aristotle's best life, in which the fear of death plays a very small role.[48] Not enough, perhaps, to make it Taylor's "inclusive view." But more than his "narrow view," insofar as he identifies that with Aristotle's.

Another type of internal transcendence enters in at this point; and once again, it is a type that lies at the heart of Greek thought about mortals and gods. It is the transcendence of creation. Homeric heroes imagine their appropriate goal to be not immortal life, but the creation of a deathless record of excellence, of deeds or works through which they do in a sense make the world as it will be ever after. This type of transcending, says Aristotle in the *De Anima,* is the "first and most common characteristic of the living, in virtue of which life belongs to all that has life."[49] In lower animals it takes the form, simply, of biological reproduction. In human life, however, as not Aristotle but Plato's Diotima points out, this desire to propagate oneself is expressed in other ways as well. Human beings make the world, and make themselves in the world, through politics, through science, through teaching, through personal love, through virtuous speech and action. In

48. In this sense, Aristotle does not seem to be a faithful recorder of the emphases of Greek popular thought.
49. *De Anima* II.4, 415a24–25. Here he is speaking of the common capability of living things (both to nourish themselves and) to produce young like themselves.

all these ways human beings seek to live on, leaving in the world some expression of themselves, some continuation of their identity.[50] Diotima plausibly says that it is only when one gives up on the aspiration to external transcendence—realizing that one is not going to be immortal—that one will begin to pursue (with good results for the world) the other sort. Odysseus' life on Ogygia would not have contained the creative deeds through which he made himself historically immortal.

This type of internal transcending supplements our other type. For, as the Greeks insisted, one does not get the immortality people seek through *bad* deeds, (even spectacular ones), or through mediocre works;[51] indeed, one does not get it through bad children either, a constant worry of ancient Greek ethics. So trying for the internal transcendence of virtue is the only way to get, as well, the internal transcendence of leaving a mark on the world. And, properly pursued, it will usually be sufficient. Here we should insist, with Thucydides' Pericles, that Achillean individual heroism is not essential.[52] Being a part of a group that, as a group, does fine deeds can be sufficient; and frequently this is a more effective way of making the world in the image of one's own virtuous action.

IV

We have said nothing so far about the place of philosophical activity in this debate—and we must now do so. For the claim I investigated in my discussion of Plato's views on transcendence, in *Fragility* chapter 5, was the claim that a certain sort of philosophical activity is the way, and apparently the only way, in which a human being transcends humanity and manages to live a divine life. This claim, as I described it, grew out of an old tradition in Greek religious thought—beginning probably with Xenophanes—according to which a truly divine and unlimited being will do just one thing: it will think. The argument goes like this. If we really, consistently, imagine a perfect unlimited being, a being truly divine and worthy of worship, we will not imagine this being as doing the usual human things that the Olympian gods do in stories—having love affairs, lying, changing shape, and so forth.[53] The godlike form of life is still further from our own than such stories imagine. Our own reasons for doing such things come from our need and our imperfection; so what reason *could* a real god have for doing them? On the other hand, so the argument goes, there is one thing we do that we can imagine an unlimited god doing, out of pure positive love of the activity. This is thinking— thinking about, probing, contemplating the nature of the universe.

There are many ways in which the thinking of god has been imagined, from Xenophanes through Plato to later Platonisms.[54] Sometimes learning is stressed.

50. For an excellent discussion of the *Symposium*'s position, see A. Kosman, "Platonic Love," in W. H. Werkmeister, ed., *Facets of Plato's Philosophy, Phronesis* Suppl. II (Assen, 1976), 53–69.

51. See G. Nagy, *The Best of the Achaeans* (Baltimore, 1979).

52. Thucydides II.41–43.

53. See Xenophanes DK B 25, and Plato, *Republic,* III, esp. 387–88.

54. For an excellent account of these debates, see R. Sorabji, "Myths about Non-Propositional Thought," in *Language and Logos,* ed. M. Schofield and M. Nussbaum (Cambridge, 1982), 295–314.

More often, as in Plato and in the Platonic part of Aristotle's account, contemplation is preferred, since learning seems too suggestive of limit and imperfection. And god's contemplation has usually been taken, quite plausibly, to be directed at universal essences, not at particulars. For the essential structure of the world, not its contingent history, would be, it is claimed, the feature that would arouse the perfect being's interest and love. And a being who didn't have experience of worldly ways of life could hardly single out or notice the salient particular features of worldly histories. (The Aristotle–Aquinas tradition holds, of course, something stronger: that a being without a body, such as an angel, would simply not be capable of the perception of particulars. This thought is used by Aquinas in a number of striking ways, in argument about the importance of the resurrection of the body.[55])

So our ability to perform abstract reasoning and to contemplate universals (as, for example, to contemplate a mathematical proof and its deductive logical structure) has been taken to be *the* feature of our current lives in which we live divinely—the one thing we do that a perfect god would also have reason to do, just out of joy and love, with no pressure of need. In *Fragility* I did express some uncertainty about this idea—for the question what motivates, and can motivate, one to think philosophically seems to me a deeply obscure one; and the question what a perfect being would find reason to pursue hardly less so. And yet, I did find it at least conceivable that philosophical thinking of the sort described might have the feature Plato ascribes to it. And I found a plausibility in the idea of a thinking god that I could not, either then or now, find in the idea of an athletic god, or an erotic god, or even (leaving to one side the Christian account of god's dual nature) a loving or a morally virtuous god. So this is, clearly, one more sort of transcending that requires investigation. I am not sure that it is the one that Charles Taylor finds appealing; nor am I sure that the idea of the philosopher/mathematician as divinity would answer at all to his conception of what is better than the human. But in order to complete the argument of this paper I need to say more about where I myself stand on this particular sort of transcending. Is the life of philosophical contemplation, or rather the life devoted to the maximal attainment of this, in which all other pursuits are viewed as merely supportive or instrumental, the best or highest life?

Now first of all, I am not sure that I should have conceded as much to this argument as I did in the book. For it now seems to me that the thought experiment that delivers the result that a perfect being would perform intellectual contemplation is more obscure and indeterminate than I suggested there. We don't clearly understand what it is that leads us to try to understand our world, to philosophize in the sense of reaching out for understanding. But it seems conceivable that it is, as Aristotle suggests in *Metaphysics* I, something specifically human about us, connected with our responses of wonder and bewilderment before the strange world in which we find ourselves.[56] And so it seems to me possible that a being for whom nothing was puzzling would not philosophize at all. A great part of the later Platonist tradition, and Plato himself, speaking as Diotima, agrees with this:

55. See n. 43.
56. Metaphysics I.1,

"No god does philosophy."[57] As for contemplation, even that may be hard to motivate, if one separates it altogether from the ongoing search for understanding. The Olympian gods did not understand serious sustained reflection any more than they understood serious sustained love. And I am now disposed to think this image of the divine at least as persuasive as the one developed by Xenophanes and Plato. Power in all things breeds *agnōmosunē* in all things. And the "over-looking" that really needless gods do in the universe seems likely to be less the intense contemplation imagined by Plato than another, more Sophoclean sort.

But let me waive these objections for the time being. Since the idea of a perfect thinking god *has* seemed coherent and persuasive to quite a few great philosophers over the ages—to Plato, Aristotle, Aquinas, and Spinoza, to name just a few—let us proceed as if they are right to find in contemplation a special case of human/divine intersection. What follows from this for Taylor's question about the best life?

In the book, I made three claims about contemplation as an ethical goal. First, I claimed that the sort of reasoning that the tradition links (plausibly or implausibly) with transcendence is an inappropriate style of reasoning for ethics: inappropriate, that is, where our aim is adequate understanding of and good action in our human social world. I defended Aristotle's claim that practical wisdom is distinct from theoretical understanding, since it is concerned with historical particulars in a way that theoretical wisdom cannot be.[58] All this is well articulated by Aristotle and even by Aquinas; I have spent a good deal of time unpacking these claims, and shall not articulate them further here. So, since we all need practical wisdom to operate well in our world, this gives us a good reason not to fail to cultivate the specifically human ends and desires and forms of perception that it requires.

Second, I argued that the best and most complete total way of life for a human being would not, in any case, be the life maximally given over to theoretical reasoning, subordinating other ends to which Aristotle ascribes intrinsic value. It would include theoretical activity as one component in a life that also ascribes intrinsic value to friendship, to morally virtuous activity, and to the other intrinsically valuable ends of a specifically human life. In other words, the transcendent character of theoretical reasoning, if and insofar as it has that character, did not seem to give a *human being* a reason to give it predominance or to subordinate to it other specifically human ends. The fact that these ends are ends only within a human and not a divine life did not count against their claim to have intrinsic value within a human life.[59] The arguments of the present paper reinforce that claim.

Third, the fact that human beings pursue theoretical reasoning, insofar as they do pursue it, along with other specifically human ends, within the context of a specifically human life, seems to alter the way in which theoretical reasoning itself will be best and most appropriately pursued. For instance, both Aristotle and

---

57. Plato, *Symposium*, 204A.
58. *Fragility*, chap. 10; see also "The Discernment" (n. 27).
59. See *Fragility*, esp. chap. 12 and Appendix. *EN* X.6–8 clearly has a different view; but I argue that these chapters are incompatible with the main line of argument in the *EN*.

Plato (in the *Phaedrus*) argue that human beings think best when they think in cooperation and affiliation with others, in the context of a relationship that is close, affectionate, and long-lasting, and is viewed as an end in itself. They appear to differ as to whether the relationship should also be erotic; but they agree that affection, as well as respect, will be an important part of its contribution to thought.[60]

All of this means that imitation of the god, even in the sense it has in this intellectualist tradition, is in a number of ways a bad and misleading goal for a human life to take for itself. It will lead to the denigration of other valuable ends, which will be downgraded because of their specific humanity; to a style of ethical understanding that is better suited to angels than to human beings; and perhaps also to an inadequate pursuit of contemplation or theoretical reasoning itself. It is a little hard to say where this conclusion fits in relation to Taylor's distinction between the "narrow view" and the "inclusive view." For we include theoretical reasoning as one component among others in a complete human life; but we include it *as* a specifically human activity, not counting its alleged divinity as a special point in its favor. And we certainly do not encourage the thought that it is good because it is a way of transcending our humanity.

V

At this point there is more to be said about philosophy's role in and toward the human good. I want to conclude this discussion of transcendence with some observations about its implications for philosophical method and style.

In the tradition of thought about transcendence that I have just briefly characterized, the fact that a certain style of human thinking was allegedly the one performed by god and thus the one in and through which we transcend our humanity seemed to many to be a powerful reason for preferring that style of thinking—abstract, detached from one's immediate context and from the bodily senses, concerned with universals, deductive and mathematical in its form—as the style best for philosophizing. It seemed to have about it a special nobility and dignity. To be sure, some unusually sensitive members of this tradition, such as Aristotle and Aquinas, did not so quickly conclude that the godlike style was always the best and most appropriate. Angelic thought was beautiful enough, but quite useless and inappropriate where ethical and political deliberation for this world was in question. Each realm and form of life demands an appropriate method and style of reasoning. Nonetheless, other thinkers, following Plato (and, later, Spinoza) did conclude that the godlike style of reasoning was always and everywhere the most philosophically appropriate. And even for those who resisted, the failure of ethics to measure up to the godlike seemed to be a point against it. Frequently it came to be ranked below mathematical and scientific reasoning, precisely because it was less easy to see how one might do it in a transcendent way.

If detached, purely intellectual, abstract, deductive reasoning about universals was the winner in this transcendence-oriented tradition, it is easy, too, to see who the losers were. The losers were stories, and the storytelling imagination and emo-

---

60. See *Fragility,* chaps. 7 and 12.

tions. As we mentioned in introducing Odysseus' story, there seemed to be an interesting connection between our preference for Odysseus' actual choice and the fact that we were viewing him as the hero of a story. As readers of stories we are deeply immersed in the messy impure world of human particularity; and we learn, as readers, to ascribe a high importance to events that befall our particular heroes and heroines as they move through the world of contingency.[61] The fact that a godlike Odysseus was not appealing to us had much to do with the fact that we were already viewing him as the hero of a story we were expecting to follow and to care about. Thus the idea of a life in which nothing happens—or rather, in which nothing that happens has importance, since the being to whom things happen is self-sufficient—was an unappealing idea. Our preference for people whose sexual life is combined with narration was not unconnected with the fact that we were ourselves, at that moment, deeply immersed in the storytelling life.

And furthermore, the very emotions with which we react to a hero's story—fear for his danger, grief at his losses, delight at his success, suspense and anxiety about uncertain outcomes—all of these reactions, central to our experiences as readers of stories and mainsprings of the interest stories generate in their readers—all these, we can now begin to see, were bound up with a view of the world according to which things that human beings do not fully control have serious importance for their lives; a view that is incompatible with the pursuit of complete transcendence as the best end. For if we really thought that the best life was a life in which the human being finally succeeded in transcending his or her human dangers and uncertainties—in which, therefore, nothing that simply happens would have any more significance than a crop failure on Olympus—we would be likely (as Plato saw) to imagine our heroes as, themselves, transcendent beings. And we therefore would not relate to them as we currently do, through our fear, our longing, our pity, our delight, our anxious concern about their unfolding story.

Numerous philosophers have objected to the use of emotion and of the storytelling imagination inside philosophy. But it is important to examine the grounds on which they have done so. There are, indeed, some philosophers who have thought of the emotions as rather like hunger and thirst—as bodily feelings that have no cognitive content and that are bad and misleading because, when one is engaged with them, one cannot think deeply or clearly. But on the whole this is a relatively superficial view—one that we usually do not find in the works of major thinkers who have devoted a great deal of their best philosophical effort to the analysis of the emotions.[62] And it is a view that has by now been shown, with compelling arguments, to be unsustainable. In philosophy, in cognitive psychology, in anthropology, and psychoanalysis—thinkers who agree on little else concur in rejecting it.[63]

---

61. On all this, see the Introduction, "Discernment," "Flawed Crystals," "'Finely Aware,'" and "Perceptive Equilibrium," this volume.

62. The most distinguished in this group is Hume; but his analysis of the passions is severely limited by the possibilities of the theory of impressions and ideas, and it does not seem to me, despite its many subtleties, to be the best part of Hume's philosophical work.

63. For references to the modern literature on this point, see "Narrative Emotions," and Introduction, this volume.

Where we do find the combination of profound, sustained reflection about the nature of the emotions with a call for their dismissal from the pursuit of wisdom and understanding, a very different line of argument predominates—an argument closely connected with our interest in transcendence. Thinkers as otherwise diverse as Plato, Aristotle, Epicurus, the Stoics, and Spinoza are in agreement that the emotions (such as fear, grief, love, pity, anger) are not simply bodily feelings or blind animal urges. They are either identical with or partly constituted by judgments of value—judgments that certain worldly items have great importance, items that the agent does not fully control. They are webs of connection and acknowledgment, linking the agent with the worth of the unstable context of objects and persons in which human life is lived. Fear involves the belief that there are big important things that may damage us, and that we are powerless to prevent that damage. Love involves the ascription of a very high value to a being who is separate from the subject and not fully controlled; it cannot be love if the response is fully controlled. When the world damages or takes from us something we love, we experience grief. When an item of great value is damaged by someone else, we feel anger. And so forth.[64]

All these are agreements between enemies of the use of emotions in practical reasoning and one supporter (Aristotle, to whom we shall return). Let us now consider the further argument of the enemies. There are many differences among Plato, the Stoics, Epicurus, and Spinoza about the precise analysis of the relationship between emotion and belief. But all agree that the emotions have at their core certain value judgments, according to which the human being is in a rather incomplete and needy position in the world, has hostages to fortune. And they agree on one thing more: that the person who aims to live a godlike life, transcending his or her humanity, must do away with them. For after all, a transcendent life has no hostages to fortune. A self-sufficient and complete person, in short, has nothing to fear, nothing to grieve for, nobody to love in the usual human sense, the sense in which love implies incompleteness and the absence of control.

In *Republic* II–III and X, Plato puts this view to work in his proposal for the education of the young, with the notorious result that all of conventional poetry—Homer and tragedy above all—must be eliminated. For as Socrates very correctly observes, these works form a relationship with the reader that teaches and nourishes emotions such as grief, fear, and pity. They represent heroes such as Achilles as grieving and fearing, and they teach the young not only to pity and fear for them, but at the same time to identify with their non–self-sufficient behavior. The Stoics follow Plato here, and repudiate the literature-making emotions just as completely. They do seem to permit a certain sort of moralizing literary depiction, in order to show "what happens when chance events befall fools"—Epictetus' definition of tragedy.[65] But the complicity between hero and reader, the emotions of hope and expectation that propel the reader on in the story—all of this is thoroughly repudiated. Spinoza, again, repudiates the emotions as acknowledgments of incompleteness: "God is free from passions, nor is he affected by any emotion

---

64. For an account of this tradition, and sympathetic argument in its favor, see "The Stoics on the Extirpation of the Passions," *Apeiron* 20 (1987), 129–75.
65. Epictetus, *Disc.* II.xvi.31.

of pleasure or pain." And he connects this view with his own decision to write about human beings *more geometrico:* "I shall regard human actions and desires exactly as if I were dealing with lines, planes, and bodies."[66]

What is especially important to see is that the rejection of stories and of emotions from philosophical thinking, in these authors, does not depend on any view that the emotions are unintelligent or unclear or merely animal. In fact such arguments against the emotions begin by establishing that they have a very important cognitive dimension, are ways in which we organize the world for ourselves. They are "irrational" *not* in the sense that they are without reasoning—but, rather, in the sense that they involve what is, from the point of view of the aspiration to transcendence, a false and pernicious reasoning.[67] They are acknowledgments of the importance of things that have no true importance. They are teachings about specifically human values that are powerful rivals to the teaching that urges us to the pursuit of godlike contemplation. Confronted with our reading of Odysseus' story, the tradition would surely say that that's the result you get, if you let stories and their emotional structures into philosophical argument. You get a merely human nontranscending philosophy. A philosophy that is mortal and thinks mortal thoughts. That, of course, was exactly what they did not want philosophy to do or to be. And they would not have supposed that anything so closely bound to the mortal, in its form as well as its statements, could really be philosophy. If we shun stories and stick with abstract intellectual argument about universals, maybe we can get back to the godlike life, and see, as complete, the values that this life discloses.

Now I happen to believe that this tradition has the correct overall view about the nature and structure of the emotions: that they are closely related to value judgments, and that the relevant judgments are judgments about the importance of things we don't fully control. This view was displaced for a while, during the ascendancy of empiricism and related psychologies. But it is firmly reestablished now, and its credentials grow stronger every day. So far, this work on cognitive dimensions of emotion has not really pursued the connection between emotions and the acknowledgment of the importance of external undependable things, preferring to pursue the general connection between emotion and belief. I have pursued a part of this other project in some historical work on Hellenistic philosophy.[68] What I want here to point out is how closely a certain ethical view is linked (or ought to be, if we think well and consistently) with a certain style of doing philosophy. If we are content to follow the tradition according to which philosophy should above all be the godlike activity, the one in and through which we transcend humanity, we should certainly follow the instructions of this same Plato–Spinoza tradition concerning how philosophy should speak to its reader. We should allow the call of theoretical reasoning about universals to draw us

---

66. Spinoza, *Ethics,* V Prop. XVII on god, III, opening, on style.

67. This distinction is missed by Galen, discussing Chrysippus' view of the emotions in *On the Doctrines of Hippocrates and Plato;* for he makes fun of the fact that Chrysippus, on the one hand, locates the passions in the rational part of the soul and, on the other hand, calls them *aloga,* "irrational." See "The Stoics on the Extirpation of the Passions" for further discussion.

68. "The Stoics on the Extirpation," "Mortal Immortals," and also "Beyond Obsession and Disgust: Lucretius' Genealogy of Love," in *Apeiron* 22 (1989). I will present a more extensive philosophical account as the Gifford Lectures for 1993.

upwards, away from the cognitive and emotional responses typical of the merely human being, and seek pure intellectual deductions such as a god might perform. Above all, we should avoid appeals to emotion, and we should eschew storytelling.

But suppose, on the other hand, we are not so enamored of the pursuit of transcendence, for some of the reasons given in this paper. Suppose we think that there is something to the suggestion that, being mortal, we should think mortal thoughts. Then we might well conclude that philosophy, as the art of our thought and the pursuer of truth about us, had better speak mortal speech and think mortal thoughts. In this case, we will instruct the philosopher not to be seduced by the lure of the unaided intellect—for one can surely speak of seduction here[69]—and to think and speak more humanly, acknowledging in speech the incompleteness and neediness of human life, its relations of dependence and love with uncontrolled people and things. The Stoics and Spinoza believed that such acknowledgment was sufficient for emotion: if emotion wasn't there, that acknowledgment was not fully there.[70] This would mean, in our argument, that the emotions, and their accomplices, the stories, would be not just permitted, but required, in a fully human philosophy.

Aristotle's approach to ethics, the one with which I have most sympathy, takes as its subject matter the human good. And its investigations into matters of value are at the same time investigations into the form of life of a being both needy and resourceful, with certain capabilities and certain sorts of incompleteness, and a certain sort of body in which all of this takes place.[71] They are attempts to describe the limits and possibilities of that species-specific form of life, saying where, within those, good is to be found. This suggests, then, that good Aristotelian writing in ethics should call upon emotions, and upon narrative structures, enlisting their illumination—for through all of this we trace the outlines of our dependence and express our attachment to things outside ourselves. Indeed, it seems that Aristotelian philosophy will be incomplete without these elements.[72]

Aristotle fulfilled this demand by turning for illumination to works of literature, whose narrative structures and emotional forms of engagement promised information concerning these aspects of a specifically human good. Our pity and fear for imperfect heroes, and our fellow feeling with their story—elements of literary experience despised by both the Platonic and Stoic traditions, in different ways—become ingredients in the recognition of human value.[73]

If we want to pursue this project in a contemporary setting, there are many ways in which we might do so. We need to attend first and foremost to our own philosophical writing, making sure that the statements made by its formal and stylistic features do not negate the insights of an Aristotelian nontranscendent inquiry. These insights, we claimed, are especially fully and fittingly expressed in the formal structures characteristic of certain types of literature; so we need to make sure that our own writing is suited to be an ally, rather than the enemy of literature. I

69. See "Reading."
70. See "The Stoics on the Extirpation" for a sympathetic defense of this.
71. See "Aristotle on Human Nature."
72. For further arguments along these lines, see Introduction, this volume.
73. See *Fragility*, Interlude 2; a remarkable discussion of these issues is in an unpublished paper by Stephen Halliwell. See also his *Aristotle's Poetics* (London, 1986).

have said much more elsewhere about what this would involve, and I have argued for the importance of such an alliance.[74]

But one very important part of the further project, closely allied to Aristotle's interest in tragedy, would surely be to bring the literary works themselves into philosophy, studying them as inquiries into the human good. Aristotle chose tragic poetry above all. And that is a valuable choice, whose implications need to be investigated further. I have argued elsewhere that, where our contemporary situation is concerned, it is perhaps the novel, above the other available genres, that will provide further illumination. For the novel as genre is committed, in its very structure and in the structure of its relationship with its reader, to the pursuit of the uncertainties and vulnerabilities, the particularity and the emotional richness, of the human form of life. The *Odyssey*, which might with some justice be said to be the first novel in the Western tradition, shows, as we have seen, that the literary project itself repudiates the choice for divine life, and invests itself in the choice to explore the values peculiar to the human form of life, the norms of practical intelligence, love, and virtue that we can expect to find and to realize within such a life. Indeed, by enlisting the reader as a concerned participant in the adventures of the characters, novels take our common humanity for their theme, implying that what is at issue is not merely some idiosyncratic event that actually happened, but a possibility or possibilities for human life. The emotional structures in which they implicate the reader involve, themselves, fellow feeling with the characters, and a sense of shared possibilities.[75]

In these ways, I suggest, novels conduct a philosophical investigation into the good of a human being. Their many more concrete Aristotelian contributions— their rich exploration of the noncommensurability of the valuable things, their concern for particular context-sensitive judgments and for particular loves, their allegiance to the emotions as sources of insight[76]—seem to derive, at some level, from the choice they make along with Odysseus, the fundamental choice to live as human, and thus to take on the riskiness and incompleteness of a mortal life. To live as *Odusseus*—a name suggestive of suffering and struggle[77]—rather than to accept the offer of *Kalupsō*, whose name means "She who conceals," and who would indeed have concealed, forever, the hero's character as hero, as the resourceful man and man of suffering. If we wish to develop a human ethical philosophy along Aristotelian lines, I suggest that we would do well to study the narrative and the emotional structures of novels, viewing them as forms of Aristotelian ethical thinking.[78]

---

74. See Introduction and essays in this volume, especially "Love's Knowledge."

75. See Introduction and the essays on James, this volume.

76. See Introduction, this volume.

77. For the etymology, connecting the name with being the recipient of anger and therefore undergoing adversity, see *Odyssey* 19.407; also 1.62, 5.340.

78. I am especially grateful to Charles Taylor for setting these thoughts in motion. This essay was delivered as the William James Lecture at the Harvard Divinity School. I am very grateful to audiences there, and also at the Atlantic Provinces Philosophical Association and the University of California, Santa Cruz, for their helpful comments. At Santa Cruz, the paper was read just after the death of John J. Winkler, one of the most extraordinary classical scholars of our generation and a wonderful friend, of complications arising from AIDS. As I did on that occasion, I dedicate this essay to his memory.

Endnote

This essay, the most recently written in the collection, links my work on Greek philosophy with my concern for novels. And it also points to a link of a different kind. In a series of papers on Aristotelian political thought (references in the endnote to "Perception and Revolution"), I have stressed, with approval, Aristotle's use of the general notion of the human being and the human form of life to provide a direction for ethical and political thinking. I have defended this emphasis against various forms of subjectivism and cultural relativism, and also against liberalisms that attempt to choose principles of justice without relying on any theory of the good. I have argued that they yield a distinctive form of social democracy. And yet, at the same time I insist on the importance of particularity for good ethical judgment. "Non-Relative Virtues: An Aristotelian Approach" (*Midwest Studies in Philosophy,* 1988) said something about how these two ideas fit together. In asking about how the good of a human being is to be promoted in a certain context, one must always be very sensitive to the historically concrete circumstances of that context. Yet, since it was always for the person *as a human being* that the good was being sought, one must not lose hold of general notions of human functioning and human capability, which can frequently be used to criticize local traditions as inimical to human flourishing. Despite these connecting remarks, one might still wonder whether there was not a tension, rather than an illuminating dialogue, between the particular and the general in such deliberations.

This essay suggests that the interest in historical particularity and the interest in focusing on the notion "human being" as the organizing ethical notion, are not opposed, but have a common root. Particularity and historical context are not visible to the godlike intelligence (see the paper's discussion of Aquinas); and the importance of context and particularity for us as we are is inseparable from the fact that we are bodily finite beings of a particular sort, beings who go through time in a particular way. In short, it is only when one focuses on the human and the differences between the human and the bestial, the human and the divine, that we begin to understand why particularity and history—and particular love—matter to us as they do.

And we see, as well, that narratives, especially novels, manifest the same connection. For they speak to the reader as a human being, not simply as a member of some local culture; and works of literature frequently cross cultural boundaries far more easily than works of religion and philosophy. And as they speak to the humanness of their readers, they immerse them in the characteristic movements of human time and the adventures of human finitude—in a form of life in which it is natural to love particular people and to have concern for the concrete events that happen to them. They cultivate the forms of vision and concern that inhabit the human form of life generally, and would be unavailable to beasts, uninteresting to gods.

In this way we see from another direction what was argued in "Perception and Revolution": that social democracy and the art of the novel are allies. Their focus is the human being, seen as both needy and resourceful; and their dominant passion is love.

Index

Hero or heroine, 17, 35, 140, 164, 199, 366–
67, 382
Hesse, Mary, 224
Hirsch, E. D., Jr., 9*n*, 228*n*
Homer, 107, 365–67, 370, 372, 374, 376–77,
381
Hope, 287–88, 297–306, 309, 367, 387. *See
also* Emotions
Howe, Irving, 197, 206, 210
"How should one live?" as starting point in
ethics, 23–29, 36, 168, 173, 232. *See also*
Aristotelian procedure; Aristotle; Ethics;
Human being; Plato
Hugo, Victor, 188
Human being: as basic notion in ethics, 16,
25, 53, 66, 95–96, 173, 389; excellences
of, 366–67, 372–75; as focus of novel, 45,
367, 385–91; as fundamentally social, 166,
373–74; good of, 66, 95–96, 368–69, 389;
life of, 366–67, 371–72, 379–85; love and,
365–67, 376–77; not an optional concept
in good deliberation, 95; philosophy's
interest in transcending, 53, 313, 382–91;
and particularity, 391. *See also*
Aristotelian procedure; Aristotle; Ethics;
How should one live?; Philosophy;
Transcendence
Hume, David, 170, 386*n*
Humor, 50, 71, 279–80, 319–20. *See also*
Comedy
Hunger and thirst, 41, 120, 201, 211–12,
340–41, 373. *See also* Appetites

Identification, 17, 35
Images, 35, 84–93, 128–29, 134, 151–52,
159–60, 181, 208, 249, 350. *See also*
Form and content; Imagination
Imagination: and body, 5, 379; and
compassion, 209; concreteness of, 5, 76–
78, 83; in education, 103–4; ethical role
of, 40*n*, 75–82, 91–92, 174, intrinsic value
of, 150–52; of literary artist, 5, 148, 150–
52, 199, 360–63; and love, 159–60; loved
person in, 254; moral and literary, 148;
political, 99, 200; public use of, 165, 193,
217; of reader of novels, 47, 91–92. *See
also* Author; Emotions; Ethics; Literature;
Novels; Rationality, practical
Immortality, xv, 365–66, 368, 374, 380–81.
See also Human being; Transcendence
Improvisation, 37, 71, 74–75, 91, 94, 96–97,
138, 155, 181. *See also* Particularity;
Perception; Rationality, practical
Indeterminacy of practical matters, 34, 38,
47, 70–71, 104, 141, 160. *See also*

Particularity; Perception; Rationality;
practical
Innocence, 126–27, 134–36, 149–50, 352,
357
Intellect, 7, 101, 238, 248–49, 262–64, 272–
74, 385, 389
Intention, 8–9
Intimacy, 187–89, 334, 343–44, 351, 353
Irwin, Terence H., 106*n*, 108*n*, 110*n*, 113*n*,
120*n*, 368–69*n*
Iser, Wolfgang, 5*n*

James, Henry, 4–10, 11, 18, 46, 123, 238,
260, 288, 315, 346–47, 377, 379; *The
Ambassadors,* 26, 31–35, 51–53, 169–93,
346; *The Art of the Novel,* 4, 133, 140,
162–63, 165, 193, 198, 377; *The Golden
Bowl,* 4–7, 11, 18, 29, 36, 43, 44, 51–52,
85–93, 125–45, 148–67, 194, 315, 346;
The Portrait of a Lady, 11, 147; *The
Princess Casamassima,* 22, 53, 133, 139–
40, 191, 195–219; *The Sacred Fount,* 81;
What Maisie Knew, 133, 163; on author's
sense of life, 4, 9, 140–41, 162, 183–85,
205; commensurability in, 89–90;
community of author and reader in, 48,
143, 145; conflicting obligations in, 134–
37; consistency in, 89–90; criticism of
authorial omniscience, 45–46; on
education, 203–4, 211–12, 217; emotions
in, 7, 91–92, 134, 153, 180, 187–90;
ethical point of view in, 52; fine attention
and perception in, 7, 84, 135–38, 148–65,
168, 179–85, 206–10; on hero or heroine,
139–40, 164, 198–99, 206–7; imagery in,
128, 159–60, 168; improvisation in, 37,
94, 138, 141, 155–56; inclusive view of
the ethical in, 50–51; love and vision in,
52–53, 136–37, 145, 187–90; moralism in,
126–33, 169, 176–79, 184; on novelist's
terms, 4–8, 149, 163, 168, 181; obtuseness
of everyday thought and speech, 47–48,
148, 156, 164–65, 207–8; particularity in,
90, 149, 197–98, 207–18; political
implications of ethical norm, 198–206;
prefaces in relation to novels, 10, 137; on
the "projected morality," 10, 46, 163, 185,
289; public use of imagination in, 165,
193, 198; on reader's activity, adventure,
and emotion, 6, 48, 140–41, 143, 157,
198–99; relation to Aristotle, 84–85, 141,
164, 201–2; sexual desire in, 128–30;
style of late novels, 149, 182. *See
also* Abstractness; Adventure; Class
distinctions; Commensurability of values;

for, 238, 256; of reader for character, 216, 335, 346–47, 353–58; and refusal of strict moral judgment, 137, 209–10, 216–17, 357–63; relation to general ethical and social concern, 4, 50–53, 96, 135–37, 187–90, 336–63; and silence, 40, 311–12, 333; and social democracy, 391; and suffering, 253–56, 264–69; transformed by change in belief, 114–17; and trust, 271–80. *See also* Emotions; Fantasy; Generosity; Judgment, refusal of strict; Memory; Mystery; Perception; Sacrifice; Sexual desire; Silence; Tenderness
Loyalty, 95, 150, 352, 361–62, 366, 376
Lucretius, x, 289, 304, 306–7, 309
Lutz, Catherine, 40*n*, 294*n*

McCarthy, Eugene, 218
McDowell, John, 36*n*
McEnroe, John, 372
MacIntyre, Alasdair, 28*n*, 370*n*
McLaughlin, Brian, xiv, 284*n*
Mailer, Norman, 235
Martin, Andrew, 134*n*
Marx, Karl, 202–3, 211, 380
Marxism, 196, 213, 295
Material conditions, 201–5
Maximization, 56, 97
Melcher, Edith, xiii
Melchior, Marthe, xiii
Memory, 252, 254, 349–50, 353, 356
Mercy, 53, 213, 301. *See also* Judgment, refusal of strict; Love
Metaphors. *See* Images
Mill, John Stuart, 109, 169, 170
Minorities, 45, 219
Minow, Martha, 43*n*
Moderation, 72, 374
Molière, 323
Moral philosophy. *See* Ethics
Moses, Paul, 232
Murdoch, Iris, 2, 23*n*, 46*n*, 93*n*, 142*n*, 151*n*, 170, 191, 251
Mutability of practical matters, 38, 71
Mutuality, 270–71, 277–80, 283, 343, 353
Mystery, 3, 29, 47, 104, 141–42, 144, 238, 258, 282, 344, 346–48, 363

Nagel, Thomas, 32*n*, 46*n*, 170, 296*n*
Nagy, Gregory, 13*n*, 382*n*
Narrative. *See* Form and content; Literature; Novels

New Criticism, 12, 21, 172. *See also* Literary theory
Newton-Smith, William, 20*n*
Nietzsche, Friedrich, 39, 169, 171, 229, 289, 306–9, 370, 380
Noncontradiction, principle of, 223, 225. *See also* Aristotle
Novels: and avoidance of love, 187–89; both friendly and erotic, 238, 353–63; and common humanity, 95–96; compared to dramas, biographies, histories, lyric poetry, 46, 236; and conflicting obligations, 37, 90; constitutive of community, 48; embody forms of desire, 290–91, 353–55; and emotions, 40, 92, 143, 230–31, 236–39, 353–63, 390–91; and imagination, 92, 143; as intelligent interpretations of experience, 47, 139, 173; and learning, 44, 211; and life, 47, 291; linked with a distinctive family of positions, 8, 26, 139–42; necessary for grasp of psychological truth, 256, 280–82; negotiate between general and particular, 95; opposition to Kantianism and Utilitarianism, 26; and perception of particularity and complexity, 5, 38–39, 90–91, 141–42, 148–65, 183–85, 197–217, 353–64, 390–91; and philosopher's examples, 46–47, 84–97; and qualitative distinctions, 36; role in ethical inquiry, 45–49, 138–43, 148–65; and universalizing, 95, 165–67
Nussbaum, Rachel, 335, 363*n*

Original sin, 127, 133, 297–306
Owen, G.E.L., 13, 223*n*

Pagels, Elaine, 370
Parfit, Derek, 170
Particularity: attention to in deliberation, 7, 38–40, 151–55, 177–82; body and, 5, 383; in characterization of ethical subjects, 34; of complex contexts, 38, 71–72, 87–88, 91, 390; and general notion of human being, 390–91; and habit, 264; in humanistic education, 103; and imagination of novelist, 360–63; lacking in philosophical examples, 46; of persons and relationships, 7, 38–40, 72–73, 90–91, 117, 157, 315–33; priority to the general, 38–40, 67–72, 82–84, 90–96, 155–57, 197–98; relation to universals, 55, 67, 72–75; and surprise, 91; and vulnerability, 67,